ANCIENT GREEK NOVELS

THE FRAGMENTS

Ancient Greek Novels
The Fragments

❖

INTRODUCTION,
TEXT, TRANSLATION, AND
COMMENTARY

EDITED BY

Susan A. Stephens and
John J. Winkler

PRINCETON UNIVERSITY PRESS

PRINCETON, NEW JERSEY

Library of Congress Cataloging-in-Publication Data

Ancient Greek novels : the fragments : introduction, text,
translation, and commentary / edited by Susan A. Stephens and
John J. Winkler.
p.   cm.
Includes bibliographical references and index.
ISBN 0–691–06941–7 (acid-free paper)
1. Greek fiction—Translations into English.   2. Lost literature—
Greece—Translations into English.   3. Lost literature—Greece—
History and criticism.   4. Greek fiction—History and criticism.
5. Lost literature—Greece.   6. Greek fiction.
I. Stephens, Susan A.   II. Winkler, John J.
PA3632.A53   1994
883′.0108—dc20   92–23526

For Cathy and Mark

CONTENTS

CONTENTS

PREFACE

Within the last decade, the discovery of new fragments, like Lollianos, *Iolaos*, and *Metiochos and Parthenope*, has dramatically increased our library catalogue of ancient novels, altering our sense of its contents and proportions, and calling for a fresh survey of the field. The last edition of novel fragments, that of Franz Zimmermann in 1936, is now hopelessly out of date. This alone was sufficient reason to undertake such a project. We also shared an interest in the postclassical world, and further, we possessed skills that complemented each other.

Deciding on the project was the easy part. Choosing what to print was more complex. We settled on all the fragments of the identifiable novels, including the fragments and epitomes of Iamblichos and Antonius Diogenes. After examining all *adespota* among the literary papyri published as "romance," "history," "oratory," "mimes," "mythography and religion," and "unidentified prose," we added a number of pieces that seem to have novellike narratives, but are too small to label with authority. There are two exceptions: we have omitted Diktys of Krete and all material associated with Alexander and the *Alexander Romance*, the latter because of the vastness of the material, the former because its Latin version raises unique problems, more suitably dealt with in a separate publication. We do not print all fragments identified as "romance" by their original editors, only those with sufficient text for us to be confident that they are more likely to belong to prose fiction than to any other genre. For a full list of fragments originally published as "romance," see Appendix A.

This book is intended to combine two normally exclusive modes of scholarship: the edition of texts, and literary interpretation. We wished to make this material available for the nonspecialist and the non-Greek reader, as well as to provide adequate and easily accessible texts. Introductions situate each text within the field of ancient fiction and present relevant background material, possible lines of interpretation, and literary parallels. Reconstructions of texts are deliberately conservative, to correct the habit of exuberant supplementation that colors much previous work. The texts themselves are printed in standard Greek; errors, spelling aberrations, and editorial marking of the original manuscripts are confined to the apparatus or discussed in the descriptions of each text that are provided. The apparatus reports all *feasible* conjectures of previous editors *in the form in which they were made*; therefore, there may be discrepancies in the matter of dots or brackets with the texts we print. Further, we have not reported readings that differ only in which letter (or letters) is dotted. Nor do we note variant readings of letters that do not form discrete words. For the most part we have relegated conjectures and supplements to the notes, since all too often, conjectures lead to erroneous interpretation. We follow standard papyrological conventions in the layout of texts. Translation of the Greek text has been provided whenever feasible.

This project could not have been completed without the assistance of a number of individuals and institutions. We wish to express our thanks first of all to those whose initial expressions of support got this project under way, and in particular, T. Rosenmeyer. We are grateful to W. Brashear, R. A. Coles, C. Gallazzi, R. Gerecke, L. Koenen, R. Pintaudi, L. Youtie, the British Library, the Instituto di Papirologia in Milan, the Universitetsbiblioteket in Oslo, the Osterreichischen Nationalbibliotek, the Smithsonian Institution, and the Staatliche Museem in Berlin for photographs; to P. Mertens, who provided us with his supplement to Pack; to R. Kussl, for providing us with a copy of his dissertation; to Kenneth Dover, for his help with *The Festival*; to Peter Parsons, for allowing us to see an unpublished Oxyrhynchus fragment and for his advice on readings in *Iolaos*; to the Guggenheim Foundation (Winkler) and the National Endowment for the Humanities (Stephens), for research support; to Denise Greaves, Nora Chapman, and especially to David Briney, for editorial assistance; and to Stanford University for ongoing research and editorial expenses. Finally, and most importantly, we wish to thank B. Reardon and L. Koenen, for their advice on various sections of the manuscript; Mark Edwards, for his painstaking care in reading the Greek translations; and most of all, James Tatum and Ewen Bowie, for undertaking to read the entire manuscript. Their comments and criticisms have been invaluable; for the idiosyncracies that remain, they should not be held responsible.

This book began as a collaboration and continued to be so until the death of Jack Winkler from complications arising from AIDS in April 1990. Although the manuscript was almost finished when he died, it has been for me to see it through its final stages to publication. The ideas and interpretations developed throughout have resulted from our constant discussion, frequent changes of opinion, and endless rewriting, and we have both contributed to every section, though not always in even proportions. The manuscript for this book was sent to press in October 1991. It has been impossible, for the most part, to incorporate scholarly material published after that date.

Susan A. Stephens

LIST OF PAPYRI

Listed below are the papyri that are discussed at length in this book. See Appendix A for other papyri mentioned within.

Antheia	PSI 726 (= P^2 2627)
Antonius Diogenes	P. Oxy. 3012
	PSI 1177 (= P^2 95)
Antonius Diogenes?	P. Dubl. inv. C3 (= P^2 2621)
Apollonios	PSI 151 (= P^2 2624) + P. Mil. Vog. 260
Apparition	P. Oxy. 416 (= P^2 168)
Chione	codex Thebanus deperditus (= P^2 244)
Chione?	P. Berol. 10535 (= P^2 2631) + P. Berol. 21234
Daulis	P. Berol. inv. 11517 (= P^2 2468)
Festival	PSI inv. 516 (= P^2 2902)
Goatherd and the Palace Guards	PSI 725 (= P^2 2626)
Initiation	P. Ant. 18 (= P^2 2466)
Inundation	P. Michael. 4 (= P^2 2271)
Iolaos	P. Oxy. 3010
Kalligone	PSI 981 (= P^2 2628)
Lollianos, *Phoinikika*	P. Colon. inv. 3328
	P. Oxy. 1368 (= P^2 2620)
Love Drug	P. Mich. inv. 5 (= P^2 2636) + P. Pilau Rib. 152 a–e
Metiochos and Parthenope	P. Berol. inv. 7927 + 9588 + 21179 (= P^2 2622)
	O. Bodl. 2.2175 (= P^2 2782)
Metiochos and Parthenope?	P. Oxy. 435 (= P^2 2623)
Nightmare or Necromancy?	P. Mich. inv. 3378 (= P^2 2629)
Ninos	P. Berol. 6926 (= P^2 2616)
	PSI 1305 (= P^2 2617)
	P. Gen. 85
Sesonchosis	P. Oxy. 1826 (= P^2 2619)
	P. Oxy. 2466 (= P^2 2259) + P. Oxy. 3319
Staphulos	PSI 1220 (= P^2 2625)
Theano	P. Oxy. 417 (= P^2 2474)
Tinouphis	P. Turner 8 (= P. Haun. inv. 400)

ABBREVIATIONS

The abbreviations for names of classical authors and their works generally follow those of the *Oxford Classical Dictionary*. Abbreviations of the form "P. Dubl." or "P. Berol." refer to inventory numbers of papyrus collections.

AT = Achilles Tatius, *Leukippe and Kleitophon*

BKT = *Berliner Klassische Texte*

Blass-Debrunner = F. Blass and A. Debrunner, *A Greek Grammar of the New Testament and Other Early Christian Literature*, translated and revised by R.W. Funk (Chicago, 1961)

BursJb = *Bursians Jahresbericht über die Fortschritte der klassischen Altertumswissenschaft* (Berlin and Leipzig, 1873–)

CAGN = B. Reardon, ed., *Collected Ancient Greek Novels* (Berkeley, 1989)

Ch. = Chariton, *Chaireas and Kallirhoe*

D-K = H. Diels and W. Kranz, *Die Fragmente der Vorsokratiker*, 3 vols. (Berlin, 1951–52)

DL = Diogenes Laertios, *Lives of Eminent Philosophers*

DS = Diodoros of Sicily, *The Library of History*

EGFP = B. Lavagnini, *Eroticorum graecorum fragmenta papyracaea* (Leipzig, 1922)

EM = T. Gaisford, ed., *Etymologicum Magnum* (Oxford, 1848)

FGrHist = F. Jacoby, ed., *Die Fragmente der griechischen Historiker* (Berlin and Leiden, 1955–69)

GCS = *Die griechischen christlichen Schriftsteller der ersten Jahrhunderte* (Berlin)

GGM = C. Müller, ed., *Geographi Graeci Minores* (Paris, 1855–61)

GLH = C. H. Roberts, *Greek Literary Hands: 350 B.C.–400 A.D.* (Oxford, 1955)

GMAW[2] = E. G. Turner, *Greek Manuscripts of the Ancient World*, 2d ed., rev. and enlarged by P. J. Parsons, Institute of Classical Studies, Bulletin Suppl. 46 (1987)

GRP = F. Zimmermann, *Griechische Roman-Papyri und verwandte Texte* (Heidelberg, 1936)

HA = *The History of Apollonius, King of Tyre*

Hld. = Heliodoros, *Aithiopika*

Kerényi = K. Kerényi, *Die griechisch-orientalische Romanliteratur in religionsgeschichtlicher Beleuchtung* (Tubingen, 1927; repr. Darmstadt, 1962)

Kock = T. Kock, ed., *Comicorum Atticorum Fragmenta*, 3 vols. (Leipzig, 1880–88)

Lampe = G.W.H. Lampe, *A Patristic Greek Lexicon* (Oxford, 1961)

LSJ = H. G. Liddell, R. Scott, and H. S. Jones, eds., *A Greek English Lexicon* (Oxford, 1968)

P^2 = R. A. Pack, *The Greek and Latin Literary Texts from Greco-Roman Egypt,* 2d ed. (Ann Arbor, 1965)

Pape-Benseler = W. Pape and G. Benseler, *Wörterbuch der Griechische Eigennamen,* 2 vols. (Braunschweig, 1911; reprint Graz, 1959)

PCG = R. Kassel and C. Austin, eds., *Poetae comici graeci* (Berlin, 1983–)

PGM = K. Preisendanz, ed., *Papyri graecae magicae: Die griechischen Zauberpapyri,* 2 vols. (Leipzig, 1928–31)

Polyb. = Polybios, *The Histories*

P. Oxy. = *The Oxyrhynchus Papyri,* Egypt Exploration Society (London, 1898–)

PSI = *Papiri greci i latini. Pubblicazioni della Società Italiana* (Florence, 1912–)

RE = A. Pauly, G. Wissowa, and W. Kroll, eds., *Real-Encyclopädie der klassischen Altertumswissenschaft* (Stuttgart, 1890–1980)

RG = Christian Walz, ed., *Rhetores graeci,* vols. 1–9 (Stuttgart, 1832–36; repr. Osnabrück, 1968)

Sp. = L. Spengel, ed., *Rhetores graeci,* vols. 1–3 (Leipzig, 1953)

Sp.-H. = L. Spengel and C. Hammer, eds., *Rhetores graeci,* vol. 1.2 (Leipzig, 1884)

Steph. Byz. = Stephen of Byzantium, *Ethnika* (Berlin, 1849; reprint Graz, 1959)

Steph. Lex. = H. Stephanus, *Thesaurus graecae linguae,* 3d ed., edited by B. Hase, G. Dindorf, and L. Dindorf (Paris, 1831–65)

Str. = Strabo, *The Geography*

TGrF = B. Snell and S. Radt, eds., *Tragicorum graecorum fragmenta,* 4 vols. (Göttingen, 1971–85)

Typology = E. G. Turner, *The Typology of the Early Codex* (Philadelphia, 1977)

XE = Xenophon of Ephesos, *Ephesiaka*

ANCIENT GREEK NOVELS

THE FRAGMENTS

General Introduction

❖

Conventional wisdom has it that English writers in the eighteenth century—Defoe, Richardson, and Fielding—invented the literary form we know as the novel, and that long fictional works in prose before that date were something else, usually called "romances." Though it may be true that in writing for an expanding and newly dominant middle class those writers produced the set of literary conventions labeled "realism," the tradition of long prose narrative with complex plots and richly developed characters is at least seventeen centuries older than that. The restriction of the term "novel" to the eighteenth century's subclass of lengthy fictions depends on the arbitrary creation of what Ian Watt calls a "definition sufficiently narrow to exclude previous types of narrative and yet broad enough to apply to whatever is usually put in the novel category" (Watt 1957: 9). But if we wish to include works that reject those fairly narrow bourgeois conventions in many different ways—such as the work of Proust, Joyce, Genet, Nabokov, or Lessing—a more up-to-date map of the terrain labeled "novel" might be drawn to cover everything fictional and in prose from Petronius to the present.

Whatever the name we choose to give to Greek and Latin fictional prose narratives, their popularity and influence down through the ages has been well established.[1] Two Roman novels have always been in fashion—Petronius's *Satyrica*[2] and Apuleius' *Golden Ass* or *Metamorphoses*. The Greek novels are less familiar nowadays, but in past centuries they have enjoyed their share of prominence. Indeed, Heliodoros's *Aithiopika* was so much the rage in the sixteenth and seventeenth centuries that Cervantes modeled his final novel, *Persiles and Sigismunda*

---

[1] Greeks themselves employed no fixed term for novels as they did for tragedy (*tragoidos*) or epic (*epos*). Chariton calls his work a "*pathos erōtikon*"; Longos uses the term "*erōtika*"; Heliodoros, "*to syntagma*"; and Photios in his epitome refers to Achilles Tatius's novel as "*ta dramata.*" Unfortunately, the novels themselves were too lately written to receive the critical imprimatur of Aristotle. We use the term "novel" for the seven extant works we discuss below and, on the principle of *similia similibus*, apply the term to the fragments we print that most clearly resemble these extant types.

[2] More usually called the *Satyricon*, where the final -*ōn* is a genitive plural.

3

on it,[3] and Goethe so admired *Daphnis and Chloe* that he recommended it be read annually.[4] Today only five complete texts survive: Chariton's *Kallirhoe* (or *Chaireas and Kallirhoe*), Xenophon of Ephesos's *Ephesiaka*,[5] Achilles Tatius's *Leukippe and Kleitophon*, Heliodoros's *Aithiopika*, and the sport of the series, Longos's *Daphnis and Chloe*.[6]

As chance has it, the "big five" Greek novels fall into a single pattern. They are set several centuries earlier than their date of composition, which is the first through the third or fourth centuries of the common era.[7] Their action tends to be located in the heyday of Greek culture—the sixth or the fifth century B.C.E.—and centers on an erotic pair of high station, scarcely postpubescent, who fall in love at first sight, may or may not be immediately married (as are Chariton's Chaireas and Kallirhoe), undergo a series of harrowing adventures and testings of their faithfulness—kidnapping, shipwreck, slavery, even marriage to another party—before being reunited, presumably to live happily ever after.

The fact that these novels share gross similarities of plot structure and sentiment has promoted the widely held assumption that they constitute the core of the "genre," and this type is usually called "ideal romantic" (see Hägg 1983: 5–80). Although the field of ancient prose fiction may be easily expanded to include other works—novellas by Lucian and Plutarch, the *Alexander Romance* (a big hit in the Middle Ages, discussed below), the *Life of Aesop* and other biographies, all of which are no less entertaining—the "big five" conventionally remain as central, and other fictions are regarded as marginal or as members of some other generic category. Fragmentary novels may well reveal, however, that the so-called ideal romantic is no more than a subclass of the whole, whose sur-

---

[3] For the relationship of Heliodoros and Cervantes, see, e.g., Wilson 1991: 20–23.

[4] See, e.g., Grumach 1949: 316–20.

[5] Although not all scholars agree, we are convinced that Xenophon of Ephesos's *Ephesiaka* (hereafter XE) is an abridgment to five books of an original ten. See "*Antheia*" below, n. 1. Another famous abridgment is the *Ass Tale*, conventionally attributed to Lucian. It is thought to be an abridged version of a now lost Greek story that was translated, adapted, or parodied by Apuleius.

[6] All five are translated in *CAGN*.

[7] Unfortunately, we have no secure dates either for the works or for their authors. Dates are conventionally assigned on stylistic grounds or on the basis of manuscript finds, which are conventionally assigned to fifty-year periods by handwriting type. Hence there is considerable margin for error. For example, Erwin Rohde wished to locate Chariton in the fifth century of the common era. Subsequently a papyrus roll of Chariton was discovered that could be no later than the third century C.E. Now, on the basis of his style, Chariton is usually taken to be the earliest of the five novelists (see, e.g., Bowie 1985: 688–90).

vival says more about the tastes of subsequent late antique and Byzantine readers than it does about the field of ancient novels itself.

Moreover, discussions of the ancient novel usually proceed from the assumption that these five novels are a unified group, shaped by increasing narrative complexity from Chariton and Xenophon of Ephesos on the one hand to Achilles Tatius and Heliodoros on the other.[8] The stylistic differences between the two groups are real enough (and Chariton, at least, may be earlier than the other four), but do the perceived differences result from linear development or from idiosyncracies of the individual authors? Even within a closed field this question deserves to be considered; but opening the field to include the fragments admits the possibility not only of development but of regression in standards of narrative complexity. *Sesonchosis*, for example, is markedly less sophisticated in its style than *Ninos*, but its fragments are to be dated much later (in the late third or early fourth century C.E.). Are we required to conclude that our *Sesonchosis* fragments are later copies of what *must have been* a very early novel, or can we concede that unsophisticated writing can exist at all times and all places, even when sophisticated models for imitation may exist?

Unlike the Greek novels, characterized by chaste lovers and the expression of noble sentiments, the two Roman novels are salacious, outrageous, and teeming with low life—the flotsam and jetsam of the ancient Mediterranean. It has been customary to divide the Greek from the Latin novels along discrete lines—"idealized" from "realistic," serious from comic, chaste from scandalous—and to understand the Roman novel both as later and as a deliberate inversion or parody of the already well-established "ideal" Greek type (see, e.g., Walsh 1970: 4–5). Whatever the merit of this thesis, the Roman novels are not discernibly later than the Greek: Petronius was a member of the court of Nero, and Apuleius lived in the middle third of the second century C.E.

These seven complete novels were by no means the only examples of this kind of writing in antiquity. There also exists the story of Apollonios, king of Tyre, in a Latin version that was extraordinarily popular in the Middle Ages. Most scholars believe it to be a translation, epitome, or free rendition of a Greek original.[9] Two other novels are known to us

---

[8] This view is widespread: see, e.g., Reardon's introduction to *CAGN* 9 or Bowie 1985: 688ff.

[9] For a translation, see *CAGN* 736–72 by G. Sandy.

from plot summaries by the Patriarch Photios—Antonius Diogenes' *The Incredible Things beyond Thule* and Iamblichos's *Babyloniaka*. To guide us in their reconstruction, in addition to Photios's epitome, we have a series of quotations from these two novels that have turned up in ancient sources—the encyclopedic lexicon known as the *Souda*, Porphyry's *Life of Pythagoras*, and the rhetorical declamations of Polemo. In contrast to the "big five," *The Incredible Things beyond Thule* is not a love story, but a narratological tour-de-force: for twenty-four books the hero and heroine do not have adventures together, they do not indulge in courtship—they narrate. So outrageous is the plot summary of the *Babyloniaka* that it is a wonder anyone could ever refer to it as an "ideal romance": its exotic entourage includes a lesbian princess of Egypt; a cannibalistic bandit; a priestess of Aphrodite whose sons, Tigris and Euphrates, and daughter, Mesopotamia, are exact doubles for the hero and heroine; a rather dignified farmer's daughter, whom the heroine forces to sleep with an executioner; and the young king of the Syrians whom the heroine marries to pique the hero.

The discoveries of fragments from hitherto unknown Greek novels on papyrus, some extending to several columns, began in 1896 with the publication of the *Ninos* fragments. The small number of papyri known earlier in this century were collected and edited first by Bruno Lavagnini in 1922 (*EGFP*), and then, with some additions, by Franz Zimmermann in 1936 (*GRP*). Numerous discoveries since Zimmermann's edition have greatly increased the corpus of texts and significantly altered our sense of the field. The present edition brings together, with translation and commentary, all published papyrus texts that have a good claim to be thought novels. We have tantalizing glimpses of at least seven other ancient Greek novels besides the "big five" (*Ninos, Metiochos and Parthenope, Kalligone, Antheia, Chione, Sesonchosis*, and Lollianos's *Phoinikika*), two to four fragments of Antonius Diogenes, and scraps of another twelve works that look to us like novels, although of these, too little has survived for certitude. They range in date—assigned on the basis of handwriting and formatting styles—from the first century C.E. (*Ninos*) to the early fourth century C.E. (*Sesonchosis*). All of them are now in very fragmentary condition; they were discovered in the refuse heaps and abandoned foundations of the larger towns and urban centers of Greco-Roman Egypt, where, thanks to the aridity of the climate, well over five thousand fragmentary rolls and codices of Greek literature have survived in the sands. Finds are not distributed evenly over the eight hundred years of Greco-Roman occupation: the bulk of these literary fragments were copied between the second and fourth centuries C.E. and were excavated from only a limited number of sites. About 75 percent of the novel fragments whose provenance is known have come from Oxyrhynchus, most of the remainder from the Fayum.

Though now only a tiny sampling of what the whole must have been, papyrus fragments of abandoned or worn-out books thus preserved may serve, in their sheer numbers, as a kind of laboratory to study ancient literary tastes.[10] Relative numbers of surviving authors give some hint, however crude, of their overall significance (or popularity), and examination of the physical presentation of ancient manuscripts can provide useful clues about the social milieus of their owners. In addition, however much we are in the dark about their scope and character, even small fragments, when taken in the aggregate, can by a careful comparison with the seven extant novels shed a good deal of light both on puzzling details and on broader concerns of literary ambition, cultural context, and readership.

To begin with a detail that will lead into the larger issues, there is in the fragments of Lollianos's *Phoinikika* an odd episode in which a band of desperadoes paints their faces and dons black or white clothing. This is a bandits' trick known also from Apuleius's *Golden Ass*: the men are dressing up as ghosts. This intersection of popular superstition, masquerade, and criminal intent had been thought limited to Latin fiction, but papyrus fragments published within the last decade make clear that language was no boundary. Apuleius and Petronius are joined now by several other Greek fragments—*Phoinikika, Daulis, Iolaos,* and *Tinouphis.* These comprise what seems to be a subgenre in the field of ancient fiction, stories that deal with criminal low-life and cult groups, often in an amusing or slightly scandalous fashion. In Latin and Greek alike, magicians, prison breaks, grisly rites, religious scandal, and sacrilege are the staples of this entertainment. The conventional division between Greek and Latin has now broken down, and it remains an open question which gave rise to the other.[11]

Another type of novelists' composition has come to light in the

---

[10] An estimate of the number of Greek books in circulation in Greco-Roman Egypt is impossible to make: unknown variables include the percentage of the population who would own books and the average number of books owned. Even estimates of the total population of Egypt and the percentage who could read Greek varies widely.

[11] For a more detailed discussion, see "*Iolaos*" below.

fragments—let us call it nationalistic drama. These are tales set (for Greeks) far in the past that center on non-Greek historical characters in their young and formative period, like Ninos, the founder of Nineveh, or Sesonchosis, the legendary Egyptian conqueror of Europe and Asia. Here we might also include the *Babyloniaka*, whose hero becomes the king of Babylon, and *Kalligone*, which features native peoples of southern Russia in a military venture (though they seem to share—or be crowded off—the stage by the young Greek warrior maiden, Kalligone, and by Themisto, the queen of the Amazons).

The characters of these nationalistic enterprises are frequently known from other traditions, which allow us to trace, delicately and cautiously, some interactions of folktale, national propaganda, scholarly investigation, and literary composition. For all the differences among these fragments, however, they all demonstrate how Hellenic culture absorbed ancient legends from the countries of the eastern Mediterranean, from Egypt to Babylon to the Crimea, assimilating the wise kings and warlords of heroic saga to the social norms of the Greek-speaking educated classes within the Roman Empire. Thus, the ferocious Semiramis known from Diodoros's account of Babylonian history becomes in the *Ninos* fragments a shy, tongue-tied maiden, too embarrassed to tell her aunt that she loves her cousin.

Fragments also reveal complicated literary relationships. The scrap we have called *Antheia* rather self-consciously recalls Xenophon's *Ephesiaka*—sharing names and occasional similarities of plot structure. An incident in Lollianos's *Phoinikika* is so similar to the scene in the robbers' cave found in Apuleius's *Golden Ass* that the two novels must be deliberately interconnected, though who can say whether one imitated the other or both followed a common ancestor? The fragment known as "Herpyllis" to previous editors, if it is not from the novel of Antonius Diogenes, may well be a later imitation, playing off the name of Antonius's heroine, Derkyllis. *Sesonchosis* looks suspiciously like *Ninos* in aspects of its plot, and *Kalligone* shares at least one character and its historical location with Lucian's *Toxaris*. This much is evident from the bits that have survived, and serves to alert us that ancient novel writers, like modern ones, expected their audience to be familiar with their fictions and to recognize and appreciate—even to expect?—the playing of allusive and interdependent textual games.

Contemplating the fragmentary novels, one is often struck by the accuracy of Bakhtin's observation about the plasticity of the novel form and the way in which it "fused together in its structure almost all genres of ancient literature" (1981: 89). The *Sesonchosis* fragments are a case in point. (This is an historical romance whose protagonist is a pharaoh of the Twelfth Dynasty—Senwosret, or Sesostris as Herodotos calls him.) A fragment of *Sesonchosis*, when first published, was identified as history. Only later was it reclassified when a new and more extensive piece of it came to light. A cogent argument was made to assign one fairly extensive fragment to a lost oration of Lysias, until it proved to be from Lucian's *Ass Tale*. A part of the *Metiochos and Parthenope* was originally labeled "philosophical" because it opens with a discourse modelled on Plato's *Symposium*, the subject of which was the power of Eros. Such examples can be multiplied. The pool of ancient narrative types seems to have been at once fluid and flexible, the absorption of other literary types more a matter of individual experiment than of generic determinatives. This dimension of ancient fiction, of course, makes the assignment of fragments hazardous: we include a number of pieces in this edition with mentally crossed fingers, prepared like our predecessors in this dangerous game for our judgments to be overturned by future finds.

Since we did not employ stylistic criteria in selecting fragments for inclusion in this collection, we were surprised to discover that the fragments we did select, in the main, are composed according to the most exacting rules of ancient rhetoric and employ a series of highly artificial conventions. Hiatus tends to be avoided (often entirely), the vocabulary is restricted to Attic words, and clauses end in a small number of favored rhythmic patterns. Many pieces boast an ornate syntax and full panoply of tropes. Narratives are often complex, but even the most straightforwardly written might contain framing devices, ekphrases, and literary allusions. We might hold up for comparison to our fragments Greek martyr acts and apocryphal writings of the New Testament, the bulk of which are written in simple declarative sentences without even the rudimentary use of connectives by authors who are either ignorant or deliberately neglectful of rhetorical refinements. From the lavishing of the highest resources of rhetorical education in the writing of ancient fictions we must infer that the intended audience was equipped—or was expected to be equipped—to appreciate them.

The elevated level of style is matched by the quality of the book production. The novel fragments are written in practiced hands ranging from workmanlike to elegant; books contain wide margins and employ the formats in vogue for the prose writing of oratory, philosophy, or history. At least one (*Kalligone*) ranks among the most attractive papyrus rolls yet found. Moreover, careful punctuation and lectional signs were employed, and many texts show signs of the corrector at work. In contrast, one may point to a large number of prose texts written in clumsily formed hands by writers who appear awkward and unskilled at the technical niceties of book production, such as layout. Other hands betray themselves as products of the schoolroom: many texts of Homer, for example, and Homeric vocabulary lists fall into this category. But novel fragments do not.

This evidence from the formatting and presentation of ancient novels tends to undermine a common misconception about them, namely, that they were targeted for a clientele qualitatively different from that for other ancient books.[12] They are often imagined as newly literate— a bourgeois class that supposedly flourished in the imperial period in the eastern Mediterranean—or as reflections of characters within the novels—women or young men approaching adulthood, or the sort of people to whom religious conversion appealed (Hägg 1983: 90). In their physical appearance, however, novel fragments are indistinguishable from the rolls or codices of classical Greek writers of high culture, like Sappho, Thucydides, Demosthenes, or Plato. But they do look different both from the early New Testament material and from less-than-literate productions. Yet it is in these latter, more widely disseminated styles that we should expect to see at least some, if not all, novel manuscripts copied, if their owners for the most part consisted of newly converted Christians or of schoolboys.[13]

Further, the relatively small number of copies of novels (compared to the number of copies of other texts of the high culture) indicates that novels were not much in demand in Greco-Roman Egypt (Harris 1989: 283). This interpretation of statistical evidence is reinforced by the notable lack of testimony about novels and novel writers in other ancient sources, and apart from a handful of references little is said about novel-reading.[14] Christian polemicists, for example, do not caution their flocks

---

[12] Among scholars of the ancient novel, proponents include, e.g., T. Hägg, B. E. Perry, and G. L. Schmeling, though recently there has been some movement away from the notion of a popular audience, e.g., Bowie 1985: 688.

[13] For a more detailed analysis see Stephens 1994.

[14] Most of this evidence is late and tends to single out the erotic; see Wesseling 1988: 67–68 for a list of passages.

against the evils of novel reading, and although Julian can admonish his priests in Asia Minor not to read "love stories" (erōtikas hypotheseis), the tenor of his letter (*Ep.* 89b) does not allow us to infer that "love stories" were any more common (or any more pernicious) than texts of high culture, like the plays of Aristophanes, which he also interdicts. The novelists themselves, unlike their eighteenth- and nineteenth-century counterparts, do not show their own characters reading novels. For all these reasons, it appears that novels attracted very little attention.

No DISCUSSION of the Greek novel can go on for very long without some consideration of the matter of its origins. As a relatively late arrival on the Greek literary scene displaying considerable flexibility in its forms and lacking a critical literature to validate its existence, the novel has been the most suspect of all categories of Greek literature. The quest for origins has taken three forms.

For some scholars (now probably the majority), the novels are essentially the progeny of common or garden-variety Greek ancestors. For example, the erotic element has been traced to Alexandrian poetry and New Comedy; the historical to Herodotos, Thucydides, and Xenophon; the overall style to the prevalance of Greek rhetorical education. While all of this, of course, is true, can it be deemed a sufficient explanation for the growth of the form?

Other scholars within the last half-century have proposed that the ancient novels were written and intended to be read as religious documents, deriving their basic structure and many details from the myths and cults of popular religions.[15] No one would deny that the ancient landscape abounded with temples and a wide variety of religious cults; supplication to the gods, temple incubation, and dream lore were part of the popular culture. But do the novels simply reflect this social condition, or were they actively the product of it?

A third set of scholars has looked to foreign sources to explain for the growth and development of the ancient novel.[16] At its least sophisti-

---

[15] See the introduction of "*Lollianos*" for a discussion of this thesis.

[16] On Indian origins, see the discussion in the introduction to "Antonius Diogenes"; for Sumerian, Babylonian, and Persian, see Anderson 1984. Anderson postulates major cycles of oriental fiction as the basis for Greek romance. In deciding whether or not a fragment of narrative should be included in this volume, we found that we could not be disinterested in the question of Egyptian origins. Our conclusions are discussed below.

cated, this is no more than a demotion in status. To say that the novel is "un-Greek" is like saying that something is "not done" or that someone is "not a gentleman"; it therefore becomes dismissable and unworthy of further consideration. Of course, implicit in the statement "un-Greek" is the restriction of what *is* Greek to fifth and fourth century B.C.E. canons and genres, and that based on what has been abstracted and selected over centuries. The elements that scholars point to are real enough, however: tales and narrative patterns that appear to be similar to those which make up Greek novels can be found written down in Egyptian, Persian, Indian, or Semitic cultures long before the Greek novels ever appear. The existence of such tales does suggest, at least in the abstract, a starting point for fiction writing in a Greek milieu, especially in view of the fact that novels do not seem to emerge as a form before the late Hellenistic or early Roman period (between the first century B.C.E. and first century C.E.), when Greeks living in the Near East had had considerable exposure to non-Greek cultures, and relatively large numbers of natives in these regions had begun to learn Greek as the language of the dominant culture.

It is of course naive to imagine that Greeks could not have developed their narrative fiction as independently as they seem to have developed Attic tragedy. Whatever they chose to write about—at whatever period—could easily have been indigenous. Equally, of course, it is unwise to underestimate the potential interaction between Greece and other cultures even if clear-cut evidence should appear to be lacking—and it is not. It is obvious, explicitly at least from the time of Herodotos, that Greek writers took great interest in foreign tales—a version of the Sesonchosis story, for example, appears in Herodotos's Egyptian book—and it is not impossible that contact with foreign literature provided the inspiration for the novel-type narrative. Certainly, the recasting of the Greek novel *Metiochos and Parthenope* as a Coptic martyr tale and later as a Persian poem is an inverse demonstration of how such transformations can occur as well as what unexpected permutations they may take.

The most successful argument for a non-Greek origin of ancient novels has been advanced by J.W.B. Barns in an influential article written in 1956. He made the suggestion—attractive on the surface—that serious consideration should be given to Egypt as the country of origin of the Greek novel, observing that novellike tales, such as the "Two Brothers" (a variant of the story of Potiphar's wife) or the "Doomed Prince" (a young man who courts a princess in a tower),[17] or the tale of devoted couple in the first Setne-Kemwe story,[18] had a long tradition in Egypt. Further, he noted that most Greek novels are set in Egypt for some part of their action, and there are identifiable examples of popular Egyptian stories translated into Greek. These are the "Dream of Nektanebos," a dream narrative that exists now in one copy assignable on paleographic grounds to the third century B.C.E., and the "Legend of Tefnut," a story perhaps best classifiable as an animal fable assignable to the second century C.E.[19] To Barns's points we might add that Greeks had prolonged contact with Egypt most likely stretching back to the Mycenaean period, but certainly from the seventh century B.C.E.; that Greek literature continued to flourish in Egyptian cities like Alexandria or even Panopolis as late as the fourth century C.E.; and that Egyptian love poetry—a flourishing genre of the New Kingdom, a type of which is the "Song of Solomon" in the Old Testament—just might have provided an erotic element some feel to have been missing from early Greek literature.

Some of this is not very substantive. The prevalence of novellike narrative in Egypt means only that the Greeks *might* have borrowed Egyptian material; it does not demonstrate that they actually did. Egypt as the setting for tales of adventure occurs in non-Greek stories as well. For example, the "Hymn of the Pearl,"[20] a travel tale, probably Semitic in origin—now with a patently religious message attached and found embedded in the apocryphal Acts of Thomas—similarly dispatches its young prince to Egypt for amatory adventure and testing. There is also, of course, the story of Joseph in the Old Testament. Conversely, in the Egyptian "Tale of the Shipwrecked Sailor" (Lichtheim 1975–80, 1: 211–15), it is only by leaving Egypt (which is not considered exotic and interesting by Egyptians) that the sailor experiences his adventures. In fact, one might go so far as to say that the location of so many novels in Egypt for at least part of the narrative time-frame militates against the hypothesis of Egyptian origin.

The consideration of Egypt does provide a clue, however, about the environment in which literary transmission was likely to occur. When

---

[17] Translations of these two stories may be found in Lichtheim 1975–80, 2: 200–211.

[18] A translation of this story may be found in Lichtheim 1975–80, 3: 127–38. Lichtheim herself points to the presence of Greco-Roman religious motifs in the second Setne story (p. 126).

[19] The influence of Barns's argument may be judged from the fact that E. L. Bowie sees fit to list these two stories in his survey of the Greek novel (1985: 684).

[20] A translation may be found in Hennecke-Schneemelcher 1963: 498–504.

the Ptolemies took control of Egypt, they imported a Macedonian-Greek elite to rule and established the Greek city of Alexandria, but they did not dismantle the native Egyptian priesthood. Rather, they adapted themselves in many respects to Egyptian custom by ruling as pharaohs and by allowing the continuation of Egyptian written high culture, which in the main reposed in the hereditary priesthoods and scribal bureaucracy. Egyptian literary texts from the Hellenistic period written in Demotic appear to be fairly numerous (Samuel 1983: 109–10) and would attest to the continuity of Egyptian literary traditions under Greek rule. Further, Egyptians appear in high administrative posts even in the early period of Ptolemaic rule. It must have been desirable, therefore, for many Egyptians to acquire the Greek language for administrative advancement.

It is not inconceivable that such men translating or freely adapting their native stories in Greek began the process that led to the development of the Greek novel. These circumstances need not be limited to Egypt; a marginal comment on the *Babyloniaka* identifies Iamblichos as a similarly multilingual type: "This Iamblichos was a Syrian by birth, both on his father's and his mother's side, not a Syrian in the sense of a Greek living in Syria but a native. He spoke Syrian and lived in that culture until a tutor, as he tells us, who was Babylonian, took charge of him and taught him the language and culture of Babylon, and their stories, of which the one he is writing is an example." The final lines of the *Aithiopika* state that the story was composed by "a Phoinikian from Emesa, whose clan is descended from the Sun, the son of Theodosios, Heliodoros." It is not important that any of these statements be true, only that such a cultural hybrid was plausible to the ancient reader. Although the existence of such figures cannot guarantee it, they increase the likelihood that such literary crossovers took place.

Can consideration of the papyrus fragments get us further? Is any obviously Egyptian novellike narrative found in Greek recensions? None of the stories Barns mentions has as yet been found in Greek versions, and neither of the two translations he points to—the "Dream of Nektanebos" and the "Legend of Tefnut"—is an impressive candidate for protonovel material. A Demotic Egyptian version of the Tefnut story actually exists, so it constitutes a true example of a written text crossing from Egyptian to Greek, but whatever its signification in Egyptian, in Greek it is an animal fable with typical moralizing tendencies. Although an argument can be made that it constitutes a very sophisticated and clever example of the genre, it is as relevant to the discussion of the novel as Aesop's fables might be—and no more. Nor, in the face of clear evidence to the contrary, should it be taken as the tip of the iceberg of a wide variety of Egypto-Greek fictional narratives in constant circulation.

The "Dream of Nektanebos" is potentially a more reasonable example: since it belongs to the Ptolemaic period, it is at least chronologically in the right place to have been an ancestor of the Greek novel, and the author, in making deliberate attempts to bridge two cultures, gives the impression of being bilingual. Nektanebos is the last native king of Egypt, around whom a variety of legends were attached. The story begins with Nektanebos in Memphis having a dream in which he sees a boat, aboard which are ranged the gods around the seated figure of Isis. To Isis one of the gods, Onouris-Ares, complains that his temple has been neglected and left half-finished. Isis makes no answer, but the king wakes up and sets out to rectify the situation, asking for the best stonecutter in the land to be sent out immediately to complete the work. The text ends in the following, most provocative way: "But Petesis [the stonecutter] took much money and left for Sebennytos, and he decided—since he was a wine drinker by nature—to take a rest before putting his hand to the job. And he happened while walking around the south part of the temple to see the daughter of . . . , the most beautiful of all in that region. . . ."

At this point, most inopportunely, the text breaks off. Can we have the beginnings of a royal historical romance, like *Ninos*, or the beginning of a picaresque tale in which the drunken stonecutter is about to have an amorous adventure? Appearances are deceiving. Alfred Hermann (1938: 39–42) has pointed out the true nature of the text: it is a type of Egyptian admonitory literature, couched in the form of a dream or report warning the pharaoh that something is amiss in the land, often with attendant predictions of disaster or the coming end of the current order, and followed by a prophecy of a new age of prosperity. Its kin includes Egyptian lamentation literature like the "Admonitions of Ipuwer" (Lichtheim 1975–80, 1: 149–63), to which Egyptians appear to have been much addicted, and the Greco-Egyptian "Oracle of the Potter," an apocalyptic set-piece predicting the end of Greek rule in Egypt.[21] At least two other

---

[21] This kind of religious material was in constant circulation in Greco-Roman Egypt. Texts appear in Demotic, Greek, and Coptic. For a discussion of their significance and an analysis of the cultural interaction, see Smith 1978: 67–87.

small papyrus fragments tentatively labeled "romance," belong in this category (see Appendix A, nos. 4 and 10). In any case, although the "Dream of Nektanebos," like the "Oracle of the Potter," is to be counted as a genuine instance of a written text transmitted from one culture to another, its real importance is its conceptualization of the ideology of apocalypse in Christian, Gnostic, and Manichean writing, not its possible role as *Ur*-material for Greek novels (Koenen 1985: 171–84).

To approach this another way: we know of only one example of a story definitively Egyptian in origin that has survived in any of the extant Greek novel material. This is another tale of Nektanebos—now called Nektanebo—that opens the *Alexander Romance*.[22] It goes like this: When the last days of his kingship are upon him, Nektanebo, who is a magician, flees to the court of Philip II of Macedon, where through trickery he gains the confidence of the queen Olympias in the absence of her husband. Predicting that she is fated to bear a son fathered by the Egyptian god Amon, he persuades her to prepare herself in her bedchamber for the god's appearance. Then, disguising himself on the awaited evening as the ram-headed Amon, he has intercourse with Olympias and fathers Alexander. At the queen's urging—on the next day she asks him, "Will the god visit me again?"—he continues the deceitful liaison until Philip's return.

The story in its current form can be understood in two opposing, almost mutually contradictory, ways:[23] to a Greek, it is a tricky and self-serving deception with chauvinistic undertones (barbarian treachery and dishonest magicians were standard fare in Greek novels); but for an Egyptian, it served to reinforce Ptolemaic claims to the throne of Egypt, because the story is a variant of the myth of divine birth that was attached to every pharaoh. This portrays the new king as the son not of the previous pharaoh, but of Amon, who impregnated his wife. The best-known example today is the frieze found in the birth hall in the

---

[22] The *Alexander Romance* is the name given to a fictionalized biography treating the birth, youth, and adventures of Alexander the Great. It was attached to the name of Alexander's court historian Kallisthenes, with the result that its anonymous author is now labeled "Pseudo-Kallisthenes." It has been translated by K. Dowden in *CAGN*, 650–735; for this anecdote, see pp. 657–59 there.

[23] In an elegant paper ("Genre of Genre") first presented at the Second International Conference on the Ancient Novel in 1989, D. Selden (1994) demonstrated that such "double determined" incidents are a salient characteristic of ancient novels. For a fuller discussion of this thesis, see the introduction to "Lollianos" below.

temple of Hatshepsut at Deir el-Bahri outside of Luxor. Here the royal wife is shown being led to the birth chamber, followed by Amon acknowledging the child as his own.[24] The circulation of this birth myth explicitly making Alexander the son of Amon, or at least of Nektanebos, must have been instigated by the Egyptian priesthood in an effort to smooth acceptance of a fait accompli, namely, the Ptolemaic takeover of Egypt. What form it originally took we can only conjecture; it too may have begun life as a temple frieze like Hatshepsut's, and only afterwards was incorporated into the *Alexander Romance*. Moreover, it provides evidence not so much of an Egyptian love story circulating in a Greek translation, but of an Egyptian political tool borrowed by the Ptolemies in their own imperial program.

Just as it was unnecessary for the story of Alexander's divine birth to have been written down, oral transmission can account for narrative types of varying levels of sophistication passing directly from one culture to another. An excellent example of such transmission is the "Hymns of Isidoros," carved in the Fayum around 96 B.C.E. (Vanderlip 1972: 63–74). The fourth hymn relates the story of Amenophis, a king of the Twelfth Dynasty, whose cult was prominent in this region, a story we are told explicitly that Isidoros got from the local Egyptian priests and translated for Greeks. His translation, moreover, is cast in the form not of its Egyptian original, but of Greek epic models, Homer and Hesiod.

We are convinced that it is to the cultural interaction of Greeks and Hellenized non-Greeks that we must look to see the transmission of novellike material from one culture to another, assuming it existed at all. But in Egypt, at least, there is very little to be seen. Although there is considerable evidence for the transmission of religious writing from Egyptian to Greek (and perhaps in the opposite direction), we were surprised to find so few examples of Egyptian tales of love and adventure in circulation in Egypt written in Greek, or, apart from Nektanebo's adventure in the court of Macedon, in the extant novels and fragments. Even the novel fragment of *Sesonchosis*, which ought to contain elements recognizably Egyptian, at least in its surviving portions, is much more reminiscent of *Ninos*, or indeed Xenophon's *Kyropaideia*, than of Egyp-

---

[24] For a discussion of the significance of this myth in the ideology of Theban kingship, see Kemp 1989: 198–200.

tian royal chronicles or the "Dream of Nektanebos." If no names in *Sesonchosis* had survived, portions of it could be easily identified as belonging to a Greek novel, but no one would guess that its protagonist was an Egyptian pharaoh.

Bowie may well be correct when he asserts that "the search for origins which dominated much earlier scholarship has now few practitioners" (1985: 687); our preceding argument has been intended not to reopen the question but, by using concrete examples, to expose the perils inherent in this mode of inquiry. A more fruitful approach, while acknowledging that the novels are indeed Greek in rhetorical style and social mores, would examine more rigorously the reasons why such stories are all too often located in non-Greek lands, populated with non-Greek characters, and preoccupied with non-Greek cultures. This fascination with the "other" may lie at the heart of the novel form or somewhere along its periphery, but in abandoning the quest for origins, we should not recede into a pro-Greek ethnocentrism that obscures or ignores the dynamics of such cultural interplay.

RECONSTRUCTING the ancient world is rather like working a jigsaw puzzle with most of the pieces missing. With only a handful of pieces we may imagine a simple landscape with earth, trees, and sky. If we find a few more we might discover a background of hills with shepherds grazing their flocks and glimpses of a distant sea. Add more and we suspect that our landscape is, in fact, a wall-painting in an urban household. An understanding of the novel fragments does not lay to rest the traditional questions about the novel's origins, its development, or its audience so much as it leaves us unsatisfied with previous answers and with the premises upon which the questions have been formulated. Like the scene painting, our picture of the novel grows more complex when we enlarge the number of texts under consideration. For example, our comfortable paradigm for stylistic development—from Chariton to Heliodoros—is not easily reconciled with the variety found in the fragments, nor is the view that the "ideal romantic novel" represents the generic norm. Reading the fragments leaves us with the suspicion that the boundary separating novels from other kinds of ancient writing and performance-text—romantic history, travel literature, utopian tales, fictional letters, or biography—may be an imposition of modern scholarship.

An appreciation of the fragmentary texts is indispensable as the study of the ancient novel grows in importance, an area that, far from being minor, repetitive, and crude (as was often alleged), is emerging as a repository of fine intelligence, style, and diversity. No longer can novels be dismissed as a late and insignificant literary sport; rather, they must be perceived as a cultural phenomenon as central to and revealing of the Greco-Roman world after Alexander as tragedy and comedy were to Athens of the fifth century.

PART I
NOVEL FRAGMENTS

Ninos

❖

Ninos holds a pride of place among the Greek novel fragments for its double primacy as the oldest in time of writing (early first century C.E.) and the first to be discovered and published in modern times (1893). Four papyrus fragments now exist: A (five columns), B (three columns), and D (a very small scrap) belong to the same Berlin roll; C is a single column from a different roll. In addition, there are two pavement mosaics depicting Ninos gazing at a woman's portrait, one from a wealthy litterateur's house in Antioch, the other in Alexandretta. These latter represent scenes from the novel or from a mime that must at least indirectly have been derived from the novel.

THE PLOT

The surviving fragments clearly display the three features that we associate with this type of ancient fiction: fine writing, chaste lovers of high station yearning for marriage, and dramatic adventures. The author avoids hiatus, uses clausulae, and generally stays within the confines of Attic vocabulary. The long speech of Ninos to his aunt Derkeia (A.II–IV) is an elaborate display of rhetorical style and compositional finesse—including neuter abstracts (A.III.28–30, 32) and a wide variation of verbal moods. The hero is, as he declares in pressing his suit, Erōs's prisoner of war, and yet he has remained exceptionally chaste (A.II.8–35); the heroine in her turn is so modest that she cannot bring herself to mention the word "marriage" (A.IV.20–V.6). The adventures are less in evidence in these fragments, but included at least a shipwreck (C), a massive military campaign across snow-covered mountains into Armenia (B), separation of the lovers (if the mosaics may be counted as evidence for the novel), and scenes of emotional distress (A.I).

Ninos is no doubt a bold enough warrior, but in our fragments more important qualities are his tenderness and sensitivity. Against a backdrop of war and physical distress (the shipwreck of Fragment C), the novelist has paid careful attention to the emotional forces at war in the souls of Ninos and his young cousin. The struggle of *tharsos* (boldness) and *aidōs* (modesty) is depicted in their conversations with their respective aunts; Ninos, in contrast to his practical companions, is in deep despair after the shipwreck. It would be rash to characterize the entire narrative on the basis of these small fragments, but it is interesting that so much of what we have focuses on the interior drama of emotional forces. As token of the relatively diminished role of external obstacles in *Ninos*, we may take the perilous crossing of the mountains into Armenia by Ninos's expedition of troops and elephants: "Most unexpectedly a gentle south wind, much more summery than the season would warrant, sprang up, and was able both to melt the snow and to make the air temperate to the travelers" (B.II.12–15). The geography of this crossing and campaign is notably vague. The author is also charmingly naive about the material and psychological lives of soldiers: the expedition suffered only a "small loss of animals and attendants" (B.II.22–23), and "having overcome the impassability of roads and the enormous breadth of rivers, they thought it but a slight labor to capture an army of mad Armenians" (B.II.27–31).

The Antioch mosaic adds an intriguing item to the *Ninos* dossier (D. Levi 1944: 420–21). It shows two couches in a bedroom, on one of which Ninos lies, looking away from the center of the room at a picture of a woman held in his right hand. From his left a young woman approaches with a cup. Hägg wonders about the maiden: "Servant or temptress? ... Or is it a scene of attempted suicide, the girl bringing Ninos a cup of poison to end his distress over the supposed death of his beloved?" (Hägg 1983: 19, fig. 4). Another possibility, aligning the scene with the adventurous disguise of the Ktesian Semiramis discussed below (Diodoros 2.6.5–6), Heliodoros's Charikleia disguised as a gypsy (7.7), and the unwilling disguise of Achilles Tatius's Leukippe (5.17), is that this mosaic depicts Ninos's wife approaching him as a servant when he thinks her dead or far away. Such a scene of unexpected reunion would certainly be memorable enough to stand for the entire novel, as it does in the two mosaics.

HISTORICAL BACKGROUND

The earliest historical source available to Greek speakers for a knowledge of Ninos and his glamorous consort Semiramis seems to have been Ktesias's *Persika*.[1] As known from Diodoros's summary (2.1–20), that

---

[1] *FGrHist* 688. There is no trace of a version of this story in Greek earlier than Ktesias, nor mention of Ninos as a national hero in cuneiform tablets.

history contained a good deal of military information[2] about Assyrian campaigns, first against Babylonia, Armenia (as in our Fragment B), and Media, then over a seventeen-year period against all the nations "from the Don to the Nile" (DS 2.2.1). Since the Ninos of our novel leads an army of immense size and speaks of "having mastered so many nations" (A.II.10), that historical tradition obviously provided at least a nominal basis for our narrative. The fact that the name our author uses for the heroine's mother, Derkeia (A.IV.14–15), is adapted from that of Semiramis's legendary mother, Derketo (DS 2.4.2), makes it virtually certain that he called Ninos's beloved Semiramis, though that name does not appear in our fragments.

Ktesias's *Persika* was a fairly "romantic" work, as histories go.[3] There are many items in his account of Ninos and Semiramis that could have afforded a good basis for "novelization": a foundling child of surpassing beauty discovered by herdsmen (DS 2.4.4–6); the long siege of Baktra (DS 2.5–6), whose king in some accounts was the archmagician Zoroaster;[4] Semiramis, in gender-ambiguous clothing, scaling the heights of the Baktran akropolis with a small band of hardy Assyrians and thus taking the supposedly impregnable city (DS 2.6.6–8); her campaign against the Indians with a large force of life-size elephant puppets (DS 2.16.8–10); the face-to-face battle of Semiramis and the Indian king Stabrobates, who wounds her with an arrow in the arm and a javelin in the back, though she escapes across the pontoon bridge while the Indian elephants are trampling her men and tossing them in the air (DS 2.19.4–8). Indeed, the Semiramis of our *Ninos* may have developed qualities of daring and independence if she accompanied her husband on an expedition to Kolchis and was there separated from him (which is one way of reading Fragment C). But the shy unnamed maiden of our Fragment A has little in common with the commanding figure of Ktesias's Semiramis.

She has even less to do with the other versions of Semiramis known from a certain Athenaios (*FGrHist* 681 = DS 2.20.3) and from Plutarch

---

[2] Or pseudo-information: Diodoros (hereafter DS) explicitly invokes the name of Ktesias to justify troop numbers and other measurements that might seem to be on the high side of credible.

[3] P. Oxy. 22.2330, which has been assigned to Ktesias on the basis of a partial coincidence with a quotation from Demetrios's *De eloc.* §§ 213ff., contains a rather torrid love letter purporting to be from Struangaios to Zarinaia.

[4] Justin 1.1.9; Kephalion (*FGrHist* 93 F 1) mentions Semiramis's war with Zoroaster; Agathias *Hist.* 2.24 cites several writers of early Assyrian history to the effect that Zoroaster "invented" magic.

Erotikos §753d–e. In this tale, Semiramis was a courtesan (or concubine) who persuaded the infatuated Ninos to let her rule in his stead for five days (or one day) and then used her royal power to imprison him. The story is obviously based on the Babylonian festival called Sakaia, at which for five days masters are ruled by slaves and one of them puts on a stole resembling the king's (known from Berossos, *FGrHist* 680 F2). That festival setting has been used as the frame to display the legendary figure of a powerful, erotic Semiramis, who in Ktesias enslaved her first husband, Onnes (DS 2.5.2), regularly slept with the most handsome of her soldiers and then eliminated them (DS 2.13.4), and buried her husband Ninos shortly after marrying him (DS 2.7.1). That Semiramis might stand behind other grand figures in Greek fiction, such as the Persian Arsake in Heliodoros, but is not visible in the timid and tearful miss of A.IV.

The likeness of Xenophon's *Kyropaideia* to this novel has led to the suggestion (Weil 1902: 90–106) that the two are intentionally similar in structure—that our novel was intended as a "Ninopaideia," that is, as the chronicle of the education and coming of age of the military and political leader. There is an element of truth in this—both Ninos and his fiancée are on the brink of adulthood, and the novel seems, at least in these two fragments, to focus on their experiences during this transitional period. And Kyros, too, is involved with Armenians. But that the whole novel was about a young man undergoing his military apprenticeship with a soupçon of the erotic thrown in—as the Pantheia and Abradatas interlude in Xenophon—is difficult to demonstrate. On the contrary, as we argue above, the *Ninos* author seems to subordinate the military incidents that were no doubt appropriated from historical sources by employing them as a backdrop for the erotic element. This interior drama, which is so characteristic of the extant novels, is quite foreign to the idealized portrait of the education of princes.

AUTHORSHIP

In its language and style and its romantic tale of teen love, *Ninos* is clearly located in the same region of the literary map as Chariton's *Kallirhoe*. The connection between the two might be even closer. Chariton's city, Aphrodisias, was earlier known as Ninoe (Steph. Byz. s.v.), from Ninos, just as it had been even earlier called Lelegopolis, from its first founders, the Pelasgian Leleges. Chariton might have written both *Kallirhoe* and *Ninos*, or another Aphrodiasian author of the same time might have written the latter. Another possibility, often suggested, is that our *Ninos* fragments are the novel known to the *Souda* as the *Babyloniaka* by one Xenophon of Antioch (L. Levi 1895: 19). "Xenophon" appears to have served as a nom de plume for at least three novelists: the author of the extant *Ephesiaka*, known to the *Souda* as Xenophon of Ephesos; the author of the *Kypriaka*, "an erotic narrative, dealing with Kinyras, Myrrha, and Adonis," called by the *Souda* Xenophon of Kypros; and the Xenophon of Antioch mentioned above. Diogenes Laertios's Xenophon, who "worked up a storied monstrosity" (DL 2.59), may also be a novelist, perhaps one of the three already mentioned (Reeve 1971: 531 n. 1).

FRAGMENTS A AND B

Fragment A opens with Ninos, at age seventeen, returned from a successful military campaign, persuading his shy cousin that they should speak with their respective aunts, who are sisters, about setting an earlier date for their marriage. In his own interview with his aunt, Derkeia, he alludes to an oath he has sworn, and to his chastity, which he regards as untypical for a young man and a soldier. He speaks to her not in terms of a man first broaching the subject of his love for her daughter, but as one to whom the girl was already promised (A.IV.8), about a union with dynastic implications (A.IV.9–11). Apparently he speaks to sympathetic ears (A.IV.13–17). The girl, in turn, is so shy that she cannot even bring herself to speak to her aunt, Thambe, who, nevertheless, shrewdly sums up the situation and promises her assistance. Fragment B opens with the someone in great distress—almost certainly the girl. Ninos apparently calms her and swears an oath, and the two spend their time in mutual affection until he leaves on a military expedition against the Armenians. This seems to have been his first independent command, though still in some ways under his father's direction (B.II.4–9), and one upon which his career and status depended (B.III.32–34). B.II–III detail the material and troop deployment. Fragment B.III breaks off as Ninos is about to address his men before battle.

Interpretation of the fragments hinges on three issues: (1) the order A and B,[5] (2) whether the pair was married before the opening of B, and (3)

---

[5] Wilcken in his editio princeps based his ordering of the fragments on the observation that the first column on the back of Frag. A has a notation dating the account in the third year of Trajan, whereas the back of Frag. B has a notation of the second as well as the

whether Ninos courted his beloved with unbecoming ardor. Gaselee, Garin, Jenistová, and Perry have argued that details of the extant narrative dovetail more neatly if Wilcken's original order is reversed. Ninos's remarks in A seem naturally to refer to events in B (betrothal, first military campaign), and the AB order seems untidily to duplicate the military campaigns.

But the order of AB can only be reversed if the couple are not married at the opening of B.I. There the couple appears to be alone—the girl is reclining and, at Ninos's approach, leaps up and is pushed back onto the couch by him. At the end of B.I they spend all day together and Eros is said to "fan the flame" of their passion. Does this necessarily mean that they are married, or only engaged? It depends—Chaireas and Kallirhoe barely speak before their marriage, whereas Theagenes and Charikleia spend several books in each other's company while unwed. Also, Ninos and the girl are cousins as well as non-Greek, which may affect the social conventions. In any case, they seem to be alone together at the beginning of A, when they are clearly unmarried. We are, for reasons of the apparent cross-references in B to events in A, disposed to reverse Wilcken's order, and propose the following scenario for the opening of B: the girl, eager for her betrothal, learns at the time of the official ceremony that Ninos must go off for several months on a military expedition; she grows distraught, either because he is leaving her or because she supposes that he will forget her. He soothes her fears by pledging his faithfulness. She readily accepts his word, and they spend their time together in growing desire until the army is ready to march. This passion then fuels the scene in A.I, when Ninos returns.

The third point is easier to resolve. Piccolomini and others have speculated that Ninos's courtship was too ardent, and that he either

---

fourth year of Trajan. Wilcken cogently observed that it is more reasonable in these kinds of accounts to refer back to the second year in the fourth year than to refer forward in the second year to the fourth (1893: 165); therefore A (with the third year on its back) should precede B (with the notation of the second/fourth year). But although reasonable, the argument is not inevitable. Furthermore, Wilcken's order would only be valid if the original roll was reused intact for the daybook; if it was cannibalized (that is, sections cut off of the original roll and reassembled randomly, whenever an additional length was necessary), then it could easily happen that an earlier portion of the Ninos text was cut off and reattached after a later portion (in fact, this would be the natural result, if the scribe writing the daybook began cutting sections from the end of the *Ninos* roll). In any case, Wilcken himself concedes that his ordering is precarious (p. 184). We wish to express our thanks to L. Koenen, who verified the condition of the back for us.

frightened the modest young girl or actually tried to rape her. Not only is such conduct unbecoming a romantic hero (as Ninos himself makes clear in his remarks to his aunt at A.III.36–IV.4), but the accusation of sexual misconduct is illusory, the combined product of imaginative restorations in B.I and the misunderstanding of Thambe's speech at A.V. Thambe's argument is primarily with herself; she seems to raise the possibility of Ninos's overbold treatment of his fiancée, only to reject it. The speech falls into two parts: lines 12–21, in which she argues that her son, although now a doughty warrior, has behaved impeccably toward her niece; and lines 21–25, in which she decides that although he is naturally eager for marriage, he has not for this reason tried to coerce her into an early marriage. Thambe concludes that tears result from the girl's own modesty and disinclination to bring up the subject of marriage, not from dislike of the marriage itself.

Fragment C

The name of Ninos in line 42 securely attaches Fragment C to the *Ninos* novel. Its discovery raises two central questions for our understanding of the plot: (1) the relationship of Fragment C to Fragments A and B, and (2) whether Semiramis was present with Ninos during any part of this misadventure. The column opens with the vocative "lady" (*gunai*), which refers either to Ninos's wife or to some other woman. Whoever she is, she does not appear to be in the company of the shipwrecked men at the column end. Clearly, if the vocative refers to Semiramis, C must follow both A and B regardless of their relative order, for the title *gunai* would be appropriate only if Ninos and Semiramis are now married. (Elsewhere in the novel fragments, Ninos's cousin is referred to either as *korē* or as *parthenos*, appropriate designations of her unmarried state.) Even if *gunai* refers to someone else, C still fits better after A and B.

Because Kolchis (line 13) is in Armenia, it is tempting to connect C closely with the incidents of B—Ninos's expedition against Armenia— but this must be rejected. B.II, which includes details of the size and configuration of the army, makes no mention of ships or marines and would appear to be describing a landlocked expedition. Further, as Wilcken observed (Norsa 1945: 194–95), this incident more appropriately suits Ninos's war against "the barbarian nations that live along the Pontus as far as Tanais" mentioned at Diodoros 2.2.3. If so, it must have taken place after Ninos's return from his first expedition against the

Armenians, and could have followed fairly rapidly upon A, in which he alludes prophetically to "sea voyages" (A.III.20–21). The fragment itself makes no mention of naval engagements or of the enemy, and though they are not much to go on, lines 9–13 suggest that the shipwreck resulted from natural phenomena.

Whether Semiramis accompanied Ninos on this adventure is more difficult to assess. Lines 18–50 appear to present the details of a shipwreck, externally narrated. If Ninos is speaking in the opening lines of the column, he must break off and the external narrative must begin in the lacunose lines 14–15. Alternatively, the narrator is the same throughout, and the whole is a report of Ninos's misadventures to a third party—the mysterious "lady." In either case, the title could refer to Ninos's wife or to another woman, but in the novelists, at least, the vocative *gunai* is normally used to refer to a woman other than one's own wife.

From Diodoros (Ktesias) there is ample testimony of Semiramis's participation in military affairs—indeed, quite apart from the presence of Ninos—but the character of the young girl with whom Ninos is in love in this novel seems scarcely suited to such hardy activity. Further, there are two mosaics plausibly linked to this novel, one from Alexandretta, the other from Daphne, which portray Ninos contemplating a small portrait of a woman who must be his beloved, whether or not they are married. This suggests to us a separation perhaps more serious in nature than Ninos merely off on his military adventures alone. If the travails of young lovers in other novels are anything to judge by, Fragment C will belong to a series of adventures and testings for the two who, as a result of this shipwreck, are forcibly separated (whether Semiramis was present on a different ship, parked in some foreign kingdom, or even at home patiently awaiting his return).

Description of A and B

P. Berol. 6926 (= P^2 2616) consists of two fragments from a well-made book roll. Fragment A (measuring 30.0 × 38.0 cm) preserves the right half of the first column, three middle columns complete, and two-thirds of a fifth column. Fragment B (measuring 30.5 × 19.3 cm) holds the right half of a first column, an intact middle column, and two-thirds of a third. Columns A.V and B.III can be restored with some confidence, A.I and B.I with only limited success.

The papyrus is light brown and of good quality; the joins between the individual sheets that made up the roll are visible at the close of A.I, the beginning of A.III, the middle of A.IV, and the beginning of B.II. Sheets average 13.5 × 30.0 cm, a dimension that appears to be at the low end of the range for sheet size (*Typology* 47–48). The columns of writing themselves average only 21 cm in height: the other 9.0 cm belong to the generous upper and lower margins; the intercolumnia average 1.5 cm. The eight columns show a pronounced tilt to the right; the last lines of the columns of Fragment A begin five letters further to the left than the first lines of the column; for Fragment B, the last lines of the column begin about three letters further to the left. (It is tempting to imagine that increasing tilt could be used as a determinant for column order, but observation of other rolls indicates that tilt does not necessarily progress at a steady rate; it can maintain itself or even decrease over several columns.) There are between twenty and twenty-four letters per line; spacing and letter size is quite regular at the beginning of the line, but the scribe frequently crowds his letters at the end. In restoring the opening of columns in particular, previous editors, with the exception of Wilcken, have taken this too little into account.

A *terminus ante quem* for the date of the manuscript is provided by the document written on the back, which bears accounts in part dated to the third year of Trajan (100–101 C.E.); *GLH* (pl. 11a and b) provides documentary parallels between 60 and 90 C.E. This of course would allow only a short period before the *Ninos* was reused (no more than the lifetime of its owner).

The condition of the text is excellent; the original scribe made several corrections, and there is some evidence of a second hand as well (e.g., A.II.12). There appears to be only one uncorrected error, the omission of ϲ on αἰϲχρῶϲ at A.II.28 (but since the papyrus is abraded at this point, it is impossible to be certain). Corrections are of three kinds: marginal addition (A.II.12, B.V.19), expunging dot (A.II.17, B.II.19), and overwriting of the original text (A.II.18). Punctuation includes paragraphi, spacing, and high and middle stops (usually in some combination); a dicolon appears at B.II.36. Iota adscript is always written, tremata occasionally. The scribe sometimes neglects elision, sometimes marks it (e.g., με ἐρεῖϲ at A.III.36, but μ' ἐκδέχονται at A.III.21; δὲ αὐ- at B.I.9, but οὐδ' αὐ- at B.I.20). The dialect is Attic, though a number of non-Attic words and forms appear (Dihle 1978–80: 55 n. 32). There are three vulgar spellings: A.I.31, V.26, B.III.6. In general, the papyrus gives the appearance of a carefully made and well-maintained book roll.

COLUMN A.I

[±11]πλουϲε[..]νον
[±12]αρεϲτι π ...
[±12] ὁ ϲφόδρα ἐρῶν
4 [±10]όμενον ῳ ̣ χα
[±10]ὑπολαμβ[άν]ων
[±10 κίν]δυνον ἐν ὧι
[±12]ν τῆϲ εὐχῆϲ α-
8 [±12]ἐλπίδα ̣[.]α̣
[±12] πολὺ καὶ ἡ ϲυγή-
[θηϲ ταῖϲ γυναι]ξὶν αἰδὼϲ ἀ[π]ε-
[ϲτέρηϲεν ±5]ν θάρϲοϲ · ὁ δὲ
12 [±8 γαμ]εῖν ἐβούλ[ε]το
[±11]ειϲ καὶ ταῦτα
[±11]κηϲαν τῶν α ̣ ̣ α
[±11]ων γονέων α[̣ ̣]
16 [±11]ω πλανήϲεϲθαι
[±11] χρόνουϲ ἐν οἷϲ
[±5 ἀδιάφθ]ορον καὶ ἀπεί-
[ρατον Ἀφροδί]τηϲ φυλάξειν
20 [±7 ὠμω]μόκει · ἀπιθα-
[±8]ϲ φυλακῇ[ϲ] τον
[±10] γενήϲεϲθαι
[±8 πρὸ]ϲ τὴν ἀναβο-
24 [λὴν ±8] ἀλλὰ δέξεϲ-
[θαι ±8] ̣ αμεν δουλω-
[±12] λέγοντα καὶ

Supplements that are clearly too long for the available space have not been printed. Supplements are those of Wilcken unless otherwise stated in apparatus or notes. Kaibel's conjectures are recorded in Wilcken, Diels's in Piccolomini 1893a and b, Schubart's in Zimmermann 1931.

A.I: 2. π]ά̣ρεϲτ̣ι Lav., γ]άρ ἐϲτι Schub. 3. ὁ Νίνοϲ] ὁ ϲφόδρα ἐρῶν Lav. 9–10. ἡ ϲυγ- ή|[θηϲ] Zimm. 10. [γυναι]ξὶν Stadtm. 10–11. ἀ[π]ε|[ϲτέρηϲεν αὐτὴ]ν Stadtm. 16. [πόρρ]ω Zimm. 18–19. suppl. Lav. 20.] ̣ οκει · pap., [διομω]μόκει Zimm. 20–21. ἀπίθα|[νον] Schub. 21. τον Schub., των Wil. 24. ἀλλ᾽ ἀδέωϲ Zimm.

] he, the intensely loving
4   ]
] he, supposing
] danger in which
] of the prayer
8   ] hope
] much and the accustomed
] modesty for women
[deprived her] of courage. But he
12   ] wanted to [marry] . . .
] and these
] of the
] of the parents'
16   ] would wander
] times in which
] unblemished and without [experi-
ence of Aphrodite] would preserve
20   ] had sworn. . . .
] of the preservation
] would become
] for the post-
24   ponement [——] but would receive
] enslave
] speaking and

[±12   ]μεν οὐδὲ το
28   [±12   ]η ὑπέμειναν
[±12   ]αυτο βουλομε-
[ν-   ±11   ]την πεῖραν
[±12   ]ς ἀνένεγκεν
32   [±10   οὔ]τε ἡ παῖς ἐτόλ-
[μ-   ±10   ]ντο δὲ τοὺς
[±12   ἐ]θάρρουν γὰρ ἀμ-
[φότεροι πρὸς τ]ὰς τηθίδας μᾶλ-
36   [λον ἢ τὰς αὐτῶν μ]ητέρας. ὁ
[μὲν οὖν Νίνος π]ρὸς τὴν Δερ-
[κείαν ἀφικόμε]νος· "ὦ μῆτερ,"

COLUMN A.II

εἶπεν· "εὐορκήςας ἀφῖγμαι
καὶ εἰς τὴν ςὴν ὄψιν καὶ εἰς
τὰς περιβολὰς τῆς ἐμοὶ τερ-
4   πνοτάτης ἀνεψιᾶς. καὶ τοῦτο ἴςτωςαν μὲν οἱ θεοὶ πρῶτον ὥςπερ δὴ καὶ ἴςαςιν· τε-
κμηριώςομαι δὲ κἀγὼ τά-
8   χα καὶ τῶι νῦν λόγωι. διελ-
θὼν γὰρ τοςαύτην γῆν καὶ
τοςούτων δεςπόςας ἐθνῶν
ἢ δορικτήτων ἢ πατρώιωι
12   κράτει θεραπευόντων με

---

27. οὐδὲν το Schub.   27–28. οὐδὲν τό|[τε] Lav.   28. ὕπε pap.   31–32. ἀλλ᾽
οὔτε ὁ Νίνο]ς ἀνένεγκεν | [πρὸς τὴν μητέρα οὔ]τε ἡ παῖς Picc.   32. ἦ παῖς Wil.
32–33. ἐτόλ|[μηςεν] Wil., ἐτόλ|[μα] Picc.   34. ἐ]θάρρουν Weil   35. [πρὸς] Picc.
36. [αὐτῶν] Picc., [ἑαυτῶν] Wil., [ἰδίας] Zimm.   ]ητερας· pap.   36–37. ὁ | [μὲν
οὖν Νίνος π]ρὸς Vit., ὁ | [δὲ Νίνος ἔλεγε π]ρὸς Wil.   38. ἀφικόμε]νος Vit., τραπόμε]νος
Levi, διαλεγόμε]νος Picc., δεόμε]νος Lav.
A.II: 4. πνο, ψιας· pap. The function of the dot above π is unclear.   5. ἴςτωςαν pap.
6. ἴςαςιν· pap.   8. χα pap.   12. κ added above κ of κρατει by second hand.

34

     ] not even the
28   ] they endured
     ] wanting it
     ] the attempt
     ] s/he referred
32   ] nor did the maiden dare
     ] and they . . .
     ] for they both felt confidence
     ] in their aunts more
36   [than in their own] mothers.
     [So Ninos came to] Der-
     keia, "O mother,"

                COLUMN A.II

     he said, "faithful to my oath I have now come
     into your sight and into
     the embraces of my
4   cousin who is so dear to me.
     And first let the gods know this,
     as indeed they are aware,
     and as I shall myself confirm
8   by this present declaration:
     Having traversed so much land and
     become master of so many peoples
     who submitted to my spear or because of my father's
12   power served me

καὶ προϲκυνούντων ἐδυνά-
μην εἰϲ κόρον ἐκπλῆϲαι πᾶϲαν ἀπόλαυϲιν· ἦν τε ἄν μοι
16 τοῦτο ποιήϲαντι δι' ἐλάττονοϲ
ἴϲωϲ ἡ ἀνεψιὰ πόθου· νῦν δὲ
ἀδιάφθοροϲ ἐληλυθὼϲ ὑπ[ὸ]
τοῦ θεοῦ νικῶμαι καὶ ὑπὸ
20 τῆϲ ἡλικίαϲ. ἑπτακαιδέ-
κατον ἔτοϲ ἄγω καθάπερ
οἶϲθαϲ καὶ ἐνεκρίθην μὲν εἰϲ
ἄνδραϲ ἤδη πρὸ ἐνιαυτοῦ· παῖϲ
24 δὲ ἄχρι νῦν εἰμι νήπιοϲ; καὶ
εἰ μὲν οὐκ ᾐϲθανόμην Ἀφροδίτηϲ μακάριοϲ ἂν ἦν τῆϲ
ϲτερρότητοϲ· νῦν δὲ τῆϲ ὑ-
28 μετέραϲ θυγατρὸϲ οὐκ [α]ἰϲχρῶ⟨ϲ⟩
ἀλλὰ ὑμῶν ἐθελη ϲάντω[ν αἰ-]
χμάλωτοϲ ἄχρι τίνοϲ ἑαλω-
κὼϲ ἀρνήϲομαι; καὶ ὅτι μὲν
32 οἱ ταύτηϲ τῆϲ ἡλικίαϲ ἄνδρεϲ
ἱκανοὶ γαμεῖν δῆλον· πόϲοι
γὰρ ἄχρι πεντεκαίδεκα ἐφυ-
λάχθηϲαν ἐτῶν ἀδιάφθοροι;
36 νόμοϲ δὲ βλάπτει με οὐ γε-
γραμμένοϲ ἄλλωϲ δὲ ἔθει
φλυάρωι πληρούμενοϲ ἐπειδὴ

---

15. ϲαναπολαυϲιν· pap.   17. ὄιϲωϲ pap.   ποθου· pap.   18. ελην υ, apparently corrected by first hand   20. τηϲηλικιαϲ· pap.   24. νηπιοϲ· pap.
27. τητοϲ· pap.   29. ϋμων pap.   31. αρνηϲομαι· pap., ἀρνήϲομαι; Lav.
33. δηλον· pap.

and paid obeisance to me, I could have
taken my full satisfaction of
every pleasure. If I had
16　done so my desire might be weaker
perhaps for my cousin. But though
I have returned in fact with my chastity intact,
I am being defeated by the god and
20　my maturing years. I am in
my seventeenth year, as
you know, and have been enrolled among
the men for a year;
24　yet to this day am I still a helpless child?
Had I not become aware of Aphrodite,
I might still have been rejoicing in my
impregnable strength. But now as
28　your daughter's prisoner of war—an honorable captivity,
of course, and blessed by your consent
—that I have been captured,
how long must I deny? That
32　men of such an age
are ready to wed, no one doubts: for how many
past fifteen
keep their purity?
36　But I am made to suffer
by a law unwritten,
one stupidly sanctioned by foolish convention, since

COLUMN A.III

παρ' ἡμῖν πεντεκαίδεκα
ὡς ἐπὶ τὸ πλεῖςτον ἐτῶν
γαμοῦνται παρθένοι. ὅτι δὲ
4   ἡ φύςις τῶν τοιούτων ςυνό-
δων κάλλιςτός ἐςτι νόμος,
τίς ἂν εὖ φρονῶν ἀντείποι;
τετρακαίδεκα ἐτῶν κυο-
8   φοροῦςιν γυναῖκες καί τινες
ν[ὴ] Δία καὶ τίκτουςιν. ἡ δὲ
ςὴ θυγάτηρ οὐδὲ γαμήςεται;
δύ' ἔτη περιμείνωμεν, εἴ-
12 ποις ἄν· ἐκδεχώμεθα, μῆτερ,
εἰ καὶ ἡ Τύχη περιμενεῖ. θνη-
τὸ[ς] δὲ ἀνὴρ θνητὴν ἡρμο-
ςάμην παρθένον· καὶ οὐδὲ
16 τοῖς κοινοῖς τούτοις ὑπευ-
[θυ]νός εἰμι μόνον, νόςοις λέ-
[γω] καὶ Τύχηι πολλάκις καὶ τοὺς
[ἐπ]ὶ τῆς οἰκείας ἑςτίας ἠρεμοῦν-
20 τας ἀν[α]ιρούςηι· ἀλλὰ ναυτιλίαι μ' ἐκδέχονται καὶ ἐκ πολέμων πόλεμοι καὶ οὐδὲ ἄτολ-
μος ἐγὼ καὶ βοηθὸν ἀςφαλεί-
24 ας δειλίαν προκαλυπτόμενος,
ἀλλ' οἷον [ο]ἶςθας, ἵνα μὴ φορτι-
κὸς ὦ λ[ε]γων· ςπευςάτω δή
τι βαςιλεία, ςπευςάτω τι ἐπι-
28 θυμία, ςπευςάτω τὸ ἀςτάθμη-
τον καὶ ἀτέκμαρτον τῶν
ἐκδεχομένων με χρόνων,

A.III: 3. παρθενοι· pap.   9. τικτουςιν· pap.   11–12. εἴποις Kaib.   13. περι
μενει· pap., περιμενεῖ Kaib.   15. παρθενον· pap.   17. νόςοις Picc., Müller,
νότοις Wil.   20. τας, ρουςηι· pap.   26. κος, ωι, λεγων· pap.   27. ἡ Wil., τι
Gronewald (twice)

our maidens
as a rule
marry when they are fifteen. But that
4 nature itself
is the best law for deciding such conjunctions,
what sensible man would deny?
Women at fourteen years can get
8 pregnant, and some
(God knows) actually bear children.
Will your daughter not even marry?
'Let us wait for two years,'
12 you might say; let us accept this condition, mother,
if Chance too will wait.
I am a mortal man and have
joined myself to a mortal maiden;
16 I am subject not only to the common calamities
—I mean diseases
and Chance, which often strikes even those
sitting quietly by their own hearth—
20 but sea journeys too
await me, and wars
upon wars; and I am certainly no coward
nor as an assistant to my safety
24 will I hide behind a veil of cravenness.
I am the man you know me to be, so I need not tiresomely
proclaim it. Let
royalty urge some haste, let strong
28 desire urge some haste, let the uncertainty
and incalculability of the
times that lie ahead of me urge haste.

προλαβέτω τι καὶ φθήτω καὶ
32 τὸ μονογενὲς ἡμῶν ἀμφο-
τέρων, ἵνα κἂν ἄλλως ἡ Τύχη
κακ[όν] τι βουλεύηται περὶ ἡ-
μῶν, καταλείπωμεν ὑμῖν ἐνέ-
36 χυρα. ἀναιδῆ τάχα με ἐρεῖς περὶ τούτων διαλεγόμενον· ἐ-
γὼ δὲ ἀναιδὴς ἂν ἤμην λάθραι

COLUMN A.IV

πειρῶν καὶ κλεπτομένην
ἀπόλαυσιν ἁρπάζων καὶ νυ-
κτὶ καὶ μέθηι καὶ θεράπον-
4 τι καὶ τιθηνῶι κοινούμενος
τὸ πάθος. οὐκ ἀναιδὴς δὲ
μητρὶ περὶ γάμων θυγατρὸς
εὐκταίων διαλεγόμενος
8 καὶ ἀπαιτῶν ἃ ἔδωκας καὶ
δεόμενος τὰς κοινὰς τῆς
[ο]ἰκίας καὶ τῆς βασιλείας ἁπά-
σης εὐχὰς μὴ εἰς τοῦτον ἀ-
12 ναβάλλεσθαι τὸν καιρόν, ὃς
ἐφ' ὑμῖν οὐκ ἔς[τ]αι." ταῦτα πρὸς
βουλομένην ἔλεγε τὴν Δερ-
κείαν καὶ τάχ[α] βραδύνας προ-
16 τέραν ἂν αὐτὴν ἐβιάσατο τοὺς
περὶ τούτων ποιήσασθαι λό-
γους· ἀκκισαμένη δ' οὖν βρα-
χέα συνηγορήσειν ὑπισχνεῖ-
20 το. τῆι κόρηι δ' ἐν ὁμοίοις πά-
θεσιν οὐχ ὁμοία παρρησία τῶν
λόγων ἦν πρὸς τὴν Θάμβην.

A.IV: 5. τοπαθος· pap.   13. εφ, ες[.]αι· pap.   18. γους· pap.

Let the fact that each of us is an
32   only child count somewhat in favor of our haste,
so that even if Chance
contrive some disaster for us,
we may leave you a token of our union.
36   You may call me shameless
for speaking of these matters,
but I truly would have been shameless if in secret

COLUMN A.IV

I had tried her virtue and stolen
my enjoyment undercover,
sharing my passion with the night, the wine-cup,
4   the trusted servant or nurse.
I am not shameless in discussing
with her mother a daughter's
longed-for marriage, nor
8   in asking you for what you have already offered,
nor in begging that the common
hopes of our house and of the entire kingdom
be not postponed
12   until the time that
will no longer be in your power." His words
to Derkeia fell on willing ears;
in fact, if he had delayed any longer in all probability
16   he would have forced her to bring
the subject up first herself.
As it was she feigned resistance briefly
and then promised to speak for him.
20   The maiden, however, though her feelings were similar,
had no eloquence comparable
to his as she stood before Thambe.

ἡ γὰρ παρθέν[οc ἐντὸc τ]ῆc γυ-
24 ναικωνίτιδ[οc ζῶcα ο]ὐκ εὐ-
πρεπεῖc ἐπο[ίει τοὺc λό]γουc
αὐτῆc · αἰτ[ουμένη] δὲ και-
ρὸν ἐδάκρυc[ε καὶ ἐβο]ύλε-
28 το τι λέγειν, [πρὶν δ' ἄρξ]αcθαι
ἀπεπαύετο · [τὴν γὰρ μ]έλ-
λῃcιν αὐτόμ[ατ]ον [cημ]ήνα-
cα λόγου, τὰ χείλη μὲν ἂν διῆι-
32 ρε καὶ ἀνέβλεψεν ὥ[cπερ τ]ι λέ-
ξουcα · ἐφθέγγετο δ[ὲ τελ]έωc
οὐδέν · κατερρήγνυ[το δὲ] αὐτῆc δάκρυα · καὶ ἠρυ[θαίνο]ν-
36 το μὲν αἱ παρειαὶ πρὸ[c τὴν] α[ἰ-]
δῶ τῶν λόγων. ἐξ ὑ[πογύου]
δὲ πάλιν ἀρχομένηc [πειρᾶ-]
cθαι λέγειν, ὠχραίνο[ντο διὰ]

COLUMN A.V

τὸ δέοc · μεταξὺ [γὰρ ἦν φόβου]
καὶ ἐπιθυμίαc καὶ [ἐλπίδοc καὶ]
αἰδοῦc, θραcυνομέ[νου μὲν οὖν]
4 τοῦ πάθουc, ἀποδερ[ύcηc δὲ]
τῆc γνώμηc, ἐκυ[. . . . .]
καὶ μετ[ὰ π]ολλοῦ κ[. . . . . ἡ Θάμ-]

23–26. ἡ γὰρ παρθέν[ων ἐντὸc τ]ῆc γυ|ναικωνίτιδ[οc ζωὴ ο]ὐκ εὐ|πρεπεῖc ἐπο[ρίζετο
λό]γουc | αὐτῆ⟨ι⟩ Weil.   26. αυτηc · pap.   28. [πρὶν δ' ἄρξ]αcθαι Kaib., [ἐν τῶι
δ' ἄρξ]αcθαι Picc., [πρὶν δὲ φθέγξ]αcθαι Vit.   29. [τάχα δὲ] Wil., [τότε δὲ] Lav.
29–30. Kaib. supplements   33. [τελε]ίωc Kaib.   38–39. [πειρᾶ]|cθαι Picc., [βού-
λε]|cθαι Wil.   39. [διὰ] Levi, [καὶ] Wil.
A.V: 1. δεοc · pap.   [γὰρ ἦν φόβου] Diels, [δ' οὖcα φόβου] Levi, [γὰρ ἦν ὁμοῦ] Lav., [δ'
ἦν ἐλπίδοc] Zimm.   2. [φόβου καὶ] Cast., [παρθενίαc] Levi, [πλήρηc μὲν] Stadtm.,
[ὀκνούcηc μὲν] Diels   3. θραcυνομέ[νου Diels, θραcυνομέ[νη Stadtm.   4. Diels
suppl.   5. ἐκύ[μαινε cφόδρα] Diels, ἔκυ[πτε cιωπῇ] Stadtm., ἐκύ[μαινεν ἅμα] Zimm.
6. κ[λόνου] Diels, κ[όcμου] Weil.   6–7. [ἡ δὲ Θάμ]|βη Diels, [ἡ Θάμ]|βη Wil.

For as a virgin [living] within the
24   women's quarters she was unable
to fashion her arguments with such finesse.
Asking for a chance
to speak to her, she burst into tears and had
28   something ready to say; [but before she could begin]
she would cut herself short. For whenever
she spontaneously signaled her desire
to speak, she would open her lips and
32   look up as if about
to say something, but no [complete] word came out.
Tears burst out
and a blush spread
36   over her cheeks as she shrunk
from what she wanted to say. When of a [sudden]
she began again to [try]
to speak, her cheeks grew pale [with]

COLUMN A.V

fear. [For she was] between [fear]
and desire and [hope and]
shame; so while her emotions were being strengthened,
4   the conviction to express them was wanting,
[. . .]
with much . . . Thambe

βη τὰ [δά]κρυα ταῖς χ[ερςὶν ἀπο-]
8 μάττο[υςα] προςέτ[αττε θαρ-]
ρεῖν [καὶ] ὅτι βούλοιτ[ο διαλέ-]
γεςθαι. ὡς δὲ οὐδὲν [ἤνυςεν,]
ἀλλὰ ὁμοίοις ἡ παρθέ[νος κατεί-]
12 χετο κακοῖς, "ἅπαν[τος," ἔφη,]
"μοι λόγου κάλλιον ἡ [ςιωπὴ]
διαλέγεται. μή τι μέ[μφηι τὸν]
ἐμὸν υ[ἱ]όν; οὐδὲν μὲ[ν γὰρ]
16 τετόλμηκεν οὐδὲ θ[ραςὺς ἡ-]
μῖν ἀπὸ τῶν κατορθω[μάτων]
καὶ τροπαίων ἐπανε[λθὼν]
οἷ[α πο]λεμιςτὴς πεπ[αρώινη-]
20 κεν εἰς ςέ. τάχα δὲ κ[οὐκ ἂν ἐςι-]
ώπας τοιούτου γενομ[ένου. ἀλλὰ]
βραδὺς ὁ νόμος τ[οῖς ἐφω-]
ρίοις γάμων. ςπεύδει δ[ὲ γαμεῖν]
24 ὁ ἐμὸς υἱός. οὐδέ, διὰ τ[οῦτ' εἰ]
κλαίεις, βιαςθῆναί ςε δ[εῖ." καὶ]
ἅμα μειδιῶςα περιέβα[λλεν]
αὐτὴν καὶ ἠςπάζετο. χ[αρᾶι δὲ]
28 φθέγξαςθαι μέν τι οὐδ[ὲ τό-]
τε ἐτόλμηςεν ἡ κόρη, [παλ-]
λομένην δὲ τὴν καρδί[αν τοῖς]
ςτέρνοις αὐτῆς προςθε[ῖςα]
32 καὶ λιπαρέςτερον κατα[φιλοῦ-]
ςα τοῖς τε πρότερον δάκ[ρυςι]
καὶ τῆι τότε χαρᾶι μόνο[ν οὐ-]

---

10. γεςθαι· pap.   12. χετοκακοις· pap.   [ἔφη] Weil, [τοῦτο] Wil., [φηςιν] Zimm.
13. ἡ [ςιωπὴ] Weil, ἡ [θάμβη] Wil.   14. μή τι μέ[μφηι τὸν] Weil, μή τι μέ[μψη] Wil.
15. υ[.]ον· pap.   19. ὡς Zimm.   πεπ·[pap. (trace of high letter before break)
19–20. πεπ[αρώινη]||κεν Picc. πεπ[είρα]||κεν Wil.   22–23. [ἐφω]||ρίοις Brink., μακα]|ρί-
οις? Wil., νυμ]|φίοις Weil, but traces more suited to ρ than φ   23. γαμων· pap.
δ[ὲ Lav., δ[ὴ τέλος Stadtm., δ' [οὖν Zimm., δ[έ τι Gronewald   24. υιος· pap.
τ[οῦτ' εἰ] Brink., τ[οῦτο] Wil.   25. δ[εῖ καὶ] Brink., δ[εῖν'] Wil.   26. μιδιωςα
pap.   περιέβα[λεν] Lav.   27. ηςπαζετο· pap.   χ[αρᾶι δὲ] Vit., δ[ι' αἰδῶ δὲ]
Garin, δ[ιὰ δέος δὲ] Diels.   32–33. Kaib. supplements

wiped away her tears with her [hands] and
8   urged her to be brave
and to talk about what she wanted.
But when [she accomplished] nothing,
but the virgin continued to be gripped by the
12   same distress, [she said:]
"Your [silence] communicates better in my opinion than any
                                                    speech.

Surely [you are] not finding fault
with my son? [For] he has done nothing
16   forward; he has not in insolence
returned to us from his victories
and triumphs. He has not
[forced himself drunkenly] on you as a proud warrior.
20   I don't suppose you [would have been] silent
if this had happened. [But]
the observance of custom is slow for [those
who are ripe] for marriage. My son is anxious [to marry],
24   but [if] you are weeping on this account,
you should not be compelled."
She smiled and embraced her
with warm affection. [In her joy]
28   not [even then] could the girl
bring herself to utter a word,
but rested her beating heart
against her aunt's breast and
32   [caressed her] more earnestly:
by her former tears
and her present joy, she

[χ]ὶ καὶ λάλος ἔδοξεν εἶνα[ι ὧν]
36 ἐβούλετο· cυνῆλθον οὗ[ν αἱ]
[ἀ]δελφαὶ καὶ προτέρα μὲν [ἡ Δερ-]
[κ]εία, "περὶ cπουδαίων," ἔφ[η]

COLUMN B.I

[. . . . . . .]ου γὰρ ἀπελείφθη.
[. . . . . τ]ῆc μητρὸc εντο-
[. . . . . . . ηκ]ολούθηcεν, ακα-
4 [. . . . . . .] καὶ περιερρηγμέ-
[ν . . . . οὐδ]αμῶc ἱεροπρεπήc,
[. . . . .]ε δακρύων καὶ κο-
[. . . . . ἐ]κ τοῦ cχήματοc
8 [. . . . .] εἰρχθεῖc' ἅτε με-
[. . . . . . ἀνα]πηδήcαcαν δὲ αὐ-
[τὴν ἀπὸ κλί]νηc καὶ βουλομέ-
[ν . . . .]αι ταῦτα, πιέcαc
12 [. . . . . χ]ερcὶν ὁ Νίνοc
[. . . . .]c," εἰπών, "cοὶ με
[. . . . .]θενων ἔcτω καὶ

B.I: 2. [ὁ Νίνοc] Weil, [χωρίc] Stadtm., [μακράν] Picc., [κἀκείνη] Zimm.   2–3. ἐν
το‖[cούτῳ] Picc., το‖[ιούτωι] Lav.   3. [ἠκο]λούθηcεν Diels, ἀλλ᾽ ἠκο]λλούθηcεν (so
pap.) Wil.   3–4. ἀκα‖[τάcχετοc] Wil., ἀκα‖[χημένοc] Weil, ἀκα‖[τάπαυcτοc] Zimm.
4–5. περιερρηγμέ‖[νη Levi, περιερρηγμέ‖[νοc Wil.   5. ἱερο pap.   6. [ἔκλαι]ε
Wil., [καὶ ἔκλαι]ε Lav., [πάντ᾽ ἔπλης]ε Stadtm., [εἴcηει δ]ὲ Weil   6–7. κο‖[ρυ-
βαντιῶν] Picc., κο‖[πετοῦ, πάνυ] Stadtm., κο‖[πτόμενοc] Zimm.   8. εἰρχθεῖc ἅτε
Stadtm., εἰρχθεῖcά τε Lav.,]ειρχθεῖc ἅτε με- Wil., [οἱονεὶ ἐξ]ειρχθεὶc Picc., [ἀλόγωc
ἐξ]ειρχθεὶc Weil   8–9. με‖[μηνυῖα] Stadtm., με‖[μηνώc] Picc., με‖[τρίος ὤν] Weil
10. [τῆc κλί]νηc Zimm.   11. [διακωλῦc]αι Vit., [ἐμποδίc]αι Levi, [ἀπέρχεcθ]αι
Picc., [ἐλέγξ]αι Weil, [ἀποκλαῦc]αι Stadtm., [ὀνειδίc]αι Zimm.   12. ταῖc χερ-
cίν Wil., [πράωc] Vit., [χεῖραc] Weil, [ἀμφοτέραιc] Stadtm., [ἐμπαθῶc] Zimm., [εἰc
τὴν κλίνην] Levi   13. [ἔλεγε· ὅτι]c? Wil., [ἆρα ἦν τι]c Levi, [ἔλεγεν· ἦν τι]c Picc.,
[ἀλλ᾽ ἔφη, παρῆν τι]c Zimm.   14. [φθορέα παρ]θένων Picc., [διαφθορέα
παρ]θένων Lav.   14–15. καὶ ‖ [τοῦτο· ἐμὲ τ]ῆc Picc., καὶ ‖ [μὴν οὐκ ἡ τῆc ἐμ]ῆc
Lav., καὶ‖[τα μειδιώcηc τ]ῆc Zimm.

46

seemed practically to be speaking

36   [her] thoughts. So the sisters met together,

and Derkeia spoke first:

"Concerning serious. . . ."

COLUMN B.I

] for she/he was left.

] of the mother

] she/he followed

4   ] and with torn garments

] and in no way fit for a sacred ceremony

] with tears and

] from the arrangement

8   ] closed in like a

] and to her leaping up

] from the couch and wanting

] to . . . these things, pushing her

12   ] hands Ninos

] having said, "For you

] virgins let there be and

[. . . . .]ῃϲ μητρὸϲ καὶ η

16 [. . . . .]ϲ οὕτωϲ ἀγομε-

[. . . . .]ϲαι. τάχα που κἀγὼ

[. . . . .]ϲ · οὐ δὴ βούλομαι

[. . . . .]ων μᾶλλον ἢ προ

20 [. . . . .] ̣ νεύεϲθαι. οὐδ᾽ αυ

[. . . . .]ϲα μ[ὴ] ὑπονοή-

[. . . . . . . π]ίϲτιϲ ἔϲτω τοῦ

[. . . . . τ]ὰ ὁμοϲθέντα · τὸ

24 [. . . . . . τοῦ ὅρ]κου πεπιϲτε-

[. . . . . . ” οὗ]τοι δὲ πανήμε-

[ροι ϲυνῆϲαν] ἀλλήλοιϲ, ὅϲα μὴ

[ὑπὸ τῶν ϲτρατ]ιωτικῶν ἀφείλ-

28 [κετο · οὐδὲ ἐλ]λιπῶϲ ὁ Ἔρωϲ ἀνερ-

[ρίπιζεν αὐτού]ϲ · κόρωι μὲν το

[. . . . .] διαιτήϲεωϲ ἀμ-

[. . . . .]τε δ᾽ εἰϲ τὰϲ ἐπι-

32 [. . . . . χ]ερϲὶ διαζεύξε-

[ωϲ . . . .]μενοϲ. οὔπω

[. . . . . ἀκ]μάζοντοϲ

15–16. ἡ | [πίϲτιϲ οὐχ] Picc., ἡ | [τῆϲ ϲῆϲ πίϲτιϲ] Lav., ἡ | [γυνὴ κατηφήϲ ·] Zimm.
18. [δηλώϲω] Vit.]ϲ · pap., [τοῖϲ λόγοι]ϲ · Picc., [ϲαφῶ]ϲ · Zimm. 19. [νυμφίοϲ
νῦν] Diels, [ἀκρατὴϲ] Picc., [ἀκρατὴϲ νῦν] Weil, γαμέτηϲ νῦν] Levi, τὰ πάντα ἡμ]ῶν
Zimm. 19–20. πρό|[τερον] Wil. 20. [πορ]νεύεϲθαι Picc., Levi, [εἰρω]νεύεϲθαι
Weil, [κινδ]υνεύεϲθαι Zimm. 20–21. οὐδ᾽ αὖ Picc., οὐδ᾽ αὐ|[τὴν Lav., οὐδ᾽ αὐ|[τὸ
Zimm. 21. [τοῦτ᾽ ἔδει]ϲα μ[ὴ] Zimm. ὗπο pap. 21–22. ὑπονοή|[ϲειν
Lav. 21–23. ὑπονοῆ|[ϲαι δ᾽ ἂν ἴϲω]ϲ τιϲ · ἔϲτω τοῦ|[το] Levi, ὑπονοῆ|[ϲαί τινα ·
πί]ϲτιϲ ἔϲτω τού|[του μηδένι] Picc., ὑπονοῆ|[ϲαι δίκαιό]ϲ τιϲ ἔϲτω · τοῦ|[το γὰρ κατὰ τὰ]
Diels, Weil, ὑπονοή|[ϲηϲ · νῦν δὲ πί]ϲτιϲ ἔϲτω · τοῦ | [τε λοιποῦ Zimm. 22. ἔϲτω · του
Wil. 23. [ἀλλὰ μὴν τ]ὰ Levi 23–24. τό|[τε δίχα ὅρ]κου Diels, τό|[τε λελυμένα
Picc., τό|[τε καὶ δίχα ὅρ]κου Levi, τό|[τε, καὶ ἐκτὸϲ ὅρ]κου Lav., τό|[τε πέρα τοῦ ὅρ]κου
Zimm. 24–25. πεπιϲτεύ|[ϲθω] Diels, πεπιϲτευ|[μένα] Picc. 25. [μοι νῦν
οὗτοι] Picc., [οὗτοι] Lav. 25–26. πανημέ|[ριοι Zimm. 27. [ἐκ τῶν] Zimm.
27–28. ἀφείλ|[κοντο Zimm. 28–29. ἀνερ|[ρίπιζεν] Zimm., ἀνερ|[ρίπιϲεν αὐτούϲ]
Picc., ἀνερ|[εθίζων]? Wil. 29–30. μὲν τὸ Wil., τό|[τε τῆϲ ἐρωτικῆϲ] Picc., τὸ | [παρὸν
τῆϲ] Zimm. 30. διαιτήϲεωϲ Picc., δι᾽ αἰτήϲεωϲ Wil., [ϲυν]διαιτήϲεωϲ Zimm.
30–31. ἀμ|[φοτερ-] Wil., ἀμ|[βλύνων Picc. 31. [ἐτάρατ]τε δ᾽ εἰϲ Picc. 31–32. τὰϲ
ἐπι|[ϲτάϲειϲ] Picc. 32–33. τῆϲ ἐν| χερϲὶ διαζεύξε|[ωϲ Picc. 33.]μενοϲ · pap.,
[ἀφηγού]μενοϲ Picc., [προτρεπό]μενοϲ Zimm. 34. [δὲ τοῦ ἦροϲ ἀκ]μάζοντοϲ Wil.,
[γὰρ τοῦ ἔαροϲ ἀκ]μάζοντοϲ Zimm., [δὲ τοῦ ὄρθρου ἀκ]μάζοντοϲ Levi

48

] of the mother and the
16] thus led
] perhaps I too
] I do not want
] rather than
20] . . . Nor yet
] do I . . . lest . . . suspect
] let it be a token of good faith of
] the things that have been sworn
24] of the oath be entrusted
[They spent] all day
] in one another's company, except
] for what was taken up in military duties.
28] And Eros did not
[cease to fan the fire they felt.]   In satiety
] of their(?) lifestyle
] into the
32] the parting
] not yet
] reached its peak

[. . . . . cτρατη]γὸc Ἀρμενι-

36 [. . . . .]μενοc η

COLUMN B.II

ἀνόπλου cυνκροτεῖν τῶν ἐ-
πιχωρίων, δοκοῦν δὴ καὶ τῶι
πατρὶ τὸ Ἑλληνικὸν καὶ Καρι-
4 κὸν ἅπαν cύνταγμα· καὶ μυρι-
άδαc Ἀccυρίων ἐπιλέκτουc
ἑπτὰ πεζὰc καὶ τρεῖc ἱππέων
ἀναλαβὼν ὁ Νίνοc ἐλέφαντάc
8 τε πεντήκοντα πρὸc τοῖc
ἑκατὸν ἤλαυνε. καὶ φόβοc
μὲν ἦν κρυμῶν καὶ χιόνων
περὶ τὰc ὀρείουc ὑπερβολάc· πα-
12 ραλογώτατα δὲ θῆλυc καὶ πολὺ θερειότεροc τῆc ὥραc ἐπι-
πεcὼν νότοc λῦcαί τε ἐδυ-
νήθη τὰc χιόναc καὶ τοῖc ὁδ[εύ-]
16 ουcιν ἐπεικῆ πέ[ρ]ᾳ πάc[ηc ἐλ-]
πίδοc τὸν ἀέρα παραcχεῖν.
ἐμόχθηcαν δὴ ταῖc διαβάcε-
cι τῶν ποταμῶν μᾶλλον
20 ἢ ταῖc διὰ τῶν ἀκρωρειῶν
πορείαιc· καὶ ὀλίγοc μέν τιc
ὑποζυγίων φθόροc καὶ τῆc
θεραπείαc ἐγένετο· ἀπαθὴc
24 δὲ ἡ cτρατιὰ καὶ ἀπ᾽ αὐτῶν ὧν
ἐκινδύνευcε θραcυτέρα κα-
τὰ τῶν πολεμίων διεcέcω-

---

35. [ὁ cτρατη]γὸc Picc.
B.II: 1. ἐνόπλου Lav.   4. cυνταγμα· και pap.   9. ηλαυνε· pap.   11. ὑπερβολαc·
pap.   16–17. πέ[ρ]ᾳ πᾳ̈[cηc ἐλ]‖πίδοc Kaib.   17. παραcχειν· pap.   19. cιν
pap.   21. πορειαιc· pap.   23. εγενετο· pap.

] of the Armenians

36   ] ...

light-armed [   ] of the natives to assemble,
at his father's decree,
Greek and Karian troops

4   in full force. Also 70,000
elite Assyrian infantry
and 30,000 cavalry
Ninos led forth, and

8   150 elephants in addition.
There was apprehension
about the frosts and snows
around the mountain passes:

12   but most unexpectedly a gentle
south wind, much more summery than the season
would warrant, sprang up, and was able both to melt
the snow and to make the air temperate to the travelers

16   beyond all that they
could dare to hope.
They actually had more trouble in crossing
the rivers than in traversing

20   the high passes:
there was a certain small
loss of animals and
attendants; but the army

24   was unharmed, and from the very
dangers they had survived were all the more bold
to meet the enemy.

ϲτο. νενικηκυῖα γὰρ ὁδῶν ἀ-
28 πορίαϲ καὶ μεγέθη ποταμῶν
ὑπερβάλλοντα βραχὺν εἶναι
πόνον ὑπελάμβανε μεμηνό-
ταϲ ἑλεῖν Ἀρμενίουϲ. εἰϲ δὲ
32 τὴν ποταμίαν ἐμβαλὼν ὁ
Νίνοϲ καὶ λείαν ἐλαϲάμενοϲ
πολλὴν ἐρυμνὸν περιβάλλε-
ται ϲτρατόπεδον ἔν τινι πε-
36 δίωι. (δέκα τε ἡμέραϲ ἀναλαβὼν μάλιϲτα τοὺϲ ἐλέφαν-
ταϲ ἐν ταῖϲ πορείαιϲ ἀποτε-

COLUMN B.III

τρυμένουϲ) ὡϲ εκ[. . . . .]
μετὰ πολλῶν ο[. . . . . μυρι-]
άδων ἐξαγαγὼ[ν τὴν δύνα-]
4 μιν παρατάττε[ι · κατέϲτηϲε]
δὲ τὴν μὲν ἵππο[ν ἐπὶ τῶν]
κεράτων, ψιλοὺ[ϲ δὲ καὶ γυ-]
μνήταϲ, τό τε ἄγ[ημα βαϲιλι-]
8 κὸν ἅπαν ἐπὶ τῶ[ν . . . .]
τῶν ἱππέων · μέ[ϲη δ’ ἡ πεζῶν φά-]
λαγξ παρέτεινεν[· προϲθὲν δὲ]
οἱ ἐλέφαντεϲ ἱκα[νὸν ἀπ’ ἀλ-]
12 λήλων μεταίχμ[ιον διαϲτάν-]
τεϲ πυργηδὸν ὡ[πλιϲμένοι]
προεβέβληντο τῆ[ϲ φάλαγγοϲ,]

29. ὑπε pap.   31. αρμενιουϲ · pap.   36. διωι: pap.
B.III: 1. ἐκ[εῖθεν ὁρᾶι Picc., ἐκ[είνουϲ ὁρᾶι Levi, ἐκ[εῖνον Vit., ἐκ[εῖνον ἀκούει Zimm., ἔκ[αϲ
ὁ Ἀρμένιοϲ Weil, ἐκ[αλλιέρει Stadtm., εἶ[δεν αὐτούϲ Lav.   2. ὁ[ρμῶνταϲ Picc., ὁ[ρ-
μῶντα Vit., ὁ[ρᾶται Weil, ὁ[μιλῶν Stadtm.   6. ψειλου[pap.   7–8. [βαϲιλι]|κὸν
Müller, [τὸ ξενι]|κὸν Picc.   8. [κεράτων]? Wil., [πλευρῶν] Picc., ἐπὶ τῶ[ν ἐϲωτέρω]
Weil, τῶ[ν ἐνδόθεν] Müller, τῶ[ν ἐφεξῆϲ Gronewald   9. ιππεων · pap.   11. ϊκα[
pap., ἱκα[νὸν Kaib.   12. μεταίχμ[ιον Kaib.

52

For having overcome the
28   impassability of roads and the enormous breadth of rivers,
they thought it but a slight
labor to capture
an army of mad Armenians.
32   Ninos invaded the river country,
taking much booty,
and in a strong position built
a camp on a piece of flat ground.
36   (And making the army rest there for ten days,
especially the elephants,
who during the journey

COLUMN B.III

had become quite worn out.) When [
with many myriads [. . .]
he led out his troops and
4   disposed them as follows:
he placed his cavalry on the
wings with the light-armed troops
and the entire [royal]
8   guard [just inside]
the cavalry; in the middle the phalanx of infantry
was deployed; [And]
the elephants, placed at considerable intervals
12   from one another and each equipped
with a turret upon its back,
were deployed in front of the phalynx;

καθ᾽ ἕκαϲτον δὲ α[ὐτῶν ἦν]
16 χώρα διεϲτηκότ[ων τῶν λό-]
χων ὡϲ, εἴ τί που τα[ραχθείη]
θηρίον, ἔχοι διελθ[εῖν τὴν]
κατόπιν, οὕτωϲ [δὲ διεκεκό-]
20 ϲμητο ἡ κατ᾽ ἐκ[εῖνα . . . . .]
ροϲ τῶν λόχων ἔ[κταξιϲ ὥϲτε]
ἐπιμῦϲαί τε ὁπότ[ε βουληθεί-]
η δύναϲθαι καὶ πά[λιν διεκ-]
24 ϲτῆναι, τὸ μὲν εἰϲ [τὴν ὑπο-]
δοχὴν τῶν θηρίω[ν, τὸ δὲ εἰϲ]
κώλυϲιν τῆϲ εἰϲδρ[ομῆϲ τῶν]
πολεμίων. τοῦτο[ν οὖν τὸν]
28 τρόπον ὁ Νίνοϲ τὴν [ὅλην δια-]
τάξαϲ δύναμιν ἵππῳ[ι . . . . .]
λαύνει. καὶ καθάπερ ε[ἰϲ ἱκεϲί-]
αν προτείνων τὰϲ [χεῖραϲ,]
32 "τὸ θεμέλιον," ἔφη, "τ[ά τε κρί-]
ϲιμα τῶν ἐμῶν ἐλπ[ίδων τάδε ἐ-]
ϲτίν. ἀπὸ τῆϲδε τῆϲ [ἡμέραϲ]
ἢ ἄρξομαί τινοϲ μεί[ζονοϲ]
36 ἢ πεπαύϲομαι καὶ τῆ[ϲ νῦν ἀρχῆϲ.]
τῶν γὰρ ἐπ᾽ Αἰγυπτίου[ϲ . . . .]
τα τῆϲ ἄλληϲ πολεμ[. . . . .]

---

15. α[ὐτῶν] Kaib. 19. κατοπιν· pap. 20. ἐκ[εῖνα] Kaib. 20–21. [ἀντίπλευ]|-
ροϲ Picc. 21. ἔ[κταξιϲ ὥϲτε] Müller, ὤ[ϲτε ταχέωϲ] Wil. 22–23. [κελευϲθεί]|η
Levi, [καιρὸϲ εἴ]|η Stadtm., [χρεὼν εἴ]|η Picc. 27. πολεμιων· pap. 29–30. [παρ-
εξε]|λαύνει Weil, [λαβὼν ἐ]|λαύνει Wil., ἱππε[ύων αὐτὸϲ ἐ]|λαύνει Lav. 30. λαυνει·
pap. 30–31. ε[ἰϲ ἱκεϲί]|αν Müller, [εἰϲ ϲταδί]|αν Weil, ο[ἴϲων or φ[έρων θυϲί]|αν
Diels 32. Kaib. suppl. 33–34. πάρε]|ϲτιν Zimm. 35. μεί[ζονοϲ γῆϲ Zimm.
36. τῆ[ϲ ἑώιαϲ Zimm. 37. [πόνων καὶ] Lav., [μαχῶν] Zimm. 38. πολεμ[ικῆϲ
Zimm.

54

and behind each there
16 was a space left between the different companies of the phalanx,
so that if the beast were frightened
it would have sufficient room
to retire between the ranks.
20 This [. . .] corridor between the ranks
was so calculated that
it could be quickly closed up [on command]
and again opened—
24 the one maneuver
to receive the retiring beasts,
the other to stop a charge of the
enemy. In this way
28 when Ninos had arranged his [whole] force,
he rode out on his horse . . .
and, as if [in supplication]
stretching out his [hands],
32 "This," he cried, "is the foundation and [turning
point] of my hopes
—for this [day] marks
either the beginning of a still greater career,
36 or I shall fall from the [power I now possess].
For the wars against the Egyptians [
and the other [. . . ."

COLUMN A.I

Column A.I has been restored with the least success. ὁ ϲφόδρα ἐρῶν (l. 3) must refer to Ninos, ἡ παῖϲ (l. 32) to his fiancée. It contains an externally narrated encounter between the two, in which Ninos tries to persuade the girl that immediate marriage is desirable. At the end of the column the two agree to speak to their respective aunts about hastening the day of the marriage. For the struggle between *tharsos* and *aidōs* that forms the psychological dynamic of the novel, see the introduction above.

3.]ὁ ϲφόδρα ἐρῶν: for the language, compare Chariton (hereafter Ch.) 6.3.2.

6. κίν]δυνον: possibly a reference to the Armenian expedition of Fragment B.

10–11. ἀποϲτερέω is apparently constructed here with two accusatives (see LSJ s.v.). Either αὐτὸ]ν or αὐτὴ]ν would fit in line 11, but αὐτὴν is more likely, since the next clause begins ὁ δὲ. For a similar sentiment expressed about the girl, see A.IV.23–26.

18–20. Compare B.I.22–25 and his remarks to his aunt at A.II.1 and 17–27. These two oaths must be connected. For the restoration, compare A.II.18 and 33–35. For Ἀφροδίτηϲ without an article, see A.II.25–26.

23–24. Wilcken's supplement, πρὸ]ϲ τὴν ἀναβο[λὴν τῶν γάμων] is compelling; if correct, "the delay of the marriage" must refer to the impediment of age (see below, A.II.36–III.10).

25. δουλῳ-: presumably a form of δουλόω, not a dative noun, since iota adscript is always written; the thought may be parallel to XE 1.4.1: νενίκημαι καὶ παρθένωι δουλεύειν ἀναγκάζομαι. See also A.II.17–20 below.

36–38. For the construction, Vitelli compares Ch. 3.9.4: ἀφικομένη τοίνυν πρὸϲ Διονύϲιον τοῦτο μόνον εἶπεν.

38. In his speech, Ninos seems to use μῆτερ as a complimentary address to his aunt; in the narrative section, however, μητέραϲ/τηθίδαϲ are distinguished. The two (Derkeia and Thambe) are sisters (so A.V.36–37).

COLUMN A.II

Ninos's speech falls into four parts: his reminder to his aunt that he has fulfilled his oath and maintained his chastity in spite of (a) temptations, (b) his age, and (c) his desire for his cousin (A.II.1–27); a critique of Assyrian marriage customs cast as a *nomos–phusis* debate (A.II.27–III.12); a conventional appeal based on the unpredictability of fortune (A.III.12–36); and a spirited peroration in which he defends his temerity in so addressing his aunt (A.III.36–IV.12). This speech (as well as that at B.I.12ff.) contains many rhetorical questions and third-person imperatives.

1. εὐορκήϲαϲ ἀφῖγμαι: cf. B.I.22–25.

7–8. κἀγὼ τάχα: again at B.I.17. For its use with a future instead of an optative + ἄν, see Blass-Debrunner § 385.

14. εἰc κόρον: cf. B.I.29.

15–16. ἦν ... δι᾽ ἐλάττονοc: LSJ, s.v. διά A.IV.

19. νικῶμαι: see above, A.I.25 note.

23–24. E. Bowie suggests punctuating as a question.

29–30: Ninos's description of himself as a captive in love is a romantic cliché: see, e.g., XE 1.3.1–2, 4.1; AT 2.16.2; and above, introduction.

COLUMN A.III

1. (sc. νόμοc) παρ᾽ ἡμῖν: the phrase betrays the non-Assyrian perspective of both the novelist and his intended audience.

14–15. ἡρμοcάμην: For the word used of bethrothal, see LSJ s.v. I 2.

20–21. ναυτιλίαι: sea voyages are *de rigueur* for Greek novels. One such ends in catastrophe in Fragment C; the plural suggests that there are at least two sea voyages in the novel.

21–22. ἐκ πολέμων πόλεμοι: for the language, compare AT 2.6.3.

26–28. Note the anaphora of cπευcάτω. (Cf. Longos 2.7.2, AT 2.24.3.)

36–IV.5. Note the repetition—ἀναιδῆ, ἐγὼ δὲ ἀναιδὴc, οὐκ ἀναιδήc. Ninos alludes to a type of sexual behavior in A.III.38–IV.5 that his audience would have recognized as typical in tragedy and New Comedy, if not in real life. By calling attention to the different standard of behavior that appears to have been favored in the Greek novels, the author may have been intentionally flagging what was perceived as a distinguishing feature of this genre.

COLUMN A.IV

The girl's conduct (A.IV.20–V.6) is in marked contrast to Ninos's, though it may be intended to reflect no more than the conventional social roles assigned to men and women. Ninos is a young man appropriately schooled in the public world of military and political affairs; his speech exudes the appropriate rhetorical education. The girl inhabits the private world of the women's quarters with a status as yet well below that of her aunt, who presumably presides over that sphere.

COLUMN A.V

5–6. ἐκυ[.........]: the sense here is fairly clear—the girl is agitated—but the exact articulation is problematic. Either the sentence ends in line 5 and καὶ μετ[ὰ π]ολλοῦ κ[describes Thambe's behavior, or the verb in line 5 is qualified by an adverb (?) + the μετὰ phrase. Considerations of space and the fact that this author tends not to end his sentences with prepositional phrases incline us to the former, e.g., ἔκυ[πτε ϲιωπῇ.] | καὶ μετ[ὰ π]ολλοῦ κ[όϲμου ἡ Θάμβη = "she was hanging her head in silence. And with much decorum Thambe. . . ."

12–25. Thambe's speech has given rise to the speculation that Ninos may have attempted to rape his cousin (though precisely when he might have accomplished this is a mystery—certainly not after the end of A.I). Her language (τετόλμηκεν, πολεμιϲτήϲ, βιαϲθῆναι) has led editors to see in the passage a stronger indictment of Ninos's behavior than is strictly necessary. See above, introduction.

25. βιαϲθῆναι: compare IV.16 for the word in a nonsexual sense. Here we take the word to mean "compel" or "coerce" by argument, not "rape."

COLUMN B.I

1–3. Restoration of these lines depends on the following considerations: ἀπελείφθη requires an object; if it is μητρὸϲ (line 2), then a connective is necessary before ηκ]ολούθηϲεν; space is insufficient, however, to account for εντο (e.g., ἐν το|[ϲούτωι] [iota adscript is always present on final omegas, so it must be restored here]) + ἀλλὰ or καὶ. Accordingly, we would locate the object earlier (λόγ]ου γὰρ or sim.) and take this phrase to be parenthetical. Supplement 2–3: [οὐδὲ ταῖϲ τ]ῆϲ μητρὸϲ ἐντο|[λαῖϲ κατηκ]ολούθηϲεν, or sim.

3–9. This passage can be (and has been) restored in a number of ways. Apart from the presence of Ninos and a woman, one of whom is in great distress, uncertainty reigns. Unfortunately, the passage is broken in such a way that either masculine or feminine forms may be consistently restored throughout. Wilcken and several others assumed it was Ninos (reading δακρύων as a participle) and restored it accordingly. But, although novel heroes have been known to indulge in fits of weeping and rending of garments, this conduct is more frequently associated with women. Further, the grammar of the passage suggests otherwise: Ninos is unlikely to be identified by name (instead of ὁ δὲ) at line 12 if he has been running around in a state of dishabille in the sentence immediately before, and if lines 3–9 describe Ninos, then the woman "leaping up from her couch"—[ἀνα]πηδήϲαϲαν δὲ—in line 9 is without a close antecedent. We agree with Stadtmüller, Lavagnini, and those who restore these lines as if Ninos's fiancée were in distress. We would restore along the following lines: ἀκά|[λυπτοϲ δὲ] καὶ περιερρηγμέ|[νη καὶ οὐδ]αμῶϲ ἱεροπρεπήϲ, | [πάντ᾽ ἔπληϲ]ε δακρύων καὶ κό|[μην ϲπάϲαϲ᾽ ἐ]κ τοῦ ϲχήματοϲ | [ἡ παῖϲ ἔκειτ᾽] εἰρχθεῖϲ᾽ ἅτε με|[μηνυῖα·] = "But unveiled and with her dress torn and in no way fit for a sacred ceremony, she filled the place with weeping, and with her hair pulled from its arrangement, the girl lay there, shut in, like a mad woman."

4–5. περιερρηγμέ|[ν . . . . : for the use of this verb without the garment expressed, see Ch. 1.3.4.

5. οὐδ]αμῶϲ ἱεροπρεπήϲ: this cannot be a casual way of referring to the girl's personal disarray. She must either have interrupted or delayed a sacrifice, quite possibly a betrothal. Marriage, of course, must be rejected if the order is BA, but also because the ceremony that must have broken off at the beginning of the column appears not to have been resumed in the remainder of B.I. Another possibility would be sacrifices for the propitious outcome of the military expedition, if they included women.

8. εἰρχθεῖϲ᾽: the word has two senses—to close out or to close in. Either she has been excluded from something (one might restore, e.g., τῶν ἱερῶν in light of οὐδα]μῶϲ ἱεροπρεπήϲ above) or she is being kept in her room, presumably as a result of her distraught appearance.

8–9. Stadtmüller's με[μηνυῖα] is not inevitable, but very tempting. Cf. Ch. 5.10.10, XE 5.13.2. Note also the μεμηνόταϲ ... Ἀρμενίουϲ of B.II.30–31, who appear to have been considerably less of a challenge for Ninos than his beloved.

13–25. Ninos's speech must be calculated to soothe the overwrought girl. Apart from lines 22–25, where some kind of an oath is alluded to, restoration is sheer guesswork.

13–14. Previous editors have assumed these lines meant something on the order of "who is it saying (εἰπών) to you that I (με) am a [——] of virgins," where the construction is εἰπών + accusative + infinitive or predicate accusative. The combined efforts of editors to supplement the lacuna as [φθορέα τῶν παρ]θένων or sim. has led to an impression of Ninos's sexual misconduct. If εἰπών acts merely as an introductory verb of speaking, however, the sentence might be less inflammatory; e.g., " ——," εἰπών, "ϲοὶ με[τὰ τῶν παρ]θένων ἔϲτω": "Let your concerns [or sim.?] be among the unmarried girls." This use of εἰπών is not uncommon in the novelists. For ϲοί directly following an introductory verb of speaking, see XE 2.10.3, 3.7.2; Longos 4.14.2.

17–18. For τάχα κἀγώ, see A.II.7–8. τάχα που κἀγὼ | [οὐκ ἀναίτιο]ϲ; or sim.?

20. Traces before]. νεύεϲθαι could suit υ or ρ. Supplements to this line have contributed to the impression of Ninos's caddish behavior. Rattenbury (1933: 217) even claims that νεα]ν⟨ι⟩εύεϲθαι "may be restored with some confidence," but correcting in the vicinity of a lacuna is dangerous. Vitelli supplies πο]ρνεύεϲθαι, but πο]ρνεύεϲθαι means to behave like a prostitute, not to frequent them, an unlikely sentiment for Ninos to express. There are, however, considerably less inflammatory supplements, e.g., κινδ]υνεύεϲθαι or παρθ]ενεύεϲθαι (the latter suggested to us by E. Bowie).

21.]ϲα μ[ὴ]: most likely μή preceded by a verb of fearing, e.g., Zimmermann's οὐδ᾽ αὐ[τὸ τοῦτο ἔδει]ϲα μ[ὴ] ὑπονοή[ϲῃϲ or sim. Alternatively, ὅ]ϲα μ[ὴ] is

possible (cf. I.26 below); if so, οὐδ' αυ- will likely be followed by another infinitive.

24–25. The verb is almost certainly an imperative, a form for which Ninos has a predilection. For Ninos's oath, cf. A.II.5ff. τέλος, ἔχυρον, or sim.?

25–26. οὗ]τοι δὲ πανήμε||ροι ϲυνῆϲαν] ἀλλήλοιϲ: see discussion above, introduction.

29. κόρωι: "satiety," not "boy"—with the latter one expects the article, and traces before do not suit. If the articulation at line 31,]τε δ' εἰϲ, is correct, then the correspondence of κόρωι μὲν and]τε δὲ (presumably a verb) is not exact, but such unbalanced μὲν–δὲ constructions occur elsewhere in this piece (see, e.g., A.II.22–24, A.IV.31–33).

36ff. The transition between the young lovers and the beginning of the campaign is abrupt, but in keeping with other scene changes in this text (e.g., A.I.34ff., A.V.36ff., B.III.1ff.). A likely scenario is that Ninos was preparing for a mid-spring or summer campaign (after the snows had melted), but hostile activities of the general of the Armenians (line 35) required more immediate attention. Hence lines 33–36 might be restored with some plausibility: οὔπω | [γὰρ τοῦ ἔαροϲ ἀκ]μάζοντοϲ, | [ἐπειδὴ ὁ ϲτρατη]γὸϲ Ἀρμενί|[ων.

COLUMN B.II

2–3. δοκοῦν δὴ καὶ τῶι πατρὶ: since Ninos's father participates in deciding the troop deployment, it seems a fair guess that this will be Ninos's first military campaign on his own. From Diodoros (Ktesias) we know that Armenia figured prominently in Ninos's military successes (see above, introduction).

3–9. The size of Ninos's army compares realistically with that of Hellenistic monarchs; its numbers are considerably smaller than those found in Diodoros (Ktesias): 1,700,000 foot-soldiers, 210,000 cavalry, and 10,600 battle chariots (2.5.4). See Jenistová 1953: 216 for comparative statistics.

9–17. For evidence of the effects of the harshness of the Armenian winter on Antony's campaigning army, which our author may have had in mind, see Plut. *Ant.* § 51 and Cassius Dio 49.31. Imperial panegyrics from a later period indulge in similar claims for the passage of an emperor: Adeo, ut res est, adversus inclementiam locorum ac siderum uestrae uos maiestatis potentia tuebatur, et ceteris hominibus atque regionibus ui frigorum adstrictis et oppressis uos solos aurae lenes uernique flatus et diductis nubibus ad itinera uestra directi solis radii sequebantur (*Panegyrici latini* XI [= III] 3.9.2–3, ed. R. Mynors). By 291 C.E., this seems to have been so familiar a theme in imperial oratory that it could easily be inverted (MacCormack 1985: 24). K. Hopkins makes a case for this kind of rhetoric at an earlier period in imperial cult (1978: 199); if his assertion is correct, then the *Ninos* author may be self-consciously adopting or imitating such a source.

32. Lavagnini (1921: 203) suggests that ποταμίαν might be either a proper name for the region through which the army was passing or an error for πολεμίαν (see B.II.26), but there is no adequate reason to emend the text.

COLUMN B.III

1–2. The comment about resting the elephants must end at ἀποτετρυμένουϲ, and the ὡϲ-clause must contain a statement about sighting the enemy.

4–11. The battle order seems to have been a usual one: compare Polybios's account of the battle of Raphia (5.82.3ff.), in which the cavalry occupies the wings and the phalanx of foot-soldiers the center, with the royal guard on the left between the foot and the horse. Elephants were placed in front of the line. Piccolomini (1893a: 328–29) compares a similar description from Heliodoros (9.14–16) and suggests that the two passages are related; Müller (1917–18: 210–12) points out, however, that both are more likely to be following the traditional Hellenistic practice. (See Jenistová 1953: 217 for schematizations of the battle order employed by several Hellenistic monarchs in comparison with that of Ninos.)

7–8. [βαϲιλι]κὸν: for a discussion of the correct supplement, see Müller 1917–18: 199–202.

8. Either ἐϲωτέρω or ἐνδόθεν will suit the space available.

11ff. The elephants were normally positioned in front of the line, with troops disposed behind them in such a way that they did not block the elephants' retreat; again, see Polyb. 5.84 for the problems with elephants in combat. See also Diodoros's description of the battle between Semiramis and Stabrobates (2.19.4–8).

12. The elephants were equipped with turrets in which an armed man sat (compare Polyb. 5.84.2 for a description of οἱ πυργομαχοῦντεϲ).

20–21. κατ' ἐκ[εῖνα (sc. θηρία) . . . . .]: the missing word must be a biform adjective ending in -ροϲ, with a meaning of "fitting," or "staggered." Compounds of -καιροϲ, -μοιροϲ, or even -ποροϲ might suit. This phrase is probably describing what Polybios refers to as troops arranged "ἐν ἐπικαμπίῳ" (5.82.9).

29–30. Possibly ἵππῳ[ι or ἱππύ[ων προεξε]λαύνει; the usual verb is ἐπιπάρειμι.

29–31. From other descriptions of a general's address to his troops before the battle, we may infer that Ninos rides along his battle line, then stops, stretches out his hands, and makes a brief speech.

31. For the content of the address and for further examples, see Müller 1917–18: 207ff.

DESCRIPTION OF C

PSI 1305 (= *P*² 2617, measuring 6.0 × 26.5 cm) was found at Oxyrhynchus in 1932. It contains one long, narrow column of a papyrus roll, with an upper margin of 3.0 cm, and a lower margin of 2.0 cm. There are fifty nearly intact lines, containing, when complete, between fifteen and nineteen letters per line. The hand is of the informal round type, very like, though not the same as, the Berlin papyrus (the upsilon and tau, for example, are different), assignable also to the last half of the first century C.E. Punctuation includes paragraphi, spacing and stops, dicola, tremata, apostrophe, and one rough breathing. Carets are used as line fillers at 35, 41, and 45, but without notable effect; line ends are very uneven, which suggests that the carets may have belonged to an exemplar and may have been copied along with the letters. There are several corrections (lines 11, 29, 38, 44, 46). The scribe neglects elision at lines 8 and 18, but marks it at 36 and 38. The back is blank. Lines 19–50 are in the main easily restored, because only a few letters are lacking from line beginnings or ends. From these lines it is possible to determine the relative tilt of the column to the right, and hence establish with some certainty the number of letters missing from the openings of lines 1–13 (in fact, almost nothing can be missing from line beginnings, although Norsa's ed. pr. conveys a different impression). Since the line ends are not right-justified, the number of missing letters could vary there between one and five. Lines 14–17 are almost completely lost.

FRAGMENT C

] . δ' ἐπ' ἀκτῆc Ἵππου . [
               ] περι[
δαcτε γύναι μοι καλ[
4   . ια, καθάπερ ἐδηλ[
ἀνειληφυῖα μετα[
. . . . . ετα[.] . . . τον . [
τ̣ο̣νεγ[. .] ἐπικουρ[
8   ναύτου καὶ ἐπιcτή[μονοc]
κυβερνήτου· οὐδ[εὶc]
[γ]ὰρ ἄλλοc ἀcφαλέc[τε-]
ροc πρὸ τῆc βορεία[c]
12   μεταβολῆc εἰc τὴν [τῆc]
[Κ]ο̣λχίδοc ἀκτὴν ε[
[. .] . . . . δερ . . ο . [
]ε̣κγαρ . . . . . . ω . . . [
16   ]ε̣τω . . . αγ κειμενο̣ [
] . . . . ουμηκ [
[ἠ]ϊὼν καὶ ἄλcοc ὑπὲρ
[α]ὐτῆc cκιερόν· οὗ κατ' [αὐ-]
20   [τὸ] τὸ μέcον εἰc ῥεῖθρον
[ἐ]παρκοῦcα πηγὴ μέ-
[χρι] τῆc κυματωγῆc κα-
[τε]ρρήγνυτο. τὸ μὲν οὖν
24   [c]κάφοc—οὐ γὰρ ἀγχιβα-
θὴc ἦν ἡ ἀκτή—πρόc τ[ι-]

Supplements are those of ed. pr. unless otherwise stated in apparatus or notes. Wilcken's conjectures are printed in ed. pr., Bartoletti's and Hartke's in Zimmermann 1953–54. 2–3. περι[cπού]]δαcτε Zimm. 3. ᾳἵμοϊ pap. 4. ἐδήλ[ωcεν] Zimm. 5. ἀνειλη-φυῖά με· Zimm. 5–6. τά[χ' ἕ]|ξεις Zimm. 6–9. δ' ἐτ[αί]ρων τὸν π[ιc]τότ]ατον ἐμ[οὶ] ἐπίκουρ[ον | τοῦ] ναύτου καὶ ἐπιcτή[μο|νοc κυβερνήτου Norsa 6–7. φ[ίλτα]-|τον Zimm. 8. ἐπιcτή[μονα] Hartke 9. κυβερνητου ου pap. 9–11. οὐδ[εὶc | γ]ὰρ ἄλ[λ]ο̣c ἀcφαλέc[τε|ρ]οc Zimm. 11. προ⳨ pap. 18.]ϊων pap., ἠ]ϊὼν S. West 19. cκιερον· ουκ pap. 19–20. κατὰ | [δὲ] Hartke, κατ[ά γε] Zimm. 21. [ἐ]παρ-κοῦcα Bart., [πάν]υ̣ ἀρκοῦcα Norsa 23.]ρρηγνυτο: pap.

on the shore of the Hippos [
  . . . [
  . . . lady, to me [
4   just as . . . made clear [
  having taken up. . . . [
  [. . .]
  an ally
8   of sailor and skilled
  navigator. For no one
  at all safer
  before the northern
12   turn into the
  shore of Kolchis
  [. . .]
  for from
16   lying
  a distance(?)
  a beach and a shady
  grove above it. Where in
20   the very middle into a stream
  an ample spring
  plashed with the
  waves. So the
24   vessel—for the beach
  was not steep—came to ground

ϲιν ὑφάλοιϲ ταινίαιϲ ἐξ[ο-]
κεῖλαν διε[ϲ]αλεύετο κα[ὶ]
28 δῆλον ἦν [ὡϲ] ταῖϲ ἐμβο-
λαῖϲ κυ[μάτω]ν ἀπολού-
μενον· οἱ δ[’ ἐ]ξέβαινον
[α]ὐτὸν εἰϲ ἄκρουϲ μαζοὺϲ
32 κλυζόμενοι· καὶ πάντα
τὰ ἐν τῇ νηὶ διαϲώϲαν-
τεϲ, ἱδρύθηϲαν ἐπὶ τῆϲ
ἠϊόνοϲ. ἐν μὲν οὖν
36 τῷ πελάγει πάντ’ ἐ[π]ε-
[ν]όουν ὑπὲρ τῆϲ ϲωτηρ[ί-]
[α]ϲ, διαϲωθέντεϲ δ’ ἐπ[ε-]
θύμουν θανάτου. καὶ ο[ἱ]
40 μὲν ἄλλοι μετριώτε-
[ρο]ν τὴν μεταβολὴν
[ἔφ]ερον· ὁ δὲ Νίνοϲ ἀ-
[θλ]ίωϲ αὐτῆϲ ᾔϲθετο· πρὸ
44 [...]ων μὲν ἡμερῶν ἡγεμὼν
[το]ϲαύτηϲ δυνάμεωϲ
[....] ηϲ ἐπὶ πᾶϲαν
[....] ... ϲτρατεῦϲαι
48 [....] .. θάλατταν· τοτε
[.........] ναυαγὸϲ
[.........]θείϲηϲ δορικτη-

27. ὀκεῖλαν Bart. 28. δ[ῆλον ἦν ὡϲ] Zimm., διεδε[ύετο] Norsa 29. κ[υ]μ[άτω]ν Bart. απολλο corrected to απολου pap. 30. μενον pap. οἱ δ’ [ἐξ]έβαινον Hartke, οἱ δ[ὲ δι]έβαινον Norsa 33. νηϊδϊα pap. 34. ειδρυθηϲαν pap. 35. ηϊο-νοϲ ενμενουν⟩ pap. 36. [τ]ῷ πελάγει Bart., τῷ ἀνελπίϲτῳ Norsa. 36–37. ἐ[π]-ε[νό]ουν Zimm., ἐ[π]ό[ν]ουν Norsa 38. υπ[corrected to επ[pap. 41. μεταβο-λην⟩ pap. 42.]φερον οδε pap. 42–43. ἀ[[θύ]μωϲ? Zimm. 43. ηϲθετο·προ pap. 44. τρι]ῶν, τίν]ων Norsa, ὀλί]γων Wil.]μεν added above ημε of ημεραν pap., ημεραν ηγεμων pap. 45. δυναμεωϲ⟩ pap. 46. [ἐτοί]μηϲ, [ἱκα]νῆϲ Norsa. Final ϲ of παϲηϲ corrected to ν by original hand. At end of line a sign of unknown func-tion, ÷ 47. [τὴν] γῆν? Norsa 48. θαλατταν· τοτε pap., θ[ά]λατταν τότε Bart. 50. [ϲυναχ]θείϲηϲ δορικτή[του]? Norsa.

on some underwater shoals and
was bobbing there, and
28   clearly by the pounding of waves,
it was going to be destroyed.
And the men disembarked from
it(?), awash up to their chests
32   in the waves, and having saved
all that was on the ship
they set up camp on the
sand. So in
36   the sea they gave thought
to achieve safety, but having achieved it,
they were desirous
of death. And the
40   others were bearing
the catastrophe
more moderately; but Ninos
bore it wretchedly. For
44   a few(?) days before, leader
of such a force
. . .] toward all
. . .] to march against
48   . . .] the sea,
. . .] shipwreck
. . .] captive

FRAGMENT C

1. ἐπ᾽ ἀκτῆς Ἵππου: according to Arrian *Per. m. Eux.* 10.2, 11.4–5 and Str. 11.3.4, the Hippos is a Kolchian river that flows into the sea near Phasis (cf. below, line 13). This is presumably the same ἀκτή as below, lines 13 and 25, the area where they run aground.

2–3. περι[....]δαςτε: Zimmermann's περι[ςπού]]δαςτε ("much desired") is attractive because it accounts for both περι and τε, and because it allows the sentence to have begun before περι. περιςπούδαςτος occurs at Longos 3.31.3, XE 1.1.3, and Ch. 2.10.1, meaning "much sought after" (as a marriage partner, in the novelists), rather than "longed for" by a loved one. (As such, it hardly seems like the kind of epithet a man would use in addressing his wife.) If correct, it must belong with γύναι; if incorrect, possibilities include (1) a verb ending,]δαςτο, and (2)]δας τε (where τε must be linking clauses).

3. γύναι μοι καλ[: no more than five letters should be missing between this line and the beginning of the next. It is uncertain how to punctuate, but there are no examples in the extant novelists of the phrase γύναι μοι, nor of γύναι plus a personal name. If περι[ςπού]δαςτε is correct, μοι ought to belong with it = "lady, much sought after by me."

3–4. καλ[....] ̣ ια: Zimmermann restores Καλ[λιγε]νία, which he takes to be vocative, and the name of Ninos's wife. Although attractive in the abstract, this presents problems. The novelist has chosen for his protagonists historical characters, Ninos and Semiramis, and he specifically employed, it would seem, a Greek variation of the name of Semiramis's mother (Derkeia for the historical Derketo). It is difficult to imagine that he would give to the Semiramis character a totally different name, like Kalligenia (even though a similarly formed name, Kalligone, does occur for the heroine of a fragmentary novel). If a proper name is the correct supplement, an option presents itself. Zimmermann himself (1953–54: 180), in restoring the subsequent lines as καθάπερ ἐδήλ[ωςεν] ἀνειληφυῖά με, assumed that the feminine participle referred to a second woman who "eine Rolle ähnlich der von Plangon bei Chariton gespielt haben sollte, wäre es denkbar, dass zwischen ihr und Kalligenia ein Eifersuchtsverhältnis bestanden hätte." The Daphne mosaic might be employed to bolster this argument, because it portrays a young woman in the scene along with Ninos contemplating the picture of his wife. (The Alexandretta mosaic does not, however.)

A sentence of the shape]δαςτο, γύναι, μοι καλ[ ] ̣ ια (verb + vocative, + indirect object + subject) is preferable to us, but plausible supplements do not easily come to mind.

4. καθάπερ ἐδήλ[ωςεν or sim.: the resulting hiatus should exclude ἐδήλ[ου, if the participle belongs with ἐδηλ[.

5. ἀνειληφυῖα: initially only one letter can be missing before nu. Conventions

of syllable division exclude, e.g., ἐδήλ[ωc]|εν. Either] . ια or με could be the object of the participle; alternatively, the participle could be used with an adverb like μετα[ξύ] to complete its meaning.

6–9. There are too many variables for fruitful speculation. Norsa and subsequent editors read δ' ἐτ[αί]ρων, supplementing the whole as: [ἕ]ξεις δ' ἐτ[αί]ρων τὸν φ[ίλτ]α|τον (or sim.) ἐμ[οὶ] ἐπίκουρ[ον] | ναύτου καὶ ἐπιcτή[νονος] | κυβερνήτου, to mean presumably, "You will have my dearest companion, to be an ally of sailor and skilled navigator." But there are several problems: (1) the expression ἐτ[αί]ρων τὸν + superlative + ἐμ[οὶ] seems unnecessarily prolix (compare, e.g., τῆς ἐμοὶ τερπνοτάτης ἀνεψιᾶς of A.II.3–4); (2) ἐπίκουρ[ον] is usually constructed with a dative, not a genitive; and (3) ἐμ[οὶ] results in hiatus.

7–9. A phrase like ἔγ[εκ'] ἐπικούρ[ου] | ναύτου καὶ ἐπιcτή[μονος] | κυβερνήτου might suit.

11. πρὸ : possibly "in defense against" rather than "before."

12. μεταβολῆc : here either "catastrophe" (as in line 4) or merely "turn."

12–13. εἰc τὴν [τῆc | Κ]ολχίδος ἀκτὴν : either with μεταβολῆc = "the northern turn into the gulf of Kolchis," or with the missing verb.

17. τ]οῦ μήκ[ουc or εἰc ——]ου μήκ[οc ? Unfortunately, the initial trace does not suit S. West's εὐμήκ[ηc.

22–23. κα|[τε]ρρήγνυτο : cf. A.IV.34.

26. ὑφάλοιc ταινίαιc : the expression is used of shoals at Gibraltar in Str. 1.3.4; ταινίαι are strips of land that cause shipwrecks along the coast of Egypt in DS 1.31.3–4.

28. Norsa's διεδε[ύετο] suits the exiguous traces, but seems too short. Zimmermann's rather longer δ[ῆλον ἦν ὡc] also suits and makes better sense with the future participle in lines 29–30.

28–29. ταῖc ἐμβολαῖc κυ[μάτω]y : for the expression, see Ch. 3.3.13.

30. Either διαβαίνω or ἐκβαίνω will fit.

31. αὐτὸν : what is the antecedent? Norsa suggested cκάφος, correcting to αὐτὸ; also Zimmermann, who demonstrates that αὐτὸν is an acceptable neuter in late Greek. The problem is the verb. While διαβαίνω takes an accusative, cκάφος as object makes no sense; one expects ἀκτὴν or sim. ἐκβαίνω usually requires a genitive, and although it may occasionally be found with an accusative object (LSJ s.v. A.3), the sense would not normally be "they left the ship." Or αὐτὸν = Ninos, in the sense of "they put him [sc. Ninos] ashore." This use of ἐκβαίνω is rare but attested (LSJ s.v. B), but Ninos is not close enough to the pronoun to be a viable antecedent. Alternatively, emend to αὐτοῦ or αὐτοί?

36–37. ἐ[π]ε[ν]όουν : the longer supplement is better suited to space available at the beginning of the line.

38. διαcωθέντεc : cf. B.II.26–27, διεcέcωcτο.

41–42. τὴν μεταβολὴν [ἔφ]ερον : cf. Plut. Tim. § 15.5.1, Cic. § 31.4.4.

44–48. Compare DS (Ktesias) 2.2.1: δεινὴν ἐπιθυμίαν ἔϲχε τοῦ καταϲτρέψαϲθαι τὴν Ἀϲίαν ἅπαϲαν τὴν ἐντὸϲ Ταναΐδοϲ καὶ Νείλου.

45. το]ϲαύτηϲ δυνάμεωϲ : cf. B.II.29.

48. τότε, τό τε, or τὸ τε- (τέλοϲ or sim.).

50.]θείϲη δορικτη[: probably of a country, as in A.II.11, not of Semiramis captured.

NINOS

DESCRIPTION OF D

P. Gen. 85 (measuring 4.0 × 5.5 cm) belongs to the Berlin roll. It preserves beginnings of ten lines with only a small portion of the left margin; the rest is broken off; punctuation is by stop and dicolon. What context remains suggests that this piece should belong to the military rather than the erotic episodes, possibly even that of Fragment B.

FRAGMENT D

- - - - - - - - - - - - - -

```
  . ωρωντε . [
  [ . ]ηϲεν ϲκε[
  ϲυνεχὲϲ αυτ[
4 ἐγένετο · πα[          4   he/it happened. [
  τοῖϲ ὁ Νίνοϲ, [           to them Ninos [spoke?
  τοὺϲ πολεμί[ουϲ           the enemy [
  καὶ τῆι μὲν ε[            and there [
8 ὥκειν · τουϲ [        8   to pursue.  Them [
  [ . ] . τατων [
  [ . . . ]ν . [
```

continuous [

- - - - - - - - - - - - - -

---

4. εγενετο ·πα[pap.   5. νινοϲ: pap.   8. ωκειν·τουϲ pap.

FRAGMENT D

1. Initially, ed. pr.'s ἑώρων is possible, but not inevitable.
4–5. Ed. pr. supplements: πά[λιν δ' ἔλεξεν αὐ]τοῖϲ ὁ Νίνοϲ.
5. After Νίνοϲ, a dicolon seems to have been used as punctuation (compare B.II.36 and C.23).
7–8. καὶ τῆι μὲν ἐ[κφεύγειν, τῆι δὲ δι]|ώκειν or sim.?
9. [κ]ατὰ τῶν [?

Metiochos and Parthenope

❖

Although it survives today in only two fragmentary columns,[1] *Metiochos and Parthenope* boasts a diverting and polymorphous *Nachleben.* Lucian testifies to its popularity as a subject for female impersonators (*De salt.* §2); there are two floor mosaics from Antioch-on-the-Orontes, one depicting Metiochos accoutered as a Roman officer, the other showing Metiochos and Parthenope sitting back to back, with heads turned towards each other,[2] a small ostracon purports to contain a letter from Metiochos to Parthenope (see below); a suitably altered version of the novel made an appearance in Coptic as the martyrdom of St. Bartanuba (Hägg 1984); and finally there is a fragment from an eleventh-century Persian version in verse—*Wamiq and 'Adhra'* by 'Unṣuri.[3]

The papyrus fragments give us the names of hero and heroine as well as Polykrates, Anaximenes, and Hegesipyle, confirming that the novel was set in early classical times (sixth century B.C.E.) and incorporated famous historical figures. Polykrates is the celebrated tyrant of Samos, Anaximenes the philosopher from Miletos, Hegesipyle the wife of Miltiades and Metiochos's stepmother. In the first column, Metiochos is explaining his distressing circumstances to Polykrates; in the second column, Polykrates instructs that the drinking should begin, and with it Anaximenes initiates a "philosophical inquiry" into the nature of eros. Metiochos ridicules the notion that Eros is a little boy who flies about causing "a breathy wind" (*pneuma ti*) in the souls of lovers. This may be

---

[1] Another papyrus scrap, P. Oxy. 3.435, has been assigned by Zimmermann to this novel, on which see below.

[2] See Stilwell 1938: 203, no. 99; Levi 1947, 1: 118–19, 2: pl. 20c; Hoffmann 1970: 112–15. The mosaics are also discussed in Maehler 1976: 1–2.

[3] See Shafi 1967: 1–8 and Utas 1984–86 for discussion of the Persian material; Hägg 1984, 1985, and 1989 deal with the relationship of Persian to Greek material. At present, only the few meager fragments that Shafi translated are available in English, though there is a Russian edition (Kaladze 1983). Ritter 1948 includes a German translation of a few fragments of the poem found in Persian compendia. Hägg states (1984: 83, 1989: 42 n. 35) that in collaboration with Bo Utas he is preparing a joint edition of the Greek and Persian material. His publications normally do not provide translations, only summaries, of the material that he discusses. Our quotations from 'Unṣuri are based on the Russian translation. We should like to express our gratitude to Michael Gorham, who translated Kaladze 1983 for us.

an oblique reference to the philosophy of Anaximenes himself, who taught that the fundamental principle of all things was "air."[4] He concludes rather that "Love is a stirring of the mind aroused by beauty and increasing with familiarity" (ll. 60–62), and he prays that it may never touch him. Parthenope bridles at his rationalizing explanation and embarks upon a spirited defense of the traditional portraits of "the poets and painters and sculptors" (l. 70) when the fragment breaks off.

Twenty-two half-pages from 'Unṣuri's poem (containing 380 verses from the original) were found glued together and used to stiffen the binding of an anonymous commentary on the *Koran*. The manuscript leaves were discovered by Mohammad Shafi and published posthumously by his son in 1967. Although the work itself is not translated into English, Shafi provides an English preface and translation of a number of verses, as well as translation of the plot summary of 'Unṣuri's poem found in the *Darab Nameh*, a twelfth-century compilation. In all, Shafi's evidence is more than sufficient to make T. Hägg's identification of the Persian poem with *Metiochos and Parthenope* beyond doubt.[5]

From 'Unṣuri's poem we learn that Polykrates of Samos was the father of 'Adhra', Syloson his brother. Polykrates is said to be a "son of Aeakos," not of Aeakes, as in Herodotos (2.43). Ibykos, the poet, was present in Polykrates' court.[6] But the names of the main characters have been changed. Metiochos is now Wamiq, which means "lover," and Parthenope is 'Adhra', which means "virgin." Of course, the latter is entirely suitable for Parthenope, who has been linked with virginity or the unmarried state as early as Herodotos. In Persian, however, the combination "the lover and the virgin" evidently came to be used as a generic title for romantic tales (Shafi 1967: 7–8). There are two other names, for which Greek analogues are not immediately apparent. The mother of 'Adhra' is Yani,[7] and Wamiq travels with a companion named Tufan.[8] In addition to the epitome and the fragments from 'Unṣuri's poem, there are a number of quotations from the poem now only found in Persian lexica. From these, B. Utas has identified two other "histori-

---

[4] "Just as our soul, being air, controls us, so breath and air surround the entire cosmos" (D–K 13B2).

[5] Hägg credits Utas for calling his attention to Shafi's publication (Hägg 1984: 83).

[6] The poet is a not-unreasonable candidate for inclusion in Polykrates' court, since he has addressed a poem to him (= *PGM* 282).

[7] Hägg (1985: 97) tentatively identifies Yani as Nanis, the name of Kroisos's daughter (Parth. 22 = Hermesianax frag. 6 Powell).

[8] Possibly the equivalent of Theophanes, so C. Bosch in H. Ritter 1948: 139.

cal" characters: Maiandrios, Polykrates' secretary, who is the "alien" of the epitome; and Anaxilaos of Rhegion, in whose court our wandering heroine finds herself at a later stage of this adventure (1984–86: 434–35).

The fragments of *Wamiq and 'Adhra'* belong to the beginning of the poem. The Persian story opens with the marriage of Folikrat (Polykrates) and Yani on the island of Samos, and the birth and upbringing of their daughter 'Adhra', who is reared as if she were a son, trained in warfare and in eloquence.[9] The scene then shifts to Wamiq, whom we find bedeviled by a stepmother who has set his father against him.[10] Wamiq therefore decides to flee his native land; as his companion he seeks out Tufan, who suggests that they travel to Samos to Polykrates' court, since ". . . you are his relation by blood, [so] he may well be a kind mentor to you" (v. 69). After arriving in Samos, Wamiq and Tufan visit the famed temple of Hera, where they encounter 'Adhra' and her mother Yani. The young couple falls deeply in love at first glance. Wamiq then gives an account of himself to Yani, who suggests that he talk with the king. After the women depart, Wamiq soliloquizes about love, saying, "Evil fate never leaves me! I What is this unhappiness that has appeared before me? Has plunged my heart into grief, set it on fire? I Who knows who this ravisher was? Was she a fairy or the moon on earth!" (vv. 104–5). Tufan, accurately sizing up the situation, prays to the goddess to protect his friend from this new disaster. 'Adhra' is equally stricken: "Unsteadily 'Adhra' went along the road, not once showing her face to her mother, I So that her mother would not notice that she had fallen in love, and her dark-complexioned face had grown pale" (vv. 102–3).

Afterwards Yani mentions Wamiq to Polykrates, who sends for the young man; they first meet at court during an evening party at which his daughter is present. Polykrates, intending to test the young man's ability in speech, has introduced a "sage" for this purpose (Mokhsinos = Anaximenes), who brings up the subject of love after closely observing the young people. Wamiq discourses on love, contrasting young Eros with the more powerful and dangerous old Eros. At the end of his speech, 'Adhra', ever more love-stricken, nevertheless argues the opposite position, namely, that love must be young. After this exchange the

[9] "With spear she moved a mountain from its place, plunged an arrow into steel. I Among the princes she had no equal, nor among the freeborn" (vv. 32–33).

[10] "He was a wise youth; his mother died, and his father married another woman. I She was a pernicious woman by the name of Mashkuliie [= Hegesipyle], aside from evil, she desired nothing. . . . I She hardened the heart of the father, gave him seeds of evil by the handful" (vv. 42–43, 45).

sage(?) asks his audience, "Who invented the *barbat*?"[11] After Folikrat expresses ignorance, Wamiq tells a story in which Hermes finds a decomposed tortoise shell with sinews intact through which the wind was sounding. He attempts to imitate nature but fails, until one day he meets an old man who shows him how to fashion a proper musical instrument.

Subsequently Wamiq would seem to have been tested "in the arena" in feats of strength. Then yet another banquet takes place during which the poet Ibykos, who sings of the young lovers, is introduced. Their passion continues to grow, and they apparently meet secretly until the girl's tutor, Falatus, discovers them and chastises 'A<u>dh</u>ra', while exacting a promise from Wamiq "that he would never look at 'A<u>dh</u>ra' with evil design" (v. 338). Whereupon the two—in predictable novel fashion—proceed to waste away from lovesickness. At this point the fragments break off.

The epitome of the poem found in the *Darab Nameh* fills in a few more details: 'A<u>dh</u>ra' attends evening parties at which Wamiq is present until her tutor reports her conduct to her mother, who rebukes her for such behavior. At this point 'A<u>dh</u>ra' confesses her love for Wamiq and threatens to kill herself if not allowed to marry him. Her father apparently consents, but changes his mind when her mother dies. Her father then goes out to fight against an enemy, is taken captive, and is executed. "An alien" then ascends the throne, and both Wamiq and 'A<u>dh</u>ra' are cast into prison. She rejects "the alien's" proposals and is sold into slavery. After four years in servitude she tells her story to her master, who recognizes her and sets her free (adapted from Shafi 1967: 3).

Although clearly unsatisfactory on a number of levels—Did the mother of 'A<u>dh</u>ra' die suddenly? Could 'A<u>dh</u>ra' have been in servitude to the same master for four years before telling her story, or was there a succession of masters? What happens to Metiochos?—the evidence confirms that *Metiochos and Parthenope* shares the conventional story line of Chariton or Xenophon of Ephesos: teen protagonists, love at first sight, initial parental opposition, travels and travails (before reunion?).

The Persian poem obviously follows its Greek original quite closely in names of characters and in narrative details like the meeting in a temple, which surely had no analogue in 'Unsuri's world. The speeches on eros are paired in both Greek and Persian versions; but in the Greek original,

---

[11] Prima facie, the lyre, but see Hägg's discussion (1989: 47–48) for the other possibilities.

Metiochos would seem to be taking a rational or untraditional stand against Parthenope's defense of poesy, whereas in the Persian, Wamiq appears to prefer age to youth in both of his speeches. Hence he may, in Persian cultural terms, be taking the more traditional position. Certainly he is praised by his listeners for his good sense. An apparent divergence between the two is that Wamiq gives the details of his background at an earlier point in the story—to Yani in the temple episode—whereas Metiochos is speaking of these matters with Polykrates as the Greek text begins. But the Greek text, which seems to have more flesh on its narrative bones than the Persian poem, may have Metiochos tell his story twice. The fact of the previous, and devastating, encounter of Metiochos and Parthenope does clear up one passage of the Greek: it makes explicable Parthenope's anger against Metiochos at the end of Column II. Since she has been smitten with eros, she is no doubt furious to hear him deny that he has undergone a similar experience, and would even find it unwelcome.

So far this only provides evidence for the beginning of the novel. A Coptic martyrium of St. Bartanuba, which looks as if it were, as Hägg put it, "the Parthenope romance decapitated,"[12] may provide some clues about further incidents. In the time of Constantine, the twelve-year-old Bartanuba (Parthenope) enters a convent in Byzantium, where her beauty and modesty both astonish and please the good sisters. The devil in jealousy brings her to the notice of the emperor, who decides to marry this model of maidenly perfection. His emissaries kidnap her and bring her into his presence, where he tries to persuade her to consent to a marriage. She cannily claims that she is already married to Christ, so the god-fearing emperor prudently returns her to the convent. The devil tries again, this time with the king of Persia, who—less devout—sends his soldiers to abduct Parthenope. When he meets her, he makes pretty much the same declaration that Constantine did. (Martyr tales are notoriously repetitive.) This time, she pretends to agree, but asks for time to rest and prepare appropriately for marriage, as well as for a fire with which to sacrifice to her God. She also receives a promise from the king that if she dies before him, her body will be returned to her convent for burial. When alone, she prays to Christ to receive her soul and throws herself into the fire, where she dies. The fire, of course, does not

---

[12] The text is listed in the Sahidic rescension of the Coptic Synaxarion for 21 Tubi (= 16 January). Coquin (1981) has edited a Coptic version of the martyr act in which the saint is explicitly identified as "Parthenope"; see Hägg 1984: 64–65.

consume her body or clothes, and after suitable lamentation, her body is returned as she requested, to the rejoicing of the faithful for her martyrdom.

The name, combined with details of a martyrdom that is in fact a suicide, along with the presence of the king of Persia, should give us pause. The girl's beauty, the envy of a potent daimon—the devil behaves not unlike Eros in Xenophon of Ephesos and Chariton or Venus in Apuleius—and lustful admirers of high station are all too familiar from Greek novels. The "death," which unlike other martyrdoms takes place in private, looks suspiciously like the "suicide" of Antheia in Xenophon of Ephesos, which she survives because she has been given a sleep-inducing drug instead of poison. Could this dimly reflect an incident in the novel in which Parthenope escapes the attentions of a would-be suitor by a feigned suicide?

Evidence from a late scholiast indicates that she would have had more than sufficient opportunity to do so. On a line from Dionysios the Periegete's geographical poem calling Naples "the home of holy Parthenope,"[13] the scholiast remarks that this does "not refer as some who are devoted to stories that are suitable for dance understand, to Parthenope the Samian, who in search of her husband wandered to Anaxilaos, but to one of the Sirens. . . . Parthenope is said, although importuned by many men, to have preserved her chastity. From Phrygia, beloved of Metiochos and having cut her hair, she came into Campania and lived there."[14] The twelfth-century bishop and exegete of Homer, Eustathios, takes the opposite line, namely that Dionysios *is* talking about our Parthenope; after providing virtually the same information, he adds that "she cut her hair and condemned herself to lack of comeliness" and that "perhaps because of such prudence [i.e., preserving her chastity], Dionysios names Parthenope 'holy.'"[15]

---

[13] Line 358. So called because one of the Sirens, whose name was Parthenope, was said to have been buried there. See Steph. Byz., s.v. *Neapolis*; Str. 1.2.13, 5.4.7.

[14] *GGM* 2: 445: οὐχ, ὥς τινες ὀρχηστικῇ προσέχοντες ἱστορίᾳ ὑπενόησαν, Παρθενόπης λέγεσθαι τῆς Σαμίας, ἢ τὸν ἄνδρα ζητοῦσα Ἀναξίλαον περιήει, ἀλλὰ μιᾶς τῶν Σειρήνων ... Παρθενόπη λέγεται διὰ τὸ πολλοῖς ὑποπεσοῦσα ἀνδράσι φυλάξαι τὴν παρθενίαν· ἀπὸ δὲ Φρυγίας ἐρασθεῖσα Μητιόχου καὶ ἀποτεμοῦσα τὰς τρίχας εἰς Καμπανίαν ἦλθε καὶ ἐκεῖ ᾤκησεν.

[15] Eustathios cited in *GGM* 2: 445: ἄλλοι δὲ περὶ Παρθενόπης οὕτω λέγουσι· Παρθενόπη πολλοῖς ἀνδράσιν ἐπιβουλευθεῖσα, καὶ τὴν παρθενίαν φυλάξασα, εἶτα Μητιόχου Φρυγὸς ἐρασθεῖσα, τάς τε τρίχας ἔτεμεν ἀκοσμίαν ἑαυτῆς καταψηφιζομένη, καὶ εἰς Καμπανοὺς ἐλθοῦσα ᾤκησε· καὶ τάχα διὰ τὴν τοιαύτην σωφροσύνην ἁγνὴν ὁ Διονύσιος τὴν Παρθενόπην

To this evidence for her wandering we should add Lucian's remark that dramatic performances in Asia include "the suffering of Polykrates and the wanderings of his daughter as far as Persia" (*De salt.* §54). This accords well with the martyr act and the Persian epitome. Parthenope and Metiochos are separated after her father's death, and she wanders around, probably because she is sold to different masters, as are Kallirhoe and Antheia. She seems to have gotten as far as Persia, perhaps to the court of the king, as Kallirhoe in Chariton's novel. The hair-cutting may have resulted from a desire to disguise herself as a man, as Thelxinoe does in Xenophon of Ephesos 5.1.7 (so Maehler 1976: 3 n. 12). But there are other possibilities: in the *Babyloniaka*, Sinonis (Phot. *Epit.* 74b9) cuts her hair in order to make a rope braid to draw water, and the farmer's daughter cuts hers in mourning for her husband (76a40). Or Parthenope may have intended it to be disfiguring in order to put off her admirers. After this, it seems probable that she then traveled west as far as Anaxilaos's court at Rhegion. And, if P. Oxy. 435 is also from this novel, she spent some time on Corcyra, in the control of one of her many admirers. Probably she returned to Samos after her adventures, since in the Persian poem her father interprets the following dream as a propitious omen for the birth of his child: an olive tree sprang up in his court, was torn from its place, passed through the island and other lands, and afterwards returned to cast its shadow over his throne (vv. 16–22).

But what happens to Metiochos? All the available testimonia concentrate on the fate of Parthenope, who seems to be cast from the same mold as novel heroines like Antheia and Sinonis. She is resourceful and determined, characteristics already visible in Herodotos, and still clearly present in the martyr tale and the epitome. She speaks out in a male gathering, contradicting Metiochos, in the Greek fragment. Since she is linked with Phaidra and Rhodope by Lucian (see below) and is the only female character from the novels to have made it to the stage,[16] she must have been one of the most powerful dramatic characters that Greek

---

ὠνόμαϲεν. The statement contained in both of these commentators that Parthenope "lived in Campania" may be erroneous, resulting from a confusion of the novel heroine with the Siren.

[16] If the two pavement mosaics featuring Ninos gazing at a woman's portrait, one from a wealthy litterateur's house in Antioch, the other in Alexandretta, are based on the novel and not a stage performance. See the discussion in "*Ninos*," above.

novelists created, dominating the book and the imaginations of its readers. Is this sufficient to have effaced Metiochos, or was the novel itself lopsided, fixed more on her travails than his? Available evidence suggests otherwise. He, too, seems to have been a fit subject for performance, and he is an equally strong character in the Greek and Persian fragments. Further, at the opening of the Persian poem, Metiochos is paired with a companion—though invisible in the Greek—whose function must have been to accompany him in misfortune, as Kleinias accompanies Kleitophon in Achilles Tatius, when he is separated from Parthenope.

HISTORICAL BACKGROUND

Metiochos and Parthenope, like *Ninos* and the novels of Chariton and Heliodoros, is self-consciously historical, its background material selected, it would seem, from the accounts of Polykrates and Miltiades found in Herodotos. Book 3.124 provides the tale of Polykrates' unnamed daughter, who, on the basis of an ominous dream, tries to dissuade her father from going to the court of Oroetes in Magnesia, a satrap of Kyros governing Sardis. Polykrates refuses to listen and threatens his daughter that if he returns safely, he will keep her unmarried. She replies only that she would prefer to remain unwed rather than lose her father. This anecdote no doubt contributed to our novelist naming his heroine Parthenope, if the name had not already been attached in some other source. The saga continues (3.140–51) with the murder of Polykrates by Oroetes; the installation of his secretary, Maiandrios, as regent of Samos in his place; and the restoration of Polykrates' brother, Syloson, with the help of Dareios. In Book 6, Herodotos gives us the details of Metiochos. He was a son of Miltiades, by his first wife (6.41); Miltiades is now married to Hegesipyle, the daughter of the Thracian king, Oloros (6.39). Finally, Parthenope in her wanderings arrives at the court of yet another tyrant known from Herodotos (6.23, 7.165), Anaxilaos of Rhegion, who is said to have had close connections with Samos. He may be the "master" of the epitome, to whom she narrates her travails and who sets her free.

Our novelist, however, was no slave to historical accuracy. Polykrates was killed by Oroetes in 522/1, whereas Metiochos's birth must have fallen somewhere between 528 and 516. It is clear from the Persian epitome that Polykrates is alive when Metiochos visits Samos. So either the author has taken liberties with the relative chronology, which is after all not entirely clear in Herodotos, or he confused Metiochos's father Miltiades with a paternal great-uncle (Hdt. 6.34–38) of the same name who was *oikistēs* of the Chersonese at an earlier period (Hägg 1985: 93). There seems to have been another confusion—or was it intended as a sly joke? The Persian poem tells us that Metiochos is a relative of Polykrates, and that Polykrates is a son of Aeakos, the son of Zeus. According to Herodotos (3.39), however, Polykrates is the son of Aeakes; it is the family of Metiochos that traces descent from Aeakos (6.35). The two, for whatever reasons, are conflated in the Persian poem, and indeed, Folikrat/Polikrates and Wamiq/Metiochos regard themselves as kin. Finally, Anaxilaos ruled Rhegion from 498 to 476. So unless Parthenope wandered for twenty-two years after her father's death, the novelist is again taking liberties with the chronology.

THE DATE OF THE NOVEL

Like *Ninos* and Chariton's novel, to which it is similar in its historical dimension and in its language, *Metiochos and Parthenope* seems to have been among the earliest Greek novels. Based on an investigation of its language, A. Dihle would locate it before the flowering of Atticism, even as early as the first century B.C.E. (1978: 54–55). Certainly it must have been written no later than the first century C.E., since it will have predated Lucian's dialogues, perhaps by some distance if by his time it had become a staple for theatrical performance. Lucian attests performances of female impersonators in soft garments who dance or mime the stories of love-stricken women—Phaidras, Parthenopes, and Rhodopes (*De salt.* §2)—and, in another dialogue, he mentions those who take the roles of Metiochos or Ninos or Achilles (*Pseudol.* §25).[17]

Our novel is also linked with *Ninos* in having its characters represented in floor mosaics as well as on the stage. Like the mosaics in which Metiochos and Parthenope are depicted, the *Ninos* mosaics must

---

[17] Kokolakis (1959: 49) cautions against identifying the Parthenope mentioned by Lucian with the novel heroine on the grounds that "she ought to be a very virtuous character," and the company of Rhodope and Phaidra suggests otherwise. His argument that she (and Metiochos) are to be rather identified with a mythological tradition mentioned in Eustathius is not cogent, however. Surely the later scholiastic material derives from the novel, not some independent source. (We are indebted to our colleague E. Courtney for calling Kokolakis's discussion of Lucian's dialogue to our attention.)

represent scenes derived directly from the novel or from a mime that at least indirectly depended on the novel. These circumstances incline us to believe that *Ninos* and *Metiochos and Parthenope* may have been near contemporaries, and perhaps the first examples in Greek of this type of writing. If so, the very fact of their novelty might account, at least in part, for their popularity.

DESCRIPTION

In 1976, H. Maehler discovered that P. Berol. 21179 (12.0 × 19.0 cm) was the missing link between two previously published fragments of a papyrus roll (= P^2 2622)—P. Berol. 7927 (12.0 × 31.0 cm) and P. Berol. 9588 (10.7 × 15.8 cm). Together they form two consecutive columns of text, thirty-eight lines in height, with between thirty-three and thirty-seven letters per line; 9588 and 21179 constitute the top and bottom of one column, 7927 the next column. The opening letters for lines 32–38 of Col. I fall at the bottom of 21179. There are five or six lines missing from the top of Column I, and its lines lack ten to fifteen letters from their beginnings. Column II is severely worn in several places, but is missing only a few letters from its line beginnings. Line ends are slightly uneven, and the columns seem to tilt slightly to the right. The text is written across the fibers on the back of an account of rents, which from the place names ought to have come from the Fayum. The scribe wrote a practiced, rapidly written hand with documentary affinities and a tendency to separate words, assigned by previous editors to the second century C.E. The text is heavily corrected by what appears to be the original hand, though there are still a number of uncorrected errors. There are numerous itacisms, but no lectional signs. The scribe sometimes marks elision, sometimes neglects it. The author himself sometimes allows hiatus.

COLUMN I [5–6 lines missing]

]. [..]ο̣λ̣[..] . [
] τίς," εἶπεν, "ὦ [
]α̣ϲ̣αι. πῶϲ Χερρο[
4   ]γ̣ . . κ̣ . ϲ εἰϲ γάμον, εἰ μὲν [...]
] . . ϲη καὶ φίλοϲ, εἰ δ' ἔπηλ[υϲ]
] . . . τοῦ πατρὸϲ ὀλιγωρία[...]
]μ̣ε̣ν̣α̣ διορθώϲομαι τὸ λοι[...]
8   κ]α̣τ̣αϲτήϲαϲ εἰϲ ὑψηλότερον
] . μᾶλλον γένηται τῇ Παρθενό-
πη "ὁ] μὲν πατήρ," εἶπεν, "βαϲιλεῦ, μα-
]γειαι καὶ οἱ θεοὶ δῷηϲαν αὐτῷ
12] . π̣οηϲειν · φ[ι]λότεκνοϲ γὰρ ὡϲ
] . τ̣ώτατον [εἰ]ϲ ἐπιβουλὴν θη-
] . τα ἀποθρ[..] . ϲ καὶ κατὰ προ-
]α Ἡγηϲι[πύ]λη τῶν ἑαυτῆϲ
16 π]αίδων οἱ [δι]ὰ νεότητα κτη-
]λειαϲ · ἐμοὶ δὲ . χ . [..]οηϲιν κατ'
] καίπερ ἀνηλέ[αϲ π]α̣ϲχων
] ἀλλ' ἐμὲ γὰρ τῷ πα[ν]τ̣ὶ ϲτάϲιν
20 ο]ὐδεὶϲ αἰτίαϲ ἐπε[.] . [.]εν . . . . .
ἤ]ρξατο κακῶν ἐπιβουλη[...] . [.]
]γ ἐνήδρευεν μεια[. . . . . .]
] τὸν ϲὸν οἶκον καὶ τὴν [. . . . .]
24]πέ̣[λ]αβον." πάντων δὲ τῶ[ν] ε[.]
θαυ]μαϲ άντων τὸ εὔθαρϲεϲ κα̣ὶ̣

The conjectures of Diels and of Kaibel and Robert (= K–R) are to be found in Krebs 1895; those of Merkelbach and Schaefer in Maehler 1976.

Col. I: 3. Χερρο[νηϲίτηϲ] Zimm.   6. ολειγωρια[pap.   7. [ἐϲφαλ]μένα̣ or [ἠδικη]-μένα Merk.   8. υψηλο~τερον pap.   10. μακρον-pap.   12. ο written above η pap.   12–13. ὡϲ | [ἀληθῶϲ] Zimm.   15.]α̅ pap.   16. [γνηϲίων π]αίδων Merk., προνοουμένη π]αίδων? Maeh.   18. [π]α̣ϲχων Maeh., [παρ]αϲχὼν Schub.   19. εμαι pap. Read ἐμὲ? Maeh.   20. [ἐκ τίνοϲ οἶδεν ο]ὐδεὶϲ αἰτίαϲ? Maeh. At end, ὅτε δὴ Maeh., ὁτὲ δὲ Zimm., Vogl.   23. [κατέφυγον ἐπὶ] Merk.   24–25. ἐ|[πιδημούντων] Merk., ἑ|[ταίρων] Schaefer

82

] as] . . .

] "Who," he said, "O[

] . . .? How . . . [

4   ] . . . for marriage, if on the one hand

] and friend, if on the other a stranger

] the contempt of my father

] I shall correct . . . for the [future?]

8   ] having set more loftily

] in order that he may be more for Parthenope

] "My father," he said, "O king

] and may the gods give him

12] to do. For loving his children as

] most . . . for a plot

] . . .

] Hegesipyle of her own

16] children, who, on account of their youth

] but me

] although suffering pitiless

] but for me at least in every respect a revolution

20] no one . . . the reasons . . .

] the plot began misfortunes

] she(?) laid a snare . . .

] your home and [

24] I took up. All those who [were present]

] marveled at the courage and

τῶν] λόγων ὁ Πολυκράτηc ὑπερ
]ν," ἔφη, "τέκνον, πότου καιρὸc
28]γειν χρὴ τὰ λυποῦντα μεθη
]υτωνομεια cχολάζομεν
]. ων εἰc τὸν Ἀναξιμένην οι
]‥c ἡμῖν," ἔφη, "cήμερον α-
32]τ[ο]υ παιδὸc ἥκοντοc ενω
] μαντεύομαι μοῦcαν, προτι-

COLUMN II

[θεὶc τ]ὴν φ[ιλ]οcόφου ζήτηcιν κατὰ τύχην τ[‥‥]."
[καὶ ἐταράχθ]ηcαν οἱ δύο τὰc ψυχὰc λαβ[όν-]
36 [τεc ‥‥‥‥]ου πάθουc ἀνάμνηcιν ἐφο[‥]
[‥‥‥‥‥] Μητίοχοc ὑποτιμηcάμεν[οc
[‥‥‥‥ εἰ]κότα ἢ μάθηcιν πρέπουc[αν
[‥‥] . [‥‥‥] . ξει. "βωμολόχοι μὲν," εἶπεν, "α[
40 [‥‥] . οι τῆ[c ἀλ]ηθοῦc παιδείαc ἀμύητοι αρ . [‥]
[‥‥] μυθ[ολ]ογίαιc ἐπακολουθοῦcι ὡc ἔcτ[ιν]
[ὁ Ἔρ]ωc Ἀφρο[δ]ίτηc υἱὸc κομιδῆ νέοc ἔχω[ν]
[πτερ]ὰ καὶ τῷ [ν]ώτῳ παρηρτημένον τόξον κα[ὶ τῇ]
44 [χειρὶ] κρατῶν λαμπάδα τούτοιc τε τοῖc ὅπλοιc ὡ[μῶc]

―――――――――――――――――――

26. [τὸ γενναῖον τῶν] λόγων? Maeh.   26–27. ὑπὲρ|[ηcθεὶc, "νῦν μὲν οὖ]ν" Maeh.,
ὑπερ|[ηcθεὶc πρὸc τὴν Παρθενόπη]ν or ὑπερ[τιθώμεθα ταῦτ᾽ εἰc αὔριο]ν Merk.   27. εφη
ꟃ pap.   28. [ἀπά]γειν Merk.   μέθη or μεθη[cομένουc]? Maeh.   29.]υτωνο
μεια pap., [ἕωc ἔτι ἐν α]ὐτονομίᾳ Merk., το]ύτων ὅμοια? Maeh.   30. [βλέ]πων or [cκώ-
π]των? Maeh.   33. [ἐρωτικὴν] μαντεύομαι μοῦcαν? Maeh.
Col. II: 34. τ[ινά] K–R, τ[ίνα] Merk., τ[αύτην] Maeh.   35. [ἐταράχθ]ηcαν Zimm.
]ηcαν καὶ pap.   35–36. λαβ[όν|τεc τοῦ καιν]οῦ πάθουc ἀνάμνηcιν? Maeh.
36. ἐφ᾽ ο[ἷc] Wil.   36–37. ἐφο[βήθηcαν] or ἐφο[βοῦντο γὰρ]? Maeh.   37–38. ὑπο-
τιμηcάμεν[οc | (τὸ?) μὴ ἔχειν λόγον εἰ]κότα? Maeh.   38–39. πρέπουc[αν | τῇ τοιαύτῃ
διαλ]έξει Merk.   39–40. ἄ[|παντεc] K–R, ἀ|[ληθῶc] Merk.   40. [ὅ]cο[ι] Zimm.
40–41. ἀρχ[αιο|τάταιc] Lav., ἀρχ[αί|αιc] Maeh.   41. επακολουθουcει pap.
42. ὁ Ἔρω]c K–R   ]ειτηcυιοcκομειτηναιοc pap., read κομιδῆ νέοc Diels   43. παρη
ρκτημενονδοξον pap., read παρηρτημένον τόξον Diels   43–44. τῇ | χειρὶ] Maeh.,
[ταῖc | χερcὶ] K–R   44. ὡ[μῶc] K–R

] of the words, Polykrates . . .
] said, "Child, it is time for drinking
28] inebriation should . . . whatever grieves us
] . . . we are at leisure
] looked to Anaximenes
] to us," he said, "today
32] the boy having come
] I predict a . . . muse, in proposing

COLUMN II

] the philosopher's inquiry as chance would have it."
[And] the two [were thrown into a turmoil?] in their souls
36] the recollection of . . . suffering
[——] Metiochos uttered a disclaimer that [he could make]
] a reasonable speech or [had] suitable knowledge
[for such a conversation?] "On the one hand," he said, "fools [
40] those uninitiated in true education
] heed the old stories, that
] Love is the son of Aphrodite, quite young, with
wings and accoutered with a bow on his back and
44 holding a torch in his hand, and with these armaments [cruelly]

[. . . . .]   blank   τὰς ψυχὰς τῶν [νέων]
[τιτρώ]ϲκει · γέλως δ᾽ ἂν εἴη τὸ τοιοῦτο · πρῶτον μ[ὲν]
[ἐντεκ]γωθὲν αἰῶϲι καὶ ἀφ᾽ οὗ ϲυνέϲτηκ[εν]
48   [. . . .] ˌον χρογοῦν βρέφος μὴ τελειωθῆναι, κ[αὶ]
[εἰ τὰ ὑ]πὸ τῶν ἀνθρώπων γεννώμενα [τέκνα]
[τοῖϲ] χρόνοιϲ τῇ ἡλικίᾳ προβαίνει τον ˌ [. . . .]
[μεμοι]ραμένον φύϲεωϲ καθάπερ τοὺϲ ἀναπ ˌ [. . . .]
52   [. . . .] ἐπὶ τῆϲ αὐτῆϲ μένειν τὰ πο[. . . . .]
[εἴη δ᾽] ἂν κἀκεῖνο παντελῶϲ ἀπίθαν̣ο̣[ν, εἰ]
[βρέφ]οϲ ἐϲτὶν ὁ Ἔρωϲ, περινοϲτεῖν αὐτ̣[ὸ]ν̣ ὅ[λη]ν̣ τὴ[ν]
[οἰκου]μένην, τοξεύειν μὲν τῶν ὑπαντών-
56   των, οὓϲ ἂν αὐτὸϲ ἐθέλῃ, κ̣α̣ὶ̣ πυρπ[ο]λεῖν
[ὥϲτ᾽ ἐ]ν̣ μὲν ταῖϲ τῶν ἐρώντων ψυχαῖϲ ἐγγίγνε-
[ϲθαι] ἱερὸν πνεῦμά τι οἷον θε[ο]φόρ̣ ˌ . . · ἴϲα-
[ϲι δ᾽ οἱ] ἤδη τοῦ παιδὸϲ πάθουϲ εἰληφότεϲ πεῖραν. ἐγὼ
60   [δέ γ᾽ οὔ]πω—μηδὲ πειραθείην τὸ ϲύγο̣λον. Ἔρωϲ
[δ᾽ ἔϲτ]ιν κίνημα διανοίαϲ ὑπὸ [κ]άλλουϲ γινόμε-
[νον] καὶ ὑπὸ ϲυνηθείαϲ αὐξόμεν̣ο̣ν.” ρ ˌ . . ν̣ ἐβου-
[. . . .]ν λόγον περαίνειν καὶ ὁ [᾽Α]γ̣[α]ξιμένηϲ δι-
64   [ελέγ]ετο πρὸϲ τὴν Παρθενόπην ἀντιλαβέϲθαι
[τῆϲ ζ]ητήϲεωϲ · κἀκείνη
δ[ι᾽ ὀ]ργῆϲ ἔχουϲα τὸν Μητίοχον δ̣ι̣ά̣ τὸ μὴ ὁμολογῆϲαι μήπω ο̣ὐ̣δεμία̣ϲ̣ ἐραϲ-

---

45. The line is blank before τὰϲ ψυχὰϲ   τῶν [νέων] K–R   46. [τιτρώ]ϲκει Krebs
47.]νωθεν—αιωϲει pap., [τοῖϲ ἄν]ωθεν αἰῶϲι K–R   47–48. ϲυνέϲτηκ[εν ὁ βίοϲ |
ἄπυϲ]τον χρόν[ιο]ν K–R   48. χρονοῦν Maeh.   48–49. κ[αὶ | εἰ] M. Maehler
49. [τά γ᾽ ὑ]πο Merk.   γεννωμεν̣ωα pap.   49–50. [τέκνα | τοῖϲ] Merk.
50. προβενει pap., read προβαίνει Krebs   50–51. τὸν [δὲ θείαϲ | μεμοι]ρα-
μένον K–R   51. ἀναπ[ήρουϲ] Merk.   52. αυτηϲαυτηϲ pap.   τὰ πό[ρρω]
M. Maehler   53. [εἴη δὲ] K–R   απειθαγο[pap., read ἀπίθ[ανον] K–R
54. περινοϲτιν pap., read περινοϲτεῖν Krebs   55. οἰκου]μένην K–R   56. [ταϲ
ψυ]χαϲ apparently deleted, των added above line   ουϲεαν pap., read οὓϲ ἂν K–R
57. νᵉ pap.   58. θε[ο]φορήτοῖϲ Maeh.   ϊϲα[pap.   58–59. ἄπ[ερ | ἴϲαϲιν οἱ]
Maeh.   61. κεινημα pap.   ὑπὸ [κ]άλλουϲ Maeh., ὑπὸ [π]άθουϲ Wil.
65. κακεινηδιοργηϲεχουϲατον pap.   66–67. ωμο|λογηϲαιτονερωτα pap.,
read ὁμολογῆϲαι

wounds the souls of the young.
This sort of thing would be absurd, first of all that
a child engendered with the ages and ageing ever since he
[first?] took form
48   has not come to maturity; [and]
[if the children] borne by mortals
in time reach adulthood, [it would be absurd] that the [young
child?]
[sharing a divine?] nature, like [stunted things?],
52   [always] remained at the same age.[. . .]
And this too would be completely unbelievable, if
Love is a child, that he wanders around the whole
world, to strike with his arrows
56   whomever he wishes of those he meets and to enflame them,
[so that] in the souls of lovers a holy
breath arises, as in the inspired. [But they know?]
who already have experienced suffering from the boy;
60   I have not yet done so—may I never experience it at all! Love
rather is a stirring of the mind aroused by beauty
and increasing with familiarity." . . . He wanted
to finish his remarks and Anaximenes urged
64   Parthenope to take part in the
inquiry. And she,
in anger at Metiochos for not admitting
that he had not yet loved a woman

68 θῆναι (καὶ εὔξατο μηδὲ μέλλειν·) " . . . . . ," ἔφη,
"κενὸ[ϲ] ὁ τοῦ ξένου λῆροϲ κα[. . .] δοκεῖ μ[οι] ὅτι
ἡμ[ῖ]ν ἐπὶ παιδείαϲ θύραν . . . . ϲ καὶ
ποιηταὶ καὶ ζωγράφοι καὶ π[λάϲτα]ι τοῦτον

---

68. μητε corrected to μηδε pap.   "μὰ τὸν" M. Maehler   69. κα[ὶ οὐ] or κα[θὼϲ]
Maeh.   70. παιδιαϲ pap.   71. [πλάϲται] K–R.

68   (and he prayed that he would not), said, "[By god],
the trifle of the stranger is hollow, [and I do not] think that
for us to the portal of education. . . .
[writers] and poets and painters and sculptors [——] this one
[Love?]

COLUMN I

2.] τίς," εἶπεν, "ὦ[: Polykrates is speaking to Metiochos. His remarks probably
end in line 7. The subject is not Parthenope's marriage, but what Polykrates
can do to aid Metiochos in straitened circumstances. Maehler would supplement "τίς," εἶπεν, "ὦ [φίλοι, δύναιτ' ἂν περὶ τούτου δικ]άσαι; or sim.

3. πῶς Χερρο[: Metiochos's father was ruler in the Thracian Chersonese (Hdt.
6.34–41). E. Bowie suggests πῶς Χερρό[νηςον κατέλιπες; or sim.

4. εἰς γάμον: this cannot refer to the marriage of Metiochos and Parthenope.
The topic is either Miltiades' marriage to Hegesipyle, which is the cause of
Metiochos's difficulties (see below, lines 13–22), or marriage in general.

6. τοῦ πατρὸς ὀλιγωρία[: probably Miltiades' spurning of his son, now that he
has remarried, rather than contempt for Miltiades. It is either the object of
διορθώςομαι or part of a phrase like [ὑπὸ τῆς] τοῦ πατρὸς ὀλιγωρία[ς with
]μενα below as object, e.g., Merkelbach's [ἠδικη]μένα. "I shall correct the
injustices done by my father's spurning of me."

7. τὸ λοι[: probably τὸ λοι[πόν = "the future," but τὸ λοι[δόρημα is also a possible restoration (so Maehler).

8. κ]αταστήςας εἰς ὑψηλότερον: probably beginning a two-line section of external narration, in which Metiochos takes a higher seat at table. (Merkelbach's
τόπον or sim. will supplement.) Hägg (1985: 102) cites v. 133 from the Persian
poem where Polykrates "had him sit in a more honored seat." But this does
not suit the Greek, which seems to be followed by a final clause. "He took a
higher seat *so that* he might be more visible to Parthenope," or sim.? See the
next note.

9–10. μᾶλλον γένηται τῇ Παρθενό|πῃ: Merkelbach suggests, e.g., ἵν]α μᾶλλον
γένηται τῇ Παρθενό|[πῃ καταφανής. Maehler takes a rather different line with
κ]αταστήςας εἰς ὑψηλότερον | [ἀξίωμα ——ἵν]α μᾶλλον γένηται τῇ Παρθε-
νό|[πῃ κεχαριςμένος.

10. "ὁ] μὲν πατήρ," εἶπεν: Metiochos begins to speak, apparently explaining that
he has left his own country because of his stepmother, but also because of
political troubles (see below). The Persian version is no help here. Not surprisingly, Greek politics has been supplanted by a series of gnomic verses on
the dangers of trusting an evil woman.
βαςιλεῦ: Polykrates.

11. οἱ θεοὶ δῷηςαν αὐτῷ: Metiochos would seem to be speaking well of his father (αὐτῷ), despite the difficulties.

12.] ˌ ποηϲειν: the text has a superlinear correction, but is still obscure. It is either an infinitive or an itacism for a noun in -ϲιν. Maehler claims παι-δ]οροποηϲεῖν is barely possible. Zimmermann's [ϲωφροϲύνην τε καὶ δι]αγόηϲιν is more attractive: "May the gods grant him prudence and good judgment."

φ[ι]λότεκνοϲ: either part of Metiochos's wish for his father or a reference to Hegesipyle, whose children are mentioned below.

13. [εἰ]ϲ ἐπιβουλὴν: plots are mentioned again below, line 21, and stasis in line 19.

13–14. θη-: Maehler suggests θῆ|[λυ γένοϲ] or sim., comparing Hld. 10.4.32.

14. ἀποθρ[..] ˌ ϲ: Maehler suggests ἀπὸ Θρ[ᾴκ]ηϲ; the region is appropriate for Metiochos as well as Hegesipyle.

15. Ἡγηϲι[πύ]λη: Hegesipyle was the daughter of King Oloros of Thrace. We might easily imagine that Hegesipyle, in the typical fashion of literary step-mothers, used her father's power to cause trouble for her stepson, in order to further the pretensions of her own children (τῶν ἑαυτῆϲ [——— π]αίδων, below, lines 15–16).

15–16. τῶν ἑαυτῆϲ [——— π]αίδων: Maehler supplements, e.g., ἡ μητρυι]ὰ Ἡγηϲι[πύ]λη τῶν ἑαυτῆϲ | [προνοουμένη π]αίδων.

17. ˌ χ ˌ [..]οηϲιν: Maehler suggests reading ὀχλ[οπ]όηϲιν, a word occurring only in Hesychios as a *varia lectio* for δημαγωγίαϲ. This would seem to indicate that Metiochos's (or his father's) difficulties included a revolution or serious political unrest, in addition to the machinations of a stepmother.

18. Either ἀνηλέ[αϲ or ἀνηλέ[α.

22. ἐνήδρευέν με: "she ensnared me. . . ." In the political upheaval?

23–24. τὸν ϲὸν οἶκον καὶ τὴν [: Metiochos is still speaking. Hägg (1985: 102) cites v. 135 of the Persian poem in which Polykrates says, "You have come to your own home and city." Obviously, one can restore τὴν [ϲὴν πόλιν], but here Polykrates cannot be speaking. A supplement along the lines of Merkelbach's and Maehler's [κατέφυγον ἐπὶ] τὸν ϲὸν οἶκον καὶ τὴν [ϲωτηρίαν | ἕξειν ὑ]πέ[λ]α-βον is more likely.

24–25. πάντων δὲ τῶ[ν] ε[——— θαυ]μαϲάντων: all the guests at the symposium.

27.]ν," ἔφη, "τέκνον, πότου καιρὸϲ: Polykrates initiates the symposium. Mixed-sex drinking parties that included wellborn wives and daughters (as opposed to *hetairai*) were not part of normal Greek behavior, but seem frequent enough in narrative fiction. Cf. AT 1.5; Hld. 6.6–7; *Apollonios*, lines 1–6, below. Maehler also lists Ath. 13.575 b–f = *FGrHist* 125 F5 (Chares of Mitylene), the story of Odatis and Zariadres. In any case, we learn from the Persian poem that 'Adhra' was reared as if she were a son, so her presence at this gathering would not be surprising.

To whom does τέκνον refer? Polykrates might be addressing his daughter, but more likely Metiochos, who is supposed to be kin.

30. τὸν Ἀναξιμένην: Anaximenes was from Miletos, and although his *floruit* coincides roughly with that of Polykrates, there is no evidence to link him with the Samian court (unlike Ibykos; see above, introduction). To judge from the Persian sources, Anaximenes was present deliberately to test Metiochos, and he introduces the subject of eros after observing the condition of the young people. But it is not obvious at which point the topic was been introduced. If it is not in lines 33–34, then the subject must have been set before Metiochos gives an account of himself.

In staging a symposium devoted to a discussion of eros, the author will expect his readers to recollect Plato's famous drinking party, and the philosophical tone of Metiochos's remarks reinforces the allusion.

31–32. E. Bowie suggests ἀ|[πὸ Χερρονήcου].

32.]τ[ο]υ παιδὸc ἥκοντοc: the arrival of Metiochos?

32–33. ενω: ἐν ᾧ (sc. Metiochos)? "In whom . . . I divine a [———] muse."

33. μαντεύομαι μοῦcον: Maehler supplements [ἐρωτικὴν], "I divine an erotic muse." This could be a sly reference to the newly kindled passions of Metiochos and Parthenope, or—restoring a different adjective—a compliment to Metiochos's skill at speaking.

COLUMN II

34. Anaximenes' remark must end before the verb in the next line.

36–37. Maehler suggests reading ἐφο[βοῦντο γὰρ.] or sim., but this kind of interjection seems never to stand at the end of a sentence in the novelists. Possibly ἐφο[βεῖ]το μὲν γὰρ ὁ] Μητίοχοc.

37–39. Metiochos begins his speech with the usual rhetorical disclaimer. ὑποτιμηcάμενο[c (τὸ ?) μὴ ἔχειν λόγον εἰ]κότα (Maeh.) ἢ μάθηcιν πρέπουc[αν τῇ τοιαύτῃ διαλ]έξει (Merk.) or sim.: "pleading that [he could not make] an appropriate speech or have sufficient learning [for such a discussion]." Cf. Wamiq's similar protest in the Persian poem: "The mature and experienced heart is more suitable for knowledge and science [sc. than mine]. | In such a difficult affair I have had no experience and there will be no reprieve for me" (vv. 153–54).

45. The scribe has left the initial two-thirds of this line blank, probably because he could not read his exemplar. Such gaps are found in a number of papyrus texts, the purpose of which—one assumes—is to leave sufficient space for the correct text, should a reader find it in another copy. Here, since the passage seems complete, we can only speculate that the missing words would have been other objects linked with τὰc ψυχάc.

91

47. ἐντεκ]νωθὲν αἰῶϲι: we owe this excellent supplement to E. Bowie. The phrase is apparently chiastic—two participles linked by καί and modifying βρέφοϲ, and two temporal phrases, αἰῶϲι and ἀφ' οὗ κτλ. Both verbs are rare and late: ἐντεκνοῦμαι occurs in Plut. *Cat. min.* §25, χρονόω in Plot. 3.7.11.

47–48. ἀφ' οὗ ϲυνέϲτηκ[εν | . . . .] . ον: cf. ἐξ ὧν ϲυνέϲτηκεν ὁ κόϲμοϲ (Arist. *Nic. eth.* 1141b2), but what is missing? M. Maehler suggests [τὸ πρῶ]τον.

For the thought, compare Longus 2.5.2, where Eros says to Philetas: οὔ τοι παῖϲ ἐγὼ καὶ εἰ δοκῶ παῖϲ, ἀλλὰ καὶ τοῦ Κρόνου πρεϲβύτεροϲ καὶ αὐτοῦ τοῦ παντὸϲ χρόνου.

50–51. τον . [. . . . | μεμοι]ραμένον φύϲεωϲ: the sense is clear—While mortal children come to adulthood in time, the child partaking of divine nature, like stunted things, always remains at the same age. But one expects τὸ, not τὸν. τὸ νέ[ον θείαϲ] is a tight squeeze, but possible.

58–59. Maehler's supplement is surely right on sense, but too long for space. Also, *tremata* stand above the iota of ιϲα at the end of line 58, which tend to indicate the beginning of a word. We suggest θε[ο]φόροιϲ . ἴϲα|[ϲι δ' οἱ], rather than θε[ο]φορήτοῖϲ ἄπ[ερ | ἴϲαϲιν οἱ].

60–62. Ἔρωϲ | [δ' ἔϲτ]ιν κίνημα διανοίαϲ ὑπὸ [κ]άλλουϲ γινόμε|[νον] καὶ ὑπὸ ϲυνηθείαϲ αὐξόμενον: see above, introduction n. 7.

62–63. αὐξόμενον." ρ . . γ εβου[[. . . .]ν λόγον: the text is corrupt. There is insufficient space for ἐβού|[λετο τὸ]ν, which sense demands, probably because a το was omitted through haplography. (Maehler would restore ἐβού[λε|το τὸ]ν, but that would make line 62 two letters longer than any other in the column.) Before that, Maehler reads ρυτιν or ρυτην (sc. ῥύδην). And whereas αὐξόμενον must be correct, the final letters are odd-looking. Most likely a haplography of some sort occurred here also, perhaps of a phrase with τρόπον; e.g., "[In such a way] he desired to finish his speech. . . ."

63–64. From the Persian poem we learn that "at two years, onto a path of learning ['Adhra'] set out, igniting her heart with knowledge. | When she turned seven, the inquisitive one became an astrologer and a clever writer" (vv. 27–28). Even allowing for the extreme hyperbole of the Persian, it seems likely that Parthenope speaks here as one already skilled in traditional male public discourse, not as a shy and tongue-tied miss normally confined to the women's quarters.

68. καὶ εὔξατο μηδὲ μέλλειν (sc. ἐραϲθῆναι), so Kaibel-Robert. The indicative following the articular infinitive is peculiar. We follow E. Bowie's suggestion that the remark is intended to be parenthetic; Maehler suggests that an ὅτι may have dropped out.

68–71. The combined restorations of H. and M. Maehler give good sense: "μὰ τὸν," ἔφη, | "κενὸ[ϲ] ὁ τοῦ ξένου λῆροϲ κα[ὶ οὐ] δοκεῖ μ[οι] ὅτι | ἡμ[ῖ]ν ἐπὶ παιδείαϲ θύραν ϲυγγραφεῖϲ καὶ | ποιηταὶ καὶ ζωγράφοι καὶ π[λάϲτα]ι τοῦτον . . . =

92

"By god," she said, "the trifle of the stranger is hollow, and I do [not] think
that writers and poets and painters and sculptors [———] us to the portal of
education."

OSTRACON

O. Bodl. 2175 (= P^2 2782) is a small pottery fragment from the Roman period
first published by J. Tait and C. Préaux in *Greek Ostraca in the Bodleian Library*
as a "literary text of uncertain character" (p. 388). It was identified and assigned
to *Metiochos and Parthenope* by M. Gronewald (1977: 21–22), who suggested
that it might belong to the novel—a letter, perhaps, written by Metiochos to
Parthenope. Given what we know about the plot, it is difficult to imagine why
Metiochos would have written such a note, and how he imagined that it could
have been delivered. If it is from the novel, it is far more likely to have been a
soliloquy. Since an ostracon is an ephemeral writing surface, however, and since
the characters from the novel were popular subjects for theatrical performance,
the ostracon is just as likely to be a derivative composition, perhaps related to
rhetorical exercise, or a quotation of a famous line from a stage performance.

- -

] . ε

] . α . . . . εν, Παρ-	Parthenope,
[θ]ενόπη, καὶ τοῦ ϲοῦ	are you forgetful
4 [Μ]ητιόχου λήϲμων	4 of your Metiochos?
[ε]ῖ · ἐγὼ μέν, ἀφ᾽ ἧϲ ἡμέραϲ	From the day
[ἀ]πῆλθεϲ, ὥϲπερ ἀνα-	you [left], as if
κεκολλημένων ἰξῷ	my eyes were glued fast,
8 τῶν ὀμμάτων ὕ-	8 without sleep . . .
πνον οὐκ [. . . . . .]	
[. . .] . . [	

- -

OSTRACON

4. λήϲμων : LSJ records only Them. *Or.* 22.268c.

6–8. ἀνα|κεκολλημένων ἰξῷ | τῶν ὀμμάτων : the reading was suggested by Peter Parsons. ἀνακολλάω, according to Gronewald, is a technical term in the medical writers describing the eyelashes gummed together with mucus. Gronewald takes this to mean that Metiochos's eyelashes were so gummed that he could no longer close his eyes.

    The comic poet Timotheos uses the expression ἰξὸϲ ὀμμάτων of Eros (frag. 2 Kock).

8–9. P. J. Parsons (Gronewald 1977: 22) suggests the supplement ὕ|πνον οὐκ [ἔχων.

Metiochos and Parthenope?

❖

Little remains of the text to which P. Oxy. 435 belongs beyond a few names and a tantalizing mention of marriage and *parthe*[. Grenfell and Hunt supposed it to be history, but Fuhr suggested that it was "romance." Zimmermann, restoring the name Parthenope in lines 6–7, attached the fragment to the novel of *Metiochos and Parthenope*. Maehler and Ziegler have rejected this on the grounds that the connection is too tenuous. Of course, the restoration itself is uncertain, and although Parthenope's travels from Samos to Naples may well have led her to stop in Corcyra, which lies along her route, there is no reason to imagine that the Corcyraeans as a group would have been concerned about her marriage. Further, the piece introduces at least two characters who do not figure in the other fragments of that novel.

There is, however, a piece of evidence that was unavailable to Maehler, and indeed to Zimmermann himself, which tends to support his identification. H. Ritter, in his discussion of lexical fragments from 'Unṣuri's *Wamiq and 'Aḏhra*', mentions a character named Damchasinos, whom he tentatively identifies as Demoxenos. He is a merchant in love with Parthenope, who gets possession of her apparently by a trick (1948: 138 [no. 17]). The Persian fragment says: "The heart of Damchasinos was aflutter. What sort of slyness should be set about in the affair of 'Aḏhra'?" Demoxenos might well be the name in lines 2–3, and such circumstances as there are tend to fit our fragment.[1] He could have gotten himself appointed Parthenope's watchdog, then stolen her away from another lover who intended to marry her (see line 8). But all this is highly speculative.

If this is not a fragment from *Metiochos and Parthenope*, it may not even belong to a novel. Of the other available options, rhetorical exercise can almost certainly be ruled out: the Corcyraeans figure in such exercises only insofar as they are at odds with the Corinthians; they would appear to have no rhetorical life independent of the tradition from Thucydides. And in the sumbouleutic speeches themselves, Cor-

---

[1] Kussl (1991: 167 n. 7) has independently made a similar observation.

cyra is scarcely mentioned beyond the fact of Timotheos's naval victory off its coast. This fragment could easily belong to a private oration, however; for sensationalism and adventure it is difficult to surpass the speech against Neaira attributed to Demosthenes (59). It might also come from a prose paraphrase or hypothesis of New Comedy.

DESCRIPTION

P. Oxy. 435 (= P^2 2623, measuring 12.5 × 10.8 cm) is a fragment from a light-colored papyrus roll preserving portions of two columns, the right of which appears to be missing only four letters from the beginning of its lines. Lines average twenty letters. An upper margin of at least 2.0 cm and an intercolumnar space of 1.5 cm remain, but the original height of the column is no longer reconstructible. The piece is so worn and broken that only a few lines from the first column can be restored with certainty. The scribe wrote in an informal round hand, upright and of medium size, though somewhat mannered in letter shape; note *e*-shaped epsilon and *h*-shaped eta. Grenfell and Hunt assigned it "to the close of the second or in the first half of the third century." We are inclined to the later date. Writing is along the fibers; the back is blank. There are no lectional signs or marks of punctuation, though spaces left in text may be intended for this purpose (see, e.g., I.1, 4). The scribe wrote iota adscript in I.1, but not elsewhere; he marked elision at I.3, 7, and almost certainly 2, but neglected it at I.11.

COLUMN I

....]μηι. οἱ δὲ Κερκυραῖοι ταῦ-
τ᾽ ἀκο]ύcαντε[c], τὸν μὲν Δημο-
....]ν ἐπή[ν]ουν καὶ δι᾽ εὐθυ-
4 μίαc] εἶχον ἔδοcάν τε τὸ τά-
λαντ]ον προθύμωc καὶ κα-
....] ον αὐτὸν τῆc παρθε-
ν ...] φυλακ[.] · τῷ δ᾽ εἶναι
8 ....]οντο υ[...] νιαν καὶ
.....]θηναι [.....] τοῦ γάμου
.....]έληcαν · [....]θεντο δὲ
.....]αλεξα[....] τὰ ἄλλα
12 ....]νεκα καὶ
......]c λαν[..., ...]θοc
......]ω δι[...........]ε
......]καὶ θυ[............]κα
16 ......]ε c[..............
- -

COLUMN II

νώτερα γενο[μεν-
ανηκουcαcπ[
.]μην[..]πα [
4 .]οι[
- - - - - - - - - - - - - - -

Rehm's and Welles's conjectures appear in Zimmermann 1935.

Col. I: 1. μηι οι pap., ἀφορ]μῆι Rehm   1–2. ταῦ|[τ᾽ ἀκο] Zimm., ταῦ|[τα ἀκο]ύcαντεc
G–H   2. τε[.] τον pap.   4. ειχον εδοcαν pap.   5–6. κα|[τέλ]αβον Zimm.
6–7. Παρθε|[νόπ]ηc Zimm.   8. κύρι]ον Rehm   τὸν Εὐ[φ]ρανίαν Zimm.
8–9. κα{ι}|[τηχη]θῆγ[αι περὶ] τοῦ γάμου Zimm., δι|[αλεχ]θῆναι Welles   10. [cυνέ]-
θεντο Zimm.   11. αλεξα[Welles, καὶ τῷ]᾽ Ἀλεξά[νδρῳ] Zimm.,᾽ Ἀλεξα[μενῶι] Rehm
12. ἕ]νεκα καὶ Zimm.   14.]ω δι[pap.
Col. II: 1. [πιθα]|νώτερα γενο[μένη Zimm., [ἵκαν]ώτερα Rehm   2. αν ἤκουcαc Zimm.,
ἀνακούcαc Lav.

COLUMN I

]... the Corcyraeans,
when they heard this,
commended Demo[xenos?] and were expectant
4 and eagerly gave him the
talent and
[left?] him as Parthenope's
watchdog, and [——]
8 ...
[——] marriage.
And they [——]
the rest [——]. ...

COLUMN I

Lines 1–11 may be restored *exempli gratia*: οἱ δὲ Κερκυραῖοι, ταῦ[τ' ἀκο]ύϲαν-
τε[ϲ], τὸν μὲν Δημό[ξενο]ν̣ ἐπή[ν]ουν καὶ δι' εὐθυ[μίαϲ] εἶχον ἔδοϲάν τε τὸ
τά[λαντ]ον προθύμωϲ καὶ κα[τέλι]π̣ο̣ν αὐτὸν τῆϲ Παρθε[νόπ]η̣ϲ φύλακα· τῷ δ'
εἶναι [κύρι]ον [name?] [.....]θῆν̣α̣ι̣ [τοιού]του γάμου [οὐκ ἠμ]έληϲαν· [παρ-
έ]θεντο δὲ [εἰϲ τὸν] Ἀλέξα[νδρον?] τὰ ἄλλα. ... In main outline, this follows
Zimmermann, who saw the shape of the sentences more clearly than ed. pr.

2–3. Δημό[[ξενο]ν? The name is otherwise unattested. Blass's supplement of
Δημο[[ϲθένη]ν is almost certainly too long, and even in oratory is no more
likely in the context of the Corcyraeans than other names. Zimmermann suggested reading Δημο[[χάρη]ν. Demochares is the *pais* of Deinias in Antonius
Diogenes, but since there is nothing in this fragment to require an allusion to
Incredible Things beyond Thule, there is no reason to prefer Demochares to
the other available options.

3–4. δι' εὐθυ[[μίαϲ] ε̣ἶχον: for a parallel, see Hld. 6.8.2.

6–7. παρθε[....]: there is space for four letters in the lacuna, but the hand is
erratic enough not to reject voπ out of hand. Even though the letter after θ is
badly broken, there are scarcely viable alternatives to παρθέ[νου or Παρθε[νό-
π]ηϲ.

7. φυλακ[: φύλακ[α? The meaning of φύλαξ is "guard," not "guardian" or the
equivalent of κύριοϲ, which may in any case occur below, line 8. Compare,
e.g., Plut. *Publ.* §5.1: φύλακα τὴν ἑαυτοῦ γυναῖκα ταῖϲ θύραιϲ ἐπιϲτήϲαϲ.
Before it (lines 5–6), the verb may be κα[τέλι]π̣ο̣ν. Zimmermann's κα[τέλα]βον
is paleographically possible, but the meaning is not apt.

7–8. The articular infinitive construction would seem to require a noun or adjective at the beginning of line 8. Rehm's κύρι]ον is attractive, but then a name following seems inevitable.

9.]θηναι [: very likely a second infinitive.

[περὶ] τοῦ γάμου, [τοιού]του γάμου, or even [τούτου] τοῦ could supplement.

10.]έλης(αν: Zimmermann's ϲυνη]έλης(αν is rare but takes the dative, and could govern the articular infinitive. Alternatively, ἀμελέω or its compounds would govern a genitive γάμου (if not περὶ τοῦ γάμου); forms of τελέω are problematic.

[. . . .]θεντο δὲ : given the limitations of the following line, this articulation is to be preferred to Grenfell-Hunt's]θεν τὸ δέ. [παρέ]θεντο or sim.

COLUMN II

2. Several articulations are possible: ἀνήκουϲαϲ π[(or ἀνήκουϲα ϲπ[ ), ἂν ἤκουϲαϲ π[(or ἂν ἤκουϲα ϲπ[ ), -αν ἤκουϲαϲ π[(or -αν ἤκουϲα ϲπ[ ). If -αν, rules of syllabification require that a vowel end the preceding line.

Antonius Diogenes
The Incredible Things beyond Thule

❖

Three papyrus fragments have been claimed for Antonius Diogenes' novel: P. Oxy. 3012, *PSI* 1177, and P. Mich. inv. 5. The first two may certainly be assigned to this novel on the basis of character names common to them and to *The Incredible Things*. The third is an elaborate magician's speech, which Reyhl (1969: 14–20) thinks was uttered by the villainous Paapis in the early books. This is a very attractive conjecture, and we are tempted to accept it; but without external corroborative evidence like a name, we hesitate. We have discussed it separately. In addition to these, P. Dubl. C3, the so-called "Herpyllis" fragment, may belong to Diogenes' novel (see below).*

Most of what we know about *The Incredible Things* comes not from these papyri but from the comments, quotations, and paraphrases of later readers. Indeed, it is far and away the most cited of the ancient novels (which is not the same as being the most read). Photios summarizes the twenty-four books of its plot; Porphyry and John Lydus quote and refer to some of its memorable passages; Epiphanios, Servius, and Synesios treat it as a benchmark of the unbelievable; and a commentator on Lucian's *True Histories* traces an episode of that fantasy back to the bizarre reports (*teratologoumena*) of Diogenes.

This relative wealth of secondary tradition, unlike that of any other novel, is due to three features: its unique character as a fictionalization of geographical facts (or what could pass for such); its downplaying of the erotic; and its superficial coating of uplifting wisdom, specifically Pythagorean. We will deal with these three features and the narrative construction of the novel before we assemble the little that can be conjectured about the author and his date.

---

* Massimo Fusillo's edition of Antonius Diogenes was unavailable to us at the time of writing.

FICTIONALIZED FACTS

Diogenes describes his own novel both as a fictional composition and as a true story. He does this, according to Photios, on whose summary we rely almost entirely for our knowledge of *The Incredible Things beyond Thule*, in the form of two letters: first, one addressed to Faustinus, which describes Diogenes' library of historians' and travelers' reports that he used in composing his saga about the world travels of Deinias and Derkyllis; second, a letter addressed to his learned sister Isidora,[1] dedicating the work to her and relating how the cypress tablets on which the novel-text was written were found in a crypt along with six mysteriously inscribed coffins. The crypt was discovered by Alexander the Great after his sack of Tyre, and the text on the tablets was copied by his general Balagros, who sent it to his wife Phila, daughter of Antipater, with a cover letter that is in turn quoted in Diogenes' letter to Isidora.

The two accounts, side by side, not only are contradictory versions of who authored the narrative and how it came into circulation but also give diametrically opposed assessments of its truth-value. To Faustinus, Diogenes describes the book sources, the difficult work of compilation, and the verification of its assembled parts.[2] To Isidora, he tells a tale justifying the literal truth of the text and in effect denying all the work of authorship so carefully communicated to Faustinus. Each is an independent strategy for asserting the veracity and believability of the novel, one by shifting the authority to the shoulders of more ancient scholars, the other by historicizing the fictional narrator and scribe and tracing the physical tradition of the text. But together they contradict each other—a contradiction that must be resolved in favor of the Faustinus version, that Diogenes is an author who has fictionalized earlier travelers' and historians' accounts of far-off peoples and places.

---

[1] She is usually understood to be Diogenes' sister, but Schissel von Fleschenberg (1912: 101) takes her to be Faustinus's sister.

[2] P. Oxy. 3012 contains the beginning of a book and shows that Photios's words (προτάττει δὲ καὶ ἑκάστου βιβλίου τοὺς ἄνδρας οἳ τὰ τοιαῦτα προαπεφήναντο, ὡς μὴ δοκεῖν μαρτυρίας χηρεύειν τὰ ἄπιστα [111a38–40]) must be understood to mean not that a list of authorities stood at the head of each book, but that the letter to Faustinus contained a complete description of his authorities broken down by book. The scholarly parallel to Diogenes' list of authorities is Pliny's *Natural History*, where the first book is devoted to listing the authors and works used for each of the subsequent thirty-six books. Schissel von Fleschenberg (1912: 102–3) imagines that only the first book was dedicated to Isidora, that the letter to her contained the sources for Book 1, and that each book was separately dedicated to a different person and prefaced by a dedicatory letter containing the authorities for that book.

There is no question of deception. Both letters were placed at the beginning of the novel.[3] Bürger (1903: 6 n. 1) suggested that Photios was carelessly describing what was in the original a single letter, addressed to Faustinus and Isidora (who were in that case probably a married couple). A better solution to the small anomaly of two prefatory epistles is to suppose that, just as the narratives of Derkyllis and others are embedded in the narrative of Deinias, and the narrative of Deinias is framed by the letter of Balagros to Phila, and that letter is quoted in Diogenes' letter to Isidora, so his letter to Isidora is contained within his letter to Faustinus. This accords better with Photios's words at 111a32–34 and 111a41–b2, and matches the complexity of boxes within boxes that he attests for the rest of the novel.

It might seem as if Diogenes has distinguished two readerships—the serious male scholars who have a higher sense of responsibility toward the truth of such accounts, and a more beguilable female audience, who will enjoy the novel's exoticism, glamour, and romance. Hence Faustinus is sent a list of the novel's legitimate sources, Isidora the mysterious tale of its discovery in a crypt. But the situation is not so simple. On the one hand, Isidora is described as "learned" (*philomathōs echousa*); on the other, Diogenes admits to Faustinus that he has fabricated incredible lies (*apista kai pseudoi plattoi*) and spun tales. Just as the two contradictory letters are juxtaposed (or embedded one in the other), so the dual nature of Diogenes' composition is variously proclaimed to the two addressees. Diogenes thereby constructs a self-presentation that is both serious and facetious: serious in that he has organized the scattered traditions of paradoxography into a single encyclopedia, citations and all; facetious in that he puts forward two verification procedures that contradict each other.

The conjectural description of *The Incredible Things beyond Thule* as an encyclopedia is based on two considerations. First, to judge by Photios's summary, its twenty-four books were almost entirely taken up with accounts of our several heroes' adventures among strange peoples. These could have been concentrated just in certain sections of the known world, but (and this is the second point) the framework sketched by

---

[3] The letter to Isidora was placed κατ' ἀρχάς (111a41). In the letter to Faustinus, which Photios outlines immediately *before* the letter to Isidora, Diogenes announced that he was dedicating the novel to her (ὅτι ... τὰ δράματα προσφωνεῖ, 111a34). That announcement of dedication would not make much sense if the letter to Faustinus came at the end of the work.

Photios contains both an extended journey across Europe and a circumnavigation of the outer Ocean. As popularly conceived by such writers as Pomponius Mela, the world's peoples are distributed in two concentric rings accessible by water—the circum-Mediterranean lands and the countries that lie on the surrounding Ocean. Deinias and Derkyllis, the two principal narrators, divide the known world of the northern temperate zone in just this fashion. Deinias travels from his native Arkadia up through the Bosporos and along the Tanais River. He then turns east and travels around the outer coasts of Asia, India, Africa, Spain, Gaul, and Britain until he reaches Thule. On his way, he picks up other travelers—Karmanes, Meniskos, and Azoulis—from whom he presumably learns their separate adventures and reports about out-of-the-way tribes. Derkyllis travels from Tyre to Krete to Etruria to northwestern Spain, then back to Italy and Sicily and on to Thrace. Her path comes close to that of Deinias at two points, the easternmost and westernmost regions of Europe, but does not overlap it. She in turn hears reports from other wanderers, Mantinias, Astraios, and probably Keryllos; Manto brings her news about the Underworld. These other travelers certainly could have covered the coast of northern Africa and the parts of the Near East not personally visited by Derkyllis. That Diogenes' novel had an encyclopedic range cannot be strictly proved, but the two considerations of the novel's sheer size and its structure of interlocked wanderings make the suggestion worth entertaining.

Balancing, and in a certain tension with, that "serious" encyclopedic range was Diogenes' facetiousness. This can be inferred from three elements provided by Photios: Antiphanes, Pytheas, and Old Comedy.

One authority cited—apparently prominently, since he is the only one recorded by Photios—was Antiphanes (Weinreich 1942: 32). In the geographical tradition, Antiphanes of Berga was a byword for fabulous lying about faraway places (Knaack 1906: 135–38). His fourth-century B.C.E. work, evidently a travelogue, included a journey to the far north, where it got so cold in winter that people's words froze as soon as they spoke them; they had to wait until the spring thaw to hear what had been said (Plutarch *De profect. in virt.* §79a). Strabo, whose strict commercial and imperial interests made him impatient with useless or unverifiable reports about distant places,[4] criticizes Poseidonios for accepting an account of

---

[4] "For purposes of administration, there would be no profit in knowing about such lands and their inhabitants" (2.5.8). Dismissing the lands of the External Sea from consideration, he maintains that their climate is intemperate and their populations are

the circumnavigation of Africa,[5] calling it a "Bergaian narrative."[6] Strabo and Antiphanes define the opposite ends of a spectrum running from the hypercritical to the unabashedly fantastic.

There were many intermediate positions on that spectrum occupied by scholars and travelers with more curiosity and tolerance than Strabo, such as Eudoxos of Kyzikos, whom Strabo describes somewhat contemptuously as "a man who marveled at local curiosities and at the same time was not uneducated" (*thaumastikon onta tōn topikōn idiōmatōn hama kai ouk apaideuton*, 2.3.4). Strabo not only frowns on catalogs of oddities (which we might instead call disinterested inquiry), he is also extremely suspicious of the narrative excellence in Eudoxos's account. "No one of his claims is strictly impossible in itself, but each is difficult to accept and would rarely occur except with the help of some good fortune; but Eudoxos is always lucky and comes out on top in a continuous series of dangerous escapes."[7] Strabo evidently had a good nose for fiction, and he will tolerate it as long as it knows its place and does not present itself "in the format of factual research" (*en historias schēmati*, 11.6.3). This automatically exempts all poets: one would not criticize Hesiod or Homer or Alkman or Aischylos for ignorance just because they mentioned dog-headed men or the like. And prose writers, too, can happily indulge their fictions as long as it is obvious that they are telling tales for their audience's wonderment and sheer pleasure, as is true for Ktesias, Herodotos, and Hellanikos. What seriously annoys Strabo is the confusion of categories when writers present entertaining stories (*muthoi*) as if they were factual research (*historia*) (1.2.35).

Of course, we should not adopt Strabo's perspective; rather, we should use it to reassemble the actual range of ancient travel narratives

---

relatively uncivilized: "We desire to know these lands [immediately surrounding the Mediterranean] in which are traditionally located more famous events and types of government and arts and everything else that contributes to practical understanding; our practical needs lead us to those lands where regular relations and associations are attainable, namely, inhabited lands, or rather lands inhabited properly" (2.5.18).

[5] By Eudoxos of Kyzikos (Pomponius Mela 3.91–2, Pliny *Nh* 2.169), or at least by certain Gaditanians whose shipwrecked prow was found by Eudoxos (Str. 2.3.4).

[6] Βεργαῖον διήγημα, 2.3.5. "Bergaian" had already been used as a put-down by Eratosthenes speaking of Euhemeros (Str. 2.4.2), and eventually someone created the verb "to *bergaize*," meaning "to speak nothing that is true" (Steph. Byz., s.v. Βέργη: βεργαΐζειν ἀντὶ τοῦ μηδὲν ἀληθὲς λέγειν), rather in the same way that Lucian announces in his *True Histories* that he will speak nothing true (μηδὲν ἀληθές).

[7] This is the same excellence that Photios admires in Diogenes (continuous escapes from danger: 109b22, 40, 112a10–12).

that variously raised the issues of truth and falsity. Another such author obviously used by Diogenes is mentioned in the next sentence of Strabo's critique: "This stuff is not much better than the lies of Pytheas, Euhemeros,[8] and Antiphanes. They, however, can be pardoned, since that is their profession—as showmen of the marvelous (*thamautopoioi*)" (2.3.5). Pytheas of Massalia was another fourth-century B.C.E. traveler who claimed to have sailed around Britain and then across the northern coastline of Europe as far as Skythia. Modern verdicts on Pytheas's veracity are still divided. Strabo's principal objection, that such northerly and necessarily cold latitudes were uninhabitable, has less weight for those who have learned of the Gulf Stream.[9] Further, the island of Thule, said to have been located six days' journey from Britain, was not described by Pytheas from personal inspection but only "from hearsay" (Strabo 2.4.1). His claim to have gone as far as the Tanais River,[10] which was believed to divide the land-masses of Europe and Asia, may only mean that he reached some major river that he took to be the Tanais. The tales of strange tribes on the islands along the northern European coast, which occur in Pythean contexts and are plausibly attributed to him,[11] might again have been reported as colorful hearsay.

The point, however, is not to vindicate Pytheas's reputation but to illustrate the kind of discourse that gathered around his book. Strabo,

---

[8] Of Messene, late fourth century B.C.E. His *Sacred Inscription* described a voyage in the southeastern ocean to the island of Panchaia, whose excellent government had been originally set up by a king named Zeus who came from Krete and whose military deeds are recorded in hieroglyphics on a golden stele (DS 5.41–46, 6.1.4–11; *FGrHist* 63; fragments edited by G. Vallauri 1956).

[9] Strabo draws the line of livability at Ireland, inhabited by "perfectly wild people who live poorly on account of the cold" (2.5.8).

[10] Strabo 2.4.1; also, "He claimed to have surveyed the entire northern coast of Europe as far as the bounds of the kosmos" (Str. 2.4.2), and "on account of our ignorance of these regions those who tell stories of the Rhipaian Mountains and the Hyperboreans have been thought worth listening to, and what Pytheas of Massalia has completely fabricated about the coast" (Str. 7.3.1). The textual tradition has helped to obscure his north-coast journey by confusing the Ostiaioi, who dwelt between the Rhine and Skythia, with the Ostimnioi in Brittany: Lasserre 1963: 107–13.

[11] "Xenophon of Lampsakos reports that there is an island of immense size three days' sail from the Skythian coast, named Balcia. Pytheas calls it Basilia. There are also said to be Oionai ['Bird'] Islands whose inhabitants live on birds' eggs and oats, others on which a people called the Hippopodes ['Horse-Feet'] are born with horse's feet, and others belonging to the Panotioi ['All-Ears'] who wear no clothes but cover their entire bodies with their own enormous ears" (Pliny *Nh* 4.95 [not in Mette]). The same three groups are mentioned by Pomponius Mela as coming from some respectable authors (*praeterquam quod fabulis traditur, apud auctores etiam quos sequi non pigeat invenio*, 3.56), after which he immediately turns to Thule.

our chief source, was adamantly hostile: Pytheas is the "lyingest" man (*anēr pseudistatos*, 1.4.3), making claims that one would not believe (*pisteusai*) coming from the mouth of Hermes himself (2.4.2). Forms of *pseud-* and *pist-* spring up like mushrooms whenever Pytheas's name is mentioned. His truthfulness was accepted by Timaios, Hipparchos, Poseidonios, and others; denied by Dikaiarchos (his first reader on record) and Polybios; accepted with qualifications by the sensible Eratosthenes. Since Thule was always identified with Pytheas and was always discussed in terms of truth and believability, the title *The Incredible Things beyond Thule* (*Apista hyper Thule*) is doubly associated with Pytheas.

Both of these associations with Antiphanes and Pytheas could be taken to suggest a certain deliberate facetiousness on Diogenes' part. To use Antiphanes, a teller of tall tales, believed by no one, as an authority can hardly be serious. To relate "incredible things" (or "unbelievable things," not simply "marvels" as it is frequently translated) *hyper Thulēn* may be an even more pointed joke, since *hyper Thulēn* can quite be constructed as "surpassing [Pytheas's tales of] Thule." The implication that Diogenes has entered into a friendly liars' contest with Pytheas need never have been pressed very hard and can easily coexist with the literal sense of the phrase. It would explain, perhaps, the somewhat unusual fact that the title, taken literally, refers to events only in the twenty-fourth book. As Photios says explicitly (110b20), the entire narrative of Derkyllis to Deinias is set on Thule and concludes in the twenty-third book. Only in the twenty-fourth do Deinias and company set off for the regions beyond Thule.

A third indication that Diogenes explicitly represented his work as a playful (and ambitious) takeoff of earlier travel-fantasy is Photios's report, from the introductory letter to Faustinus (111a34–35), that "he calls himself a poet of Old Comedy." There is no need to reject the literal sense of this, as Rohde does (251–70 n. 2). Diogenes means that he is a writer of works comparable to those of Aristophanes, who sent his heroes to far-off lands of fantasy such as Cloudcuckooland.[12] So, too, Lucian in his *True Histories*, a travel-fantasy whose intellectual premises (not its content) have many points of contact with Diogenes, praises Aristophanes: "On the next day we hoisted sail and sailed near the clouds. There we saw and marveled at the city of Cloudcuckooland, but

---

[12] Di Gregorio (1968: 200 n. 1), who also suspects a satiric or parodic element in Diogenes missed by Photios.

we did not disembark there since the wind wouldn't let us. . . . And I called to mind Aristophanes the poet, a wise and truthful man, whose writings were wrongly disbelieved" (*Vh* 1.29). Diogenes, however, also provided a complete and respectable scholarly apparatus, as Photios's sentence about Old Comedy goes on say. Again the parallel with Lucian's *True Histories* is apt: "Each of these episodes contains hints and allusions, not without humor, in the direction of certain ancient poets and writers and philosophers who composed many bizarre fictions, whom I would mention by name except that they will be obvious to you upon reading" (*Vh* 1.2).

To say that Diogenes' conception and presentation of his work had a facetious side is not to say that his scholarship was bogus or that his "library of authorities" was nonexistent. In this respect he is to be distinguished from an author like Ptolemy Chennos, whose *Novel Research* (*Kainē historia*) was an anthology of truly bizarre items, such as the claim that Odysseus's real name was Outis, which he was given because at birth he had enormous ears (*ōta*).[13] Ptolemy's game was to construct ingenious jokes that made fun of rarefied scholarship and ignorant half-learning alike. He belongs in the world known to us from Petronius's picture of Trimalchio, who thinks that Odysseus twisted off the Cyclops's thumb with a pincers (*Satyrica* §48), or Lucian's vicious account of a wealthy book-collector (*adversus indoctum*) or of the fate of tame scholars kept for amusement by wealthy ignoramuses (*de mercede conductis*).

Diogenes' program seems rather to have been the construction of a continuous narrative set among strange peoples and places that had been described by earlier authors, many of whom clustered at Antiphanes' end of the spectrum sketched above (see below). This is very similar to the plan of Lucian's *True Histories*, except that Lucian freely invents and exaggerates in order to parody his exemplars.[14] Diogenes, who went to

---

[13] Photios *Bibl.* cod. 190. Other facts about Ptolemy, who lived under Trajan and Hadrian, might remind us, at least distantly, of Diogenes: he dedicated the seven books of his *Novel Research* to a certain Tertulla; he also wrote a novel (δρᾶμα ἱϲτορικῶν, *Souda*) entitled *Sphinx* and a twenty-four book epic (ποίηϲιϲ ῥαψωιδῶν, *Souda*) entitled Ἀνθό-μηροϲ, "Anti-Homer." The *Souda* gives the title of his "*Novel Research*" as "*Unconventional Research*" (*Paradoxos historia*; cf. Chatzis 1914: xviii–xix), which is a title employed by another second-century rationalizing scholar, Philo of Byblos (Eusebios *Prep. ev.* 1.9.28).

[14] The characters of and relationships between *The Incredible Things* and the *True Histories* are excellently analyzed by Morgan (1985).

the trouble of recording the authorities used for each of his twenty-four books, seems to have been both facetious and serious in his scholarship, without Lucian's one-note insistence on parody. At least, Photios's summary stresses the melodrama and the variety of characters, continuing through the twenty-four books; Lucian wisely stops his *True Histories* after two books, since its repetition of essentially the same joke could not be carried much further without palling.

The details of Diogenes' playful scholarship cannot be recovered, given the unfortunate loss of most of the travel literature he could have known, which we have only heard of. One item that may be worth noting is that two Hellenistic historians who worked on the records of Argos were named Deinias and Derkylos (*FGrHist* 305 and 306). Their extremely scanty surviving output show no outstanding connection with the known material of Diogenes' novel.[15] But the close association of two such distinctive names, parallel to the names of Diogenes' two principal narrators, is very striking.[16] If Diogenes himself were from Argos, we could say that the names were a sort of private joke. But speculation of this sort brings us to the farthest edge of our chartable knowledge about Diogenes, and we are in danger of falling off.

NOT A LOVE STORY

As has often been observed, *The Incredible Things beyond Thule* does not begin with two teenagers falling in love and follow the course of their adventures over land and sea—though, to judge from the papyrus fragments, it certainly included falling in love, adventures, and land and sea. There is no reason why it should have. Though several authors found it useful and attractive, the teen-romance framework was not an essential feature of long prose fiction in the ancient world.

The mistake of regarding it as such stems from the fact that many ancient novels employed it. But many is not all. The consequences of that stereotyping are serious. If teen romance is regarded as the core of

[15] Except for *FGrHist* 306 F7, which traces the name of Red Sea to Erythras, son of Argive Perseus. But the source of the fragment actually reads "Kleinias"; "Deinias" is at best a likely conjecture. Mention should also be made of a two-lambda Derkyllos who is cited eight times in the pseudo-Plutarchan "Schwindelwerke" *De fluviis* and *Parallela minora* (*FGrHist* 288). The last of those citations is also picked up by John Lydus and concerns a mineral found in the river Hydaspes that sings when the moon is waxing.

[16] Demochares, Deinias's *pais*, is homonymous with a fourth-century historian, a nephew of Demosthenes (*FGrHist* 75). But the name is not uncommon.

the novel-writing project, then Diogenes' work is by definition a marginal work, not a central masterpiece. This assumption about romance led many scholars to see Diogenes' novel as an early work, the "root and source" and "paradigm" both of fantasy-fiction and of romantic dramas (Photios 111b32–42), before the two categories diverged.[17]

The significance of the marginal role of eros in Diogenes' work is that it allowed the novel to be read and cited with approval by "serious" scholars such as Epiphanios, Porphyry, John Lydus, and the Vergil commentators who stand behind Servius. Teen-romance was not an approved subject for legitimate writing, any more than other erotic or popular-narrative material, such as the amorous *jeux d'esprit* for which Pliny and others apologized.

Romantic elements were certainly present in *The Incredible Things beyond Thule*. Derkyllis is ardently loved by Throuskanos, who kills himself when he thinks that she is dead; by Deinias, who may be much older than she is; probably by Keryllos, judging from Photios's list at 111b41; and perhaps even by Paapis (see the commentary on *The Love Drug*). But none of these is a happily ending teen-love story, and Derkyllis's relation to Deinias seems to have consisted entirely in trading stories on Thule: they underwent no adventures together, only met when everything except the final leg of Deinias's journey was finished, and went their separate ways from Thule.

Her brother Mantinias did fall in love with a woman of Thule. She can probably be identified as Lysilla, whose epitaph is one of the six in the Tyrian crypt discovered by Alexander. There are three men and three women, four of whom fall into married pairs. Mnason and Aristion are the parents unwittingly killed by Derkyllis and Mantinias; they both lay dead for five years until their children returned home with the remedy to undo Paapis's magic spell. Hence their epitaphs read "lived sixty-six years from seventy-one" and "lived forty-seven years from fifty-two." Derkyllis and Deinias are evidently a married pair. This leaves Mantinias and Lysilla. Symmetry suggests that Lysilla was the woman Mantinias wooed on Thule and then brought back with him to Tyre.

---

[17] Rohde saw the novels as a commingling of two previously separate streams, travel literature and passionate love-tales, which were first combined by Diogenes (1974: 294–96). Rohde's simplistic stemma has remained oddly authoritative, even though neither side of it is valid. The surviving novels often have settings in a variety of lands, but they are by no means travel literature. On the other hand, the Hellenistic tales and poetry about lovers were almost uniformly tragic, not romantic—fated from the beginning not to succeed and unhappy in outcome.

Mantinias and Lysilla represent the one identifiable strand of young love in Diogenes' novel. But Deinias and Derkyllis deserve further discussion, particularly in light of the epitaph that says that he died at the age of 125. It is implied at 111a27–29 that Derkyllis survived him, and since she lived "39 years and 760 nights," theirs must have been an extreme case of a Day-December match. Must we accept the improbable picture that Deinias was traveling around the world at the age of ±100, married Derkyllis at ±105, and died after ±20 years of wedded bliss with his beloved? This would be the implication of putting Derkyllis's age at about 17 when she begins her adventures, 22 when she marries Deinias, and 42+ when she dies shortly after burying him.

Conceivably the age difference was a piquant takeoff on the usual formula of young lovers. But other possibilities ought at least to be mentioned. One line of thought that springs to mind is that the riddling epitaph, "39 years and 760 nights," might be read in terms of Thule nights, which can last up to six months each. Could the 760 nights stand for dozens of years, so that Derkyllis is in fact almost as old as Deinias? An amusing thought, but it must be rejected, since the parents' epitaphs clearly say that they were dead for five years, which must be the measure of Derkyllis's wanderings between her leaving Tyre and returning to it.

Another possibility is that John Lydus is still quoting Diogenes in the sentence immediately after his reference to *The Incredible Things* at *De mensibus* 3.5 (concerning long-lived mortals: see below) where he says, "The Arkadians counted a year as consisting of three months." The sense of this is not that each of their "months" lasted as long as four of ours, but rather that they counted three lunar months as a "year," just as the Egyptians in the previous sentence managed to tot up incredible numbers of years in a life by using a smaller unit for their "year." If Deinias as an Arkadian counts each period of three lunar months as one "year" of his life, then his 125 years could stand for more than 41 years, about the same as Derkyllis.

But there is a major objection to this picture of coeval lovers who simply celebrate a different number of birthdays per annum. Deinias refuses the request of a delegation from the Arkadian commonwealth to return to Arkadia because "the weight of old age prevented him" (109b7). This is an obstacle to either the purely literal or the purely "Arkadian" interpretation of his years, since 41 years old is not conventionally regarded as old age and 125 years old is well past the conventional age of political participation (or do the Arkadians regard him as an extreme case of the "elder statesman"?). Perhaps Deinias's 125 years comprise both some Arkadian-years (those lived in Arkadia) and some year-years (those lived outside Arkadia). This would still make him significantly beyond his teen years when he falls in love with Derkyllis, for if we count backwards from 125, giving him 20 year-years of marriage in Tyre and 10 year-years of wandering, he would have left Arkadia at the age of 95 Arkadian-years, which equals over 31 year-years. If we translate his entire life span into year-years, he would have been over 61 year-years old at death. If the Arkadian delegation visited him not too long before his death, the about 60 year-year-old Deinias might be able to refer to "the burden of old age."

Such a reconstruction, put forward in the serious-facetious spirit of Diogenes himself, rescues us from the image of a nonagenarian or centenarian traveler and suitor. But it also deprives us of a hero/lover who, like Ninos, Chaireas, Theagenes, and so forth, has barely begun to grow a beard.

PYTHAGOREANISM?

A third feature of *The Incredible Things beyond Thule* that gave it a measure of respectability among "serious" readers and writers was its patina of Pythagorean lore. John Lydus's quotation concerning the bean taboo comes from Book 13 and is therefore centrally placed. The entire description of the Pythagorean life-style in Porphyry *Life of Pythagoras* §§ 32–45, which includes Lydus's passage about the bean taboo (§ 44), in all probability also came from Book 13, and quite possibly Astraios's account of his own life with Pythagoras (§§ 10–17). Since Diogenes seems to be remarkably careful about structure, this central position may be significant. One might compare the almost terminal position of Pythagoras's lecture in Ovid's *Metamorphoses*.

But significant of what? A dedicated Pythagorean propaganda text? Modern scholars, who frequently experience the same anxieties about popular or entertaining or romantic literature that ancient scholars did, have sometimes suggested that Diogenes was a committed Pythagorean and that his book promoted the truth of that philosophy.[18] There are certainly strings of Pythagorean images that occur in Photios's summary, in

---

[18] Bürger 1903: 13; Merkelbach 1962: 225–33; di Gregorio 1968: 211, "opera di un neopitagorico, che pone al servizio di un'idea religioso-morale la paradossografia, l'aretalogia, la favolistica dei viaggi e il vero e proprio δραματικόν erotico."

particular the image of things waxing and waning in phase with the moon. Astraios's eyes are the chief instance, used to reconcile feuding kings and regulate their phases of alternate ruling. Astraios is certainly a Pythagorean in Diogenes' novel, but he is nowhere else mentioned in Pythagorean traditions, and his eyes seem to be a sign of his wondrous birth and nature (Porphyry *VP* §10; see below), not of any Pythagorean principle. Deinias and Kymbas, the principal narrator and his audience, are Arkadians, who are sometimes called *Prouselēnoi*, older than the moon. Could curiosity about the relation of Arkadia and the moon originally have inspired Deinias's journey?

There is a connection between the moon Sibyl in Diogenes' Book 24 and certain animal and plant wonders known on earth. Plutarch (*De Pyth. orac.* §398c–d) refers to verses of the Delphic Sibyl that claimed that after her death she would become the face in the moon and that her body would infuse the earth and affect the inward organs of animals when they ate grass so as to form them into prophetic shapes. This is particularly attested for the livers of field mice, for oysters, moonstones, and cats' eyes.[19] The onion is condemned for following a counterrhythm in its waxing and waning.[20] But all this was common lore, not patented by Pythagoreans.

Keltic and Thracian beliefs about reincarnation or immortality were sometimes interpreted as "Pythagorean" (DS 5.28.6; Hdt. 4.94–6), and Diogenes may have done this too, though there is no trace of it in Photios's summary. Grasping at other straws, one might notice that in *PSI* 1177 the slave Myrto is strangely silent. Could this be somehow connected with the famous Pythagorean silence? Is the discovery of coffins and encased text together modeled on the supposed discovery of Numa's Pythagorean writings in 181 B.C.E.? (Cassius Hemina *ap.* Pliny *Nh* 13.84; Livy 40.29). Readers determined to find a *Tendenz* in Diogenes' novel can of course make a case, but not a compelling one.

Counterindications to a committed and consistent Pythagorean perspective are just as telling. It is difficult to reconcile Diogenes' overriding facetiousness with Pythagorean morality. For one thing, the Pythagorean injunction to truth-telling was absolute. Further, Pythagoras is praised precisely for his stability: "His bodily condition was invariant,"

---

[19] Mice: Plutarch *Q. conv.* §670b; oysters: Aulus Gellius 20.8.3–4, citing Lucilius; moonstones: Damaskios *Life of Isidore* pp. 119–20 Westermann; cats' eyes: Plutarch *De Iside* §376e, Aulus Gellius 20.8.6; Demetrios *De elocutione* §158. For other such beliefs, see Riess 1894: 39–41.

[20] Plutarch *De Iside* §353f; Aulus Gellius 20.8.7.

not sometimes waxing fatter, other times waning thinner, and his soul too was always in the same state, not sometimes relaxed in pleasure, other times tense with pain. "In fact, no one ever saw him laughing or crying" (Porphyry *VP* §35; see below).[21] These characteristics do not sit easily with Diogenes' admission of fabrication or with the theme of lunar-influenced waxing and waning. Myrto teaches Derkyllis about the Underworld, presumably about a doctrine of afterlife. Does this square with well-known Pythagorean beliefs that the Isle of the Blessed was in the sky?[22] "The planets are the dogs of Persephone," a Pythagorean saying (Porphyry *VP* §41; see below), seems to mean that what is traditionally said of an Underworld is more correctly affirmed of an Aboveworld.

There is no denying that Pythagorean elements of some sort were present in *The Incredible Things*, and they were probably important enough to assist the difficult transition of this novel, unlike any other, to an honored status. But it is an elementary confusion of modern criticism to leap from the mere mention or use of a philosophical belief to an assertion that the work was formed and ruled by adherence to that belief. For the works we now call the ancient novels, this has been an especially strong temptation. It is no enhancement of our appreciation of Diogenes' work as an encyclopedic, serious-facetious novel to force it to pledge allegiance to a philosophical or religious system. To worry about philosophical or religious schools, heresies, and commitments distracts from the really interesting and significant achievements of ancient fiction in general, and of Diogenes in particular.

THE FIRST PERSONS

One of the most striking features of Diogenes' novel is the fact that there are so many narrators re-telling each others' stories. It is fortunate that ancient texts did not use quotation marks, since some narratives in *The*

---

[21] Lucian cites an oracular verse by Alexander of Abonouteichos claiming identity with Pythagoras: "Sometimes the soul of Pythagoras wanes, other times it waxes" (*Alex.* §40). But this is simply an elegant way of saying that his soul reappears on earth at various times—a different doctrine and not a "Pythagorean" manner of speaking.

[22] Two sayings known as Pythagorean might be taken to imply some belief in an Underworld: the point of thunder is to frighten those in Tartaros (Arist. *Anal. post.* 94b33); an earthquake is a town-meeting of the dead (Ailian *Vh* 4.17). But both of these belong in contexts of folk-science—like our "thunder is the giants playing ten-pins above the clouds"—rather than theology.

Incredible Things would have to be packed in as many as seven pairs, like the inset narratives of "Menelaiad" in John Barthes's *Lost in the Funhouse.* The structure is as follows:

A. Diogenes writes to Faustinus, quoting or prefacing

  B. Diogenes' letter to Isidora, which quotes

   C. Balagros's letter to Phila, which includes a transcript of

    D. Erasinides' text[23] of Kymbas's account of his visit to Tyre and meeting with

     E. Deinias, who recounts his journey from Arkadia around the world, meeting and hearing the accounts of

      F1. Karmanes,

      F2. Meniskos, and

      F3. Azoulis, until they reach Thule and meet

      F4. Derkyllis, whose long account includes reports by

        G1. Myrto about the Underworld,

        G2. Astraios about Pythagoras (Book 13) and what he heard from

          H1. Philotis, and later

          H2. his "separate adventure" among the Astyroi; also

        G3. Mantinias's many wanderings,

        G4. Astraios's encounter with Zalmoxis on Derkyllis's behalf,

        G5. someone's report of how Throuskanos killed Paapis after Paapis put Derkyllis and Mantinias into a death-like trance, and probably

        G6. Mantinias's love affair on Thule.

      F5. Azoulis completes the story of Derkyllis's daytime death by telling how he deciphered Paapis's spell.

     E. Deinias continues the tale of his travels beyond Thule and instructs

    D. Erasinides to write two copies of the entire narrative on cypress tablets, taking one home to Arkadia and leaving the other in Tyre, where Derkyllis will bury it, someday to be found by

   C. Alexander the Great and his soldiers, one of whom, Balagros, copies the text and sends it to his wife Phila.

[23] The presence of an Athenian scribe may serve to account for the Attic language of Kymbas's narrative. Diktys of Knossos, putative author of a diary of the Trojan War, was scribe to Idomeneus (*FGrHist* 49 T2).

The narratological sophistication of this structure must have forced the reader—at least it did Photios—continuously to be aware of the presence of a narrating I. In a fairly strong sense, we may say that this is a novel in which many things happened but nothing happens: the only present-time events are acts of narrating and listening. The lovers Deinias and Derkyllis do not have adventures together, they do not woo, they narrate.

The justification for this view of *The Incredible Things* is that Photios repeatedly reminds himself of the structural complexity of Diogenes' narratives-within-narratives, whereas he takes no notice of the flashbacks-within-flashbacks of Heliodoros' *Aithiopika* (cod. 73). Photios simply rearranges the events of the *Aithiopika* into chronological sequence and presents them as if there was no inversion and no chain of subnarrators. His pains to put Diogenes' narrators in their correct frame suggest not only that the novel had a complex structure but also that the reader was reminded of the presence of listeners. Kymbas may have intruded remarks on Deinias's narrative just as Heliodoros's Knemon so frequently does during Kalasiris's long recital. They would have the same intrusive effect that Photios's reiterations of that outer structure do in his summary.

The complexity of Diogenes' structure was used by Lacôte (1911) to argue that the Greco-Roman novel came from India. The argument, like others of its kind, will not withstand close scrutiny. Pisani (1940) pointed out that the extant Indian narratives are no earlier than the Greek novels and that there are plentiful examples of complex structure within the traditions of sophisticated Greek writing. To that polite and conservative rebuttal other, stronger arguments could be added. Even if *The Incredible Things beyond Thule* were the first extended prose fiction in Greece, antedating the other novels (which it does not), it would be a curious proposition in the annals of literary history to maintain that the first instance of a generic type in Greece was modeled on an Indian literary practice, but that all succeeding Greek instances of that genre forsook the essential feature (complex structure of narratives within narratives) used to prove the dependence. What narrators adopt and adapt from any source available to them is not structure but storyline, not form but content. So, what R. F. Burton called "The History of the First Larrikin" (Burton 1887: 281–90) is also found on an Assyrian tablet from Sultantepe dated 701 B.C.E. (Gurney 1956: 147). Plots certainly circulate without patent or copyright from one language and culture to another.

Connections of that sort, which may be close or loose, are fascinating to trace. But wholesale derivations of narrative practice from one culture to another cannot be sensibly based on considerations of formal structure. With the concatenation of first persons in Diogenes' novel we may contrast the narrative of Chariton, which begins, "I shall tell you the story of ...," and at no point alludes to the chain of transmission that might have imparted the events, including private thoughts and monologues, to him. The traditional name for Chariton's type of narrative is "third-person," but as Genette has pointed out, all narratives are in the first person.[24] Chariton, Homer, and Thucydides can all say "I," even though their narratives are about "third persons" and not at all about themselves. What that older narratology was trying to distinguish was not grammatical form, "I" versus "they," but rather the fact that some ego-narrators claim, implicitly or explicitly, that the events they narrate really took place, whereas others (Homer and Chariton) make no such claim. Narrators who make such a claim (whether seriously or not is another issue) may reinforce it by describing themselves and the situation that brought them into contact with the narrated events. Just how central or peripheral the narrator is to the story makes little difference: what matters is that he or she tells us something that he could have experienced or learned about, and because it is presented as something he could have experienced or learned about, it is implicitly affirmed as something that could have happened.

The boxed structure of Diogenes' novel brings this common sense about the nature of narratives to the foreground. Deinias's narrative scrupulously segregates his personal experiences from the reports given to him by others. The operating rule seems to be that every reported event should be clearly attached to the "I" who experienced it, not relayed for its own sake as an impersonal fact but tagged with a personal name. Since Diogenes began with an account of the books from which he drew his "facts," it seems as if what he has done is to invent a set of persons who could have experienced those facts and hence are entitled to narrate them.

This again brings him very close to Lucian, who prefaced his *True Histories* by saying that he turned to lying "since I had nothing true to relate—for I had never experienced anything worth telling," and "I write

---

[24] Genette 1980: 244–45. The present account, modified from Genette, is explained in Winkler 1985: 73–75.

about things that I neither saw nor experienced nor learned from others" (1.4). If Lucian had personally experienced something worth telling, he would be justified in narrating it. A narrative is thus implicitly analyzed as a compound entity: an event plus an "I" who relates it. Diogenes seems to have taken his "events" (places, peoples, natural history) from preexisting accounts, some of them intrinsically doubtable (like that of Antiphanes), and to have invented the characters necessary to convert those "events" into a narrative. Theoretically, it could have been a single invented character who traveled to all the places mentioned in Diogenes' library of geographers and paradoxographers. But that would have been . . . unbelievable.

AUTHOR AND DATE

The analysis above would suggest, using the magical principle of *similia similibus* so often invoked in literary history, that Diogenes should be placed in the second century C.E., the time of Lucian and Ptolemy Chennos. There is nothing to speak against that hypothesis, and some minimal facts that are consistent with it. The combination of an interest in neo-Pythagoreanism (however serious) and what Kerényi describes as an anti-Egyptian *Tendenz* is more likely to have occurred in the first century C.E. or after.[25] The names Faustinus[26] and Antonius[27] put us in a Roman context. The references to Diogenes' novel begin perhaps as early as Serenus Sammonicus (d. 212: see Servius's testimony below), certainly as early as Porphyry (234–c. 304), and the papyri provide a *terminus ante quem* of the end of the second century C.E. *PSI* 1177 and P. Oxy. 3012 are both written in hands usually assigned to the late second or early third centuries C.E., and P. Dubl. C3 should belong in

---

[25] Rohde (1974: 277) would place him in the first century C.E., Kerényi (1962: 239) and Sinko (1940–46: 25) in the second. Though the depth of Antonius Diogenes' commitment to Pythagoreanism is debatable (see above), he is unlikely to have devoted such a substantial part of his narrative to it if it were not a relatively popular topic.

[26] Hallström (1910: 200–201) identifies Faustinus with a well-to-do member of Martial's circle.

[27] In the papyri, Antonius in combination with a Greek name does not much occur before the end of the second century C.E. But E. Bowie (in a letter) has made the attractive observation that "the name-form Antonius Diogenes (as opposed to Diogenes) might suggest a time when Roman *gentilicia* had not yet become common enough among the Greek upper classes to be no longer worth flaunting." This would give us a rather earlier period, late first through early second century C.E.

the second century, some time after the reign of Trajan (see discussion below).

But how much before second century can this author be placed? Photios's guess that Antonius Diogenes lived soon after Alexander is by his own admission only a stray thought, and not a very acute one, obviously based on the fiction of Alexander finding the text. Although Strabo cited numerous authors whose vivid imaginations irritated him, he does not include Diogenes. Some have seen Lucian's *True Histories* as a parody of *The Incredible Things*, but the relation could be reversed. Indeed, J. R. Morgan (1985: 475–90) presents a strong argument that it should be: if the *True Histories* are intended to parody those writers who pass off tall tales as true, then more appropriate targets for Lucian's humor would be "serious" writers like Ktesias, Iamboulos, and even Herodotos, instead of the work of a writer who declares himself "a poet . . . of Old Comedy." Morgan can find traces of such writers, but no clear-cut resemblances between Lucian's leg-pull and *The Incredible Things*. But this does not help with dates. If Diogenes was not a suitable target, his work could easily have preceded Lucian without necessarily being mentioned by him.

Arguments about the relationship of *The Incredible Things* to the other novels and fragments is precarious at best. Kerényi (1962: 239–40) points to Derkyllis as a deliberate play on *Ninos*'s Derketo. But it is difficult to imagine what effect would be gained by the evocation of Ninos's aunt. Achilles Tatius has a narrator who travels and encounters another narrator who tells his story of love and adventure; Longos invents his tale. This consciousness about fictionality sets up a kind of gravitational field drawing Diogenes to the second century, but it does not prove that he was not earlier. Although the supposedly earlier novels are simpler in structure (Chariton, Xenophon) and without the "encyclopedic" interests found in Achilles Tatius and in a small way in Heliodoros, the notion that there must have been a linear progression in "complexity" is difficult to maintain. After all, narrative complexity and the telling of tall tales is already present in Plato.

TESTIMONIA

1. Epiphanios (c. 315–403, bishop of Constantia/Salamis on Cyprus), *Adv. haer.* 1.33.8 (Migne 1857–66: 41.568 = GCS 25.458)

Who will endure these words and the madness of this charlatan and his followers?—I mean of Ptolemaios and his disciples who mix up and patch together fictions (*plasmata*) to such an extent! None of the ancient tragedians nor the writers in a fictional style (*miméloi ton tropon*) who followed them—I mean such as Philistion,[28] and Diogenes, who wrote *The Incredible Things*—or all the rest who recorded and stitched together the myths were able to fantasize (*ektupósai*) so great a lie as these people.

2. Servius (fl. 400 C.E.), Commentary on Vergil *Georgics* 1.30 (*tibi serviat ultima Thule*)

Thule is an island in the Ocean between the northern and western regions, beyond Britain, Spain, and the Orkneys. On Thule, when the sun is in Cancer, it is said that the day is continuous, without nights. Many other wonders are reported concerning this island, as for instance by Ktesias[29] and Diogenes among the Greeks and Sammonicus[30] among the Latins.

3. Synesios (c. 370–413, pagan scholar, bishop of Cyrene), *Letter* 148

[The Cyreneans who live in the interior] regularly adopt an attitude like ours whenever we hear of the things beyond Thule, whatever in the world Thule is, which grants those who visit it the right to tell unrefuted and uncriticized lies.

4. Scholiast to Lucian *True History* 2.12. This is written by the original scribe in the margin of Marcianus 840 (formerly 434), fol. 47a, where Lucian's text concerning the Isle of the Blessed reads: "For clothing they use fine spider webs, dyed purple. They themselves do not have bodies

---

[28] A writer of "mimes," i.e., little dramas about daily life, who flourished in the time of Augustus and remained popular for several centuries. The yoking of Diogenes with a mime-writer shows how ancient novels were not sharply segregated from texts for stage performance.

[29] Ms. reads Etesias. "Ktesias" is the easiest correction, though Müllenhoff, cited and accepted by Knaack (1906: 138), would read "Pytheas." Ktesias is not known to have said anything about Thule—indeed, it is highly improbable that he did—but his name is regular in contexts of far-off wonders. Servius's error may be due to a misreading of his source, probably Sammonicus.

[30] Serenus Sammonicus was a scholar of the second century C.E. (d. 212). If he is Servius's authority for citing Ktesias and Diogenes, then he is the earliest reader of record for *The Incredible Things beyond Thule.*

but are intangible[31] and without flesh, showing only a form and a shape. Though bodiless, they nonetheless cohere and move about and think and speak. All in all it is as if their soul was a naked entity walking about wearing the likeness of their body; at least, if you did not touch one, you would not be able to prove that what you saw was not a body, for they are just like shadow-outlines walking upright, not dark shadows. None grows older; each stays at the age it was when it arrived. Further, there is no nighttime there, nor is the day ever very bright. Just as the early light begins to glimmer towards dawn when the sun has not yet risen, that was the sort of light that always shone over their land. And further, they know only a single season of the year; among them it is always spring-time and the western zephyr is the only breeze that ever blows their way."[32]

He is mocking the bizarre tales told of the regions beyond Thule.

5. Photios (c. 810–893 or shortly thereafter, a wealthy layman, twice appointed patriarch of Constantinople), *Bibliothēkē* codex 166 (pp. 109a6–112a12 Bekker).[33] Our translation is based on the Budé edition of R. Henry.

[109a6] The twenty-four books of Antonius Diogenes' *The Incredible Things beyond Thule* were read. The books are a dramatic work; the style is clear and so pure as to want nothing in exactitude even in the digressions from the narratives. As regards sentiments, it contains much that is pleasing, since its narrative material, verging on the mythical and marvelous, is cast in a most credible format and structure.

---

[31] ἀναφεῖς (the reading of the beta family of mss., Marcianus 840, and a correction by the original scribe in Vaticanus 90); ἀφανεῖς ("invisible," Vat. 90); ἀσαφεῖς ("indistinct," a later hand in Vat. 90); διαφανεῖς ("translucent," Rohde).

[32] Though the scholion is written opposite the sentence, "All in all it is as if their soul was a naked entity walking about wearing the likeness of their body," Rohde is probably correct in referring the comment to the climatological description, since the peculiar cast of light in far northern latitudes and the odd mingling of and the lack of differentiation for night and day were a regular feature of descriptions of that region (1974: 206 n. 4: the relevant part of the note is printed on 207–8).

[33] According to Treadgold's reconstruction of the *Bibliothēkē* (not Photios's title), Photios's method in "codices" 1–233 was to dictate his summary to a secretary with the book in front of him, working quite rapidly (about fifteen folios per day, less than three weeks for cod. 1–233, Treadgold 1980: 51). The probable date of composition is 845 (ibid., 16–36). Though the *Bibliothēkē* reviews more theological works than secular ones, Photios devotes more space to writing about the secular works (57%, so ibid., 7–8, 99). *The Incredible Things beyond Thule* fits nicely with Photios's interest in the outré, whether in far-off lands (Ktesias, cod. 72) or nearer to home (hermaphrodites in Diodoros, cod. 244) (Treadgold 1980: 101).

ANTONIUS DIOGENES, *INCREDIBLE THINGS*

[109a13] We are introduced to one Deinias, who has undertaken a quest for knowledge with his servant[34] Demochares and has wandered far from his homeland, across the Pontos, across the Kaspian and Hyrkanian[35] Sea towards the so-called Rhipaian Mountains,[36] and has reached the sources of the Tanais River; then, because of the overwhelming cold,[37] they have turned their course along the Skythian Ocean and ultimately reach the Oriental Ocean[38] and the place where the sun rises, then traveling in an arc along the outer sea over a long period of time and with various wanderings. On this wandering voyage he is joined by Karmanes and Meniskos and Azoulis.[39] They also sojourn for a time on the island of Thule as a sort of

[34] Previous translators have taken παῖς here to mean "son." See the discussion of the characters' ages (above, introduction). Even on a literal reading of the epitaphs, if Deinias is 125 years old at death when his wife Derkyllis is only at most 41, his travels must have occurred when he was roughly 100 years old. If he had a son by a prior marriage, could that already-senior citizen be called a παῖς rather than υἱός?

[35] The Kaspian (also called Hyrkanian) Sea was sometimes taken to be self-enclosed (Hdt. 1.202; Aristotle *Meteor.* 2.1: 354a3), but the majority of geographers considered it to be an inlet from the Ocean (Str. 2.5.18, Pomponius Mela 3.39, Pliny *Nh* 6.36), relying in good measure on the authority of the Seleucid admiral Patrokles (*FGrHist* 712), who described his sea journey from there to India.

[36] The supposed northernmost range of Europe, fancifully mentioned from early times in poetry and legend (Alkman, Aristeas of Prokonnesos). "From the so-called Rhipaian Mountains" there swoops down a cloud of singing swans into the temple of Apollo among the Hyperboreans, according to Hekataios of Abdera (late fourth century B.C.E., *FGrHist* 264 F12 = Ailian *Na* 11.1). Hekataios's *On the Hyperboreans*, which describes a far northern island about the size of Sicily, evidently stood somewhere in the family tree of Diogenes' *The Incredible Things*. In it, Hekataios described how the moon comes very close to the earth at that point and hence can be seen perfectly from that island (*FGrHist* 264 F7 = DS 2.47). "In the extreme north, beyond furthest Skythia, are the so-called Rhipaian Mountains, about whose size quite mythical tales are told" (Aristotle *Meteor.* 1.13: 350b7).

[37] *Inde Asiae confinia nisi ubi perpetuae hiemes sedent et intolerabilis rigor* (Pomponius Mela *De chorographia* 3.5 [36]).

[38] The Ocean as it goes around Asia is divided into three regions. It is called the Oriental Ocean along the eastern coast of Asia, the Indian Ocean along the southern, the Skythian Ocean along the northern: Pomponius Mela 1.9; Ronconi 1931: 193–242, 257–331, esp. 298–331. Since the Don (Tanais) River is the conventional divider between Europe and Asia (Pomponius Mela 1.8), Deinias enters the ocean where it is called Skythian and follows it to the far east where its name changes to the Oriental.

[39] Photios tells below something of the roles of Karmanes and Azoulis in the novel (110b20–37, 111a11–12); of Meniskos, however, he says nothing else, except that he got his wish from the moon Sibyl (111a12–13). Since Deinias circumnavigated the three continents from the extreme northeast to extreme northwest, it may well be that he picked up these three in different places, each representing an interpolated narrative and no doubt the geographical lore of his region. Azoulis is an Egyptian name; he may have been displaced in the same disturbances that drove Paapis from Egypt. Karmanes' name might derive from an Arabian coastal people, the Karmanii, a hairy race that dresses in fish scales, who are mentioned in geographical accounts of the world's outer limits (Pomponius Mela 3.75).

resting place on their journey. Here on Thule Deinias falls in love with a woman named Derkyllis, who came from an aristocratic family in Tyre and who is accompanied by her brother Mantinias.

[109a29] Deinias learns from her the tale of their wanderings: how Paapis,[40] an Egyptian priest, came to live in Tyre after his own country was vanquished and plundered, and received hospitality from the parents of Derkyllis and Mantinias and seemed at first to be grateful to his benefactors and to their entire household, but then wrought so many evils on the family, the brother and sister and their parents, and how she was brought to Rhodes with her brother after the family's disaster, and from there she wandered to Krete, then to Etruria, then to the people called Kimmerians,[41] where she saw the Underworld and learned many of its secrets, her teacher being a woman named Myrto, a family servant who had died long ago and now from the dead instructs her mistress.

[109b3] This then is what Deinias begins to narrate to a man named Kymbas, a native of Arkadia, sent to Tyre by the Arkadian commonwealth to ask Deinias to return home to his native land. But as the burden of old age effectively prevented him from doing so, Deinias is introduced telling the stories both of what he himself saw on his wanderings and of what was seen by others and told to him, in particular what he knew from Derkyllis's narrative—I mean the aforementioned wanderings and how after her return from Hades with Keryllos[42] and Astraios, now that she had been separated from her brother, they come to the tomb of the Siren,[43] and then how she listened to Astraios discoursing about Pythagoras and Mnesarchos,[44] and the things he heard from Philotis and the fabulous spectacle in respect to his eyes, and then again Derkyllis resuming the tale of her own wanderings, how in Iberia she came to a city where the people could see in the dark but were blind by

[40] Paapis was the name of a famous prophet in Egyptian history, the father of Amenophis (*FGrHist* 609 F10 = Manetho).

[41] Homer's Kimmerians (*Od.* 11.13–19) are located at the boundaries of the Ocean, a land of perpetual night where Odysseus draws up the shades of the Underworld. Later writers, such as Ephoros (fourth century B.C.E., *FGrHist* 70 F134 = Str. 5.4.5) placed the Kimmerians in Campania at Lake Avernus, a well-known connecting point with the Underworld.

[42] Evidently a lover of Derkyllis: he is mentioned by Photios along with Derkyllis's other lovers, Deinias and Throuskanos, below (111b41).

[43] Near Naples (see Steph. Byz., s.v. *Neapolis*). The Siren's name was Parthenope; she is often confused by later scholiasts with the novel heroine (see *Metiochos and Parthenope* above, introduction).

[44] Pythagoras's father. The paraphrases and quotations of Astraios's Pythagorean lore in Porphyry and John Lydus (see below) are cited by Lydus from Diogenes' thirteenth book. Astraios's lecture, therefore, was centrally placed in the twenty-four books.

day,[45] and what Astraios did by piping to their enemies. After a gracious farewell, they fall in with the Kelts, a crude and senseless race, from whom they flee on horseback, and their adventure when the horses change color.[46] They then come to the Akutanoi, where great honor is accorded to Derkyllis and Keryllos and even more to Astraios because of the way his eyes grow larger and smaller indicating the waxing and waning of the moon. Astraios reconciles the two kings who are at odds over their rule and who take successive turns to power according to the phases of the moon, all of which makes the local people wax enthusiastic over Astraios.

[109b34] Then the story is told of Derkyllis's further adventures and misfortunres, particularly how she was led to the Artabroi,[47] where the women conduct war, the men stay at home and do women's work. Then what happened to Derkyllis and Keryllos among the Astyroi,[48] and the separate adventures of Astraios, and how Keryllos, though with Derkyllis he had escaped a long list of dangers among the Astyroi contrary to every hope, nevertheless did not escape the penalty that he owed for an old crime: as against all expectation he had been rescued from dangers, so too [i.e., against all expectation] was he butchered.

[110a3] Next, Derkyllis's adventures as she wandered through Italy and Sicily and how in the Sicilian city of Eryx she was arrested and brought to Ainesidemos,[49] the then-tyrant of Leontinoi. There she again encounters the thrice-wicked Paapis, friend of the tyrant, and in her unexpected misfortune she finds an unhoped-for consolation—her brother Mantinias, who has wandered over many places and seen many marvelous things involving people and other animals, about the sun itself and the moon and plants and islands,[50] all of which he explains to her, providing her a rich fund of mythi-

---

[45] "Eudoxos of Rhodes writing about the Kelts says there is a certain tribe that is blind by day but has sight at night" (Apollonios *Hist. mirab.* 24 Westermann). Cf. Pliny *Nh* 7.12; Aulus Gellius 9.4.6. "Germara, a Keltic tribe, which is blind by day, as Aristotle says in his *On Marvels*, and the Lotos-Eaters sleep for six months" (Steph. Byz., s.v. *Germara*).

[46] "According to Poseidonios, . . . the horses of the Keltiberians are slightly dappled but when they are taken to outer Iberia they change their color" (Str. 3.4.15).

[47] A people of extreme northwestern Spain, living about the promontory of Nerium and a bay named for them. Strabo relates from Poseidonios that the land there was rich in tin and silver, which was carried down in the rivers and sifted in pans by women (3.2.9). The Keltic tribes of northwestern Spain maintained native forms of social organization even when Roman rule was well established (so Nicols 1987: 129–51).

[48] Also in northwestern Spain, famous for their gold mines, horses, and warlike character.

[49] Said to have ruled about 490 B.C.E. This is consistent with an historical setting for the novel in the first generation of Pythagorean disciples and the conquest of Egypt, which sends Paapis packing.

[50] Since Derkyllis's wanderings take her over western and eastern Europe whereas Deinias's voyage is directed in the first instance towards Asia, perhaps Mantinias traveled

cal lore that she later relates to Deinias, whose cat's-cradle narration of all this to Kymbas the Arkadian we are hearing.

[110a16] Then how Mantinias and Derkyllis take Paapis's satchel of books and his herb-chest and leave Leontinoi for Rhegion and then for Metapontion, where Astraios catches up with them to say that Paapis is following on their heels. And how they accompany him to Thrace and the Getai[51] when he visits his friend Zalmoxis,[52] and all that they saw on their journey, and how Astraios finds Zalmoxis already worshiped as a god by the Getai. And the message and request that Derkyllis and Mantinias asked Astraios to convey to Zalmoxis on their behalf. And how they received an oracle saying they were fated to travel to Thule and that they would in fact see their homeland in a time to come, but not before they went through various sufferings and requited their impiety towards their parents (involuntary though it had been) by a division of their life into life and death—they would live at night but be corpses by day. After these predictions they depart, leaving Astraios behind with Zalmoxis to be worshiped by the Getai. And there are all the marvels they see and hear in the North.

[110a39] All this Deinias heard in Thule from Derkyllis and is shown in the present time relating it to Kymbas of Arkady.

[110a41] After this, Paapis, hot on their trail, catches up with them on the island and by his magic art condemns them to death each day and revivification the following night. He casts the enchantment by spitting in their faces in public. Then Throuskanos[53] of Thule, who is desperately in love with Derkyllis, sees her collapse under the curse of Paapis, and overwhelmed by grief suddenly attacks Paapis, striking him with his sword and killing him, and so he comes at long last to the end of his interminable career of wickedness. Throuskanos, when he sees Derkyllis lying there, apparently dead, kills himself as well.

[110b11] All this and many other related matters, their burial, their emergence from the tomb, the love affair of Mantinias and all its dreadful repercussions, and other adventures of like kind on the island of Thule are related by Derkyllis to Deinias, who is now presented weaving the tale for the Arka-

---

through the fabulous regions of Africa, the third continent of the land-circle known to Greco-Roman geographers.

[51] Ms. "Massegetai," corrected by all editors.

[52] Zalmoxis or Salmoxis (later often Zamolxis) was a Thracian, especially Getic, god or prophet. Greek accounts early described him as a charlatan and linked him, unflatteringly, with Pythagoras (Hellanikos *FGrHist* 4 F73, Hdt. 4.94–6; Strabo 7.3.5). His name was of fairly common cultural currency, at least among the educated: Plato *Charm.* §156d–e; DS 1.94.2; Lucian *Vh* 2.17, *Iup. trag.* §42.

[53] Neumann (1953: 53–55) argues that Throuskanos is a properly formed North German name, the oldest such, and possibly an argument for identifying Thule with some territory in the North German linguistic region, such as Norway.

dian Kymbas. So comes to an end the twenty-third book of Antonius Diogenes' *The Incredible Things beyond Thule.*

[110b24] The twenty-fourth book brings on Azoulis as a narrator, and Deinias tying in Azoulis's narrative with his own previous account—how Azoulis realized the kind of spell that Paapis had cast to make Derkyllis and Mantinias live by night and die by day, and how he released them from that state when he discovered the nature of this curse and its cure from the satchel of Paapis, which Mantinias and Derkyllis carried with them.[54] Not only this, but he discovered how Derkyllis and Mantinias might release their parents from the great affliction that they themselves had caused them to suffer, duped by Paapis into believing it would actually help them, namely, then they had caused their parents to fall into an extended deathlike trance.

[110b33] Thereafter Derkyllis, along with Mantinias, hastens homeward to revivify and rescue their parents. Deinias, along with Karmanes and Meniskos—Azoulis has gone his own way—extend his journey to the regions beyond Thule.[55] And he now relates to Kymbas all the marvels he saw on his journey beyond Thule, saying that he actually saw what the devotees of the art of star-gazing conjecture, such as the possibility that for some people the Bear is directly overhead at the zenith,[56] and the nights there a month long, some shorter, some longer, and even six months long and ultimately a year long. Not only does the night last so long, but the days, too, in proportion.[57]

[111a4] And he tells of seeing other similar things—people and various marvels that no one has seen or heard or even imagined. Most incredible of all, that in their progress northwards they came close to the moon, as to a very pure land, and there they saw what you would expect a person to see who had previously made up lies out of all proportion. Then how the

---

[54] It might seem more romantic for Deinias to undo the magic binding his beloved, but Azoulis, whose name is Egyptian, is presumably brought into the story because he knows the language used in Paapis's curse and can read his Egyptian magic books. His presence, then, is more likely to be a modest token of verisimilitude than a sign that the "original" tale adapted by Diogenes was Egyptian and featured Azoulis as Derkyllis's lover (Reyhl 1969: 78) or that in the putative original tale the lovers were brother and sister (Fauth 1978b: 59).

[55] On the journey of Deinias and Karmanes, Thule is not a goal but a resting-place or stopover (cταθμόc, 109a24). Perhaps they go on beyond Thule because Karmanes must reach the moon Sibyl, as Derkyllis and Mantinias have been instructed by an oracle to reach Thule (110a28).

[56] We owe our translation of this phrase to J. T. Romm, by letter.

[57] Among the Hyperboreans, "sol non cotidie ut nobis sed primum verno aequinoctio exortus autumnali demum occidit; ideo sex mensibus dies et totidem aliis nox usque continua est" (Pomponius Mela 3.5[36]).

Sibyl[58] took the opportunity provided by Karmanes to prophesy again. Next, each one prayed his own prayer and each got what he prayed for, and Deinias himself fell asleep and was carried from there to Tyre to the temple of Herakles, and from there went out and found Derkyllis and Mantinias alive and well and also their parents recovered from their long sleep, or rather doom, and prospering.

[111a20] Deinias completes this tale for Kymbas and then brings out tablets of cypress and bids Kymbas's companion Erasinides of Athens to write the story of them—for he was skilled in writing. He also introduces them to Derkyllis: she is in fact the woman who brings in the cypress tablets. And he further bids Kymbas to inscribe the tale in two copies, to keep one tablet himself, and the other one Derkyllis, at the end of his life, would place in a chest and bury near his tomb.[59]

[111a30] Diogenes then, also called Antonius, presents Deinias performing wonders of narrative legerdemain for Kymbas, and yet writes to Faustinus that he has composed *The Incredible Things beyond Thule* and that he is dedicating his novel (*ta dramata*) to his learned sister Isidora. He calls himself a poet of Old Comedy, and says that, even if his incredible fictions seem to lack the ring of truth, he has a library of ancient testimonials about the greater part of his fabulations and has laboriously compiled his *Incredible Things* from these. He brings forward a list of authorities for the contents of each book, so that the unbelievable things will not be left unvouched for.

[111a41] A prefatory epistle is addressed to his sister Isidora that both announces the dedication of the work to her and brings in Balagros writing to his wife Phila (she is the daughter of Antipater) to say that when Tyre was captured by Alexander, king of Macedon, and largely destroyed by fire, a soldier came to Alexander with word of something strange and even startling, something to see outside the city. The king took Hephaistion and Parmenio and followed the soldier, and they came upon some buried stone coffins, one of which was inscribed

Lysilla: lived 35 years;

another,

---

[58] Plutarch's Aridaios heard the Sibyl on the moon during his celestial journey (*De sera numinis vindicta* § 566d–e).

[59] Compare the similar phenomenon in Diktys of Krete: "igitur de toto bello novem volumina in tilias digessit Phoeniceis litteris. quae iam reversus senior in Cretam praecepit moriens, ut secum sepelirentur. itaque, ut ille iusserat, memoratas tilias in stagnea arcula repositas eius tumulo condiderunt" (Prol. 12–16 Eisenhut).

Mnasōn, son of Mantinias: lived 66 years from 71;

another,

Aristion, daughter of Philokles: lived 47 years from 52;

and another,

Mantinias, son of Mnasōn: lived 42 years and 760[60] nights;

and another,

Derkyllis, daughter of Mnasōn, lived 39 years and 760 nights;

and the sixth coffin,

Deinias of Arkadia: lived 125 years.

[111b18] Puzzled by these inscriptions, except for the first, which was clear enough, they found by the wall a small chest of cypress with the inscription, "Stranger, whoever you are, open, so that you may learn marvelous things." When Alexander's companions opened the chest, they found the cypress tablets that Derkyllis apparently buried at Deinias's request. He presents Balagros writing this to his wife and saying that he transcribed the tablets and was sending the transcription to her. And then the story plunges into the reading of the writing on the cypress tablets, and Deinias is narrating to Kymbas what has been given above. Such is the manner and occasion of Antonius Diogenes structuring his dramatic fiction (*hē tōn dramatōn plasis*).

[111b32] He appears to be older than the other novelists, such as Lucian, Lucius, Iamblichos, Achilles Tatius, Heliodoros, and Damaskios.[61] For this work is the root and source of Lucian's *True History* and Lucius's *Metamorphoses*; and not only of these, but also of Sinonis and Rhodanes, Leukippe and Kleitophon, Charikleia and Theagenes, their adventures and wanderings and loves and capture and perils are evidently modeled after Derkyllis and Keryllos and Throuskanos and Deinias.

[111b42] As for the age in which Antonius Diogenes, father of such fictions (*plasmata*), flourished, we have no clear indication, though we may suggest that it was not very far from the time of King Alexander. He mentions an older author named Antiphanes, whom he says devoted himself to the recording of bizarre things.

---

[60] R. Henry's text misprints zeta for xi, that is, 7 for 60; his translation compounds the error: "sept cents et six nuits."

[61] Photios's canon of ancient fiction consists in Lucian's *True Histories* (cod. 128); Lucius of Patras's *Metamorphoses* (cod. 129); Iamblichos's *Babyloniaka*, starring Sinonis and Rhodanes (cod. 94); Achilles Tatius's *Leukippē and Kleitophōn* (cod. 87); Heliodoros's *Aithiopika*, concerning Charikleia and Theagenes (cod. 73), and Damaskios (cod. 130). Damaskios was a late Neoplatonist (c. 458–533) whose writings included a collection of occult lore (see below, App. B).

[112a6] Two things stand out, as in all such works, as worthy of notice: the villain, even if he seems to get away a thousand times, is caught in the end; and many innocent people undergo great perils but are often saved against all hope.

BOOK FRAGMENTS

1. JOHN LYDUS, ON MONTHS

a. *De mensibus* 3.5

Αἰγύπτιοι δὲ λέγονται ἀριθμῆςαι τὸν ἐνιαυτὸν τεccάρων μηνῶν, ὅθεν καὶ χιλετεῖc τιναc βιῶναί ποτε παρ' αὐτοῖc ἀναγράφουcιν· Ἡcίοδοc δὲ καὶ Ἑκαταῖοc, Ἑλλάνικοc καὶ Ἀκουcίλαοc καὶ Ἔφοροc καὶ Νικόλαόc φαcι τοὺc μακραίωναc καὶ ὑπὲρ χιλίουc διαζῆcαι χρόνουc, καὶ οὐκ αὐτοὺc μόνουc ὡc ἡρωικὰc ἀνημμένουc ψυχάc, ἀλλὰ καὶ ἀνθρώπουc τινάc, ὡc Διο-γένηc ἐν τοῖc ὑπὲρ Θούλην ἀξιοῖ.

b. *De mensibus* 4.42

Διογένηc δὲ ἐν τοῖc τριcκαιδεκάτῃ ἀπίcτων ταῦτά φηcιν· τότε ἀπὸ τῆc αὐτῆc cηπεδόνοc ἄνθρωπον cυcτῆναι καὶ κύαμον βλαcτῆcαι. τούτου δὲ φανερὰ ἐπῆγε τεκμήρια· εἰ γάρ τιc διατραγὼν κύαμον καὶ τοῖc ὀδοῦcι λεάναc ἐν ἀλέᾳ τῆc τοῦ ἡλίου βολῆc καταθείη πρὸc ὀλίγον, εἶτα ἀναcτὰc ἐπανέλθοι μετ' οὐ πολύ, εὕροι ἂν ὀδωδότα ἀνθρωπείου φόνου· εἰ δὲ καὶ ἀνθοῦντοc ἐν τῷ βλαcτάνειν τοῦ κυάμου λαβών τιc περκάζοντοc τοῦ ἄνθουc βραχὺ ἐνθείη ἀγγείῳ κεραμεῷ καὶ ἐπίθεμα ἐπιθεὶc ἐν τῇ γῇ τε κατορύξειε καὶ ἐννενήκοντα παραφυλάξειεν ἡμέραc μετὰ τὸ κατορυχθῆ-ναι, εἶτα μετὰ ταῦτα ὀρύξειε καὶ λάβοι καὶ ἀφέλοι τὸ πῶμα, εὕροι ἂν ἀντὶ τοῦ κυάμου ἢ παιδὸc κεφαλὴν cυνεcτῶcαν ἢ γυναικὸc αἰδοῖον.

1. JOHN LYDUS, *ON MONTHS*[62]

a. *On Months* 3.5

Egyptians are said to count the year as consisting of four months, whence they record that some thousand-year-old people once lived among them. Hesiod and Hekataios, Hellanikos and Akousilaos and Ephoros and Nikolaos say that long-lived people once lived more than a thousand years,[63] and not only those with the brightly burning souls of heroes but also some ordinary mortals, as Diogenes claims in his *Things beyond Thule*.

b. *On Months* 4.42 [64]

Diogenes in the thirteenth book of his *Incredible Things* says: "At that time from the same putrescence human beings were formed and beans sprouted. He adduces evident proofs of this. For if one thoroughly chews a bean and mashes it into a paste with one's teeth and leaves it for a little while in a spot warmed by the sun's rays and then returns after a short interval, he would find it smelling of human gore. And if when the bean plant is blossoming one takes a bit of its ripening floweret and places it in a covered ceramic vessel and buries it in the earth and returns to dig it up after ninety days, then one would find on taking off the lid that instead of a bean there had been formed either a child's head or a woman's genitals."

[62] The Greek text is taken from Ricardus Wünsch, *Joannis Laurentii Lydi liber de mensibus* (Leipzig, 1898). The text is in sufficiently good condition that we have chosen not to reproduce the apparatus criticus.

[63] The same list of six experts is cited for this belief by Josephus *J. Ant.* 1.108.

[64] This extract is also found, without explicit attribution to Antonius Diogenes, in §44 of Porphyry's *Life of Pythagoras* (see below). Since Lydus cites the book number, which is not in Porphyry, he did not take his extract from Porphyry; but since the text he gives is identical to that in Porphyry, we evidently have here a direct quotation from Diogenes and not merely a paraphrase.

2. PORPHYRY (234–c. 304), *LIFE OF PYTHAGORAS*,

from his *History of Philosophy*, Book 1

a. *Vita Pythagorae* §§ 10–17

(10) Διογένουϲ δ᾽ ἐν τοῖϲ ὑπὲρ Θούλην ἀπίϲτοιϲ τὰ κατὰ τὸν φιλόϲοφον ἀκριβῶϲ διελθόντοϲ, ἔκρινα μηδαμῶϲ τὰ τούτου παρελθεῖν. φηϲὶ δὴ Μνή-ϲαρχον Τυρρηνὸν ὄντα κατὰ γένοϲ τῶν Λῆμνον καὶ Ἴμβρον καὶ ϲκῦρον κατοικηϲάντων Τυρρηνῶν κἀκεῖθεν μεταϲτάντα πολλὰϲ μὲν πόλειϲ πολλὰ δὲ χωρία ἐπιόντα ἐπιτυχεῖν ποτὲ παιδὶ νηπίῳ ὑπὸ λεύκῃ μεγάλῃ καὶ εὐφυεῖ κειμένῳ· ἐπιϲτάντα δὲ θεάϲαϲθαι ὕπτιον εἰϲ τὸν οὐρανὸν ἀναβλέποντα πρὸϲ ἥλιον ἀϲκαρδαμυκτὶ καὶ τῷ ϲτόματι ἐνιέντα κάλαμον ϲμικρὸν καὶ λεπτὸν καθάπερ αὐλόν. θαυμάϲαντα δὲ καὶ δρόϲῳ ἐκ τῆϲ λεύκηϲ καταϲτα-ζούϲῃ θεαϲάμενον τρεφόμενον ἀναλαβεῖν, θείαν τινὰ νομίζοντα τὴν τοῦ παιδίου εἶναι γένεϲιν· ἱδρυθέντα δ᾽ ἐν ϲάμῳ ἀναληφθῆναι ὑπὸ τοῦ Ἀνδρο-κλέουϲ ἐπιχωρίου, ὃϲ τὴν ἐπιμέλειαν αὐτῷ τῆϲ οἰκίαϲ ἐνεχείριϲεν. βιοῦντα δ᾽ ἐν ἀφθόνοιϲ ἀνατρέφειν τὸ παιδίον Ἀϲτραῖον καλέϲαντα μετὰ τῶν αὐτοῦ παίδων τριῶν ὄντων, Εὐνόϲτου καὶ Τυρρηνοῦ καὶ Πυθαγόρου· ὃν καὶ υἱὸν ἔθετο Ἀνδροκλῆϲ ὄντα νεώτατον.

2. PORPHYRY, *LIFE OF PYTHAGORAS*[65]

a. *Life of Pythagoras* § 10–17[66]

(10) Since Diogenes in his *Incredible Things beyond Thule* gives an accurate account of Pythagoras's circumstances, one should not, in my judgment, pass over what he says. He says that Mnesarchos, an Etruscan[67] by descent, and belonging to the Etruscans who colonized Lemnos and Imbros and Skyros, emigrated from there and traveled to many cities and many regions. He says that once Mnesarchos came upon a baby lying under a large and noble white poplar. Standing over the child, he saw that it lay on its back looking up at the heavens and staring at the sun without blinking and with a delicate little straw in its mouth like a reed-pipe. He says that Mnesarchos marveled at the event, seeing that the babe was nourished by the dew dripping from the poplar, and reckoned that its birth was something divine.[68] He says that Mnesarchos settled on Samos and was taken in by a certain native-born Samian named Androkles, who put him in charge of his household. Mnesarchos then lived in some luxury and raised the child, whom he named Astraios,[69] along with his own three sons, Eunostos, Tyrrenos, and Pythagoras. Androkles adopted Pythagoras, the youngest, as his own son.

[65] The Greek text is taken from Augustus Nauck, *Porphyrii philosophi platonici opuscula selecta* (Leipzig, 1866). This text is in sufficiently good condition that we have chosen not to reproduce the apparatus criticus. Porphyry's citations of Diogenes begin at § 10 and § 32, but it is not clear where they end. Principal discussions are Rohde 1871–72, 1: 554–76, 2: 23–61; Rohde 1974: 272 n. 2; Jäger 1919; Burkert 1962: 88; and Reyhl 1969: 20–31. We print here only those sections which may plausibly be assigned to Diogenes.

[66] This section concerns Pythagoras's life and travels and includes the tale of the wonder-child Astraios, not elsewhere found in the Pythagorean traditions.

[67] Neanthes (*FGrHist* 84 F29 = Porphyry *VP* §§ 1–2, where the name is mistakenly given as Kleanthes [Jäger 1919: 5–6]), records the belief of others that Mnesarchos was Etruscan (Tyrrhenos), but says that in truth he was from Tyre and that he sent his son Pythagoras there to study with the Chaldaians. This may be a scholarly correction, Tyros for Tyrrhenos, intended to bring Pythagoras closer to the wisdom of the orient. (Porphyry himself was from Tyre.) In any case, it is interesting that in the pre-Diogenes Pythagorean material there was a connection between Pythagoras and Tyre, which is the site of the narration of *The Incredible Things*, a connection that Diogenes apparently did not know or did not use, since Porphyry's summary of Diogenes here mentions Tyrrhenos but not Tyros.

[68] Real gods don't blink, explains Kalasiris, and their feet don't touch the ground (Hld. 3.13). These are the signs by which John knows that Jesus is divine (apocrophal *Acts of John* 89, 93). One Pythagorean tradition held that souls of the dead do not blink (Plutarch *Q. Gr.* § 300c).

[69] Astraios's name may have been fashioned from that of Pythagoras' star pupil and successor Aristaios: "Pythagoras's successor, as all accounts agree, was Aristaios son of Damophon of Kroton, who lived in the time of Pythagoras, at least seven generations before Plato. He was judged worthy not only of membership in Pythagoras's school but

(11) παῖδα μὲν οὖν ὄντα ἔπεμπεν εἴς τε κιθαριϲτοῦ καὶ παιδοτρίβου καὶ ζωγράφου, νεανίαν δὲ γενόμενον εἰς Μίλητον πρὸς Ἀναξίμανδρον, μαθηϲόμενον τὰ γεωμετρικὰ καὶ ἀϲτρονομικά. ἀφίκετο δὲ καὶ πρὸϲ Αἰγυπτίουϲ, φηϲίν, ὁ Πυθαγόραϲ καὶ πρὸϲ Ἄραβαϲ καὶ Χαλδαίουϲ καὶ Ἑβραίουϲ, παρ' ὧν καὶ τὴν περὶ ὀνείρων γνῶϲιν ἠκριβώϲατο· καὶ τῇ διὰ λιβανωτοῦ μαντείᾳ πρῶτοϲ ἐχρήϲατο.

καὶ ἐν Αἰγύπτῳ μὲν τοῖϲ ἱερεῦϲι ϲυνῆν καὶ τὴν ϲοφίαν ἐξέμαθε καὶ τὴν Αἰγυπτίων φωνήν, (12) γραμμάτων τε τριϲϲὰϲ διαφοράϲ, ἐπιϲτολογραφικῶν τε καὶ ἱερογλυφικῶν καὶ ϲυμβολικῶν, τῶν μὲν κυριολογουμένων κατὰ μίμηϲιν, τῶν δ' ἀλληγορουμένων κατά τιναϲ αἰνιγμούϲ· καὶ περὶ θεῶν πλέον τι ἔμαθεν.

ἐν δὲ Ἀραβίᾳ τῷ βαϲιλεῖ ϲυνῆν ἔν τε Βαβυλῶνι τοῖϲ τ' ἄλλοιϲ Χαλδαίοιϲ ϲυνεγένετο καὶ πρὸϲ Ζάρατον ἀφίκετο, παρ' οὗ καὶ ἐκαθάρθη τὰ τοῦ προτέρου βίου λύματα καὶ ἐδιδάχθη ἀφ' οὗ ἀγνεύειν προϲήκει τοῖϲ ϲπουδαίοιϲ, τόν τε περὶ φύϲεωϲ λόγον ἤκουϲε καὶ τίνεϲ αἱ τῶν ὅλων ἀρχαί. ἐκ γὰρ τῆϲ περὶ ταῦτα τὰ ἔθνη πλάνηϲ ὁ Πυθαγόραϲ τὸ πλεῖϲτον τῆϲ ϲοφίαϲ ἐνεπορεύϲατο.

(13) τὸν δὴ Ἀϲτραῖον τῷ Πυθαγόρᾳ χαρίζεται Μνήϲαρχοϲ. ὁ δὲ λαβὼν καὶ φυϲιογνωμονήϲαϲ καὶ τὰϲ κινήϲειϲ καὶ τὰϲ ἠρεμίαϲ τοῦ ϲώματοϲ ἐπιϲκεψάμενοϲ ἐπαίδευεν. ταύτην γὰρ ἠκρίβου πρῶτοϲ τὴν περὶ ἀνθρώπων ἐπιϲτήμην, ὁποῖοϲ τὴν φύϲιν ἕκαϲτοϲ εἴη μανθάνων. καὶ οὔτ' ἂν φίλον οὔτε γνώριμον ἐποιήϲατο οὐδένα πρὶν πρότερον φυϲιογνωμονῆϲαι τὸν ἄνδρα, ὁποῖόϲ ποτ' ἔϲτιν.

(14) ἦν δ' αὐτῷ καὶ ἕτερον μειράκιον ὃ ἐκ Θρᾴκηϲ ἐκτήϲατο, ᾧ Ζάμολξιϲ ἦν ὄνομα, ἐπεὶ γεννηθέντι αὐτῷ δορὰ ἄρκτου ἐπεβλήθη· τὴν γὰρ δορὰν οἱ Θρᾷκεϲ ζαλμὸν καλοῦϲιν. ἀγαπῶν δ' αὐτὸν ὁ Πυθαγόραϲ τὴν μετέωρον θεωρίαν ἐπαίδευε τά τε περὶ ἱερουργίαϲ καὶ τὰϲ ἄλλαϲ εἰϲ θεοὺϲ θρηϲκείαϲ· (τινὲϲ δὲ καὶ Θαλῆν τοῦτον φαϲὶν ὀνομάζεϲθαι. ὡϲ Ἡρακλέα δ' αὐτὸν προϲκυνοῦϲιν οἱ βάρβαροι. (15) Διονυϲοφάνηϲ δὲ λέγει δουλεῦϲαι μὲν αὐτὸν τῷ Πυθαγόρᾳ, ἐμπεϲόντα δ' εἰϲ ληϲτὰϲ καὶ ϲτιχθέντα, ὅτε κατε-

---

also of being raised as his child (*paidotrophia*) and marrying Theano, because of his preeminent mastery of the doctrines. Pythagoras himself is said to have been the school's leader for thirty-nine years and to have lived for nearly a hundred, so that Aristaios, when Pythagoras handed over the school to him, was already an old man" (Iamblichos *VP* §265). Rohde (1974: 284 n. 3) conjectures a connection with a mythical consort of Dawn (Hesiod *Theog.* 378) and father of the stars (Aratos *Phain.* 98). The astral ring of the name undoubtedly should be connected with the lunar and calendrical lore that features so prominently in the novel, but a specific allusion to those shadowy ogygian figures seems far-fetched. The adoption (*paidotrophia*) common to Diogenes and to Iamblichos's source strongly supports the close relation of Astraios and Aristaios.

(11) He sent him as a boy to the teachers of music, gymnastic, and drawing, and as a young man to Anaximander in Miletos to learn geometry and astronomy. Pythagoras also journeyed to the Egyptians, Diogenes says, and to the Arabs and Chaldaians and Hebrews, from whom he obtained an exact knowledge of dream interpretation; and he was the first to employ divination by frankincense.

In Egypt he associated with the priests and learned their wisdom and the Egyptian language, (12) and the three categories of writing—the epistolographic, the hieroglyphic, and the symbolic, of which the former is directly imitative and used in the literal sense, the latter employ enigmas and are used allegorically. And he learned much more concerning the gods.

In Arabia he associated with the king. In Babylon he spent time with the Chaldaians and in particular visited Zaratos,[70] by whom he was purified of the defilement of his former life and was taught the source of serious men's sanctity. He heard the discourse on nature and the origins of the universe. For it was from his wanderings to these nations that Pythagoras imported most of his wisdom.

(13) Mnesarchos entrusted Astraios to Pythagoras. Pythagoras accepted him, determined his character by studying the way his body naturally moved and rested, and oversaw his education. Pythagoras was the first to attain an accurate knowledge of this scientific physiognomy,[71] searching out the individual nature of each person. He would accept no one as his friend or even acquaintance without first reaching a physiognomic analysis of his character.

(14) There was another youth in his company whom he acquired from Thrace, named Zamolxis from the fact that at his birth he was wrapped in a bear hide, since the Thracians call a hide a *zalmos*. Pythagoras cherished him and taught him the theory of the heavens and about sacred rites and others matters pertaining to the cult of the gods. (Some say[72] that he was also called Thales. The barbarians worship him as Herakles. [15] Dionysophanes says that he was Pythagoras's slave and that he fell into the hands of brigands and was tattooed, when Pythagoras

---

[70] Zoroaster is meant.

[71] The first physiognomic texts belong to the fourth century B.C.E.

[72] The introduction of alternative accounts, "some say" and the like, should be attributed to Porphyry, not to Astraios or Diogenes.

cτακιάκθη ὁ Πυθαγόρας καὶ ἔφευγεν, δῆκαι τὸ μέτωπον διὰ τὰ κτίγματα. τινὲς δ᾽ ἑρμηνεύεκθαι τὸ ὄνομα φακὶ Ζάλμοξιν ξένος ἀνήρ.)

νοκήκαντα δὲ τὸν Φερεκύδην ἐν Δήλῳ θεραπεύκας ὁ Πυθαγόρας καὶ ἀποθανόντα θάψας εἰς Cάμον ἐπανῆλθε πόθῳ τοῦ κυγγενέκθαι Ἑρμοδάμαντι τῷ Κρεοφυλείῳ.

χρόνον δέ τινα αὐτοῦ διατρίβων Εὐρυμένους τοῦ Cαμίου ἀθλητοῦ ἐπεμελεῖτο, ὃς τῇ Πυθαγόρου κοφίᾳ καίτοι κμικρὸς τὸ κῶμα ὢν πολλῶν καὶ μεγάλων ἐκράτει καὶ ἐνίκα Ὀλυμπίακιν. τῶν γὰρ ἄλλων ἀθλητῶν κατὰ τὸν ἀρχαῖον ἔτι τρόπον τυρὸν καὶ κῦκα κιτουμένων, οὗτος Πυθαγόρᾳ πειθόμενος πρῶτος κρέας τεταγμένον ἐκθίων ἐφ᾽ ἑκάστην τὴν ἡμέραν ἰκχὺν τῷ κώματι περιεποιήκατο. καίτοι γε προϊὼν τῇ κοφίᾳ ὁ Πυθαγόρας ἀθλεῖν μὲν παρῄνει, νικᾶν δὲ μή, ὡς δέον τοὺς μὲν πόνους ὑπομένειν, τοὺς δ᾽ ἐκ τοῦ νικᾶν φθόνους φεύγειν· κυμβαίνειν γὰρ καὶ ἄλλως μηδ᾽ εὐαγεῖς εἶναι τοὺς νικῶντας καὶ φυλλοβολουμένους.

(16) μετὰ δὲ ταῦτα τῆς Πολυκράτους τυραννίδος Cαμίους καταλαβούκης, οὐ πρέπον ἡγούμενος ὁ Πυθαγόρας ἐν τοιαύτῃ πολιτείᾳ βιοῦν ἀνδρὶ φιλοσόφῳ, διενοήθη εἰς Ἰταλίαν ἀπαίρειν. ὡς δὲ πλέων Δελφοῖς προκέκχε, τὸ ἐλεγεῖον τῷ τοῦ Ἀπόλλωνος τάφῳ ἐπέγραψε, δι᾽ οὗ ἐδήλου ὡς Cειληνοῦ μὲν ἦν υἱὸς Ἀπόλλων, ἀνῃρέθη δὲ ὑπὸ Πύθωνος, ἐκηδεύθη δ᾽ ἐν τῷ καλουμένῳ Τρίποδι, ὃς ταύτης ἔτυχε τῆς ἐπωνυμίας διὰ τὸ τὰς τρεῖς κόρας τὰς Τριόπου θυγατέρας ἐνταῦθα θρηνῆσαι τὸν Ἀπόλλωνα.

(17) Κρήτης δ᾽ ἐπιβὰς τοῖς Μόργου μύσταις προκῄει ἑνὸς τῶν Ἰδαίων Δακτύλων, ὑφ᾽ ὧν καὶ ἐκαθάρθη τῇ κεραυνίᾳ λίθῳ, ἕωθεν μὲν παρὰ θαλάττῃ πρηνὴς ἐκταθείς, νύκτωρ δὲ παρὰ ποταμῷ ἀρνειοῦ μέλανος μαλλοῖς ἐκτεφανωμένος. εἰς δὲ τὸ Ἰδαῖον καλούμενον ἄντρον καταβὰς ἔρια ἔχων μέλανα τὰς νομιζομένας τρὶς ἐννέα ἡμέρας ἐκεῖ διέτριψεν καὶ καθήγικεν τῷ Διὶ τόν τε κτορνύμενον αὐτῷ κατ᾽ ἔτος θρόνον ἐθεάκατο, ἐπίγραμμά τ᾽ ἐνεχάραξεν ἐπὶ τῷ τάφῳ ἐπιγράψας "Πυθαγόρας τῷ Διί," οὗ ἡ ἀρχή·

ὧδε θανὼν κεῖται Ζάν, ὃν Δία κικλήκκουκιν.

was defeated by a rival faction and sent into exile and that he later bound his forehead to cover the tattoo. Some interpret the name Zalmoxis as meaning "stranger.")

Pythagoras nursed Pherekydes when he was sick on Delos and when he died buried him. Then he returned to Samos, with a desire to study with Hermodamas the descendant of Kreophylos.[73]

After spending a certain amount of time, there he took charge of Eurymenes the Samian athlete, who, thanks to Pythagoras's wisdom, in spite of his small stature, prevailed over many large opponents and was victorious at the Olympics. For while the other athletes followed the archaic diet of cheese and figs, Eurymenes took Pythagoras's advice and was the first to eat a set amount of meat each day and thus built up his bodily strength. Advancing in wisdom, however, Pythagoras recommended that he compete but not win, since one needed to endure labors (*ponous*) but flee the enviousness (*phthonous*) that arises from winning. For it is a simple fact that victors, who are celebrated with applause, are not free of pollution.[74]

(16) After this the Samians were overpowered by Polykrates' tyranny. Pythagoras did not think it proper for a philosopher to live in such a state and decided to move to Italy. On his journey he put in at Delphi and inscribed an elegiac couplet on Apollo's tomb that declared that Apollo was the son of Seilenos, that he was killed by Python and buried in the place called "Tripod" (*Tripous*), which received its name from the fact that the three daughters of Triopas mourned for Apollo there.

(17) Arriving at Krete, he visited the initiates of Morgos, one of the Idaian Daktyls; they purified him using a thunder-struck stone, requiring him to stretch out prone by the seashore at dawn and by night at the riverside crowned with black sheep's wool. He descended into the so-called Idaian cave carrying black wool and spent the assigned twenty-seven days there; he made offerings to Zeus, and he saw the throne that was furnished there for him annually. He inscribed an epigram on the tomb headed "Pythagoras to Zeus," which begins "Here lies the dead Zan, whom they call Zeus."[75]

---

[73] Porphyry *VP* § 1.1 (from Kleanthes); Diog. Laert. 8.2; Iamblichos *VP* §§ 9, 11. Kreophylos figures in the Homer legends variously as a friend or rival; his "school" of epic rhapsodes evidently flourished on Samos: Rzach 1913: 2150–52, Davies 1988: 149–53.

[74] The themes of this paragraph—healthy regimen, moderate meat-eating, enduring πόνος while avoiding φθόνος—all recur in Porphyry's second Diogenes passage below, supporting the attribution of this section to *The Incredible Things beyond Thule*.

[75] The awkwardness of stopping first at Delphi and then at Krete on route from Samos

b. *Vita Pythagorae* §§ 32–45

(32) τὴν δὲ καθ᾽ ἡμέραν αὐτοῦ διαγωγὴν ἀφηγούμενος ὁ Διογένης φησὶν
ὡς ἅπασι μὲν παρηγγύα φιλοτιμίαν φεύγειν καὶ φιλοδοξίαν, ὥπερ μάλιστα
φθόνον ἐργάζεσθαι, ἐκτρέπεσθαι δὲ τὰς μετὰ τῶν πολλῶν ὁμιλίας. τὰς γοῦν
διατριβὰς καὶ αὐτὸς ἕωθεν μὲν ἐπὶ τῆς οἰκίας ἐποιεῖτο, ἁρμοζόμενος πρὸς
λύραν τὴν ἑαυτοῦ φωνὴν καὶ ᾄδων παιᾶνας ἀρχαίους τινὰς τῶν Θάλητος.
καὶ ἐπῇδε τῶν Ὁμήρου καὶ Ἡσιόδου ὅσα καθημεροῦν τὴν ψυχὴν ἐδόξαζε.
καὶ ὀρχήσεις δέ τινας ὑπωρχεῖτο ὁπόσας εὐκινησίαν καὶ ὑγείαν τῷ σώματι
παρασκευάζειν ᾤετο. τοὺς δὲ περιπάτους οὐδ᾽ αὐτὸς ἐπιφθόνως μετὰ
πολλῶν ἐποιεῖτο, ἀλλὰ δεύτερος ἢ τρίτος ἐν ἱεροῖς ἢ ἄλσεσιν, ἐπιλεγόμενος
τῶν χωρίων τὰ ἡσυχαίτατα καὶ περικαλλέστατα.

(33) τοὺς δὲ φίλους ὑπερηγάπα, κοινὰ μὲν τὰ τῶν φίλων εἶναι πρῶτος
ἀποφηνάμενος, τὸν δὲ φίλον ἄλλον ἑαυτοῦ. καὶ ὑγιαίνουσι μὲν αὐτοῖς ἀεὶ
συνδιέτριβεν, κάμνοντας δὲ τὰ σώματα ἐθεράπευεν, καὶ τὰς ψυχὰς δὲ
νοσοῦντας παρεμυθεῖτο, καθάπερ ἔφαμεν, τοὺς μὲν ἐπῳδαῖς καὶ μαγείαις
τοὺς δὲ μουσικῇ. ἦν γὰρ αὐτῷ μέλη καὶ πρὸς νόσους σωμάτων παιώνια, ἃ
ἐπᾴδων ἀνίστη τοὺς κάμνοντας. ἦν (δ᾽) ἃ καὶ λύπης λήθην εἰργάζετο καὶ
ὀργὰς ἐπράυνε καὶ ἐπιθυμίας ἀτόπους ἐξῄρει.

(34) τῆς δὲ διαίτης τὸ μὲν ἄριστον ἦν κηρίον ἢ μέλι, δεῖπνον δ᾽ ἄρτος ἐκ
κέγχρων ἢ μᾶζα καὶ λάχανα ἑφθὰ καὶ ὠμά, σπανίως δὲ κρέας ἱερείων θυσί-
μων καὶ τοῦτο οὐδ᾽ ἐκ παντὸς μέρους. τά γε μὴν πλεῖστα ὁπότε θεῶν
ἀδύτοις ἐγκαταδύσεσθαι μέλλοι καὶ ἐνταῦθα χρόνου τινὸς ἐνδιατρίψειν,
ἀλίμοις ἐχρῆτο καὶ ἀδίψοις τροφαῖς, τὴν μὲν ἄλιμον συντιθεὶς ἐκ μήκωνος
σπέρματος καὶ σησάμου καὶ φλοιοῦ σκίλλης πλυθείσης ἀκριβῶς ἔστ᾽ ἂν τοῦ
περὶ αὐτὴν ὀποῦ καθαρθείη, καὶ ἀσφοδέλων ἀνθερίκων καὶ μαλάχης φύλ-
λων καὶ ἀλφίτων καὶ κριθῶν καὶ ἐρεβίνθων, ἅπερ κατ᾽ ἴσον πάντα σταθμὸν
κοπέντα μέλιτι ἀνέδευεν Ὑμηττίῳ· τὴν δ᾽ ἄδιψον ἐκ σικύων σπέρματος καὶ
ἀσταφίδος λιπαρᾶς, ἐξελὼν αὐτῆς τὰ γίγαρτα, καὶ ἄνθους κορίου καὶ
μαλάχης ὁμοίως σπέρματος καὶ ἀνδράχνης καὶ τυροῦ κνήσεως καὶ ἀλεύ-
ρου πάλης καὶ γάλακτος λίπους, ἅπερ πάντα ἀνέμιγνυ μέλιτι νησιωτικῷ.
(35) ταῦτα δ᾽ Ἡρακλέα παρὰ Δήμητρος ἔφασκε μαθεῖν στελλόμενον εἰς τὴν
Λιβύην τὴν ἄνυδρον.

ὅθεν αὐτῷ καὶ τὸ σῶμα ὥσπερ ἐπὶ στάθμῃ τὴν αὐτὴν ἕξιν διεφύλαττεν, οὐ
ποτὲ μὲν ὑγιαῖνον ποτὲ δὲ νοσοῦν, οὐδ᾽ αὖ ποτὲ μὲν πιαινόμενον καὶ αὐξα-

---

to Italy might be due to some author-editor who here drew from an account of
Pythagorean inscriptions not arranged geographically. It seems unlikely that Diogenes
would have invented or tolerated such a haphazard itinerary. Further, the euhemeristic
tendency of the inscriptions is unlike anything we know of Diogenes. On the other hand,
purification is a theme in *The Incredible Things* (Porphyry *VP* §§ 12, 45).

b. *Life of Pythagoras* §§ 32–45 [76]

(32) In describing Pythagoras's everyday conduct, Diogenes says that he advised everyone to flee from the pursuit of honor and glory, which principally arouses envy (*phthonos*), and to avoid encounters with most people. He himself, at any rate, spent his time at home in the early morning, tuning his soul to a lyre and singing some ancient paeans composed by Thales. And he chanted those parts of Homer and Hesiod which he judged suitable to pacify the soul. He also danced certain dances that he thought imparted good motion and health to his body. He had a powerful aversion to taking walks in the company of a crowd, though he would stroll with one or two companions in sacred places and groves, choosing always the most serene and lovely locations.

(33) He had a surpassing affection for his comrades, and was the first to declare that "friends should share" and that "a friend is another self." He spent time with his healthy friends and nursed those whose bodies were suffering and consoled those whose souls were ill (just as we said), some with chants and formulas of the magi, some with music. For he possessed healing melodies even for bodily illnesses: when he chanted them, he made the sick rise up. And he had melodies that effected forgetfulness of sorrow and calmed anger and removed improper desires.

(34) As to his diet, his breakfast was honeycomb or honey; his dinner was millet bread or barley bread and vegetables, cooked and raw, rarely meat from sacrificed animals, and not from every part of the animal. For the most part, whenever he was about to enter into the inner sancta of the gods and spend a certain time there, he used no-hunger and no-thirst foods. He prepared the no-hunger from poppy seeds and sesame and squill bark carefully washed until it is purified of all its sap and asphodel stalk and mallow leaves and barley meal and barley corns and garbanzos, all mashed together in equal amounts by weight and moistened with Hymettan honey. He made the no-thirst from squirting cucumber seeds and glistening raisins with the seeds removed and coriander blossom and also mallow seed and purslane and grated cheese and fine wheat meal and pure cream, all mixed together with island honey. (35) He said that Herakles learned these recipes from Demeter when he was sent to waterless Libya.

As a result of this regimen, even his bodily condition was invariant, as if measured by a carpenter's rule: it was not at one time healthy, at another time sick, nor some times waxing fat, other times waning thin.

---

[76] This section describes Pythagoras's teachings and moral practice.

νόμενον, ποτὲ δὲ λεπτυνόμενον καὶ ἰςχναινόμενον, ἥ τε ψυχὴ τὸ ὅμοιον ἦθος ἀεὶ διὰ τῆς ὄψεως παρεδήλου. οὔτε γὰρ ὑφ' ἡδονῆς διεχεῖτο πλέον οὔθ' ὑπ' ἀνίας ςυνεςτέλλετο, οὐδ' ἐπίδηλος ἦν χαρᾷ ἢ λύπῃ κάτοχος, ἀλλ' οὐδὲ γελάςαντα ἢ κλαύςαντά τίς ποτ' ἐκεῖνον ἐθεάςατο.

(36) θύων τε θεοῖς ἀνεπαχθὴς ἦν, ἀλφίτοις τε καὶ ποπάνῳ καὶ λιβανωτῷ καὶ μυρρίνῃ τοὺς θεοὺς ἐξιλαςκόμενος, ἐμψύχοις δ' ἥκιςτα, πλὴν εἰ μή ποτε ἀλεκτορίςιν καὶ τῶν χοίρων τοῖς ἁπαλωτάτοις. ἐβουθύτηςεν δέ ποτε ςταίτινον ὥς φαςι βοῦν οἱ ἀκριβέςτεροι, ἐξευρὼν τοῦ ὀρθογωνίου τὴν ὑποτείνουςαν ἴςον δυναμένην ταῖς περιεχούςαις.

ὅςα γε μὴν τοῖς προςιοῦςι διελέγετο, ἢ διεξοδικῶς ἢ ςυμβολικῶς παρῄνει. (37) διττὸν γὰρ ἦν αὐτοῦ τῆς διδαςκαλίας τὸ ςχῆμα. καὶ τῶν προςιόντων οἳ μὲν ἐκαλοῦντο μαθηματικοί, οἳ δ' ἀκουςματικοί· καὶ μαθηματικοὶ μὲν οἱ τὸν περιττότερον καὶ πρὸς ἀκρίβειαν διαπεπονημένον τῆς ἐπιςτήμης λόγον ἐκμεμαθηκότες, ἀκουςματικοὶ δ' οἱ μόνας τὰς κεφαλαιώδεις ὑποθήκας τῶν γραμμάτων ἄνευ ἀκριβεςτέρας διηγήςεως ἀκηκοότες.

(38) παρῄνει δὲ περὶ μὲν τοῦ θείου καὶ δαιμονίου καὶ ἡρῴου γένους εὔφημον εἶναι καὶ ἀγαθὴν ἔχειν διάνοιαν, γονεῦςι δὲ καὶ εὐεργέταις εὔνουν· νόμοις δὲ πείθεςθαι· προςκυνεῖν δὲ μὴ ἐκ παρέργου τοὺς θεούς, ἀλλ' οἴκοθεν ἐπὶ τοῦτο ὡρμημένοις· καὶ τοῖς μὲν οὐρανίοις θεοῖς περιττὰ θύειν, τοῖς δὲ χθονίοις ἄρτια. ἐκάλει γὰρ τῶν ἀντικειμένων δυνάμεων τὴν μὲν βελτίονα μονάδα καὶ φῶς καὶ δεξιὸν καὶ ἴςον καὶ μένον καὶ εὐθύ, τὴν δὲ χείρονα δυάδα καὶ ςκότος καὶ ἀριςτερὸν καὶ ἄνιςον καὶ περιφερὲς καὶ φερόμενον.

(39) παρῄνει δὲ καὶ τοιάδε. φυτὸν ἥμερον καὶ ἔγκαρπον, ἀλλὰ μηδὲ ζῷον ὃ μὴ βλαβερὸν εἶναι πέφυκε τῷ ἀνθρωπείῳ γένει, μήτε φθείρειν μήτε βλάπτειν. παρακαταθήκην δὲ μὴ χρημάτων μόνον ἀλλὰ καὶ λόγων πιςτῶς τῷ παρακαταθεμένῳ φυλάςςειν. τριςςὰς δ' ἡγεῖςθαι διαφορὰς τῶν ἀξίων ςπουδῆς πραγμάτων, ἃ καὶ μετιτέον καὶ μεταχειριςτέον· πρῶτον μὲν τῶν εὐκλεῶν καὶ καλῶν, εἶτα τῶν πρὸς τὸν βίον ςυμφερόντων, τρίτην δὲ καὶ τελευταίαν τὴν τῶν ἡδέων. ἡδονὴν δὲ οὐ προςίετο τὴν δημώδη καὶ γοητευτικήν, ἀλλὰ τὴν βέβαιον καὶ ςεμνοτάτην καὶ καθαρεύουςαν διαβολῆς. διττὴν γὰρ εἶναι διαφορὰν ἡδονῶν· τὴν μὲν γὰρ γαςτρὶ καὶ ἀφροδιςίοις διὰ πολυτελείας κεχαριςμένην ἀπείκαζε ταῖς ἀνδροφόνοις τῶν ςειρήνων ᾠδαῖς· τὴν δ' ἐπὶ καλοῖς καὶ δικαίοις τοῖς πρὸς τὸ ζῆν ἀναγκαίοις, ὁμοίως καὶ παραχρῆμα ἡδεῖαν καὶ εἰς τὸ ἐπιὸν ἀμεταμέλητον, ἣν ἔφαςκεν ἐοικέναι μουςῶν τινι ἁρμονίᾳ.

His soul, too, always displayed the same disposition through his face: it was not more relaxed in pleasure nor contracted in pain, and never showed him possessed by joy or sorrow—in fact, no one ever saw him laughing or crying.

(36) In sacrificing to the gods he gave no offense, propitiating them with barley meal and cakes and frankincense and myrtle, seldom with living creatures except for an occasional cock or suckling pig. When he discovered the formula for the equivalence of a right-angled hypotenuse with the adjacent sides, he sacrificed a cow, but one that the most careful authorities say was made of wheat dough.

In conversing with those who came to him, his advice was either discursive or symbolic, (37) for his teaching had a double format. Some of his disciples were known as *mathēmatikoi*, others as *akousmatikoi*: the *mathēmatikoi* were those who more fully learned his teaching in all its ramifications and carefully worked out details, the *akousmatikoi* were those who heard only the summary counsels of his writings without more accurate explanation.

(38) He recommended that one maintain auspicious language and good thoughts concerning what is divine and daimonic and heroic, and kindly attitudes towards parents and benefactors; that one should obey the laws; that one's worship of the gods should be not casual but deliberate and heartfelt; that one should sacrifice odd things to the celestial gods, even things to the chthonic gods. For he called the better of the two opposite forces monad, light, right, equal, enduring, and straight; the worse dyad, darkness, left, unequal, mobile and curved.

(39) He also recommended the following: not to destroy or injure any domestic, fruit-bearing plant, nor any animal that is not naturally hostile to humans; faithfully to guard deposits, not only of money but of words; to acknowledge three classes of serious pursuits that should be undertaken and followed through: first, those which are noble and fine; second, those which are useful to life; third and last, those which are pleasant. He did not approve pleasure that was popular and seductive but only that which was lasting and most holy and untouched by accusation. For he said that pleasure was of two sorts: the one that gladdened the stomach and genitals through extravagant expenditures he likened to the man-killing songs of the Sirens; the other, which aimed at the fine and just and at life's necessities and which was equally pleasurable at the moment and brought no regrets in its wake, he likened to a harmony of the Muses.

(40) δύο δὲ μάλιϲτα καιροὺϲ παρηγγύα ἐν φροντίδι θέϲθαι, τὸν μὲν ὅτε εἰϲ ὕπνον τρέποιτο, τὸν δ᾽ ὅτε ἐξ ὕπνου διανίϲταιτο. ἐπιϲκοπεῖν γὰρ προϲήκειν ἐν ἑκατέρῳ τούτοιν τά τε ἤδη πεπραγμένα καὶ τὰ μέλλοντα, τῶν μὲν γενομένων εὐθύναϲ παρ᾽ ἑαυτοῦ ἕκαϲτον λαμβάνοντα, τῶν δὲ μελλόντων πρόνοιαν ποιούμενον. πρὸ μὲν οὖν τοῦ ὕπνου ταῦτα ἑαυτῷ τὰ ἔπη ἐπᾴδειν ἕκαϲτον·

> μηδ᾽ ὕπνον μαλακοῖϲιν ἐπ᾽ ὄμμαϲι προϲδέξαϲθαι
> πρὶν τῶν ἡμερινῶν ἔργων τρὶϲ ἕκαϲτον ἐπελθεῖν,
> πῇ παρέβην; τί δ᾽ ἔρεξα; τί μοι δέον οὐκ ἐτελέϲθη;

πρὸ δὲ τῆϲ ἐξαναϲτάϲεωϲ ἐκεῖνα·

> πρῶτα μὲν ἐξ ὕπνοιο μελίφρονοϲ ἐξυπαναϲτὰϲ
> εὖ μάλ᾽ ὀπιπεύειν ὅϲ᾽ ἐν ἤματι ἔργα τελέϲϲειϲ.

(41) τοιαῦτα παρῄνει· μάλιϲτα δ᾽ ἀληθεύειν· τοῦτο γὰρ μόνον δύναϲθαι τοὺϲ ἀνθρώπουϲ ποιεῖν θεῷ παραπληϲίουϲ. ἐπεὶ καὶ τοῦ θεοῦ, ὡϲ παρὰ τῶν μάγων ἐπυνθάνετο, ὃν Ὡρομάζην καλοῦϲιν ἐκεῖνοι, ἐοικέναι τὸ μὲν ϲῶμα φωτί, τὴν δὲ ψυχὴν ἀληθείᾳ. καὶ ἄλλ᾽ ἄττα ἐπαίδευεν ὅϲα παρὰ Ἀριϲτοκλείαϲ τῆϲ ἐν Δελφοῖϲ ἔλεγεν ἀκηκοέναι.

ἔλεγε δέ τινα καὶ μυϲτικῷ τρόπῳ ϲυμβολικῶϲ, ἃ δὴ ἐπὶ πλέον Ἀριϲτοτέληϲ ἀνέγραψεν· οἷον ὅτι τὴν θάλατταν μὲν ἐκάλει εἶναι δάκρυον, τὰϲ δ᾽ ἄρκτουϲ Ῥέαϲ χεῖραϲ, τὴν δὲ πλειάδα μουϲῶν λύραν, τοὺϲ δὲ πλανήταϲ κύναϲ τῆϲ Φερϲεφόνηϲ. τὸν δ᾽ ἐκ χαλκοῦ κρουομένου γινόμενον ἦχον φωνὴν εἶναί τινοϲ τῶν δαιμόνων ἐναπειλημμένου τῷ χαλκῷ. (42) ἦν δὲ καὶ ἄλλο εἶδοϲ τῶν ϲυμβόλων τοιοῦτον. ζυγὸν μὴ ὑπερβαίνειν, τοῦτ᾽ ἔϲτι μὴ πλεονεκτεῖν. μὴ τὸ πῦρ τῇ μαχαίρᾳ ϲκαλεύειν, ὅπερ ἦν μὴ τὸν ἀνοιδοῦντα καὶ ὀργιζόμενον κινεῖν λόγοιϲ τεθηγμένοιϲ. ϲτέφανόν τε μὴ τίλλειν, τοῦτ᾽ ἔϲτι τοὺϲ νόμουϲ μὴ λυμαίνεϲθαι· ϲτέφανοι γὰρ πόλεων οὗτοι. πάλιν δ᾽ αὖ ἕτερα τοιαῦτα. μὴ καρδίαν ἐϲθίειν, οἷον μὴ λυπεῖν ἑαυτὸν ἀνίαιϲ. μηδ᾽ ἐπὶ χοίνικοϲ καθέζεϲθαι, οἷον μὴ ἀργὸν ζῆν. μηδ᾽ ἀποδημοῦντα ἐπιϲτρέφεϲθαι, μὴ ἔχεϲθαι τοῦ βίου τούτου ἀποθνήϲκοντα· τάϲ τε λεωφόρουϲ μὴ βαδίζειν, δι᾽ οὗ ταῖϲ τῶν πολλῶν ἕπεϲθαι γνώμαιϲ ἐκώλυεν, τὰϲ δὲ τῶν λογίων καὶ πεπαιδευμένων μεταθεῖν. μηδὲ χελιδόναϲ ἐν οἰκίᾳ δέχεϲθαι, τοῦτ᾽ ἔϲτι λάλουϲ ἀνθρώπουϲ καὶ περὶ γλῶτταν ἀκρατεῖϲ ὁμωροφίουϲ μὴ ποιεῖϲθαι. φορτίον δὲ ϲυνανατιθέναι μὲν τοῖϲ βαϲτάζουϲιν, ϲυγκαθαιρεῖν

(40) He recommended that one pay careful attention to two times of the day in particular: when turning to sleep and when rising from sleep. At both of these times one should consider one's past and future actions, rendering an accounting to oneself for the past and taking counsel for the future. So before sleep everyone should chant the following verses:

Let no sleep fall on my tender eyes
Before three times reviewing each of the day's deeds:
Where did I go wrong? What did I do? What should I have
done but didn't?

And before rising:

First of all on rising from honey-sweet sleep
Carefully scrutinize what actions you will accomplish that day.

(41) He gave the following advice: above all to tell the truth, for this alone can make human beings like god. For god (as he learned from the magi, who call him Horomazos) has a body like light and a soul like truth. And he taught certain other doctrines, which he said he heard from Aristokleia in Delphi.

Some of his sayings were symbolic, uttered in a mystical style, which Aristotle has recorded at greater length,[77] e.g., "The sea is a tear [of Kronos]," "The Bears are the arms of Rhea," "The Pleiad is the Muses' lyre," "The planets are the dogs of Persephone." He said that the sound made when brass is struck is the voice of one of the daimons trapped in the brass. (42) Another type of his symbolic utterances ran as follows: do not cross over a yoke, i.e., do not be greedy; do not poke the fire with a sword, i.e., do not provoke by sharpened words a person swollen with anger; do not pluck a garland, i.e., do not sully the laws, since they are the garlands of cities. And there are others of the same type: do not eat a heart, i.e., do not grieve yourself with pain; do not sit on a bushel, i.e., do not live a lazy life; do not turn back when emigrating, i.e., do not cling to life when you are dying; do not walk on the public thoroughfares, whereby he advised against following the opinions of the common majority, instead pursuing those of the intelligent and well educated; do not welcome swallows into your house, i.e., do not let talkative and loose-tongued people dwell under the same roof with you; help those who are carrying a burden, do not help them put it down, whereby he

---

[77] In Aristotle's *On the Pythagoreans*, a lost work used by many later writers. The comment must be Porphyry's, not Astraios's or Diogenes'.

δὲ μή, δι' οὗ παρήνει μηδενὶ πρὸς ῥᾳςτώνην, ἀλλὰ πρὸς ἀρετὴν ςυμπράττειν. θεῶν τ' εἰκόνας ἐν δακτυλίοις μὴ φορεῖν, τοῦτ' ἔςτι τὴν περὶ θεῶν δόξαν καὶ λόγον μὴ πρόχειρον μηδὲ φανερὸν ἔχειν μηδὲ εἰς πολλοὺς προφέρειν. ςπονδάς τε ποιεῖςθαι τοῖς θεοῖς κατὰ τὸ οὖς τῶν ἐκπωμάτων· ἐντεῦθεν γὰρ ᾐνίττετο τιμᾶν τοὺς θεοὺς καὶ ὑμνεῖν τῇ μουςικῇ· αὕτη γὰρ διὰ ὤτων χωρεῖ. μηδ' ἐςθίειν ὅςα μὴ θέμις, γένεςιν, αὔξηςιν, ἀρχήν, τελευτήν, μηδ' ἐξ ὧν ἡ πρώτη τῶν πάντων ὑπόθεςις γίνεται. (43) ἔλεγε δ' ἀπέχεςθαι τῶν καταθυομένων ὀςφύος καὶ διδύμων καὶ αἰδοίων καὶ μυελοῦ καὶ ποδῶν καὶ κεφαλῆς. ὑπόθεςιν μὲν γὰρ τὴν ὀςφῦν ἐκάλει, διότι ἐπὶ ταύτῃ ὡς ἐπὶ θεμελίῳ ςυνίςταται τὰ ζῷα· γένεςιν δὲ τοὺς διδύμους καὶ αἰδοῖα, ἄνευ γὰρ τῆς τούτων ἐνεργείας οὐ γίνεται ζῷον· αὔξηςιν δὲ τὸν μυελὸν ἐκάλει, ὃς τοῦ αὔξεςθαι πᾶςιν ζῴοις αἴτιος· ἀρχὴν δὲ τοὺς πόδας, τὴν δὲ κεφαλὴν τελευτᾶν· ἅπερ τὰς μεγίςτας ἡγεμονίας ἔχει τοῦ ςώματος.

ἴςα δὲ κυάμων παρήνει ἀπέχεςθαι καθάπερ ἀνθρωπίνων ςαρκῶν. (44) ἱςτοροῦςι δ' αὐτὸν ἀπαγορεύειν τὸ τοιοῦτο ὅτι τῆς πρώτης τῶν ὅλων ἀρχῆς καὶ γενέςεως ταραττομένης καὶ πολλῶν ἅμα ςυνηνεγμένων καὶ ςυςπειρομένων καὶ ςυςςηπομένων ἐν τῇ γῇ κατ' ὀλίγον γένεςις καὶ διάκριςις ςυνέςτη ζῴων τε ὁμοῦ γεννωμένων καὶ φυτῶν ἀναδιδομένων, τότε δὴ ἀπὸ τῆς αὐτῆς ςηπεδόνος ἀνθρώους ςυςτῆναι καὶ κύαμον βλαςτῆςαι. τούτου τε φανερὰ ἐπῆγε τεκμήρια. εἰ γάρ τις διατραγὼν κύαμον καὶ τοῖς ὀδοῦςι λεάνας ἐν ἀλέᾳ τῆς τοῦ ἡλίου βολῆς καταθείη πρὸς ὀλίγον, εἶτ' ἀποςτὰς ἐπανέλθοι μετ' οὐ πολύ, εὕροι ἂν ὀδωδότα ἀνθρωπείου γόνου· εἰ δὲ καὶ ἀνθοῦντος ἐν τῷ βλαςτάνειν τοῦ κυάμου λαβών τις περκάζοντος τοῦ ἄνθους βραχὺ ἐνθείη ἀγγείῳ κεραμέῳ καὶ ἐπίθεμα ἐπιθεὶς ἐν τῇ γῇ κατορύξειεν καὶ ἐνενήκοντα παρφυλάξειεν ἡμέρας μετὰ τὸ κατορυχθῆναι, εἶτα μετὰ ταῦτα ὀρύξας λάβοι καὶ ἀφέλοι τὸ πῶμα, εὕροι ἂν ἀντὶ τοῦ κυάμου ἢ παιδὸς κεφαλὴν ςυνεςτῶςαν ἢ γυναικὸς αἰδοῖον.

(45) ἀπέχεςθαι δὲ καὶ ἄλλων παρήνει, οἷον μήτρας τε καὶ τριγλίδος καὶ ἀκαλήφης, ςχεδὸν δὲ καὶ τῶν ἄλλων θαλαςςίων ξυμπάντων. ἀνέφερεν δ' αὐτὸν εἰς τοὺς πρότερον γεγονότας, πρῶτον μὲν Εὔφορβος λέγων γενέςθαι, δεύτερον δ' Αἰθαλίδης, τρίτον Ἑρμότιμος, τέταρτον δὲ Πύρρος, νῦν δὲ

advised cooperating toward excellence, not toward leisure; do not wear images of gods on rings, i.e., do not display your opinions and doctrines concerning the gods ready to hand or in the open and do not expose them to many people; make libations to the gods along the ear of drinking cups, whereby he hinted that one should honor and hymn the gods with music, for this goes through the ears; do not eat what is not allowed—birth, growth, beginning, end, nor those things from which the first foundation of all things arises; (43) he meant that one should abstain from certain parts of sacrificed animals—loin, testicles, genitals, marrow, feet, and head. For he called the loin the "foundation" since it is as it were what underlies and supports the structure of the animal; "birth" means the testicles and genitals, without whose activity no animal comes into being; "growth" was his name for marrow, which is the cause of growth for all animals; "beginning" means the feet, "end" the head, which two have the greatest leadership in the body.

He advised his followers to abstain from beans as they would from human flesh. (44) They report that he issued such a ban because when the first principle of generation was all in a confusion and many things had been combined together and their various seeds and putrescences were coming together in the earth, there gradually occurred a generation and a separating out of living creatures that had been generated together and plants that had sprung up. At that time from the same putrescence human beings were formed and beans sprouted. He adduces evident proofs of this. For if one thoroughly chews a bean and mashes it into a paste with one's teeth and leaves it for a little while in a spot warmed by the sun's rays and then returns after a short interval, he will find it smelling of human gore. And if when the bean plant is blossoming one takes a bit of its ripening floweret and places it in a covered ceramic vessel and buries it in the earth and returns to dig it up after ninety days, then one will find on taking off the lid that instead of a bean there had been formed either a child's head or a woman's genitals.

(45) He also recommended abstinence from other foods, such as wombs, red mullet, sea anemones and practically all seafood.

He related himself to prior lives, saying that first he had been Euphorbos, second Aithalides, third Hermotimos, fourth Pyrrhos, and now

Πυθαγόρας. δι᾽ ὧν ἐδείκνυεν ὡς ἀθάνατος ἡ ψυχὴ καὶ τοῖς κεκαθαρμένοις εἰς μνήμην τοῦ παλαιοῦ βίου ἀφικνεῖται.

c. *Vita Pythagorae* §§ 54–55

(54) Πυθαγόρας δ᾽ ἄχρι πολλοῦ κατὰ τὴν Ἰταλίαν οὕτως ἐθαυμάζετο αὐτός τε καὶ οἱ συνόντες αὐτῷ ἑταῖροι, ὥςτε καὶ τὰς πολιτείας τοῖς ἀπ᾽ αὐτοῦ ἐπιτρέπειν τὰς πόλεις. ὀψὲ δέ ποτε ἐφθονήθηςαν, καὶ συνέςτη κατ᾽ αὐτῶν ἐπιβουλὴ τοιάδε τις. Κύλων ἀνὴρ Κροτωνιάτης, κατὰ μὲν τὸ γένος καὶ δόξαν προγονικὴν καὶ βίου περιουσίαν πάντας ὑπερβάλλων τοὺς πολίτας, χαλεπὸς δ᾽ ἄλλως καὶ βίαιος καὶ τυραννικός, τῇ τε τῶν φίλων περιβολῇ καὶ τῇ τοῦ πλούτου δυνάμει πρὸς ἰσχὺν ἀδικημάτων χρώμενος, οὗτος τῶν τ᾽ ἄλλων ἁπάντων ἃ ἐδόκει καλὰ ἑαυτὸν ἠξίου, ἡγεῖτο δὲ καὶ τῆς Πυθαγόρου φιλοσοφίας ἀξιώτατον εἶναι μετασχεῖν. πρόςειςι τῷ Πυθαγόρᾳ ἑαυτὸν ἐπαινῶν καὶ βουλόμενος συνεῖναι αὐτῷ. ὁ δ᾽ εὐθὺς φυσιογνωμονήςας τὸν ἄνδρα καὶ ὁποῖος ἦν συνιδὼν ἐκ τῶν σημείων ἃ διὰ τοῦ σώματος ἐθήρα [τῶν προσιόντων], ἀπιέναι ἐκέλευεν καὶ τὰ ἑαυτοῦ πράττειν. τοῦτο τὸν Κύλωνα οὐ μετρίως ἐλύπησεν ὥσπερ ὑβρισμένον καὶ τὰ ἄλλα χαλεπὸν ὄντα καὶ ὀργῆς ἀκρατῆ. (55) συναγαγὼν οὖν τοὺς φίλους διέβαλλε τὸν Πυθαγόραν καὶ παρεσκεύαζεν ὡς ἐπιβουλεύςων αὐτῷ τε καὶ τοῖς γνωρίμοις.

Pythagoras.[78] By these means he showed that the soul was immortal and, in the case of those who had been purified, could arrive at a memory of earlier life.

c. *Life of Pythagoras* §§ 54–55 [79]

(54) For a long time Pythagoras and his companions were admired in Italy, so much so that cities entrusted their constitutions to his disciples. At length, however, they became objects of envy and a conspiracy arose against them as follows. Kylon, a man of Kroton who surpassed all his fellow-citizens in birth and ancestral honor and wealth but was in other respects a harsh and violent and tyrannical man, used his network of friends and the power of his wealth to practice injustice by force. He thought he deserved everything that seemed to him fine, and in particular he held himself most worthy to share in Pythagoras's philosophy. He approached Pythagoras, praising himself as one who was willing to associate with him. But Pythagoras instantly read the man's character, perceiving what kind of person he was from the indications he ferreted out on the bodies [of those who approached him], and he told Kylon to go away and mind his own business. Kylon was immoderately upset by this, as if he had been insulted, and he was in any case a bitter person and had a quick temper. (55) So, gathering together his friends, he made accusations against Pythagoras and contrived a plot against him and his associates.

[78] The "and now" is a good sign that this passage is still derived from Diogenes, where the speaker was Pythagoras's contemporary Astraios (Reyhl 1969: 24).

[79] This section deals with the Kylonian conspiracy. The reference to Pythagoras's physiognomic knowledge, firmly associated with Astraios in §13 above, strongly indicates that this paragraph is also derived from Diogenes (so Reyhl 1969: 25). In the paragraphs following this section (not reproduced), Porphyry's own voice is recognizable from the phrases "some say," "according to Neanthes," and "Dikaiarchos and the more accurate scholars say." He relates several variant endings for the story. It is not clear which of them, if any, Diogenes used.

PAPYRI

PSI 1177

In *PSI* 1177, a dramatic scene is in progress between two women: one is named Myrto (line 9); the other, addressed by Myrto as "mistress" (line 22), is the narrator. The subject matter is intriguing: Myrto, who is unable to speak, is given the sort of writing tablets that schoolchildren use and told to write down what she cannot say. She writes a warning to her mistress to leave before her (Myrto's?) lover visits, "lest you too enjoy the attentions of a cruel [demon]." At this point the column breaks off.

On the basis of the name Myrto, previous editors have been quick to identify this fragment as part of Antonius Diogenes' *The Incredible Things beyond Thule*, because, according to Photios, Derkyllis "saw the Underworld and learned many of its secrets, her teacher being a woman named Myrto, a family servant who had died long ago and now from the dead instructed her mistress" (109a38–109b2). As Crönert pointed out (in Zimmermann 1935: 475), Myrto is not usually a slave name, yet in Photios she is said to be a *therapainis* (a female slave) and in this piece a *therapainidion*—an unlikely coincidence if the two are unrelated.[80]

Although the fragment does not quite match Photios's epitome, this is not necessarily an obstacle to attribution to Diogenes. The solution proposed by Gallavotti and others is quite plausible: Photios's compression of twenty-four books into the equivalent of about ten pages of a modern text must have omitted a number of details. The scene may be understood in two ways: Myrto was alive in the household in Tyre at the time that Mantinias's and Derkyllis's parents were placed in a sleep simulating death through the malicious devising of the Egyptian magician Paapis. Paapis could be the lover of Myrto as well as the one responsible for her silence though a magic spell. (Hence the cryptic warning about attentions of evil spirits?) He may also have contrived her death. Another possibility is that Myrto is indeed dead and she is sending back a note for Derkyllis's nurse. Apparently Myrto's letter to the nurse contained some information that the nurse would have found distressing and eye-opening. Was Paapis her lover too? The specific occasion for this narrative must surely be Derkyllis recounting the vicissitudes of her life

---

[80] In fact, the most famous bearer of this name was a daughter of Aristides the Just and the second wife of Socrates (Plut. *Arist.* §27.5; [Luc.] *Halcyon* §8).

to Deinias—with, no doubt, an embedded tale of Myrto's woes or of Paapis's malignancy (or both) written on the tablets.

The assignment of this fragment to *The Incredible Things* is attractive for another reason. This scene displays a self-consciousness about writing and about the physical media involved that borders on the frivolous, which would suit well our understanding of Diogenes' novel: a novel that, from the summary, seems to indicate rather more than an occasional interest in the forms available for written as opposed to spoken means of narration. The cypress tablets themselves (on which the tale is said to have been written down and buried nearby Deinias' tomb) are part of the game of incredible things the reader is asked to play—imagine how much wood would be necessary, what quantity of cypress tablets would be required, to inscribe twenty-four books of adventures, however minute the writing?

DESCRIPTION

The papyrus *PSI* 1177 (= P^2 95) measures 8.5 × 20.3 cm. The front contains an account of arable land from several villages in the Arsinoite nome; it bears no date, but the hand is assignable to the second century C.E. Writing on the back is across the fibers and upside down in respect to that of the front. One fragmentary column remains, preserving parts of thirty lines (of which lines 5–30 are nearly complete), a small left margin (c. 1.0 cm), and a substantial lower margin (to 4.5 cm). The hand is a fluently formed Severe style of medium size. There were originally between twenty-nine and thirty-one letters per line (about twenty-four of which survive); the original column height is unknown. Punctuation includes a paragraphos used with dicola (l. 12), dicola alone (lines 20, 22), and what appears to be a middle stop (line 5). An apostrophe separating doubled consonants seems to have been used at line 16, a practice that indicates a date for the hand no earlier than 200 C.E. (see *GMAW*^{2}, introd. 11 n. 50). There are no corrections, additions, or visible errors. Iota adscript is not written; elision is marked occasionally (e.g., lines 9, 14). Note that in the lacunae we have restored *scriptio plena* following δὲ ἀν[(line 21). The text itself does not always avoid hiatus, however, note διδαϲκάλου ἐπεφερόμεθα (line 8) and]ρι ἐξιέναι (line 20). There is one peculiarity of dialect: ἐξῖναι for ἐξιέναι (line 20). The scribe writes both ἠβούλετο (line 17) and ἐβουλόμην (line 30).

149

PSI 1177

```
- - - - - - - - - - - - - - - - - - - - - - - - - - -
      πλεον[........................]
      και τω[........................]
      και εν[........................]
  4   γαι τυχη πλε . [........................]
      ρουcη · ἐcιώπα γὰρ ἀχρε[ίωc · ἄκουcον]
      οὖν, ὅπερ τότε ἐπὶ νοῦ[ν ἦλθέ μοι · γραμ-]
      ματεῖον δίθυρον τῶν [τοιούτων, οἷα ἐc]
  8   διδαcκάλου ἐπεφερόμεθα, ἀπ[ολαβοῦcα]
      δίδωμι τῇ Μυρτοῖ · "κεὶ cὺ ἀλλ᾿ ἔ[τι μοι μὴ]
      δύναcαι λαλεῖν," ἔφην, "ἀλλ᾿ ἕν [γε τούτῳ χά-]
      ραξον ὅcα εἰπεῖν ἐθέλειc. ἐγὼ δ[ὲ ἀναγνοῦ-]
 12   cα εἴcομαι." ᾔcθη τὸ θεραπαιν[ίδιον · δήλη]
      γὰρ διὰ τῆc ὄψεωc ὡc αὐτίκα [μάλα ἐκδι-]
      κίαc ἐφ᾿ οἷc πέπονθε καὶ θεραπ[είαc τευ-]
      ξομένη. λαβοῦcα οὖν τὸ γραμμα[τεῖον καὶ]
 16   τῷ λύχνῳ προcελθοῦcα χαράτ[τει τῷ γρα-]
      φείῳ πάνυ cπουδῇ ὅcα ἠβούλε[το ἐν μι-]
      κροῖc πάνυ γράμμαcι τ[ο]ῦ πλέο[ν ἐγγρά-]
      ψαι, καί μοι δίδωcιν ἄμ[α] διανεύ[ουcα τῇ χει-]
```

Supplements are those of Gallavotti unless otherwise indicated. Those of Maas and Crönert may be found in Vitelli. We have omitted all supplements that do not suit the space available.
3–5. καὶ εἶ[πον · "ἄρ᾿ οὖν, ὦ Μυρτοῖ, λαλεῖν οὐ δύνα]|cαι τύχη πλεο[νεκτουμένη δυcτυχεῖ τῇ πα]|ρούcη." Vit.   4–5. πλεο[νεκτεῖcθαι οὕτω τῇ πα]|ρούcη Gal.   5. ρουcη : pap.   γὰρ ἀχρε[ίωc] Vit., ἀχρε[ῖον] Zimm., ἄρα κρε[μαcθεῖcα] Gal.   5–6. [ἄκου-cον]| οὖν Crön., [ἀλλὰ] | οὖν Gal., [εὐθὺc] | οὖν Zimm.   6. [ἐπῆλθεν] Zimm.   7. τῶν [τοιούτων, οἷα ἐc] Zimm., τῶν [μικροτέρων, ἃ ἐc] Gal., [πρόχειρον] Crön., [κηρίνων] Maas   8. ἀπ[οξέcαcα] Maas, ἀπ[αρτίζουcα] Crön., ἀπ[ορουμένηι] Zimm.   9. "κεὶ cὺ ἀλλ᾿ ἔ[τι μοι μὴ] Vit., καὶ "cὺ ἃ λέ[γουcα οὐ] Gal., ἀδε[ῶc μοι μὴ] Crön., cὺ ἀλ⟨λα⟩λε, εἰ[ἱ ἀληθῶc μὴ] Zimm.   10. ἕν [γε τούτῳ] Vit., ἐν [τούτῳ χά-] Gal.   12. cαειcομαι : pap.   13–14. [μάλα ἐκδι]|κίαc Vit., [τῆc μαλα]|κίαc Gal., [τῶν τῆc ἐκδι]|κίαc, [δὴ καὶ ἐκδι]|κίαc Zimm., [βλα]|κίαc Crön.   14–15. θεραπ[είαc τευ]|ξομένη Vit., θεραπ[είαν παρε]|ξομένη Gal.   17–18. [μι]|κροῖc Körte, [ἐν cμι]-|κροῖc Zimm. (1935)   19–20. [τῇ χει]|ρὶ Zimm., [αὐθω]|ρὶ Gal.

150

4   luck more [
She continued to be silent [helplessly. Hear]
now, what [came] into my mind [
the double-leaved tablet of [the sort that]
8   we used to carry to school, I [took]
and gave it to Myrto, "If you cannot
say anything else to me," I said, "on [this tablet at least]
scratch as much as you want to say. And I [after reading]
12   will know." My servant was delighted; [for she showed]
from her face that she would at once [obtain re-]
venge and comfort for what she suffered.
Now she took the [tablet and]
16   moved to the lamp and scratched with the stylus
in much haste all that she wished [in very small]
letters in order to inscribe more,
and she gave it to me, at the same time motioning with her [hand]

20 ρὶ ἐξιέναι. ἐγὼ δὲ λαβοῦ[c]α ἐξῆλθ[ον μὲν εὐ-]
θὺc οὐδαμῶc, πρότερ[ο]ν δὲ ἀν[έγνων αὐτὸ]
καὶ ἐδήλ[ο]υ τάδε · "ἄπιθι, ὦ δέcπο[ινα, αὐτί-]
κα πρὸc τὴν τροφόν, καὶ ἀκουού[cηc ἀνά-]
24 γνωθι τὰ λοιπά, ὡc ἂν κἀκείνη [μάθοι τὰ]
ἑαυτῆc κακὰ μηδὲ ἐc τὸν πάντ[α χρόνον]
ἀγνοοῦcα ἥδοιτο, ὡc ἂν καὶ τὰ ἐμ[ὰ γνοίη-]
τε. ἄπιθι, ἤδη, πρὶν φοιτῆcαι π[αρὰ . . .]
28 τὸν cυγκοιμώμενον μὴ καὶ α[ὐτὴ δαίμο-]
νοc ἀπολαύcηc χαλεποῦ." ταῦτα [δὲ ὡc ἀνέ-]
γνων, ἐβουλόμην μὲν ἐπιcκ[. . . . . .]

---

20. εξιναι: pap.   20–21. [μὲν εὐ]‖θὺc Zimm., [παρευ]‖θὺc Gal.   21. ἀν[έγνων τινά]
Vit., ἀν[έωιξα ἀτρέμα] Zimm.   22. ταδε: pap.   23. ἀκουού[cηc (sc. ἐκείνηc)
ἀνά-] Maas, ἀκουού[cη] Gal.   27. π[αρ᾽ ἐμὲ] Maas, π[αρά cοι] Gal., Π[άαπιν]
Zimm.   28–29. α[ὐτὴ δαίμο]‖νοc Vit., δ[ὴ δαίμο]‖νοc Gal. Vitelli also suggests
[λυμεῶ]νοc   29–30. [ἐπεὶ ἀνέ]‖γνων Zimm.

20   to go away. I took it, but did not depart im-
     mediately, but first [read it
     and it read thus: "Go away, Mistress, immed-
     iately to your nurse and in her hearing
24   read the rest so that she too [may learn]
     of her own misfortunes and not for the future
     be happy in her ignorance—so that you too [might know about]
     my misfortunes. Go away now before he visits,
28   my(?) bedmate, lest you too
     enjoy a cruel [demon.]" These things, [when I]
     read, I wanted on the one hand to . . . [

PSI 1177

1–4. A variety of restorations are possible, but filling lacunae of this size is no
more than speculation.

4–5. No doubt πα]|ρούϲῃ or a compound, which suggests that we should restore
τύχῃ in line 4 above.

6–7. γραμ]|ματεῖον δίθυρον: for the expression, see Libanios 51.11. Double-
leaved school tablets were usually made of wax; no doubt our tablets were the
type called *pugillares* in Latin, because they were small enough to fit in the fist.
Although the supplements of both Crönert and Maas are technically appropriate for such tablets, both expressions seem rather more labored than necessary
to describe such a common item.

7–8. ἐϲ]| διδαϲκάλου: for the expression, see LSJ s.v. διδάϲκαλοϲ.

12. Although it is tempting to restore the form Photios has, θεραπαινίϲ (as Zimmermann does), the article is definitely neuter.

20. ἐξιέναι: the papyrus reads εξῖναι, a variant of ἐξιέναι that occurs in Machon
302 (= Ath. 13.580c), on which see Gow's note; it is attested also in *EM*
467.19. The form may have been introduced by the scribe, who will almost
certainly have been responsible for the ε-/η- variation in the augment of
βούλομαι (lines 17 and 30).

23. Although ἀκουού[ϲῃ is more attractive grammatically than the genitive abso-
lute, ἀκουού[ϲηϲ, it does introduce hiatus with the following ἀνά]|γνωθι;
though perhaps this should not be a serious consideration, in light of the hiatus
in lines 8 and 20.

27–28. Zimmermann's conjecture of Π[άαπιν] is attractive, especially since he
must in fact be the lover, but, as Vitelli points out, this construction with
φοιτῆϲαι requires παρά. We assume π[αρ᾽ ἐμέ is the correct restoration, and
this must mean that Myrto is alive, not a resident of the Underworld. If it is
the nurse who is expecting a lover, Myrto might well be dead.

P. OXY. 3012

P. Oxy. 3012 contains the name Deinias (line 3), and a female narrator (line 9). Line 5 contains a portion of her name, Derkyllis, from which this piece can be securely identified as Diogenes' *The Incredible Things beyond Thule*. Little context remains: there is mention of a letter that "made these things clear," the narrator's troubles and haste. If [. .]Δ is a book number[81] the best location for the fragment is in Book 4, an early part of the narrative where Derkyllis may be explaining to Deinias the family woes. "My own troubles" (lines 9–10) will surely refer to her innocently inflicting her parents with a deathlike trance, through the wiles of Paapis, as well as her punishment—to live only by night, to enter a condition similar to that of her parents by day. Book 14 probably can be excluded, because it surely continued the Pythagorean material begun in Book 13 (see Reyhl 1969: 121), and although Book 24 is theoretically a possible location (Borgogno 1979b: 241–42), Photios claims that "the twenty-fourth book brings on Azoulis as a narrator, and Deinias tying in Azoulis's narrative with his own previous account" (Photios *Epit.* 110b24). Yet nothing absolutely excludes the possibility that Book 24 opened with Derkyllis and Deinias still conversing about her troubles, especially since it is in this book that Derkyllis and her brother are finally released from the evil spell that has held them, through the efforts of Azoulis.

Finally, it should be noted that a suprising number of words or phrases in this scrap are also to be found in *PSI* 1177—ταῦτα ἐδήλου and ἐδήλου τάδε, τοῖc ἐμαυτῆc κακ[οῖ]c and τὰ ἑαυτῆc κακά, cπουδῆι (used adverbially?) in both as well as ἤδη used postpositively, προεῖμαι (if that is the correct reading) ἤδη and ἄπιθι ἤδη. Although all of these words are common or garden-variety Greek, to find four such repetitions within the space of twenty lines is worthy of note, even when the pieces are related, and even when the subject matter is similar. In fact, in both the narrator is the same—Derkyllis. It is worth entertaining the possibility that the two papyri were part of the same scene, or at least the same narrative sequence.

[81] It is difficult to imagine what else it might be. In theory it could be a roll number, but unless Diogenes' books were incredibly long or the papyrus rolls used to transcribe the novel abnormally short, normal practice suggests that roll and book would coincide.

DESCRIPTION

P. Oxy. 3012 measures 11.0×12.0 cm. It is a fragment apparently from the beginning of a very handsomely set out book roll; parts of fourteen lines survive, averaging fifteen letters per line. There is a deep upper margin of about 5 cm; a left margin of 4 cm, which suggests the beginning of the roll; and an intercolumnium of 2.0 cm. The scribe wrote an elegant Severe style, using carets as line fillers (lines 2, 9, 10, 14), but no marks of punctuation appear. Iota adscript is written at line 13, elision is unmarked at line 2. The hand is of a type generally assigned to the end of the second or early third century C.E. A second hand is responsible for the number 4 placed at the top of the column, which will be either a book or a roll number. (It cannot be a column number, since it stands over what appears to be the first column of the roll.) A lacuna (thus, [. .]Δ) occurs before the number, which raises the possibility that a larger number may originally have been written (either I]Δ or K]Δ). The back is blank.

P. OXY. 3012

"ἡ μὲν ἐπιϲτολὴ ταῦ-
τα ἐδήλου. ἐγὼ δὲ
πῶϲ ἄ[ν ϲ]οι, ὦ Δεινία,
4 τὸ μέ[γ]α λέξα[ιμ]ι," ἔ-
φη [ἡ Δ]ερκυ[λλίϲ, "τί-]
γα [καρ]δίαν λα[βοῦ-]
ϲ[α] τίνα φωνὴ[ν οὔ-]
8 τω γενναίαν · προεῖ-
μαι ἤδη τοῖϲ ἐμαυ-
τῆϲ κακ[οῖ]ϲ π . . [ ] .
τ[. .]τε, [ἐ]ὰν [μ]ένῳ[μ]εν
12]ν εὐθὺϲ κατε-
] . ϲπουδῆι βου-
] . . . [.] . .

- - - - - - - - - - - - - - - - - - - -

Supplements are those of ed. pr. unless otherwise noted. Upper margin: [. .] Δ, either a roll or a book number.

2. δε⟩ pap.   4. τί μέ[γ]α M. Gronewald   λέξα[ιμ]ι J. R. Rea (in ed. pr.)   5–8. So Gronewald   8–9. προει[ ]|με pap.   Read προεῖ|μαι? Parsons. There is a small hole at the end of line 8, sufficient for one letter. προεῖ[ϲ]? Parsons, προεῖ[ο] Gronewald   9. εμαυ⟩ pap.   10.] . ⟩ pap.

The letter made
these things clear, but I,
how should I tell you, Deinias,
4   about the important matter,"
said Derkyllis, "what
attitude can I find,
what form of words
8   noble enough?
Now I am abandoned (?)
to my own evils . . . ;
if we remain (?)
12   ] immediately
] in haste

P. OXY. 3012

1–2. This initial sentence with its μέν-δέ clause would appear to be contrasting the coherence of the letter with what Derkyllis feels is her inability to express herself to Deinias; the μέν clause probably refers to something from the end of the preceding book, whereas the δέ clause begins to set out the new situation. For a similiar opening of a book, see that of Heliodoros, Book 2. The phrase ταῦτα μὲν ἐδήλου ἡ ἐπιστολή occurs also in Lucian *Vh* 2.35; the context is a letter purporting to be from Odysseus to Kalypso.

4. τὸ μέ[γ]α: Presumably "the weighty matter" refers to events from a preceding book.

5. For hiatus after ἔφη, see Reeve 1971: 517.

5–9. The shape of this phrase, as Gronewald has seen, appears to be two nouns linked asyndetically and qualified by οὕτω γενναίαν. Between them λα[. . .]ι c[.] almost certainly belongs to a participle, since space is insufficient for another optative + coι or cε. Traces suit a form in -ουcα but not -οντι. Gronewald's supplement τί]ινα [καρ]δίαν λα[βοῦ]ι c[α] τίνα φωνὴ[ν suits both traces and sense. E. Bowie points out the tragedy queen aspect of Derkyllis's speech, comparing Eur. *Hipp.* 825–26.

8–9. If not προεῖμαι, προεῖc with a verb to follow? πεπ[or sim. could well contain a perfect form, πέπ[υc]ι[τ[αι] or sim., though traces in the rest of the line are intractable. Gronewald restores the middle optative προεῖο, presumably taking it as a polite imperative. Possible, but this does not persuade.

157

Antonius Diogenes?

— ❖ —

At first glance the surviving story in the so-called Herpyllis fragment is relatively straightforward ego-narration: there are two main characters, who are stopping either with friends or with hospitable strangers, and they are about to begin a journey on two different ships: the woman on a larger vessel, the man on a smaller one. The pilots of these ships argue about weather conditions, but decide to sail in spite of the signs of a rising storm. The narrator—a man—and a woman speak their farewells, then each sets off on his own ship. The bulk of the column is taken up in an elaborate and ominous description of the onslaught of the storm, during which the two ships are separated. The location for this activity is in the vicinity of Kos; the ships intend to hug the Turkish coastline when the storm blows the narrator's ship off course and into the Kretan sea. Although descriptions of storms at sea can occur in virtually any genre of ancient literature, there is little doubt that this one belongs to narrative fiction: the separated couple and the elegantly wrought description of the storm, which takes up the bulk of the column, are the formulaic prelude to an adventure about to happen.[1]

The man and woman in this piece are usually taken as lovers, but there is no evidence for this. The extreme emotion of the farewell contrasts oddly with the narrator's expressed desire to stay on "for merriment," without a word about postponing the imminent separation from his beloved. And their adieus are in fact rather curious for lovers—"so bidding each other a fond farewell and raising a halcyon wail of grief, each of us boarded our own ship, mourning all the while, watching each other at a distance and throwing kisses with our hands" (lines 11–14). None of the language is specifically erotic,[2] and the terms used are more

---

[1] The one demurrer to consensus has been Crusius (1897: 1–2), who argued that it might be a private letter (comparing a letter of Synesios in which the bishop describes a storm at sea in very similar language) or a philosophical tractate. The flaw in Crusius's argument is his focus on details, like the storm or St. Elmo's fire and the epiphany of the Dioscuri, rather than the narrative as a whole.

[2] The terms ἀcπάcομαι ἀλλήλουc and φιλήματα would be quite natural in a description of the parting of kin or friends.

appropriate for mourning the dead,[3] which seem out of place to describe the sentiments of even the most passion-crazed of lovers on being forced to part. What other conclusions we can draw about this piece depend on the name of the woman, which occurs in only one place in a nearly complete form. Previous editors have read it as "Herpyllis." No such heroine is recorded in ancient fiction, but the name itself is well attested; in contrast, the orthographically similar Derkyllis is a character in Antonius Diogenes, but rare otherwise as a proper name. The reading of the name is not wholly secure. Indeed, Gallavotti suggested reading the traces as "Derkyllis" and assigning the fragment to *The Incredible Things beyond Thulē*.[4] Zimmermann dismissed Gallavotti's suggestion (*GRP* 72 n. 21), in part because the style of this piece seemed to him to differ from a fragment of *The Incredible Things* (*PSI* 1177). But stylistic arguments are often unconvincing. Both are intricate and polished narratives, well above the level of *Sesonchosis*, for example; both avoid hiatus, for the most part, but permit a few examples. Beyond this, the stylistic differences are not easy to assess. Although both fragments are ego-narrations—a woman in *PSI* 1177, a man here—the woman, Derkyllis, relates an incident with her nurse Myrto, whereas this narrator presents us with a highly rhetorical set piece on a storm at sea; vocabulary and diction will necessarily vary. The real question is whether such different modes of narration would occur within a single text. The answer to that is surely, yes. Achilles Tatius and Heliodoros, for example, are capable of a considerable stylistic variety within their novels, and Antonius Diogenes seems to us similarly deft.

Bury (Smyly 1909: 330) was sufficiently struck by the similarity of the names Herpyllis and Derkyllis—which are like each other, but unlike names of other novel heroines—to argue that there must be a connection between this fragment and *The Incredible Things*. He proposed that since Antonius Diogenes (according to Photios) claimed Antiphanes of Berga as a predecessor, this fragment might belong to his work, and that the name Derkyllis was deliberately chosen to echo Herpyllis. Bury's argument is dubious at best. There is no reason to suppose that Anti-

[3] θρῆνον ἀλκυόνειον and ὠλοφυρόμεθα; the latter is almost a technical term for mourning the dead. See below, note on lines 13–14.

[4] Gallavotti 1931: 257. Since the letter identified as pi in line I.12 is badly broken and the letters read as Eρ are anomalous in shape for this hand, it is just possible that the papyrus had Δε[ρ]|κυλλίδος.

159

phanes could have served as a model for anything more than outrageous mendacities—the verb "to *bergaize*," after all, meant "to tell tall tales" (see above, "Antonius Diogenes," introduction). And apart from their orthographic similarity, the names Herpyllis and Derkyllis have nothing in common, so that an imitation would have been of the Annie-Frannie variety,[5] lacking the bite of Pamela-Shamela that we would expect from Antonius Diogenes. But Bury's instincts are surely correct. If this is not a fragment of *The Incredible Things*, it is worth questioning whether it bears some relationship to it.

We begin by considering whether this scrap might fit into Diogenes' narrative. From Photios's epitome we know that Derkyllis and her brother Mantinias went to Rhodes upon leaving their family's home in Tyre because, as a result of the machinations of Paapis, they believed that they had caused the destruction of their parents (*Epit.* 109a29ff.). The brother and sister are later separated, have a series of adventures, and meet again in Leontini. Photios does not relate how or when their separation took place, but it must have been shortly after the pair left Rhodes, because his language suggests that Derkyllis was in the company of Keryllos and Astaios at the time of her adventures in the underworld.[6] Rhodes is very close to the geographical markers in this piece—Lakter and Nisyros. Although our couple probably did not start out from there, they could have been at most only a bit north in either Knidos or Kos. And certainly the lamentations of the couple at parting would well suit a brother and sister in flight, mourning the death of their parents and their own perilous fate.

In this hypothetical reconstruction, who could be the narrator? The most reasonable guess is Mantinias, but Photios claims that his adventures were related indirectly to Deinias by Derkyllis, who in turn is relating them to Kymbas (*Epit.* 110a14). Since our narrator refers to the woman in the third person, it is difficult to imagine him talking directly to her. But if the woman—that is, Derkyllis—is the narrator, she is unlikely to have related the events that took place only between her brother and herself in this manner. If the narrator is Mantinias, he is more likely to be represented as speaking before a group—perhaps even

---

[5] This is not to say that such deliberate imitations did not exist. Antheia in Xenophon of Ephesos is deliberately named to allude to Pantheia in Xenophon's *Kyropaideia*.

[6] 109b10–13: "I mean the aforementioned wanderings and how after her return from Hades with Keryllos and Astraios, now that she had been separated from her brother, they come to the tomb of the Siren. . . ."

giving an official account of himself to the tyrant of the Leontinoi. His whole account might then have been related to Deinias as direct narration after "and he said."[7]

This scrap is even more intriguing if the name is in fact Herpyllis, and we have a fragment of a totally different narrative. We have two ego narratives, involving a couple not obviously lovers, separated by a storm in a region where Diogenes' unlucky siblings were known to have traveled and where they may well have been separated. One of the pair has a name remarkably similar to Diogenes' heroine. Though most of these parallels are trivial, the name seems telling, and raises the suspicion that we are dealing either with a predecessor to Diogenes (as Bury believed) or a later imitator. We are inclined to reject the former because, as we have suggested above, Diogenes' choice of the names of his protagonists, Deinias and Derkyllis, would seem to echo those of two Hellenistic historians who worked on the records of Argos—Deinias and Derkylos. Moreover, Photios presents us with two pieces of information that may be relevant: he imagined that Antonius Diogenes was among the earliest novelists, the *fons et origo* of adventure narrative,[8] and he mentioned no predecessors other than Antiphanes of Berga. While the good bishop is clearly wrong in many of his particulars, he may be correct about Diogenes' relatively early date. This fragment on paleographical grounds is probably no later than mid-second century B.C.E.; if it does consciously imitate *The Incredible Things*, then Diogenes' novel can be no later than the end of the first or beginning of the second century. If he is as central to the development of the novel as Photios believes, then we should not be surprised to find that he had imitators.

[7] Alternatively, Mantinias may have been speaking to Deinias directly. Mantinias and Deinias were both present on Thule, and it is possible that his adventures were related partially by his sister, partially by himself. Photios's brief summary will have necessarily omitted some of the narrative vagaries of Antonius Diogenes, as his epitome of Heliodoros abundantly demonstrates.

[8] "He appears to be older than the other novelists, such as Lucian, Lucius, Iamblichos, Achilles Tatius, Heliodoros, and Damaskios. For this work is the root and source of Lucian's *True Histories* and Lucius's *Metamorphoses*; and not only of these, but also of Sinonis and Rhodanes, Leukippe and Kleitophon, Charikleia and Theagenes, their adventures and wanderings and loves and capture and perils are evidently modeled after Derkyllis and Keryllos and Throuskanos and Deinias" (111b32).

ANTONIUS DIOGENES?

DESCRIPTION

P. Dubl. C3 (= P^2 2621), measuring 18.5 × 34.5 cm, was written on the back of a papyrus roll. It preserves one complete column of sixty lines, upper and lower margins to 3.0 cm, a left intercolumnium with up to eight letters from the end of the preceding column, as well as a right intercolumnium with one or two letters from the column following. The front contains two different texts: the larger is an account written right side up with respect to our text; it bears a dating formula that should belong to Trajan—Αὐτοκράτοροc Καί[caροc | Νερούα Τρ]αιανοῦ Cεβαcτοῦ Γερμανικοῦ; the smaller, which occupies the bottom right corner of the account and is upside down with respect to it, looks as if, at the time of reuse, it was intended to patch a flaw in the original roll. It contains § 126 from Demosthenes' *Against Meidias* written in an upright rounded type that can be assigned to the first century C.E. (Note that the *Antheia* fragment is also written on the back of a Demosthenes text; see below.) The hand of our text is rapidly written, with documentary affinities, assigned by Kenyon, Grenfell, and Wilcken to the second century C.E. Column II is now badly abraded along its left edge, and the whole is stained and worn, so that readings in some cases are problematic. Infrequent tremata and carets to fill out line ends occur; there is at least one error and two supralinear additions (ll. 24, 48), as well as a number of itacisms. The author usually avoids hiatus, but there is one clear (II.16) and two other probable exceptions (II.40–41, 53). Although iota adscript does not appear to have been written elsewhere, the hypercorrect καγωι occurs in II.8. At the top of column II, there is probably a column number. Wilcken read this as κθ = 29, but Smyly (1909: 325) thought the letters were χ°, the purpose of which is obscure. He rejected the reading $χ^ρ$ = χρηcτόc or sim. (on which siglum see *GMAW*^{2}, 14–15.). But what Smyly must have taken as omicron looks more like a decorative loop on the upper right arm of the kappa, so we are inclined to accept Wilcken's column number.

ANTONIUS DIOGENES?

COLUMN I

```
     ] . πιθ[ . . ]αν
     ]ηϲονοϲτα
     ]ν θάτερον
4    ]λλ . . . ηϲ
     ]ατωνε . .
     ]αν . . . ϲεν
     ]θερα[π]είαϲ
8    ]ορ . μενῃ
              ] . . .
              ]πε . .
              ]γων
12   ]υ[λ]λίδ .
     τ]ηϲ πολλῆϲ
     ]ναι[ . . ]ανει
     ]ειϲ . [ . . ]ατε
16   ]πλο[ι]ον ὑπε-
     ]ειϲ γ[ . ]φητ[ . ]
     ]αν ἑορταζο-
     ]ρονταϲ
20   ]υϲ εἶπεν ε-
     ]νωμαξον
     ]ωνηνῃ
     ] . θιϲ ἐγγυ-
24   ἄ]λλο ἐκτὸϲ
     ]ϲοφοϲ
              ] . . . . .
     ] . . ειϲ και
28   ] . . ελω
     ]βάντεϲ
     ] . ρ . θυ
```

Col. I: 12.]υ[λ]λίδ . : the name of the heroine? At end, apparently an abbreviation stroke. If so, it could represent any termination.]υ[λ]λίδ(οϲ), (α) or sim.   13. or [ἐ]κ πολλῆϲ
17.]ειϲ γ[έ]φη τὰ Zimm.   19. π]αρόνταϲ Zimm.   20. εἶπεν : εἶπαν Schub., ϲει-
ληνέ Wil.   22. [φ]ωνὴν ῃ Zimm.   29. [ἐκ]βάντεϲ Zimm., or [ἐμ]βάντεϲ, see II.13.

COLUMN II

ε[. .] ἐποχαῖϲ παραλίαιϲ δ[.]ξ . . . . παρεκάλουν,
δυϲώρου τῆϲ καταϲτάϲ[εωϲ οὔϲηϲ] καὶ γὰρ ἐλάν-
θα[ν]εν ἐν ἐπιϲημαϲία[ιϲ] γ[. . . . . .] καθεϲτῶϲα,
4   μέγειν αὐτόθι τὴν ἐπ[ιοῦϲαν] ἡμέ[ρ]αν, ἐπιδοῦναί
τ᾽ ε[ἰϲ] εὐφροϲύνην· [. . . . .]ϲτατοϲ δὲ εἰϲ κατοχὴν
ἀπ[ο]δημίαϲ οἰωνὸ[ϲ] ἀγ[δρὸϲ εὐ]φροϲύνου με-
τά[κ]ληϲιϲ· κἀγὼ μὲν [ἐβ]ου[λόμη]ν μένειν· τῶν
8   δὲ κυβερνητῶν ϲταϲι[αζόντων, ὁ μὲν ἡ]μέτεροϲ
ἠπείγετο πλεῖν, [ὁ δὲ τῆϲ μεγάληϲ νεὼϲ] ϲυνε-
τεκμαίρετο χειμῶνα πλεῖϲ[τον καὶ ἴϲ]ωϲ ἀνίκη-
τον. ἔδοξεν οὖν πλεῖν· ἀϲπαϲάμεν[οι] τοίνυν ἀλ-
12   λήλ[ο]υϲ καὶ θρῆνον ἀλκυόνειον ἐγεί[ροντ]εϲ, εἰϲ τὴν
ο[ἰ]κε[ί]αν ἑκάτεροϲ ἐμβάντε[ϲ] ναῦν ὠ[λο]φυρόμε-
θα, [ϲκ]οποῦντεϲ ἀλλήλουϲ φι[λή]ματά τε ταῖϲ χερϲὶ
β[άλλο]ντεϲ. ἡ μὲν οὖν με[γ]άλη ναῦϲ βραδύτερόν
16   τι ἐ[ξ]ωπλίζετο, τάχιον δ᾽ ἡμεῖϲ ἐξ[επ]λεύϲαμεν.
ἡλίου δ᾽ ὑπὸ μὲν τὸν ἔκπλ[ου]ν φ[α]νέν[τοϲ, αὐτίκα
δὲ ζοφεραῖϲ ἐγκρυβέντοϲ νεφέλ[αι]ϲ, α[ἰ]φνίδιον
κο[ῖ]λόν τε καὶ βραχὺ βροντήϲα[ν]τοϲ, ἡμεῖϲ μὲν
20   οὐκέτ᾽ ἀναϲτρέψαι μεταγοοῦντεϲ ἐδυνάμεθα,
πυκνὸν γὰρ εἵπετο πνεῦμ[α] κατόπιν· ἡ δὲ τῆϲ . . [.]
. υλλίδοϲ ἄκατοϲ οὐκέτ᾽ ἀνήχθη, κατέϲτη δ᾽ ἀπὸ
τοῦ τείχουϲ ἀνακαλουμέν[η]. πρὸϲ βραχὺ δ᾽ ὁρῶν-

Col. II: Supplements throughout are those of Smyly unless otherwise noted. The conjectures of Bury and Purser are to be found in Smyly.
1. ἐ[ν δ᾽] . . . δ[ε]ξ[άμενοι] Lav. δ[ε]ξ[ιῶϲ] Zimm.   3. γ[εφέλη] Lav., γ[ηνεμία] Schmid.,
κ[νηκὶϲ] Zimm.   5. [ϲαφέ]ϲτατοϲ Vit., [χαριέ]ϲτατοϲ Crön., [πανύ]ϲτατοϲ Purser,
[εὐπρεπέ]ϲτατοϲ Lav., [ἐνεργέ]ϲτατοϲ, [εὐφυέ]ϲτατοϲ Schmid   6. οἰωνὸ[ϲ] ἀγ[δρὸϲ]
Vit.   οἰωνὸ[ϲ ἦν δαιτὸϲ]? Lav., οἰωνὸ[ϲ ἐφαίνετο] Crön., οἰωνὸ[ϲ ἢ φίλου] Schmid
[φιλο]φροϲύνου Zimm.   7. καγωι, μενειν·των pap.   8. [ἡμ]έτεροϲ Wil.   9. ϲυνε⟨
pap.   10. πλιϲ[, ανεικη pap.   12. ἐγεί[ραντ]εϲ Ratt.   15.]ντεϲ·η pap.
16. προ[ϲ]ωπλίζετο Wil.   ταχειον pap.   ἐ[ξ]επλεύϲαμεν Wil.   18. ενκρυβεντοϲ
pap.   19. βραχυ pap., βαρύ Zimm.   21–22. Ἐρπυλλίδοϲ Smyly, Δερκυλλίδοϲ
Gal.   22. κατεϲτουδαπο pap., κατέϲτη Schmid, κατέϲτη δ᾽ οὖν, κατέϲτ⟨η γ)οῦν Zimm.
23. ἀνακαλουμέν[η] Bury

coastal checkpoints . . . I was encouraging [them]—since the disposition of the weather was unseasonable and in fact he had not noticed
the [cloud] that had come up among the weather signs—(4) to
remain right there for the coming day and to spend the time making
merry; the most . . . omen for a postponement of the journey was an
invitation of a cheerful man; so I at least was planning to wait; (8)
but the pilots were arguing with each other—ours was urging that
we sail, the [pilot of the big ship] reckoned that an enormous,
perhaps unsurvivable, storm was brewing. Then a decision was
reached to sail. So bidding each other a fond farewell and (12) raising a halcyon wail of grief, each of us boarded our own ship, mourning all the while, watching each other at a distance and blowing
kisses with our hands.

Now the large ship was rather slow about (16) gearing up,
whereas we set sail more quickly. Though the sun was shining while
we sailed out, it was soon hidden in misty clouds; suddenly there
was a short, hollow peal of thunder. (20) It was no longer possible
for us to change our minds and turn back, for a forceful wind was
blowing behind us. ——yllis's craft was no longer under weigh, but
had stopped, since it was being summoned back from the wall. We
watched them for a short time and

24 τέ[ϲ ϲ]φαϲ ἀφηρπαζόμεθα, πνεῦμα γὰρ ἄθρουν ἐγ-
κ[ατέ]ρρηξεν ἀπηλιωτικὸν ἀπ' αὐτοῦ τοῦ ἀκρω-
τ[ηρίου] καὶ τὴν μὲν κεραίαν οὐκ ἦν παραβαλεῖν,
ἐ[ναντ]ίαν γὰρ οὐκ ἴϲχυε φέρειν ἡ πορθμὶϲ τὴν
28 [θάλα]τταν· . . . . . . δὲ τὸ κέραϲ οὔριον ἔχοντεϲ
τ[ετα]μένοιϲ τοῖϲ ἀκατίοιϲ τοῦ προκειμένου μὲν
. [. .] . τομεν δρόμου, παρὰ [δὲ] τὸν Λακτῆρα, χαλεπώ-
[τατον] ἀκρωτήριον, κατὰ τὸ Κρητικὸν ἐϲυρό-
32 μ[ε]θα πέλαγοϲ, οὐδὲ τὴν Νίϲυρον καθορᾶν ἔτι
[δυν]άμενοι διὰ τὴν ϲυννέφειαν· ἧϲ ἐφιέμε-
[νοι] . . . . . . βλέπειν ἀπετύχομεν. μετὰ
[δὲ] νοϲώδει παραδόντεϲ πελάγει τῶν μὲν ε[ἰ]ϲ
36 [ϲωτ]ηρίαν οὐδ[ὲ]ν παρὸν ἐωρῶμεν, ὀλέθρου [δ' οὐ
[προ]ϲδοκία μόνον ἀλλὰ καὶ πόθοϲ ἦν ἅπαϲιν.
[ἤδη] γὰρ θ[ά]λαττα ἄγαν ἐκ πολλοῦ διαϲτήματοϲ ϲυ-
ρ[ομ]ένη, πυκνῷ μὲν οὐκ [ἐτ]ραχύνε-
40 τ[ο π]νεύματι, κοιλα[ι]νομένη δ' εἰϲ ἄπειρον ἐξ ἴϲου
[ὄρεϲ]ιν ἐκορυφοῦτο, μέλαινά τ' ἦν ὑπὸ ζόφου τοῦ πε-
ρ[ιέχ]οντοϲ ἐϲκιαϲμένη· τὸ πνεῦμα τ' ἐ⟨ϲ⟩ ϲτάϲιν οὐ
[. . πο]λεμίαν, γνοφ[ο]ειδῆ δέ, κυκλόθεν ἀδοκήτοιϲ
44 ἐ[ρρί]πιζον ἀῆται πνοιαῖϲ, οἱ μὲν ψιλοὺϲ πνεύμα-
τ[οϲ] πρηϲτῆραϲ, οἱ δ' ὄμβρουϲ καθιέντεϲ. ἅπαϲ
δ[ὲ κ]όϲμοϲ ἐν κύκλῳ περιεβροντᾶτο, πυκναὶ δὲ
ἀγ[τ]ήϲτραπτον ἀλλήλαιϲ ἀπ' οὐρανοῦ λαμπάδεϲ, ἀγ-
48 χο[.] δὲ πολλάκιϲ ἐωρ[ώ]με[ν] οὐρανόθεν πῦρ ἀπ[οτ]οξευ-
όμ[ε]νον· ἦν δ' ἄδηλ[ο]ν εἴτε νὺξ εἴθ' ἡμέρα καθειϲ-
τή[κ]ει ϲκότουϲ ὁμοι[ό]τητι· ϲυνεπληρούμεθα [δ' ὑ]πὸ
τῆ[ϲ τ]ῶν κυμάτων ἐπιβολῆϲ καὶ τῆϲ τῶν γνόφων

---

24. αφ added above ηρ pap. 25. ἀγρίωϲ πνέον Bury 27. ἐ[ναντ]ίαν Zimm.,
ἐ[γκαρϲί]αν Smyly, [τραχεῖ]αν Lav., [τὸ παράπ]αν Crön. ειϲχυε, προθμιϲ pap., read
πορθμίϲ Wil. 28. ἐπιζ[αὲ]ϲ Zimm. 29. τετα]μένοιϲ Bury, ἐ[ντετα]μένοιϲ Smyly,
ε[ἱλκυϲ]μένοιϲ Zimm. 30. λακτηρα pap. 32. οὐδέτι ὂν Wil. 33. εφειεμε
pap. 33–34. [ἐφιέμε]νοι τότε μὲν] Lav., [τότε τοῦ] Zimm. 37. [προ]ϲδοκία Bury
39.]ϲνηειϲαπειρ[.]ν pap., εἰϲ ἄπειρ[ο]ν deleted by Lav. οὐκ⟨έτ'⟩ Zimm. 40. ἐξ
ἴϲη[ϲ] Zimm. 41–42. πε[ρ]ιέχ]οντοϲ Bury 42. τ' ἐ⟨ϲ⟩ ϲτάϲιν or τε ϲτάϲιν Smyly
42–43. οὐ[ἴ|τι γε] Zimm. 44. ψειλουϲ pap. 46. δ' [ὁ κ]όϲμοϲ Zimm. 48. ἐν
added above πυρ pap. 49. ειτημερα pap.

(24) then were snatched away, for a powerful east wind broke over us from the headland itself, and it was impossible to turn the yardarm, for the boat was not strong enough to endure the opposing sea. (28) [When] we held the yardarm in a favorable position for the outstretched sails, we were losing our intended course and being swept alongside Lakter, that most dangerous headland, and towards the sea of Krete, (32) Nisyros no longer visible to us through the cloud banks. This we missed, although we tried to catch a glimpse of it.

Thereafter we surrendered ourselves to the pestilent ocean, since (36) not a single thing could we see around us that might portend safety: all of us not only expected to be destroyed but desired it. For the sea by now was being viciously raked in all directions [to infinity], not merely roughed up by the strong winds but (40) scooped out in bottomless pits, leaving peaks like mountain tops, and it had turned black in the shadow of the surrounding darkness. The blasts of unexpected wind from all sides were stirring up a revolution in the air current, not [yet] in outright hostility, but with darkening visage, (44) sometimes bringing only whirlwinds, sometimes drenching us in showers. The whole cosmos thundered all around us; fires from the sky were constantly flashing back and forth at each other; (48) often we watched an arrow of fire shoot down from the heaven close beside us. It was not possible to tell whether it was actually night or merely a day indistinguishable from darkness. We were being swamped by the volleys of waves and showers

ANTONIUS DIOGENES?

52 ἐ[πομ]βρίας · ἦν δ᾽ οὔτε γῆν [ἰ]δεῖν οὔτε οὐρανόν · πε-
    πυ[κας]μένη δὲ νυκτ[ὶ . . . . .] ϲυνείχετο, καὶ ποτὲ
    μ[ὲ]ν κατόπιν ἡ μεγ[άλη πνοὴ] ἐφίϲτατ[ο, π]οτὲ δ᾽ ἐν-
    [ηρεί]δετο κῦμα · πολλά[κιϲ δὲ κα]ὶ τῆϲ κεραίας ἐβάλ-
56 λον[το] πυρϲοὶ βραχεῖϲ [μέροϲ] ἐϲ ἑκάτερον. εἴτ᾽ ἀϲ-
    τρ᾽, ὡϲ] ἔφαϲκον οἱ να[ῦται Διοϲ]κόρων προϲωνυμί-
    αν [βο]ῶντεϲ, εἴτ᾽ ἀϲτρ[οειδεῖϲ ϲ]πινθῆρεϲ ὑπὸ τοῦ
    πνεύματος ῥιπιζό[μενοι, τὸ ϲα]φὲϲ μὲν ἀδύνατον
60 εἰπ[εῖ]ν · προϲεκύνου[ν δὲ καὶ] προϲεύχοντο πάντεϲ.

52–53. πε|πυ[κνω]μένη Zimm. 53. [πάντα] Zimm., [τὸ πλοῖον] Crön. [θάλαϲϲα]
Vogliano 54. ἡ μεγ[άλη πνοὴ] Bury, ἡμερ[ινὸν φῶϲ] Smyly 54–55. ἐν|[ηρεί]δετο
Bury 55. δ᾽ ἐπ]ὶ Wil. 58. [βο]ῶντεϲ Zimm., [λέγ]οντεϲ Smyly 59. ρηπιζο[
pap. 60. [τε καὶ] Mahaffy.
Col. III is too fragmentary to reproduce.

168

from the gloom. (52) Neither land nor sky could be seen. [The ship] was trapped by a thick wall of night, and sometimes a great blast came up suddenly behind us, sometimes the wave bore us down. Frequently quick flashes of light danced on either side of the yard-arm, either the stars, as the sailors were saying, calling them the Dioscuri, or star[like] sparks fanned by the wind—it was impossible to say. (60) Everyone was worshiping them and praying to them.

COLUMN II

1. ε[..]: Lavagnini's restoration of ἐ[ν δ'] forces the sentence or phrase to begin in this line, but if it does, there is insufficient space for an object of the main verb and nothing to which the datives seem connected. Possibly just ἐ[ν] or ἐ[πὶ] .

δ[.]ξ . . . . : δ[ε]ξάμενοι is too long; Zimmermann's δ[ε]ξ[ιῶϲ] is possible, but not helpful for the datives.

παρεκάλουν : either "I was urging [them = the helmsmen]" or "they were urging [us] to stay." The former makes more sense, because there seems to be a single person issuing the invitation to stay in line 6.

2–3. S. West argues that a negative with ἐλάν|θα[ν]εν must have dropped out, but that is not necessary. It would depend on context (which is now largely missing), the word restored, and the speaker's tone. If the speaker is urging the helmsman not to sail because he desired to stay on for pleasure, his argument may not necessarily be an accurate depiction of the actual conditions.

3. γ[. . . . . .] καθεϲτῶϲα : the missing noun must be a weather phenomenon—either γ[εφέλη] or γ[ηνεμία] ("cloud" or "calm") would suit the sense and the space.

The second perfect occurs in the novelists as well as other late Greek authors.

5. εὐφροϲύνην : Kussl (1991: 111–12) finds in this passage an allusion to *Od.* 9.5–6: οὐ γὰρ ἐγώ γέ τί φημι τέλος χαριέϲτερον εἶναι | ἢ ὅτ' ἐϋφροϲύνη μὲν ἔχῃ κατὰ δῆμον ἅπαντα, and would restore Crönert's [χαριέ]ϲτατοϲ as the next word.

[. . . . .]ϲτατοϲ : the space can hold no more than four or five letters, therefore [ϲαφέ]ϲτατοϲ or [χαριέ]ϲτατοϲ are the most likely supplements.

6. εὐ]φροϲύνου : presumably this is a calculated variation of εὐφροϲύνην above. But the masculine (or neuter) adjective must surely have had a noun with it to make the shift intelligible.

9. [ὁ δὲ τῆϲ μεγάληϲ νεὼϲ] : the restoration is conditioned by line 15 below.

12. θρῆνον ἀλκυόνειον ἐγεί[ροντ]εϲ : for the phrase compare Ch. 8.3.6: ἤγειρε θρῆνον (where the context is Statira learning that she has become a captive).

ἀλκυόνειον: the adjective is rare, though the reference to the halcyon is certainly explicable. Alkyone's mourning for the death of her husband Keyx at sea was a well-known mythological exemplum of grief. In Greek sources, the story occurs in Hesiod (frag. 16 Merkelbach-West), in Nikander (frag. 64 Gow), and in the pseudo-Lucianic *Halcyon*, but the best known and most extensive is the Latin version of Ovid in *Metamorphoses* 11.410–582. Indeed, Wilcken (1901: 269 n. 1) suggested that there were similarities to be found between Ovid's treatment of the story—or his source's—and details in this fragment. Kussl (1991: 138–40) tries to flesh out the argument, but the principal points of parallel he adduces belong to ordinary narrative fare for departure on a sea journey—fitting out the ship, embracing, waving good-byes, followed by a description of a storm. The only telling point of comparison is Alkyone's proleptic lament for her not-yet-dead husband in Ovid and the curious language of mourning at the time of departure in this piece. But how to evaluate this? In this piece, both parties (not just the prescient Alkyone) indulge in the "halcyon wail of grief," but the storm at sea—to judge from the omen of St. Elmo's fire (see below, note 55–56)—should have a propitious outcome. We are more inclined to believe that the reference to Alkyone is intended as a general reference to grieving, rather than to a specifically derived set of references to a particular version of the story—one that does not quite seem to fit.

13–14. ὠ[λο]φυρόμε]θα: in the Attic funeral oration, the word is regularly used to signal the beginning of public mourning (see, e.g., Thuc. 2.44, Lys. 2.37), and imitations of these funeral orations were common in later rhetorical literature. For its use in the novels, see AT 3.5.6: εἶτα ὠλοφυρόμεθα τὸν Κλεινίαν καὶ τὸν Cάτυρον, νομίζοντες αὐτοὺς ἀπολωλέναι.

14–15. φι[λή]ματά τε ταῖς χερcὶ | β[άλλο]ντες: the expression is unattested elsewhere in Greek, but compare the Latin *oscula* (or *blanda*) *iacere* (Juv. 4.118, Tact. *Hist.* 1.36). Note that the term in Latin, at least, appears to occur in crowd scenes, not between lovers.

16ff. The description is elaborate, often employing poetic vocabulary. But the elements of the storm are standard issue. Compare, e.g., the even longer description in AT 3.1–4, or Lucian, *Vh* 1.5–6.

21–22. . .|. υλλίδοc: see above, introduction for the possibilities. If the name here is Herpyllis, it means "cicada" according to Hesychios, and occurs as a name for *hetairai* (see Pape-Benseler, s.v. Ἑρπυλλίc).

22. κατέcτη: the papyrus's κατεcτου must result from scribal error. Correcting to κατέcτη is the simplest solution; Zimmermann's κατέcτ⟨η γ⟩οῦν and κατέcτη δ' οὖν attempt to account for ου, but the letters are too fragmentary to identify with certainty.

23. ἀνακαλουμέν[η: Beare's suggestion, recorded in Smyly, that this comes from a hitherto unattested verb formed from κάλωc seems unnecessary; the standard meaning of "call back" fits well with the circumstances—the woman's ship

was being called back by people on the wall who had noticed the sudden squall coming up. The helmsman of this ship, after all, was more reluctant to sail out than that of the narrator's ship. Further, οὐκέτ᾽ (line 22) will have a meaning parallel to οὐκέτ᾽ above, line 20; but if the participle is taken to mean "tied up," then one expects something like οὔπω ἀνέχθη. Alternatively, the subject may shift from ship to woman, and the verb may be middle, i.e., "she stood calling us."

25. ἀπηλιωτικὸν: in spite of Smyly's caution, the reading of the first four letters seems clear.

27. πορθμὶc: rare in the Classical period, but it does occur in Ch. 5.1.7 and Hld. 1.30.1. The metathesized spelling of the papyrus is not uncommon.

27–28. ἐ[ναντ]ίαν γὰρ οὐκ ἴcχυε φέρειν ἡ πορθμὶc τὴν | θάλα] τταν: the phrase is similar in shape to line 21 above (πυκνὸν γὰρ εἴπετο πνεῦμ[α] κατόπιν)— adjective + γάρ + verb + noun, with the whole interrupting a μέν–δέ construction. A number of adjectives will suit the lacuna.

28–30. This is the δέ-clause responding to καὶ τὴν μὲν κεραίαν above, line 26. τὸ κέραc here is presumably the equivalent of ἡ κεραία, though this is not elsewhere attested. Since the usual meaning of ἀκάτιον is "small boat," and the meaning here must be "sail," we are tempted to read ἀκατείοιc. But note Xen. *Hell.* 6.2.27 where ἀκατίοιc means "small sails" (unless this passage is also to be emended). The sense is, "by holding the yardarm in a favorable position for the outstretched sails. . . ." Lavagnini's conjecture of ἔπειτα to fill the initial lacuna is more attractive grammatically than another adjective, but it does not suit the traces.

30. .[..] τομεν: Smyly and subsequent editors have accepted the restoration of ἡ[μβρ]ότομεν, a form of ἁμαρτάνω otherwise confined to Epic-Aeolic. Clearly context demands a verb like ἁμαρτάνω, but the omicron is not certain enough to restore such an anomalous form. Read ἡ[μά]ρτομεν? This second aorist at least occurs in Herodotos.

τὸν Λακτῆρα: the southern promontory of Kos (Str. 14.2.19). According to Smyly's note ad loc., the better manuscripts of Strabo and Plutarch (*Q. Gr.* § 304c) prefer the spelling Λακητήρ.

32. τὴν Νίcυρον: a small island, north of Tenos and sixty stades from Kos, according to Strabo 10.5.16. The ship is apparently running between the promontory of Lakter and this small, rocky island when it loses sight of it. The closest departure points would have been Knidos or Kos itself, further east of Lakter. Smyly suggests Halikarnassos, and even the northwestern part of Rhodes is a possibility.

33–34. ἧc ἐφιέμε|[νοι] .... βλέπειν ἀπετύχομέν: compare Hld. 6.12.1: τὸν Θεαγένην καὶ τὸν Θύαμιν εὑρήcειν ἐλπίcαντεc ἀπετύγχανον. Here ἧc must be the object of ἀπετύχομεν, and the infinitive must belong with the participle. The missing word(s) is likely to be an adverb.

38. διαcτήματοc: technically a point on the circumference of a circle.

39. Lavagnini deletes εἰ‹ ἄπειρ[ο]ν, which adds nothing to the sense here and could easily have crept in from the following line by a dittography. Note that there, too, εἰ‹ ἄπειρον follows -μένη. Hiatus results if it is allowed to stand in this line.

40. Smyly compares Pollux 1.108: θάλαττα τραχεῖα, κοίλη θάλαττα, καὶ κοιλαι-νομένη καὶ τραχυνομένη.

40–41. For the thought compare AT 3.2.5: ἡ δὲ ναῦ‹ ἀεὶ πρὸ‹ μὲν τὸ κυρτούμενον τῆ‹ θαλάccη‹ ἠγείρετο, πρὸ‹ δὲ τὸ παράδρομον ἤδη καὶ χθαμαλὸν τοῦ κύματο‹ κατεδύετο. ἐῴκει δὲ τῶν κυμάτων τὰ μὲν ὄρεcι, τὰ δὲ χάcμαcιν.

42. τ' ἐ‹‹› cτάcιν : Smyly's emendation is preferable to the reading of the papyrus. The variation of ἐc with εἰc is not infrequent in the novelists.

42–44. ἀῆται is the subject, τὸ πνεῦμα the object of ἐ[ρρί]πιζον.

42–43. οὔ|[τι], οὔ|[πω] or sim. The sense is that the air mass is in revolt, but not yet in outright warfare. The "battle" of the winds was a topos familiar from the time of Homer, the most famous example, perhaps, being that in Alkaios 326 (L-P). Smyly's οὐ | [μὲν] would require the δέ-clause to be negated also.

43. γνοφ[ο]ειδῆ : the form is *hapax legomenon*, probably a virtual equivalent of γνοφώδη‹.

45. πρηcτῆρα‹ : also in Hld. 1.2.5 and 1.22.4.

47–48. ἀγ|χο[.]: space seems insufficient for Smyly's ἀγ|χό[θι]. Perhaps ἄγ|χο[υ].

52–53. πε|πυ[καc]μένη δὲ νυκτ[ὶ . . . . .] cυνείχετο : Smyly, restoring [ἡ ναῦc], suggests this is an imitation of Homer *Il*. 17.551: πορφυρέη νεφέλη πυκάcαcα ἓ αὐτήν. Since the supplement ἡ ναῦc results in hiatus, Zimmermann preferred to read πε|πυ[κνω]μένη δὲ νυκτ[ὶ πάντα] cυνείχετο.

53–54. καὶ ποτὲ μὲν . . . ποτὲ δὲ occurs also in Longos 1.23.2.

54. ἡ μεγ[άλη πνοή] : Bury's reading has a slight palaeographic edge over Smyly's ἡμερ[ινὸν φῶc], and sense seems better served by it. Line 49 establishes the total gloom in which these events were taking place, the only alleviation of which seems to have been the flashes of starlike lights. A "daylike" light can only intrude into this studied description of the terrifying dark.

55–56. The phenomenon is St. Elmo's fire. Rattenbury (1933: 236) observes that "the elaborate description of storms was a favorite theme for the writer of a Greek romance, and natural phenomena such as St. Elmo's Fires, which were capable of alternative explanations, were dear to his heart." St. Elmo's fire was often connected with the appearance of the Dioscuri (see Burkert 1985: 213), a phenomenon that normally heralded a propitious outcome for the voyage, rather than a shipwreck (Crusius 1897: 2). E. Bowie suggests an echo here of Alkaios 34 (L-P).

57–58. Here Zimmermann is probably correct in thinking that the sailors were invoking the Dioscuri by name as the flashes of light occurred.

The Love Drug

❖

P. Mich. inv. 5 opens with the speaker describing his or her magical powers in affected and incantatory language. Apparently the speaker's companion has consulted this magic practitioner because a fair apparition has visited his daughter, and she has fallen in love with it. Although the incantatory style of the opening can be paralleled in the magic papyri, its extreme elegance guarantees that this piece is to be located in a literary genre. Also, as E. R. Dodds argues (1952: 135), claims to cure love abound in magic texts, so that the magician's confession of helplessness in the face of love is a sure indication that this piece belongs to the realm of fiction.

Of course, magicians and their practices, especially those involving *pharmaka*, do occasionally serve as subjects for rhetorical exercise. For example, see Quintilian's animadversions on the matter (2.10.5), or the display speech mentioned in Philostratos on the topic of "a magician asking to die, since he is unable to kill another magician who was an adulterer" (*Vit. soph.* §619), or Libanios 41, which gives us a magician who offers to save the city by magic means in exchange for his son's life. The complaint that magicians cannot cure love, however, is most familiar as a topos in erotic elegy, where it is found in the mouths of love's victims, not of the magicians themselves. If this is a rhetorical piece, then, it would seem to run counter to the usual cultural expectations.

Campbell Bonner assumed the speaker, whom he identified with "your daughter" (lines 18–19), to be female. Dodds's repunctuation of the text makes it clear that this is not the case, but he also assumes the speaker to be female (a witch), very possibly because a chief attribute of Thessalian witches seems to have been the ability to draw down the moon (see below, line 2 and note). If the speaker is male, the possibility exists that he is the apparition with whom the girl is in love, and that what is involved is not magic and dreams, but trickery. The story of Nektanebos's deception of Olympias in the *Alexander Romance* comes to mind, or the less salacious duping in the *Phasma* of Menander. If the lover and the magician are two different people, this story may be something like the romantic tale of Zariadres, the brother of Hystaspes, the king of Media, who fell in love with the princess Odatis, whom he first saw in a dream (Athenaios 13.575a = *FGrHist* 125 F5 [Chares]).

Reyhl, in his study of Antonius Diogenes, has made the intriguing suggestion that this fragment belongs to *The Incredible Things beyond Thule* (1969: 14–20). The magician, of course, would be Paapis, the father Mnason, and his daughter Derkyllis. Indeed, it might fit very well as a sequence to the incident in *PSI* 1177 where Myrto warns her mistress against the attentions of an evil spirit who would seem to be her lover. But there is no positive evidence to support the conjecture, and we have thought it better to print the fragment separately.

Five small fragments written in the same hand as this papyrus were published by S. Daris (1986: 110–14; P. Pilau Rib. 152 *a–e*). They are unfortunately very abraded and contain at most only a few identifiable words. None can be located with respect to the nearly complete Michigan column, nor, for the most part, even with respect to each other. For these reasons, we have not included a complete transcription here.[1] In Fragment *a* we seem to have dialogue—*a*.3: (ἡμῶν χρηcαμε[ν-, Daris suggests reading χριcαμέ[νων, comparing P. Mich. 5.17), *a*.10: probably "you were bewitched" ([μ]εμάγε[υc]θε)—and there is probably dialogue in Fragment *b* as well—*b*.3: "I am afraid that" (δέδοικα μ[ή). Talk about day and night in lines *a*.10–12 could indicate a connection with the magician's claim to control time (see below, lines 2–8).[2] More intriguingly, if P. Mich. 5 is from Antonius Diogenes, it could refer to the fate of Mantineas and Derkyllis, who are condemned to live by night and sleep by day having been "bewitched" by the magic spell Paapis placed upon them.[3]

---

[1] Those so inclined should see Stramaglia (1991: 76–78), who reproduces Daris's diplomatic transcription and attempts with little success to make sense of the pitiful remains. Daris, Kussl, and Stramaglia all assume that the words in *a*.10 (]εμαγε[) and *b*.6 (]. τουτουμαγ[) must be forms of μάγοc.

[2] Fragment *a*.11–13: ν]ὺξ οὐδέπω φα[ίνεται (so Daris) ±5] ἡμέρα κ[αὶ] φῶc[±10]ν καὶ πε[ποί]η[ται or sim.

[3] In Fragment *b*.2–6, magic practices are also the subject. One might restore along the following lines, for example: δέδοικα μ[ὴ μάθῃ | τὴν α]ὐτὴν τέχνην [καὶ τὸ | βιβλίο]ν τούτου μαγ[ικὸν | εὑρὼν] καὶ τὰc ποιή[cειc (so Daris) | τῶν c]οφῶν αὐτὰc [("I am afraid that [he may learn the] same art, [since he discovered] both this man's magic [book] and the very procedures [of the sages]"), though a number of other schemes are possible. Whether Fragment *b* follows or precedes Fragment *a* is unknown.

DESCRIPTION

P. Mich. inv. 5 (= P^2 2636, measuring 8.5 × 16.2 cm) contains the upper portion of a column from a papyrus roll preserving twenty-three nearly intact lines. The papyrus is light-colored and of good quality; the back is blank. Writing is along the fibers in an informal round style assignable to the mid-second century C.E. For the type, compare *Tinouphis* (= P. Turner 8). Lines contain between sixteen and nineteen letters. A generous upper margin (about 3.0 cm) and the right intercolumnar space survive; the left break occurred just before the initial letters of the lines, and the bottom is broken off. There are no marks of punctuation, nor are there lectional signs; there are occasional gaps between words or phrases, but these are not consistent enough to be intended to punctuate. Iota adscript is not written, and there are two itacistic variations of spelling (lines 4, 17). The piece is composed in the Attic dialect (see line 8), and hiatus is avoided absolutely. The language is ordered with extreme elegance in attention to rhetorical detail, whereas the sentiments are set out in nearly identical clausulae.

P. MICH. INV. 5

ϲτήϲεται · κἂν ϲελήνῃ κε-
λεύϲω, καταβήϲεται · κἂν
κωλῦϲαι θελ[ή]ϲω τὴν ἡμέ-
4 ραν, ἡ νύξ μοι μενεῖ · κἂν
δεήθωμεν πάλιν ἡμέ-
ραϲ, τὸ φῶϲ οὐκ ἀπελεύϲε-
ται · κἂν πλεῦϲαι θελήϲω
8 τὴν θάλατταν, οὐ δέομαι
νεώϲ · κἂν δι᾽ ἀέροϲ ἐλθεῖν,
κουφιϲθήϲομαι. ἐρωτικὸν
μόνον οὐχ εὑρίϲκω φάρ-
12 μακον—οὐ ποιῆϲαι δυνάμενον, οὐ παῦϲαι δυνάμενον.
ἡ γῆ γὰρ φοβουμένη τὸν
θεὸν οὐ φέρει. εἰ δέ τιϲ ἔχει
16 καὶ δίδωϲιν, αἰτῶ, δέομαι,
"δότε · πιεῖν θέλω, χρίϲαϲθαι
θέλω." φαίνεϲθαί ϲου τῇ θυ-
γατρὶ καλὸν εἴδωλον λέ-
20 γειϲ καὶ τοῦτό ϲοι παράδοξον εἶναι δοκεῖ. πόϲοι δὲ
ἄλλοι παραλόγων ἡράϲθη-
[ϲ]αν ϲωμάτων [. . . .] νικαϲ
24 [. .] ṇδε̣ ω̣[. . . . . .]λịμ[. .
- -

3. κυλωϲαι pap., κωλῦϲαι or κολοῦϲαι Bonner, κυλῶϲαι Eitrem 4. μενεῖ Dodds,
μένει Bonner 17. χρηϲαϲθαι pap., read χρίϲαϲθαι S. West 22. παραλόγων
Eitrem, παρ᾽ ἀλόγων Bonner.

] it will stand still; if I order the moon,
it will descend; if
I wish to prevent the day,
4   night will linger on for me;
and again, if we demand the day,
the light will not depart;
if I wish to sail
8   the sea, I have no need
of a ship; if I wish to move through the air,
I shall become weightless. For love
alone I find no drug,
12   none with power to create it,
none with power to abate it.
For the earth in fear
of that god bears no such plant. But if anyone has it
16   to give, I beseech, I implore,
"Give it to me—I wish to drink it down, I wish to rub it on."
A fair image is appearing
to your daughter you say,
20   and this seems strange to you?
But how many
others have fallen in love with outlandish
creatures . . . [

P. MICH. INV. 5

1–10. These lines contain an elaborately wrought topos consisting of three or more pairs detailing the magician's powers and climaxing in an unexpected inversion. Normally magicians do claim to cure love, not to be defeated by it. See, e.g., Phot. *Bibl.* 184.128a–129.

1.]cτήcεται: Bonner suggests [ὁ ἥλιος] cτήcεται, comparing *PGM* 13.873: ὃ (sc. τὸ ὄνομα θεοῦ) ἐὰν εἴπω τέλειον, ὁ ἥλιος cτήcεται. But the other pairs are parallel, and drawing down the moon is not normally linked with stopping the sun, which would in any case be a duplication of lines 3–7. More likely, staying the course of rivers or summoning Hekate. Compare Lucian *Philopseudes* §13: τὴν Ἑκάτην αὐτὴν ἐναργῆ παριcτὰc καὶ τὴν Cελήνην καθαιρῶν. One might restore, e.g., κἂν τὴν Ἑκάτην ἐπικαλεῖν θελήcω, παρα]cτήcεται, and the longer παρα]cτήcεται provides a better rhythmic balance for καταβήcεται (line 2).

1–2. The ability to draw down the moon is most often in literature attributed to Thessalian witches, cf. Plato *Gorg.* §513a, Aristoph. *Clouds* 750, Prop. 1.19, Hor. *Ep.* 5.46, Tib. 1.2.43, Verg. *Ecl.* 8.69.

3–7. The claims are typical; Bonner compares Simon the magician's speech in pseudo-Clement *Recognitiones* 2.9, or Lucian *Anach.* §13.

10–13. For the rhetorical balances as well as the sentiment, compare Longos *Daphnis and Chloe* 2.7: ἔρωτος γὰρ οὐδὲν φάρμακον, οὐ πινόμενον, οὐκ ἐcθιόμενον, οὐκ ἐν ᾠδαῖc λεγόμενον.

17–18. Again, a conventional sentiment. S. West provides as parallels Eur. *Hipp.* 516 (πότερα δὲ χριcτὸν ἢ πότον τὸ φάρμακον) and Theok. 11.2 (on which see Gow's commentary).

19. καλὸν εἴδωλον: "fair image" could be a painting, which figured in *Ninos* (shown in the Antioch mosaic); or it could be an apparition in a dream, as in the story of Zariadres (see introduction above); or a ghost, as in Phlegon of Tralles' Περὶ θαυμαcιῶν I (*FGrHist* 257 F36).

22–23. παραλόγων ἠράcθη]|[c]αν cωμάτων: Eros brings about strange conjunctions, familiar in Greek folktales and known from various authors who collected them. The collections of erotica attributed to Theophrastos and Klearchos are said to have contained stories of animals in love with people—goose, dolphin, rooster, peacock, elephant (Athenaios *Deipnosophists* 13.606b–607b), men and animals in love with statues or pictures ([Plut.] *Paral. min.* §29, Ant. Lib. 21, Phaedrus 3.3, Plut. *Sept. Sap. Conv.* §149c–e), and of course Pasiphae, though these last are sheer wayward lust, not "romantic" as the former tales are.

23. [. . . .]νικαc: Dodds's conjecture, [ἐξ ἐνυπ]νίου, does not suit traces.

Iamblichos
Babyloniaka

❖

The extraordinary plot of Iamblichos's *Babyloniaka* is summarized by Photios in codex 94 of his *Bibliothēkē*. If there were any suspicion that the patriarch was capable of pulling our leg, this would be the place to exercise it. According to him, the hero and heroine roam throughout the Near East pursued by two eunuchs whose noses and ears have been cut off. They encounter bees with poisoned honey, a Lesbian princess of Egypt, a cannibalistic brigand, look-alike brothers named Tigris and Euphrates who happen to be exact doubles for the hero, and a rather dignified farmer's daughter whom the heroine forces to sleep with an executioner who is really a priest of Aphrodite who helps his son Euphrates break jail by dressing in the farmer's daughter's clothes. Considering the emotional tension that is constantly breaking out between the hero and heroine, culminating in her leaving him to marry another man before their final reconciliation, it is a wonder that anyone could ever refer to this work as an "ideal romance."

The fragments of the *Babyloniaka* come not from papyrus discoveries but from manuscript excerpts[1] and from short quotations used to illustrate interesting words in the massive tenth-century dictionary-cum-encyclopedia known as the *Souda*. Indeed, until recently, the principal scholarly attention devoted to Iamblichos has concerned itself with which of the many hundreds of unattributed quotations floating through-

---

[1] Three long passages, one (Frag. 61) in Vaticanus Graecus rescriptus 73, two (Frags. 1 and 35) found both in Laurentianus 57,12 and in Vaticanus 1354. These last two mss. also contain six shorter sentences, apparently from Iamblichos, and one longer passage in which mercenaries argue their cases for extra wages before the Amphiktyonic Council. This last seems to have nothing to do with the *Babyloniaka* and was only attributed to Iamblichos on the basis of a marginal note placed near the end of the passage. M. Naechster (1908) reasonably argues that the note refers only to the passages that follow, and that the excerpt comes, like its predecessor, from the rhetor Hadrianos. Habrich also rejected its authenticity, printing it as frag. 101 of the "dubious fragments."

out that lexicon might have come from the *Babyloniaka*.[2] The quotations usually just consist in a short sentence; but the fact that the illustrative quotations in the *Souda* tend to be drawn from a short list of favorite authors[3] and that some anonymous quotations contain distinctive proper names from the *Babyloniaka*[4] while others fit easily into the plot as summarized by Photios,[5] form together a strong argument for attributing at least some of the 116 claimants in Elmar Habrich's edition to Iamblichos.[6]

IAMBLICHOS

Our information about the author comes from three sources: the *Souda*, a scholion in ms. A of Photios, and Photios's own account of what Iamblichos says of himself in the novel. But, ultimately, all three must derive from the novel itself. Together they give us more detail than we have for any other novelist, but there are the usual small contradictions to be ironed out.

The *Souda* article reads: "Iamblichos: this man, so they say, was born of slaves. He wrote the work called *Babyloniaka*, which is about the passion of Rhodanes and Sinonis, in thirty-nine books. He tells of Zobaras the eunuch, lover of the supremely beautiful Mesopotamia."

Thirty-nine (that is, λθ) is probably a mistake. The other novels are much more compact: Chariton's has eight books, Xenophon's ten, Achilles Tatius's eight, Longos's four, Heliodoros's ten. Only Antonius Diogenes' novel, with twenty-four books, comes close to such a length.[7]

---

[2] The fragments explicitly attributed to Iamblichos are 30, 54, 56, 59, 70, 84, 89, 90, 91, 93, 97, 98, and 99.

[3] Constantine Porphyrogennetos's excerpts: Adler 1928–, 1:19–20.

[4] Sinonis: Frags. 3, 13, 61, 78; Sinonis and Soraichos: Frag. 78; Garmos: Frag. 9; Damas: Frag. 18.

[5] E.g., the thirty-stade-long cave with two entrances (Frag. 11), the sentry who drops his shield so that the hollow reverberation reveals the location of the underground cave (Frag. 14), the bees with poisoned honey (Frag. 16), the priest wearing the clothing of a public executioner (Frag. 55).

[6] Hercher (1858–59, 1866, 1875) identified sixty-one *Souda* fragments as coming from Iamblichos (in his *Erotici scriptores graeci* vol. 1 (1858): 220, frag. 27 has been assigned two numbers by the printer; cf. p. xxxiv). Bruhn (1890) suggested another seventeen, and Adler tentatively mentioned another thirty-eight candidates, many of them also assignable to Ailian (index to her edition of the *Souda* 5:87–88).

[7] Is it an accident that these are all even numbers? Would Iamblichos have organized a massive work into exactly thirty-nine books when forty was easily possible? Apuleius's eleventh book, of course, is deliberately excrescent.

Photios ends his summary of Iamblichos's novel with the sixteenth (that is, ιϛ') book, at a point that seems to be the conclusion of the entire story, and that is more likely to be the length of the *Babyloniaka*.

A second probable error in the *Souda* entry can be detected by comparing the other two sources: Iamblichos learned his Babylonian tales from a slave, but if his parents could afford to buy a highly educated slave as a tutor, Iamblichos was probably not a slave himself. The scholion in Photios runs as follows:

> This Iamblichos was a Syrian by birth, both on his father's and his mother's side, not a Syrian in the sense of a Greek living in Syria but a native. He spoke Syrian and lived in that culture until a tutor, as he tells us, who was Babylonian, took charge of him and taught him the language and culture of Babylon, and their stories, of which the one he is writing is an example. The Babylonian was taken prisoner in the time when Trajan entered Babylonia and the booty merchants sold him to a Syrian. He was learned in the wisdom of the barbarians, enough to have been one of the king's scribes when he was living in his fatherland. So this Iamblichos, speaking his native Syrian, learned Babylonian as well, and after that he says that he worked hard practicing Greek too, so as to be an accomplished rhetor.

How much of this is fictional framing, constructed by Iamblichos as an authorial mask, is hard to say. That Iamblichos, like Lucian,[8] was a Syrian native who acquired his Greek as a second language is probable enough. His name is of Arabic derivation and is found in Palmyra and among the tribes around Apameia.[9] The Babylonian tutor is harder to judge. The chronology is reasonable, but many elements of the narrative seem thoroughly Greek, at least as Greek as Chariton and Xenophon of Ephesos. The author has fully embedded himself in the Greek culture of the Roman Empire and declares as much in the course of the novel. For this we rely on Photios's summary, which contains at least one mistake:

> The writer says that he himself is a Babylonian and has learned magic, that he also had a Greek education, and that he flourished under Sohaimos the Achaimenid and Arsakid, a king from a line of kings, and who became a member of the Senate at Rome and then a consul and then a king again of

---

[8] "For while he just a lad, still a barbarian in speech practically wearing a burnoose (kandys) in the Syrian style . . ." (*Bis accus.* §27).

[9] Schneider-Menzel 1948: 91 n. 18 cites H. Wuthnow 1930: 56, 148. Iamblichos, son of Sampsikeramos, was chieftain of the tribe of the Emisenoi in the stronghold of Arethousa near Apameia (Str. 16.2.10).

Greater Armenia. This was the period in which he says he lived. He expressly states that Antoninus was ruling the Romans. And when Antoninus (he says) sent the emperor Verus, his brother and kinsman, to make war on Vologaeses the Parthian, he himself foretold that the war would occur and how it would end. And he tells how Vologaeses fled beyond the Euphrates and Tigris and how the land of the Parthians became subject to Rome. (75b27–41)

The more exact and insistent information in the scholion should be preferred to Photios's casual mention that Iamblichos was Babylonian. If Iamblichos is being tutored not long after the fall of Babylon to Trajan (115/6), he may have been born about the turn of the century, later if the Babylonian served more than one master.

This autobiographical digression in the novel—indeed, if we can trust Photios, in the midst of a digression on the forms of magic—is very interesting. The only comparable performance on our shelf of novels is that of Apuleius, whose autobiographical references at beginning and end are deliberate riddles (1.1, 11.27). Apuleius also shares with Iamblichos both the claim to be a latecomer to the language he is writing and a personal involvement with magic. Is this mere coincidence—not remarkable in a period when the entire Mediterranean basin has been brought into a comprehensive economic and administrative framework such that diverse cultural traditions may more easily be investigated and blended? Or is it a convention of the genre—that is, an authorial stance appropriate to narrative or similar material that is somewhat exotic, elaborate and intense? (see Winkler 1985: 257–73). The two explanations are more than compatible: the one is simply a more distant and material description of what the other views close up and in more literary terms.

But Apuleius does not associate himself with the grand course of history as Iamblichos does. Verus campaigned against the Parthian king Vologaeses III (148–92) from 164 to 166. Since Iamblichos describes the flight of Vologaeses, the novel was completed after that date, because, whatever we think of his claim to have predicted the Roman victory, its publication would not constitute a proof of the author's powers until after the event.

The fulsome praise of (C. Iulius?) Sohaimos argues some connection of the author to that Syrian member of the Roman Senate, who was king of Armenia from 164.[10] The immediate implications of that fact are

---

[10] Possibly a descendant of the C. Iulius Sohaimos who was king of Emesa from 54 C.E. until at least the Vespasian period (Halfmann 1979: 175–76; Cass. Dio 71.2–4).

difficult to assess. Iamblichos himself is Syrian, of course, and Syria figures prominently in the denouement of the *Babyloniaka*. The heroine Sinonis, feeling betrayed by her lover Rhodanes, leaves him and marries the young king of Syria; the Babylonian king sends Rhodanes with an army to fight that king, "lover against rival." We could wish that Photios had been a bit more informative about the conclusion: "Rhodanes is victorious, recovers Sinonis, and rules over the Babylonians." Did this leave Syria defeated and humiliated or in a state of honorable alliance, allowed to maintain at least the forms of independence and native rule? The latter would seem more probable in a text that so proclaimed its current Syrian connections.

Further, Sohaimos is praised specifically as both an Achaimenid and an Arsakid, that is, as a member of the ruling dynasties both of Persia (descendant of Kyros, Dareios, and Xerxes) and of Parthia. Between the two great powers of Rome and Parthia, Armenia functioned at times as a sort of buffer zone. The Parthian king Vologaeses I had installed his brother Tiridates on the throne of Armenia, and Tiridates diplomatically confirmed his rule by allowing Nero to crown him in Rome in 66 C.E. The balance of power seemed to sway seriously with Trajan's conquest of Mesopotamia and the Parthian capital of Ktesiphon in 115/6 (Cassius Dio 68.30.3; Ziegler 1964: 97ff.), but Hadrian backed off from Trajan's extensions and in 117 made peace with the Parthian king Osroes. A different Osroes, set on the throne of Armenia by Vologaeses III, defeated a small Roman force and invaded Syria in 162, prompting a major Roman expedition under the nominal leadership of the playboy Verus that resulted in the burning of Ktesiphon and the annexation of Mesopotamia as a Roman province.

Iamblichos locates his *Babyloniaka* by reference to these events: the story material was putatively acquired from a Babylonian royal scribe brought to Syria as a slave after Trajan's sack of "Babylonia," and its publication postdates the expulsion of the Parthian ruling class from Mesopotamia. It is clear that Iamblichos, like Sohaimos, cast his loyalties on the side of Roman rule, and that his chosen audience was the Greek-speaking elite (of many races and places) who administered the empire. The "nationalist" inspiration that Braun (1938) sees in the earlier folk stories of Ninos and Sesostris cannot apply to Iamblichos.

The larger implication of Iamblichos's proclaimed connection with Sohaimos is that it reinforces the obvious first impression generated by the stylistic level of this and many other novel texts, that they were aimed at an audience trained in the fine arts of language. As Lucian devoted two essays to the praise of Verus' mistress Pantheia (*Imagines, Pro imaginibis*), so too, Iamblichos moved, or hoped that he might move, in the high circles of the Greek-speaking social elite in the eastern Roman Empire.

THE *BABYLONIAKA*

For all the striking originality of its content and the fact that Photios found it a "worthy model of writerly skill and power," modern critics have scarcely expended any words on Iamblichos's novel as a complex and stylish literary performance. Yet even Photios's frequently opaque and gappy summary lets us see that the *Babyloniaka* was a work of remarkable energy and artful contrivance. Its two outstanding features are the jealousy of Sinonis, which breaks up the unanimity ordinarily maintained by the central couple in this genre, and the insistent doublings—of episodes with similar structure and of characters with identical features.

More than any other novelist, Iamblichos has exploited the possibilities of twins and look-alikes. Heliodoros's Charikleia is mistaken for Thisbe, and Achilles Tatius's Kalligone is literally taken for Leukippe, but the misapprehension of a character's identity through actual physical resemblance to someone else is virtually Iamblichos's signature. The hero Rhodanes is mistaken for the dead Tigris by the lad's own mother. Since the brothers "Tigris and Euphrates resembled each other, and Rhodanes resembled both of them," it is not surprising that Euphrates is arrested in Rhodanes' place. What is surprising is that the arrest is brought about by Euphrates' own father, who denounces him, thinking he is Rhodanes. Both parents misidentify one of their sons, and both mistakes work in Rhodanes' favor. Euphrates' father corrects his mistake later when, as public executioner, he is about to put his son to death but recognizes him in time.

Sinonis has two doublets as well. The farmer's daughter is suspected to be Sinonis because her hair is shorn and she is trying to sell some of the gold chain that Sinonis had been forced to wear in prison. Mesopotamia is arrested in Sinonis's place, not necessarily because they resemble each other but because circumstances have forced Euphrates to refer to his sister Mesopotamia as Sinonis. Two pairs of boy and girl look-alikes are mentioned in Fragment 92, which, if it is from the *Babyloniaka*, probably belongs to a lie told by a character.

The grandest and grisliest of these misidentifications occurs when Rhodanes' dog eats some of a maiden's corpse in an inn. Sinonis's father recognizes the dog, thinks the maiden is Sinonis, kills the dog, buries the maiden's body with an inscription identifying the grave as that of Sinonis, and then hangs himself. Rhodanes and Soraichos then arrive and take the accumulated evidence—dog's corpse, father swinging in a noose, grave marker for Sinonis—as cogent proof that Sinonis really is dead, so Soraichos hangs himself, Rhodanes draws enough blood to complete the inscription with his own name and then prepares to strike the sword into his chest.

The two older men dangling in nooses at that point are another doublet, since Soraichos accompanies the couple as a kind of protective father: "O Sinonis," he says in Fragment 61, "I cherish both of you, since Fortune has given me to you as father. You became my daughter before Rhodanes became my son."

Though these various episodes can be grouped together under the category of doublets or twins, they do not seem repetitious. Each is quite different from the rest in its structure and local effects. The premises of this genre, of course, not only tolerate but encourage and aim at scenes displaying the stunning effects of coincidence: these are not just any old events but "storied" events. In a series of *sententiae*, such as the showpieces of Iamblichos's contemporary Polemo,[11] paradox may wear out its welcome quickly, but narrative paradox palls only in summary or when one closes the book and puts on one's official hat. The detail and variety of a long narrative easily palliate the effect of contrivance; or rather, the addition of so many other literary structures—description, dialogue, digressions— allows one to avoid confronting the fact that the concatenation of events is quite simply incredible.

Bryan Reardon (1982) has analyzed the essential plot of Chariton's *Kallirhoe* as a single situation—a triangle of Lover, Beloved, and Rival—which is repeated in different locales with a series of different Rivals, each a notch up the social scale. A skeleton almost that simple can be seen in stretches of the *Babyloniaka*. The early books are constructed as a sequence of scenes or stage sets—Prison, Meadow, Cave, Inn, Brigand's House, and Cemetery—on which rather similar events take place. In each location, Rhodanes and Sinonis are brought very

---

[11] Whose two speeches contesting for the prize of valor at Marathon were transcribed along with the two longish rhetorical excerpts from Iamblichos in Vat. 1354 and Laur. 57,12 (H. Hinck 1873).

near death, in three of them they are actually mistaken for dead. The soldiers pursuing them (a) toss burial gifts in their direction when they see them lying by the road in a stupor from the poisoned honey; (b) flee from them as ghosts after the fire at the brigand's house; and (c) see them lying asleep in the tomb of the girl whose funeral procession was interrupted and assume them, once more, to be real corpses. At the inn, they are accused of a murder, which would have resulted in their death, and in the palace prison (this geography is vague) Rhodanes is actually hanging on a cross. In each succeeding episode other people die while the central couple either is thought to have died or narrowly escapes death.

Yet if each of these settings reenacts what is in some sense the same basic situation, they are very different from each other in color and characters. Further, none is expendable, for each (with the possible exception of the cannibalistic brigand) contributes an item that is later used in the novel. From the meadow Rhodanes takes some of the gold treasure he has discovered, and later uses it to free Soraichos; in the cave Sinonis cuts her hair to draw up water (her shorn head will later lead to confusion with the widowed farmer's daughter); at the inn Rhodanes acquires a flask of poison, which he will later use to attempt suicide; from the cemetery Sinonis takes some funeral clothing, which leads to her arrest later when she tries to sell it.

Certainly there was an architecture of the whole governing at least the coincidence of beginning and end: Soraichos is sent to execution in the same meadow where Rhodanes had found the buried treasure at the beginning; Rhodanes is crucified on the very same cross from which he had been hanging in the first episode reported by Photios. Beyond that, some elements of broad design may be discerned. If the first six major settings can be called a unit, all involving variations on near-death and apparent death, the next block of episodes introduces the look-alike characters and begins to play with the possibilities of misidentification. On the island we meet Euphrates and Mesopotamia, soon after that the farmer's daughter. This cast of interchangeable characters combines and recombines in various permutations and in various locales.

As a fulcrum between these two sections of the novel occurs a scene that is crucial to the psychology and motivation of the heroine. From this episode on, the plotting shifts emphasis from reiterated near-death to mistaken identity. To this end, the episode introduces the new paternal protector Soraichos (who is like Kalasiris in the *Aithiopika*) and leads directly to the three look-alikes on the island. Arrested for grave-robbing and brought to justice, Sinonis is being conveyed by Soraichos to King Garmos. She and Rhodanes take poison, but Soraichos has substituted a sleeping drug, so they simply fall into a coma. Rhodanes' sharp cry during a nightmare wakes Sinonis, she realizes that she is being taken to Garmos, and she tries to commit suicide by plunging a sword in her breast. The wound is serious but not fatal. Soraichos is so impressed with her determination that he decides to help the couple to escape. He takes Sinonis to the temple of Aphrodite on the island and commissions a doctor to attend her there.

This fulcrum scene also shows Sinonis at her most courageous, ready to kill herself with a sword rather than marry another man. She has from the beginning been a remarkably daring and energetic heroine, showing initiative in escaping from prison and engineering Rhodanes' liberation, cutting her long hair to make a rope to draw up water in the cave and leading the way in the darkness with a lamp (Fragment 13, not securely attributed). Her character is consistently drawn in terms of determination and initiative, so we should not wonder that when she sees Rhodanes and the farmer's daughter kissing she feels seriously aggrieved.

In the long fragment 61 she makes her motivation perfectly clear: "Displaying the wound she had once inflicted on herself she said, 'Do you see this [wound], O [——]? Do you see how Sinonis does not spare her own life?'" Rhodanes has not lived up to her example of single-minded and uncompromising commitment to one lover. In the same fragment, Soraichos injects a small touch of realism: "You are not the only one, my child, who finds Rhodanes attractive. . . ." But such worldly realism is exactly what Sinonis will not tolerate: "She flared up at this last remark and did not wait for the rest of his speech. 'Soraichos, I have indulged this wicked windiness of yours, and grudgingly at that. I should have died before hearing you say that any other woman finds Rhodanes attractive.'"

Jealousy is too narrow a description of Sinonis's motivation in this last section of the novel, making her seem capricious and irrational. Her standards for Rhodanes' behavior are arguably too high, but they are the standards she has consistently applied to herself, and her perception of the meaning of his kiss is accurate.[12]

This highly original turn of events dominates the last stretch of the novel, in which Sinonis kills another would-be suitor, engages herself to

---

[12] Borgogno (1975b: 164) suggests that the doubling of the farmer's daughter and Sinonis is not merely a narrative device but serves to ground Sinonis's fears of rejection.

be married to the young king of Syria, and uses her new position to take vengeance on the farmer's daughter.

What might have been a climactic scene bringing on a resolution occurs in the inn, where Rhodanes finds his dead dog, Sinonis's father hanging in a noose, and a tombstone for Sinonis. At this point his courage at last matches that of Sinonis and he turns his sword on himself. Like the hapless Chaireas in Chariton's novel, the hero is at first a moral failure, or at least a second-rater, but later redeems himself. Rhodanes' suicide is interrupted, however, by the farmer's daughter rushing up with the news that the buried woman is not Sinonis. Unfortunately, Sinonis then arrives to see the farmer's daughter nursing Rhodanes' chest wound. This forestalls any reconciliation that might have occurred if the farmer's daughter had not been there and Sinonis had realized that Rhodanes' courage could on occasion equal hers.

STYLE

Any assessment of Iamblichos's style must, of course, take into account the unorthodox nature of the excerpts. If, as is more than likely, the selections were chosen for the presence of rare words or unusual locutions, the rest of the novel could easily have been written in a mainstream Atticizing style. Indeed, the longer fragments display the habits of Greek rhetorical training, and would not disgrace more classical writers. Reeve (1971: 534–35) points out, for example, that in the long fragments Iamblichos's avoidance of hiatus conforms to that of the other Greek novelists, whereas there is a higher incidence of hiatus in the lexical fragments, where no doubt strict attention to word order would have been of less concern than the grammatical construction or an unusual usage. Explanations are given of Babylonian words and customs, as one would expect in a work directed to a Greek audience. Some of the proper names and customs may be Babylonian, but the plot and characterization seems wholly Greek, both melodramatic and rhetorical and with bold female characters. In fact, Photios's assessment of Iamblichos's style as "fluent and gentle; and if there is an occasional jolt, it creates not so much a tension but ... an undercurrent of languid excitement" (*Epit.* 73b32) suits well these contrasting elements.

Those who have worked on the quotation question are Hercher (1858–59, 1866, 1867, 1875, 1876), Rohde ([1876] 1974), Bruhn (1890), Adler (1928–), Schneider-Menzel (1948), Habrich (1960), Barigazzi (1961), Di Gregorio (1963), and Borgogno (1975a, 1975b). They of course disagree about the relative probabilities in this artful guessing game. Without entering too deeply into such debates, we have translated most of the quotations that have been claimed for the *Babyloniaka*, indicating the section where they might fit into Photios's summary along with information about where to find discussions of their authenticity and position. We include the fragment numbers used in Habrich's edition (though we do not include all the fragments Habrich claimed for the *Babyloniaka*). The fragments whose authenticity or position are quite doubtful are translated last.

TESTIMONIA

Photios (c. 810–893), *Bibliothēkē* codex 94. Our translation is based on the Budé edition of R. Henry.

[73b24] The novel (δραματικόν) of Iamblichos was read, which acts out affairs of passion. He does not flaunt indecent language to the same degree as Achilles Tatius, but his attitude is rather more shameless than that of the Phoenician Heliodoros. For these three authors have set themselves roughly the same goal—the enactment of plots involving erotic dramas—but Heliodoros is very dignified and pure-spoken, Iamblichos less so, and Achilles is shameless and indecent.

[73b32] His style on the whole is fluent and gentle; and if there is an occasional jolt, it creates not so much a tension but rather a tickle (as one might say) and an undercurrent of languid excitement.

[73b35] Iamblichos then, because he is excellent in style and composition and in the arrangement of narratives that represent highly serious matters rather than fictitious horseplay, is a worthy model of the writer's art and power.

[74a4] The cast of characters he has devised includes Sinonis and Rhodanes, beautiful and handsome respectively, deeply in love with each other within the bounds of matrimony, and they are in fact being married [or betrothed?]; and Garmos, king of Babylon, who at his wife's death falls in love with Sinonis and is trying to force her to marry him.[13]

[74a9] Sinonis refuses and is thrown into bondage, her chain being plaited with gold.[14] Rhodanes on this account is tied onto a cross, with the royal eunuchs Damas and Sakas assigned to oversee the operation. But he is taken down from it thanks to Sinonis's intervention, and both manage to escape—he the cross, she the marriage. Sakas and Damas for this get their ears and noses cut off[15] and are then sent in pursuit of the couple. They split up and go their separate ways on the trail.

[74a17] The party of Rhodanes[16] is nearly caught by its pursuer Damas in

---

[13] Garmos is the supposed writer of the fifty-ninth letter in the epistles of Apollonios of Tyana. The subject of the letter, however, has no connection with what we know of the *Babyloniaka*.

[14] Though Aithiopians are said to use golden chains on prisoners as a matter of course, since gold is not as precious to them as other metals (Hdt., Hld.), Sinonis's chains are specially made for her by a goldsmith who later appears in the novel (76b6)—presumably as a sign of honor from Garmos.

[15] The Persian noble Intaphrenes inflicts a similar penalty on two chamberlains who refuse him entrance to Dareios (Hdt. 3.118).

[16] This locution (οἱ περὶ Ῥοδάνην) refers only to Rhodanes and Sinonis, not to a larger crowd. We retain the odd expression, which seems to have been Iamblichos's (cf. Frag. 61

a meadow. There was a fisherman who informed against the shepherds, who, under torture, reluctantly reveal the location of the meadow in which Rhodanes actually found gold, whose hiding place was hinted at by the inscription on a pillar of a lion.[17] And an apparition in the form of a billy goat lusts after Sinonis—for which reason the party of Rhodanes depart from the meadow. Damas finds the garland that Sinonis made in the meadow and sends it to Garmos as a consolation.

[74a27] Rhodanes' party meets in its flight an old woman in a hut,[18] and they hide themselves in a cave that had been dug straight through to a length of thirty stades.[19] Its mouth had been plugged by shrubby brush. Damas's party arrives and the old woman is examined. At the sight of a naked sword she faints. The horses that Rhodanes and Sinonis had been riding are seized,[20] and troops surround the area in which Sinonis and Rhodanes are hiding. A bronze shield of one of the sentries crashes down on the ground above the tunnel, and the hollow reverberation reveals their hiding place. The tunnel is excavated, while Damas shouts continuously. The people inside it become aware of the activity and flee into the cave's recesses, and they come out at the other opening.

[74a40] A swarm of wild bees from that place attacks the men digging, and some of their honey also drips onto the fugitives. The bees in fact have distilled their honey like a drug from the plants eaten by serpents:[21] stinging the diggers, they mutilate some, others they actually kill. Overcome by hunger, the party of Rhodanes licked up the honey, suffered stomach cramps and collapsed by the roadside like corpses.

---

below, line 20), modeling the English on such uses as "the party of the first part." In some authors, the plural article with periphrastic περί even refers to single individuals (as τοὺϲ περὶ τὸν Ὄϲιριν = Osiris, DS 1.16.2; τοῖϲ περὶ Ῥωμύλον καὶ Ῥῆμον = Romulus and Remus, Plut. *Q. Rom.* §268f.

[17] The hiding place was apparently underground in or near a spring (see 78a13–14, 20–21). Rhodanes takes some of the gold but probably leaves the bulk of it there, for it is later found and used by Soraichos (78a15–22). Perhaps the lustful apparition of a billy goat who leaps out of a well (Frag. 10) is a Babylonian demon guarding the golden treasure there. Soraichos recovers it by some clever ruse that makes him appear supernaturally gifted; perhaps he tricks the demon/jinni.

[18] This is no doubt intended as a reminiscence of Hekale, the old woman in whose hut Theseus takes shelter in Kallimachos' poem.

[19] This is presumably a natural phenomenon.

[20] Damas may suspect the old woman of harboring the fugitives because he recognizes the king's horses (Borgogno 1975a: 120).

[21] The thistle blossoms are especially sought out by bees, according to Columella 9.4.4 (Schneider-Menzel 1948: 59 n. 13). For the various types of poisonous honey and their effects on man and beast, see Pliny *Nh* 21.74–78; cf. Dioskourides Περὶ ἁπλῶν φαρμάκων 2.142 (vol. 2, p. 310 Wellmann).

[74b5] The army fled, hard pressed by the bees' warfare. And they were still pursuing the party of Rhodanes, and when they saw the persons they were pursuing lying by the road they rode on by, thinking they were in truth some corpses.

[74b9] Now in this cave Sinonis had cut her locks in order to draw up water for themselves. Damas finds her rope of hair there and sends it to Garmos as a sign that he is near to actually capturing them.

[74b12] As Rhodanes and Sinonis are lying by the roadside, the army, riding by, throws down some clothes to cover the corpses, and other soldiers throw various items, including meat and bread—this being their ancestral custom. And so the army rode on.

[74b17] Still stunned and groggy from the honey, they rise with great difficulty, Rhodanes being wakened by the noisy crows fighting over the meat, Sinonis by Rhodanes. Rising, then, they turn back in the opposite direction to that of the army, the more to seem unpursued. They find and mount two asses and load on the goods that they had gathered from the offerings scattered over their corpses by the army.

[74b24] They stop at an inn, but escape from there, and at about the filling of the agora they reach another public house, where occurs the adventure of the two brothers. They are accused of murder, and acquitted: the older brother, who had poisoned his younger brother, accused them of the crime, but he acquitted them by his suicide. Rhodanes, unnoticed, takes possession of the poison.

[74b31] They stop at the house of a brigand who waylays wayfarers and makes them his dinner. But soldiers sent by Damas arrest the brigand and set fire to his house. They are engulfed by the flames but barely escape destruction by killing the asses and using them as a causeway to make their way through the fire.[22] They are spotted—it is late at night—by the soldiers who set the fire, and when challenged as to their identity, they reply, "shades of those murdered by the brigand." Because of their pale color and emaciated features[23] and thin voices, they convince the soldiers and strike them with terror. And they flee from that place too.

[74b42] Now they come upon a maiden being carried to the grave and they mingle with the crowd attending the spectacle. An old Chaldaian man stands up and forbids the burial, saying the maiden is still alive and breathing— and she was shown to be so. He also prophesies to Rhodanes that he will be king. The maiden's tomb is left empty, along with many of the robes which were to be burnt on it, and food and drink as well. The

---

[22] Herodotos tells a similar story about Sesostris (2.108), who effected his escape from a burning building, not with the bodies of asses, but with two of his own sons.

[23] For a discussion of the color of ghosts, see Winkler (1980: 160–65).

party of Rhodanes feasts on these and takes some clothes too, and sleeps that night in the maiden's tomb.

[75a8] When day comes, the soldiers who had set fire to the brigand's house realize that they have been deceived and follow the tracks of Rhodanes and Sinonis, supposing them to be the brigand's accomplices. Following their trail to the tomb and seeing them lying inside, but motionless in the bonds of sleep and wine, they presume them dead and leave them there, puzzled, however, that the tracks led to that place.

[75a16] The party of Rhodanes leaves that place and crosses a river whose waters are sweet and crystal clear and reserved for the king of the Babylonians to drink. Sinonis sells the garments and is arrested as a tomb-robber and is remanded to Soraichos, the son of Soraichos the tax-collector, who is surnamed the Just. He plans to send her to King Garmos on account of her beauty, and this leads to the mixing of the brothers' poison for Rhodanes and Sinonis, for they would choose rather to die than to see Garmos. Soraichos is informed by a servant of the deed that Rhodanes and Sinonis intend and he secretly empties out the drug of death and fills the cup with a somniferous drug.[24] And once they have drunk and fallen into a deep sleep, he places them on a covered carriage and drives to the king.

[75a30] As they are drawing near, Rhodanes takes fright from a dream and cries out and wakes Sinonis. She wounds herself in the breast with a sword.[25] Soraichos enquires about their entire story, and they accept his guarantees and tell him, and he releases them. He shows them the temple of Aphrodite on the island, in which Sinonis would be cured of her wound.

[75a36] As a digression, the story is told of the temple and the island: how the Euphrates and the Tigris run on either side and so make it an island, and how the priestess of Aphrodite there had three children—Euphrates and Tigris, and Mesopotamia, who was ugly to look at from birth but was transformed by Aphrodite into a beauty. For her sake there was a contest of three lovers and a judgment in the case. The judge was Bokchoris,[26] and of all the judges in those days he was the best. The three lovers competed and submitted to judgment because to one of them Mesopotamia had given the cup from which she drank, to another she had taken the garland of flowers from her head and placed it on him, and the third she had kissed. The one who had been kissed won the judgment, but their strife nonetheless rose to a pitch until they killed each other. He tells this, then, as a digression

---

[24] XE 3.6–8; Plutarch *De sollertia anim.* §§ 973e–974a (the Canine Mime).

[25] The summary gives the impression that her wound is an accident, due to the confusion of waking up suddenly, but she reminds Soraichos in Frag. 61 that it was a courageous and deliberate act, an almost successful suicide.

[26] His reputation for wisdom was legendary among the Greeks: see, e.g., DS 1.65.

about Aphrodite's temple, and how women who visit there must publicly announce the dreams that they have in the temple.

[75b11] In this digression the tales of Pharnouchos and Pharsiris and Tanais,[27] after whom the river Tanais is named, are minutely related, and also it is explained that the mysteries of Aphrodite for those who dwell around the region and countryside of the Tanais are mysteries of Tanais and Pharsiris.

[75b16] On the aforementioned island, Tigris eats a rose and dies, for a blister beetle lurked in the folded petals of the rose.[28] The boy's mother performs a magic ceremony and is convinced that he has become a hero. And Iamblichos goes through various types of skills of the *magos*—the *magos* who works with locusts and the *magos* of lions and the *magos* of mice, which is where the word "mystery" takes its name, from "mouse,"[29] for mouse-magic was the original type—and he says there is a *magos* of hail and a *magos* of serpents and of necromancy and a ventriloquist, whom (as he says) the Greeks call Eurykles[30] and the Babylonians Sacchouras.

[75b27] The writer says that he himself is a Babylonian and has learned magic, that he also had a Greek education, and that he flourished under Sohaimos the Achaimenid and Arsakid, a king from a line of kings, and who became a member of the Senate at Rome and then a consul and then a king again of Greater Armenia. This was the period in which he says he lived. He expressly states that Antoninus was ruling the Romans. And when Antoninus (he says) sent the emperor Verus, his brother and kinsman, to make war on Vologaeses the Parthian, he himself foretold that the war would occur and how it would end. And he tells how Vologaeses fled beyond the Euphrates and Tigris and how the land of the Parthians became subject to Rome.

[75b41] But the two youngsters Tigris and Euphrates resembled each other, and Rhodanes resembled both of them. After the one son, as we said, died from the rose, Rhodanes journeyed to the island with Sinonis. And when their mother saw Rhodanes, she cried out that her dead son had returned to life and that the Maiden had come with him. Rhodanes plays along with this, taking advantage of the naivete of the islanders.

[76a7] Damas is informed about Rhodanes' situation and about all that Soraichos had done for them. The informer is the very physician whom

---

[27] Or perhaps Tanaitis, as Merkelbach suggests (in Habrich).

[28] Trencsényi-Waldapfel 1969: 512–17.

[29] μῦς, "mouse"; μυστήριον, "mystery." The pun also occurred in the tragedies of Dionysios, tyrant of Sicily, who called mouse holes "mysteries" because they protect mice, τοὺς μῦς τηρεῖ (*TGrF* 1: 76 F12 = Ath. 3.98d).

[30] Eurykles was a famous ventriloquist; cf. Plato *Sophist* §252c, Aristophanes *Wasps* 1019 (and scholium), and Plut. *De. def. orac.* §414e.

Soraichos secretly sent to cure the wound of Sinonis. For this reason Soraichos is arrested and brought to Garmos. The informer himself is commissioned to take a letter of Damas to the priest of Aphrodite, with orders to arrest the party of Sinonis. The doctor tries to cross the river in the customary way, tying himself fast to the holy camel and placing the letter in its right ear. But in the end the informer is drowned in the river, the camel crosses over to the island, and the party of Rhodanes recovers the letter from the camel's ear and learns everything.

[76a20] So they flee from there and they encounter Soraichos being led to Garmos: they put up at the same inn. At night Rhodanes persuades [some people] through their desire for gold and the guards of Soraichos are killed. Soraichos flees with them, thus rewarded for his previous benefaction to them. Damas arrests the priest of Aphrodite and interrogates him about Sinonis. The result is that the old man is condemned to be a public executioner instead of a priest. Then follows a description of the character and lifestyle of a public executioner.

[76a29] Next Euphrates is arrested because his father the priest thinks he is actually Rhodanes and accuses him. But his sister Mesopotamia escapes. Euphrates is led to Sakas and interrogated about Sinonis, in the belief that he is Rhodanes. Sakas sends a message to Garmos that Rhodanes has been captured and Sinonis soon will be. For Euphrates, when on trial as Rhodanes, said that at the time he was arrested Sinonis had fled, being forced by circumstances to identify his sister Mesopotamia as Sinonis.

[76a40] Then the party of Rhodanes and Sinonis, escaping with Soraichos, lodge at the house of a farmer. He has a young daughter, beautiful of face, who has been recently widowed and in devotion to her husband has cut her hair. She is sent to sell some of the golden chain that the party of Rhodanes has kept from its bondage. The farmer's daughter goes off to the goldsmith. When he sees how beautiful she is and recognizes the segment of chain that he himself had fashioned and notes that her hair is shorn, he suspects that she is Sinonis and sends word to Damas and follows her secretly with some guards when she leaves. But she suspects him and takes up refuge in a deserted lodging.

[76b10] Here we have the adventures of the maiden known as Trophime and the slave who is her lover and murderer, and the golden ornament, and the slave's extralegal activities, and his suicide, and the blood splattering on the farmer's daughter when he did away with himself, and the maiden's fright and flight, and the guards' terror and flight, and the maiden's arrival back at her father's, and her account of the adventures, and the flight from there of the party of Rhodanes, and before that the letter of the goldsmith to Garmos saying that he had found Sinonis, the warrant whereof was the enclosed section of chain that they had sold to him and the rest of his suspicions about the farmer's daughter.

[76b22] Rhodanes on leaving for his escape kisses the farmer's daughter and Sinonis flares up in anger. At first she comes to suspect the kiss, and then, when she wipes from his lips the blood that had been smeared on him when he kissed her, her suspicions are confirmed. Sinonis therefore seeks to kill the girl: she violently turned on her like a madwoman. Soraichos then followed her, since he was unable to restrain her maniacal energy.

[76b31] They lodge at the house of a rich man of dissolute character, whose name is Setapos. He falls in love with Sinonis and presses his suit. She pretends to love him in return, and on that very night at the beginning of their lovemaking when Setapos is quite drunk, she kills him with a sword. She asked that the courtyard door be opened and, leaving Soraichos behind in ignorance of her deed, she hastened towards the farmer's daughter. When Soraichos learned that she had left, he pursued her and caught up with her, accompanied by some of Setapos's servants whom he had hired to help him prevent the murder of the farmer's daughter. Apprehending her, he puts her on the wagon (which he had brought along for this purpose) and drives back. But as they were returning, Setapos's men met them, enraged from seeing their master slain, and they arrested Sinonis and bound her and led her to Garmos as a murderess to be punished.

[77a5] Soraichos is the bearer of these bad tidings to Rhodanes, having sprinkled his head with dust and having torn his burnoose (*kandus*). Rhodanes tries to kill himself, but Soraichos prevented him. When Garmos received the letter of Sakas saying that Rhodanes had been captured and the letter of the goldsmith saying that Sinonis was in custody, he rejoiced and conducted a sacrifice and made preparations for his wedding. He published an announcement to all parts of the land that all prisoners were to be released and let go. Sinonis, who is being led a prisoner by the men of Setapos, is released according to the general proclamation and let go.

[77a14] Garmos orders Damas to be put to death, and he is placed in the charge of the executioner whom he himself had forced to be executioner instead of priest. Garmos was angry with Damas because Rhodanes (or so he thought) and Sinonis had been arrested by others. Damas's brother Monasos succeeds to his place.

[77a20] A digression about Berenike,[31] daughter of the king of Egypt, and about her seething, unnatural passion; and how she consorted with Mesopo-

---

[31] Berenike was the name borne by a number of Ptolemaic Egyptian queens, to one of whom Kallimachos addressed a poem, which was subsequently imitated by Catullus. A number could be called "daughter of the king of Egypt"—the daughter of Ptolemy II, the daughter of Ptolemy Soter II, and the daughter of Ptolemy XI Auletes. All of these women were involved in intrigue and political coups, and given the proclivity of the Ptolemies for brother-sister marriage, any one might be regarded as engaging in outré sexual practices. See Macurdy 1932.

tamia; and how afterwards Mesopotamia was arrested by Sakas and led to Garmos along with her brother Euphrates.

[77a24] Garmos receives a letter from the goldsmith saying that Sinonis has escaped. He orders the goldsmith to be slain and the men who were sent to guard and escort her to be buried alive with their wives and children.

[77a29] Rhodanes' Hyrkanian dog[32] discovers in that accursed inn the bodies of the unfortunate maiden and the murderous, lovelorn slave. The dog first eats the slave's body and then, bit by bit, the girl's too.[33] Sinonis's father arrives and, recognizing the dog as Rhodanes' and seeing the half-eaten maiden he slaughters the dog, as if to avenge Sinonis, and hangs himself in a noose, after burying what remained of the maiden and inscribing with the dog's blood: "Here lies Sinonis the fair." Soraichos and Rhodanes arrive at that place and, seeing the dog slaughtered on the grave and Sinonis's father hanging, and the inscription, Rhodanes strikes a first blow against himself and writes with his own blood after Sinonis' inscription, "and Rhodanes the fair." Soraichos hangs himself in a noose. Just as Rhodanes was beginning to strike the final blow, the farmer's daughter arrived and cried out, "The dead woman, O Rhodanes, is not Sinonis." And running up she cuts Soraichos's noose and takes the sword from Rhodanes and persuades them finally by telling the adventure of the unfortunate girl and about the buried gold[34] and how she was coming to recover this.

[77b9] Sinonis, released from arrest, ran to the farmer's house, still furious against the daughter. Not finding her she asked the father and he pointed down the road. She followed that direction with her sword drawn. When she came upon Rhodanes lying helpless and the daughter sitting with him alone and nursing his chest wound—for Soraichos had gone off in search of a doctor—she is filled with even greater rage and jealousy and rushes at the woman. Rhodanes, at the prospect of violence, overcame his weakness and blocked her and took the sword away from her. She is furious and leaps out of the inn, running away wildly, and flinging over her shoulder the words, "I invite you to Garmos's wedding, today!" Soraichos arrives and learns all and consoles Rhodanes. After nursing his wound they send the daughter back to her father with the goods.[35]

---

[32] Hyrkanian dogs were noted for their fierceness (Ail. *Na* 7.38, Lucr. 3.750). Cicero (*Tusc. disp.* 1.45.108) connects them with a burial practice involving mutilation of the dead by dogs, mentioned also in Herodotos (1.140).

[33] In the Coptic Acts of Andrew and Paul, a mother butchers her newborn infant and gives it to a dog to eat to conceal her crime. The dog tells Andrew what happened and the child is (regurgitated and?) resurrected (see James 1963: 473).

[34] The golden ornament (76b12).

[35] Presumably the golden ornament of Trophime, buried in the inn, which the farmer's daughter had returned to get.

[77b27] Euphrates, thought to be Rhodanes, and Mesopotamia, thought to be Sinonis, have been led to Garmos. Now Soraichos and the real Rhodanes are brought in too. Garmos recognizes that Mesopotamia is not Sinonis and gives her to Zobaras to have her beheaded by the river Euphrates, saying, "So that no other woman will take on herself the name Sinonis." Zobaras, having drunk deep from the wellspring of passion[36] and falling in love with Mesopotamia, rescues her. He departs to Berenike, who is now queen of Egypt after her father's death, and takes Mesopotamia with him. Berenike celebrates Mesopotamia's marriage,[37] and because of Mesopotamia war is threatened between Garmos and Berenike.

[77b38] Euphrates is handed over to the executioner, who is actually his father, and he is recognized and saved. Then he himself performs his father's office—so the father is not defiled by human blood[38]—and later, in the guise of the executioner's daughter, he leaves the building and is safe.[39] At this point we also hear about the woman who slept with the executioner (the customs and habits in regard to her) and how the farmer's daughter was dragged away when Sinonis, now married to the king of Syria, had the power to fulfill her anger against her, and how she condemned her to sleep with the executioner.[40] Actually, when she went to the executioners' compound, she slept with Euphrates,[41] and he pretended to be her and left the compound. She, in Euphrates' place, performed the duties of the executioner.

[78a10] And that was the point to which things had advanced. Soraichos, too, was handed over for crucifixion. The place selected for the execution is the very one where Rhodanes and Sinonis first encamped, in the meadow and at the spring where the hidden treasure was discovered by Rhodanes, who tells Soraichos about it as he is being led away to crucifixion. And it so happens that an army of unpaid and disgruntled Alanoi, mercenaries for King Garmos, are encamped in the region where Soraichos is about to be

---

[36] It is not clear from the Greek whether this is meant as a metaphor or a real spring connected with the island of Aphrodite.

[37] Though the veil of Photios's language makes certainty impossible, it appears that Berenike, like Zobaras, is in love with Mesopotamia. At 77a20–23, he mentions Berenike's "seething, unnatural passion, and how she consorted with Mesopotamia."

[38] Presumably the execution of Damas.

[39] For men escaping from prison in women's clothing, see AT 6.1–2, Polyainos 8.34.

[40] Maidens who are condemned to sexual servitude but manage to preserve themselves include Antheia (Xenophon of Ephesos), Tarsia (*HA*), and Trophima (Acts of Andrew 23 in James 1963: 345), who is sent to a brothel by her lover's wife and protects herself from lustful clients by the gospel she wears on her bosom.

[41] The executioner turned lover is another interesting variant on the sympathetic executioner (XE 4.6.4–7, *HA* § 31) as well as on the lover turned executioner (Pausanias 7.21.1).

crucified. They drive off Soraichos's captors and liberate him. He finds the treasure, drawing it up from the pit by a certain clever trick, and convinces the Alanoi that he knows this and other things from the gods.

[78a22] Little by little he maneuvers them into the habit of treating him as their king. Then he makes war on Garmos and wins. But all this happened later.

[78a24] When Soraichos was being led to the cross, at the very same time Rhodanes was being brought again to the same cross he had been tied to before, and Garmos is garlanded and dancing, drunk and delirious with joy, dancing around the cross with his flutegirls. While this is going on, Sakas sends a letter to Garmos saying that Sinonis is about to be married to the king of the Syrians, a young man. Rhodanes up on the cross is delighted; Garmos tries to kill himself. But halting, he has Rhodanes—who is unwilling, for he chose rather to die—brought down from the cross and outfits him as a general and sends him to lead the war that he has declared against the Syrian king, so that lover and rival will fight it out. He treats him with favor that conceals evil in sending a private letter to the lieutenants with instructions that if they win and Sinonis is captured, Rhodanes is to be killed.

[78a39] Rhodanes in fact wins the battle and recovers Sinonis and becomes king of the Babylonians. This had been prophesied by a swallow: for in the presence of Garmos, when he was sending Rhodanes off to the war, an eagle and a kite were chasing the swallow.[42] She eluded the eagle but the kite caught up with her. Thus ends the sixteenth book.

---

[42] If the name Sinonis is derived from Akkadian *sinuntu*, Aramaic *senunit*, meaning "swallow" (Schneider-Menzel 1948: 79–80), then the bird sign is very appropriate. Garmos the king is the eagle, Rhodanes the kite. In Babylonian divination, the eagle has royal associations similar to those it had in Greece; the swallow, which does not particularly figure in Greek omenry, was also significant, usually for where it built its nest: Hunger 1909: 37–39, 40–42. We are indebted to C. Faraone for the reference.

FRAGMENTS ASSIGNABLE TO SECTIONS OF
PHOTIOS'S *EPITOME*

[74a4]

[74a9]
τὴν γενομένην ἀπόρρησιν τοῦ γάμου
(Fragment 2 = *Souda* 1.316.3, s.v. ἀπόρρησιν)

"ἀλλὰ καὶ τῶν Cινωνίδος γάμων προθυσάσθω καὶ προτέλεια τοῦ
μοιχοῦ ὁ ἀνὴρ γενέσθω"
(Fragment 3 = *Souda* 4.237.19, s.v. προτέλειον)

ὅταν ὁ ἔρως ζηλοτυπίαν προσλάβῃ, τύραννος ἐκ βασιλέως γίνεται
(Fragment 4 = codd. laur. 57,12 and Vat. 1354)

ἡ δὲ ἐπὶ τὸ τέγος ἀναβᾶσα ταχέως, ἅτε τῆς ἐπιβάθρας ἐμπείρως ἔχουσα
(Fragment 5 = *Souda* 2.348.29, s.v. ἐπιβάθρας)

πρώτη δὲ ἤδη ἀπέβη, οἱονεὶ ἐπιβάθραν αὐτῷ κατασκευάζουσα καὶ
κατακόλπισιν
(Fragment 6 = *Souda* 2.348.25, s.v. ἐπιβάθρα)

τὴν κεφαλὴν αὐτοῦ ἄξειν, καὶ ὅσοι κοινῶνες αὐτῷ τῆς φυγῆς ἐγένοντο
(Fragment 7 = *Souda* 3.202.10, s.v. κοινῶνας; see Borgogno 1975a: 113)

[74a17]
"ἔναγχος οὖν ποιμέσι τισὶν ὀψοποιουμένοις ἰχθῦς ἀπεδόμην"
(Fragment 8 = *Souda* 3.602.28, s.v. ὀψοποιουμένοις)

[Although most scholars would now locate the excerpt entitled "concerning the Procession of the King of the Babylonians" contained in two manuscripts (Laurentianus 57,12 and Vaticanus 1354) at the beginning of the novel, its position is by no means certain. We have translated below.]

The actual refusal of marriage

"But let him be the preliminary sacrifice for Sinonis's marriage; let the husband become the ceremonial offering for the adulterer."[43]

Whenever jealousy is added to *erōs*, a king turns into a tyrant.

She quickly made her way up to the roof, since she was familiar with the stairways.

At this point she was the first to retreat, as if to prepare for him a stairway and a harboring place.[44]

Would bring his head, and those of all who became commonsharers of his flight.

"Just lately I sold fish to some shepherds who were fixing a fancy meal."

[43] If this is spoken by Garmos of Rhodanes' crucifixion at this point in the novel, his reference to himself as an adulterer is ironic. Possibly Rhodanes is speaking of himself in the third person (as Sinonis does in Fragment 61). Schneider-Menzel (1948: 68) and Borgogno (1975a: 111) would place this fragment in the second crucifixion of Rhodanes, toward the end of the novel.

[44] "Stairway" may be used here, like "harboring place," in its metaphorical sense of "a means of progress to the next stage": LSJ, s.v. ἐπιβάθρα 2.

Ἰάμβλιχος· ὄντας ὡραίους καὶ καλοὺς τοὺς παῖδας ὁ πατὴρ ὑπεξέπεμψεν εἰς τοὺς ποιμένας φοβούμενος τύραννον ὑβριςτήν
(Fragment 90 = *Souda* 4.649.6, s.v. ὑπεξέπεμψεν)

ὁ δὲ ἐμφερεῖς παῖδας τοῖς ἐπιζητηθεῖςι κοςμήςας ὑπὸ πεπλαςμένης
τιμῆς καὶ ςηρικῆς ἐςθῆτος
(Fragment 92 = *Souda* 2.265.28, s.v. ἐμφερεῖς)

Ἰάμβλιχος· ἐπειδὴ διακωδωνίζων ἕκαςτον τῶν ποιμένων οὐχ οἷός τε
ἦν ἀκοῦςαι καὶ μαθεῖν, οἵτινες ἦςαν οἱ παῖδες
(Fragment 91 = *Souda* 2.60.26, s.v. διακωδωνίςω)

ὁ δὲ ἕτερος ταῦρος ἐμυκήςατο, κακὸν φώνημα Γάρμῳ· καὶ ἔδοξε
τράγος εἶναι, μὴ ταῦρος ἐκεῖνο τὸ φάςμα
(Fragment 9 = *Souda* 4.703.20, s.v. φάςμα; 1.509.4, s.v. Γάρμος)

ὁ δὲ τράγος ἐκ τοῦ φρέατος ἀπεπήδηςε τὸ αὐτὸ φωνήςας εὐά
(Fragment 10 = *Souda* 2.439.18, s.v. εὐά)

[Borgogno (1975a: 115) suggests this as one possible site for Fragment 18 (see below, 74b9).]

[74a27]
ὁ δὲ διῆγεν αὐτοὺς ἐπί τι ὄρυγμα, ὃ διαμπερὲς μὲν ἦν ὀρωρυγμένον ἐπὶ
ςταδίους λ′, εἶχε δὲ ἔξοδον ἐπὶ θάτερα τοῦ ὀρύγματος
(Fragment 11 = *Souda* 2.67.1, s.v. διαμπερές)

Iamblichos. Since they were beautiful and in their youthful prime, their father secretly sent the youngsters to the shepherds, fearing a tyrant who was insolent.[45]

He, adorning in false grandeur and silk clothing youngsters who resembled the ones being pursued[46]

Iamblichos. After sounding each of the shepherds he was unable to hear and learn the identity of the youngsters.[47]

And the other bull bellowed, an ill sound for Garmos; and that apparition seemed to be a billy goat, not a bull.

The billy goat leaped out of the well, uttering the same "εὐά."[48]

He led them to a tunnel, which had been dug straight through to a depth of thirty stades and which had an exit on the opposite end of the tunnel.[49]

[45] This fragment cannot, of course, be spoken by the same narrator of the main characters, who do not have the same father and are not secretly sent to the shepherds, and whose beauty would not be described at this point in the novel (Bruhn 1890: 280). But the sentence could be uttered by a character such as the fisherman, who was falsely told such a story by Rhodanes and Sinonis themselves (Borgogno 1975a: 114–15), or (with emendation) by one of the shepherds who is attempting to mislead Damas (Di Gregorio 1963: 394). Unmarried persons in their late teens can still be called παῖδες, "youngsters." The lie apparently represents the lovers as brother and sister, as in Hld. 1.21.3.

[46] Perhaps part of the same misleading story as the preceding fragment (Di Gregorio 1963: 394). Borgogno (1975a: 115) suggests that the story or lie contains a switch: the father is a wealthy man who saves his son and daughter from the unwelcome attentions of the tyrant (Fragment 90) by disguising them in poor clothing and sending them to the countryside to stay with shepherds; he substitutes two similar-looking youngsters, dressing them in the fine clothing of his own offspring.

[47] Either said of the fisherman, who has noticed the handsome couple and is fishing for useful information, or of Damas, who knows that the shepherds have helped two youngsters and wants to verify that they are indeed Rhodanes and Sinonis.

[48] It seems that Sinonis has a nightmare, as Rhodanes does later (75a31), which symbolizes her situation, since Garmos figures in it. Perhaps the two bulls, one of which looks like a billy goat, represent Garmos and the king of Syria, both of whom are rivals of Rhodanes for the hand of Sinonis. Garmos later sends Rhodanes to fight against the king of Syria, "as lover against rival" (78a36).

[49] Schneider-Menzel (1948: 58) notes the possibility that the old woman handed the fugitives over to someone else; Habrich (1960) emends to "she" (ἡ δὲ), observing that when the soldiers later arrive, they interrogate only the old woman.

"ἆρά γε ὀρθῶϲ ζῶμεν καὶ ὑπὸ φωτὶ δέ, ἢ ἐν ἀϲελήνῳ καὶ ἀνάϲτρῳ πλέομεν;"
(Fragment 12 = *Souda* 1.189.20, s.v. ἀνάϲτρῳ)

πῦρ δὲ αὐτοῖϲ ὑπέφαινεν ἡ Ϲινωνὶϲ καὶ περιηγεῖτο
(Fragment 13 = *Souda* 4.98.19, s.v. περιηγεῖτο)

[74a40]
τῶν δὲ περιπόλων τιϲ περιθέων ἀποβάλλει χαλκῆν ἀϲπίδα ὕπερθεν τοῦ ὀρύγματοϲ· ἡ δὲ οὖϲα μὴ πλατεῖα, ἀλλὰ κυρτή, οὐ ϲτερεὸν ἐκτύπηϲεν, ἀλλὰ κοῖλον καὶ διάκενον
(Fragment 14 = *Souda* 4.106.28, s.v. περιπόλων)

αἱ δὲ μέλιτται ἐμπεφωλεύκειϲαν ὥϲπερ ἐν κυψέλη τῷ φωλεῷ· τὸ μέλι δὲ ἐλείβετο κατὰ τῶν κεφαλῶν
(Fragment 15 = *Souda* 3.223.18, s.v. κυψέλη)

τὸ δὲ μέλι, ἄτε οὐκ ἀκέραιον
(Fragment 16 = *Souda* 1.78.22, s.v. ἀκέραιοϲ)

[74b5]
ἀπεκείρατο τὴν κόμην· ἦν δὲ πολλὴ καὶ ξανθὴ καὶ βαθεῖα
(Fragment 17 = *Souda* 1.447.13, s.v. βαθεῖα κόμη)

"Are we truly alive and neath the light? Or do we sail in a moonless and starless night?"[50]

Sinonis revealed the fire and began to lead them about.[51]

One of the sentries, running about, drops his bronze shield above the tunnel; since it was not flat but convex, it did not thud firmly but sounded hollow and empty.[52]

The bees had lain in the lair as if in a hive; and the honey was dripping onto their heads.[53]

The honey, inasmuch as it was impure and not from thistles but from serpents drawn, upset their entrails.

She cut her hair: it was thick and blond and long.

[50] In the pitch darkness of the cave, they compare their experience first to that of shades in the Underworld, then to that of sailors in a fog-bound night. ὑπό with the dative is poetic, as is the entire expression; compare, "He lives and sees the light of the sun," *Il.* 18.61. Bruhn (1890: 282) prefers to locate this fragment at Photios 74b17, when Rhodanes is just waking up from the poisoned honey.

[51] Against earlier editors who had placed this fragment in the cave scene, Di Gregorio (1963: 395) wonders where Sinonis got the fire and who are the "them." He prefers to see it as Sinonis's pretending to be a ghost after the fiery destruction of the brigand's house. Sinonis faces the soldiers and points to the fire. It is possible to answer Di Gregorio's objections by translating, "Sinonis exposed some of the flame [i.e., in a lamp she was carrying] for themselves and began to lead the way around." This requires reading ἑαυτοῖς for αὐτοῖς, as at Photios 74b10, "She drew up water for themselves," also in the cave scene. Sinonis apparently also carries a bucket, with which she draws up that water (74b10). Borgogno (1975a: 119) wonders how she can act as a guide when she is not familiar with the cave, but she simply leads the way because she is holding the lamp. Neither location is entirely satisfactory.

[52] The *Souda* reads κοῖλον καὶ διάκοιλον. τάχα διάκενον, "Hollow and quite hollow. Perhaps quite empty." The last words are some scholar-copyist's correction of the very odd repetition of κοιλ-. A more difficult textual problem is οὖcα μέν, for which editors have suggested οὖcα μή (Hemsterhuis), οὖcα μὲν οὐ (Hercher 1858–59, 1: 33), and οὐκ οὖcα μέν (Küster). The sentry accidentally uses the traditional device for detecting the movement of sappers digging under city walls: a bronze shield magnifies the underground sounds (Hdt. 4.200; Plut. *De gen. Soc.* §589d; Aeneas Tact. 36.6–7).

[53] The word order ὥσπερ + comparison + compared is common in the novelists and other prose writers: Ch. 7.5.6, 6.18.3; Hld. 1.29.3, 1.30.7; Plut. *An seni resp.* §785b, §790c, §791e. An early poetic example is Euripides *Kyklops* 433.

ὡc ἂν θηρώcηc κόρηc καὶ θυραυλούcηc, τρεφομένη μὲν ὄμβροιc, τινιαccομένη δὲ ἀνέμοιc κόμη πολλὴ ἦν καὶ βαθεῖα
(Fragment 17 = *Souda* 2.739.6, s.v. θυραυλεῖν)

[74b9]

αὐτὸc δὲ πάλιν ἐκουφίζετο καὶ τὸν Δάμαν ἐπῄνει καὶ προὔπινεν αὐτῷ καὶ μεcτὸc ἦν ἐλπίδων ἐρωτικῶν
(Fragment 18 = *Souda* 4.240.24, s.v. προὔπινεν αὐτῷ)

[74b12]

οἱ δὲ cτρατιῶται ἐλθόντεc cκοταῖοι εἶδον τὰ cώματα, καὶ νόμῳ τῶν Βαβυλωνίων ἐπέρριψαν αὐτοῖc ὁ μὲν κάνδυν, ὁ δὲ χλαμύδα, ὁ δὲ ψωμούc, ὁ δὲ ἀκρόδρυα· καὶ μέγα κεφάλαιον ἠθροίcθη μικρῶν κερματίων
(Fragment 19 = *Souda* 4.386.26, s.v. cκοταῖοc ἐλθών; also in 1.92.12, s.v. ἀκρόδρυα; 3.101.19, s.v. κερματίζει; and 3.104.12, s.v. κεφαλαῖον)

[74b17]

οἱ δὲ κόρακεc περιιπτάμενοι ἄνω καὶ κάτω, θορυβούμενοι καὶ κεκραγότεc μετὰ πολλῆc ἀcελγείαc, οἷον οἱ κόρακεc λαρυγγίζουcι
(Fragment 20 = *Souda* 3.236.3, s.v. λαρυγγίζειν)

206

Since she was a maiden who hunted and spent time outdoors, her hair, nurtured by showers and brushed out by winds, was thick and long.[54]

He for his part became lighthearted once more, and he praised Damas and toasted him and was full of erotic hopes.[55]

The soldiers coming in the darkness saw the bodies and, following the custom of the Babylonians, threw down various items for them—one a burnoose, one a cloak, one chunks of food, one fruits; and a great summation was aggregated from small fragments.[56]

Fluttering around, up and down, the crows, noisily complaining and squawking with brassy insolence—as crows do[57]—utter hoarse, throat-splitting cries.

---

[54] Habrich, following Rohde (1974: 367 n. 4) and Hercher (1858–59, 1: 33), combines these two quotations from the *Souda* to produce a single fragment. Schneider-Menzel (1948: 64 n. 49) and Borgogno (1975a: 123) see the two quotations as separate descriptions of Sinonis and the farmer's daughter but disagree about which describes whom. Both characters do cut their hair short, which leads to one being mistaken for the other. The former quotation, if it is from Iamblichos, would be apt to describe the locks that are both used as a makeshift rope to draw up water and sent as a present to Garmos. The second quotation is less appropriate to Sinonis, since she seems not to be an outdoors type. It also contains a hiatus (πολλὴ ἦν), which is avoided in the former quote (ἦν δὲ πολλή) and ought not to have been accepted in Habrich's text. But is the farmer's daughter a huntress? Furthermore, she is a recent widow, not a maiden (κόρη), even though Photios calls her a κόρη θυγάτηρ, "maiden daughter," in relation to her father at 76a42. There is nothing distinctively Iamblichan about the subject matter, which could well describe an Amazonian heroine like Daphne (Parthenios 15), perhaps reported by another of the *Souda*'s favorite authors, such as Ailian.

[55] Damas need not be present at the court for the king to toast him (Habrich 1960: 17). Schneider-Menzel (1948) locates this fragment at Photios 76a10, where Damas sends information to the king through the physician. Borgogno (1975a: 115, 124) suggests other possible locations for it; see above, 74a17, and below, 76a7.

[56] There is no need to take κερματίων as "coins" (Borgogno 1975a: 125–26). Babylonians held that ghosts of the unburied would haunt those who saw an unburied corpse without at least giving it funeral gifts. The case of a corpse lying "on the steppe" or "by the highway" is actually mentioned in some incantations. (See Thompson 1971: 24–27. We are grateful to C. Faraone for this observation and the reference.)

[57] "Like crows," οἷον οἱ κόρακες, is not a simile but a factual comment, "wie Raben schreien" (Schneider-Menzel 1948: 59–60).

περιδεεῖς δὲ ἦςαν ὡς ἐν ἐρημίᾳ τά τε ἄλλα καὶ ἄφιπποι γενόμενοι
(Fragment 21 = *Souda* 1.431.25, s.v. ἄφιπποι; see Bruhn 1890: 283)

[74b24]

ὁρῶν δὲ τὸν ἀδελφὸν πάντα δυςωπούμενον καὶ οὐδὲν ὅ τι τῶν ὄψων
οὐχ ὑφορώμενον
(Fragment 22 = *Souda* 2.152.7, s.v. δυςωπεῖςθαι)

εἶχε δὲ ἐν τῇ ζώνῃ ληκύθιον παρηρτημένον, ἐν ᾧ τὸ φάρμακον ἦν τὸ
θανάςιμον
(Fragment 23 = *Souda* 3.262.5, s.v. ληκύθιον)

[75a8]

εὖρον δὲ τὴν θύραν τοῦ μνήματος ἀραιῶς ἐπικειμένην
(Fragment 24 = *Souda* 1.344.7, s.v. ἀραιῶς)

ὁρῶςιν ἐν τῇ λάρνακι ςώματα ἀλλήλοιν περικείμενα
(Fragment 25 = *Souda* 1.110.3, s.v. ἀλλήλοιν)

οἱ δὲ ἀνακλῖναι μὲν τὴν θύραν οὐκ ἐτόλμηςαν οὐδ᾽ εἴςω παρελθεῖν
ἴςχυςαν
(Fragment 26 = *Souda* 1.170.27, s.v. ἀνακλῖναι; wrongly attributed to
Herodotos)

οὐκ ἔξεςτι γὰρ Βαβυλωνίοις ἀωρίᾳ τάφον ὑπερβῆναι
(Fragment 27 = *Souda* 1.257.23, s.v. ἀωρίαι)

[75a16]

οἱ δὲ ἐπορεύοντο τὴν αὐτὴν τῷ ποταμῷ διὰ τῆς κυματωγῆς βρέχοντες
τοὺς πόδας, ὅπου μηδὲ ἴχνος ἔμελλε ςυμβαίνειν
(Fragment 28 = *Souda* 3.211.11, s.v. κυματωγή)

ἦν γὰρ ἐνταφίων πωλητής
(Fragment 29 = *Souda* 4.184.12, s.v. πωλητής; cf. Petronius *Sat.* §§ 12–16)

They were very frightened inasmuch as they were in a deserted place and particularly because they were horseless.

Seeing that his brother was extremely upset and was casting suspicious looks on each of the dishes[58]

He had a little vial hanging on his cincture, in which was the fatal poison.[59]

They found the door of the tomb not firmly closed.

They see in the coffin bodies lying entangled.[60]

They did not have the courage to open the door wide nor the strength to pass within.

It is not allowed that Babylonians walk over a grave in the dead of night.

They were following the same course as the river, wetting their feet along its edge, where there would be no footprints.

For s/he was a merchant of grave-goods.

---

[58] Bruhn (1890: 280) detached this fragment from Ailian (frag. 182 Hercher) and added it here to Iamblichos, where it certainly fits. But, like Schneider-Menzel (1948: 60 n. 18) and Habrich (1960), we see no grounds for a confident decision.

[59] Schneider-Menzel (1948: 61) prefers to put this fragment at Photios 75a23, where Rhodanes and Sinonis plan to use the poison to kill themselves.

[60] The alternate reading, παρακείμενα "lying next to one another," would present a more decent picture.

Ἰάμβλιχος· ἀνὴρ ἐπιϲτάμενοϲ ἥκιϲτα ψεύδεϲθαι, φίλοϲ δὲ εἴπερ τιϲ ἄλλοϲ ἀληθείᾳ
(Fragment 30 = *Souda* 2.558.9, s.v. ἥκιϲτα)

ἥκιϲτα δ' ἄν τιϲ αὐτὸν ἐθεάϲατο παρεκβαίνοντα τὸ ἀληθὲϲ ἔργῳ ἢ λόγῳ ποτέ, ἤτοι πρὸϲ τὸ εἰρωνικώτερον ἢ ἀλαζονέϲτερον
(Fragment 31 = *Souda* 2.558.4, s.v. ἥκιϲτα + 2.534.21, s.v. εἴρων)

[75a30]
"ὄμνυμι τοὺϲ βαϲιλείουϲ θεούϲ· ἦ μὴν ἐγὼ ὑμᾶϲ ϲώϲω"
(Fragment 33 = *Souda* 2.569.9, s.v. ἦ μήν)

[75a36]
ὁ δὲ εἶπεν· "ἀλλὰ πιϲτεύω· πάνυ γάρ ϲου κλέοϲ ἐπ' ἀρετῇ διήκει"
(Fragment 32 = *Souda* 2.90.11, s.v. διήκει)

τὰ ἐνύπνια ὑπὸ μὲν τοῦ δαιμονίου πέμπεται, ὑπὸ δὲ τῆϲ ἑκάϲτου ψυχῆϲ τῶν ὁρώντων πλάττεται· καὶ τῆϲ μὲν φύϲεωϲ αὐτῶν ὁ θεόϲ ἐϲτι χορηγόϲ, τῆϲ δὲ ἰδέαϲ ἡμεῖϲ αὐτοὶ δημιουργοί
(Fragment 34 = codd. Laur. 57,12 and Vat. 1354)

[Here too belongs the long Fragment 35 (see below), concerning the man who brought his wife and slave to trial because she dreamed that she had sex with the slave. Conceivably that husband is the Pharnouchos who is mentioned in the next sentence.]

[75b41]
ἀντιλαμβανομένηϲ τῆϲ γυναικὸϲ καὶ βοώϲηϲ ὡϲ ἂν ὑπὲρ τηλικούτων
(Fragment 39 = *Souda* 3.624.23, s.v. ὡϲ ἂν ὑπὲρ τηλικούτων)

"ἤδη γάρ ϲε γινώϲκω, καὶ ὧν εἶπαϲ ἀκούϲαϲα καὶ τὴν ὄψιν ἰδοῦϲα"
(Fragment 40 = *Souda* 1.525.14, s.v. γινώϲκω)

οὐκέτι οὖν ἦν ἀμφιϲβητήϲιμα τὸ μὴ οὐ τοῦτον ἐκεῖνον εἶναι τὸν τεθνηκότα
(Fragment 41 = *Souda* 1.157.15, s.v. ἀμφιϲβητεῖν)

προϲιόντεϲ δὲ αὐτῷ ἐταινίαζον οἱ νηϲιῶται καὶ ἀνέδουν
(Fragment 42 = *Souda* 1.200.24, s.v. ἀνέδουν, and 4.514.14, s.v. ταινιοῦντοϲ)

Iamblichos: A man who least understood how to lie, and a friend if ever there was one of the truth.[61]

Least of all would one ever have seen him transgressing the truth in deed or word, in the direction either of irony or of exaggeration.[62]

"I swear by the royal gods—I shall in very truth save you."

He said, "But I trust you, for your reputation for excellence has spread far."[63]

Dreams are sent by the divine, but the soul of each individual dreamer shapes them. God is the principal patron of their nature,[64] but we ourselves are the fashioners of their form.

The woman tried to hold him and cried out, as on matters of great urgency.

"For now I recognize you, hearing your words and seeing your face."

There was no longer any doubt but that this was the one who had died.

The islanders came forward and headbanded and wreathed him.

[61] Without the *Souda*'s explicit attribution to Iamblichos, this fragment probably would not have found its way into the present dossier.

[62] This fragment combines two other fragments of similar tendency.

[63] There is not much that is distinctive about this fragment, which might also describe Soraichos the Just (Di Gregorio 1963: 396).

[64] God is the χορηγός, the sponsor behind the scenes—in modern theatrical language, the "angel."

[76a7]

οἱ δὲ ἀποπέμπουςι τὸν ἰατρὸν ἐπιθέντες γράμματα πρὸς τὸν τελώνην
(Fragment 45 = *Souda* 2.356.14, s.v. ἐπιθέντες)

"ἐθεραπεύθη δέ," ἔφη, "δαιμονίῳ τρόπῳ"
(Fragment 46 = *Souda* 2.12.22, s.v. δαιμονίως)

[Schneider-Menzel (1948: 63) and Borgogno (1975a: 124) see this
as a possible site for Fragment 18 (see above, 74a17 and 74b9).]

ἄρτι γὰρ αὐτῇ παρεβέβλητο τροφή {τουτέςτι τῇ καμήλῳ}
(Fragment 48 = *Souda* 4.48.6, s.v. παρεβέβλητο)

οὐδὲ γὰρ πρόςοιτο ἀναβάτην ἡ κάμηλος οὐδένα ὑπ᾽ αὐθαδείας καὶ
ἀςυνηθείας
(Fragment 49 = *Souda* 4.235.10, s.v. πρόςοιτο)

εἶδε φορτίον χλωρῶν ἀκανθῶν, ἃ καμήλοις ἐςτὶ φαγήματα· ἡ δὲ τὴν
κεφαλὴν καθῆκε
(Fragment 50 = *Souda* 4.691.17, s.v. φαγήματα)

ἡ μὲν κάμηλος ἐγεύετο τοῦ χιλοῦ, ὁ δὲ ἔπινε ποτὸν τοῦ ποταμοῦ
ἀκούςιος, καὶ ἅτε κάτωθεν τοῦ πνεύματος ὠθουμένου, ἄνωθεν δὲ τοῦ
ὕδατος ἐπιφερομένου, ἡ φάρυγξ ἐκελάρυζε, καὶ πολὺς ἐν τῷ ςτόματι
ἦν βορβορυγμός
(Fragment 51 = *Souda* 3.91.6, s.v. κελαρύζει, and 1.481.3, s.v. βορβορυγμός)

ἡ δὲ κάμηλος ὑφῆκε τὰ κῶλα καὶ ἑαυτὴν ἐκάθιςεν εἰς τὰ ςτέρνα
(Fragment 52 = *Souda* 3.171.11, s.v. κῶλα)

ὁ δὲ εὑρίςκει τὰ γεγραμμένα, καὶ ἐπιλεξάμενος ἐλέγχει τὸ πᾶν ὡς
ἐγένετο
(Fragment 53 = *Souda* 2.367.23, s.v. ἐπιλεξάμενος)

[76a20]

καὶ Ἰάμβλιχος· βιαζομένους δὲ τοὺς κολυμβητὰς ςυμψήςας ὁ ποταμὸς
ἔφερε κάτω, καὶ οὐκέτι ἀπενόςτηςαν
(Fragment 54 = *Souda* 4.462.19, s.v. ςυμψήςας)

ὁ δὲ ἱερεὺς ςκευὴν ἐςκευάζετο τὴν τοῦ δημίου, μεταλαβὼν ἀντὶ τῶν
ςεμνοτάτων τὰ οἴκτιςτα
(Fragment 55 = *Souda* 4.375.5, s.v. ςκευή)

They sent away the doctor, giving him letters to the tax-collector.

"And s/he was cured," he said, "in a divine manner."

For fodder had recently been put beside it [that is, the camel].

For the camel would not tolerate any rider, due to its independence and unfamiliarity.

It saw a load of green thistles, which are comestible for camels. It lowered its head.

The camel for its part was tasting the green fodder while he unwillingly drank in water from the river, and since his breath rushed up from below while the water weighed down from above, his pharynx gurgled and in his mouth there was a mighty belching.

The camel bent its legs and rested itself on its chest.

He finds the writing and after reading it exposes everything as it actually happened.

And Iamblichos: The river overpowered the divers, jumbled them together and carried them down—and they no longer came home.[65]

The priest outfitted himself in the garb of the public executioner, changing the most august for the most abject.

---

[65] Habrich refers this to policemen accompanying Damas to the island, Schneider-Menzel to companions of the doctor who is drowned earlier. In either case it would appear that we have to posit both a boat wreck (surely they would not swim to the island?) and an ironic reference to the people in the water as "divers."

[76b10]

Ἰάμβλιχος· ἐπεὶ δὲ τοῦτο χαλεπὸν ἦν καὶ cπάνιόν τι τῆc τε οἰκουροῦ φυλαττούcηc καὶ ἄβραc τινὸc ἄλληc cυμπαρούcηc, ἀναπείθει τὴν κόρην λαθοῦcαν τοὺc γονεῖc ἀποδρᾶναι
(Fragment 56 = *Souda* 1.9.14, s.v. ἄβρα)

ἀποcφαγεῖcαν γὰρ αὐτὴν ὑπὸ ἐραcτοῦ δυcέρωτοc
(Fragment 58 = *Souda* 2.149.12, s.v. δύcερωc)

Ἰάμβλιχος· "τὴν δὲ ἄλυcιν—οὐ γάρ ἐcτιν ἡμῖν ἀναγκαία—προcέπεμψά cοι"
(Fragment 59 = *Souda* 1.163.21, s.v. ἀναγκαία τράπεζα)

[76b22]

ὀξεῖc οἱ τῶν ἐρώντων λογιcμοὶ καὶ πρόχειροι ὑποπτεῦcαι, δεινοὶ δὲ εἰκάcαι, ἔνθεοι δὲ μαντεύcαcθαι
(Fragment 60 = codd. Laur. 57,12 and Vat. 1354

[The long Fragment 61, an excerpt from this portion of the *Babyloniaka*, copied in Vaticanus Graecus rescriptus 73, belongs here. It is printed below.]

[76b31]

ἐπείρα χρήματα πέμπων τῆc διαφθορᾶc δέλεαρ
(Fragment 64 = *Souda* 2.343.13, s.v. ἐπείρα)

πρὸc τὴν ἐπιπλοκὴν τῆc κόρηc ἔχαιρεν ἐκτόπωc
(Fragment 65 = *Souda* 2.234.21, s.v. ἐκτόπωc)

αὐτή γε μὴν κλεψιποτοῦcα καὶ cωφρονοῦcα
(Fragment 66 = *Souda* 3.130.4, s.v. κλεψιποτῶ)

ὁ δὲ παίεται κοπίδι τὴν κεφαλὴν ὡc οὐ βιωcόμενοc {εἶναι}
(Fragment 67 = *Souda* 3.155.9, s.v. κοπίc)

Iamblichos: Since this was a difficult and infrequent thing, while the housekeeper was keeping watch and another favorite maid-slave was present, he persuaded the maiden secretly to run away from her parents.

For she had been slain by an unhappy lover.[66]

Iamblichos: "The chain—since I have no compelling need of it—I have sent along to you."

The reasoning powers of lovers are sharp and quick to suspicion, vigorous in conjecture, inspired in divination.

He tried her virtue by sending her goods—a bait for her debauchment.[67]

He rejoiced extraordinarily at his involvement with the maiden.

But she for her part, trick-drinking and keeping sober[68]

He is smitten in the head with a cleaver, as one who is not going to live.

---

[66] Photios later calls this slave δύcεϱωc, "unhappy in love" (77a31); if this fragment comes from the *Babyloniaka*, it might come from another place in the novel where that set of events is narrated, such as 77b7–8.

[67] This looks rather more distant and formal than Photios's summary suggests. Habrich suggests that χϱήματα, "things" or "money," are gifts before dinner.

[68] The only other heroine who compromises the perfection of her honor by affecting a form of shyness is Charikleia (Hld. 5.26).

τὸ ϲτόμα τῇ χειρὶ φιμώϲαϲα τοῦ ἐϲφαγμένου, μήτινα τῇ ψυχῇ ϲυνεκπέμψειε φωνήν
(Fragment 68 = *Souda* 4.739.7, s.v. φιμοῖ)

ἡ δὲ φεύγει, ἐπιθυμοῦϲα ἀμείψαϲθαί ποτε χρηϲτουργίᾳ τὸν ἄνθρωπον
(Fragment 69 = *Souda* 4.826.7, s.v. χρηϲτουργία)

Ἰάμβλιχοϲ· ἡ δὲ μεϲτὴ μὲν ἦν καὶ τῆϲ ἔμπροϲθεν ζηλοτυπίαϲ, προϲείληφε δὲ καὶ τὴν ἀπὸ τῆϲ πράξεωϲ εὐτολμίαν· ὡϲ οὖν ἐλάβετο τῆϲ ὁδοῦ, "ὁ μὲν πρῶτοϲ ἀγών," ἔφη, "διηγώνιϲται· ἐχώμεθα δὲ καὶ τοῦ δευτέρου· καὶ γὰρ ἐν καιρῷ γεγυμνάϲμεθα"
(Fragment 70 = *Souda* 2.504.27, s.v. ζηλοτυπία)

[77a29]

ὁ δὲ ἤδη μεμηχανημένοϲ ἀγχόνην, τὸν βρόχον ἐνδεδυμένοϲ
(Fragment 74 = *Souda* 1.497.27, s.v. βρόχοϲ)

ὁ δ᾽ ἐπιϲυράμενοϲ εὐπρόϲωπον λίθον ϲτήλην ἔϲτηϲεν
(Fragment 71 = *Souda* 2.466.13, s.v. εὐπρόϲωποϲ)

ὁ δὲ λαβὼν τὸ ξίφοϲ πατάϲϲει τοῦ ϲτέρνου
(Fragment 72 = *Souda* 4.67.1, s.v. πατάϲϲει)

ὁ δὲ δεύϲαϲ τοῦ αἵματοϲ τοὺϲ δακτύλουϲ προϲέγραψεν
(Fragment 73 = *Souda* 2.27.12, s.v. δεύϲαϲ; also assigned to Ailian as frag. 277 by Hercher)

ὁ δὲ ἔκειτο πνευϲτιῶν ἡμίπνουϲ ὑπὸ τοῦ βρόχου
(Fragment 75 = *Souda* 4.153.21, s.v. πνευϲτιῶν)

ὁ δὲ καὶ ἐταινίωϲε τὸ τραῦμα τῇ ζώνῃ
(Fragment 77 = *Souda* 2.433.20, s.v. ἐταινίωϲε)

[77b9]

ὁ δὲ ὀλίγον φθέγγεται πρὸϲ τὴν κόρην καὶ αἰτεῖ πιεῖν
(Fragment 80 = *Souda* 3.518.1, s.v. ὀλίγον)

She muzzled the slain man's mouth with her hand lest he emit, along with his soul, some sound.

She flees, desiring to repay the man for his good deed some time.[69]

Iamblichos: She was full of her former jealousy and she had also added to it the boldness that followed from her deed. So when she took to the road, she said, "The first contest has been fought through. Let us grapple with the second. For we have had a timely exercise."[70]

Having already contrived a way to hang himself, having put the noose around his neck[71]

He dragged over a smooth-faced stone and set it up as a pillar.

He took the sword and struck himself in the breast.[72]

He wet his fingers in the blood and wrote further.

He lay gasping, half-breathing from the noose.

He bandaged his wound with a cincture.[73]

He uttered a few words to the maiden and asked her for a drink.

[69] Hercher (1875: 4) referred this to the farmer's daughter and Soraichos, though there is nothing quite like it in Photios; Schneider-Menzel (1948: 65 n. 55) put it at the moment when Soraichos first releases the pair from arrest (75a34), but one might expect "they fled" rather than just "she."

[70] Sinonis regards her murder of Setapos as a trial run for that of the farmer's daughter.

[71] Or possibly around that of Soraichos below.

[72] Or possibly, translating "her" rather than "himself," of the slave murdering Trophime (Schneider-Menzel 1948: 65 n. 53). The genitive is used of the area within which the blow lands.

[73] Schneider-Menzel (1948: 67 n. 73) objects to the active voice of the verb and to the contrast with Rhodanes' weakness described below. She suggests that this fragment describes Sinonis's wound in Soraichos's covered carriage (75a32).

"ὤμοι τάλαινα, ὡς κακῶς διάκεισαι, γενναιότατος περὶ ἐμὲ γενόμενος καὶ θανάτου με ῥυσάμενος"
(Fragment 81 = *Souda* 1.513.26, s.v. γενναιότατος)

"μὴ γὰρ οὕτως ὑφ᾿ ἡλίῳ δυσκλεὴς εἴην, ὥστε τὸν ἐμὲ ςώςαντα μὴ ἀντιςῶςαι"
(Fragment 82 = *Souda* 2.150.22, s.v. δυςκλεές)

ἄρτι δὲ ἀπηρκότος τοῦ Ϲοραίχου ἡ Ϲινωνὶς ἐφίςταται
(Fragment 78 = *Souda* 1.285.3, s.v. ἀπηρκότος, and 4.398.10, s.v. Ϲόραιχος)

ὁ δὲ ἄγχων τὴν αὐτῆς δεξιὰν καὶ περιάγων περιαιρεῖται τὸ ξίφος
(Fragment 79 = *Souda* 1.42.24, s.v. ἄγχων)

[77b27]
ὁ δὲ ἐλειποψύχηςεν· ἀνενεγκόντα δὲ αὐτὸν ἀράμενοι οἱ φύλακες παρὰ τὸν βαςιλέα φέρουςιν ἐκ τῆς νόςου περιςωθέντα
(Fragment 83 = *Souda* 1.204.12, s.v. ἀνενεγκών)

πάντας μὲν ἀνθρώπους ἐξίςτηςιν ἔρως, εὐνούχους δὲ ποιεῖ φονικωτέρους ὥςπερ οἶνος Ϲκύθας· φονᾷ γὰρ Ϲκύθης μὲν πιών, εὐνοῦχος δὲ ἐρῶν
(Fragment 96 = codd. Laur. 57,12 and Vat. 1354)

καὶ ἅμα τῇ κόρῃ παρεςκεύαςε πομπὴν ἐπιφανῆ, ἁρμάμαξάν τε λαμπρὰν καὶ ἐςθῆτα ςοβαρὰν καὶ θεραπείαν ςυχνὴν εὐνούχων τε καὶ θεραπαινίδων
(Fragment 84 = *Souda* 4.170.9, s.v. πομπήν, and 4.483.3, s.v. ςυχναῖς)

[78a10]
φιλαίτιοι τὰς φύςεις εἰςὶν οἱ βάρβαροι καὶ πρόχειροι τὰς ὁρμάς, ὀλίγα μὲν χρώμενοι τοῖς λογιςμοῖς, τὰ πολλὰ δὲ τοῖς πάθεςιν εἴκοντες
(Fragment 85 = codd. Laur. 57,12 and Vat. 1354)

θανάτου καταφρονήςας ἄνθρωπος δεςπότην οὐκ ἔχει
(Fragment 86 = codd. Laur. 57,12 and Vat. 1354)

"O wretched woman that I am! How miserably you lie there, who showed yourself so noble in my case and saved me from death."

"For I may never gain so foul a reputation under the sun—that I would not save in return the one who saved me."

As soon as Soraichos had departed, Sinonis arrives at the scene.

He seized her right arm, twisted it around, and took away the sword.

He lost consciousness; when he came to, the guards hoisted him up and carried him to the king, saved from his illness.

Passionate love stimulates all human beings, but it makes eunuchs more murderous, just as wine does to Skythians. A Skythian commits murder under the influence of drink, a eunuch under the influence of passionate love.[74]

And at the same time, for the maiden s/he prepared a splendid procession: a gleaming covered carriage and stunning clothes and a thronging retinue of eunuchs and maidservants.[75]

Barbarians by nature are contentious and exuberantly impulsive; they make little use of reason but mainly yield to their emotions.

The person who despises death has no master.

---

[74] The collocation of eunuch, passion, and murder suggests that the following excerpt belongs here. Zobaras, however, is not a lover of Mesopotamia turned murderous against her (Di Gregorio 1963: 393); he is simply ordered by the king to kill her. He might turn murderous later, in Egypt, when Berenike tries to steal her away from him.

[75] This fragment might also be placed in the wedding of Sinonis with the young king of Syria, below. Di Gregorio (1963: 395–96) would put it at Soraichos's arrest of Sinonis (75a22).

[78a24]

"κέλευϲόν με ἀποθνήϲκειν ἐπιτεμόμενοϲ τοῦ ϲταυροῦ τὴν περίοδον"
(Fragment 87 = *Souda* 2.386.10, s.v. ἐπιτεμόμενοϲ)

οὕτωϲ ἄγαν αὐτοῖϲ ϲυμβεβήκει τὸν μὲν φονᾶν, τὸν δὲ θανατιᾶν
(Fragment 88 = *Souda* 2.683.22, s.v. θανατιᾶν)

[Schneider-Menzel (1948: 68) places Fragment 3 (see below) here, spoken in rage by Garmos; Borgogno (1975a: 111) agrees as to the location but reads it as spoken ironically by Rhodanes.]

"ἤδη γὰρ ἐλεῶ ϲε, ὅτι τὰ αὐτά ϲοι δυϲτυχῶ"
(Fragment 89 = *Souda* 2.552.4, s.v. ἤδη)

"Bid me die, cutting short the cross's slow cycle."

Very much thus had it happened in their case: the one thirsting for blood, the other desiring to die.

"for now I pity you, since I suffer the same misfortunes as you."[76]

[76] If these words belong to Garmos, he is speaking hypocritically.

LARGE FRAGMENTS

Fragments 1 and 35 are found in two manuscripts (Laurentianus 57,12, folio 118–19, and Vaticanus 1354, folio 113–14, both of the fifteenth century), along with a work of Philo, letter collections attributed to Pythagoras, Euripides, Chion of Heraklea and others, a rhetorical excerpt from Diodoros (two soldiers each arguing after a battle that he deserves the prize for bravery), and excerpts from three rhetoricians of the Second Sophistic—Polemo (two fathers argue that their respective sons deserve the prize for greatest valor after the battles of Salamis and Marathon), Hadrianos (on the burning of a reputed witch), and Kallinikos (in praise of Rome). The first page of Laurentianus 57,12 lists among its contents "extracts (παρεκβολαί) from Kallinikos; from Hadrianos the rhetor; from Iamblichos's *Histories*" (Hercher 1866: 363), and it has a marginal note identifying Fragment 35 as "[from] Iamblichos's *Babylonian Histories*." Fragment 35 is followed by Fragment 1 and then by six shorter sentences (Fragments 86, 34, 85, 4, 60, and 96), all of which are reasonably (but not indubitably) attributed to Iamblichos.

We provide only minimal information about the condition of the text of these fragments: readers desiring further details of manuscript variants should consult Habrich.

FRAGMENT 1

The text of Fragment 1 is from Hinck, reprinted by Habrich as Fragment 1, pp. 5–9. Hercher 1858–59, 2: 66–67 also prints a text of this fragment; Borgogno (1975a: 107) has verified Hinck's reading of cod. Laur. 57,12.

This passage contains many echoes of Xenophon's *Kyropaidia*, especially of Kyros's procession at 8.3.9. Details may be found in Naechster 1908: 57–59, endorsed by Münscher 1920: 146. Persian processions are also described by Herodotos (7.40, 55) and Chariton (6.3.9–4.3), though the latter is really a hunting party, like Vergil *Aen.* 4.130–50, not a parade. Iamblichos's procession, or at least the king's costume, is explicitly distinguished from that of a hunt or a judgment or a sacrifice. Some have compared this description to that of the theoric and sacrificial procession of the Ainianes at Delphi, described by Heliodoros 3.1–4, but the two have virtually nothing in common except the colors red and gold.

Those who agree that this passage comes from the *Babyloniaka* disagree about its position in the novel. Schneider-Menzel (1948: 68) suggests that because Garmos is a wicked tyrant, he would not be described so appreciatively, and that the description comes from the end of the novel when Rhodanes has become king. Hefti ([1940] 1950: [144] 455) proposes that it comes from the middle of the novel, when Garmos is making preparations for his wedding with the farmer's daughter, thinking her to be Sinonis. Both of those are less likely than the majority opinion, which holds that the passage comes from the beginning of the novel, perhaps when Garmos is wooing Sinonis and trying to make a good impression on her (Habrich ad loc., Borgogno 1975a: 106).

FRAGMENT 1

Περὶ προόδου τοῦ Βαβυλωνίων Βασιλέως

Τὸ ἅρμα, ἐφ᾽ ᾧ φέρεται ὁ βασιλεύς, ἅπαν ἐλέφαντός ἐστιν εἰρ-
γασμένον ἐγγύτατα ἀπήνης Ἑλληνικῆς· αἱ δὲ ἡνίαι τῶν ἵππων εἰςὶ
πορφυραῖ ταινίαι. ἐφέςτηκε δὲ ὁ βασιλεὺς ςκευὴν ἐςκευαςμένος
4 ἐξαίρετον, ἐν ᾗ μήτε θηρᾷ μήτε δικάζει μήτε θύει, ἀλλὰ πομπεύει
μόνον. ἔςτι δὲ ἁλουργὶς χρυςῆ· ἐξ ἴςου γὰρ ὁ χρυςὸς ὕφανται τῇ
πορφύρᾳ. φέρει δὲ καὶ ςκῆπτρον ἐλεφάντινον, ᾧ τὴν χεῖρα τὴν
δεξιὰν μετέωρον ἐρείδεται.

8 Ἡγοῦνται δ᾽ ἱππεῖς ςκηπτοῦχοί τε καὶ ςατράπαι καὶ ἱππάρχαι
καὶ χιλιάρχαι, οἷς τι μέτεςτι τοῦ ἔργου· οἱ μὲν πεζοὶ ἀργυράςπι-
δες, ἔτι δὲ ἀργυροθώρακες καὶ χρυςοθώρακες, ψελλίοις μὲν τὰς
χεῖρας, ςτρεπτοῖς δὲ τοὺς τραχήλους κεκοςμημένοι· περὶ δὲ ταῖς
12 κεφαλαῖς οὐ κράνη περιτίθενται, ἀλλὰ ἐπάλξεων ςημεῖα καὶ
πύργων ςτεφανοῦντα τὴν κεφαλὴν καὶ ςκέποντα. καὶ ταῦτα μὲν
ἀργύρου καὶ χρυςοῦ πεποιημένα· ἔςτι δὲ ἄλλα καὶ λιθοκόλλητα
τοῖς κρείττοςιν, ὀλίγοι δὲ καὶ ςτεφάνοις χρυςοῖς ἀναδέδενται, οἷς
16 ἂν ἐκ βασιλέως δοθῇ. οἱ δ᾽ ἐφ᾽ ἵππων ἐλαύνουςι Νιςαίων, τῶν μὲν
τὸν πολεμικὸν τρόπον ἐςκευαςμένων προμετωπιδίοις τε καὶ ςτερ-
νιδίοις καὶ παραπλευριδίοις καὶ παραμηρίδια τοῖς ἱππεῦςι περίκειται, τῶν δὲ εἰς πομπὴν ἠςκημένων χρυςοχαλίνων πάντων
20 ὥςπερ εὐδαιμόνων γυναικῶν. ζωςτῆρές τε καὶ τελαμῶνες καὶ
ἐφίππια οὐδὲν οὐδὲ τούτων ἐςτίν, ὃ μὴ χρυςήλατόν ἐςτιν ἢ χρυςό-
παςτον.

Τρίχες δὲ τῶν ἵππων οὐραῖαι διαπλέκονται καθάπερ πλόκαμοι
24 γυναικῶν καὶ διαδοῦνται καὶ περιςφίγγονται πορφυραῖς τε καὶ
ποικίλαις ζώναις, αἱ δὲ ἐν ταῖς ἱππολοφίαις ἔνθεν τε καὶ ἔνθεν
αἰωροῦνται καὶ καθίενται κατὰ τῶν αὐχένων, αἱ μὲν ἁπαλαί, αἱ

---

1. ἐφ᾽ οὗ Hercher 1876   9. οἷςτιςι Hercher 1876   οἱ μὲν πολλοί Hercher 1876
18–19. Hab. deletes καὶ παραμηρίδια τοῖς ἱππεῦςι περίκειται as an explanation of the
scholiast   19. χρυςοχλαίνων Rohde   23. οὐραῖαι Rohde, οὖλαι codd.

Concerning the Procession of the King of the Babylonians

The chariot on which the king rides is wrought entirely of ivory, its construction very like that of a Greek wagon. The horses' reins are crimson ribbons. The king rides standing on it, wearing a special costume, (4) not used when he hunts or judges or sacrifices but only when he rides in parade. It is a golden robe of sea-crimson—for gold has been woven into it in equal parts to the red. He holds an ivory scepter as well, on which he rests his raised right arm.

(8) The procession is led by scepter-carriers on horseback and satraps and cavalry commanders and infantry commanders, who have a share in the work. The soldiers on foot carry shields of silver and of gold and wear body armor of silver and of gold, their forearms adorned with metal bands and their necks with collars of twisted metal; on their (12) heads they wear not helmets but figures of battlements and towers, encircling and covering the head, and these are fashioned of silver and gold, while others, those of the more prominent, are studded with jewels too, and a very few wear golden crowns (16) awarded by the king. Those who are mounted rode on Nisaian horses, some of which are outfitted as for battle with frontlets and breastplates and side-armor—and the riders wore thigh-guards—and others were dressed for parade, their reins all of gold (20) as if they belonged to aristocratic ladies. Their cinches and straps and other harness—none of these but was chased or stitched with gold.

The hair of the horses' tails was braided like women's locks (24) and was interwoven and bound around with crimson and multicolored ribands; the hair of their manes was gathered in bunches that rose up and then flowed down along their necks: some were simple, some straight,

δὲ ὀρθαί, αἱ δὲ οὖλαι, αἱ μὲν φύϲει πεφυκυῖαι, αἱ δὲ διὰ τέχνηϲ
28 ἠναγκαϲμέναι.

Πλάττουϲι δὲ αὐτῶν καὶ βαδίϲματα καὶ βλέμματα καὶ νεύματα
καὶ φρονήματα, ἐνίων δὲ καὶ τὰ φρυάγματα καὶ χρεμετίϲματα.
πομπευτὴϲ γὰρ ἵπποϲ πάντα διδάϲκεται. πρῶτον μὲν γὰρ αὐτό-
32 〈ματο〉ϲ ἐκτείναϲ εἰϲ τὸ ἔδαφοϲ τοὺϲ πόδαϲ καὶ χαμαιπετὴϲ γενόμε-
νοϲ ἀναβάτην λαμβάνει καὶ τρυφῶντα καὶ κάμνοντα· ὁ δὲ ἐπὶ τὸ
ϲοβαρώτερον πεπαιδευμένοϲ οὐκ εἰϲ γαϲτέρα καθίεται, ἀλλ' εἰϲ
γόνατα πίπτει, ἵνα δοκῇ τὸν ἱππέα δέχεϲθαι καὶ προϲκυνεῖν,
36 ἔπειτα παρέχει ὑγρὰν τὴν ῥάχιν καὶ κραδαινομένην ἐν τῷ δρόμῳ
δίκην ἑρπετοῦ. διδάϲκεται δὲ καὶ ῥυθμίζειν ἑαυτὸν καὶ ϲχηματί-
ζειν καὶ ταῖϲ ῥιϲὶν ἐμπνεῖν καὶ τοῖϲ ὀφθαλμοῖϲ ἐμβλέπειν καὶ
ὑψαυχενεῖν καὶ ϲοβεῖν καὶ γαυριᾶν καὶ πάντα, ὅϲα καὶ ἀθλητὴϲ
40 ἐπιδείκνυϲι τῷ θεάτρῳ. ἐκ δὲ τούτων ὁ μὲν ἵπποϲ εὐειδέϲτεροϲ φαί-
νεται, ὁ δὲ ἱππεὺϲ ϲοβαρώτεροϲ γίνεται

---

31. διδάϲκεται Rohde, διδάϲκει V Allatius, διδάϲκοι L   31–32 αὐτό〈ματο〉ϲ Hab., αὐτόϲ
codd.   33. κάμνοντα codd., λάμποντα Hab.   36. παρέχειν L   38. Hab. adds
ἀπὸ νεύματοϲ before ταῖϲ ῥιϲὶν.

some curly; some were as they naturally grew, (28) others constrained by artful technique. And they also train their steppings and glancings and noddings and sprightly sportings, in some cases even their neighings and whinneyings, for a processional horse is taught everything. First the horse by itself (32) stretches its legs out along the ground and thus close to the earth takes on a rider who is too fastidious and languorous to climb up. A horse trained to a greater degree of pride does not lie down on its stomach but falls to its knees, so that it seems to accept the rider and do him obeisance, (36) then it displays the suppleness of its spine, flexing and curving as it canters, serpent fashion. It is taught, too, to move in rhythm and to hold poses and to control the breath from its nostrils and to look in a certain direction and to hold its neck high and prance and be proud, and all the attitudes that an athlete (40) displays to the crowd. These performances enhance the pure beauty of the horse and the proud bearing of the horseman.

FRAGMENT 1

8. cκηπτοῦχοι: the scepter-carriers were important officers of the Persian court: Xen. *Kyr.* 8.1.38, 3.19. Good objections have been raised against the word ἱππεῖc by Reeve (1971: 534 n. 2). But since three hundred of the scepter-carriers in the king's procession at *Kyr.* 8.3.15 are riding ἐφ' ἵππων, we might understand ἱππεῖc cκηπτοῦχοι as "scepter-carriers on horseback."

9. οἷc τι μέτεcτι τοῦ ἔργου: this means either that they were not just for show or that they are participating in the parade in contrast to those king's men who were lining the streets, as in Xen. *Kyr.* 8.3.9–10.

10–11. ψελλίοιc μὲν τὰc χεῖραc: cf. Xen. *Kyr.* 6.4.2.

16. ἐφ' ἵππων ... Νιcαίων: "Next came ten sacred horses, the so-called Nesaian horses, most beautifully adorned. They are called Nesaian horses for the following reason: there is a large plain in Media called Nesaion; this plain breeds those huge horses" (Hdt. 7.40). "Some writers say that the breed of Nesaian horses, which the kings used because they were the best and the biggest, come from Media, others say from Armenia" (Str. 11.13.7, cf. 11.14.9, "used by the kings of Persia"). These Clydesdales of the ancient world are a well-known feature of novelistic pageantry (Ch. 6.4.2) and battle (Hld. 9.19.1). Their name may be spelled Νιc- or Νηc-.

18. παραμηρίδια: Xen. *Kyr.* 7.1.2, *De re equestri* 12.8; cf. *Kyr.* 6.4.1, Naechster 1908: 58.

19. χρυcοχαλίνων: Rohde suggested "golden robes" for "golden reins," χρυcο-

χλαίνων for χρυϲοχαλίνων; but the comparison with golden earrings and ornaments is apt and realistic, whereas the notion of golden clothing, even for very wealthy women, is far-fetched. Horses in the king's parade in Xen. *Kyr.* 8.3.16 are χρυϲοχάλινοι, and the king's horse in the procession at Chariton 6.4.2 has a χρύϲεον χαλινόν.

21. ἐφίππια (cod. ἔφιππα): the usual generic word for equine equipment is ἐφίππια; ἔφιπποϲ is used exclusively of people on horseback, cf. ἄφιπποϲ. The hiatus is explained by pause—a noun series followed by a collective description.

30. φρονήματα: "proud thoughts"; cf. Xen. *De re equestri* 11.1: a horse good for showing off in parade should have a proud soul, ψυχὴ μεγαλόφρων.

32. For κάμνοντα Habrich would read λάμποντα, so that the rider is luxurious and splendid: we take κάμνοντα as an ironic interpretation of why the horse is trained to bring itself down to ground level.

36. παρέχει ὑγρὰν introduces hiatus, but no obvious solution comes to mind.

FRAGMENT 35

The text of Fragment 35 is from Hinck, which is reprinted by Habrich as Fragment 35, pp. 27–31. Hercher (1858–59, 2: 67) also prints a text of this fragment. It has been located in the digression on the island of Aphrodite. The argument is spoken before a "king," who in this novel could be Garmos. It may also be the famous judge Bokchoris, an Egyptian king from the eighth century B.C.E. (Twenty-fourth dynasty, 720–715), who decided among Mesopotamia's three lovers. Could the speaker be that Pharnouchos mentioned by Photios immediately after his reference to women announcing to the public their dreams in the temple of Aphrodite? Attempts have been made to identify Pharnouchos[77] as a divine or heroic figure, either Men Pharnakes or Baal Pharnak, but the name is a common one among the Persians (Aischylos *Persai* 313; Xen. *Kyr.* 6.3.32, 7.1.22, 8.6.7). The temptation to divinize Pharnouchos is that Photios speaks of Iamblichos's "detailed exposition of the material concerning Pharnouchos and Pharsiris and Tanais" and says that the people who live near the Tanais River interpret the mysteries of Aphrodite in terms of Tanais and Pharsiris. The phrase τὰ περί may refer simply to interpolated tales, both occasioned by the "digression concerning the temple of

[77] Wüst 1938: 1856–57.

Aphrodite"—one about Pharnouchos's accusation of his wife's adultery, another concerning Tanais and Pharsiris. Many folktales are "Just-So" stories, attached to festival days, places, and rites as a putative explanation of them. The story of Pharsiris and Tanais may have been just such a tale.

For the nexus of dreams and trials, note that under Claudius two Roman knights, suspected of lending their house to Poppaea as a meeting place with her lover Mnester, were brought up on a capital charge that one of them had had a dream of ill omen for Claudius (Tacitus *Ann.* 11.4). There is also the example in Sopatros of a man who saw the rites of the mysteries in a dream, asked a friend about it, and was tried for impiety (see Innes and Winterbottom 1988: 93–101 and *Initiation* below).

FRAGMENT 35

Δεσπότης δούλου κατηγορεῖ ἐπὶ μοιχείᾳ τῆς οἰκείας γαμετῆς
ἐξηγηςαμένης, ὡς ὄναρ τούτῳ ἐν τῷ τῆς Ἀφροδίτης ἱερῷ ἐμίγη

Ὅτι μὲν οὐδεὶς ἂν ἑκὼν ἐπὶ τοιαύτην δίκην ἔλθοι καὶ ταῦτα
coὶ μέλλων, βαςιλεῦ, χρήςεςθαι δικαςτῇ, ὃς οὐ μόνον τοὺς τῶν
κρινομένων ἐξετάζεις βίους, ἀλλὰ καὶ τοὺς τῶν κατηγορούντων
4 τρόπους, οὐκ ἔςτιν ὅςτις οὐκ ἂν ςυνομολογήςειέ μοι. ἔςτω δὲ καὶ
τοῦτο τεκμήριον τοῦ τὴν κατηγορίαν εἶναι τὴν γινομένην
ἀληθῆ, τὸ καὶ τὴν ὑπόθεσιν εἶναι τῷ μέλλοντι κατηγορεῖν ἀηδῆ·
τὴν γὰρ τοιαύτην δίκην ἡ νικηθεῖςα μὲν ἀδικεῖ, ἀτυχεῖ δὲ ὁ
8 νικήςας.

Παραιτοῦμαι δὲ ςυγγνώμην ἔχειν μοι οὐ κατηγορεῖν βεβου-
λευμένῳ, ἀλλὰ ςιγᾶν μὴ δυναμένῳ, οὐ μόνον ὅτι ἀφόρητόν ἐςτιν
ἀδίκημα μοιχεία, ἀλλὰ καὶ ὅτι τῷ κοινῷ τῆς αὐτῆς ὕβρεως ἴδιόν
12 τι τὸ ταύτης πρόςεςτιν. ὁ γὰρ μοιχὸς δοῦλός ἐςτι καὶ τὴν ψυχὴν
ταπεινός, κἂν ταύτῃ καλὸς εἶναι δοκῇ· δοῦλος δὲ οὐδὲ ἄλλου
τινὸς ἀλλ᾿ ἐμός· ἔδει δὲ καὶ ταύτης δοῦλον αὐτόν, ἀλλὰ μὴ
δεςπότην εἶναι. ποιεῖ δὲ τὴν μοιχείαν περιττὴν καὶ μᾶλλον
16 αἰςχρὰν ἄμφω ςυνελθόντα, ἡ τῆς μεμοιχευμένης δόξα καὶ ἡ τοῦ
μοιχεύςαντος ἀδοξία.

Δέομαι δὲ ςοῦ, βαςιλεῦ, πρὸς ταῦτά μοι βοηθῆςαι ὑπὸ μὲν
γυναικὸς ὑβριςμένῳ, ὑπὸ δὲ δούλου παρευδοκιμημένῳ, νεμεςῆ-
20 ςαι δὲ καὶ τούτοις, ἐν μὲν τοῖς ἔργοις λαθεῖν δεδυνημένοις, ὑπὸ
δὲ τῶν θεῶν μεμηνυμένοις.

Ἀπορῶ δὲ πότερον αἰτιάςωμαι θατέρῳ ςυμβουλον καὶ διδάς-
καλον γεγονέναι τῶν ἁμαρτημάτων. οὗτος μὲν γὰρ μειράκιόν
24 ἐςτιν· ὁ δὲ τοιοῦτος πειςθῆναι μᾶλλον ἢ πεῖςαι πιθανὸς εἶναι
δοκεῖ καὶ διεφθάρθαι μᾶλλον ἢ διεφθαρκέναι· αὕτη δέ ἐςτι
γυνή· εὐεξαπάτητον δὲ εἶναι δοκεῖ γυνή. ὥςτε τῷ μὲν τὸ τῆς ἡλι-
κίας ἀςθενές, τῇ δὲ τὸ τῆς φύςεως τοιοῦτον ςυναγωνίζεται.

28 Ϲυνελὼν οὖν λέγω· ςυναμφότεροι καλοί. δοῦλον δὲ τίς προετί-
μηςεν ἀνδρός; ὡραῖος γάρ ἐςτι καὶ καλὸς εἶναι, βαςιλεῦ, κἀμοὶ
δοκεῖ, καὶ πολλάκις αὐτὸν ὁ μωρὸς πρὸς ταύτην ἐπήνεςα, ὡς εὖ

---

27. τοιοῦτον codd., κοῦφον Hercher 1866: 365

A Master Accuses His Slave of Adultery with His Wife, Who Told How in a Dream She Had Had Intercourse with Him in the Temple of Aphrodite

To say that no one would willingly come to such a trial, particularly when he is going to have you, O King, as his judge, you who not only examine the lives of those being tried but also the behavior of those who accuse—(4) with this there is no one who would not agree. But let this, too, be counted as a proof that the present accusation is true, the fact that the very subject is distressing to him who would bring the charge. For in such a case she who loses is proved unjust, he who wins proves to be unfortunate.

(8) I beseech the court to sympathize with my plight: I am unwilling to prosecute but unable to remain silent, not merely because adultery is an intolerable crime but also because in addition to the outrage commonly accompanying this act the present case adds its own peculiar twist. (12) For the adulterer is a slave, a soul of low status—even if he does appear handsome in her eyes—and he is not another's slave but my own. He ought to have been her slave too, not her master. What makes this adultery extraordinary and the more (16) shameful is the coincidence of these opposites: the adulteress's social distinction, the adulterer's lowly station.

I beg you, O King, to assist me in the face of this situation—disgraced by my wife, dishonored by my slave—and punish (20) these two, whose wrongdoing was long able to escape detection, but has been revealed at last by the gods.

I am uncertain which of these two I should charge as the other's instigator and instructor in crime. For this one is still a lad, (24) at an age where he seems more likely to be persuaded than to persuade, to be corrupted rather than to corrupt. But she is a woman, and a woman is evidently a being easily deceived. The decision in this contest is between the weakness of his age and the suchness of her nature.

(28) In sum then I say: both are beautiful. But who could prefer a slave to a husband? He is certainly in his youthful prime, and to my eyes too, O King, he seems handsome. Often enough I praised him to her—fool that I was—

231

μὲν τὸ πρόϲωπον ἱϲτάντα, ὑγροῖϲ δὲ τοῖϲ ὄμμαϲιν ἐμβλέποντα.
32 ἐπήνεϲα δὲ αὐτοῦ πολλάκιϲ καὶ χεῖραϲ ἄκραϲ ὡϲ λευκὰϲ καὶ
κόμαϲ ταύταϲ ὡϲ ξανθάϲ. καὶ ταῦτα ἄρα λέγων ἐδίδαϲκον
ταύτην ἐρᾶν. οἶδαϲ δὲ καὶ ϲύ, βαϲιλεῦ, ὡϲ ἔϲτι ταῦτα ἀληθῆ.
οὐδὲ γὰρ κατέλιπεν αὐτὸν τὸ κάλλοϲ οὐδὲ φοβούμενον, ἀλλ᾽
36 ἔλαμψε μὲν ὑπὸ τοῦ δέουϲ ἡ παρειά, τὸ βλέμμα δὲ οὐκ ἀπήνθη-
ϲεν οὐδὲ λυπουμένου. παρέϲτηκε δέ ϲοι δεδεμένοϲ, ἀλλ᾽ ἐπέπρεψεν
αὐτῷ καὶ τὰ δεϲμά. φθόνοϲ ϲοι καταρᾶται, καὶ τῶν κακῶν ὁ κίν-
δυνόϲ ϲε κοϲμεῖ, πονηρὲ καὶ καλέ. ὀκνῶ, δέϲποτα, λέγειν,
40 ὅτι ϲήμερον καὶ καλλίων ἐγένετο. οὐκ ἐλεεῖϲ με, βαϲιλεῦ; μοιχὸν
ἀνὴρ ἐπαινῶ, καὶ ταῦτα τῆϲ μεμοιχευμένηϲ ἀκουούϲηϲ. φοβοῦμαι δὲ μὴ καὶ ϲήμερον τὸ κάλλοϲ αὐτῷ βοηθήϲῃ. Ἐπήνουν
αὐτὸν οὕτωϲ. ὑπώπτευον δὲ αὐτοῦ τῶν ὀφθαλμῶν τὴν πλάνην
44 καὶ τὰ πολλὰ κινήματα καὶ τὸ ἀποβλέπειν τῆϲ κύλικοϲ ἔξω καὶ
τὸ τοὺϲ ὅρουϲ τῶν οἰνοχόων ὑπερβαίνειν. τηρήϲαϲ δὲ εἶδον ἀμφο-
τέρων αὐτῶν νεύματα, τὸ μέν παρ᾽ αὐτοῦ πεμπόμενον, τὸ δὲ
παρ᾽ ἐκείνηϲ ϲυναντῶν· πάντα δὲ ὁμοῦ παρῆν ἐπ᾽ αὐτούϲ,
48 νεότηϲ, οἶνοϲ, κάλλοϲ. προϲῆν δὲ τούτοιϲ ἐγὼ τῆϲ μοιχείαϲ ϲυν-
αγωγεύϲ, ὁ τοῦ κάλλουϲ ἑρμηνεύϲ.

Ὤιμην δὲ αὐτοὺϲ νουθετήϲειν τὴν μὲν ἀνυπόδητον ἐκπέμψαϲ,
τὸν δὲ πατεῖϲθαι καταβαλών. ὁ δέ, ὡϲ ἔοικεν, οὐκ ἠτι-
52 μάϲθη πατούμενοϲ, ἀλλ᾽ ἐπατήθη μᾶλλον ἐλεούμενοϲ ... καὶ
γυναικῶν ἐν ὕπνοιϲ ἡ μὲν φίλανδροϲ οἰκουρεῖ, ἡ δὲ φιλότεκνοϲ
ὠδίνει, ἡ δὲ ἔριθοϲ ἐργάζεται, ἡ δὲ ἐρῶϲα μοιχεύεται. εἰ δὲ μή γε,
ἕκαϲτοϲ ἡμῶν τῶν ὀνείρων ἑαυτὸν ἀναμνηϲάτω, τί μὲν
56 ὀνειροπολεῖ τὰ πολλά, τί δ᾽ ὁρᾷ· τοξότηϲ τόξον, ἱππότηϲ ἵππον,
βαϲιλεὺϲ θρόνον, αὕτη δὲ μοιχόν. ἑάλωκαϲ, ὦ πανουργοτάτη
γυναικῶν· εὕρηκά ϲε αὐτῷ τῷ μειρακίῳ περικειμένην. τὰ γὰρ
νυκτερινά ϲου φιλήματα τῶν μεθ᾽ ἡμέραν ἐϲτὶν ὑπομνήματα· ἃ
60 ποιεῖϲ ἐγρηγορυῖα, ταῦτα καθεύδουϲα μελετᾷϲ. ἐνύπνιον γὰρ
ἀνθρωπίνηϲ ϲπουδῆϲ εἴδωλόν ἐϲτι. καὶ ϲυγκατάκειϲαι μὲν ἐμοί,
ϲχολάζειϲ δὲ ἐκείνῳ, καὶ παρ᾽ ἐμοὶ μὲν τὸ ϲῶμα, παρ᾽ ἐκείνῳ δὲ ἡ
ψυχή· κἀμοὶ μὲν καθεύδειϲ, ἐκείνῳ δὲ οὔ.

---

44. τὸ Hab. deletes   50. ἀνυπόδητον Hab., ἀνυπόδετον codd.   58. περικειμένην
codd., παρακειμένην Hinck.

remarking how well-set-up he was in the face, how moist and glowing was his gaze. (32) Often I praised his hands for their whiteness and his locks for their golden hue, and in so saying I taught her to desire him. You yourself know, O King, that this is true, for his beauty has not abandoned him, even in his terror. (36) Rather his cheek glows with fear, in grief his glance has not lost its luster. He stands before you bound, but even his bonds enhance his beauty. Envy calls curses down on you and danger of death adorns you, wicked and handsome at once. I could almost, Lord, bring myself to say that (40) he has become even more handsome today. Do you not pity me, O King? The husband praises the adulterer—and in the hearing of the adulteress. I am afraid that today, too, his beauty will serve him well. Thus I praised him. And I did have some suspicions—of his wandering eyes, (44) their restless movement, his glance outside the cup, his overstepping of the determined bounds of a wine-pourer. I watched and observed their nods: first one sent by him, then one answering from her. Everything conspired together for them— (48) youth, wine, beauty—to which was added I myself, the facilitator of her adultery, the exponent of his beauty.

I supposed I could correct them by sending her forth without shoes, by hurling him down to be walked on. But he, it seems, was not (52) ashamed to be walked on, and when trodden upon was all the more to be pitied. . . . In the dreams of women, the loving wife keeps her house, the loving mother gives birth to her children, the spinster works her wool, the lustful woman commits adultery. If you doubt it, let each of us remind himself of his own dreams. (56) What does he regularly dream of? A bowman dreams of his bow, a horseman of his horse, a king of his throne, and she of her adulterer. You have been caught, O most wicked of women! I have found you with your arms around the lad himself. For your kisses in the night are testimonials to those in the day. What (60) you do in your waking hours you contemplate in your sleep. For a dream is an image of human desire. You sleep alongside me, but you are spending your time with him; your body is with me, your soul is with him. You sleep when you are with me, but not with him.

FRAGMENT 35

Title: The Greek indicates that she slept with the slave in the temple, but from the context in Iamblichos, one expects rather that the dream took place in the temple.

44–47. This type of amatory behavior is almost a cliché; see, e.g., Ovid *Amores* 1.4.17–18.

50–51. This has the look of a proverb about it, but we have not succeeded in finding any parallels.

52. Previous editors have suspected a lacuna after ἐλεούμενοϲ.

58. περικειμένην: in this instance "with arms around" seems preferable to "alongside." (See above, 75a8, Frag. 25, for a similar confusion.)

Fragment 61 (Habrich 1960: 45–53; Hercher 1858–59, 2: 64–66) is found in one palimpsest, Vaticanus Graecus rescriptus 73, folio 61–62. It is, we are informed, very difficult to read, even more so since it was treated with chemicals by Cardinal Mai. Since there is considerable uncertainty about the readings, we have not attempted to supply the illegible portions beyond a few obvious suggestions of previous editors (Borgogno 1975b). We only indicate where lacunae are present; we have not given accurate estimates for their sizes (nor does Habrich).

This is the only extended fragment to which no shred of doubt concerning its Iamblichan authenticity clings. It begins in the middle of a speech by Sinonis after she has become aware that Rhodanes has accepted a grateful kiss from the farmer's daughter. She rages against his weakness.

FRAGMENT 61

[Two fragmentary lines] κινδύνους οὐκ ἀναγκαίους ἔξεςτι ζῆν,
εἰ μὴ φιλεῖς· ἀλλ' ἴθι μᾶλλον καὶ κάθευδε παρ' ἐκείνην τὴν
ξένην· ...ςιου κηδεςτοῦ καὶ τὸν χρυςὸν καὶ διδ...ου ξενίας
4 δῶρον. ...μεν εἴτε τυχὸν ἤδη καὶ τὸ πρόςωπον κεκαθαρμένη
[καὶ] κεκοςμημένη τὴν ὀλίγην ἐκείνην κόμην. τί γὰρ ἔτι Cινωνίδος χρήζεις; ἔχεις κόμην κεκαρμένην ὡς ἐγώ, εὐτυχέςτερον δὲ
τῆς...ς οὐκ ἀνδρὶ χαριζομένη τὴν ἐνεν...."
8   Ταῦτα λεγούςης τῆς Cινωνίδος ὁ Ῥοδάνης οὐκ ἀνείχετο, ἀλλ'
ἐγε[.]ενει θυμωθεὶς ... ἡ Cινωνὶς ὀργῆς ἀνεπίμπλατο καὶ τιςαπο-
νιτον ...το, καὶ χεῖρας ἀντήρατο καὶ πολλὰς ἀπειλὰς ἐνε[δα-
τεῖτο] καὶ δείξαςα τὸ τραῦμα, ὅ ποτε ἔτρωςεν αὐτήν,
12 "ὁρᾷς," ἔφη, "τοῦτο, ὦ ... ὁρᾷς, ὅτι τῆς ψυχῆς Cινωνὶς οὐ φεί-
δεται· ἔχεις μεν ...δειγματι ...ταχυτερα δέ ἐςτιν ἐρωτι...ζο-
μενη... μαρτύρομαί ςε, Ῥοδάνη, ἄρξεις ςήμερον μεγάλου κακοῦ
... θυγάτηρ γεωργοῦ αλλο τρι[one fragmentary line]δειλης
16 τετρωμένης [two fragmentary lines]τοῦ φόνου τῆς θυγατ[two
fragmentary lines] μεν ἀριςτερας ... ν τὴν δὲ δεξιὰν ... ἐφ' ὅςον [
three fragmentary lines]οντος καὶ λοιδοροῦντος ...τατης...
τικῶς ἡ Cινωνὶς ὑπεξέρχεται καὶ δραμοῦςα διὰ τῆς
20 ςελήνης ἔθει εὐθὺς τῆς ἐπ[αύλε]ως τῆς τοῦ γεωργοῦ, [ἧπερ] παρε-
τύγχανεν προτερον, ἐν νῷ ἔχουςα εἰςδραμεῖν καὶ φονεύειν τοῦ
γεωργοῦ τὴν θυγατέρα...χωραν...ταις θηραις εχε και....
    Ὡς δὲ ἔγνωςαν τὴν διάνοιαν αὐτῆς οἱ περὶ τὸν Ῥοδάνην, "cὺ
24 μέν," εἶπεν ὁ Cόραιχος, "ὦ Ῥοδάνη, κατὰ χώραν μένε καὶ μὴ
παρεξ[έλθῃς], μὴ καὶ δόξῃς ἐπαμύνειν τὴν ἐρωμένην
{ῥύςαςθαι} · ἀλλὰ φυλαξώμεθα κόρην ἐρῶςαν καὶ φονῶςαν· ἐγὼ
δὲ ἐκείνην μετελεύςομαι· πείθω δὲ ἐμαυτὸν ὅτι ταχέως αὐτὴν
28 ἐπανάξω· θάρρηςον ...ςε... οἶδα νικᾶν ρ... τοὺς Cινωνίδος

---

3. δίδ[ου π]ου Hab., δίδ[ου αὐτῇ] Boissevain   6. κόμην Hab., κόρην codd.   8. δὲ
Cινωνίδος Mai   8–9. ἐνέκειτο θυμωθείς[η Boiss., ἐθρήνει θαμβηθείς Hab.   10. τιςα
πονιτον Boiss.   11. ἐνε[δατεῖτο] Hab.   13. ἔχεις μὲν [ἰςχυρότατον] δεῖγμά τι
[τούτου.] ταχυτέρα δέ ἐςτιν ἐρωτι [κεντρι]ζομένη [ψυχή] Hab.   20. ἐπ[αύλε]ως Hab.
22. θυγατέρα ὑπάρξαςθαι Mai   θύραις? Boiss.   26. Borgogno 1975b omits
ῥύςαςθαι as a doublet of ἐπαμύνειν.   28. ῥ[ᾷςτα] Boiss.

. . . [How] is it possible [for me] to live [enduring] unnecessary dangers, if you do not love me? But go, rather, and sleep by that stranger woman. [Take the necklace?] of one who is close to you, and the gold, and give [it to her?] as a pledge of closeness. . . . (4) Or by accident now with her face scrubbed clean and that short hair of hers prettied up. For what further need do you have of Sinonis? You have a maiden whose hair has been shorn like mine, more fortunately than . . . not gratifying a husband. . . ."

(8) While Sinonis said this, Rhodanes did not wait patiently but angered. . . . Sinonis was filled with anger and . . . and raised her arms and [hurled] many threats, and displaying the wound she had once inflicted on herself (12) she said, "Do you see this [sc. wound], O [———]? Do you see how Sinonis does not spare her own life? You have . . . demonstration . . . but swifter is [———] with passion. I call you to witness, Rhodanes, you are beginning today a great misfortune . . . farmer's daughter . . . cowardly woman (16) wounded . . . daughter's murder . . . left . . . right . . . insofar as . . . but since . . . -ing and abusing . . . Sinonis left and (20) raced in the moonlight directly towards the house of the farmer's daughter, where she had happened to stay before, intending to run in and kill the farmer's daughter. . . .

When Rhodanes' party realized her intention, (24) Soraichos said, "You, Rhodanes, must wait right here and not [go out], lest you seem to be defending your girlfriend. Let us take precautions against a maiden who is passionate and murderous. I will follow after her. I am convinced that I will quickly (28) bring her back. Courage! [For] I know [that in time] you will conquer Sinonis's

θυμούς· τί κλάεις, ὦ 'Ροδάνη; μένε, εἰ Cινωνίδα θέλεις ἀπολα-
βεῖν, εἰ πιστεύεις Cοραίχῳ τῷ δι' ὑμᾶς πλανωμένῳ." τοcαῦτα ὁ
Cόραιχος εἰπὼν μόλις {μὲν} ἔπεισε τὸν 'Ροδάνην μένειν, μάλιστα
32 μὲν ὑπὲρ τῆς Cινωνίδος φοβούμενον, ἔμελε δὲ αὐτῷ καὶ τῆς κιν-
δυνευούσης κόρης, μή τι δεινὸν ἀπολήψεται τῆς ζηλοτυπίας.

Καὶ τὸ μὲν οὖν πρῶτον οὐδὲ ἐν καταλήψει τῷ Cοραίχῳ ἡ Cινωνὶς ἐφαίνετο· καὶ γὰρ προεῖχε πολὺ καὶ θεῖν ἦν ὀξυτέρα τοῦ
36 Cοραίχου, ἦν δὲ καὶ ὑπὸ τῆς ὀργῆς ἐλαφροτέρα· τὸ γὰρ τοῦ
θυμοῦ τάχος κουφοτέραν αὐτὴν εἰργάζετο τῷ cώματι. ὅμως δὲ
cυντεινόμενος ὁ Cόραιχος καὶ παρὰ δύναμιν ἁμιλλώμενος ὡς
ὁρᾷ τὴν [χλαῖν]αν τῆς Cινωνίδος πόρρωθεν βοᾷ· "μεῖνον
40 Cινωνί· Cόραιχος ἐγὼ μόνος· 'Ροδάνης οὐ πάρεστιν, οὐ μὰ τὸν
Βῆλον."

Ἡ δὲ ἐπέσχε τοῦ δρόμου καὶ τὸν ὅρκον πιστὸν ἡγουμένη καὶ
τὸν Cόραιχον αἰδουμένη. ἐπελθὼν δὲ ὁ Cόραιχος πρῶτον αὐτὴν
44 ἐκέλευε προσιέναι καὶ λέγει· "ὦ Cινωνί, ἀμφοτέρους μὲν ὑμᾶς
φιλῶ, ἐπείπερ ἀπὸ τῆς τύχης ἐδόθην ὑμῖν πατήρ· cὲ δὲ πρότερον
ἢ 'Ροδάνην ἐκτησάμην· ἀλλὰ 'Ροδάνην μὲν οὐκ ἀπολύω τῆς
αἰτίας, cὲ δὲ οὐκ ἀξιῶ πάντα τῷ θυμῷ χαρίζεcθαι, οὐδὲ δίκην
48 τοcαύτην λαμβάνειν παρὰ γυναικὸς καὶ ξένης, ἀφ' ἧς τάχα μὲν
καὶ κινδυνεύcομεν, πάντως δὲ εἰς Δία τὸν Ξένιον ἀcεβήcομεν·
αὐτὴ γὰρ καὶ τράπεζαν παρέθηκεν ὑμῖν καὶ ξενίοις ὑπεδέξατο·
καὶ τάχα μὲν ἐβιάcθη, τάχα δὲ ἐξηπατήθη ἢ ἐψυχαγωγήθη. οὐ
52 cοὶ μόνη, τέκνον, 'Ροδάνης ἐcτὶ καλός."

Ἡ δὲ πρὸς αὐτὸ τοῦτο ἀνεφλέχθη καὶ οὐχ ὑπέμεινε τὸν λοιπὸν
λόγον, ἀλλ' εἶπεν· "ὦ Cόραιχε, τοῦτό cοι τὸ δύcτηνον πνεῦμα
κεχάριcμαι καὶ τότε κακῶς· ὤφελον γὰρ ἀποθανεῖν πρὶν
56 ἀκοῦcαι, ὅτι ἐcτὶ καὶ ἄλλη τινὶ 'Ροδάνης καλός. μή με κωλύcῃς
μηδὲ θελήcῃς φόνον ἰδεῖν ἐν ἐρημίᾳ. οἶδας δὲ ὅτι οὐ ψεύδομαι·
cὲ γὰρ μάρτυρα τῆς τόλμης ἔχω. ὁρᾷς δὲ ὅτι ἔχω μὲν ξίφος, ἔχω
δὲ τραῦμα· καὶ 'Ροδάνης μὲν ἀνεσταυρώθη μόνον, ἐγὼ δὲ καὶ

---

31. μὲν deleted by Hercher   39. [χλαῖν]αν Hab., cκιὰν Boissevain   44. προcιέναι
Hercher, προιέναι codd.   45. ἀπὸ cod., ὑπὸ Rohde   48. παρὰ Hercher, περὶ
codd.   52. μόνη cod., μόνον Hercher   56. ἐcτὶ καὶ Hercher, καί ἐcτιν codd.
57. θελήcῃς φόνον ἰδεῖν ἐν ἐρημίᾳ codd., θελήcῃς φόνου εἴργειν ἐν ἐρημίᾳ Hab.

anger. Why are you crying, Rhodanes? Wait, if you want to recover Sinonis, if you trust Soraichos who has become a wanderer for your sake." With this long speech Soraichos barely persuaded Rhodanes not to rush out, which he would do mainly (32) because he feared for Sinonis but also because he was concerned for the maiden's danger, lest she suffer some terrible harm from Sinonis's jealousy.

At first Sinonis seemed not within Soraichos's range at all, for she had a good head start and was faster than (36) Soraichos. She was also filled with energy from her anger, for the speed of her heart's rage lent lightness to her body. Nevertheless, Soraichos, concentrating his strength and competing beyond his powers, when he saw the cloak of Sinonis he shouted from afar, "Wait, (40) Sinonis. It is Soraichos, I am alone. Rhodanes is not with me, I swear by Ba'al!"

She stopped running, both because she thought his oath trustworthy and because she respected Soraichos. Soraichos first approached her and (44) bid her to come closer and said, "O Sinonis, I cherish both of you, since Fortune has given me to you as father. You became my daughter before Rhodanes became my son. But while I do not absolve Rhodanes of all blame, I do not think it right for you to give in completely to your anger nor to exact (48) so great a penalty from a woman, a stranger, from whom we may perhaps expect some danger, and in any case we will be insulting Zeus the protector of hospitality. For she did give us food and received us with hospitality. And perhaps she was compelled, perhaps she was deceived or misled by her own imagination. You are not (52) the only one, my child, who finds Rhodanes attractive—"

She flared up at this last remark and did not wait for the rest of his speech. "Soraichos, I have indulged this wicked windiness of yours, and grudgingly at that. I should have died before (56) hearing you say that any other woman finds Rhodanes attractive. Do not get in my way, unless you want to see murder here in the deserted countryside. You know that I do not lie. I have you as witness of my courage. You see that I have a sword—and I have a wound. Rhodanes has only been hung

60 ἡψάμην τοῦ θανάτου καὶ πεῖραν ἔλαβον, ὅτι ἀποθνήϲκοντεϲ οὐκ
ἀλγοῦϲιν ἄνθρωποι, οὐδέ ἐϲτιν ἀηδὴϲ ὁ θάνατοϲ · τοῖϲ δὲ ἐρῶϲι
καὶ ἡδύϲ ἐϲτιν. τί μου λαμβάνῃ, Ϲόραιχε; μαρτύρομαι, Ῥοδάνῃ
τὴν ἐρωμένην ϲῶϲαι θέλειϲ · μηδέ μοι κινδύνουϲ ἀπείλει μηδὲ
64 ϲυλλήψειϲ μηδὲ τιμωρίαν · οὐδένα φοβοῦμαι ἢ μὴ φοβηθεῖϲα
νύξειϲ μηδὲ ϲταυρούϲ.

[Here ends the page.]

---

65. νύκταϲ codd.

from the cross, I have actually (60) touched death and know from my own experience that people dying feel no pain, nor is death distressing. For lovers it may actually be sweet. Why do you hold onto me, Soraichos? I protest—you want to save Rhodanes' girlfriend for him. Threaten me with no dangers, no (64) arrests, no punishment. I who did not fear stabbings or crosses fear no one!'"

FRAGMENT 61

57. If the reading of the codd. stands, φόνον ἰδεῖν, Sinonis would seem to be threatening Soraichos; Habrich's φόνου εἴργειν will instead refer to murder of the farmer's daughter.

62. For μαρτύρομαι used in this way Habrich compares Ch. 5.7.7.

65. νύκτας has displeased most editors. We propose νύξεις, accusative plural of the rare word νύξις: Sinonis has, as she said prominently a moment ago, jabbed herself courageously, and that self-stabbing was parallel to Rhodanes' crucifixion. The rareness of the word would lead to its misreading. Borgogno (1975b: 171) proposes δέςμα or πληγάς.

UNPLACED FRAGMENTS

The following fragments are explicitly attributed to Iamblichos in the *Souda*, but they do not correspond exactly to any portion of Photios's summary.

1. Ἰάμβλιχος· ἔδωκε τὸν ὅρμον ὁ τελώνης τῷ ἐμπόρῳ. οὐκ ἤδη καὶ λύκοι θήςουςιν ἄρνας ἐκ τῶν ςτομάτων καὶ λέοντες ἀπὸ τῶν ὀδόντων ἀπολύςουςι νεβροὺς ταῖς μητράςιν, ὁπότε καὶ τελώνης ἀφῆκεν ἄγραν τηλικαύτην;
(Fragment 93 = *Souda* 4.521.4, s.v. τελώνης)

Iamblichos. The tax-collector gave the necklace to the merchant. Will not wolves set down lambs from their jaws and lions release fawns from their teeth back to their mothers when a tax-collector actually parts with so great a prize?

2. Ἰάμβλιχος· περιβαλὼν δὲ περὶ τὰς χεῖρας αὐτοῦ τοὺς τελαμῶνας προςέδηςε τῇ κλίνῃ.
(Fragment 97 = *Souda* 4.517.12, s.v. τελαμών)

Iamblichos. Putting the straps around his arms he tied him to the bed.

3. Ἰάμβλιχος· ἡ δὲ νῦν μὲν ἐγέλα ἰταμόν τε καὶ ἀκόλαςτον γέλωτα, νῦν δὲ ἐφθέγγετο ῥήματα αὐθάδη.
(Fragment 98 = *Souda* 1.85.3, s.v. ἀκόλαςτος, with attribution; *Souda* 2.676.9, s.v. ἰταμός, without attribution)

Iamblichos. She was at one moment laughing recklessly and without restraint, the next moment she was speaking audacious words.

4. Ἰάμβλιχος· "εἶτα ἐάςατε οὕτως ἀπραγμόνως ἀποθανεῖν."
(Fragment 99 = *Souda* 1.332.2, s.v. ἀπραγμόνως)

Iamblichos. "Then allow [her/him/them] to die thus without trouble."

IAMBLICHOS, *BABYLONIAKA*

DOUBTFUL FRAGMENTS

1. Fragment 100 is not explicitly attributed to Iamblichos in the *Souda* (4.94.14, s.v. περιδινοῦντες) and does not correspond to anything in Photios's summary, but its Babylonian subject makes it a strong candidate. (Besides, it is too amusing to omit.)

οἱ δὲ Βαβυλώνιοι ἐντιθέντες εἰς ϲφενδόναϲ ᾠὰ καὶ περιδινοῦντεϲ ἐν κύκλῳ, ἅτε οὐκ ἄπειροι τῶν αὐτοϲχεδίων καὶ κυνηγετικῶν διαιτημάτων, ἀλλὰ μεμελετηκότεϲ τὰ ἐν ἐρημίᾳ μηχανήματα, ἐφθὸν {καὶ ὠμὸν} τῇ ῥύμῃ τὸ ᾠὸν κατεϲκεύαζον.
(καὶ ὠμὸν del. Hercher)

The Babylonians, placing eggs into their quivers and whirling them around in a circle—inasmuch as they are not unfamiliar with improvised and hunters' usages but have carefully studied the contrivances employed in the desert countryside—cook the egg by centrifugal force.

2. The marginal note in Laur. 57,12 identifying Fragment 35 as from Iamblichos's "Babylonian Histories" is placed not directly at the head of the excerpt but in the margin towards the end of the previous excerpt (Fragment 101), evidently an afterthought, as Naechster argues. The position of the note—and his estimate of its style—misled Hercher into attributing it, too, to Iamblichos, but it is extremely difficult to integrate the contents of that excerpt with the plot of the *Babyloniaka*. It is translated here for the curious. (Schneider-Menzel 1948: 69 n. 88 cites Norden, *Antike Kunstprosa* 1.385, for the theme "sea-battle on land.")

FRAGMENT 101

Μιϲθοφόροι τὸν ποταμὸν τοῖϲ πολεμίοιϲ ἐπήγαγον,
καὶ ἀπαιτοῦϲι τὸν μιϲθὸν παρ᾽ Ἀμφικτύοϲι δικαζόμενοι.

Οὐκ ἐπαναλώϲαμεν τῷ πολέμῳ χρόνον, ἀλλὰ προϲέθεμεν τῇ νίκῃ τάχοϲ· ὑμεῖϲ δὲ ἀποϲτερῆϲαι τὸν μιϲθὸν διεγνώκατε, τὸ πλεονέκτημα τῆϲ εὐτυχίαϲ ἔγκλημα ποιούμενοι, καὶ οὐδὲ ἐκεῖνο ϲυνίετε,
4 ὅτι πολλοὶ ϲυμμαχήϲαντεϲ, οὐ μέντοι κρατήϲαντεϲ τὰ ϲυνωμολογη-

μένα χρήματα παρὰ τῶν ϲυμμαχίαϲ τυχόντων κομίζονται, διότι τῶν ϲυμμαχούντων ἕκαϲτοϲ ϲυμβαλλόμενοϲ τὴν γνώμην οὐκ ἐπαγγέλλεται τὴν τύχην.

8   Ὦ τὸ παράδοξον τοῦτο τόλμημα ἡμῶν. ϲτρατόπεδον ὅλον ποταμῷ βάλλεται καὶ κλύδωνι χερϲαίῳ παραϲύρεται καὶ χειροποιήτῳ
χειμῶνι βαπτίζεται. ὦ μὴ πεζομαχήϲαντεϲ ἡμεῖϲ μόνον, ἀλλὰ καὶ
χωρὶϲ νεῶν ναυμαχήϲαντεϲ. αὔτανδρον οἴχεται τὸ τῶν πολεμίων
12 ϲτρατόπεδον, καὶ πάνδημοϲ ἐν ἠπείρῳ μέϲῃ τοὺϲ ἐχθροὺϲ κατείληφε
ναυαγία· κῦμα δεδιδαγμένον ἠγείρετο καὶ ῥοῦϲ κεκελευϲμένοϲ ἐγίνετο
καὶ ποταμὸϲ ἀπὸ ϲυνθήματοϲ ῥεῖν προϲετάττετο. ὦ μὴ μόνον ἀνδρῶν,
ἀλλὰ καὶ ποταμῶν ἐϲτρατηγηκότεϲ.

Mercenaries Directed a River against the Enemy, and They
Demand Their Pay in a Case before the Amphiktyonic Council

We have not spent extra time on the war, we have added speed to
the victory. You have decided to dock our pay, turning the excess of
your success into an accusation against us, and you do not understand (4) the fact that many men undertake to fight a common cause
and when they do not win they still collect the pay promised by
those who commissioned them, because each man fighting contributes his best judgment but none can promise success.

(8) O this unexpected boldness on our part! A whole army was
struck by a river and swept off their feet by a tidal wave on land and
drowned in a man-made storm. O how we fought not only a land
battle but also a sea battle—without ships! The enemy army has
been eliminated to a man, (12) and a shipwreck with all hands has
destroyed them in mid-continent. A wave carefully trained was
raised on high, an obedient stream came into being, a river was
ordered to flow on signal. O how we have commanded not only
men but even rivers!

3. The hiatus (κόρη ὑπακούει) in Fragment 57 (= *Souda* 2.453.10, s.v.
εὐκαρδίωϲ) adds to the doubt about the attribution of this fragment.

ἡ δὲ κόρη ὑπακούει προθύμωϲ τε καὶ εὐκαρδίωϲ.

The maiden agrees eagerly and with all her heart.

4. At some point in the novel, the following fragment (*Souda* 4.260.17, s.v. ποινήν, identified by Hercher [1867: 95], not in Habrich) referring to Sakas may have been introduced. Di Gregorio (1963: 392–93) argues for the meaning "hang from a cross" rather than "impale" for ἀνεϲκολόπιζε. It is possible, however, that Sakas is not the character in Iamblichos, since the name simply means "men of the Sakai," a well-known Iranian tribe, sometimes interchangeable with the Skythians (Hdt. 7.64, Str. 11.8.2).

οὓϲ δὲ λάβοι Ϲάκαϲ αἰχμαλώτουϲ, ἀνεϲκολόπιζε καὶ ᾐκίζετο, καὶ αὖθιϲ ποινὰϲ τοῦ πατρὸϲ φόνου πράξαϲθαι θέλων.

Whatever prisoners Sakas would capture, he would impale them and treat them shamefully, wishing to exact revenge for his father's murder.

Sesonchosis

❖

The legend of Sesonchosis was a staple of Greek lore about Egypt from at least the fifth century B.C.E.[1] Its subject is an Egyptian king, variously named,[2] who comes to stand in Greek versions of the Egyptian past as their greatest military leader, a conqueror of both Asia and Europe whose deeds surpass those of Cambyses and rival Alexander's. Several pharaohs from several dynasties have been conflated to produce both the name and the achievements. The historical original must have been Senwosret I of the Twelfth Dynasty, who added Nubia to Egypt and pushed into Syria, with accreted elements from the reigns of Senwosret III (of the same dynasty); Rameses II (of the Nineteenth Dynasty), Shelley's "Ozymandias, king of kings," whose colossal statuary are one of Egypt's most remarkable architectural features, and Sheshonk I (of the Twenty-Second Dynasty), the Shishak of the Old Testament,[3] who captured Jerusalem and sacked the temple of Solomon in 930 B.C.E.

This skeleton of "historical" facts has been amply fleshed out with folktale (the machinations of the evil brother), Greek ideals of kingship (the king as lawgiver and as inventor or facilitator of agriculture),[4] and Egyptian political propaganda stemming from the Persian conquest (Lloyd 1988: 16–18). Indeed, much of the story has the look of material confected by the Egyptians themselves around the time of the Persian invasion for reasons of nationalist pride, since Sesonchosis's military prowess seems particularly designed to outdo that of the Achmaeonids or of Kyros. Conscious reworkings in the Ptolemaic period by the Egyptian priesthood and under the auspices of the Ptolemies turned this legendary king into a prototype for Alexander, who in the *Alexander Romance* is

---

[1] The most extensive Greek versions of this story are found in Herodotos and later Diodoros, whose narrative with its details of the prince's youthful training and the first campaign against the Arabians is closer to events in the novel.

[2] Sesostris (Herodotos, Aristotle, Theopompos, Strabo, Plutarch), Sesoosis (Diodoros and doubtless his source, Hekataios of Abdera), Sesonchosis (Manetho, the *Alexander Romance*).

[3] 1 Kings 14.25, 2 Chron. 12; Josephus (*J. Ant.* 8.10.2) remarks that Herodotos mistakenly attributed Shishak's activities against the Jews to Sesostris.

[4] See, e.g., DS 1.54–58, or Aristotle *Pol.* 7.1329a40.

called "young Sesonchosis," and whose achievements Alexander sets out to rival (Murray 1970: 162–63).

The publication of P. Oxy. 3319 in 1980 has made it clear that in addition to histories, a novelized version of the Sesonchosis legend circulated in antiquity. This fragment, which combines romance and intrigue, opens in a courtyard or garden, where Sesonchosis and an associate named Pamounis discuss his plight. Sesonchosis announces that he had been engaged to the girl whom they see in the distance and that he intends to reveal himself to her in order to recover his former position. From Pamounis's remarks it follows that they are somewhere outside of Egypt with Sesonchosis's real identity unknown to his host. As they talk, the girl, who is named Meameris, approaches to look at him; she is obviously in love, though she does not appear to know his true identity. Immediately a banquet takes place, and whether Sesonchosis is present or not is unclear, though parallel scenes from other novels suggest that he would be.

Meameris is the daughter of Sesonchosis's former vassal, whom Pamounis depicts as a potential danger now that Sesonchosis's fortunes have suffered a reversal. Since Sesonchosis, who is described as a "youth," is handsome enough that Meameris falls in love at his good looks, he can hardly have been in heavy disguise. These circumstances suggest either that the pledge of fealty and engagement took place over some distance without the three actually meeting, or, if they had met in the past, that her father is not now in the immediate vicinity, because he surely would have recognized his former overlord and potential son-in-law after several years even if his daughter did not. (The language of III.1–6 is ambiguous enough to support either interpretation.)

In addition to 3319, there are two other fragments from this novel: P. Oxy. 1826, which features the young prince as he comes of age beginning an address to his father; and P. Oxy. 2466 (which was originally identified as Egyptian history), in which the Egyptians, after prolonged combat, put a band of Arabians led by Webelis to flight. P. Oxy. 1826 and 2466 are likely to be closely connected because Diodoros (1.53.5) tells us that Sesonchosis's first military expedition was against the Arabians. But the order of the two fragments is not immediately apparent. In 1826, Sesonchosis could be approaching his father to ask for his first command, the events of which are detailed in 2466. Sesonchosis does not appear to take part in that battle, however, but only learns the details afterwards from one Thaïmos (2466.27–28), so we might equally well conjecture that the events of 2466 should precede 1826, and that it is Webelis's escape that emboldens him to ask his father for command. Whatever the truth of this, P. Oxy. 3319 must follow these two, since Sesonchosis has already been off to war and has for some time been engaged. It is also possible that either Thaïmos, who appears to be an ally, or Webelis, the enemy of 2466, is Meameris's father.

Even in their fragmentary states, *Sesonchosis* displays remarkable structural similarity to *Ninos*. Both novels focus on national heroes of the Hellenized East—of Egypt and of Assyria. Both include (1) events at the time of the young prince's coming of age; (2) a first military adventure—Ninos against the Armenians, Sesonchosis against the Arabians; (3) an engagement to a girl who is described as a "child" (παῖc) that is interrupted by military adventures; and (4) a reversal of fortune that, although a *sine qua non* of novelistic adventure, is not a noticeable part of the extant historical traditions associated with these kings. But whereas *Ninos* in its compositional finesse and interior drama links itself securely with Chariton or Achilles Tatius, *Sesonchosis* belongs to the rather more mundane world of the New Testament, the apocryphal Acts, or the *Alexander Romance*. Its language is often pedestrian and devoid of stylistic embellishment, its author revealing little acquaintance with the rhetorical niceties like avoidance of hiatus, the use of clausulae or even the careful use of connectives.

The actual date of the novel and its origins are matters for speculation. Martin Braun has argued cogently that obscure local heroes like Ninos, Semiramis, Nektanebos and Moses became prominent in the Hellenistic period as focal points of native resistance to Greek rule and that these local legends grew into subjects for Greek history as well as popular romantic fiction (1938: 1–31). *Sesonchosis* certainly fits Braun's thesis. The pseudo-historical, propagandistic material out of which it was fashioned stems from the period of the Persian conquest and was reworked by the Egyptian priests at the time of Alexander. So the novel could be as old as *Ninos*. But it could also be much later, and not an independently derived piece of fiction, but a weak imitation of *Ninos* written any time after the first century C.E.

The use of words or phrases with meanings restricted to Egypt (see below, 1826.8 front and 2466.25), as well as names like Pamounis and Thaïmos that do not occur in the historical material, suggest that this might have been an Egyptian product, intended predominantly for local consumption. The name Sesonchosis itself could be enlisted in this argument. This form, which must ultimately be a Greek derivation from Sheshonk, would seem to be firmly attached to Egypt, as well as to a romantic rather than an historical tradition. It is already attested as a personal name in an Egyptian document of the third century B.C.E. (West 1980: 12 n. 1). Apart from papyri, this form of the name occurs only in this novel, the *Alexander Romance*, which must have originated in Egypt (Merkelbach 1954: 25ff., Braun 1938:31–42), and Manetho.

Does the origin of Sesonchosis's name support the direction for the origin of the novel suggested by J.W.B. Barns (1956: 29–34), namely from Egypt into the Greek world, or does it reverse it? Do we have an Egyptian tale acting as a seed for the embryonic Greek novel, or do we see the already developed Greek novel producing a later Greco-Egyptian imitation? We are inclined to the latter view, because the structural parallels with *Ninos* do not seem fortuitous, and it is easier for us to believe that the more elegantly written text—for which an early date has been sufficiently established—was the original. But our inclinations can hardly be given the status of fact.

This novel raises a further question that can perhaps be more easily answered. Scholars have detected similarities between the educations of Kyros, Ninos, Sesonchosis, and Alexander, and have occasionally accorded the fictionalized *paideia* of princes the status of "genre" (e.g., Weil 1902: 90–106; Perry 1967: 167–69; O'Sullivan 1984: 40). Clearly Xenophon's model for the education of princes was an extremely influential text for both historians and novelists (Tatum 1989: 9–12 and n. 23). In fact, Murray argues cogently (1970: 164) that the idealizing portrait of Sesoosis's (Sesonchosis's) education was adopted from Xenophon by Hekataios of Abdera, and subsequently by his epitomizer, Diodoros. The popularity of the *Kyropaideia* suggests that subsequent writers of histories would feel compelled to show at least a notional concern with a future king's education, and this tendency could have influenced the novelizations of king's lives as well as Xenophon's own writings.

The differences, however, between the *Kyropaideia* and the *Alexander Romance* on the one hand and *Sesonchosis* and *Ninos* on the other—even when allowance is made for the fragmentary status of these latter—militate against believing that all four texts constitute a unified field. The extant Greek novels are preoccupied with the emotional state of teenagers, so it is not surprising to find that *Sesonchosis* and *Ninos* emphasize the young-adult status of their protagonists. But these same novels are barely interested in education (as opposed to youth), whereas it is central in the *Kyropaideia* and of considerable importance in the *Alexander Romance*. Conversely, Xenophon and Pseudo-Kallisthenes have no interest in the psychodynamics of teen love, though it is an obsession of the extant novelists. (We have argued above in our discussion of the *Ninos* novel that it is no *Ninopaideia*.)

DESCRIPTION

P. Oxy. 1826 (= P^2 2619), measuring 9.0 ×7.3 cm, is a leaf from a papyrus codex (= *Typology* no. 412), now faded and broken on all sides, so that line length and order of recto and verso is not recoverable. The handwriting is of the Biblical type, a mixture of narrow and broad letters, mainly upright but with some occasional tilting. The original editors assigned it to the end of the third or early fourth century C.E.; we are inclined to the later date. There are no lectional signs or iota adscripts visible; there is one correction, but no obvious errors. We have employed the term "front" to refer to the side with writing along the fibers, and "back" to the side with writing against the fibers.

1826 FRONT

1826 BACK

- -

]νη . . [
] περικρατῆ ε . [
] τὸν παῖδα ν[ο]ῦν ε[
4] Cεcόγχωcιc ἀνῆλθε[
]εια λοιπὸν μετὰ τῶ[ν
] ἱππομαχων καὶ ὁπλομ[αχων
εἰω]θότα βαcιλεῦcιν ἐπὶ τ[
8 ἐν]νόμου ἡλικίαc γε[νομεν
τῷ] πατρὶ εἶπεν, "κ[
] ὑπὸ τῶν πατρῴω[ν
κε]χαρ[ί]cθαι τὴν ο . [
12]αλ[. .] . ο . [.] ἀηδῶc α[
]γ[.]εc . [.] . θυμ[
τε]λειοῦcθαι c[

- -

Cεc]όγχωcιc π[
]και τυγχανου[
] . πάντωc ἀλλ᾽ ἔχου[cι
4] ὅπερ ἐπέκλωcαν του[
] μὴ βουλόμενοc τὰ τα[
]ειν ὅταν ἐκεῖνα ἀδεη[
] τότε αὐτὸc ἐπιφανε . [
8]ρι δὲ ἕνα τῶν μορμ[
] ἀνθρώπουc οθ . . [
]δαιμονίαν τὴν δω[
] τὸν θεὸν βοηθὸν τ[
12 Cε]cόγχω[cι]c εἰc χώρα[ν
]ρτων ἔξω γε ὅλου . [
]υτα δο . . που . . . . [
]ε . . τ . [

- -

Supplements are those of Grenfell and Hunt unless otherwise indicated.
Front: 3. ἔ[χειν Zimm. 7. κατὰ τὰ εἰω]θότα G–H 7–9. Zimm. supplements ἐπί
τ[ε τῆc ἀκμῆc τῆc | καὶ ἐν]νόμου ἡλικίαc γε[νόμενοc ὁ παῖc προcελθὼν τῷ] πατρὶ εἶπεν,
"κ[ύριέ μου, πατήρ.
Back: 2. τύγχαν᾽ οὗ Zimm. 5. τὰ τα[ττόμενα Zimm. 8. πε]ρὶ G–H 10. εὐ]-
δαιμονίαν G–H. Final ν corrected by original scribe δω[ρεὰν Zimm. 13. ἑο]ρ-
τῶν Zimm.

252

]
] having full command over [
] his son has sense [
4   ] Sesonchosis arrived [
] for the rest, with the [
] training as cavalry and infantry [as is
] customary for kings. [
8   ] having reached(?) the legal age [
] to his father he said [
] by paternal (or "hereditary") [
] have pleased the [
12   ] . . . unwillingly [
      ] . . . [
] to be fulfilled [

] Sesonchosis [
] and they(?) happen [
] completely, but they(?) have [
4   ] whatever fate they allotted [
] unwilling [
] whenever those things fearless [
] Then he appeared [
8   ] one of the [
] men [
] happy(?) [
] the god assisting [
12   ] Sesonchosis into the country [
      ] outside the whole [

P. OXY. 1826 FRONT

3. τὸν παῖδα ν[ο]ῦν ε[: ἔ[χειν or ἔ[χοντα? These are probably the father's thoughts about his son, expressed as indirect statement.

6.] ἱππομαχων καὶ ὁπλομ[αχων : ed. pr. takes as nouns ἱππομάχων καὶ ὁπλομάχων to be construed with μετὰ τῶ[ν. Alternatively, they could be participles agreeing with Cεcόγχωcιc. Compare, e.g., Luc. *Makr.* §17: Ἄcανδρος δὲ ... βαcιλεὺc ἀναγορευθεὶc Βοcπόρου περὶ ἔτη ὢν ἐνενήκοντα ἱππομαχῶν καὶ πεζομαχῶν οὐδενὸc ἥττων ἐφάνη. This is likely to detail the military training that the young prince underwent: compare Diodoros's description, 1.53.2–4.

6–7. The shortest supplement necessary to fill the lacuna between the lines is [κατὰ τὰ εἰω]θότα. If correct, then the line length is around thirty letters. Zimmermann's supplement for lines 8–9, which is attractive on independent grounds, also suits this spacing.

7. ἐπὶ τ[: if this begins a new phrase, as seems likely, Zimmermann's ἐπί τ[ε is attractive. But note that elsewhere this piece occasionally omits connectives.

8. ἐν]νόμου ἡλικίαc : the phrase is used in documentary papyri to mean the age at which men must pay the poll tax. Here presumably it means the legal age at which Sesonchosis will be considered a man. Compare *Ninos* A.II.22–23: ἐνεκρίθην μὲν εἰc ἄνδραc.

γε[νομεν : either γε[νόμενοc or γε[νομένηc. If the construction is ἐπί + genitive + γενόμενοc, compare below, 3319.III.9: παρ[εγένε]το ἐπὶ τοῦ τ[όπου.

8–9. Zimmermann's προc[ελθὼν τῷ] πατρὶ provides a verb on which the dative may depend (normal usage in the novelists militates against it belonging with εἶπεν).

10. ὑπὸ τῶν πατρῴω[ν : Compare *Ninos* A.II.11–12: πατρῴωι κράτει, or Ps.-Kall. β 2.17.12: τῶν πατρῴων ἐλπίδων.

12. Perhaps] ἀλλ᾿ οὐκ ἀηδῶc. Note also 3319.III.19.

P. OXY. 1826 BACK

4. ὅπερ ἐπέκλωcαν : the verb is used of the fate that gods assign to men. Possibly this is meant to echo Homer *Od.* 3.208: οὔ μοι τοιοῦτον ἐπέκλωcαν θεοὶ ὄλβον. Again, this may be similar to Ninos's argument that since he is only mortal, he should not be constrained by arbitrary age limits (*Ninos* A.II.13–24), but should be allowed full adult responsibilities.

5. If μή belongs with the participle, it is not necessarily conditional. In New Testament Greek, for example, μὴ has supplanted οὐ.

8. μορμ[: if the letter before the break is μ, options are limited. μορμολυκείων or sim.? Compare Hld. 6.2.1.

DESCRIPTION

P. Oxy. 2466 (= *P*² 2259) and 3319 belong to the same papyrus roll. In both pieces, the name of the king is spelled Ϲεϲόγγωϲιϲ (in contrast to Ϲεϲόγχωϲιϲ in 1826). P. Oxy. 2466, measuring 12.5 × 20.5 cm, consists of six fragments joined to form one nearly complete column with twenty-eight lines of text of about twenty-four letters per line. Although there is no trace of an upper margin, the column can be missing at most only a line or two. A lower margin to 4.0 cm and intercolumnia of 2.0 cm survive. P. Oxy. 3319, measuring 17.5 × 20.7 cm, contains three columns, reconstructed from three fragments. Columns II and III are virtually complete, along with their upper and lower margins. These columns hold twenty-three lines per column and average twenty letters per line. Although the variation found in the formatting of the two pieces is well within the acceptable variation for a single roll, it does suggest that they were situated at some distance from each other. This papyrus uses a caret as a line filler, and is inconsistent about *scriptio plena*. P. Oxy. 2466 shows no lectional signs or iota adscript, and writes nu in suspension at lines 9 and 26, and tremata at line 18; a roughened vertical fiber near to the right margin apparently caused the scribe to leave a slight gap between letters in lines 18–28. P. Oxy. 3319 shows high stops, and inconsistent adscript iotas (note the hypercorrect use in I.4). Writing is along the fibers, and the backs of both pieces are blank. The hand is a medium-sized, rightward sloping Severe style, of the type usually assigned to the third century C.E. Rea (1962: 134) suggests that P. Oxy. 2177 might also have been written in the same hand.

P. O X Y. 2 4 6 6

. . . .] . τ[
μ[. . . . .] γενναίως οὖν ὁμοδυ-
γα[μή]ϲαντεϲ ἐφ᾽ ἱκανὸν χρό-
4   ν[ον . . .] . ϲταντεϲ ἐμάχοντο, πολλοὶ μ[ὲ]ν αὐτῶν ἀπώλλυντο, πολ-
λοὺϲ δὲ [κ]αὶ τῶν ἐναντίων ἔκτ[ει-]
ναγ· [ϲφ]ᾶϲ δ᾽ ὁρῶντεϲ αὐτοὺϲ οἱ Ἄ-
8   ραβεϲ [ἑκά]ϲτηϲ ἡμέραϲ μειουμέ-
νοῡϲ, τ[οὺϲ] δὲ Αἰγυπτίουϲ ἔτι μᾶλλον
ἐκ τῶν ἄλλων νομῶν ἐπερχο-
μένων πληθύ⟨ο⟩νταϲ ἐτροπώθη-
12   ϲαγ ὥϲτε μηδὲ τὸ πέμπτον μέ-
ροϲ ἀναϲ[ωθ]ῆναι τῆϲ ϲτρατείαϲ,
ἀλλὰ τοὺϲ μὲν διωκομένο[υ]ϲ, τοὺ[ϲ]
δὲ φεύγονταϲ ὑπ᾽ ἀλλήλων ϲυμ-
16   πα[τ]εῖϲθαῑ, μόνον δὲ τὸν Οὐέβηλιν
μετ᾽ ὀλίγων τῶν περὶ αὐτὸν εἰϲ τοὺϲ
ἰδίουϲ ἀνακομιϲθῆναι τόπουϲ· οἱ
δὲ Αἰγύπτιοι μετὰ τὴν ἧτταν τῶν
20   ἐναγτίων εὐλαβηθέντεϲ μὴ
ϲτρατολο[γ]ήϲαϲ ὁ Οὐέβηλιϲ ἐκ τῶν
ἄλλ[ων ἐ]θνῶν τῶν ὁμορούντ[ων]
αὐτῶ τ[ὸ] δεύ[τε]ρον ἐπ᾽ αὐτοὺϲ ἔλθῃ
24   γεν[ό]μεν[οϲ ἰϲ]χυρότεροϲ τὰϲ πόλειϲ τὰϲ [ἐπὶ] τ[ῆ]ϲ ϲυνορίαϲ τῆϲ Ἀρα-
βίαϲ ἱκαγ[οῖϲ] ἄνδραϲιν ὠχυρώϲαν-
το εἰϲ [. . . .] . πᾱγτα. Ϲεϲόγγωϲιϲ δὲ
28   δῑαϟ[ο]ῡϲαϲ παρ[ὰ] τοῦ Θαίμου τὰ ϲυμ-

Supplements are those of J. Rea unless otherwise indicated.

2. μ[αχεῖν] Ruiz-Montero   3. χρο⟩ pap.   4. ἀντ]ιϲτάντεϲ R–M   8. μιουμε
pap.   9. μαλλο͞ pap.   10. χο⟩ pap.   11. πληθυνταϲ pap.   13. ϲτρατειαϲ⟩
pap.   15. ϲυμ⟩ pap.   18. ϊδ pap.   25. αρα⟩ pap.   26. ωχυρωϲα͞ pap.
28. ϲυμ|[βεβηκότα] Rea.

           . . . Now valiantly
on an equal footing for a considerable time,
4   . . . they were fighting; while many
of them perished, they also killed
many of the enemy.
The Arabs, who saw themselves
8   dwindling in number each day,
and the Egyptians gaining
in even greater numbers from men
coming in from the other nomes, were routed
12   so that not even a fifth part
of their army could return safely;
some while being pursued,
others in flight were trampled by one another,
16   and only Webelis
with a few of his contingent
came safely to his own country.
And the Egyptians, after the defeat of their
20   enemy, taking precautions
against Webelis gathering troops
from the other tribes on his borders
and attacking them a second time,
24   when he had become stronger,
fortified the cities on the
Arabian border with sufficient men
for every contingency(?). And when Sesonchosis
28   heard from Thaïmos [what had happened]. . . .

P. O X Y. 2 4 6 6

2–3. ὁμοδυ|γα[μή]ςαντες : Rea (1962: 136) noted that this verb was a possible reading, but he added that it "seems to be used only as a mathematical technical term." Its meaning, however, is entirely suited to this context, and ὁμο-δύναμος is used regularly in patristic texts to mean "of equal strength" (see Lampe s.v.). ὁμοδύ|γα[μοι] πάντες is another possibility. Ruiz-Montero's ὁμο-θυ|μα[δὸν ἅ]παντες does not suit traces.

7–8. οἱ Ἄ|ραβες : according to Diodoros (1.53.5), the conquest of the Arabs was Sesoosis's (Sesonchosis's) first military feat. This seems to parallel Ninos's expedition against the Armenians.

16. τὸν Οὐέβηλιν: for the name Webelis, see Wuthnow 1930, s.v. Οὐέβηλις, though no entry encourages identification with this Webelis, who must be a leader of tribes in the region of the Sinai or Palestine. Rea (1962: 134–35) canvasses other possibilities.

25. τ[ῆ]ς ςυνορίας : the noun seems restricted in use to designate the frontier regions of Egypt; see LSJ s.v. So Rea 1962: 136.

27–28. These lines were read by Rea after the publication of 3319; see West 1980: 11 n. 1.

28. τοῦ Θαΐμου : for the name, see Wuthnow 1930, s.v. Θαΐμος.

COLUMN I

```
      ]γεπω
   Μεα]μῆρις
     ]αυτης
 4 Μεα]μῆρις
      ]υναρχι-
      ]ἐπιστο-
      ]αργουϲ
 8    ]οραπαρ
      ]˛ρϲικω
      ]ενηι
      ]α˛λογχο-
12    ]ϲ καὶ
      ]τικην
      ]ι˛θερα
      ]αϲα
16 Ϲεϲόγ]γωϲιϲ
      ]ϲτω[˛]
      ] Παμου-
      ]ε˛ αρ˛˛
20    ]˛ βαϲι-
      ]δε ε-
      ]˛˛χα
      ]γὰρ
```

COLUMN II

```
    ἐνταυ ...η...[..........
    ξια δοῦλον εἴλ[η]φα [τὸν]
    ταύτης πατέρα, ἔκδοτόν
 4  μοι δίδωϲιν ἣν ὁρᾷϲ παῖ-
    δα, πιϲτωϲάμενοϲ δὲ αὐ-
    τὴν πρὸϲ γάμουϲ ἐπὶ τοὺϲ
    πολέμουϲ ὥρμηϲα· δέον
 8  οὖν ἐϲτιν ἐμφανιϲθῆναι
    αὐτῇ τίϲ [ε]ἰμὶ καὶ τυχὸν ἀ-
    ναλήψομαί μου τὴν πα-
    λαιὰν ἀξίαν." εἶπεν ὁ Πα-
12  μοῦνιϲ· "μηδαμῶϲ, ἀλλὰ
    χρῆϲαί μου ἣ⟨ν⟩ προεῖπον
    ϲοι ϲκῆ[ψ]ι˛ν· εἰ γὰρ ὑπέτα-
    ξεν [αὐτόν] ϲοι ὁ βαϲιλεὺϲ
16  δυγ[αμικώ]τερον εὑρών,
    νῦν [.......]˛ δυναμι-
    κώ[τερο ....]ηι ὑποχείρι-
    ον ε[........] ὅθεν ἐπί-
20  μεγ[ε ἐπὶ τῇ τα]πεινότητι
    [κ]αὶ φά[ϲκε ἐξ Α]ἰγύπτου
    πεμ[......ελ]ηλυθέναι
    χρυϲ[ίον .....θ]ῆγαι ὑπὸ
```

Supplements are those of S. West unless otherwise indicated.

Col. I: 1. επω⟩ pap.   4.]μηⁱρις pap.   6.]επιστο⟩ pap.   12.]ϲκαι⟩ pap.
15.]αϲα⟩ pap.   21. δεε⟩ pap.   23–II.2. [ἐπει(δὴ)] γὰρ | ἐνταῦθα τῇ[ϲ λώβηϲ
ἐπά]|ξια Luppe (exempli gratia)

Col. II: 7. μηϲα·δεον pap.   9. τυχ˛ω˛ν O'S-Beck   11. αξιαν·ει pap.   13. ειπον⟩ pap.
13–14. ἣ...ϲκῆ[ψ]ει O'S-Beck   14. ·ει, τα⟩ pap.   16. δ˛υ pap.   17. δυναμι⟩
pap.   17–18. δυναμι|κώ[τερον or δυναμι|κώ[τατον]? West.   17–19. νῦν, [ἐὰν αὐ-
τὸ]ϲ δυναμι|κώ[τεροϲ φαν]ῇ, ὑποχείρι|ον ἕ[ξει ϲε αὐτῷ.] O'S-Beck, νῦν [δέ ϲε αὐτὸ]ϲ (or
[ἂν ϲε μηκέτ]ι˛) δυναμι|κώ[τεροϲ ὑπάρχω]γ, ὑποχείρι|ον ἐ[ποιεῖτο ἄν.] Luppe   20. τα]-
πεινότητι Luppe, O'S-Beck, δ]εινότητι κ]οινότητι? West   21–III.3. φά[ϲκε ἐξ Α]ἰ-
γύπτου | πέμ[πων προϲελ]ηλυθέναι | χρυϲ[ία καὶ ληφθ]ῆγαι ὑπὸ | κακ[ού]ργων πλαν[ητῶν
καὶ] | εἰϲ τ[ού]τουϲ τοὺϲ τ[όπουϲ] | πεπλανῆϲθαι μ[ετ] ὀλίγων? Luppe, φα[θὶ ἐκ τῆϲ
Α]ἰγύπτου | πεμ[φθεὶϲ παρελ]ηλυθέναι· | χρυϲ[ίον ἀφαιρεθ]ῆγαι ὑπὸ | κακ[ού]ργων,
πλαν[ώμενοϲ δὲ] | εἰϲ τ[ού]τουϲ τοὺϲ τ[όπουϲ] | πεπλανῆϲθαι μ[όνοϲ·ἐπὶ O'S-Beck

COLUMN I

```
     ]
     ] Meameris
     ] her
 4   ] Meameris
     ]
     ] letter?
     ]
 8   ] s/he saw?
     ] Persian?
     ]
     ]
12   ] and
     ]
     ]
     ]
16   ] Sesonchosis
     ]
     ] Pamounis
     ]
20   ] king
     ]
     ]
     ] for
```

COLUMN II

```
     then [
     I took her father as a vassal,
     he betrothed to me
 4   the girl whom you see;
     and when I secured
     her pledge to marriage,
     I set out for the wars.  It must
 8   now be revealed
     to her who I am and perhaps
     I shall resume my
     former position.  Pa-
12   mounis spoke: "No way, but
     use what I told you before
     as an excuse.  For if
     the king subordinated himself to you
16   when he found you more powerful,
     now . . .
     powerful, . . . subjugate
     So
20   remain in your low position
     and say that sent [from] Egypt
     you have come
     money [
```

COLUMN III

κακ[ού]ργων πλαν[
εἰc τ[ού]τουc τοὺc τ[όπουc]
πεπλανῆcθαι μ[. . . . . .
4 ταύτηι τῆι διαcτολῆ[ι ὁ Cε-]
cόγγωcιc ἐξαγγέλλε[ι τὰc
αὐτοῦ ἁ[μ]αρτίαc τοῖc . [
καί πο[τε ἡ Μεαμῆρ[ιc ἐπὶ]
8 περίπ[ατο]ν ἐρχομέν[η]
παρ[εγένε]το ἐπὶ τοῦ τ[όπου]
οὗ ἦν [ὁ Cεc]όγγωcιc · ἔcτ[η-]
κεν δὲ [καθ]ορῶcα τὴν τ[οῦ]
12 ὕδατοc [ἐπί]ρροιαν · ἀπέ-
βλεπεν [δὲ] εἰc τὸν Cεcόγ[γω-]
cιν κ[αὶ . . .]ον ἑώρα τὸ[ν ἄν-]
δρα · ἐπ[ὶ τού]τωι πονέcα[cα]
16 τὴν ψυχ[ὴν] ἀπέρχετα[ι].
καὶ τημ[ελ]ηθεῖcα κατ[ε-]
κλίθ[η ἐπὶ] τὴν εὐωχ[ίαν.]
ἀηδῶc [μετ]ελάμβαν[ε τῶν]
20 [π]αρακε[ιμ]ένων · ἐμ[νη-]
μόνευε τὴν τοῦ νεα[νί-]
cκ[ου] εὐείδειαν · ὡc δ[ὲ οὐκ ἔ-]
cτεγεν ἑνὶ τῶν cυνδ[είπνων]

Col. III: 7. πο[τε] Luppe   7–9. Supplemented by J. Rea   9. letter added above ρ of
παρ[10.]ογγωcιc ·εcτ[pap.   11. [ὡc] ὁρῶcα O'S-Beck   12.]ρροιαν ·απε[
pap.   14. αὐτ]ὸν, ἱλαρ]ὸν, ἀθυμ]ὸν? West, καλ]ὸν O'S-Beck   15. δρα ·επ[pap.
20.]ενων ·εμ[pap.   22. ι added above what appears to be a deleted letter before
δειαν.

COLUMN III

by criminals [
into these places [
have been forced to wander."
4   At this communication, Sesonchosis announced
his mistakes to his [companions?].
And at length Meameris,
8   coming into the walk,
arrived at the place
where Sesonchosis was.
And she stood looking [down]
12   at the flow of the water.
And she glanced at Sesonchosis
and saw that the man was [———]
Grieving at this
16   in her soul, she went away.
After she had been attended,
she reclined at the feast;
reluctantly she took what
20   was placed before her; she
kept remembering the youth's
handsomeness. And when [she did not]
succeed in covering her feelings, to one of her fellow
                 [banqueters]. . . .

P. O X Y. 3 3 1 9, C O L U M N I

2. Μεα]μῆριϲ : the beginning of the name is unbroken in III.7. It is unattested as a name, though Ἀμῆριϲ and Μῆριϲ both occur as masculine Egyptian names.

9.] . ριϲκω : West suggests Π]ερϲικῷ or sim.

11. West suggests λογχο|[φόροϲ or sim. Cf. Xen. *Kyr.* 2.1.5; Ps.-Kall. 1.46.8: λογχοβόλοϲ.

14. θερα[πεύω or sim.

16–18. Since Sesonchosis is already speaking to Pamounis in Col. II, his speech will have begun in this column, probably between lines 16 and 23.

18.] Παμου-: for the full name, see Col. II.11–12. It is a well-attested Egyptian name.

20. βαϲι|[λεὺϲ or sim. Presumably the same person as in II.15, who seems to be the father of Meameris. For βαϲιλεύϲ used of vassal kings, see DS 1.58.2.

23. Initially Luppe's ἐπεὶ or ἐπειδὴ γάρ is quite plausible, since εἴλ[η]φα should belong to a dependent clause.

P. O X Y. 3 3 1 9, C O L U M N II

2. δοῦλον : O'Sullivan and Beck point out that this should mean "vassal" rather than "slave," since Sesonchosis is unlikely to have betrothed himself to the daughter of a common slave. This no doubt describes a situation familiar in Egypt from the time of the New Kingdom, and associated with Alexander as well, in which daughters of the newly subject princes are sent off to become wives of the conqueror or his chosen favorites as a way of solidifying the status change. For this usage of δοῦλοϲ, O'Sullivan and Beck compare Hdt. 1.89.1, Ps.-Kall. 1.38.1.

3–5. ταύτηϲ ... ἣν ὁρᾷϲ παῖδα : how many women are involved? West assumed there were two—the girl who is betrothed to the speaker, and a female slave given to Sesonchosis by his future wife. Luppe also argued that ταύτηϲ and ἣν ὁρᾷϲ παῖδα must refer to two separate women. We agree with O'Sullivan and Beck, who believe the two to be the same, with the following scenario: Seson-chosis and Pamounis are talking at some distance from the girl (ἣν ὁρᾷϲ παῖδα) to whom, at some time in the past, he was betrothed, probably when she was little more than a child. She draws nearer to them as they speak, though she does not address them. She does not recognize Sesonchosis, nor apparently does he expect that she would.

11–III.3. Pamounis disagrees with Sesonchosis's plan and outlines an alternative—to maintain his disguise and create a fictitious background to account for his presence—presumably so he can apprise himself of the situation before revealing his true identity. His advice is introduced by three imperatives: χρῆϲαι (line 13), ἐπίμευ[ε (lines 19–20) and φά[ϲκε (line 21). This last introduces the fiction that Pamounis advises Sesonchosis to employ as a series of infinitives; see below lines 21–III.3.

11–12. εἶπεν ὁ Πα|μοῦνις : the lack of connective is common in Ps.-Kall. or in the *Acta Alexandrinorum* when there is a change of speaker between two sections of dialogue.

13–14. ἢ⟨ν⟩ προεῖπον | ϲοι ϲκῆ[ψ]ιν : West's reading with her correction best suits the traces.

14–20. The exact nature of the construction is in doubt. εἰ γὰρ will introduce either a condition or a wish. At stake is the nature of the first assertion. If a wish, it is contrary-to-fact: "Would that the king had subjected himself to you when he found you the more powerful." If a condition, it could be open: "For if he submitted himself to you, etc." How to decide? The paragraphos under line 16, which usually marks a change of speaker or a new section, argues for εἰ γὰρ through εὑρών being a complete construction, hence a wish (so Luppe). Further, νῦν (or νῦν [δὲ]) is more likely to introduce a new thought than an apodosis. Against this is the fact that the language of this papyrus is closer in style to that of the New Testament than to that of the extant novels, and the normal expression of wish is not εἰ γὰρ, but ὤφελον / ὄφελον. Further, if the king in question is the vassal of II.2 (as is likely), then he must actually have become subject to Sesonchosis, so lines 14–16 will express a fact, not an unfulfilled possibility. Though the exact supplements are in doubt, we think O'Sullivan and Beck's line of restoration basically correct.

17.] . : trace does not encourage reading O'Sullivan and Beck's μηκέτ]ι; αὐτὸ]ϲ is the most probable supplement.

18.]ηι : traces suit ηι rather than Luppe's ν. This suggests a subjunctive, e.g., φαν]ῆι or εὕρ]ηι (to match εὑρών above?), which in turn encourages a supplement like νῦν [δὲ, ἂν αὐτὸ]ϲ δυναμι|κώ[τεροϲ φαν]ῆι . For the expresion δυναμικὸν ἐφάνη, see Ps.-Kall. 2.10.5.

19. ὅθεν : for the use of ὅθεν with the imperative, O'Sullivan and Beck cite Ps.-Kall. 2.8.6, 3.22.15.

20. τα]πεινότητι : although other supplements are possible, this is admirably suited to context. For Ninos' reversal of fortune, see above, *Ninos* Frag. C.41.

21. Obviously an imperative of a verb of speaking is necessary. Either φάϲ[κε or φα[θί might be restored, but the former seems slightly more common as an imperative.

21–III.3. Three infinitives would seem to depend on the imperative: -ελ]ηλυθέναι, -θ]ῆναι, and πεπλανῆϲθαι. The limited space indicates that Sesonchosis will be the subject of all three infinitives. The gist of this confected tale seems to be that he came into his present location from Egypt, after his money or his person or both was taken captive by criminals. Two lines of restoration have been suggested: either "say you have come here having been sent from Egypt; that you were robbed of your money by criminals and, wandering about, have

265

wandered into these parts on your own" (so O'Sullivan and Beck), or Luppe's "say that you have come from Egypt conveying money, and you were captured by wandering criminals and you wandered into these parts with a few companions." Luppe's restorations are better suited to the available space, and his connectives are welcome (O'Sullivan and Beck's restored asyndeton in line 23 seems especially harsh). But neither seems obviously correct to us without further context. For the thought, compare Ps.-Kall. 5.21.49: ἐνταῦθα δὲ παρε-πέμφθην δέϲμωϲ τοῖϲ ἐρήμοιϲ πλανᾶϲθαι τόποιϲ.

P. O X Y. 3319, COLUMN III

3. Although O'Sullivan and Beck's μ[όνοϲ is plausible in the abstract, it seems incompatible with the fact that Sesonchosis is in the company of at least two people in a public place (III.6).

6. ἁ[μ]αρτίαϲ: Sesonchosis's admission to his companions that his original plan was a mistake (so O'Sullivan and Beck).

τοῖϲ ̣[: the slight horizontal trace after τοῖϲ does not suit φ[ίλοιϲ, though the idea is obviously correct. θ[εράπουϲιν seems too long (but cf. above, I.14); perhaps ξ[ένοιϲ?

7–8. ἐπὶ | περίπ[ατο]ν ἐρχομέν[η]: O'Sullivan and Beck note Ps.-Kall. 1.18.5: ἐπὶ περίπατον ἐξῄει.

11–12. [καθ]ορῶϲα τὴν τ[οῦ] | ὕδατοϲ [ἐπί]ρροιαν: cf. Ps.-Kall. 2.9.3: ὁρῶντεϲ τὴν ἐπίρροιαν τοῦ ποταμοῦ.

14.]ον: the restoration is in doubt. O'Sullivan and Beck's καλ]ὸν is supported by ἐμ[νη]‖μόνευε τὴν τοῦ νεα[νί]‖ϲκ[ου] εὐείδειαν below, but the girl may have fallen in love with his good looks earlier and now be disturbed by his downcast spirits (restoring [ἄθυμ]ον with West). Though the *Sesonchosis* narrative is not as elaborate as many of the extant novels, it is difficult to believe that the details of the girl falling in love with Sesonchosis can be told as baldly as lines 10–22 would require, if this was the only description of the onset of her passion. The mention of her name in Column I leads us to suspect that she has already seen him and fallen in love, and in this scene steals closer for a further chance to gaze on him. Love at first sight is a standard cliché in the novels, as is the resulting loss of appetite (lines 19–20), and the inability to keep one's passion a secret (lines 22–23), or how else would the plot progress?

22. West points out that a negative is necessary in this line.

Kalligone

❖

The raw dramatic power of the *Kalligone* fragment is evident, in spite of numerous ambiguities. Its force may even be somewhat enhanced for us because the situation that motivates it remains mysterious. The column opens with Kalligone entering a tent in a destructive fury, which is explained by one Eubiotos to those at hand as her reaction to some distressing news she has received about the Sauromatians. Since the tent distinctly suggests a military atmosphere, we may guess that the Sauromatians are involved in a war, probably as allies of Eubiotos in a distant field of operations. What relation does Kalligone have to the Sauromatians, not shared by Eubiotos and the rest, that could explain why she would react hysterically to news concerning them—news that does not appear to have been passed on to Eubiotos's other companions?

That public explanation, of course, has only been invented by Eubiotos to clear the room. The Sauromatians must exist in the novel but they have nothing to do with Kalligone's frenzy at this moment. The real reason concerns a certain Eraseinos, whom Kalligone regrets ever having set eyes on. The easiest interpretation of this is that she saw him ("at the hunt") and fell in love with him at first sight: hence the emphasis on her eyes (lines 19–20). What throws her into turmoil now will be his misfortune—with her lover dead she wants to die herself—or, perhaps, his rejection—he loves another, or at least does not respond to her.

The quality of her violence is noteworthy. The modern stereotype of "Greek romance" leaves out the moments of passionate discord and outright hatred between the lovers that sometimes occur. Chaireas out of jealousy kicks his wife in the stomach (Ch. 1.4); Sinonis in a frenzy of rage against the farmer's daughter attacks her with a sword and struggles with her lover for possession of it (Phot. *Epit.* 76b22–31, 77b9–23). For passionate anger, Kalligone is matched only by Sinonis among the novel heroines.

Kalligone seems to have a relation of equality with Eubiotos, who is evidently a commander; she carries a weapon; her very spirited talk includes a death threat by the superior strength of her bare arms; she singles out Artemis and a hunting scene from her past; she only speaks after the others have been sent from the tent on false pretenses. And at the end of our fragment she cries, "Though I am no Amazon, no Themisto, but a Greek, Kalligone. ...." In contrast, Eubiotos acts protectively by clearing the room and removing her dagger to prevent her from suicide. Is he guarding her true identity, which in her turmoil she might reveal to those who should not know it? Is he protecting the secret of her love for Eraseinos? Or is he merely giving her the privacy to express her feelings freely?

An Oxyrhynchus papyrus containing two more fragmentary columns from this novel[1] sheds light on some of this. In the Oxyrhynchus piece—the action of which surely takes place before our text—Kalligone's ship runs into difficulty on an Amazonian beach (*ton Amazonikon aigialon*). She and her crew are overwhelmed and taken before the Amazon queen, who is named Themisto,[2] and who "admires Kalligone for her beauty and stature."[3] In the queen's presence, Kalligone would seem to give the details of her lineage, mentioning the Milesian settlement of Borysthenes (Olbia). The fragment also mentions the Maiotai, a people living in the region of Lake Maiotis who were frequently subject to the king of the Bosporans, another people whom it is said "a woman also rules," (*archei de kakeinōn gunē*), and an impending military expedition.

Since our novel heroine insists to Eubiotos that she is a Greek, which is what we would expect if she came from Olbia, we must assume from her costume that she is either disguised as an Amazon herself or as a female commander, perhaps of the peoples ruled by a woman (the Sauromatians?).

About Eubiotos we may be more certain. According to Lucian's *Toxaris*, he was an illegitimate brother of Leukanor, king of the Bosporans

---

[1] P. Oxy. ined. 112/130 (a) is a roll written along the fibers; the hand, which differs from this text, is assignable to the third century C.E. We are most grateful to Peter Parsons for calling it to our attention in advance of its publication in a forthcoming volume of *The Oxyrhynchus Papyri*.

[2] That Themisto was an actual character in the novel rather than a mythological allusion was first suggested by Körte (1927: 271). The presence of such a mythic people in what otherwise appears to be an historical romance should occasion little surprise. After all, the Amazons do occur in Herodotos, to whom many of the novelists seem indebted for their historical "facts." For a discussion of sometimes nonexistent boundaries between fact and fiction in ancient prose writings, see the introduction to "Antonius Diogenes" above.

[3] ἰδοῦσα δὲ τὴν | [Καλλιγό]νην ἐθαύμασεν | [τοῦ κάλλου]ς καὶ τοῦ μεγέθους. Assuming the restoration to be correct, it calls to mind Arsakomas's reaction to Mazaia in Luc. *Tox.* §44: ἰδὼν τὴν Μαζαίαν μεγάλην καὶ καλὴν παρθένον ἤρα ("When he saw Mazaia, a tall and beautiful girl, he fell in love with her").

(§ 51), who lived amongst the Sauromatians and on the death of his half-brother became king. While leading a force of Greeks, Alans, and Sauromatians against the Skythians, he died in battle (§ 54).

Apart from a structural similarity of doubtful significance observed by Rostovtzeff (see below, lines 9–10 and note), there appear to be no further points of overlap between *Toxaris* and *Kalligone*, though the rest of Lucian's tale is exciting enough and might well fit into romance: Arsakomas, a Skythian, falls in love with Mazaia, the daughter of Leukanor, Eubiotos's half-brother. Leukanor rejects Arsakomas and bestows his daughter on Adyrmachos, the king of the Machlyans. The point of Lucian's tale is friendship: when insulted by the rejection of his suit, Arsakomas enlists the help of two friends to avenge him. One brings him the head of Leukanor; the other tricks Adyrmachos into entrusting him with Mazaia, whom he promptly carries off to Arsakomas. Mazaia herself has no active role in the story; if she loves either man, Lucian has no interest in revealing this to his audience. In contrast, Kalligone is a volatile actor—stirred by her passion for Eraseinos into a murderous rage against Eubiotos. Although it is possible that friendship between Eubiotos and Eraseinos figured in the plot of the novel, this is not obvious from what remains.

Kalligone must be located, at least in part, in South Russia, around the Sea of Azov (Lake Maiotis), and its cast includes Greeks—Kalligone (and Erasinos?); a Bosporan king—Eubiotos; Amazons—Themisto et al.; Maiotai; and Sauromatians.

Sauromatians were often equated with Amazons in Greek historical writings: indeed Herodotos identifies them as a hybrid race of Amazon women and Skythian men (4.110–17), an identification resulting in part because they occupied the territories that mythology most often assigned to Amazons, but also because their women—at least according to Greek sources—took part in male activities like hunting and war, and even wore clothing similar to men's. In this vein, Polyainos (8.56) records a story of a Sarmatian queen, Amage, to whom the Greeks of the Chersonese appealed for help against an incursion of Skythians.

Though clearly related to the Skythians, most Greek historians and geographers seem to regard Sauromatians as a distinct group of nomadic peoples. The spelling "Sauromatian" was applied (though by no means consistently) to those nomads living on the Asian side of the Tanais River, whereas "Sarmatian" was preferred for the European tribes of these same peoples. After the time of Herodotos, these tribes appear to have begun a westward migration that brought them by the middle of the second century B.C.E. into continuous contact with Greeks settled in the region of the Bosporos. Harmatta (1950: 16–17) argues that their growing power threatened the Greek cities, who eventually applied to Mithridates for aid. Mithridates succeeded in stemming their advance and effectively curbing the power of these tribes, eventually enlisting them as allies in his wars against the Romans.

This same alliance of Greeks and Sauromatians against Skythians occurs, of course, in the Lucian episode, and, according to Harmatta, must belong to the period of 165–140 B.C.E., when the Skythian power in the Bosporan region was on the wane, and Skythian tribes had become vassals of a Sarmatian confederacy that had moved westward into the Pontus region. This, then, would have been a period in which these peoples were most conspicuous to Greek settlers in the Thracian Bosporos, and hence a period from which tales about them would be most likely to have been written down and transmitted by Greek writers. Rostovtzeff posits the existence of a number of "Bosporan-Skythian" romances based on events of the Hellenistic period that would have been available to Lucian as he wrote his dialogues. Whatever the merit of this hypothesis, it is clear that there must have been at least one famous story, perhaps first popularized in legend and subsequently written down, which served as source for Lucian and this novel—and perhaps Polyainos—in much the same way that incidents from the life of the "historical" Ninos and Semiramis were able to serve as material both for Ktesias and his epitomizers as well as for the *Ninos* novelist.

DESCRIPTION

PSI 981 (= *P*² 2628) consists of two pieces (measuring 9.5 × 15 cm + 7.5 × 15 cm), evidently the top and bottom halves of a forty-two-line column, with unusually large upper (7.0 cm) and lower (8.0 cm) margins and intercolumnia (2.0 cm). A few letters (never more than four) from the left edge of the preceding column are visible opposite lines 3–10, and from the right edge of the following column opposite lines 19–21 and 34–42. The lines average between seventeen and twenty-two letters per line. No punctuation or lectional signs occur; iota adscript was written occasionally; the scribe usually writes *scriptio plena*, but the text itself generally avoids hiatus. The hand itself is a small and extremely elegant formal round hand of a type assigned to the second century C.E. The back is blank, and the whole conveys the impression of a most luxurious edition. Originally the pieces were published as separate fragments from the same roll, but O. Guéraud (reported in *GRP*) subsequently joined the pieces and improved the readings. In terms of language and style, *Kalligone* falls into conventional novel patterns. The language of the opening lines, for example, can be easily paralleled in Chariton and Achilles Tatius (see notes ad loc.). We do not print the fragmentary columns.

PSI 981

παντελῶϲ τὴν γνώμην
διαϲεϲειϲμένη. ἐλθοῦϲα
δὴ ἐπὶ ϲκηνὴν καὶ ῥίψα-
4 ϲα ἑαυτὴν ἐπὶ τῆϲ ϲτιβάδοϲ
ἀνωλόλυξεν μέγα καὶ διω-
λύγιον, καὶ δάκρυα ἐξέρ[ρ]εον
ἀθρόα· κατερρήξατό τε τὸν χι-
8 τῶνα. ἐπεμελεῖτο δὲ ὁ Εὐ-
βίοτοϲ μηδένα παρεῖναι
ἐν τῇ ϲκηνῇ, ἀλλ' ἐξήλαυ-
νεν ἅπανταϲ ὡϲ ἄν τινων
12 δυϲχερῶν αὐτῇ περὶ Ϲαυ-
ρομ̣ατῶν ἠγγελμέν̣ω̣ν.
ἡ δὲ ἀνωλοφύρετο καὶ ἐ-
κώκυεν καὶ ἐλοιδορεῖτο
16 μὲν ἐκείνῃ τῇι ἡμέρῃι,
ἐν ᾗ τὸν Ἐραϲεῖνον εἶδεν
ἐν τῇι θήρᾳ, ἐλ̣ο̣ι̣δορεῖ̣τ̣ο
δὲ καὶ αὐτὴ τοῖϲ αὐτῆϲ ὀ-
20 φθαλμοῖϲ· ἐ[μ]έμφετο δὲ
κ]α̣ὶ τὴν ['Άρ]τεμιν . [. .] . μ̣ε̣
.] . [. . . . .]α
. . . .]υ
24 . . . .]ι̣ρ̣[.
. .] . κ̣αὶ ἐν τοιαύτ[αι]ϲ ξ[υμ-
φο]ραῖϲ ϲτρεφομένη ἵε̣ι̣

Supplements are those of ed. pr. unless otherwise indicated. Schubart's conjectures are in
GRP.
3. ρειψα pap.   7. κατερηξατο pap.   11. ὡϲ ἄν Zimm., ὡϲεί ed. pr.   18–19. ἐν
τῇι θήρᾳ, ἐλ̣οι̣δορεῖτ̣ο | δὲ κ̣αὶ Guér.   19. αὐτὴ ed. pr., αὐτῇ Guér.   20. ἐ[μ]έμ-
φετο Guér.   21. κ]α̣ὶ τὴν ['Άρ]τεμιν Guér.   23–24. One line missing between, so
Guér.   25. ἐν τ̣οιαύτ[αι]ϲ Schub., ἐν τῶι αὐτ[ῇ]ϲ ed. pr.   26. ειει pap., ἵει Zimm.

272

... her mind being
in complete turmoil. Having come
into the tent and
4   hurled herself onto the mattress,
she gave a loud piercing cry;
her tears flowed
abundantly; she ripped her clothing.
8   Eubiotos saw to it that
no one stayed
in the tent: he drove
everyone out on the pretext that some
12   devastating news concerning the Sauromatians had been brought to her.
She was mourning and
screaming and cursing
16   that day
when she had seen Eraseinos
at the hunt, cursing
her own eyes as well.
20   She was railing even
at Artemis ...
       ...
       ...
24   ...
While she was flailing about in such
torments she reached

τὴ]ν χεῖρα ἐπὶ τὸ ἐγχειρί-

28 διον· ἐτύγχανεν δὲ αὐτὸ

ὁ] Εὐβίοτος ε[ὐθ]ὺ κατὰ τὴν

ἔφ]οδον cπαcάμενοc ἐκ

το]ῦ κολεοῦ καὶ λαθών· ἡ δὲ

32 ἐπ]ιβλέψαcα πρὸc αὐτὸν

λέ]γει· "ὦ πάντων ἀνθρώ-

π]ων κάκιcτε, ὃc ἔτληc [ἄ]ψα-

cθ]αι τοῦ ἐμοῦ ξίφουc· εἰμὶ

36 μ]ὲν γὰρ οὐκ Ἀμαζὼν οὐ-

δὲ] Θεμιcτώ, ἀλλ' Ἑλληνὶc

καὶ] Καλλιγόνη, οὐδεμιᾶc

δὲ] Ἀμαζόνων τὸν θυμὸν

40 ἀc]θενεcτέρα. ἴθι μοι τὸ ξί-

φο]c κόμιζε, μὴ [κ]αὶ cὲ ταῖc

χε]ρcὶν ἄγχουc' ἀποκτει-

---

29. ε[ὐθ]ὺ κατὰ τὴν Schub.   30. ἔφ]οδον Schub.,]ολον ed. pr.   41. μὴ [κ]αὶ Edgar,
μ[ή τ]ί ed. pr.

her hand out for her dagger;
28 but in fact,
Eubiotos, at her
entry, had slipped it from
the sheath unnoticed.
32 She glanced towards him and
said, "O most wicked of all men—
you dared to touch
my sword! Though I am
36 no Amazon, no
Themisto, but a Greek,
Kalligone,
yet my spirit is
40 no weaker than that of any Amazon. Come,
bring me my sword, lest even you
I throttle to death with my bare hands. . . ."

PSI 981

3–4. ῥίψα|cα ἑαυτὴν τῆc cτιβάδοc : cf. Ch. 3.6.6; XE 2.8.1, 3.9.3.

5–6. ἀνωλόλυξεν μέγα καὶ διω|λύγιον: cf. Ch. 3.3.15, 3.7.4; AT 1.13.1; XE 1.11.5. Rattenbury (1933: 244) points out that the adverbial use of διωλύγιον was particularly common in the novels.

6. δάκρυα ἐξέρ[ρ]εον : cf. Ch. 2.5.7, 3.6.6, 5.2.4; AT 3.11.1.

7–8. κατερρήξατό τε τὸν χι|τῶνα: cf. Ch. 5.2.4, 7.1.5; XE 3.10.1; AT 5.3.6; Hld. 6.9.2; *Ninos* B.I.4–5.

8–9. Εὐ|βίοτοc : see above, introduction.

9–10. μηδένα παρεῖναι | ἐν τῇ cκηνῇ : cf. Luc. *Tox.* § 50 when Leukanor advises his retinue to withdraw: μηδεὶc δὲ παρέcτω ἐc τὸν νεών. . . . Rostovtzeff (1931: 33) has noted the general similarity of the scene in the Ares temple to that in our fragment—dismissal of attendants, a story made up to divert attention from the real event, the pulling of a sword or dagger.

14. ἀνωλοφύρετο : note Xen. *Kyr.* 7.3.14, where Pantheia kills herself over the corpse of her dead husband and the nurse "cries out in mourning." Cf. also Hld. 7.14: ἀπωλοφύροντο, and above, "Antonius Diogenes?" II.13–14: ὠλοφυρόμεθα. The use of this verb may well indicate that Kalligone has received news of Eraseinos's death.

275

14–15. ἐ|κώκυεν: cf. AT 1.13.1, 1.14.1, 3.5.2.

15. ἐλοιδορεῖτο: cf. AT 1.6.5.

17. Ἐραςεῖνον: the name mainly occurs as that of a river, variously located (see, e.g., Str. 8.6.8); as a man's name only in Hippocrates *De morb.* 3.13 (8). But Stephen of Byzantium (s.v. Ἄρνη) notes a Thracian people called "Erasinioi" (if the reading is correct). If Eraseinos derived his name from that source, he could be a commander of Thracian Greeks.

24. The goddess Artemis is of course appropriately mentioned in connection with the hunt, but she was also worshiped among the Skythians.

27–28. ἐγχειρί|διον: As she enters the tent, Kalligone is apparently wearing a dagger or short sword (which she refers to as τοῦ ἐμοῦ ξίφους below, line 35). Sword belts and daggers could not have been a normal part of the fashionable Greek woman's costume even in the outer reaches of the Bosporos. We assume, therefore, that she is in some sort of disguise, and that her weapon was the *akinakē*—a Persian short sword, worn by Skythians (Luc. *Tox.* §38) and venerated by the Alanoi (according to Ammianus Marcellinus 31.2.23) and by the Sauromatians (according to Clem. Alex. *Protr.* 5.64.5).

29–31. Cf. Luc. *Tox.* §50: οἱ μὲν εἰςῆλθον … ςπαςάμενος (sc. Lonchates) τὸν ἀκινάκην.

37. Θεμιςτώ: the named is otherwise unattested in connection with Amazons. A chief area of Amazon habitation in the Pontus region, however, was the plain of Themiskura on the Thermodon, which was said to have been named after an Amazon queen (App. *Mithr.* §78). Therefore, a name with a *themis*-root is not inappropriate for such a lady.

42. Doubtless ἀποκτεί|[νω] is to be restored. The missing syllable will have come at the top of the following column.

Antheia and a
Cast of Thousands

❖

The *Antheia* fragment begins with a scene in a temple, with what seems to be a description of its functions and cult objects. The narrative shifts at line 16 to a woman entering (or leaving) a small town or fortress. (The Greek word, *polichnē*, is ambiguous.) She is concealing something in the folds of her garments. The second column contains a dialogue between two unnamed persons, at least one of whom is male. One tells the other about a bewildering series of events, naming seven characters in fourteen lines. The column breaks off with speaker A remarking—appropriately—"the rest is conjecture and talk, mingled with [———] holding the unbelievable and astonishing." Only a few words remain from Column III, where the dialogue apparently continues and Artemis is mentioned.

Antheia would appear to be the central character in this fragment. She has a drug secreted about her person, which a woman named Thalassia, evidently a political supporter of Thraseas, has taken away and hidden from her. These events are cast against an historical or pseudo-historical backdrop: the condition of a *politeia* is at issue; Thraseas seems to be in control, while Thalassia, having appropriated a ship from one Kleander, has sailed off in Thraseas's support (whether to join him or to protect his flank is unclear). Subsequently she succeeds in eluding her entourage, and would appear to be in Antheia's company. Meanwhile, Lysippos and Euxeinos are off on a fact-finding expedition. What relationship the speakers have to all these persons and events is unknown, but possibly lines II.9–10 indicate that they intend to support Thalassia (and hence Thraseas).

The temple description, narrative of events, report, and dialogue suggest a relatively complex narrative, and although the language is not elaborate, neither is it unpolished. Note, for example, the *homoioteleuton* and balance of II.18–19. The nature of the discussion is curious. One calls the other "friend," so it cannot be a slave or servant giving a report. Nor is the main speaker recounting an adventure that has taken place in his past. Both seem acquainted with and interested in the fates of the participants of the enclosed narrative. It sounds almost as if one speaker is recounting the plot of a particularly exciting novel to the other, but without yet having read its final pages.

Moreover, the names suggest that this piece belongs in some rather self-conscious relationship to Xenophon's *Ephesiaka*: (1) Antheia and Euxeinos are characters in the *Ephesiaka*; names of other characters are borrowed from either Herodotos or Xenophon (as are characters in the *Ephesiaka*). (2) Artemis and a temple (if not a temple of Artemis) figure in this fragment; in the *Ephesiaka*, the lovers meet during a festival of Artemis in Ephesos, and the goddess acts as a protectress throughout. (3) Both Antheias find themselves in possession of poison. In the *Ephesiaka*, Antheia begs a poison from the doctor Eudoxos, to commit suicide on the eve of her marriage to Perilaos; this Antheia appears to want poison for similar reasons—to avoid further sexual harassment.

There is already considerable speculation about the extant version of the *Ephesiaka*. Was it written in the form in which we now have it? Or is what survives in part an epitome of a more complex narrative?[1] Zimmermann has conjectured that our scrap may be a predecessor to the extant manuscript version of the *Ephesiaka*, but this is hard to swallow. Although we are convinced that the extant *Ephesiaka* is to some extent the handiwork of an epitomizer, we can find nothing to support Zimmermann's suggestion. The plots, apart from the general similarities outlined above, are not alike. We might of course fantasize that the epitomizer left out the particular section that our fragment recounts (along with seven characters!), but one might equally well suppose that this fragment came from a novel deliberately borrowing from the *Ephesiaka*, perhaps in ways similar to which that novel has borrowed from Chariton.[2] At the very least, however, the existence of the *Antheia* fragment increases our appreciation for the way in which these novels may have been interdependent.

[1] See Bürger 1892: 36–67, Reeve 1971: 531–34 (who argues that our current version contains sections of epitome, based on the presence or absence of hiatus), and Schmeling 1980: 76–77 for a summary of other positions.

[2] Papanikolaou (1964: 305–20) has studied the degree to which Xenophon's novel has appropriated the language of Chariton.

Description

PSI 6.726 (= *P*^{2} 2627, measuring 11.5 ×20.0 cm) preserves three columns from the top of a papyrus roll; only the middle column is intact. The left is lacking between two and eight letters from the beginnings of the lines, the right lacking two-thirds from the ends. There are between twenty-seven and thirty letters per line. This text was written across the fibers on the back of a roll containing Demosthenes 51.7–10 (*On the Crown of the Trierarch*), right side up in relation to that speech. Four columns of the Demosthenes survive, written in a narrow format—about twelve letters to the line, twenty-nine or thirty lines to the column—familiar from the second century C.E. If the papyrus roll contained only this speech, its complete dimensions would have been about 1.60 meters long by 30 cm high. This is relatively small: approximately two-thirds the size of Xenophon's *Ephesiaka*, Book 1, shorter than most of the dialogues of Lucian. The roll might have contained more than this one speech, however; for example, *P*^{2} 337 (= Demosthenes *Epistle* 3) is part of the same roll as *P*^{2} 1234 (= Hyperides). To judge from the Demosthenes on the front, the lower two-thirds of each column of our text will be missing. The handwriting on the back is quickly written and practiced, but shows little consistency in spacing of letters or in their inclination relative to each other. In this respect it resembles Herodas (*GMAW*^{2}, pl. 39). We are inclined to place it in the latter half of the second century C.E., though the ed. pr. placed it rather later. The surface of the papyrus has been severely abraded in places, but the whole has a pleasing workmanlike quality. There is one correction made in the text and repeated in the margin (I.1); both high stop and dicolon are used for punctuation; a paragraphos appears below the first line of Column II, an apostrophe at II.1. No itacisms or uncorrected errors are visible. Iota adscript appears to have been written (II.17, but not elsewhere). There are three examples of hiatus (I.7, 13; II.19). Subsequent to the ed. pr., the papyrus was reread by W. Crönert and T. Lodi; Zimmermann prints this improved text in *GRP*, though it is often difficult to distinguish genuine new readings from Zimmermann's conjectures.

COLUMN I

```
   .. ]εις δ᾽ ἦςαν [ 10–12 ]ον [ . . . ] ροτε-
   ρ . ] . · τοὺς μητ[ 10–12 ]πους . . κον-
   .. ]αν ὥσπερ . . . [ . . . . . . ]ςεχ . ος ἐρρω-
4  μέ]νοι · μήτε ς . [ . ]εν . [ . . . ]των διεμεν[ . .
   μήτ]ε ἀναστῆναι . . . . . ντας [ . . . . . .
   . . . . . ] . . τες τὸν νεὼν καὶ χεῖρ[ας νί]ψαγ-
   τες καὶ] πόδας καὶ εἴ τι ἄλλο ἦν ἄκρον · ενι
8  . . . . . δ]εςποτικῶν ἀναθημάτ[ων] κα-
   . . . . . . ] . . . . πον προ . . ο . . . .
   . . . . . . ] . . β . . δ[ . ]φρου . . . . τ[ . . . .
   . . . . . . . τες δίφρο[υ] τοῦ τῆς . . . . .
12 . . . . . . ]ταις ἡλίκαις π[άς]αις ρ . ω . . . .
   . . . . . . ]τα . η[ . ]ικου ἀνέςτρεφε . εκ . .
   . . . . . ]τοξαρην ὡς δια . . αςιαυτ . . . . ρα
   . . . . . . ]περ πολλῶν ἀπολογηςαμεν . ν
16 . . . . . . ]ηςιν φόνων. ἡ δὲ ἐπεὶ κατά-
   . . . . . . εἰς] τὴν πολίχνην ἔμελλεν, τὸ μὲν
   . . . . . . . . ] τοῖς κόλποις κατέθετο, μή τις αὐ-
   τὴν ἀφέλη]ται πάλιν. αὐτὴ δὲ ἀνατείναςα
```

- -

Col. I: 1.]ειςηςαν corrected to]εις δ᾽ ἦςαν in text and added again in the margin, τρ]εῖς
Zimm.   2.] . · pap.   4.]ναι · corrected to]νοι · pap.   τῶν δε[δε]μέγ[ων
Zimm.   5. μήτ]ε ἀναςτῆναι [ε]ὐνηθέντας Crönert-Lodi   6. ςήρ]αντες Crön. χεῖ-
ρ[ας Lav.   νί]ψαγ[τες Crön., νί]ψαι Lav.   9. τὸν πρό[πολ]ο[ν Crön.   11. δί-
φρο[ν Lav.   12. π[άς]αις Zimm.   12–13. ῥ[ύ]μ̣[αι δὲ ἦ]ςαν μες]ταὶ ἐπινίκου
Zimm.   13. ἐπ[ιν]ίκου ἀνέςτεφεν Norsa   14. τοξάρ⟨χ⟩ην Zimm.   ταῦτ[α
Lav.   15. καθά]περ Lav., καί]περ Zimm.   ἀπολογηςαμένων ed. pr.   16. ἔγκλ]η-
ςιν Wil., ἀπείλη]ςιν Crön.   φονων : pap.   16–17. κατα|[λύειν εἰς Lav., κατα|[λεί-
πειν Zimm.   18. [φάρμακον ἐν] Lav.   18–19. αὐ|[τὴν Lav.   19. [ἀφέλη]ται
Zimm., [ἀφαιρῆ]ται Lav.   παλιν · pap.

] and there were
] some . . .
] just as . . . the strong . . .
4   ] nor to
] nor cause to leave
] ——ing the temple and washing their hands
[and] feet and any other extremity.
8   ] of the despot's dedications
]
]
] . . . chair . . .
12   ] to all women of like age
] . . . he was overthrowing
] . . . on the grounds that
] having defended himself
16   [against a charge] of many murders. But when she
was going [to lodge in] the village, she
[put the poison?] in her clothes, lest someone
[capture her] again; and she, stretching out

COLUMN II

ἐγγραψάτω· Λύcιπποc δ᾽ ἐ[λ]θὼν ἐπὶ θάλατταν cὺν Εὐξείνῳ πυνθάνεται τῶν γνω-
[ρί]μων τὴν κατάcταcιν [π]ᾶcαν . . . . ωcα
4 [2–3] πολιτ . . . . · Θραcέαc μὲν ἄρχει . . ωνιc
[.] . τοc. Θαλαccία δὲ ἀναρπάcαcα τὸ πλοῖ-
[ο]ν Κλεάνδρου Θραcέαν περιέπει καὶ . . [
. . . . . ειcιν ἀλλ . . . . ὅτε ἐξέ-
8 [π]λευcεν λαθοῦcα αὐτὰ[c ὦ]ν αὐτῇ με-
λ[εῖ .]—ἀcφαλὲc γὰρ δοῦναι . . . τὰc Θαλαc-
cίαc βουλάc—τὰ δὲ Ἀνθ[εί]αc ἑλομένη,
[.] . . [.]ρεc . [. .]ν Ἀνθείαν ἰδοῦcα τὸ φάρ-
12 [μ]ακον καὶ κατακρύψαcα ὡc μάλιcτα ὑ . . [.]
. . . εc . . . περιεγένετο.” “τὰ δὲ Ἀνθείαc,
[ο]ὐδ᾽ ἔχ[ει] λέγειν, φίλτατε;” “οὐκ οἶδα,” ἔφη,
“cαφῶ[c . ὁ] μὲν γὰρ Λύcανδροc αὐτὴν ὑπ[ὸ ἁ]ρ-
16 παγῆc παρέδωκεν δ . [. .] . . . καὶ Θραcέα[c]
ἐξῄρητο ἐπ᾽ αὐτῆι. δ[ῆλ]α ταῦτα ἅπαcιν·
[τὰ δὲ] ἄλλα εἰκαcία καὶ λόγοc μεμιγμένοc
[. . . . . .]ατι ἔχοντι τὸ ἄπιcτον καὶ παράδο-
20 [ξον.”]

- -

COLUMN III

ἐcωζόμην [
ταύρων ορ[
ἐκεῖνοι κ[
4 ανο . . . αυ[
ωρα α . . . [
θαι καὶ κτ . [
Ἄρτεμιν. ο[
8 ψευcαμεν[
. . λ[. .]ενο[
μήτε αὐτὸc . [
ἐκείνην ατ[
12 [. . . .]cαφη[
[. . . .]ηδε
. [. . . . . .] . [
[. . . . .] . [
16 . [
. ο . [
τα[
ραc κακιc[τ-

- - - - - - - - - -

Col. II.1. _ενγραψατω· pap.   ἐ[λ]θὼν Zimm., πλ]έων Lav.   3–4. τ[ῆc ἔ]ωc ἄ|[ρτι]
πολιτ[ε]ί[αc Zimm.   4. [μὲ]ν Zimm.   ἄρχει Lav.   μό]νοc ? Zimm.
5.] . τοc· pap., [ο]υτοc ed. pr., α]ὐτόc ? Zimm.   5–6. πλοῖ[ον] ed. pr.   6. περι-
έπε[ι] Lav.   7. τε πάρ]ειcιν ? Zimm.   7–8. δὲ ἐξέ|[π]λευcεν ed. pr.   8–9. αὐ-
τὰ[c ὦ]ν αὐτῇ με|[λεῖ.] Zimm.   9. δ᾽ οὖν [ὅθ]εν Zimm.   10. [β]ουλάc Lav., δούλαc
Zimm.   τὰ δε[ῖπ]να Zimm.   ἀφελομένη ed. pr.   μενη· pap.   11. καὶ
τ]ρέcα[cα]ν Zimm.   12. μαλιcταῡ pap.   13. ἔ]cεcθαι Lav.   περιέπειν ἐ[ὰν]
Lav., περιέπειν ε[ἴα] Zimm.   14. [cο]ὶ δέχ[ου] Lav., [ἐπ]ὶ δέχ[ου] Zimm.   φιλτατε :
pap.   15–16. ἀφ᾽ ἁρ|[παγῆc] Crön.   16. δὴ [ἴκ]α[ν]ά· Zimm.   Θραcέα[c δ᾽
Zimm.   17. ἐξ[επτό]ητο ἐπ᾽ α[ὐ]τῆι. Zimm., Lodi   δ[ῆλ]α Crön.   18. τὰ δὲ]
Zimm., τὰ δ᾽] Lav.   ικαcια pap.   19. πλάcμ]ατι Zimm., μυθεύμ]ατι Lav.   ἄ[πι-
c]τον Zimm., ἄπληcτον? ed. pr., ἀ[δύνα]τον Lav.   19–20. παράδο|[ξον] Lav.
Col. III: 1. [κἀγὼ μὲν] | ἐcωζόμην Zimm.   2. Ταύρων Crön.   6. κτᾶ[cθαι
Crön.   7. αρτεμιν : pap. Possibly a paragraphos below; traces too broken for
certainty   7–8. ἔ]|ψευcα μὲν Lav.   18–19. [cυμφο]|ρᾶc κακίc[τηc ? Zimm.

A: "let him write it down. Lysippos, having come to the sea
with Euxeinos, asks the people he knows
about the whole situation . . .

4   government; Thraseas is ruling . . .
Thalassia, having commandeered Kleandros'
boat is aiding Thraseas . . .

. . .

8   when she sailed out having escaped notice of those in her care—
for it is safe to give out . . . Thalassia's devisings—
having taken Antheia's affairs in hand,
she . . . Antheia, after she saw the poison

12   and concealed it certainly
. . . she escaped" (?) B: "About Antheia's affairs,
is it not possible to speak, friend?" A: "I'm not sure," he said.
"Lysander betrayed her by a rape . . . and Thraseas

16   has been removed because of her(?). These things are clear to everyone.

The rest is conjecture and talk, mingled with
[——] holding the unbelievable and astonishing."

COLUMN I

1–2. Perhaps πρότε|ρ[ο]γ·.

2–7. The construction appears to be]ειϲ δ' ἦϲαν … μήτε … μήτε … μήτε ἀναϲτῆ-
ναι. If Zimmermann's τρ]εῖϲ is correct, three prohibitions? Compare, e.g.,
Lollianos B.1 recto 15–17.

6–7.] ̣ ̣τεϲ τὸν νεὼν καὶ χεῖρ[αϲ νί]ψαγ|[τεϲ καὶ] πόδαϲ καὶ εἴ τι ἄλλο ἦν ἄκρον:
"[——]ing the temple and washing both the hands and feet and any other pro-
jection [of the statues]?" Crönert's [ϲήρ]αγτε ̣ϲ is attractive as a supplement for
the opening participle in this context.

Although in theory it may be desirable to connect καὶ χεῖρ[αϲ νί]ψαγ|[τεϲ
καὶ] πόδαϲ καὶ εἴ τι ἄλλο ἦν ἄκρον with the following genitive, ενι is fairly cer-
tain and space at the beginning of the next line is limited. Articulate either ἐνὶ |
[δὲ] or ἔνι|[οι τῶν]?

νί]ψαγ|[τεϲ]: there is not room to restore, e.g., ἐνί]ψαγ|[το]. If the form is
active, then "they" must have been washing statues or some other object;
washing themselves would require a middle. Washing statues in connection
with bloodshed of some sort (lines 15–16) faintly suggests the *Iphigenia in
Tauris*.

8. δ]εϲποτικῶν ἀναθημάτ[ων]: the temple dedications of a tyrant? ἀναθήματα is
the standard term for both public and private dedications found in every
ancient temple.

9. προ ̣ ̣ο ̣: πρόναοϲ would suit traces.

11. δίφρο[υ]: for a similar object among temple dedications, see Paus. 1.27.1 (a
chair).

13. Norsa's ἐπι[ν]ίκου would be a tight fit.

ἀνέϲτρεφε: others have read ἀνέϲτεφε, but there is space as well as a trace of
ink before εφ. Given that this passage continues with a mention of bloodshed,
and that the status of a government is at issue in the next column, "he was
overthrowing" might suit context better than "he was crowning." The verb
requires an object, which is presumably]τοξαρην in the next line.

At end, δ' ἐκεῖ|[νοϲ] or sim.?

14.]τοξάρην: the letters are quite legible. If the reading is to stand (and emending in the vicinity of a lacuna is a dubious practice), there seem to be two possibilities: (1)]τοξάρηϲ as an unattested variant of τοξήρηϲ, itself rare and poetic,
or (2) the name Ἀρτοξάρηϲ, attested as the name of a eunuch of Artaxerxes in
Ktesias (Photios *Epit.* 72.42ff.). Either could do. A statue, for example, might
be described as "holding a bow." Alternatively, an Artoxares could be one of
the characters. Note, for example, that Artaxerxes and his eunuch Artaxates
figure prominently in Chariton.

ὡϲ δια ̣ ̣αϲιαυτ ̣ ̣ ̣ ̣ρα: independently, elements of Zimmermann's conjec-
ture ὡϲ διὰ βίαϲ ταῦτα πεπρα|[χό]τα are attractive, but the whole does not quite
fit (as Zimmermann realized). Perhaps ὡϲ διαϲ̣ταϲι (=διαϲτάϲει) or διὰ

ϲτάϲι⟨ν⟩ αὐτὰ πεπρα|[χότα = "on the grounds that he had accomplished these things by dissention [or through faction]"?

15–16. πολλῶν ἀπολογηϲαμεν . ν|[. . . . .]ηϲιν φόνων: previous editors have read ἀπολογηϲαμένων, but the final vowel is either η, or more likely o—to agree with]τοξαρην? The missing noun is likely to be a word meaning "charge" or "complaint." "He made a defence against [the charge] of many murders"?

16. The dicolon to indicate a change of speaker is used here after φόνων. If this is indeed a dialogue, the participants are not clearly marked. Normal narrative style would demand at least ὁ δ' ἔφη. Dicola, however, may also mark the end of a speech with the resumption of narrative or simply a shift from one scene to another, without dialogue.

17. τὴν πολίχνην: originally a proper noun, after which it came to mean a small town or a fort. Without context it could be either. The accusative requires a verb with the sense of "enter into" or "stop at." Lavagnini's καταλύειν is acceptable, or κατάγεϲθαι εἰϲ (if she has a ship), or sim.

17–19. The woman conceals something about her person. From II.8 we learn that Antheia apparently has poison, which Thalassia hides away. It is tempting, therefore, to restore φάρμακον here and assume that ἡ in line 16 is Antheia. This restoration, though, is a tight squeeze, especially since τοῖϲ κόλποιϲ would seem to require a preposition. (It is difficult to imagine τοῖϲ κόλποιϲ as a dative of instrument following κατατιθέναι = "to deposit or store up"). Alternatively, e.g., τὸ μὲν | [ξίφοϲ ἐν]. Cf. Photios's epitome of Iamblichos 74b30: Ῥοδάνηϲ ἀνελόμενοϲ τὸ φάρμακον.

COLUMN II

1. ἐγγραψάτω: ἐγγράφω may mean to inscribe in a letter or record or to inscribe in stone for a public dedication. The third-person imperative implies the presence of a third party serving as an amanuensis to one or both of the speakers. The imperative may equally well refer to what preceded as to the account that follows it. Presumably the present tenses throughout are historical.

Lysippos and Euxeinos below are both found in Xenophon's *Hellenika*; the former was a Spartan governor in Epitalios (3.2.29ff.), the latter a Spartan governor in Asia (4.2.5). Euxeinos is the name of a character in the *Ephesiaka*.

It is possible that Lysippos or Euxeinos is the speaker of this report, referring to himself in the third-person.

δ' ἐ[λ]θών: elsewhere δὲ is unelided. There is insufficient space for δὲ [ἐλ]θών. The expression is frequent in the novelists.

1–2. θάλατ|ταν: both this Attic spelling and θάλαϲϲα are used by the extant novelists, in no discernible pattern.

3–4. τὴν κατάϲταϲιν [π]ᾶϲαν . . . . ωϲα|[. . .] πολιτ . . . . : the simplest solution is a genitive following κατάϲταϲιν [π]ᾶϲαν, τῆϲ . ωϲα|[. . .] πολιτείαϲ·, but ωϲα has proved intractable. τὴν κατάϲταϲιν [π]ᾶϲαν ἵγ[α γ]νῷ ϲα|[φῶϲ τὰ] πολιτικά might do, but there is no room for a definite article. Zimmermann's ἕ]ωϲ ἄ|[ρτι] is a solution, but that phrase is almost never used in the attributive position; rather, one expects τῆϲ πολιτείαϲ ἕωϲ ἄρτι.

4. Θραϲέαϲ μὲν ἄρχει : presumably he governs the state in question (after a take-over?). The most famous bearer of the name held consular rank under Nero (Plut. *Cat. min.* §25.1, §37.1, Cassius Dio 61.15, 20, 66.12), but none with this name seem to have been prominent in the Classical period. It is perhaps worth noting that the passage in the *Hellenika* that features Lysippos also involves one Thrasudaios (3.2.27–30).

4–5. ‸‸ωνιϲ[.]‸ τοϲ : at the end, traces could suit either τηϲ or υτοϲ. An agent noun like ἀγωνιϲ|[ ]τήϲ suits the space well, but the meaning seems hardly apt. Zimmermann's [μό]νοϲ, [α]ὐτόϲ is tempting, but looks too short to account for all existing traces.

5–13. We take the shape of these lines to be as follows: Θαλαϲϲία δὲ (responding to Θραϲέαϲ μὲν) + participle + περιέπει … ὅτε [Thalassia] ἐξέπλευϲεν + participle—an aside—three participles + περιεγένετο. The subject throughout must be Thalassia, unless there is yet another woman sailing about—a circumstance we refuse to contemplate.

5. Θαλαϲϲία: unattested elsewhere as a proper name.

6. Κλεάνδρου: Kleander is quite a common Greek name, borne by historical figures in both Herodotos and Xenophon.

7. ειϲιν: if this forms part of a compound of εἶμι, then it will be paired with περιέπει. If a compound of εἰμί, then the subject will change from Thalassia, to "they," then back to Thalassia in the next sentence (see above, 5–13 note).

αλλ‸‸‸‸‸‸‸‸ : previous editors have read ἀλλ[α]παϲι (variously articulated), but there is insufficient space for this to begin a new phrase. Alternatively, an object of some kind for the preceding, ϲύγειϲιν ἀλλήλοιϲ, "and … they are in each other's company" or sim.? Cf. XE 2.3.6: καὶ ϲυνῆϲαν ἀλλήλοιϲ ἔτι ἐν Ἐφέϲῳ.

8–9. αὐτὰ[ϲ ὦ]ν αὐτῇ με|λ[εῖ] : doubtless the phrase refers to Thalassia's female attendants.

9–10. ἀϲφαλὲϲ γὰρ δοῦναι ‸‸‸ τὰϲ Θαλαϲ|ϲίαϲ βουλάϲ : this appears to be a break in the report, addressed to the hearer: "For it is safe to give [you?] Thalassia's devisings." Letters before τὰϲ are too broken to identify, but ϲοι or νῦν are possibilities.

10. τὰ δὲ Ἀγθ[εί]αϲ ἑλομένη : Previous editors have restored τὰ δε … α ἀφελομένη, and have had no success in finding a supplement for the second word. In fact, phi is almost impossible to read (no vertical), and the change from ἀφαιρέω to αἱρέω is easy. τὰ δὲ Ἀνθείαϲ below then becomes the second speaker's request for elaboration of a subject already introduced.

Antheia (often spelled Anthia) is the name of the heroine in the *Ephesiaka*, in which novel the names of the lovers, Habrokomes and Antheia, are modelled on Abradatas and Pantheia of Xenophon's *Kyropaideia*. Indeed, the *Ephesiaka*'s storyline would seem to be indebted to this earlier work, namely, a wife faithful in the absence of her husband and a third party who falls violently in love with her to his detriment against inclination (and expectation). Elsewhere the name Antheia is rarely found, so prima facie, the Antheia in this fragment is deliberately borrowed from the *Ephesiaka*. Alternatively, it is possible for this fragment to have been the original imitator of the *Kyropaideia*, and for the *Ephesiaka* to have been based on it; certainly there are a number of other names borrowed from Xenophon that cannot have been accidental. This piece (insofar as we can tell) makes no mention of a husband for Antheia to whom she is faithful at all costs—the prime ingredient of the Abradatas-Pantheia tale—but so little remains that it is impossible to be dogmatic about this.

11-12. .].. [.]ρες.[..]ν Ἀνθείαν ἰδοῦϲα τὸ φάρ|[μ]ακον καὶ κατακρύψαϲα: the syntax is not wholly clear. We take Thalassia to be the subject of the participles and, because of the position of καί, we take the φάρμακον to be the object of both. Initially another main verb with Antheia as its object?

13-14. The punctuation after φίλτατε marks a change of speaker. Here, either speaker A speaks lines 1–14 and finishes the report with a request for information about Antheia's affairs, or speaker B interjects the question τὰ δὲ Ἀνθείας ... φίλτατε into A's recital. If the restoration in line 10 is correct, then the latter is more probable.

φίλτατε may be used for same-sex conversations as well as for a woman to a man. For φίλτατε used by one man to another, note Ch. 7.1.7 (Polycharmos to Chaireas) and XE 3.2.15 (Hippothoos to Habrokomes).

14. ο]ὐδ' ἔχ[ει] λέγειν, φίλτατε;" : previous editors restore δέχ[ου] or ἐπ]ιδέχ[ου], influenced by the presence of χ, but the resulting Greek scarcely seems idiomatic, whereas ἔχω λέγειν is common in the novels. For δὲ ... οὐδὲ, compare AT 8.11.3: τὸ δὲ μέγιϲτον, οὐδὲ εἶδον τὸ παράπαν....

15. ὁ] μὲν γὰρ Λύϲανδρος should correspond with τὰ δὲ] ἄλλα in line 18, contrasting what is known with what is not; Zimmermann's Θραϲέα[ϲ δ' is unnecessary.

Lysander is the name, of course, of the famous Spartan admiral found, like Lysippos and Euxeinos above, in Xen. *Hell.* 1.5.1 and throughout.

15-16. ὑπ[ὸ ἁ]ρ|παγῆϲ : a variant of a reading suggested by Crönert. Apart from the fact that such doings are commonplace in the novels (see. e.g., AT 8.17.2, Longos 2.23.5), this seems to fit with I.17–19 where the woman (surely Antheia?) fears a further assault or capture.

16. δ.[..]... : an adverb? Initially δη or δε, and after break, ναϲ or νωϲ seems possible.

17. ἐξῄρητο : options would appear to be limited to a pluperfect middle/pas-

sive of an ἐξ-compound. Zimmermann's ἐξ[επτό]ητο is too long, and the tail of a letter is visible before -ητο. Either ἐξῄρητο or ἐξέριπτο (= ἐξέρριπτο) are possibilities. Presumably Thraseas is the subject, not Antheia (who would seem to be ἐπ᾽ αὐτῆι below?).

ἐπ᾽ αὐτῆι: the reading is anomalous on two counts: elsewhere in the body of the text, when the readings are not in doubt, there is *scriptio plena*, and iota adscript was not written. Since this section of the report is about Antheia's circumstances, however, we are inclined to accept the reading, though the sense is not altogether clear. Has Thraseas been removed from Antheia's presence so that he cannot fall in love with her?

ἅπαϲιν: who are "all"—the audience of the novel or yet other characters within?

19–20. [......]ατι ἔχοντι τὸ ἄπιϲτον καὶ παράδο|[ξον]: a variety of nouns will fit the lacuna. Cf. XE 5.10.4: διηγήματα ἴϲωϲ ἄπιϲτα.

COLUMN III

2. ταύρων: Crönert (in *GRP*) conjectures that this is a proper name connecting it with a passage in Strabo (16.4.7) that describes the Tauri as two mountains in the Arabian desert. They are so called because their shape resembles these animals from a distance. Near them is another mountain with a temple to Isis on it. He locates this adventure in that region. But there were a number of other people as well as places named Tauri: e.g., the famous Skythian Taurians of Euripides' play, and the Taurus Mountains that divided Europe and Asia. Further, the cult of Artemis Tauropolos was celebrated in Attika as well as other parts of Greece and Asia Minor, and there was a well-known temple of Artemis Tauropolion in Samos (see Pape-Beneseler s.v. for references). Without further details it is chancy to pick one location over another.

288

Chione

❖

In November 1898, Ulrich Wilcken was offered for sale in Thebes a stack of parchment pages that the seller claimed had belonged to a monastery in upper Egypt. They were Coptic sermons, according to his co-worker Heinrich Schaefer, and late ones at that—so he had little interest in them until he noticed some traces of Greek under-writing. From the pile he purchased seven palimpsest leaves and then spent what he later recalled as the happiest days of his trip drifting in his felucca on the Nile, retrieving the (as he put it) fine, light-yellow uncial letters from under the thick, black coptic hand. Six of the leaves came from the same codex, four of them containing text from the last book of Chariton's *Kallirhoe*, the other two from a hitherto unknown work concerning a princess named Chione. The seventh page was never identified. Unfortunately, the ship that was transporting the papyri that Wilcken and Schaefer had dug up at Ehnas-Herakleopolis caught fire the following spring when it had just reached the harbor of Hamburg, and the cargo was destroyed. Hence it is that those pages from a seventh-century book that contained at least *Kallirhoe* and another novel, which we will refer to as *Chione* ("Snow White"), are now known as codex Thebanus deperditus, or "lost Theban codex," and we now rely on Wilcken's incomplete transcription.

Even in these small fractured pieces, however, the excellence of this narrative is apparent. Like Chariton, the author of *Chione* tells his story very rapidly, dramatically, and with a constant eye to feelings— apprehension, hatred, fear, determination. Columns I and III consist mostly of direct speech; Column II appears to be a transition from one scene in direct speech to another. The style is elegant and unobtrusive with carefully phrased rhythms and clausulae and the avoidance of hiatus. Since it was copied into the same codex as *Kallirhoe*, it is tempting to imagine that it, too, may have been written by Chariton, but though the style is not dissimilar, there is really nothing to sustain the conjecture.

The chief problem in the way of understanding the story is to identify the referents of the plural pronouns. "They" have granted thirty days for some people to think things over (I.12); "they" have uttered a crude threat that upsets the general populace (II.12); and "they" have laid claim to the princess in such a way that the powerful young citizens who might have been her suitors are frightened away. Previous interpretations have relied on the mention of Chione's potential suitors in Column II and on the role of the rude suitors in Chariton's opening scenes to reconstruct the plot of *Chione* as one involving hubristic suitors. In the first reconstruction, the king has announced that in thirty days he will choose a husband for his daughter. A group of nobles gathers and discusses in Column I what their joint strategy will be; they decide to unite behind one of their number and to frighten off all others. One of them, Megamedes, is chosen by the king, but Chione has already fallen in love with another and in an intimate conversation with him about their common crisis declares that she will take some drastic action (no longer visible) rather than live with Megamedes (Wilcken). In the second scenario, a group of bold suitors has frightened off potential rivals and delivered an ultimatum to the king: you must choose one of us within thirty days. They do this in the absence of Chione's intended, Megamedes (Garin 1920, Lavagnini 1922a). In Lavagnini's view, the king is dead, I and III are spoken by the queen mother to her daughter in the company of others, and the order of the columns is I–III–II. A third reconstruction has the king, pressured by ardent suitors, gaining thirty days' grace, hoping for the speedy return of Megamedes, to whom he has already betrothed his daughter. Chione then reveals that she has fallen in love with someone else, which puts the king in the predicament of having all the suitors and Megamedes angry with him. In this view, both I and III are spoken by the king (Rattenbury). In a fourth hypothesis, the king has chosen Megamedes as husband for his daughter and given her thirty days to change her mind about the lover she has already set her heart on. In the meantime, a group of rivals for her hand holds a meeting (Col. I) in which they plan to use the thirty days to shut out Megamedes and frighten away other competitors (Zimmermann).

The only basis in this text for imagining a group of villainous suitors is the plural pronouns designating those who crudely threaten, demand the maiden, and (in some interpretations) allow a thirty-day grace period. Though familiar enough from the *Odyssey* and *Kallirhoe*, there is good reason to expel these suitors from a reconstruction of *Chione*. In II.14–19, those who now will not dare to ask for Chione's hand are described as "those powerful citizens, at the beginning of their political careers who had themselves been intending to woo Chione." The phrase seems to be an absolute description of all young men of good family—the proper social class from which a consort might be chosen for a king's daughter. Nothing in the phrase sets these men apart from another group of potential suitors: *hosoi* means "all who," not "some others who." The imagined suitors can in fact be dismissed from our reconstruction with no loss. The following hypothesis lays no claim to certainty, only to economy and accuracy.

Megamedes is a powerful king or tyrant who has some diplomatic or family claim to Chione's hand (III.7–10). The king, her father, may know that she is already in love with another young man; he is certainly aware that suitors are available in his own city (II.13–22), with no need for more distant offers, and he is reluctant to honor whatever commitment has been made to, or is being claimed by, Megamedes. Megamedes sends ambassadors to the king's city with an ultimatum: I will arrive in thirty days at the head of an army to claim my rightful bride. The ambassadors' address to the king and his council is a crude display of arrogance; they demand Chione with no show of respect for the king or allowance for face-saving negotiations. Column I is the reaction, probably of the king and his councillors, to the ambassadors' presentation. Their problem is that, no matter what they decide, Megamedes may end up controlling the kingdom: either they resist, in which case he will try to take the city by force, or they will concede the legitimacy of his claim, in which case "the kingship devolves upon her and her future spouse." Column II follows immediately with the spread of the report of the ambassadors' rude deportment; their undisguised threats dissuade all the usual eligible bachelors from wanting to be known as the rival of Megamedes. In Column III, Megamedes' arrival is imminent; Chione and X (her lover) are at their wits' end. It is still perceived as something of a diplomatic problem: "Megamedes has given you no cause to abandon him" (III.7–10). Her lover leaves the decision to Chione, and she unhesitatingly declares that she prefers [——] to separation from X, provided that it be done with due propriety.

DESCRIPTION

The codex Thebanus deperditus (= P^2 244) measures 20.0 × 15.0 cm. Wilcken's initial transcription, on which we now rely, was limited to the better preserved portions on the skin sides of the pages, which he described as approximately 20 cm high by 15 cm broad, each containing two columns of twenty-eight lines and averaging between fourteen and sixteen letters per line. The hand was a finely made, careful uncial, slightly inclined to the right. This he tentatively assigned to the sixth or seventh centuries C.E., likening it to the Bobsienus mathematical fragment. Some of the lines ended with a small dot, but there were no accents, punctuation or lectional signs; spacing seems to have been used to separate paragraphs. The only abbreviation was an occasional macron for nu at line end. Wilcken himself realized that his transcription contained some obvious errors (Col. II.2 and 14–15), which he tried to emend on publication; Crönert at once offered three palmary emendations in Column III and Wilamowitz later noted two probable ones in column I. And in 1935 Wilcken informed F. Zimmermann by letter that his autograph of III.19–20 was in fact slightly different from what he had published. In the absence of the original parchment, discussion of the constitution of text must rely heavily on Wilcken's notes and recollections, however imperfect. These are referred to as "trans." in the apparatus criticus below.

The eight columns of Chariton, compared to the unique thirteenth century manuscript on which our knowledge of *Kallirhoe* depends, show a fairly large number of minor transpositions, additions, and omissions. From *Chione*, Wilcken deciphered parts of three columns, two of which must be from the same page. Regrettably, he failed to record the order of the three fragments. Since Wilcken's columns of *Kallirhoe* come from the concluding pages of the novel, it is tempting to suppose that the *Chione* columns followed immediately in the codex and therefore represent its opening scenes. This could easily fit the situation described there of suitors newly disappointed (Col. II.14–22) and lovers forced by external threat to take a desperate action, perhaps flight and subsequent adventures (Col. III). But measurement of the Wilcken *Kallirhoe* passages against the extant text shows that, even allowing for numerous small differences, at least three more leaves were required to reach the end of the novel. Therefore the leaves holding *Chione* do not follow *Kallirhoe* consecutively, and once this is acknowledged, there is no reason to assume that these leaves must have come from the opening of the novel. Further, each of the three columns partially transcribed by Wilcken from *Chione* presupposes so much information about the actors that it is hard to imagine any of them standing on the very first page. From this we conclude that at least three full leaves, probably more, intervened between Wilcken's four leaves of *Kallirhoe* and his two leaves of *Chione*.

Wilcken could not recall the order of the three partially transcribed columns, though he thought they were as he published them (we follow his order here). He maintained that two of the columns were from the same page, but whether III followed immediately is unclear. Since Wilcken only transcribed the flesh side of the leaves, there are numerous possibilities: (1) I–II and III are contiguous, since they came from two facing flesh sides; (2) one column intervenes between I–II and III, since III is the *second* column on the contiguous flesh side (Rattenbury); (3) at least four columns intervene between I–II and III because hair side faced hair side, placing flesh sides of the leaf on the outside; (4) the two leaves were not contiguous; and III is separated from I–II by at least eight columns.

COLUMN I

"
.... ας ἡ
[β]αϲιλεία εἰϲ ταύτην
καὶ τὸν ϲυνοικήϲον-
4 τα αὐτῇ μετέρχε-
ται, διόπερ οὕτω χρὴ
βουλεύϲαϲθαι νῦν
ἡμᾶϲ ὡϲ μὴ μετα-
8 γνῶναί ποτε δύνα-
ϲθαι. ἔχομεν δὲ εἰϲ
ϲκέψιν χρόνον ἡμε-
ρῶν τριάκοντα ἃϲ
12 εἰϲ τοῦτο παρ' αὐτῶν
⟨.............⟩
πλεῖον." ταῦτ' ἀκου-

[4 more lines were left untranscribed]

COLUMN II

-ρουϲαν. οὗτοι μὲν
ἦϲαν πρὸϲ τ[ῷ] περ[ὶ αὐ-
τῶν βουλεύεϲθαι · τα-
4 χέωϲ δὲ διεφοίτηϲε
ἀνὰ τὴν πόλιν ἅπαϲαν
. . . .
φαϲ φήμ[η καὶ] οὐθε[ὶϲ
8 ἄλλο οὐδὲν ἐλάλει [ἢ
περὶ τοῦ γάμου. πάν-

Trans. = Wilcken's original transcript. Lav. refers to 1922b. Zimm. without date refers to
GRP.
Col. I: 2. Read βαϲίλεια? Reeve   3. οικηϲο trans.   12. αυτῶ trans.   13. Wila-
mowitz suggests a lacuna between last two lines of transcribed text   14. ταῦτ' ἀκου-
Wilam., ταῦτα κου- Wil., ταῦτα κού|[φωϲ] Zimm. 1931
Col. II: 1. πα]ροῦϲαν? Zimm.   2. προετ‿περ trans., read πρὸϲ τ[ῷ] περ[ὶ Wil.
5. απαϲᾱ trans.   6–7. Zimm. supplements [ἡ ἀγγέλλουϲα τὰϲ ϲτρο]|φάϲ

CHIONE

. . . the kingship devolves upon her
and her
4 future spouse,
therefore we must
now lay our plans
in such a way that
8 we will never have occasion to repent.
We have for
our inquiry a period of
thirty days that [has been granted?]
12 for this purpose by them
. . .
more." Having heard these things. . . .

These persons
were at the point
of making plans concerning them.
4 But quickly there spread
through the entire city
. . .
rumor [and] no one
8 spoke of anything else
but the marriage. Everyone

τεϲ δὲ ἤχθοντο λογι-
ζόμενοι τὸ περὶ τῆϲ
ἀπειλῆϲ αὐτῶν ἀπαί-
δευτον καὶ μάλιϲτα
ὅϲοι δύνατοι τῶν πο-
λιτῶν ὑπάρχοντεϲ
καὶ αὐτοὶ πολιτεύε-
ϲθαι τὴν Χιόνην ἔ-
μελλον μνηϲτεύε-
ϲθαι. οὐ μέντοι γε αὐ-
τῶν τιϲ ἐτόλμα μετ᾽ ἐ-
κείνουϲ αἰτεῖν τὴν
κόρην. ἡ δὲ Χιόνη
παρὰ τῆϲ μητρὸϲ μα-
θοῦϲα ταῦτα οὐκ ετ .

[4 more lines were left untranscribed]

COLUMN III

"[Με-]
γαμήδηϲ τε προϲδό-
κιμόϲ ἐϲτιν, ἡμεῖϲ
δὲ μέχρι νῦν πάντα
κάλων κινοῦντεϲ,
ὡϲ εἰπεῖν, οὐδὲν ἐπὶ
ϲωτηρίαν νενοήκα-
μεν. αἰτίαν δ᾽ οὐδεμί-
αν παρέϲχηκέ ϲοι Με-
γαμήδηϲ ἵνα ἀπολί-
πηϲ αὐτόν. ὥϲτε δια-
λογίζου τι δραϲτέον

14. πα|ντων trans., read π⟨ο|λι⟩τῶν Wil., Πανιτῶν Wilam., πα|ν⟨ιών⟩των Lav. 24. ετ. trans., perhaps οὐκέτι Wil.

Col. III: 2. κειμοϲ, ημιϲ trans. 4. καλον trans., κάλων Crönert, Naber κειν ουντεϲ trans. 5. εἰπεῖν Crön., εἶπεν Wil.

was upset when
they thought about the
12 crudity of their threat,
especially
those powerful citizens
at the beginning
16 of their political careers
who had themselves been intending
to woo Chione.
But no one of them
20 dared, after
those persons, to ask
for the maiden. Chione,
having learned these facts from her mother,
24 no longer. . . .

COLUMN III

"Megamedes is
expected to arrive;
but though up till now we have been
4 pulling every rope,
as the saying goes,
still we have not devised
any scheme to save ourselves.
8 Megamedes has given you no cause
to abandon
him. So then,
discuss what we must do.

12 ἡμῖν. ἐγὼ μὲν γὰρ
ἀπορῶ.” ἡ δὲ Χιόνη, “οὐ-
δ’ ἐγὼ μέν,” φησιν, “εἰϲ
ϲωτηρίαν τι εὑρίϲκω.
16 ἓν δὲ τοῦτό ϲοι λέγω,
εἰ μὴ δυνάμεθα ζῆν
μετ’ ἀλλήλων, προϲτά-
ξαντεϲ τουτω . . . . ἐπω-
20 δυνω . . . .
. . . . τὸ γὰρ
τελευταῖον ἡμῖν
ἀπολείπεται. χρὴ δὲ
24 οὐδὲν [4–8 letters] καὶ ὅ-
πωϲ εὐϲχημόνωϲ
γενηθῇ ϲκοπεῖν · λε-
ληθόταϲ γὰρ ἡμῖν το

[1 line was left untranscribed]

---

16. ἓν δὲ τοῦτο Crön., Naber, ἐν δὲ τούτῳ Wil.   17. ζῆ trans.   18–22. trans., προϲτά|ξαντεϲ τούτ[οιϲ] ἐπ[ὶ] | δύ[ω ἡμέραϲ ἀνοχὰϲ δοῦναι, ϲυναποθνήϲκειν τὸ] | τελευ-ταῖον Wilam., (ἀποθνήϲκειν τὸ Lav.; ϲυναποθανεῖν Zimm. 1931); προϲτά|ξαντοϲ τούτ[ῳ] ἐπ[ὶ] | δύ[ω ἡμέραϲ περιμεῖναι, ϲυναποθανεῖν] | τελευταῖον Rattenbury; προϲτά|ξαντεϲ τούτ[ου] ἐπ[ω]|δύνω[ν εἶρξαί με δακ|ρύων, ϲυναποθανεῖν] | τελευταῖον Zimm. 1936a
23. χρὴ [δὲ Wilam., χρῆ[ϲτε] Wil.   24. οὐδὲν [ἄλλο · δεῖ δὲ?] Wil., οὐδεν[ὸϲ ὕϲτερον] Wilam., οὐδὲν [ἧττον, ὦ παῖ,] Lav., οὐδὲν [πρότερον ἢ] Ratt., οὐδὲν [ἕτερον ἢ] Zimm.

12   I for one am
at a loss." Chione
replied, "Nor have I
discovered any way to save us.
16   But this one thing I declare to you,
that if we are not able to live
with each other,
commanding him . . .
20   . . .
. . .
ultimately
is left to us. We must
24   . . . nothing and,
with due propriety,
consider how this may be done.
For if we secretly. . . ."

CHIONE

COLUMN I

The speaker might, as Wilcken and others have supposed, be a rhetor addressing an assembly, but the scene might also be a more private one, involving as few as two persons. Clearly some political intrigue is afoot revolving around the king's daughter Chione and her future marriage.

2. [β]αςιλεία: Reeve (1971: 536) makes the comment, "Why not βαςίλεια?" This would presumably mean: "The queen is joining her and her intended," neatly removing the kingdom as the bone of contention.

εἰς ταύτην: the demonstrative hardly seems the normal way for a father or mother to refer to their daughter, even in this clearly political context, but it would be the natural way for a foreign ambassador or a member of the king's cabinet to speak.

3–4. τὸν ςυνοικής(ο(ν)|τα: the future participle should indicate that a marriage has not yet taken place, and the periphrasis might suggest that the identity of her consort is still, at least in some minds, an open question.

6. βουλεύςαςθαι: if the suitors are issuing an ultimatum to the king to choose one of them as husband for Chione within thirty days (so Garin, Lavignini; see above, introduction), the verb is an odd one. One expects a form of αἱροῦμαι. The more natural interpretation is that the king is deliberating about some matter with his court.

10–11. ἡμε|ρῶν τριάκοντα: the thirty-day period of grace before some momentous event occurs seems almost to have been a cliché, see, e.g., Ch. 5.3.11.1, 5.4.4.1, 6.2.3.1; and XE 2.13.8.5, 3.3.7.2.

14. Wilamowitz's ταῦτ' ἀκού|[ςαντες or sim. is surely correct.

COLUMN II

2–3. ἦςαν πρὸς τ[ῷ] περ[ὶ αὐ]|τῶν βουλεύεςθαι: for the idiom, see LSJ, s.v. πρός B.II.

3–9. For the sentiment, see, e.g., XE 1.12.1: ταχὺ δὲ δι' ὅλης τῆς πόλεως διεπε- φοιτήκει τὸ ὄνομα Ἁβροκόμου καὶ Ἀνθίας.

7. οὐθε[ὶς: the spelling only here in this text. But as Crönert points out, this is hardly normal in the fifth century C.E. If not an aberration of Wilcken, it serves to indicate a fairly early date for the original composition of which this codex could only have been a late copy. Theta is found in place of delta in negatives from the Ptolemaic period into the first century C.E.

14–15. δύνατοι τῶν πο|λιτῶν: Wilcken's correction of his own transcript is eminently sensible, fitting well with what follows. "Powerful citizens" should be the equivalent of ὀλίγοι or ἄριςτοι, in fact, the usual group to provide suitors for romantic heroines.

COLUMN III

1. [Με]|γαμήδης : the beginning of the name will have occurred at the bottom of the preceding column. It occurs elsewhere only as the name of Antheia's father in Xenophon of Ephesos. Here, if he is the arrogant suitor of Chione, perhaps his name is meant to suggest powerful Persians like Megabates or Megabazos.

3–4. πάντα | κάλων κινοῦντες : for the idiom, which means roughly "exhausting the options," Naber cites Zenobios *Prov.* 5.62: πάντα κάλων ςεῖε—παροιμία ἐπὶ τῶν πάςῃ προθυμίᾳ χρωμένων· παρῆκται δὲ ἀπὸ τῶν τὰ ἄρμενα χαλώντων; and Gregory of Cyprus 2.27 in Cod. Mosq.: πάντα κάλων κινεῖς.

19–20. ἐπω|δυνω : Wilcken in a letter to Zimmermann in 1935 claimed that his original publication differed from his transcript at this point and that the word must be a form of ἐπώδυνος or ἐπωδύνω, hence Zimm.'s restoration above.

24–26. καὶ ὅ|πως εὐςχημόνως | γενηθῆ ςκοπεῖν : previous commentators have assumed that Chione is speaking about committing suicide with her lover. But we question whether propriety would have been a significant issue in that event. More likely she is thinking of fleeing with him, a necessarily improper course of action, unless some ruse can be devised.

γενηθῆ : the form is Hellenistic.

Chione?

❖

P. Berol. 10535 (= P^2 2631) and P. Berol. 21234 are two fragments from the same roll. The former was first edited by F. Zimmermann in 1935; the latter fragment was identified by H. Maehler and edited by M. Gronewald in 1979, who placed it immediately below the second column of 10535. Interpretation of the events depends in part upon the accuracy of his placement. The first column appears to contain a discussion between one man, called "leader" (*hēgemōn*), and a group. Details are difficult to sort out, but this man seems to be recounting military adventures. He refers to "our" in line 12, and possibly in lines 6–7 to "our many travails." The others address him in an exchange that does not suggest a hostile relationship. There is mention of homecoming, the ninth [——] and a woman's girdle (*zōnē*). The discernible contents of Column II involve a procession in progress—there is a crush and bystanders are gaping at something or someone. The verb *egameito* in lines 12–13 has naturally led editors to suppose that a marriage was in progress (though the imperfect tense is cause for concern). Someone's mother (line 21) arrives and and takes a seat when 10535 breaks off. Gronewald locates the new fragment at this point, arguing that the bride herself is speaking and that all is not well ("whether I am a happy bride or these things [have] come upon me . . ."). The relation of the people in Column I to those in Column II is unknown, though it is tempting to identify Column I's "leader" with "O master" of the second fragment.

Gronewald has suggested (as *ein müssiges Spiel?*) that this might well be part of *Chione*, coming from a scene in which Chione is forcibly married to Megamedes (who would then be "leader" of Column I). He points to similarity in language and style, the prominence of the mother in this scrap and in *Chione*, but in none of the other extant novels, and the time period of thirty days in *Chione* and the "ninth [and twentieth]" here. Further, there are phrases throughout reminiscent of Chariton.[1]

---

[1] P. Berol. 10535 shows clear verbal echoes of Chariton at II.7–9 and 18–20, as well as several others that Gronewald points out, i.e., [οἱ μ]ὲν ἄλλοι (II.8) and οὐδεὶς ἀπελείφθη (II.18). But this may be insignificant, because the topic of crowd behavior may be quite standardized. Although the extant fragments of *Chione* themselves do not show such

On the surface this is quite an attractive suggestion, and there are admittedly close parallels between Gronewald's restoration and interpretation of this scrap and what seems to be happening in *Chione*. But perhaps an equally plausible case can be made for identification with Ninos. In Column I, Ninos might be returning home from one of his military adventures and requesting marriage to his preternaturally shy cousin. That might be the "marriage" of Column II. Remember that in the extant fragments of *Ninos*, his aunt played an important role; she would then be the mother so prominent in this scrap. The girl's hesitancy and fear at marriage might account for the odd speech (whoever makes it). But this too is *ein müssiges Spiel*.

In any case, Lucke (1984), for reasons we believe to be cogent, has rejected the placement of the new fragment and questioned the exact nature of the events in Column II. On grammatical grounds alone the two pieces cannot be continuous. At the very least, an explanation of who or what the mother's chair was near to and a subject for the verb "coming to a halt" ([*an*]*epaueto*) are necessary, and this cannot be the "bride," if she is named in the following temporal clause (as Gronewald suggests). Further, the parallels from Chariton adduced for Column II, for the most part, do not describe wedding processions, but other events, such as Kallirhoe's entrance into the temple of Aphrodite (2.5.4), or the trial before the king for the hand of Kallirhoe (5.5.8). Since a mother is prominent at the end of 10535 col. II and a woman is speaking in 21234, we are tempted, as previous editors were, to locate these scraps in close proximity, but with the intervention of some lines. We suggest: (1) Column II describes the "leader" coming to an assembly, the subject of which is someone's marriage. (2) The mother of the girl destined to be the bride arrives first and seats herself near to the presiding official's throne—the king? her husband? (3) It is she who speaks in the second fragment, addressing the "leader" and expressing concern over the marriage. Oddly enough, identification with *Chione* is strengthened with such a reconstruction: Megamedes could be the "leader," addressed by Chione's mother as "O master." Has he performed some military service for which he is to be rewarded with the girl's hand?

---

parallels, they were found in a codex that also contained *Kallirhoe*, so it is possible to argue prima facie that Chariton had written both novels.

DESCRIPTION

P. Berol. 10535 (= P^2 2631, measuring 11.0 × 14.3 cm) and P. Berol 21234 (measuring 6.5 × 5.0 cm) together contain portions of two columns, lacking all margins, but with an intercolumnium of 1.5 cm. The smaller piece (21234) has lines that are complete to the right edge, but without a margin, from which it is clear that the original lines held between eighteen and twenty letters. The whole, which now presents a tattered and worn appearance, must have been an elegantly set-out roll. Column height is unknown, but to judge from comparable formats, like that of *Kalligone*, there would have been at least forty lines to the column. The hand is a small, carefully executed rounded upright, of the type assignable to the second century C.E. There are three corrections (I.4, II.8, 19), which appear to be in a different hand. No lectional signs appear; there is insufficient evidence for the presence or absence of iota adscript. Hiatus seems to have been admitted at 10535.I.22 and 21234.II.29. The backs of both fragments are blank.

P. BEROL. 10535

COLUMN I

- -

```
                                        ] .
                                        ] . .
[. . . . . . . . . . . . ]η . [. . ] . . αι ϲοὶ
4   [. . . . . . . . . . . . . ]εϲεηγι
[. . . . . . . . . . ] . . . . [. . ]ϲ ψευ-
[. . . . . . . . . ] μόχθων ἡμῖν
[. . . . . . . . . ]πολλῶν εἴτε τιϲ
8   [. . . . . . . . . . ] . ιε . ϲι[ . ] . [ . ]ει
[. . . . . . . . . ] . . . . . . . α . α
[. . . . . . . . . ]απειραι π . . [ . ]οι
[. . . . . . ἡμε]τέρων ἐϲώθη
12  [. . . . . . . . . ]οιων δὲ ἔφη · "τί
[. . . . . ] ἡμετέρων;" οἱ δέ · "ϲοῦ
[. . . . . ] οὖν ε[. . . . ] ἵνα τί καὶ
[. . . . . ] . [ . ] . . . . ιεναι; ϲοὶ δὲ
16  [. . . . . ] . . . . [. . ἡ]μῖν αὐ-
[τ- . . . ἡ]γεμὼν γίνεϲθαι τῆϲ
[. . . . . . . οἴ]καδε ἀπονοϲτη-
[ϲ . . . . . . . . ] κα[ὶ] τὰ ἡμέτερα
20  [. . . . . . . . ] . . . διᾳ ἀναλα-
[β- . . . . . . . . ] . . . περ ἀπέλιπεϲ
[. . . . . . . . . ]γηδη ἡ [ἐ]νάτη
```

Schubart's and Zimmerman's conjectures are to be found in *GRP*. Maehler's are in Gronewald.

Col. I: 3. ϲοὶ Maeh. 4.]εϲ^εηγι pap. 6. μόχθων Gron., μοχλῶν Schub. 8–10. εἴ |[τε γεγόναϲιν τινεϲ] κατὰ | [θάλατταν κατ]άπειραι ἢ ϲά[λ]οι Gron. 9. κατὰ Schub. 10. κατ]άπειραι Zimm. at end, πλ[ο]οι Maeh. 12. πρ]οιὼν Schub. 12–13. τί, | [φῇϲ, τῶν] Maeh., "τί|[να τῶν] ἡμετέρων;" Gron. 13–14. οἱ δέ · "ϲοῦ | [ταῦτα] οὖν [ἐϲτιν;]" Gron. 15. Perhaps κ]ατιέναι Maeh. ϲοὶ δὲ Maeh. 16. αυ) pap. 16–17. αὐ|[τοῖϲ or αὐ|[τὸϲ Maeh. 17. ἡ]γεμὼν Zimm. γεινεϲθαι pap. 18–19. οἴ]καδε ἀπονοϲτή|[ϲεωϲ Zimm. 20. γα]μήλιᾳ or κει]μήλιᾳ Gron. 22. Perhaps νῦν ἤδη Gron. ἡ [ἐ]νάτη (sc. ἡμέρα or νύξ) Maeh.

306

COLUMN I

6   ] weariness for us
     ] many whether a
8   ] . . .
     ] . . .
     ] attacks or . . .
     ] one of our [——] has been saved
12   ] he said "What
     ] of ours?" They said, "Of you
     ] now [——] why even
     ] to go? But for you
16   ] for us
     ] to become leader of the
     ] return home
     ] and our affairs
20   ] accounting?
     ] you left
     ] the ninth

[. . . . .] ̣ ̣ε̣δ[. . .]ντε‹

[. . . . .] ̣ ̣ ̣ τῇ ζώνῃ

- -

COLUMN II

- -

[. .] ̣ [

[. .]νηρ[

[̣]χ̣ρ̣η̣[

4   [

[. .] ̣ ̣ λ̣[

π̣ρ̣ο̣ . . . [

‹ ̣ ̣ ̣ ο̣‹[. .] προύπεμπον δὲ [αὐ-]

8   [τ- . . . οἱ μ]ὲν ἄλλοι θαυμά[ζον-]

τε̣[‹ κ]αὶ ἐκπεπληγμέν[οι . . .]

[

[

12   [ἐ-]

γαμεῖτο κ[. . . . .]

εἰ‹ τὸν ἑαυτ̣[

δὲ ἀνεπαύ‹α̣τ̣ο δ ̣ [. . . . . .]

16   γενομένη‹ ἀνῆλ̣θ̣[ον . . . .]

‹κεψόμενοι τὴν ̣ υ̣[. . . . .]

καὶ οὐδεὶ‹ ἀπελείφθη · κ̣α̣[ὶ ἦν]

ὠθι‹μὸ‹ περὶ τὸ δωμά̣[τι-]

20   ον πάντων εἰ‹τρεχόντω[ν.]

ἡ δὲ μήτηρ φθά‹α‹α πρ[ώ-]

τη μὲν εἰ‹ῆλθεν, πρώτη δ[ὲ ἐ-]

κάθι‹εν ἐπί τινο‹ δίφρου

24   πλη̣‹[ί]ον κει̣μ̣[ένου . . . . .]

- -

Col. II: 2. ἀ]νήρ Zimm.   7–8. δὲ [αὐ|τοὺ‹] Zimm.   8. -ε̣θαυμα pap.   8–9. so
Schub.   12–13. ἐ]|γαμεῖτο Zimm.   14. ἑαυ[τῶν οἶκον Zimm., ἑαυ[τοῦ Schub.
15. δε[ιλῆ‹ δὲ Schub., perhaps δη[Maeh.   18. κ̣α̣[ὶ ἦν Zimm.   19. –νωθι‹μο‹
pap.   19–22. so Schub.   24. at end, [ἐν ᾧ δὲ or [ὅτε δὲ Gron.

]...

24   ] by her girdle

COLUMN II

They escorted [?]

8   The rest marveled and
      were aghast [
      [
      [
12   [
      was being married [
      into . . . own . . . [
      ] stopped, [and since]
16   it was [?] they arrived [
      in order to consider the [
      and no one was left out. And there [was]
      a crush around the house,
20   with everyone rushing in.
      [Someone's] mother was the first
      to arrive, and was the first
      to sit upon a chair [throne?]
24   placed nearby.

CHIONE?

COLUMN I

[ἀν]επαύετο καὶ ὡς εἶδεν η
[. . . . .] ἀνέστη καὶ "ὦ δέσπο-
[τα . . . .]τιον," εἶπε, "πάρεστί co[ι]
4   [. . . . . .] πότερον εὐτυχῶ
[καὶ μ]ακαρία τίς εἰμι γυνὴ α-
[. . . . .] χουσα ἢ καὶ ταυ-
[. . . . .] ἦλθε πρὸς ἐμὲ
8   [. . . . .] ̣ ϲτα τεκμηρι-
[. . . . .]ωϲε ̣ [. . .]

----

1. [ἀν]επαύετο Gron., [. .] ἐπαύετο Lucke   1–2. ἡ | [Χιόνη] ? Gron., ἡ|[γεμόνα] Maeh.
2–3. ὦ δέϲπο|[τα] Maeh.   3–4. "ἐναν]τίον," εἶπε, "πάρεστί co[ι | ἐρωτᾶν] Maeh.,
ἐρωτᾷϲ με] or ἀγνοῶ δὲ] Maeh., εἰδέναι] ? Gron.   4. ποτερα°ν pap.   5. so
Maeh.   5–6. ἄ|[νδρα Maeh., ἄ|[νδρα ϲὲ λα]βοῦσα Gron.   6. ἔ]χουσα ? Maeh.
6–7. τὰ ὕ|[ϲτατα παρ]ῆλθε Maeh.   8. μέγ]ιϲτα Maeh.   8–9. τεκμήρι|[α] Gron.

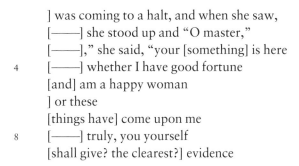

      ] was coming to a halt, and when she saw,
      [——] she stood up and "O master,"
      [——]," she said, "your [something] is here
4   [——] whether I have good fortune
      [and] am a happy woman
      ] or these
      [things have] come upon me
8   [——] truly, you yourself
      [shall give? the clearest?] evidence

CHIONE?

6ff. See above, introduction.

18–19. οἴ]καδε ἀπονοϲτη|[ϲ-: if not the rare ἀπονοϲτή|[ϲεωϲ as Schubart suggests, surely a form of ἀπονοϲτέω. In either case, the issue seems to be a homecoming, for the leader and his army.

22. ἡ [ἐ]νάτη: while it is possible to restore ἡ [ἐ]νάτη | [καὶ εἰκοϲτή], as Gronewald suggests, there is no room for ἡμέρα or for a verb. More likely ἡμέρα or νύξ was actually written, and the ninth [day?] is at issue, not the twenty-ninth.

23.] . . . εδ[. . .]γτεϲ : τότε δ[ὲ πά]γτεϲ ?

24. τῇ ζώνῃ: the presence of this item of women's apparel is intriguing. Though we are attracted by Zimmermann's suggestion that she was about to hang herself in despair at being abandoned, nothing supports this supposition, though it may tend to reinforce the identification with *Chione*, who may have been plotting a suicide with her lover rather than endure marriage to Megamedes. Lucke suggests, somewhat more plausibly, that this item of clothing has its place in the description of a beautiful woman (as all heroines are), e.g., AT 1.1.11, 8.12.1, 8.13.1. Gronewald connects it with the coming "marriage." Whatever its significance, it would seem to require the presence of another woman besides the mother of Column II. Either the mother or this woman could be the γυνή of 21234.

7. προύπεμπον: the verb can be used for the bringing of the bride to the house of the bridegroom; see, e.g., Ch. 5.5.5, where Kallirhoe sees in a dream Χαιρέαν καὶ τὴν τῶν γάμων ἡμέραν· ἐϲτεφανωμένην τὴν πόλιν ὅλην καὶ προπεμπομένην αὐτὴν ὑπὸ πατρὸϲ καὶ μητρὸϲ εἰϲ τὴν οἰκίαν τοῦ νυμφίου. But this usage is hardly exclusive. Note that here only the mother seems to be present.

8. οἱ μ]ὲν ἄλλοι: Gronewald points out that the expression is frequent in Chariton, with the δέ clause (here in the lacuna) indicating an exception. See, e.g., Ch. 5.8.10: οἱ μ]ὲν ἄλλοι πάντεϲ ϲκυθρωποί, μόνοϲ δὲ Μιθριδάτηϲ γεγηθώϲ.

8–9. Bystanders can be counted on to marvel at the beauty of the heroine as well as other things. Compare Ch. 2.5.4: αὐτὴν [sc. Kallirhoe] ἐθαύμαϲαν ἅπαντεϲ· καταπλαγεὶϲ οὖν ὁ Διονύϲιοϲ ἄφωνοϲ ἦν.

12–13. The imperfect is difficult. Gronewald points out that the tense might be an expression of sadness and inevitability from an interested bystander. Alternatively, it could belong to a contrary-to-fact condition.

15. Schubart's δε[ιλῆϲ δέ is not unreasonable; the word can refer to the late afternoon, just before sunset. Kallirhoe is brought in procession to Dionysios περὶ τὴν ἑϲπέραν (Ch. 3.2.11).

312

17. τὴν ̣υ[: not γύ[μφην. Maehler suggests either τὴν δυ[cτυχῆ or δύ[cτηνον.

19. ὠθιcμὸc : in the extant novels, only once before in Ch. 5.5.8: ἔωθεν οὖν ὠθιcμὸc ἦν περὶ τὰ βαcίλεια . . . πάντεc γὰρ cυνέτρεχον . . . εἰcῆλθεν οὖν εἰc τὸ δικαcτήριον. Nu was deleted from the beginning of the line (either to eliminate dittography or to correct the word division or both.)

P. BEROL. 21234

1–2. Although it is obvious that these two fragments do belong together, Gronewald's join is impossible. At the very least another line or two must intervene before the second fragment begins to make the events coherent.

ὡc εἶδεν η : ἡ μήτηρ, the name of the girl (Gronewald's ἡ Χιόνη) would fit, or, e.g., ἡ νύμφη. Maehler's ἡγεμόνα, or indeed any object, should require an article.

2. ἀνέcτη : someone "stands up" to speak. This could easily be the mother, who takes a seat near the end of Column II. In this case, has the person addressed as ὦ δέcποτα just entered the chamber and come to a stop?

2–3. ὦ δέcπο|[τα] is hardly the customary way for women in the novels to address their betrothed, however reluctant they may be about the marriage. A different supplement (e.g., ὦ δέcπο|[ινα]) would violate normal rules for syllable division.

5. γυνὴ : the word must refer to a married woman; it is unsuitable for an unmarried girl, even if she is betrothed.

Lollianos
Phoinikika

Fragments of the *Phoinikika* recall Spencer Tracy's classic remark about Katherine Hepburn in *Pat and Mike*: "There's not much meat on 'er, but what's there is cherce."[1] The now pitifully mangled fragments include the appearance of a ghost, a deflowering, human sacrifice, cannibalism, and a masquerade in white and black costume that takes place at midnight, events that have inspired interpretations as sensational and as controversial as the material itself.

The central question raised by these fragments is how to assess the relative importance of religious and literary parallels. Can this text be regarded as a document in reconstructing religious or literary history, or does it inhabit the borderland between them both? There has been a lively discussion in the last half-century of the thesis that the ancient novels were written and read as religious documents, deriving their basic structure and many details from the myths and cults of popular religions. Albert Henrichs, in his *editio princeps* of the *Phoinikika*, argues that the sacrifice scene in Lollianos is inspired by actual rite, probably of a Dionysian character, and employs the literary text to illuminate a little-known corner of religious history. His edition contains an extensive collection of liturgical, mythological, and ethnographic parallels concerning oath rituals, the sacrifice of children, cannibalism, and face-painting to support his views. Without postulating a religious message for the novel as a whole, he claims that Lollianos's description of a ritual murder represents, more or less accurately, the cult practices of the Egyptian *boukoloi*. He argues that this scene yields valuable information about the structure of ancient mystery rituals (1972: 78 n. 6) and that these new fragments support the methodological correctness of Kerényi's and Merkelbach's interpretations of the ancient novels.

In contrast, G. Sandy, C. Jones, and J. Winkler have argued on the

---

[1] We would like to express our gratitude to Catherine Evans for verifying this quotation for us.

basis of the extensive literary parallels with the other novels, especially Apuleius and Achilles Tatius, that the piece is to be located in the seamier regions of criminal-satiric fiction. All three would read the sensational elements as confected for entertainment; and while attributing to the author the capability of appropriating and incorporating within his narrative the rites and religious beliefs that would have been a natural part of the texture of daily life, they would deny that the text was intended to convey an overt (or covert) religious message.

Recently, the possibility of a middle ground has suggested itself. D. Selden (1994) has demonstrated that the wall painting described in the opening pages of Achilles Tatius's novel is capable of being "read" in two quite different ways: the iconography of the girl riding on the back of a bull a Greek viewer would identify as the victimized Europe being carried off by Zeus; but a worshipper of Astarte—that is, a non-Greek native of the region of Sidon—would see that same picture as representing the dominion of the marine goddess Astarte over Baal (symbolized as the bull). Selden is interested in exploring those areas so common within the novels that would seem to be "double determined," that is, capable of being decoded in two opposing, often mutually contradictory ways, and suggests, quite cogently, that this habit of mind—or as he has it, the rhetorical figure of *syllepsis*—may be a significant characteristic of the fiction of late antiquity. The fragments of Lollianos, Iolaos, and Tinouphis, like Apuleius, are striking for their determined conjunction of the sacred and the scurrilous. Selden's thesis holds out the possibility that the authors of ancient novels deliberately selected material and presented it to offer a coherent experience not of one or the other mode of activity, but of both. Many incidents in the text become, thereby, optical illusions; viewed from one angle they present the reader with dangerous criminal behavior, from another a complete religious ritual. Of course, ultimately this kind of double determination is a matter of narrative strategy, not of religious belief; but just as the bicultural interpretation of the painting at the opening of Achilles Tatius's novel must reflect "real" beliefs of that world's inhabitants in order to gain its effect, so too—in so far as these texts are truly double determined—the religious world of ancient fiction must represent "real" beliefs and a coherent set of activities of its inhabitants.

THE AUTHOR

The subscription of the papyrus obligingly gives us the name of the author, Lollianos. Although it does not occur frequently, this name is familiar enough in documents from Greco-Roman Egypt for the notion that the *Phoinikika* was a product of a local but now otherwise unknown writer to be not unduly disturbing. But a more intriguing potential author is P. Hordeonius Lollianos, a sophist, who was the "first to have held the chair of rhetoric in Athens," probably under Antoninus Pius.[2] The basic information about him comes from Philostratos (*Vit. soph.* §§ 526–27), augmented by a few inscriptions and notices in the rhetorical theorists,[3] in the grammarian Phrynichos, and in the *Souda*.[4] Besides providing anecdotal material about his political life in Athens, Philostratos mentions that he was the student of Isaios the Assyrian, a master of the plain style (*Vit. soph.* § 514), and like him, his writing was free from excess. Two samples from his oeuvre that clearly impressed Philostratos remain. One comes from a popular type of set piece modeled on Demosthenes' *Against Leptines*:[5] "The mouth of the Pontus is closed by a law and a few syllables halt the Athenian food supply; Lysander, sparring with ships (*naumachōn*), and Leptines, sparring with statutes (*nomomachōn*) are equal in might."[6] The other comes from a speech against the sale of the sacred island of Delos: "Take back, O Poseidon, your favor to Delos! Since she is being sold, allow her to make an escape."[7]

---

[2] For discussion of Lollianos's life and position in rhetoric, see Schissel von Fleschenberg 1926: 181–201 and Keil 1953: 5ff. Henrichs discusses the inscriptional evidence for Lollianos' dates, concluding "Mann kann ... annehmen, dass Lollianos bereits unter Hadrian in Athen Privatunterricht erteilt hat, aber erst unter Antoninus Pius die öffentliche Professur bekommen hat" (1972: 24 n. 2).

[3] Principally he is cited for his position on stasis theory; for a collection of his statements and a discussion of their significance, see Schissel von Fleschenberg 1926: 185–92.

[4] "Lollianos the Ephesian, a sophist, a student of Isaios the Assyrian, born in the time of Hadrian Caesar. He wrote many things" (*Souda*, s.v. *Lollianos*).

[5] This was a popular exercise: further examples include orations 53 and 54 attributed to Ailios Aristides, a reference in Apsines 232.16 (Sp.-H.), and an anonymous speech of the third century B.C.E. found on papyrus (BKT 7.4–13 = P^2 2511).

[6] κέκλειϲται τὸ ϲτόμα τοῦ Πόντου νόμῳ καὶ τὰϲ Ἀθηναίων τροφὰϲ ὀλίγαι κωλύουϲι ϲυλλαβαί, καὶ ταὐτὸν δύναται Λύϲανδροϲ ναυμαχῶν καὶ Λεπτίνηϲ νομομαχῶν.

[7] "λῦϲον, ὦ Πόϲειδον, τὴν ἐπὶ Δήλῳ χάριν, ϲυγχώρηϲον αὐτῇ πωλουμένῃ φυγεῖν." The passage depends on the hearer's knowledge that Delos was originally a floating island, to whom Poseidon granted the "favor" of remaining stationary in the ocean. This, too, might be a rhetorical exercise rather than a political speech on a live issue; see Kohl 1915: no. 210.

Hordeonius Lollianos's *floruit* was early enough for him to have authored the *Phoinikika*, but unfortunately there is no positive reason to attribute the piece to him, apart from the fact that he is the only Lollianos for whom we have evidence of literary prominence. Negative evidence is equally inconclusive. Henrichs has argued that (1) the style of the *Phoinikika* is incompatible with what we know of Lollianos, and (2) the sophists supposedly did not write novels. His second point is based on an assumption that novel-writing would have been less than socially acceptable for men of status, which cannot be justified by the ancient evidence. The incident that he cites from Philostratos, namely that Celer wrote an "erotic novel" on the subject of "Araspes the lover of Pantheia"[8] and circulated it under the name of Dionysios—to the latter's detriment—is subject to more than one interpretation. In fact, Philostratos's language[9] suggests that it is the style of the piece, not its erotic theme, that he regards as unworthy of Dionysios, and the work in question was more likely to have been a rhetorical composition than a novel.[10]

It is more difficult to judge the quality of Lollianos's style from such a small sample. Clearly he writes in Attic[11] and avoids hiatus. While the balance and wit found in Philostratos's two illustrations may not be typical of Lollianos's every sentence, he is obviously capable of such elegancies. But these are far from the intricate and artifical style of Heliodoros or even the studied simplicity of Longos. In contrast, the *Phoinikika* permits hiatus, and lacks the artifice of Λύϲανδροϲ ναυμαχῶν καὶ Λεπτίνηϲ νομομαχῶν. But its overall quality is unusally difficult to judge, because the middle portion of every line is missing. And the dialogues, which are

---

[8] The original story is found in Xenophon's *Kyropaideia*, where it already shows its novelistic potential, for a discussion of which see Tatum 1989: 163–88. The names Antheia and Habrokomes in the *Ephesiaka* are deliberately modeled on Xenophon's husband and wife, Pantheia and Abradatas. The story of Pantheia is also told in Philostr. *Imag.* 2.9.

[9] *Vit. Soph.* §524. For a translation, see below, App. B, no. 15.

[10] So Jones 1980: 254 n. 61. Erotic themes occur in *progymnasmata*; for a list see Rohde 1974: 344–72. Further, Lucian remarks in the opening of *Alex.* §2 that Arrian wrote a life of Tillorobos (or Tilloboros) the bandit, and that this is sufficient justification for Lucian's embarking on his own biography of a scoundrel. This suggests that low-life topics were not unpopular and that authorial disclaimers for choosing such unsavory topics were a stylized part of the literary practice.

[11] Phrynichos objects to Lollianos's lapses from pure Attic. Whether this indicates that the two men were on opposite sides in a lively academic controversy or that Lollianos's Attic was not as good as it should have been is moot. See Fischer 1974: nos. 140, 141, 152 (= pp. 15, 170, 180 Lobeck).

vital in producing variety and a fix on character suffer the most—speakers and contexts are all but impossible to determine. In spite of these obstacles, the Greek appears lucid enough, consistently Attic and free from gross syntactical or morphological anomalies.[12] Indeed, there are some stylistic pretensions: in B.1 verso 19–21, the phrases are nearly equal in number of syllables, and the asyndeton ("they sang, they drank, they had sex with the women") is quite effective; and in P. Oxy. 1368.3–6 we find alliteration and a balanced and artificial word order ("I am lying beneath that plane tree, and with me a fair maiden, both of us slain"). Henrichs himself, after all, linked the *Phoinikika* stylistically with Chariton, a text written presumably before the heyday of Atticism in plain but not inelegant Greek, not with such unprepossessing narratives as the apocryphal *Acta* or the *Alexander Romance* (1972: 27).

Two features of the narrative are especially striking: its rapidity (the sacrifice scene, for example, is presented without any of the repetitions that build to a climax or rhetorical outpourings found in Achilles Tatius), and an undoubtedly related phenomenon, the placid surface of the text, which glosses over horrors like the appearance of a ghost or the disposal of corpses with the blandest prose. Should this be deliberate choice rather than ineptitude, we would not find it impossible to imagine that the rhetor had produced such a text, if he was intent on writing a novel of low life and chose to abandon some of the niceties of Atticism. But this is not to say that he did.

THE TITLE

The *Phoinikika* provides us with our earliest manuscript title for an ancient novel.[13] Our novel is called "Phoenician Matters." It conforms to a type—neuter plural of a geographical location—that was in vogue for fictional (e.g., *Babyloniaka, Ephesiaka, Milesiaka*) as well as historical (e.g., *Persika, Skythika, Indika*) material,[14] though without any firm

---

[12] Though there are a few unclassical usages, the one real oddity Henrichs can point to is the expression "to swear in the blood of the heart"; but that occurs in a broken passage, and how we evaluate it depends on whether it is a semitism or an imitation of Latin usage. See below, B.1 recto 14–15 note.

[13] We may have an earlier reference to ancient fiction by title, Persius 1.133: "post prandia Calliroen do." But it is not absolutely certain that Persius means Chariton's novel. Plutarch's reference to the *Milesiaka* (*Crass.* §32.3) is more or less contemporary with Lollianos. For other examples of this type, see App. B.

[14] Henrichs (1972: 11) remarks that there were several local histories called

indication of contents: the *Milesiaka* was apparently a collection of salacious short stories; Ktesias's *Persika* a romanticized history of the earlier
Assyrian and Medean empires, then the Persian Empire from its foundation in 398 B.C.E. Indeed, the form of the title was so standardized that
Petronius could play off of expectations by calling his novel "Satyrika,"
or as Perry translates it, "A Tale from the Land of Lascivious" (192).

If we judge from other novels with similar titles, no consistent pattern
for the relationship of the title to the actual location of the novel
emerges. If Lollianos's novel was like Xenophon's *Ephesiaka*, its characters might have originated on some part of the Phoenician coast, most
probably Sidon or Tyre, or a few incidents may have taken place there,
but the major part of the novelistic adventures could easily have been
located elsewhere in the Greco-Roman world. Most of Xenophon's
"Ephesian Matters," after all, takes place in Egypt. If it was like
Iamblichos's *Babyloniaka*, which, according to Photios's *Epitome*, not
only took place in the area of ancient Babylonia, but even included the
characters Mesopotamia and her twin brothers Tigris and Euphrates,
then the whole of it would have been located in that part of the ancient
world to which the term "Phoinikia" could be applied. The limits of this
region were rather flexible in antiquity. According to the geographer
Strabo writing in the second century C.E., who may therefore be taken as
a near contemporary source, Phoinikia extended from the area around
Tripolis in the north along the coast to Pelusium on the eastern border of
Egypt (16.2.12–22).

THE LOCATION OF THE NOVEL

Henrichs would locate the activities of B.1 in the eastern marshes near
Pelusium, because he identified those performers of the sacrifice of the
pais with the Egyptian *boukoloi*. These so-called "herdsmen" were
apparently social outcasts who retired to the more inaccessible regions of
the Delta and survived by preying on the shipwrecked and on unwary
travelers. Both Achilles Tatius and Heliodoros, as well as supposedly less
imaginative sources like Cassius Dio (72.4), described their behavior in
detail. The identification is based on the similarity of the narrative of the

---

"Phoinikika" that can be assigned to the first or second century C.E., those of Klaudios
Iolaos (= *FGrHist* 788, 1–3), Herennios Philon (= *FGrHist* 790 F5), and Mochos
(= *FGrHist* 784 F3–5).

sacrifice of the *pais* in Lollianos to the *Scheintod* of Leukippe in Achilles Tatius and the murder of a Roman centurian in Cassius Dio, but not on any overt indications from the text itself.

We agree that the parallels between the three texts are quite striking, but we question whether the fact that those performing the sacrifice in Achilles Tatius and Cassius Dio are *boukoloi* requires that the same group be responsible in the *Phoinikika*. After all, the *boukoloi* in Heliodoros and Xenophon of Ephesos do *not* engage in human sacrifice, and the outlaws in Xenophon who attempt to sacrifice Antheia to Ares are not *boukoloi*. Further *boukoloi* are swamp dwellers, their natural habitat reed huts cunningly hidden throughout the marshes or boats (Hld. 1.5–7). In Heliodoros, they store their loot in a cave, but in none of the extant novels do they have the kind of building that the group in the *Phoinikika* would seem to inhabit—one large enough for a considerable number of people[15] with windows raised above ground level.

This building is a puzzle: most ancient urban centers or villages did not run to such large structures, apart from the temple, which would not have had windows, or a bath. The rooms in private dwellings, even in the houses of the well-to-do, would usually have been too small, as would stables, which in any case did not have windows.[16]

But wherever they were, they were clearly not in the open, in a cave, or in a reed hut—the three areas associated with the nefarious activities of the *boukoloi*. Further, the very end of B.1 verso mentions the "workshop of a goldsmith" as if it were the destination of at least some of the outlaws who leave after the party. If they had planned to rob his shop (and this is by no means certain), then they must have been fairly close to an urban center, which is the only place a goldsmith's shop could have been located; in staging a robbery within a populated area, they are behaving in a manner anomalous for *boukoloi*, if our literary sources are

---

[15] Eleven guards are mentioned, plus the remainder of the band, plus a number of women, plus corpses, all within the enclosed space. Without being dogmatic, it does seem to us that the precise number of guards was meant to be taken literally, and so may imply the presence of a relatively large number of captives. Even if the function of the guards was to protect the corpses from being looted by their fellows, the large number again requires a similarly large number of bandits.

[16] Several of the private dwellings in the Egyptian village of Karanis seem to have had subterranean basements sufficiently large to have held around thirty people; from the inside, they would have had high windows located at the ground level (Husson 1983: 109–18). Alternatively, the outlaws might be in possession of a bath, which normally had high narrow windows and could have been privately owned. (We are indebted to S. C. Herbert for this information.)

accurate. Since banditry was common to all regions of the Greco-Roman world, we are inclined to think these men were not *boukoloi* at all, but closer in kin to the robber band in Apuleius. If so, their exact location could be anywhere near an urban center in the eastern Mediterranean.

THE CHARACTERS AND PLOT

The plot contains several incidents bound together in no obvious way: three would seem to be externally narrated, one scene certainly has an ego-narrator, another seems to. We have (1) the celebration of a festival or party, during which a nameless narrating-I loses his virginity (this is to be located at the end of Book 1 or the beginning of Book 2), (2) an apparent ritual murder of either a child or a servant (*pais*) by a group of outlaws, who proceed to cook the victim's heart, swear an oath upon it, and eat it, followed immediately by (3) a feast, after which the outlaws indulge in communal sex, sleep for a while, then dress up in white or black costume and exit into the night. Both prisoners and corpses are mentioned in this third scene. The events of (2) and (3) must occur after (1), but whether they come in Book 2, Book 3, or some even later book is not known (see below for a discussion of the placement of the fragments). We also have episode (4), wherein a ghost appears to Glauketes as he rides along a path, but he continues to ride until he reaches a stable, where it looks as if he is about to have an amatory adventure. This episode cannot be located with respect to the other events.

That they are all to be located within the one novel depends on the presence of a most enigmatic character named Glauketes, who acts as if he is the slave or the servant of Persis (or perhaps Persis's inexperienced companion?). He does not speak in the extant parts, and would seem to have some independence, because he is alone when he meets the ghost. To judge by appearances, Persis is a woman of the world, if not a courtesan. She has a secret room in her establishment, operates without a duenna, and possesses sufficient social independence to send to her steward for money. The fact that she has a mother does not necessarily contradict this picture. A number of the ladies in Lucian's *Dialogues of the Courtesans* have mothers who launch them in their careers. The names of Glauketes and Persis occur on two small scraps that are to be located at the top of page B.1 recto, so these two may be participants in the scene of human sacrifice.

The third named character is Androtimos, whose presence can only be securely fixed during the party following the human sacrifice. He may be one of the prisoners of the outlaw band, or indeed he might be its leader; such a figure would seem to be involved in sacrificing the *pais*, although his name does not occur. There has been a tendency to identify Andro-timos as the main character—the novel's hero—and he may be, but he does not appear in the Oxyrhynchus fragment. (Is it only coincidence that the names Persis and Androtimos sound like Perseus and Andromeda?)

In addition to these characters, there is an ego-narrator—a man—in one of the fragments who has "his first experience of sexual intercourse" with Persis. He might be Androtimos, or he might not. There also seems to be an ego narrator in the human sacrifice cum party scene, who cannot be Androtimos—but the text is too broken to be dogmatic. If there is, we are tempted identify him with Persis's boyfriend, and assume that he is telling an involved anecdote, encompassing the Cologne A and B frag-ments, and embedded within the larger external narration. But he is just as likely to be Glauketes.

There is also the sacrificial victim designated only by the term *pais*, which can be used for a child, a servant, or a male lover. Henrichs (1972) took the victim to be a child; Winkler (1980: 173–74) discusses the possibility of the *pais* being the boyfriend of another male character; and at B.1 verso 13, *pais* is used of a servant.

Other characters include Persis's mother, someone's sister, the uniden-tified man wearing nothing more than a scarlet loincloth who performs the sacrifice, a girl who appears to be dead, and a ghost and his dead female companion, who appear to Glauketes.

LOLLIANOS AND APULEIUS

Previous commentators[17] have been struck by the similarity between events of B.1 verso and Lucius's captivity in the robbers' cave (Apuleius 4.8 and 4.22), which we schematize as follows:

LOLLIANOS	APULEIUS
The group is feasting (8–11).	A new group arrives with booty (4.8.1.).

[17] Jones (1980: 251–53), whose schematization of the relationship between the two passages we have adapted with a few additions; and Winkler (1980: 158–59).

LOLLIANOS	APULEIUS
They drink from a cup chased with a design of Lapiths (and Centaurs?) (14–15).	The group is feasting (4.8.5).
A new group arrives (18–19).	They are compared to Lapiths and Centaurs (4.8.5).
They indulge in singing, drinking, sex, then go to sleep (20–21).	They pour libations to dead comrades, sing songs to Mars, then go to sleep (4.22.1).
At midnight (23) they wake up, dress themselves in black or white garments, and go out (26–29).	When the night had advanced, some with swords, some dressed as *Lemures* go out (4.22.5).
There seem to be plans for an escape (31–33).	The ass escapes with the girl (6.26).

The parallels are even more striking when we consider that Apuleius 4.9–21 consists of three robber's tales inserted into the main narrative and 4.28–6.24 is another, much longer insert, the tale of Cupid and Psyche. There may also be a scatological parallel: the episode of the ass distracting his attackers by spattering them with noxious feces (Apuleius 4.3.10) shows linguistic similarities with Androtimos's complaint that he is overwhelmed by the smell of belching and flatulence (B.1 verso 10–11)—an incident we believe was meant to function as a distraction. A final point of overlap may be the presence of a girl in both tales, the apparently dead girl at B.1 verso 24 and the captive brought into the cave at 4.23.3. The overwhelming difference between these two, of course, is the absence of ritual murder—or even *Scheintod*—in the relevant section of Apuleius; nor do his robbers have a woman available for sexual purposes. And although they are not particularly adverse to killing, they have not littered their cave with corpses.

In contrast to Apuleius, the version of the ass tale attributed to Lucian contains only the details of the arrival of a group with booty followed by feasting and drinking (§ 21), several days later the report of a sentry followed by an attack on a passing stranger in the predawn hours (§ 22), then the ass's attempt to escape (§ 23). The allusion to Lapiths and Centaurs, the pouring of libations and singing songs to Mars, and the masquerade are all missing from the Lucian; but these are precisely the sort of specific details that an epitome might omit. The incident of the ass defecating on his attackers is present (§ 18), however, and the outlaws in [Lucian] are based in a dwelling (*ta oikeia*) with a forecourt (*pro-domos*), not a cave, as in Apuleius. In this one particular, Lollianos and [Lucian] agree against Apuleius.

Too many peculiar and memorable details of the *Phoinikika* and of Apuleius converge in too small a space for the pattern be accidental. Nor is it possible to explain their convergence as naturally deriving from the circumstances of the story itself. For example, by way of a test, if we compare Lollianos's account of the activities after the murder of the *pais* and the actions of the *boukoloi* in Achilles Tatius and Cassius Dio, who engage in equally antisocial acts—murder and cannibalism—we find no similarities. If the parallels are not accidental, then the two texts must bear some literary relationship to each other—either one imitated the other or both share a common ancestor. Obviously, if the author of the *Phoinikika* was P. Hordeonius Lollianos, he could easily have produced his tale in time for Apuleius to have known it; equally, Apuleius could have been the inspiration for the scene in the outlaws' lair, if the *Phoinikika* belongs not to the early, but to the later second century. And of course, both writers could have been borrowing from the original Greek ass tale, which Photios knew and compared—favorably—with the version attributed to Lucian (*Cod.* 129).

Any allusive interdependence between these two hinges on the fact that what the ass narrates in Apuleius seems in Lollianos to be communicated by a human narrator. Naturally this raises the question: could the narrator of the B.1 incidents be an ass? B.1 verso 14–15 gives a tantalizing glimpse of an ego-narrator, elsewhere unsuspected, whose species is unknown. The earlier scene with Persis, for which there is also a narrating-I, might then begin to look similar to Lucius's dalliance with Fotis (in Apuleius) or Palaistra (in Lucian), after which the narrator is transformed into the beast and falls in with the characters of B.1 verso. But the location of the B.1 verso events within a large building with high windows should preclude the presence of animals (unless the ego-narrator is without, gazing in through one of the windows?). And the scatological incidents—if they are indeed related to each other—suggest that any imitation stopped short of metamorphosis: what was in the one bestial behavior is firmly located in human action in the other. Lollianos is not, therefore, the author of the original Greek ass tale; if he imitates it, he does so while omitting its most salient feature—the metamorphosis.

An answer to the related question of who imitates whom, considering the precarious state of our text and at least one missing link, we cannot give. It is interesting, however, that Lollianos's narrative has points of overlap with the seamier aspects not only of Apuleius but also of Achilles Tatius. Of course, the elements of similarity with Achilles Tatius—ritual murder or *Scheintod*—almost certainly cannot have been part of an original ass tale, because they are not to be found either in the Lucianic version or in Apuleius. One wonders, therefore, if Lollianos might not be a later and derivative writer who quite consciously set out to exploit the sensationalism of his predecessors. Unfortunately, whatever messages the pointed allusions to earlier tales must have carried to the reader are now lost in the lacunae.

Description

P. Oxy. 1368 (= P^2 2620, measuring 19.2 × 9.6 cm) consists of twenty-nine lines from the top of a column from a papyrus roll, with a few traces of a preceding column visible to the left. It was written on the back of a register of persons, probably drawn up for taxation. The register was assigned on the basis of its handwriting to the end of the second century C.E.; the hand that has written the *Phoinikika* is medium-sized and shows some affinity for the Severe style, as well as cursive characteristics. Grenfell and Hunt's date of "no later than about the middle of the third century" seems correct (1915: 119). The original scribe made several corrections by adding words above the line and by using expunging dots above and below the text to be deleted. There seems to be a paragraphos at line II.9, nu in suspension at II.15, and tremata, but iota adscript is not written. The scribe tends to mark elisions (II.15, 18), but the text itself has freely admitted hiatus. M. Reeve assigned this piece to the *Phoinikika* on the basis of the name Glauketes, after the Cologne fragment was identified (Henrichs 1970c: 42, n. 1); certainly the two fragments are stylistically consistent (see Henrichs 1970c: 42–43 and Henrichs 1972: 9–10 for details).

P. OXY. 1368, COLUMN II

νι ειϲ τὴν αὐτὴν θαψα[. . .]
μικρὸν ἀπὸ τῆϲ ὁδοῦ ἐκ[τρα-]
πείϲ. κεῖμαι δὴ ὑπὸ τῇ π[λα-]
4   τανίϲτῳ ἐκείνῃ καὶ μετ’ ἐ-
μοῦ κόρη καλή, ἄμφω ἀνῃρη-
μένοι. ” ὁ δὲ Γλαυκέτηϲ ἐκ-
πλαγείϲ, ὥϲπερ εἰκόϲ, ἐφθέγ-
8   ξατο μὲν οὐδὲν πρὸϲ ταῦτα, ἐπένευεν δὲ μόνον καὶ
[ἄμ]α ἤλαυνεν. ὁ δὲ νεάνι-
[ϲκοϲ] ἠφανίϲθη ἐπινεύϲαν-
12   [τοϲ, ὁ] δὲ Γλαυκέτηϲ κατὰ κρά-
[τ]οϲ ἤλαυνεν καὶ ἅμα ἐπε-
ϲτρέφετο, εἴ που αὖθιϲ ἴδοι
ἐκεῖνον, ἀλλ’ οὐκέτι ἔβλεπεν.
16   ἀφικνεῖται οὖν νυκτὸϲ ἔτι
ε[ἰ]ϲ τὴν κώμην καὶ ἦν παρ-
ρ’ αὐτῇ ποταμόϲ · τοῦτον δι-
αβὰϲ ὁρᾷ τινα ἱππόϲτα-
20   ϲιν ἀνεῳγμένην καὶ ἐν
αὐτῇ ϲτιβάδα εὐτελῆ καὶ
φαύλην. καταδήϲαϲ οὖν
πρὸϲ τῇ φάτνῃ τὸν ἵππον
24   βαλὼν αὐτὸϲ ἐπὶ τῆϲ ϲτιβά-
δ[ο]ϲ ἐπεχείρει καθεύδειν ·
κἂν τούτῳ κάτειϲι γυνὴ δι-
ὰ κλίμακοϲ ἣ ἦν ἐξ ὑπερώ-
28   [ου ἄ]γουϲα κάτω εἰϲ τὴν ἱπ-
[πόϲταϲιν . . .

- - - - - - - - - - - - - - - - -

We do not print the fragmentary first column.
Col. II: 1. νιοιϲ, θάψα[ι or θάψε[ιν ed. pr.   2. μεικρον pap.   5. καλη · αμφω pap.?
9. τα̣ pap.?   14. ἴδοι pap.   15. εβλεπε̄ pap.   18. ποχᵗαμοϲ pap.   19. παρ
αυτη deleted with expunging dots, τινα added above line   27. κλειμακοϲ pap.

"... to the same ... bury,
having turned aside a little from the path.
There I am lying beneath that
4   plane tree, and with me
a fair maiden, both of us slain."
Glauketes, astonished
(as one would expect) said
8   nothing in reply to this,
but merely nodded his assent
and rode on. The young man
vanished after Glauketes nodded.
12   Glauketes
hurried on and at the same
time turned in case he might see
him again. But he could no longer see him.
16   While it was yet night he arrived
at the village, beside which
ran a river. Crossing this
he saw a horse stable
20   lying open and
inside a cheap and scruffy pile of hay.
So having tied up
his horse at the manger,
24   he threw himself down on the pile of hay
and tried to sleep.
Meanwhile, a woman came down
by a ladder that led down from the upper story
28   into the stable. . . .

P. OXY. 1368, COLUMN II

As the column opens in P. Oxy. 1368, the ghost of a dead man is addressing a passerby. But any frisson of terror that the reader might normally expect to feel about this solitary, nocturnal encounter with a ghost is curiously absent. The dead man, in a highly artificial style—"I am lying beneath that plane tree, and with me a fair maiden, both of us slain"—would seem to be requesting burial for himself and his female companion. The passerby, Glauketes, is surprisingly unmoved by this event; we learn only that "he was astonished (as one would expect)," and although he agrees to do the apparition's bidding, he does not stop his journey. One wonders, therefore, where the bodies were supposed to be in relation to the place of the ghost's appearance. Later on, Glauketes stops for the night without ostensible trepidation, so that the apparition seems to have been neither urgent nor menacing.

1. νι εἰς τὴν αὐτὴν θαψα[...]: has there simply been an ellipse of ὁδόν, or should some other antecedent be understood—ταφήν or sim.?

3-4. κεῖμαι δὴ ὑπὸ τῆ π[λα]|τανίςτῳ ἐκείνη: Jones (1980: 252) notes a possible parallel with Apuleius 1.18.8: iuxta platanum istam residamus. In Apuleius, the narrator of the tale, Aristomenes, proposes to his companion, Socrates, that they should pause under the plane tree. A little while later, Socrates falls dead. The incident in Apuleius of course evokes the opening of Plato's *Phaidros*.

π[λα]|τανίςτῳ: this is the earlier form of the noun (see LSJ s.v.); πλατανός is used in the novelists. The plane was a broad-leafed deciduous tree common in both the northern and southern Mediterranean, so it gives no clue about location. In Achilles Tatius, it grows in Sidon in what appear to have been cultivated gardens (1.2.3, 15.3, 16.3).

5-6. Economy tempts us to connect these two dead with the sacrificial victim of Cologne B.1 recto 10-11 and/or the apparently dead girl and B.1 verso 23-25: πρῶτον μὲν τὰ ςώμ[α]τα τῶν ἀποτε[θνηκότων ἀ]πέδυςαν μ[η]δὲ τὴν ταινίαν ἐν ἧι ἡ κόρη τοὺς μαςτοὺς ἐδέδετ[ο παρέντες]. But nothing positively requires this.

ἀνηρη|μένοι: compare AT 7.7.6: ἔμαθον ἀνηρημένην.

6. ὁ δὲ Γλαυκέτης: it is this name that links this fragment with the Cologne codex. This proper name occurs infrequently in Greek literature, though it is borne by a number of Athenians who appear in the Attic orators.

9-10. ἐπένευεν δὲ μόνον καὶ | [ἄμ]α ἤλαυνεν: note that nearly the same phrase occurs below, lines 13-14: ἤλαυνεν καὶ ἄμα ἐπε|ςτρέφετο.

12-13. κατὰ κρά|[τ]ος: this phrase is classical, but it is not in the extant novelists, and occurs only once in the New Testament (Acts 19.20).

16. νυκτὸς ἔτι: the ghostly encounter must also have taken place at night.

24-25. βαλὼν ... καθεύδειν: ed. pr. compares Arrian *Epict.* 2.20.10: βαλὼν κάθευδε.

26. κἀν τούτῳ : this adverbial expression is frequent in the Cologne fragment.

γυνὴ : is this woman Persis, who seems to be linked with Glauketes in the Cologne C fragments as well as in A.1 and A.2 recto?

28. ἄ]γουϲα κάτω εἰϲ : cf. the phrase at B.1 verso 26: ἀφῆκαν κάτω εἰϲ το ̣ [.

DESCRIPTION

P. Colon. inv. 3328 consists of forty-six fragments from at least three separate leaves (labeled A, B, and C recto and verso) of a papyrus codex. The act of reconstructing these leaves from individual fragments is like working a jigsaw puzzle with patterns on both sides, but with more than half of the pieces missing or damaged—the location of some pieces is easily identifiable, others are impossible. For the convenience of the reader, the original numbering of the papyrus has been followed here. The terms recto and verso, as used by ed. pr., have been applied to fiber direction with respect to the writing (that is, writing is *along* the fiber on the recto, *across* the fiber on the verso). In order of reading, however, recto will not necessarily precede verso.

The page labeled A recto consists of three large pieces: A.1 recto is one fragment, lacking all margins, which must be situated in the upper half of the page; A.2 recto is the label given to five fragments (*a–e*) that combine to form left and right portions of the bottom of A recto. The section between them is missing. A.1 recto and A.2 recto do not obviously overlap in any of their lines; therefore, the original column height of the codex must have been at least fifty-five lines (A.1 recto + A.2 recto). Four other small scraps can be placed with some certainty, though they do not join other pieces: A.16 recto must belong to the upper right corner; A.3 and 4 recto, because they retain right margins, will probably lie along the upper right somewhat below A.16 recto, opposite A.1 recto and above A.2 recto; A.15 recto contains a bit of left margin and should fit into the upper left corner. Fragments A.5–14 recto retain no margins and offer no clues about their placement.

The back of this fragment (A verso) must have contained the last two or possibly three lines of Book 1, marked with a coronis at the left margin. The name of the author, the title, and the book number—Lollianos's *Phoinikika*, Book 1 (Λολλιανοῦ Φοινεικικῶ[ν] α)—has been written about midpage, slightly to the right of center. The rest of this page is blank.

B.1 recto consists of two large fragments (*a* and *b*), each with a substantial lower margin; Fragment *a* retains a left margin, Fragment *b* a right margin, but again the middle section is missing. At its bottom, the page has the title of another book, but its number has disappeared. The backs of these fragments (B.1 verso *a* and *b*) must therefore contain the beginning of a third book (see below). B.4–6 recto and verso are very small fragments with an upper margin, so they are to be located at the top of B recto/verso. Fragments B.7–16 are unplaced.

C recto and verso consists of nine tiny scraps, some of which contain the names of Glauketes and Persis. C.1 and 2 contain an upper margin on both sides, C.9 a lower margin on both sides. Other C scraps remain unplaced.[18]

Since no page is intact, dimensions can only be estimated at 20–25 cm breadth by 35–40 cm height including margins, which gives a ratio of height to breadth of 3 to 2 (Henrichs 1972: 3 n. 12). The formatting of the pages on either side of the leaf shows a slight variation; the original line length now appears to have been between fifty and fifty-seven letters for A.2 recto, between fifty-six and sixty-three letters for B.1 recto, between fifty and fifty-nine for B.1 verso.[19] Because all lines are missing at least ten letters between their left and right halves, their original length must be established on the basis of plausible supplements, combined with an estimate of the length of the end title on B.1 recto, where the phi and final nu of Φοινικικῶν are visible on two separate fragments. Therefore estimates are always subject to a margin of error.[20]

Two different writing styles (if not different hands) were employed in the codex. The first line of A.1 recto as well as A.1 verso and the C fragments are written in a slightly larger, broadly formed cursive that tilts slightly to the right, though the letter shapes are in general similar to those of the second style (or hand) that copies the rest of A.1 recto, A.2 recto, and the B fragments. The latter is a medium-sized upright, rather irregularly formed informal round hand, which on the basis of parallels should be assigned to the end of second century C.E. This makes it a very early example of the codex format (*Typology* no. 223a).

About the format three points are certain: (1) the A fragment contains the end of Book 1 and the beginning of Book 2; (2) the B fragments contain the end of a book (2 or higher) and the beginning of another (3 or higher); (3) the C fragments, the end of Book 1 and its title, and part of Book 2 are written in one style (or hand), the rest of the A fragment and the B fragments in another. The codex can be assembled in several ways: if we assume that the first writing style consistently preceded the second, then the C fragments will form the earliest leaf from Book 1, A.1 verso will end Book 1, and A.1 recto will begin Book 2. The scribe will have changed his style after the first line (or few lines) of Book 2. Since the narrative itself guarantees that B recto must precede B verso, in the most economical reconstruction, Book 2 would end on B recto and Book 3 begin on B verso. If the writing styles alternate inconsistently throughout the codex, however, then the C fragments could be located anywhere, and the B fragments could belong to any two consecutive books (2–3, 3–4, 4–5, etc.).

---

[18] For greater detail about the condition and placement of these fragments, consult Henrichs 1972: 4–5, and pls. II–XIV.

[19] Browne (1982: 142) and O'Sullivan (1983: 9) who, although applying a different criterion, concludes that Browne's estimates "were very near the truth on the width of the gap."

[20] Although the length of this title certainly provides limits, it is neither a totally accurate gauge nor is it as objective a measure as O'Sullivan claims (1983: 8), since the exact spelling of the title (Φ[οινικικῶ]ν or Φ[οινεικικῶ]ν), the size of the letters, and the tightness of the writing are matters for editorial judgment.

Lectional aids include accents, apostrophe to mark elision, tremata, and stops. Nu in suspension, carets as line fillers, and the coronis to mark book ends also occur. Iota adscript is consistently written. Corrections are by the original scribe, but there are a few uncorrected errors and itacisms.

We do not print texts of the very fragmentary scraps. Interested readers should consult Henrichs 1972 for text and plates.

A.1 RECTO

⌐].την εχο[.].. [
]ομένουϲ · καὶ τοὔνομ[α
]εκέ[λ]ευεν · ὡϲ δὲ οὐδεὶϲ αὐ[τῶν
4   ]ωϲ ἀνατρέψοντεϲ · κἂν το[ύτωι
].παῖδεϲ οἱ ἀκόλουθοι ἐξεβ.[
.]πέβαλλον ἀπὸ τοῦ τέγουϲ · οἱ.[
].ἀνατετραμμέναιϲ · ἀμυν[
8   κ]αὶ ἅμα νήφοντεϲ · καὶ ὁ μὲν [
]χώρηϲεν· αἱ δὲ γυναῖκεϲ αὖθι[ϲ
]αι καὶ διετελοῦ[ν] ὀρχούμενα[ι
τῆ]ι ὀρχήϲει ἀλλήλαϲ. ἡ δὲ [
12   ]το · ἀλλὰ πρῶτον μὲν [
ἐκ]είνηϲ · ἔπειτα ἐϲιωπ[
τ]ῶι Γλαυκ[έ]τηι ἄλλο τε κ[αὶ
].ν · ἡ δὲ ὄψε ἀνεϲτη[
16   ν]υκτὸϲ πρ[..].γι.[
].ουϲια · νιϲ.[
ἡ] δὲ Περϲὶ[ϲ
τὴ]ν κεφ[αλὴν
20   ]ν ὅτε π[
]ἔλεγον [
]ειϲαν· [
].ηϲτω[
24   ]ατο[.].[
].[

A.1 recto: The supplements are those of Henrichs 1972 unless otherwise indicated.

3.]ευεν· pap.   4.]ὼϲ Hen.   ανατρεψοντεϲ· pap.   5. ἐξέβα[ινον] or ἐξέβη-
[ϲαν] Hen.   6. [ἐ]πέβαλλον Reeve, [ἀ]πέβαλλον Hen.   τεγουϲ· pap.   8. νη
φοντεϲ· pap.   9. χωρηϲεν· pap.   11. αλληλαϲ · pap.   12.]το· pap.   13.]ει
νηϲ· pap.   ἐϲιώπ[ηϲεν]? Hen.   15.]ν· ἥδε pap.   16. ν]υκτὸϲ or ἐκτόϲ Hen.
17.].ουϲια· pap.   22.]ειϲαν· pap.

] and the name [
] ordered. But when none of them [
4   ] overturning. Meanwhile [
] the accompanying slaves went out? [
] . . . from the roof. The [
] overturned. Warding off [
8   ] and at the same time sober. So he [
] went, while the women again [
] and they kept on dancing [
] each other in the dance. And she [
12   ] . . . But first [
] . . . Thereafter was silent [
] to Glauketes especially [
] and at length she arose [
16   ] at night [
] . . . [
] And Persis [
] head [
20   ] when [
] I (or they) said [

...] κελ[...................] . [
...]ζειν · ν[.................ἔ]φη δ[
...] . ειντ[....................] . ωι χ . [.............] . [
4   ...]ηγαγε[.................]τοϲ κα[...........]μεν[.] . [. . . .]δε
...] . ενδιε[................Π]ερϲίδι τ[.......]ι̣ πείθοντεϲ καὶ τε-
...]ανεπ[.................]ει με εἰϲ [οἴκ]ημα ἀποκεκρυμμένον
θ]εραπαιν[................]κ̣ελημένων καὶ καταλαμβάνω τὴν
8   Π]ερϲίδα ἐγ̣ [τῶι οἰκήματί με ἀν]α̣μένουϲα[ν]. καὶ τότε πρῶτον ἐπειρά-
θ]ην ϲυνου[ϲίαϲ..........] περιελομένη μοι ἐδίδου τὰ χρυϲία ἃ πε-
ρι]έκειτο μ[.............]ϲ διακορήϲεωϲ · ἐγὼ δ᾽ οὐκ ἂν ἔφην λαβεῖν.
ἡ] δὲ τὸν Γλα[υκέτην πρὸϲ αὐτὴν] καλεῖ, καὶ ἐπεὶ παρῆλθεν ἐκείνωι δίδω-
12   ϲι] καὶ κελε[ύει .... τῶι τα]μίαι κομίϲαντα παρ᾽ αὐτ[ὴ]ν
δ[ιϲ]χιλίαϲ ἀ-
ρι]θμήϲαϲ[θαι δραχμάϲ. ἔπειτα] ἐπ᾽ [ἐ]μὲ ἐτράπ[ετ]ο καὶ οὐ πρότερον ἐ-
π]αύϲατο π[ρὶν .... ἡμᾶϲ ἄ]μφω ἔλαβε[ν] καὶ ἡμέρα ἐπέλαμψεν.
ἦγ οὖν . [...................]ϲ ἔξω καὶ τὴν θύραν ἄμφω ἔκοπτον
16   καὶ μόγ[ιϲ ....]ιν. ἐγὼ μὲν αὐτόθι ὑπέμενον, ἡ
δὲ Περϲὶϲ α[........................] . ωϲ ἡ μήτηρ ἐπανίου-
ϲα ἐκ τῆϲ π[.......................] . η καθορᾷ αὐτὴν καὶ τ[ὸ
παραχρῆμ[α ....] καὶ τότε μὲν ἐϲιώ[πηϲεν
20   ἐπειδὴ κ[.......................] ἄμφω παρ[........

A.2 recto: Estimates for the number of letters missing are approximations. The supplements are those of Browne 1982: 142 unless otherwise indicated; supplements of Merkelbach and Dihle are to be found in Henrichs 1972.
2. ζειν · pap.   5–6. τε|[λει]αν? Hen.   6. ἄγ]ει με εἰϲ [οἴκ]ημα Hen.   μενō pap.
7. θεράπαιν[ά τιϲ]? Hen.   κε⟨ι⟩ϑ̣λη̣μενων pap.   8. ἔγ[δον με ἀν]αμένουϲαν Hen.
] · και, επειρα⟨ pap.   8–9. ἐπειρά|[θ]ην ϲυνου[ϲίαϲ Dihle   9. [ἔπειτα] Browne
10. μ[ιϲθὸν] Hen., μ[νημεῖα τῆϲ ἑαυτῆ]ϲ Browne   διακορηϲεωϲ ·, λαβεῖ · pap.
12. κελε[ύει, τῶι τα]μίαι Hen., κελε[ύει παραχρῆμα τῶι τα]μίαι Browne   12–13. ἀ|[ρι]
θμήϲαϲ[θαι] Hen.   14. π[ρὶν κόροϲ (or ὕπνοϲ)] Hen., [κόροϲ ἔρωτοϲ ἡμᾶϲ] Browne
[ἄ]μφω Hen.   λαμψε̄ · pap.   15. ⟨- left marg., κοπτō pap.   16.]ιν · εγω,
αυτοθὶ ϋπε pap.   17. ἡμητηρ pap.   19. παραχρῆμ[α ἐρράπιϲε] Merk.

334

A.2 RECTO

5   ] to Persis [ ] (they) persuading and
                                   ] me into a hidden [chamber?]
female servants [——   ] and I found

8   Persis waiting for me in the chamber. And then I had my first experience
                                              of
sexual intercourse. [—— she] removed the gold ornaments she was
                                         wearing and
was going to give them to me [——] deflowering. But I said I wouldn't
                                        take them.
And she calls Glauketes [to her] and when he arrived, she gave [them to]
                                        him

12 and ordered him when he had brought [——] to her steward to count
                                        out
two thousand drachmas for her. [Then she] turned to me and did not
cease before [——] both, and the day shone forth.
There was then [   ] outside and they both struck
   the door,

16 and scarcely [   ]. While I remained there,
Persis [   ] so that(?) her mother returning
from the [   ] might not(?) see her and
immediately [   ] and then s/he was silent.

20 When [   ] both

ἠρωτ[.............................]ουντο ομγ[..]ι̣[.....
παιδ[.............................]εἰ μὴ ἕκαϲτα κατ[.....
.] ε̣τ[.............................. ἀ]μφοτέρουϲ · ω[....
24 ....] ε̣ιχ̣ει̣ϲ [.............................]ϲεν · ἐμοὶ δὲ [.....
....]εν · ἀλλά μοι αλ[.....................] διδαϲκαλεια[.....
...]η τὰ ἀνθρωπ[.........................]ε ἀδελφὴ [.........
...] παρὰ τῆϲ νοτίδ[οϲ ....]εν · ἔλεγε[.........
28 ..]εν πρὸϲ ἐμὲ τη̣ [.......................] ̣φερεν καὶ διαλεγ[...
...]υ οὐκ ἀπεκριν[..........................]πολὺ χεῖρον [α]ὑτου[...
....]γούμενοϲ ὑπ[.........................] ̣ϲτριτηιαπα[.]ϲ[...
....]μοϲ ὁρῶν ενα[.........................]ετάττετο ωϲ[..]αι̣[...
32 ....] ̣ἐκ τῆϲ παλ[.........................]ϲ καὶ βίαι παϲ[...
....] ̣[.]η̣ν δέ τιϲ [..........................] τῶν ἐραϲτῶν [...
..........]ηντ[.........................]ο ὄμμα ἔρωτοϲ ω[...

B.1 RECTO

- -

　　　　　　　　　　　　　　　　　　　　　　　]νηϲε[
　　　　　　　　　　　　　　　　　　　τ]α πρῶτα ἀγενν[
　　]ι̣[　　　　　　　　　　　　　　　　ρ̣]α̣δίωϲ ἀνθρω[
4 　]αμ[....]γ̣δ[　　　　　　　　　]λέγει αὐτῶι προ[

_____

21. οὖν τὸ ὀμν[ύε]ι̣[ν] Hen.　　23. α]ϲμφοτερουϲ · pap.　　24.]ϲεν · pap.　　25.]εν ·
αλλα, καλει α̣[pap.　　27. παρὰ τῆϲ νοτίδ[οϲ] Hen.　　]εν · ελεγε pap.　　29. απε
κρειν[pap.　　30. ϋπ pap.　　34. τ]ὸ ὄμμα ἔρωτοϲ ὡ[ραίου μεϲτόν] Hen.

B.1 recto: In the main, supplements follow Browne 1982 unless otherwise indicated. The
supplements of Burkert and Reeve are to be found in Henrichs 1972.
3.]αιδιωϲ pap.　　4–9. ὁ δὲ] λέγει αὐτῶι · "πρό[βηθι | ὦ ταλαίπ]ωρε ἄνθρω[πε · ὥρα γάρ
ἐϲτι τῶι παιδὶ νῦν (τούτωι τῶι παιδὶ Koen.)] ἀποθανεῖν." ὡϲ δ᾽ ἀ[κούει,] | λέγ[ει πρὸ]ϲ ἐκεί-
νουϲ · "ὦ [ἄνδρεϲ, τί ὄφελοϲ ἀποκτείναϲιν] ὑμῖν [τὸ]ν παῖδα ἔϲ[ται;"] | "αὐτὸ[ϲ," δ᾽ ἔφ]α-
ϲαν, "ἐμπειρό[τατοϲ εἶ παραμυθεῖϲθαι (τοῦ παραμυθεῖϲθαι Koen.) αὐτόν], ὅπωϲ [φανῇ
γ]ενναῖ[οϲ." "τί] | δ᾽ οὐ μέλλει," ἔφη, "ἐπεί γε Ἀγ[δρότιμοϲ πολλάκιϲ προϲιὼν εἰρήκε]ι̣
(Ἀγ[δρότιμοϲ ὡϲ ἤδη πρότερον ἐρε]ῖ Koen.) εὔψυχ[ον ῥῆ]μα πρὸϲ [τού]|τον ·" "ὁ μιϲητόϲ,"
ἔφη, "ἐγώ. τί [πεποίηκα; ἀλλ᾽ ὑμεῖϲ κακ]ῶϲ ἀ[π]ολεῖϲθε." Henrichs, *exempli gratia*

336

asked [
slave [

24

] but to me [
] human [
] from the moisture [
28   ] to me [
] not answer [
] thinking(?) [
] seeing [
32   ] from the [
] someone [

] they
] unless each
] both
] And to me
] an instruction [
] sister [
]s/he said[
] s/he bore and conversing
] much worse than it/he [
]   [
] ordered [
] and by force [
] of the lovers [
] eye of love [

B.1 RECTO

] first baseness [
] easily human [
4   ] he says [approaching?] him:

"ὦ ταλαίπ]ωρε ἄνθρω[πε . . . .]ἀποθανεῖν." ὡς

δ' α[. . . .]

λέγ[ει πρὸ]ς ἐκείνους, "ᾧ[. . . .] ὑμῖν [τὸ]ν

παῖδα ες[. . . "]

αυτο[. . . .]ασαν ἐμπειρο[. . . .] ὅπως [. . . .

γ]ενναι[. . τί]

8   δ' οὐ μέλλει," ἔφη, "ἐπεί γε α . [. . . . .]ι εὔψυχ[ον

ῥῆ]μα πρὸς [αὐ-]

τόν· "ὁ μισητός," ἔφη, "ἐγώ. τί [. . . . .] . ως ἀ[π]ολεῖςθε."

ἐ[ν τού]τωι παρέρ-

χεται ἄλλος γυμνὸς περίζ[ωμα περὶ ἑαυτῶι] ἔχων φοινικοῦ[ν, καὶ

β]αλὼν τὸ ςῶ-

μα ὕπτιον τοῦ παιδὸς τυ[θέντος ἀνατέμνε]ι. καὶ τὴν [κ]αρδίαν ἐξεῖλεν

καὶ ἐπὶ τοῦ

12 πυρὸς κατέθηκεν. ἔπε[ιτα τὴν ὠπτημένη]ν ἀνελόμενος ἀποτέμνει αὐτῆς ἕ-

ως ἐφ' ἥμισυ. ἐς τὸ ἄκρον [δὲ τῶν τόμων ἄλφιτ]α ἐπέπασεν καὶ ἐλαίωι

ἔδευςεν καὶ

ὡς μετρίως ἐς[κ]εύαςτο, [ἔδωκεν αὐτοὺς τοῖ]ς μυουμένοις καὶ ἔχοντας

ἐν τῶι

αἵ]ματι τῆς καρ[δί]ας ὀμ[όςαι ἐκέλευςεν . . .]κιςην μήτε ἐγκαταλείψειν

μήτε

16 π]ροδώςειν μη[δὲ ἐὰν εἰς τὸ δεςμωτήριον] ἄγωντ[αι] μηδὲ ἐὰν

βαςανίζων[τα]ι

μηδὲ ἐὰν ἐξορύττω[νται . . . .]ηςαν τὸ μὲν ἥμιςυ [τῆς καρ-

δίας τὸ λοιπὸν [. .] . π[. . . . . τὸ]ν δὲ Ἀνδρό[τ]ιμο[ν . . . .

ταν καὶ τοὺς α . [.] . ςου[. . . . .] . . [. . . . . .]πίνοντα

καὶ . [. . . .

---

5. ωςδ'α[pap.   6. ὕμιν pap.   7. [ἔφ]αςαν Burkert   7–8. ["τί] | δ' οὐ μέλλει,
Burkert   8. δ'ου pap.   εὔψυχ[ον ῥῆ]μα Hen., [λῆ]μα Burkert   10. περίζ[ωμα
περὶ τῆι κοιλίαι] Hen.   11. μαϋπ pap.   τυ[θέντος] Koen., τυ[θέντα] Hen.   [ἀνα-
τέμνε]ι Hen.   12. ἔπε[ιτα ὠπτημένην αὐτὴ]ν Reeve, ἔπε[ιτα δ' ἔτι ἡμίοπτον αὐτὴ]ν
Koen., ἔπε[ιτα δὲ ἔτι ὀπτομένη]ν Browne   13. ἐς τὸ ἄκρον [δὲ αὐτῆς ἄλφιτ]α Hen., [δὲ
τῆς ἡμιςεία ἄλφιτ]α Koen., [δὲ μετ' ὄξους ἄλφιτ]α Browne   14. [ἔδωκεν αὐτοὺς τοῖ]ς
Koen., [μετέδωκεν αὐτῆς τοῖ]ς Hen., [δι- (or μετ)έδωκεν αὐτοῖς ὠ]ς Browne   15. ὀμ[ό-
ςαι ἐκέλευςεν Hen.   πολλά]κις? Hen.   ἢ ⟨μὴ⟩ν Lloyd-Jones, Reeve, ὀρ]κιςς⟨τ⟩ὴν
Koen.   ενκατα, μητε) pap.   16. [ἐὰν εἰς τὸ δεςμωτήριον ἀπ]άγωντ[αι] Hen.
17. ἐξορύττω[νται τοὺς ὀφθαλμούς] Hen.   17–18. [τῆς καρ]δίας τὸ λοιπὸν [κα]τ[α]-
π[ιεῖν] Hen.   18–19. [ἐρω]τᾶν? Hen.   19. ἀν[αμ]έςου[ς] Hen.

338

"O wretched man [   ] to die." When [

says to them, "O [   ] to you, the *pais* ["

[And] they themselves said that experience [——] so that [——]

            noble [. "Why]

8 shouldn't it" he said, "seeing as [——"] a courageous remark to

him: "I am despised," he said, "[——] you will perish." Meanwhile

another man, who was naked, walked by, wearing a crimson loin-

            cloth, and throwing the

body of the *pais* on its back, he cut it up, and tore out its heart

12 and placed it upon the fire. Then, he took up [the cooked heart]

            and sliced it up

to the middle. And on the surface [of the slices] he sprinkled

        [barley groats] and wet it with oil;

and when he had sufficiently prepared them, [he gave them to the]

          initiates, and those who held

(a slice?) [he ordered] to swear in the blood of the heart that they

         would neither give up nor

16 betray [——], not [even if they are led off to prison], nor yet if

          they be tortured

nor yet if [their eyes] be gouged out [   ]the remaining half of

the heart [   ] And Androtimos [

and those in the midst [   ] him drinking and [

20 καὶ πιεῖν εν[.] ˌ ι καια ˌ[. . . . . ἀ]λλοϲκ[. .] ˌ ϲ ἔφερεν ἅπαντα
ἐκε[ῖ]νοϲ

ἀνθρώπων [ ]εδοκει.

[Λολλιανο]ῦ
Φ[οινεικικῶ]ν
24 [   ]

B.1 VERSO

ϲτερ[
κατακτ[
ρη αλ[λ]ο[   ]ρ ˌ [. . . .] ˌ ωϲ[
4 ποδαϲ αὐ[. .] ˌ [   ] ἐξ ὠιδῆ[ϲ] κο[
μουο[.]ι ὅπερ [   ] ˌ ϲ καταφερομ[. . . . .] ˌ [ ]
ν[. . . .]ᾳ τὴν [   ]
κ[. . ε]ϲτι απ[   ]ι τῆϲ καρδίαϲ τοῦ παιδὸϲ ὅπερ
8 ετ[. . .] καταπι[. .]ν κα ˌ [. . . . . ἐπὶ τῆϲ τρα]πέζηϲ ἐξεμεθέν. οἱ μὲν δὲ αὐ-
θ[ιϲ ἐ]πέπανον, ὁ δὲ Ἀν[δρότιμοϲ · "βδελυρ]όν τι," ἔφη, "ἔπαθον ἀπέπτου
μ[ο]ι τῆϲ τροφῆϲ ἔτι οὔϲη[ϲ," . . . .] ˌ ατο καὶ ἅμα πολύν · "τὸ κακῶϲ
ἀπολούμενον τοῦτο κορ[. . . . .] τινα διὰ τοῦ ϲτόματοϲ, τὸν
12 δὲ κἀκ τοῦ ὄπιϲθεν ἐπιπε[. . . . .] πρὸς τὴν ἀηδίαν τῆϲ ὀϲμῆϲ

B.1 recto: 20. πιεῖν ἐν[έχ]ει Burkert.

B.1 verso: The supplements are those of Browne 1982 unless otherwise indicated. The original estimates for the size of the gap between left and right pieces of the column were incorrect in ed. pr. We have therefore omitted all supplements that do not suit the space available. The supplements of Burkert, Reeve, and West are to be found in Henrichs 1972.

8. καταπι[εῖ]ν Hen., καταπί[νειν] Koen.   [τὸ ἐπὶ τῆϲ τρα]πέζηϲ Hen., [τὸ αἷμα ἐπὶ τῆϲ τρα]πέζηϲ Browne   9. Ἀν[δρότιμοϲ] Hen.   10. [ἐβ]οᾶτο Koen., [γόον δὲ μέγαν ἐγ]οᾶτο Browne   11. κορ[άϲιον] Burkert, κόρ[ιον] Browne   [παύϲαϲθε βρῶμόν] τινα Hen., [οὐ παύεται βρῶμόν] Koen.   τō pap.   12. ἐπιπέ[μποντεϲ] Hen., ἐπιπέ[μπον] Koen.   [ἱκανῶϲ γὰρ] Browne, [οὐκέτι] Winkler

LOLLIANOS, *PHOINIKIKA*

20 and to drink [   ] but the [——] was bearing everything
                                                          which that one

of men had given(?).

[Lolliano]s's
P[hoinikik]a

B.1 VERSO

] other [
4   feet [   ] from song [
    which [   ] I am brought down [
    ] is [   ] of the *pais*'s heart which
8   ] drink down and [——] vomited out upon the table. While some were
    warming (sc. the food) again, Androtimos said, "I have suffered a
                                        [terrible thing], seeing as
    my food is still uncooked." [——] and at the same time . . .
                                        "This damned
    . . . [——] pouring forth a [stench?] from the mouth, another(?)
12 from the backside. [——] I have held out against the unpleasant-
                                        ness of the odor.

341

ἀντέϲχον. ἀλλ’ ἔγχει, παῖ, δὸ[ϲ .... εἰ]ϲ ποτ[ή]ριον ὃ μέγιϲτον
[ἦν.]

ἐκάλουν δ’ αὐτὸ [ἐ]κεῖνοι κ[..... Κενταύρων ὡ]ϲ ἐμο[ὶ δ]οκεῖ, καὶ
Λαπιθ[ῶν μά-]

χη ἐν τούτωι ἐπ[ε]ποίητο [   ] πρὸϲ αὐτὸν ἐγιν[

16 ὁ δὲ Ἀνδρότιμο[ϲ   ] καὶ ἀχθόμενοϲ ἐπεὶ [

..] ̣̣ ἐν τούτω[ι   ]την [..]νον ζώνην αρ[

.]ιου ἔχουϲαν κ[.......]αγ[   ]περ[ι]ῆψαν. ἄλλοι δὲ εἰϲ-

ήεϲαν οὐδὲν ἀ[γορ]εῦϲαι ἀ[νειπόντεϲ. ἐπεὶ δὲ] πάντεϲ [πα]ρεληλύθεϲαν

20 καὶ ἦν οὐδεὶϲ ἔτ[ι ἔ]ξω, τὰϲ θυρ[.... κλείϲαντ]εϲ ἦιδον, ἔπινον, ταῖϲ γυ-
ναιξὶ ϲυνήεϲα[ν ἐ]ν ὄψει τῆι Ἀ[νδροτίμου. οἱ μ]ὲν καθεῦδον ἀπαγορεύ-
ϲαντεϲ, οἱ δ’ ἐπ[ὶ τῶ]ν νεκρῶν [ταχθέντεϲ ἕ]νδεκα οὐ πολὺ μὲν ἔπιον,
ἀλλὰ ὅϲον ἀποθ[ερ]μανθῆναι [....... ἐπ]εὶ δὲ νύκτεϲ μέϲαι ἦϲαν, πρῶ-

24 τον μὲν τὰ ϲώμ[α]τα τῶν ἀποτε[θνηκότων ἀ]πέδυϲαν μ[η]δὲ τὴν ταινίαν
ἐν ἧι ἡ κόρη τοὺϲ μαϲτοὺϲ ἐδέδετ[ο παρέντεϲ,] ἔπειτα ἀνελόμενοι ὑπὲρ
τὰϲ θυρίδαϲ ἀφῆκαν κάτω εἰϲ το ̣[.......] ̣. καὶ μετὰ ταῦτα χιτῶναϲ ἐν-
δύονται οἱ μὲν λευκούϲ, οἱ δὲ μέλα[ναϲ τελ]αμῶϲιν ὁμοίωϲ τὰϲ κεφαλὰϲ

28 περιειλήϲαντεϲ · καὶ τὰ πρόϲωπα [οἱ μὲν τὰ] μέλανα ἔχοντεϲ ἀϲβόληι, οἱ δὲ
[τὰ λε]υκὰ ψιμυθίωι ἐχρείοντο. καὶ οὕ[τωϲ αὐτοὺ]ϲ κοϲμήϲαντεϲ ἐξήεϲαν ἔξω.
⟨οἱ⟩ μὲν τὰ λευκὰ ἔχοντεϲ διὰ τοῦ ̣̣̣[.......... οἱ δὲ τὰ μ]έλανα διὰ τῆϲ ϲε-
λήνηϲ ἐπορεύοντο. ὁ δὲ Ἀγ[δ]ρ[ό]τιμοϲ   ] ̣ οὐ γὰρ ἦν ἀπαλλα-

32 γὴ ἀπ’ αὐτῶν [κα]ὶ γὰρ ἐφρουρο[ῦντο   ]μηνύϲειν ἐδοκο[ῦν

13. αντεϲχον : ι changed to ε, αλλ’ εγχει pap.   παῖ, δὸ[ϲ Hen., Reeve, παιδὸ[ϲ αἷμα,
ἔφη, καὶ δόϲ. ἐνέχει δὲ εἰ]ϲ ποτ[ή]ριον ὃ μέγιϲτον [ἦ(ν)] Koen. (in ed. pr.), "παῖ δὸ[ϲ τὸ
αἷμα." ἐνέχει δ’] Koen.   14. εκαλουν corrected from ελαλουν? pap.   δ’αυτο pap.
14–15. [Κενταύρων, ὡϲ] ἐμο[ὶ δ]όκει, καὶ Λαπιθ[ῶν μά]|χη ἐν τούτωι ἐπ[ε]ποίητο Bur-
kert   19. θεϲαν⟩ pap.   20. τὰϲ θυρ[ίδαϲ] Hen.   [κλείϲαντ]εϲ Koen.   γυ⟩
pap.   21. ϲυνήεϲαν Hen.   Ἀ[νδροτίμου] Hen.   [οἱ μ]ὲν Jones   22. δ’επ[
pap.   [ταχθέντεϲ] Hen.   23. [ἐπ’ ὀλίγον. ἐπ]εὶ Browne   24. ἀποτε[θνηκότων,
ἀ]πέδυϲαν Hen.   25. [παρέντεϲ] or [ἐάϲαντεϲ] Jones, [λιπόντεϲ] Browne   26. β[ά-
ραθρον or φ[ρέαρ] Jones, β[αθὺ φρέα]ρ Browne   27. [τελ]αμῶϲιν O’Sullivan,
[δρ]άμωϲιν Hen., [πᾶν το]λμῶϲιν Browne   28. [οἱ μὲν τὰ] μέλανα Jones   29. οὕ[τωϲ
ἑαυτοὺϲ] κοϲμήϲαντεϲ Reeve   30. ⟨οἱ⟩ μὲν or ⟨καὶ οἱ⟩ μὲν Reeve   διὰ το[ῦ]
ἡλίου Burkert, Reeve, διὰ το[ῦ] ϲκό[τουϲ Jones, Winkler, διὰ το[ῦ] ϲκο[τεινοῦ Jones

But, boy, pour out and give [me. . . . into] a cup that was the largest.
And they were accustomed to call it [. . . a battle of Centaurs,] as I
thought, and Lapiths

had been wrought on it [   ] became to him . . .

16 and Androtimos [   ] . . . and annoyed when

. . . meanwhile [   ] the . . . cincture [

having [   ] they bound around, others

went in, . . . to say nothing. When all had passed in

20 and there was no longer anyone outside, closing the [———], they sang,
drank,

had intercourse with the women in full view of Androtimos. [Some] slept
exhausted,

while the eleven [stationed] by the corpses did not drink very much
—just enough to get warm (cool off?) [———] When it was midnight, first

24 they stripped the bodies of the dead and not even leaving the band
with which the girl bound her breasts; then hoisting them up
over the windows, they let them down into [———] . And after this they
put on robes

—some white, some black—and bound similarly colored bands around
their heads;

28 and those with the black robes smeared their faces with soot, those
with the white with white chalk. And [having thus adorned themselves]
they went outside,

those with the white through the [———], those with the black through
the

moonlight. But Androtimos [———] for there was no escape

32 from them for they were guarded [———] but they seemed about to reveal [

εἰ ἀπέλθοιεν ὥϲτε ὑπ' ἀναγ[   ] . [
χρυϲοχόου ἐργαϲτήριον γ[
πρεϲβύτην ἄνδρα κ[
36   .]η ϲῶϲαι ην πεμ[
      .] . ϲε[

_____

33. ϋπ pap.   ὑπ' ἀνάγ[κηϲ or ὑπαναγ[καζ- Hen.

if they went out, so that necessarily [
workshop of the goldsmith [
an aged man [
36   to save [

A.1 RECTO

The mentions of the rooftop, women dancing, and sobriety—which always brings to mind its opposite—suggest the celebration of the Adonia. This festival, which commemorated the untimely death of Aphrodite's young lover Adonis, involved nocturnal festivities on the rooftops, and seems to have permitted women of various social categories to mix freely. From Aristophanes we learn that the goings-on were public (*Lys.* 387–96), and from Menander (*Sam.* 35–50) that young women of the citizen class might be sufficiently unattended at these events for their boyfriends to get them pregnant. This would suit admirably the circumstances in the rest of the column, where Persis and an unnamed man spend most of the night engaged in sexual activity and, after the event, are interrupted by her mother. (For a recent discussion of the evidence for the Adonia festival, see Winkler 1990: 189–93 and n. 1.)

5-10. Frag. A.3 recto might belong to the far right of these lines. ταῖς γυναι[ξίν could be an antecedent for ἀνατετραμμέναις (line 7) and]ατο the verb for ὁ μὲν (line 8). But it should be noted that ἀνατετραμμένος is more often predicated of objects than of people.

6.   .]πέβαλλον ἀπὸ τοῦ τέγους : people either watch from or throw something from the roof. For the former, cf. Xen. *Kyr.* 7.5.22: μὴ ἐπὶ τὰ τέγη ἀναβάντες βάλλωσιν ἔνθεν καὶ ἔνθεν, or Lys. 3.11.

οἱ .[: either μ[έν or δ[έ would suit trace before the break.

7. ἀνατετραμμέναις : cf., e.g., Hld. 1.1.4: κρατῆρες ἀνατετραμμένοι.

αμυν[: ἀμυνόμενοι or sim.?

8. νήφοντες : cf., e.g., Ch. 4.3.12; 1 Peter 1.13, 4.7.

ὁ μὲν [: ὁ μὲν would seem to be contrasted with αἱ δὲ γυναῖκες (line 9) and ἡ δὲ [Περςίς ? (line 11). This is either Persis's inexperienced friend from A.2 recto 8–9, or Glauketes, who is mentioned in line 14 here.

17.] .ουςια : although [υ]γουςία is an obvious supplement (see A.2 recto 9), the trace before does not inspire confidence. Henrichs suggests rather [ἀ]ρουςία or [με]τουςία, and further that the punctuation of the papyrus must be wrong, preferring] .ουςίαν.

18. ἡ] δὲ Περςὶ[ς : the name is an ethnic one, of the sort usually attached to slaves, or prostitutes. Persis's generosity with her sexual favors is a pretty clear indication that she is not a novel heroine cut from the same cloth as Charikleia or Kallirhoe, but then the world of the *Phoinikika* seems closer to that of Apuleius than that of Heliodoros.

18–19. ἡ] δὲ Περςὶ[ς ... τὴ]ν κεφ[αλὴν: Henrichs suggests locating Frag. A.4 recto opposite these lines, supplementing καταφιλή[ςαςα or sim. Cf. Ch. 8.4.11: καὶ κεφαλὴν καὶ χεῖρας αὐτοῦ κατεφίληςε, as a mode of greeting.

A.2 RECTO

The broad outline of this scene is clear, but the details may be filled in a variety of ways. In the course of the festivities described in A.1 recto, our ego-narrator is led into a hidden chamber where he finds Persis and with her has his first experience of sexual intercourse. Either before or after these proceedings, Persis attempts to give her lover the gold necklace she is wearing; when he refuses, she summons Glauketes to bring her some money for him. Although it is not explicitly stated, he probably accepts the money, because she is sufficiently pleased with him either to begin or to continue the lovemaking, after which they probably fall asleep in exhaustion. The next day brings the arrival of Persis's mother. The bottom of the column, which is badly broken, seems to have been taken up with a conversation between the servants (ἄμφω?), the mother, and possibly Persis. Line 26 mentions a sister. This combination of a deflowering, an exchange of gifts or money, and the girl's mother are more familiar from Lucian's *Dialogues of the Courtesans* than the extant Greek novels. In the latter, girls with mothers are virgins, and mothers arrive in the knick of time, not a day later; if the man and woman are the teen lovers, they should not succeed in consummating their passions, at least with each other, until properly married. The hero, however, occasionally succumbs to the importunings of a sexually experienced woman.

5–6. The text is very broken, but a possible reconstruction would be that some friends or guests have persuaded Persis to undertake the sexual education of the narrator.

 τε][...]ανεπ[: this could refer to Persis's favors, e.g., τε][[λεῖ]αν ἐπ[ίδειξιν] or sim.?

6. καὶ ἄγ]ει or sim. will supplement.

7. θ]εραπαιν[: this is either the subject of ἄγ]ει in line 6 (e.g., [θ]εράπαιν[ά τις]) or part of the genitive absolute construction with]κελημένων (e.g., [θ]εραπαίν[ων] or [θ]εραπαιν[ίδων]).

]κελημένων: the text was corrected, but remains problematic. Most likely the scribe intended κεκλημένων or κεκλημένων (= κεκλειςμένων). If the former, one might restore, e.g., καὶ ἄγ]ει με εἰς [οἴκ]ημα ἀποκεκρυμμένον | [θ]εράπαιν[[ά τις, ἀπιόντων τῶν] κε⟨κ⟩λημένων, i.e., "and a servant led me into a hidden chamber while the guests were leaving." For κεκλημένος with this meaning, see LSJ, s.v. καλέω 1.2, and Hld. 5.13.1. If κεκλημένων, e.g., τῶν ἄλλων θύρων] κε⟨κ⟩λημένων, i.e., "after the other doors were locked." Cf. Ch. 1.12.5 (κεκλειςμέναι τὰς θύρας) or 7.6.7.

8–9. καὶ τότε πρῶτον ἐπειρά|[θ]ην ϲυνου[ϲίαϲ: Lucainon's initiation of Daphnis into the rites of erōs (Longos 3.19.3) provides the clearest parallel from the extant Greek novels. Young men customarily had their first sexual experiences with prostitutes: see, for example, Kleitophon's remark in AT 2.37.5: ἐγὼ μὲν πρωτόπειροϲ ὢν εἰϲ γυναῖκαϲ, ὅϲον ὁμιλῆϲαι ταῖϲ εἰϲ Ἀφροδίτην πωλουμέναιϲ.

9. The scene can be reconstructed in two ways: if ἔπειτα is restored in the lacuna to begin the sentence (so Browne) it would mean that the narrator had had his first experience of intercourse, then Persis gave him a gift, and then at line 13 they continued their activities. Alternatively, one can restore, e.g., ἡ μὲν δὴ κόρη. In this case the young woman will have given him a gift *before* the love-making commences, καὶ τότε πρῶτον κτλ. will introduce the entire anecdote, and Glauketes will not have intruded on the couple in the act, as it were.

ἐδίδου τὰ χρυϲία: women give men gifts or money for a variety of reasons—an experienced partner may pay a reluctant lover (see AT 6.1.4: δίδωϲι δέ μοι καὶ χρυϲοῦϲ ἕκατον), or an inexperienced lover (see Luc. *Dial. mer.* 5.4, where the suppliant is a woman disguised as a man attempting to make love to another woman!); or a girl may take an impecunious lover whom she subsidizes with gifts because he is "handsome and beardless, and says he loves me and he weeps" (Luc. *Dial. mer.* 7.2).

Henrichs (1972: 22–23) connects Persis's jewelry with the bedecked goddesses of the Near East, many of whom were associated with Aphrodite and whose cults practiced ritual prostitution: "Wir dürfen annehmen, dass auch auf Lollianos diese orientalische Tradition direkt eingewirkt hat. Die Goldkette, die Persis trägt, hat also ihre Entsprechung im Schmuck der Gottes-braut und Hierodule bzw. der Liebesgöttin selbst."

10. μ[±13 letters]ϲ διακορήϲεωϲ: restorations have included μιϲθὸν = "payment" or μνημεῖα = "memento." Browne cites AT 6.1.3 (τὴν ἐϲθῆτα ταύτην φύλαττε μνήμην) as a possible parallel. Normally διακόρηϲιϲ and its cognate verb are used of the deflowering of women; see Steph. *Lex.* s.v. for examples. For a literary use, Henrichs notes τὴν ἄρτι διακεκορευμένην (Luc. *Dial. mer.* 11.2). Some commentators have balked at διακορήϲεωϲ applied to the man (Jones 1980: 244; Henrichs 1969: 212–13; Browne 1982: 142), and have assumed therefore that Persis gives a gift to her lover in gratitude for her own deflowering. But virginity and Persis's *modus vivendi* would seem incompatible, unless she encountered the narrator before she was officially launched upon a career as a courtesan by her mother. Since it is evident from lines 8–9 that the narrator was a virgin, we are inclined to assume that διακόρηϲιϲ is being ironically applied to the man's condition, not Persis's. (So Henrichs 1970a: 22, 1972: 23; and Sandy 1979: 368). But see below, line 25.

οὐκ ἂν ἔφην λαβεῖν: the ἂν belongs with the infinitive.

12. κελε[ύει .... τῶι τα]μίαι: we take the construction to be κελε[ύει + accusative (κομίϲαντα) + infinitive (ἀ|[ρι]θμήϲαϲ[θαι), with τῶι τα]μίαι + a

direct object (restore τὰ χρυcία?) dependent on κομίcαντα. "She orders [Glauketes] when he has brought [the necklace] to the steward to count out two thousand drachmas for her."

14. Browne's κόροc ἔρωτοc is attractive, but not inevitable. For the phrase, Henrichs (1972: 110) compares Hld. 1.15.8; for the sentiments, Luc. *Dial. mer.* §3, AT 4.8.2.

ἡμέρα ἐπέλαμψεν: Henrichs points out that this is a variation of a phrase in Herodotos (1972: 110).

15. καὶ τὴν θύραν ἄμφω ἔκοπτον: presumably two of Persis's servants had slept outside her door and warned her of the mother's approach (so Jones 1980: 244). Certainly the servant woman of line 7 and Glauketes seem to be her supporters.

16. καὶ μόγ[ιc ±18 letters]ιν: Jones (1980: 244) would supplement καὶ μόγ[ιc ἐγείρουc]ιν. Though about eight letters short, the idea is clearly right.

16-17. ἐγὼ μὲν αὐτόθι ὑπέμενον, ἡ | δὲ Περcὶc: Persis presumably goes out to speak with her mother, while the narrator remains within the hidden chamber.

17-18.]̣ ὡc ἡ μήτηρ ἐπανίου]cα κτλ. The construction of these lines could be ὅ]πωc ἡ μήτηρ ... [———] μὴ καθορᾷ κτλ.

18. ἐκ τῆc π[: Henrichs's π[όλεωc is very plausible.

25. διδαcκαλεια: Jones takes the noun to be διδαcκαλεῖα, arguing that it means "teacher's fee" and that "it could ... be an urbane reference to the payment which Persis has just made for her first lesson in love" (1980: 244). But if our reconstruction is correct, it will be an itacism for διδαcκαλία = "instruction."

26.]ε ἀδελφὴ [: ἡ δ]ὲ ἀδελφὴ or sim.?

27. παρὰ τῆc νοτίδ[οc: prima facie, the word is νοτίc, which means "moisture," but Henrichs's suggestion (1972: 111) that this might be a hitherto unattested feminine name—Notis—is attractive, considering the "sister" above in line 26. Note the similarity to Apuleius's Fotis.

30. cτριτηιαπα[.]̣ c[: the articulation is difficult: a dative τριτηι embedded within a genitive phrase seems unlikely; possibly]̣ cτρι τηι απα[.]̣ c[.

32. ἐκ τῆc παλ[: παλ[αιᾶc or one of its cognates are of course possible supplements, but παλ[suggests also παλ[αιcτρᾶc] or παλ[ῆc], and both wrestling terms are connected with sexual activity; see, e.g., [Luc.] *Asin.* §10 (and note that the name of Lucian's maid is Παλαίcτρα) and AT 5.3.5 and 6.18.5.

34. ὄμμα ἔρωτοc: the "eye of love" is a cliché, since it is through the eye that passion takes hold. See, e.g., Plato *Sym.* §210.

B.1 RECTO

2-9. The dialogue in progress can be reconstructed in a number of ways. Henrichs's *exempli gratia* restorations require three speakers—the subject of λέγει (line 4), whom he takes to be the leader of the outlaw band; his addressee (ὦ ταλαίπ]ωρε ἄνθρω[πε, line 5), whom he takes to be Androtimos; and the band itself, the plural subject of [ἔφ]αcαν (line 7). Alternatively, there might be only two speakers—the leader of the band who addresses first the victim (ὦ ταλαίπ]ωρε ἄνθρω[πε) and then the band itself (λέγ[ει πρὸ]c ἐκείνουc); and the victim, who speaks at line 9. Or again three speakers, if the text is reconstructed to give the gang a speaking part in line 7. The subject of discussion is the impending sacrifice of the *pais*. The relationship between the dialogue and subsequent action is not obvious; another man, who is identified as "naked, but wearing a scarlet loincloth," abruptly appears to perform the sacrifice.

Henrichs has supplemented line 8 with the name Androtimos. If correct, he must be the speaker of line 9 (and identical with αὐτῶι, line 4). But this is not without difficulty. The name, apart from the first letter, is completely restored, and Androtimos's subsequent behavior (B.1 verso 8–12) does not lead us readily to imagine that he would publicly object to the sacrifice, refer to himself as "hated," and curse the outlaws—[κακ]ῶc ἀ[π]ολεῖcθε (as Henrichs restores it). Henrichs suggests the curse was delivered "zu sich selber," but this is not apparent from the text itself.

4–5.]λέγει αὐτῶι προ[: normal usage requires πρὸc + accusative (as below, line 6, line 9?) to express the addressee after λέγω. Therefore, we should restore either a compound of λέγω or a participle like προ[cιών (= "approaching him, he says") to govern the dative.

5. ὦ ταλαίπ]ωρε ἄνθρω[πε: prima facie, it is the victim who ought to be "wretched." Henrichs assumes the addressee to be Androtimos, no doubt because elsewhere the victim is referred to as a *pais*. But the generic ἄνθρω[πε is not necessarily an inappropriate term of address in these circumstances, especially if the *pais* is a servant, not a child. If the "wretched man" is other than the victim, we can only speculate that he was a friend or master of the victim. Certainly the tone of this section does not convey the impression that anyone was a parent of the victim.

Whoever the actual addressee, the sentiment expressed here must be close to Henrichs's [ὥρα γάρ ἐcτι τῶι παιδὶ (αὐτῶι, cοι, or sim.)] ἀποθανεῖν.

5–6. ὡc δ' ἀ[. . . .] | λέγ[ει πρὸ]c ἐκείνουc: options are circumscribed by space and the construction. One might restore ὡc δ' ἄ[γει,] | λέγ[ει πρὸ]c ἐκείνουc (= "when he brings [the victim], he says to them"), which does not require a change of speaker.

6.] ὑμῖν τ[ὸν] παῖδα: interpretation of this passage hinges on who is assumed to speak this line, if they do indeed belong to the dialogue and not intervening narrative. The speaker cannot be the victim. If it is not the gang leader, then (as Henrichs has it) it must be a third party.

7. αὐτο[ὶ . . .]αcαν: αὐτο[ὶ δ' ἔφ]αcαν or sim. This is almost certainly another speaker change, since the addressee of the gang speaks in line 6 and again at 7–8, apparently in reply to something ("τί] | δ' οὐ μέλλει," ἔφη).

ἐμπειρο[and γ]εννᾱι[probably refer to the impending sacrifice, though who or what the actual referent is can only be guessed at. For noble language to describe a dastardly deed, compare [Luc.] *Asin.* §23: τόλμημα γενναῖον καὶ ἄξιον, or Satyros's remark about their hoax as ὁ χρηςτὸς οὗτος (AT 3.22.1)

9. "ὁ μιςητός," ἔφη, "ἐγώ. τί [. . . . .] ̣ ὡς ἀ[π]ολεῖςθε" : these lines would seem to come more naturally from the mouth of the victim, who is then immediately sacrificed. Note that in this text each new sentence or change of speaker (see lines 5, 8) seems to be marked. If the change begins with "ὁ μιςητός," ἔφη, one would expect rather ὁ δὲ ἔφη or sim. A change in speaker could easily fall in line 8, however, restoring, e.g., [καὶ ὁ παῖς λέγε]ι εὔψυχ[ον ῥῆ]μα πρὸς [αὐ]|τόν = "And the *pais* makes a spirited remark to him (sc. the bandit leader)."

Previous editors have restored κακ]ῶς ἀ[π]ολεῖςθε as if a curse. Alternatively, ὅπως + future? One might restore, e.g., τί [δὴ μέλοι μοι ὅ]πως ἀ[π]ολεῖςθε = "But why should I care that you will perish?"

For the expression ὁ μιςητός . . . ἐγώ, Henrichs (1972: 113) compares [Luc.] *Asin.* §45, Men. *Perik.* 348.

10. The executioner's costume and the detail with which it is recorded have struck previous interpreters of the scene. Henrichs's evidence for the wearing of a crimson loincloth or sash in a variety of cults (1972: 114–15) suggests that at the very least the sacrificial scene is intended to have an aura of authenticity about it. Winkler has argued that "this is just the sort of detail which is both memorable and apparently significant—an ideal clue" for an impending *Scheintod* (1980: 173).

11. The only other example of human sacrifice cum cannibalism in the extant Greek novels is in AT 3.15.4–6, where Leukippe is apparently disemboweled in full view of a band of *boukoloi* and her entrails cooked, then consumed by the group. There are notable similarities of language: for β]αλὼν τὸ ςῶ|μα ὕπτιον (lines 10–11), compare ἀνακλίνας αὐτὴν ὑπτίαν (AT 3.15.4), and to lines 11–13 here, compare τὰ ςπλάγχνα δὲ εὐθὺς ἐξεπήδηςεν, ἃ ταῖς χερςὶν ἐξελ- κύςαντες ἐπιτιθέαςι τῷ βωμῷ, καὶ ἐπεὶ ὠπτήθη, κατατεμόντες ἅπαντες εἰς μοίρας ἔφαγον (AT 3.15.5). The fact that Leukippe's death was a *Scheintod* may influence our interpretation of this scene from the *Phoinikika*. For the rela- tionship of the two novels, see above, introduction.

12. ἔπε[ιτα τὴν ὠπτημένη]ν : since the food (τροφῆς) is later described as ἀπέπτου (B.1 verso 9), restorations here have tended to assume that the heart, too, was undercooked. But not necessarily: we take Androtimos' complaint to be about the food they have eaten, which must have consisted of more than the heart, if it ever included it. Reeve's supplement is therefore preferable on sense, but rather long for the space; the shorter supplements ἔπε[ιτα τὴν ὠπτημένη]ν or ἄρτι ὠπτημένη]ν (= "just cooked") are preferable.

12–13. ἔ|ωϲ ἐφ᾽ ἥμιϲυ: for the use of ἔωϲ with a preposition, compare Hld. 2.28.3: ἔωϲ ἐπί; Ch. 3.3.18: ἔωϲ εἰϲ.

13. ἐϲ τὸ ἄκρον [δὲ τῶν τόμων: we are indebted to L. Koenen for this supplement. The sense of the passage is that he sliced the heart up to the halfway point, and then sprinkled barley groats and oil on the surface of the slices.

ἄλφιτ]α ἐπέπαϲεν καὶ ἐλαίωι ἔδευϲεν: the addition of ingredients like wine or barley groats to sacrificial offerings is well attested. Henrichs (1972: 117) provides parallels from a variety of sources. This addition could have been the means of producing the vomiting and flatulence experienced in B.1 verso. If so, the person performing the sacrifice must have been part of a conspiracy.

14. τοῖϲ μυουμένοιϲ: cf. AT 3.22.4 where the same language is used of Menelaos and Satyros, who are "initiated" into the band of *boukoloi* by performing the sacrifice of Leukippe. Jones (1980: 252–53) argues that the use of this term in the Hellenistic and Roman period does not necessarily imply a religious initiation or shared religious beliefs of the participants. See Henrichs 1972: 56, 63–64, 117, 127–28 for the opposite view.

ἔχονταϲ: the participle lacks an object. The most obvious solution is an ellipse of τὴν καρδίαν. If correct, the initiates will be holding a small slice of the heart while they swear the oath. Alternatively, the object may have dropped out of the text, and they are holding something "in the blood of the heart." In this case, ἐν τῶι | [αἵ]ματι belongs not with ὀμ[όϲαι] but with ἔχονταϲ.

14–15. ἐν τῶι | [αἵ]ματι τῆϲ καρ[δί]αϲ ὀμ[όϲαι ἐκέλευϲεν: if they swear "in the blood of the heart," they do not appear to be holding cups of blood or to drink blood as part of the ritual. In fact, in neither of the literary parallels—the *boukoloi* engaging in cannibalism in AT 3.15ff. and in Cassius Dio 72.4—is the blood of the sacrificial victim drunk; rather, the group cooks and eats the victim's entrails (τὰ ϲπλάγχνα).

Henrichs remarks that the construction ὄμνυμι ἔν τινι is not Greek, though it could be a semitism (1972: 117–18). He further provides the intriguing Latin parallel from Statius *Theb.* 5.162–63: in sanguine vivo coniurant.

15. ...]κιϲην: the reading is corrupt in some way. Prima facie, it will be the object of the verbs in the oath—μήτε ἐγκαταλείψειν μήτε | [π]ροδώϲειν. Browne's suggestion that this may be a personal name (1982: 139) is attractive, but names in]κιϲην are difficult to find. Alternatively, it could be a miscopying of a noun that meant "band" or "group," e.g., κοινωνίαν, ϲυνουϲίαν, or as Koenen suggests, "leader," e.g., οἱ]κιϲ⟨τ⟩ήν. But if a noun of some kind, there is insufficient space in the lacuna for an article.

17. μηδὲ ἐὰν ἐξορύττω[νται: τοὺϲ ὀφθαλμοὺϲ] or sim. will supplement. Henrichs (1972: 118) compares AT 7.14.3, Ch. 6.5.8.

17–18. B.1 verso 7–8 would indicate that the oath-swearers consumed the bits they were holding. But what happens to the rest of the heart is not clear. The construction—τὸ μὲν ἥμιcυ … τὸν δὲ Ἀνδρό[τ]ιμο[ν—suggests an opposition between the disposal of the rest of the heart and what Androtimos and the others (the prisoners?) are doing. The division of the heart into two distinct parts and its distribution at two distinct times is a curious and noteworthy feature. Henrichs has adduced no parallels from ritual, nor are there literary parallels. The explanation that most readily comes to mind, of course, is that half of the heart was doctored for consumption by the bad guys, the other half left untreated to be eaten by those perpetrating the hoax.

18. τὸ]ν δὲ Ἀνδρό[τ]ιμο[ν: this is the first certain appearance of this name in the *Phoinikika*. Its occurrence in other ancient sources is rare; see *RE* 1: 1, 2, col. 2173.

20–21. ἀ]λλοcκ[. .] ̣ c ἔφερεν ἅπαντα ἐκε[ῖ]νοc | ἀνθρώπων [ ]εδο̣κει : a modicum of sense can be made of this by articulating ἀ]λλ᾽ ὁ cκ[. .] ̣ c (or ἄ]λλοc κ[. . .]c) ἔφερεν ἅπαντ᾽ ἃ ἐκε[ῖ]νοc | ἀνθρώπων ἐδόκει (sc. φέρειν, or read [δ]εδώκει), "But the [———] (or Another [———]) was bearing everything which that man seemed to" (or "which that man had given"). Though without a context, it is still obscure. An unaugmented pluperfect is not uncommon at this period, though ἐπεποίητο at B.1 verso 15 is augmented.

If ὁ cκ[. .] ̣ c, the word might be cκ[οπ]ός; cf. [Luc.] *Asin.* §22, quoted below, note B.1 verso 19.

We suggest the following scenario for the events in this column: The heart, which was previously cut up and consumed by some of the group, presumably those who swore the oath, has been doctored, so that those who ate it were at least temporarily incapacitated or distracted, perhaps from examining the corpse of the sacrificial victim too closely. After the sacrifice, there is a meal in which the bandits, at least, partake. At this point, Androtimos publicly complains about the belching and flatulence, and attributes it to a failure to cook the food properly. Then he calls for a large cup from which to drink. The cup appears and afterwards other bandits enter the house, and join in singing, drinking, and communal sex. Most of the men settle down to sleep after appointing eleven of their number as guards. At midnight, they wake up, strip the corpses, and dump the bodies (or their possessions) out of the windows, dress up, some in black, others in white garments, and go out into the night. Although it is not specifically stated, some must have been left to guard the prisoners. The final, broken lines of the column suggest that there is a plan for escape.

The character of Androtimos remains a puzzle. He might be the bandit chief: nothing in this scene is inconsistent with this supposition and a minimal amount of evidence supports it—he alone complains about the meal and the flatulence, and he calls for the drinking cup. The fact that the group has sex "in sight of Androtimos" and that he does not leave with the rest does not necessarily vitiate the argument. No bandit chief is designated as leaving within the extant narrative, and the fact that he was their leader may be the reason that having sex in his presence is notable. He might, of course, be a character like Thrasyllus in Apuleius, who only pretends to be a bandit in order to rescue his girlfriend, or like the pair of "initiates" in AT, who pretend to sacrifice Leukippe, that is, someone trusted by the bandits but really on the side of their victims. Alternatively, he could simply be a prisoner. If he is a prisoner of the bandits, he will doubtless be involved in the escape that would seem to be brewing at the end of this column.

4. ἐξ ᾠδῆ[ϲ]: cf. AT 3.15.3: καὶ ὁ ἱερεὺϲ ᾖδεν ὡϲ εἰκὸϲ ᾠδὴν Αἰγυπτίαν. If the Achilles Tatius passage is an apt parallel, this song may be connected with the ritual and the oath-swearing. Note below, line 20, where the subsequent singing seems rather to be part of the general jollifications.

7–8. τῆϲ καρδίαϲ τοῦ παιδὸϲ ὅπερ | ετ[. . .] καταπι[. .]ν κα . [. . . . . ἐπὶ τῆϲ τρα]πέζηϲ ἐξεμεθέν: context and traces suggest, e.g., ὅπερ | ἔτ[υχε] καταπι[ώ]ν, κατ[έφανη ἐπὶ τῆϲ τρα]πέζηϲ ἐξεμεθέν. = ". . . of the the the *pais*'s heart, whatever he happened to swallow, had clearly been vomited up on the table." For the general shape, cf. Thuc. 3.83: τὸ εὔηθεϲ, οὗ τὸ γενναῖον πλεῖϲτον μετέχει, κατα-γελαϲθὲν ἠφανίϲθη. For the thought, compare [Luc.] *Asin.* §18: πάντα τὰ λάχανα κάτωθεν ἐξεμέϲαι (so Henrichs 1972: 119).

8–9. οἱ μὲν δὲ αὖ|θ[ιϲ ἐ]πέπανον: Henrichs (1972: 119) has suggested that the initiates are forced to consume again what they had regurgitated, noting that ἀπέπτου may mean "undigested." This is surely far fetched—at the very least we should expect a verb like "swallow" or "eat." But [ἐ]πέπανον normally means to "ripen" or "grow warm." We think it much more likely that some of the men are reheating their meal, in the mistaken assumption that uncooked food has made them ill.

10.] . ατο καὶ ἅμα πολύν: the third-person verb termination suggests that this phrase may belong to intervening narrative rather than to Androtimos's complaint. The sentence requires a noun object + adjective to be linked with καὶ ἅμα πολύν. It is possible, of course, that the subject of the verb is τὸ κακῶϲ κτλ., but the word order would be unusual for this author. Browne's [γόον δὲ μέγαν ἐγ]οᾶτο is probably on the right track.

10–11. "τὸ κακῶϲ | ἀπολούμενον τοῦτο κορ[: for the word order, compare [Luc.] *Asin.* §23: τὸν δὲ ἄθλιον τοῦτον ὄνον, ἔφη τιϲ αὐτῶν. But what is the noun here? Previous editors have restored κορ[άϲιον] or κόρ[ιον]. The usual term for "girl" in the novelists is κόρη; note that κόρη is used in line 25 here of one of the victims, and again in P. Oxy. 1368.5. If a diminutive or pejorative form of κόρη was written here, Androtimos must be cursing her because she has

353

failed to cook the meal properly. If this line of argument is right, it is tempting to identify her with Persis, who might well be a participant in this adventure, since her name occurs in a tiny fragment (B.5 recto) located at the top of B recto. For κορ[άϲιον], see [Luc.] *Asin.* §6: ἰταμὸν καὶ χαρίτων μεϲτὸν τὸ κοράϲιον (sc. Palaistra).

Alternatively, he might be cursing an ingredient, e.g., κορίαννον (= coriander), or the food itself, e.g., κόρημα (= garbage).

11. Henrichs's βρῶμον is attractive—perhaps [βρῶμον μέν] τινα.

11–12.] τινα διὰ τοῦ ϲτόματοϲ, τὸ(ν) | δὲ κἀκ τοῦ ὄπιϲθεν ἐπιπε[: while a variety of restorations are possible, the sense is clear—Androtimos complains that the food has induced belching and flatulence, either in himself or in the others. Apuleius provides a provocative parallel: when Lucius (as the ass) is in danger of being beaten to death, he distracts his attackers by spattering them with a noxious stream of watery feces: nisi dolore plagarum alvus artata crudisque illis oleribus abundans et lubrico fluxu saucia fimo fistulatim excusso quosdam extremi liquoris aspergine alios putore nidoris faetidi a meis iam quassis scapulis abegisset (4.3.10).

These lines must belong to Androtimos's speech, because there is no room to mark a change of speaker before ἀντέϲχον and ἔγχει in line 13.

ἐπιπε[: a form of ἐπιπέμπω is the most likely supplement.

12–13.] πρὸς τὴν ἀηδίαν τῆϲ ὀϲμῆϲ | ἀντέϲχον : the subject must be "I" = Androtimos, not "they," for reasons given above, 11–12. Cf. Apul. 4.3.10: putore nidoris faetidi.

13. ἀλλ' ἔγχει, παῖ, δὸ[ϲ : Androtimos calls for the largest drinking cup they have. If παῖ, δὸ[ϲ is the correct articulation instead of παιδὸ[ϲ, then there is no reason to assume they are drinking blood (as previous editors have it). They are much more likely to be drinking wine; hence the remark in lines 22–23 that the guards only "drink enough to get warm (or cool off)." That is, they do not get drunk.

εἰ]ϲ ποτ[ή]ριον ὃ μέγιϲτον [ἦν.] : this could belong to Androtimos's remarks or to intervening narrative, like the beginning of line 14.

[ἦν] : the supplement is Koenen's, who suggests, considering the space available, that it must have been written ἦ.

14. ἐκάλουν δ' αὐτὸ [ἐ]κεῖνοι : this must be interjected narrative. The sense is either "they were accustomed to summoning it [the cup]," or "they were accustomed to call it [the cup] a k[——]," where the missing noun will be a type of drinking vessel, possibly a foreign or non-Greek word (so S. West, Henrichs 1972: 121). If Burkert's supplement of lines 14–15 is correct, then this word must have been quite short—at most five letters long. Such a philological note, however, would not be inappropriately coupled with a brief description of the object.

14–15. Burkert's Κενταύρων, ὡ]c ἐμο[ὶ δ]οκεῖ, καὶ Λαπιθ[ῶν μά]|χη ἐν τούτωι
ἐπ[ε]ποίητο is admirable, but raises some questions.

ὡ]c ἐμο[ὶ δ]οκεῖ requires either that Androtimos resume his remarks after
ἐκάλουν δ' αὐτὸ [ἐ]κεῖνοι, or that there is an ego-narrator telling the entire
story. The pluperfect, ἐπ[ε]ποίητο, does not instill confidence that this could be
a comment made by Androtimos upon the appearance of the cup; surely following the present δ]οκεῖ, he would have said π[ε]ποίηται. It is possible that ἐν
τούτωι ἐπ[ε]ποίητο begins a new sentence, since elsewhere ἐν τούτωι is used
adverbially at the beginning of sentences to mean "meanwhile." But this
would mean that Κενταύρων could not have been written, since the lacuna
would then necessarily contain a notice of change of speaker (ὁ δὲ ἔφη or sim.)
as well as a main verb for the phrase Λαπιθ[ῶν μά]|χη. Further, the only two
examples of ἐπ[ε]ποίητο in the Greek novels do refer to works of art (AT 1.1.9
and Longos 1.4.2). If ἐπ[ε]ποίητο is part of the description of the cup, ἐν τούτῳ
must mean "on it," since "meanwhile it had been engraved" is scarcely intelligible as narrative, especially after the subject of the engraving has been stated
by one of the characters. We are left to conclude that there *is* an
ego-narrator in this scene who is reporting events as well as the remarks of
Androtimos, and that this piece is somewhat more complex than it seems on
the surface.

Other references to Lapiths and Centaurs in the novels are Hld. 3.3.5, a
description of the embroidery on Theagenes' cloak, and Apuleius 4.8.ff.,
where a robbers' banquet is compared to that of the Lapiths and Centaurs.
The likening of the men's behavior to Lapiths and Centaurs in Apuleius would
seem to find its narrative equivalent in Lollianos in ornamentation on a cup.
This allusion functions more subtly within the Greek scene; it allows the reader
to make the comparison, but does not require it.

17–18.]την [. .]νον ζώνην αρ[. . | .]ιου ἔχουcαν: is [. .]νον a biform adjective
modifying ζώνην? Or does ἔχουcαν modify [. .]νον with ζώνην as an object?
Possibly ζώνην ἀρ[γυ|ρ]ίου. Henrichs suggests that this ζώνην may be con-
nected with the περίζωμα of the sacrificer above B.1 recto 10. We are tempted
to connect this with the description of the cup, taking ζώνη to refer to the band
on which the frieze of Lapiths and Centaurs was carved (for this meaning, see
LSJ, s.v., 3.3), but the only word that comes to mind for την [. .]νον is ληνόν
(= wine vat).

19. ἀ[νειπόντεc]: Browne's supplement is attractive because it provides a participle to govern the infinitive and would appear to be an accurate description of
the situation = "And the others came in announcing that there was nothing to
report." Cf. [Luc.] *Asin.* §22: τῶν cκοπῶν τιc . . . ἔρχεται ἀγγέλλων. . . .

20. τὰc θυρ[. . . . κλείcαντ]εc: while θυρίδαc are mentioned below (line 26),
these appear to have been sufficiently elevated that the text describes men as
"hoisting [the bodies?] up over the windows." This does not suggest that the

windows were a normal means of entrance. Surely, the arriving group will have used the doors, and these, rather than the windows, are more likely to need closing to prevent unwanted interruptions. Restore, e.g., τὰϲ θύρ[αϲ ϲυγκλείϲαντ]εϲ or sim.? Cf. [Luc.] *Asin.* §47.

ἦιδον: see above, note on line 4; compare Apuleius 4.22.1, where the robbers sing "canticis quibusdam Marti deo."

21. ἐ]ν ὄψει τῆι Ἀ[νδροτίμου: although ὄψει τοῦ Ἀ[νδροτίμου would be a more common expression, sufficient parallels for this construction exist (see Henrichs 1972: 122, whose example from Xen. *Anab.* 2.5.31—ἐπὶ ταῖϲ θύραιϲ ταῖϲ Τιϲϲαφέρνουϲ—is most apt).

23. ἀποθ[ερ]μανθῆναι: the verb is hapax legomenon. Whereas θερμαίνω and ὑποθερμαίνω mean "warm" and "grow somewhat warm," Henrichs suggests that this ἀπο-compound is ambiguous, and could mean either "cool down" or "warm up" (1972: 122–23 and 1969: 209 note 11).

νύκτεϲ μέϲαι: the plural is Attic; Henrichs (1972: 123) cites Lucian *Dial. mer.* 4.2, 12.3; AT 2.26.1; and Hld. 9.10.2. Cf. also [Luc.] *Asin.* §22: μεϲούϲηϲ ϲχέδον τῆϲ νυκτόϲ.

24. ἀποτε[θνηκότων: although Jones (1980: 247, n. 26) objects to this form in prose, Browne (1982: 140) provides sufficient parallels.

24–25. μ[η]δὲ τὴν ταινίαν | ἐν ἧι ἡ κόρη τοὺϲ μαϲτοὺϲ ἐδέδετ[ο: Henrichs compares the language of Apuleius 10.21.1, "taenia quoque qua decoras devinxerat papillas," noting that a parallel passage is lacking in [Luc.] *Asin.*

26. Stramaglia (1992: 62–63) suggests reading εἰϲ τοὺ[ϲ κρημνού]ϲ, citing as a parallel [Luc.] *Asin.* §24 where the robbers throw down over a cliff the body of the old crone who has hanged herself (ἐϲ τὸν κρημνὸν κάτω ἀφῆκαν). If correct, the supplement makes it even less than the location of the action could be Egypt, and it adds to the series of parallels between Lollianos and Apuleius (6.30.7) outlined above.

26–29. καὶ μετὰ ταῦτα χιτῶναϲ ἐν[δύονται οἱ μὲν λευκούϲ, οἱ δὲ μέλα[ναϲ: the group now garb themselves, some in white garments, some in black; those with white garments then smear their faces with white chalk (ψιμυθίωι), those with black use soot (ἀϲβόληι). See Henrichs 1972: 124–26 for the potential ritual significance of these acts.

30–31. ⟨οἱ⟩ μὲν τὰ λευκὰ ἔχοντεϲ διὰ τοῦ . . . [. . . . . οἱ δὲ τὰ μ]έλανα διὰ τῆϲ ϲε[λήνηϲ ἐπορεύοντο: this line has occasioned considerable debate. The men go out over a period of time—those dressed in white "through the . . . [" and those in black "through the moonlight." For the first half of the line, Reeve and Burkert have suggested διὰ τοῦ ἡλί[ου. Both Jones and Winkler, perceiving the problem with ἡλί[ου, suggest ϲκό[τουϲ, which does not quite suit the traces. Although no better conjecture comes to mind, we think the interpretation of the passage requires that those in white-face depart in darkness (not sunlight or the light at dawn) for their disguises to be most effectively spooky.

31–32. οὐ γὰρ ἦν ἀπαλλα|γὴ ἀπ' αὐτῶν: the first indication that some of those present were not willingly part of the band.

32. ἐφρουρο[ῦντο: the plural is a further indication that there must have been several prisoners. Are the guards here the same eleven chosen above, line 22?

32–33.]μηνύcειν ἐδοκο[ῦν] | εἰ ἀπέλθοιεν: the subject is presumably the guards who have been left.

Iolaos

———— ❖ ————

Iolaos mixes together conventionally incompatible items—mystical and vulgar, noble and obscene, verse and prose. The plot at the point where the papyrus begins seems to be that suggested by E. R. Dodds in a foot-note to Parsons (1974), namely that a young man of sound body tries to gain access to a woman by pretending to be a religious castrato. Although the general tenor seems provisionally clear, the details remain obscure. The prose narrative before and after a verse inset of Sotadeans describes the action of at least two characters—one character who learns and subsequently teaches ineffable things as a favor to his friend; and Iolaos, the friend who receives that mystic teaching. The first character is referred to as the "mystic" (35). The "mystic" appears to have learned his secrets from a friend named Neikon, who might be the guileless(?) *kinaidos* of line 26. The friendship between the "mystic" and Neikon is praised with a quotation adapted from Euripides *Orestes* 1155–57. The action consists in the "mystic" learning from Neikon what he is to teach to Iolaos, his meeting with Iolaos ("by chance," 12), and his speech to Iolaos in Sotadean verse. The speech begins: "O noble Iolaos, hail, and shut up, *kinaidos*!" It is possible that the first line of the speech is addressed only to Iolaos, who is alternately praised as noble and insulted as *kinaidos*—a rapid and unexpected shift of attitude, but not out of keeping with a facetious style. The *kinaidos*, who is told to shut up, does not appear elsewhere in the scene (though Neikon is called a *kinaidos* in the "mystic's" speech, 26).

The plot which Dodds suggests, if we omit the obscenity or the reli-giosity, has a dignified pedigree, going back to Euripides' *Skyrioi*, in which Achilles dresses as a maiden and gets Deidameia pregnant; to Menander's *Androgynos*, in which Pyrrhos dons his sister's clothing to become the friend and confidant of a well-chaperoned maiden, whom he gets pregnant (Neumann 1953); and to Terence's *Eunuch*, which was first acted in 161 B.C.E. at the Megalesia, the commemoration of the Great Mother's arrival in Rome. The motif was incorporated into Daphne's story by one Diodoros of Elaia and by Phylarchos: Leukippos dresses as a maiden and joins Daphne's band of huntresses to be near her; Apollo, who is also in love with Daphne, puts it into her mind that they should all bathe together; Leukippos, exposed, is killed by the group (Parthenios 15). This motif was also used in the story of Hymenaios, who dressed as a maiden to be near his beloved; when a group of maidens, including him, was kidnapped by bandits, he was able to kill their captors (Schmidt 1886: 12–15). Eumolpus, in Petronius's *Satyrica*, adopts the strategy of seduction by assuming the role of perfect chastity when he is billeted in Pergamum: "As often as the conversation at dinner turned to the enjoyment of beautiful boys, so angrily did I flare up and with such stern melancholy did I refuse to let my ears be violated by the mention of impure things that the mother in particular regarded me as a philosophical saint" (§ 85).[1]

To this old plot our author has added the piquancy of making the hero not merely a sham-female or a sham-eunuch but a sham-*gallus*. The *gallus* was a castrated devotee of Cybele (the Great Mother) or of Atargatis, the Syrian goddess. On the one hand, his religious associations allow mystical and exalted language to be introduced. But the extravagance of his devotional behavior (whirling, slashing with knives, effeminate dress, castration) was viewed with contempt by those who adhered to the conventions of Greco-Roman piety; hence the *gallus* in unfriendly and satirical portrayals, which are virtually all that we have left, is frequently identified as a *kinaidos* (Graillot 1912: 318), an adult male who enjoys being the sexual object of other adult males, no longer a real man but not exactly a woman (ita amputatur uirilitas ut nec conuertatur in feminam nec uir relinquatur, Augustine *Civ. Dei* 7.24).[2] In such a deliberately ridiculous and shocking composition, one should not expect to find much in the way of reliable information about either the sex lives or the religious practices of actual *galli*. Yet the secrecy surrounding

---

[1] Quotienscumque enim in conuiuio de usu formosorum mentio facta est, tam uehementer excandui, tam seuera tristitia uiolari aures meas obsceno sermone nolui, ut me mater praecipue tamquam unum ex philosophis intueretur. The motif of cross-dressing also occurs in the extant fragments of the *Satyrica*: "On the day when Giton would have assumed the toga of virility, he donned instead a woman's robe, persuaded by his mother not to be a man, and he set about doing women's work in the slave section" (die togae virilis stolam sumpsit, qui ne vir esset, a matre persuasus est, qui opus muliebre in ergastulo fecit [§ 81]).

[2] In 77 B.C.E., the consul Mamercus reversed a lower-court decision and declared that a *gallus* named Genucius was not entitled to inherit an estate, since "having voluntarily amputated the genital parts of his own body he should be reckoned neither as a man nor as a woman" (Val. Max. 7.7.6). On *galli* as a "third sex," see Sanders 1978: 1080–81. On the generalized use of "*gallus*" to mean any eunuch, see Carcopino 1942: 86–87.

ancient mysteries and initiations has ever whetted the curiosity of modern scholars, and hence some have tried to find in *Iolaos* usable scraps of religious information (Merkelbach 1973, Macleod 1974). Unfortunately, the fundamental item in *Iolaos*, the initiation of a *gallus*, appears to be a mare's nest: there is evidence about Mater initiations and there is evidence about *galli*, but the two do not overlap.

Alongside the very public celebrations of the Great Mother in the last two weeks of March,[3] at which *galli* were highly visible, there were private initiations of individual worshipers. No information survives that would fix such initiations to any definite date in the sacred calendar, and it seems that, like the *taurobolium* ceremony, to which mystic connotations were attached in the fourth century, initiation could occur by private arrangement on any day of the year.[4] Nothing ties the practice of special initiation into the Mater's mysteries to the public ceremonies of carrying reeds, bringing in the pine tree hung with an effigy of Attis and purple ribbons, mourning on the Day of Blood, burying the pine tree, and bathing the statue of the goddess. Initiation appears to have been a private dedication undertaken on occasion by some of the lay faithful, not systematically connected either to the public cult or to the permanent status-change of the *galli*.

Concrete references, as opposed to Christian ranting, to mysteries of the Magna Mater are never plentiful, but they do exist, beginning with three Hellenistic inscriptions and a bas-relief (Sfameni Gasparro 1985: 21–23; Vermaseren 1982: nos. 432, 469, 479, 650). About the content of such initiations we are told little beyond the refrain, "From the tambourine I have eaten, from the cymbal I have drunk, I have carried the chest, I have descended into the chamber."[5] Initiates are never said to be castrated or to become *galli*, nor are *galli* said to be initiated.[6]

---

[3] Vermaseren 1977: 113–24.

[4] Some taurobolic ceremonies are described as performed on the celebrant's "birthday," which probably indicates a symbolic rebirth (Sfameni Gasparro 1985: 113–14). Lucius's first initiation, described as a birthday, is performed on a day arranged by him and the priest (Apuleius 11.24.4).

[5] Clement of Alexandria (himself an initiate) *Protrep.* 2.13; Firmicus Maternus (*De err. prof. rel.* 18.1) reports the first two clauses, then "I have learned the religious secrets" (Latin) or "I have become an initiate of Attis" (Greek). Even if the first two clauses refer to a period of fasting, as seems probable (Boyancé 1935), that is not enough to associate the initiation with the community fasting of March 16–24.

[6] The *galli* at Hierapolis described by Lucian (*De Syria dea* §60) may represent an extreme form of the dedication undergone by every Syrian youth. As he describes it from his own experience, boys let one lock of their hair grow long, which they cut off and offer

Galli are regularly portrayed as mendicant devotees[7] rather than as temple personnel.[8] They of course play a prominent role in the March celebrations, but at other times of the year, for all we know, they are wandering in bands from shrine to shrine, from town to town. In the Roman Empire the chief priest of a Mater shrine was called the *archigallus*, but he was not a *gallus*: Roman priests had to be whole men (Sanders 1972: 1012, 1978: 1087). Further, his consecration (and that of priestesses) was a consecration to office and to the duties of the temple liturgy, not an initiation to a higher spiritual life per se. The official cult and the activities of the *galli* seem to be relatively independent worlds, moving to the same mystic music but along separate paths. The physician Aretaios speaks of the ecstasy experienced by *galli*, using a metaphor of initation (3.6.11), but direct testimony to initiation ceremonies or "secrets" of *galli* do not otherwise exist.[9]

Iolaos seems therefore to be a fictional scene in every sense, and does not appear to offer us a new peephole onto the shuttered darkness of ancient initiations. But if modern interpreters of a pious bent are thwarted in their search for new light on ancient ecstacy, that is not to deny that there is any relation at all between criminal-satiric fiction and actual bandits or cults or conspiracies. As the picture of unspeakable rites and a terrible oath in Lollianos's *Phoinikika* picks up popular fears

---

to the goddess when their beard begins to grow. The lock is placed in a silver or gold vessel, inscribed with the dedicator's name, and lodged in the temple. This rite of passage might be regarded as the ordinary level of dedicating one's manhood to the goddess, whereas the *galli*'s act is an extraordinary version of the same. On the general reliability of *De Syria dea*, see Oden 1977.

[7] Mainly of the Great Mother and the Dea Syria, but Plutarch (*De Pyth. orac.* §407c) notes the presence of similar characters around the temples of Sarapis. Such "itinerant specialists," as Burkert calls them, are known in Greece from the fifth century and "must have been responsible for the spreading of votive monuments for Mētēr through the Greek world as early as the archaic period, from Cyzicus in Asia Minor to Locri in southern Italy" (Burkert 1987: 35–36; see also Graillot 1912: 312–17).

[8] The Syrian *galli* described by Lucian are actually forbidden to come inside the sacred precinct (*De Syria dea* §50). Occasionally western writers speak of *galli* in the Mater's temple, but never with the authority and clarity that we would like, e.g., "he amputates his masculine parts, he slashes his arms . . . they butcher themselves in temples, they worship with their own wounds and blood" (Seneca *De superstitione* frag. 34 Haase = Aug. *Civ. Dei* 6.10).

[9] Sfameni Gasparro (1985: 77 n. 75) cites a scholium on Aristophanes *Birds* 877 and Paulinus of Nola 19.186 and 32.88 as the closest anyone comes to speaking of the *galli*'s practices as "mysteries," but the language is vague and the attitude distinctly hostile.

and may resonate in its fictional way with actual social practices, so the fascination of Imperial poets and theologians with the missing *phalloi* of the *galli* may echo popular, and very partial, perceptions of the cult, and may even correspond to a facet of the Mother-worshipers' own humor. *Gallus* is also the common word for cock (that is, rooster)—a bird with prominent and widespread phallic associations. A rooster is occasionally employed in monuments commemorating *galli* (Vermaseren 1977: 108, pl. 64). A devotee's conception of his own role may include symbolic and amusing play with presence or absence of the phallos: as the rooster's name indicates the profession of the *gallus*, so the rooster's associations indicate the precious loss that established that profession.

Further, in the initiation story, known from one who himself underwent the process, Zeus, after he had raped Demeter, pretended to be contrite and threw into her lap a ram's testicles, saying that he had castrated himself (Clem. Alex. *Protrep.* 2.13).[10] This false castration is close in spirit to the criminal-satiric genre—a sexual joke involving both real violence and pretended violence, horror and humor intermingled. No doubt Clement singles it out to make the initiation seem sillier than it appeared to those undergoing it, and we should not take the surprised horror of Demeter as the testicles land in her lap as the essence of pious feeling for the Great Mother. But it does seem to show that the experience of initiation was (or could be) many-sided, that its frightening aspects were balanced by an awareness of contrivance, that following its often-mentioned terrors there could supervene a feeling of release tinged with humor and embarrassment.[11] In this one sense, *Iolaos* might be entered as a document in the dossier of the Mother's mysteries—not as a serious or even a warped portrayal, but as an independently constructed cartoon that happens to correspond to an underappreciated facet of the emotional complexity of initiation. Similarly, the popular actors presenting a skit on *The Loves of Cybele*, in which a young Attis rejected the favors of an aging and decrepit Mother Goddess, may have touched on themes and tones actually present in some part of her worship.[12]

[10] Pausanias (2.3.4) knew, but did not reveal, an initiation story concerning the Great Mother, Hermes, and a ram.

[11] "We have the word of Diodoros that Priapos Ithyphallos played a role in nearly all the mysteries, though it was 'with laughter and in a playful mood' [DS 4.6.4] that he was introduced, and this was hardly the core of the mystery" (Burkert 1987: 104–5).

[12] Tertullian *Ad nat.* 1.10.45 = *Apol.* 15.2; Min. Felix *Oct.* 22.4: quoniam et ipsa deformis et uetula, ut multorum deorum mater; Hepding [1903] 1967: 116.

PROSIMETRIC TEXTS AND MENIPPEAN SATIRE

With the publication of P. Oxy. 3010, scholars have felt the need to assess two questions, possibly interlinked: what, if any, is the relationship of the *Iolaos* fragment to Menippean satire, and what, if any, is its relationship to Petronius's *Satyrica*? Answers have differed and, without further data, will no doubt continue to do so, depending on the a priori assumptions, stated or implicit, that an individual scholar brings to the questions.

About Menippos we know the following: he was a Syrian-born Greek who settled in Boiotian Thebes, whose *floruit* is located in the third century B.C.E. He is said to have composed a variant of the Cynic diatribe, characterized as "not at all serious" (DL 6.99) or "seriocomic" (Str. 16.2.29) on a wide range of subjects. Diogenes Laertios lists necromancy, wills, epistles composed as if by the gods, remarks to physicists, mathematicians and grammarians, the birth of Epicurus, and the School's reverence for the twentieth day (DL 6.101). From Probus, a much later source, Menippos is said to have written in a mixture of prose and verse,[13] perhaps in imitation of near eastern models (Perry 1967: 208–9). Nothing of Menippos survives, but we have the *Saturae Menippeae* of Varro in Latin and Lucian's Menippean dialogues in Greek.[14] Both mix prose and verse, both produce narratives whose purpose is to satirize or lampoon human foibles and which may be characterized as "seriocomic," and both paint themselves as adapting or imitating Menippos.[15] But Roman would seem to differ from Greek: Varro employs a wide variety of metrical types, including Sotadeans, on an astonishing number of themes, and a vigorous colloquial language, whereas Lucian writes in a refined Attic, incorporates quotations from Homer or tragedy, but does not compose his own verse, and the verse serves to adorn rather than to advance the plot. His range of themes is also rather confined— apparently dependent on the necromantic works attested for Menippos.

[13] On Verg. *Ecl.* 6.31: Varro qui sit Menippeus non a magistro, cuius aetas longe praecesserat, nominatus, sed a societate ingenii, quod is quoque omnigeno carmine saturas suas expoliverat (Servius, vol. 3, pt. 2, 336.22).

[14] The *Apocolocyntosis* attributed to Seneca, though clearly in the Menippean mold, is irrelevant to this discussion, since it is derived from Varro. Note, however, Parsons (1971: 65), who cites the prophecy of the reign of Nero as the closest example of a poetic narrative that "is an integral part of the story, it continues the narrative and does not merely adorn it."

[15] For Varro's relationship to Menippos, see Astbury 1977: 22–23. For Lucian and Menippos, see Helm 1906; and for an opposite view, McCarthy 1934: 3–55.

Either or neither may represent the original form of Menippos; it is not possible to judge. Of the two, *Iolaos* (and *Tinouphis*) is closer in style to Varro. But although both Varro and Lucian are "seriocomic," they are not obscene—*Iolaos* is, and one suspects *Tinouphis* could be. What does all this mean? There are several possibilities.

1. Menippos is the direct ancestor of Varro in Latin (who accurately represents his model), and *Iolaos* and *Tinouphis* represent his true Greek descendants (however close or remote). Lucian represents an Atticizing dead end.

2. Varro was not an imitator so much as innovator. If *Iolaos* and *Tinouphis* resemble Varro, they are more likely to be descendants of the Latin models than the Greek. Although one assumes a priori that in the second century C.E. no Greek texts will yet be influenced by Roman, this has the status of editorial convention, not demonstrable fact—in a society in which the literate must necessarily be elite, it is not impossible for some few to have been exposed to Roman texts even at this early date.[16]

3. The criteria of "seriocomic" and prosimetry are insufficient to connect these Greek texts with either Menippos or Varro. The former in varying degrees must be a criterion of all social satire and much philosophical discourse, at least from Plato. And in any case, while *Iolaos* and *Tinouphis* are comic, are they also serious? Not discernibly so from what remains. Texts that sport a counterfeit *gallus* out for "a crafty fuck" or a condemned prophet saved by an executioner with a trick brick do not instill confidence that their principal intent is moral edification. The question comes down, then, to how much weight to give to the prosimetry. Prosimetry that is sustained and integrated into the text is found in Greek only in mime, and neither of these Greek texts is mime. Though poetry is occasionally quoted in the extant Greek novels, no true parallel for these texts exists. The parallel that does exist is Petronius's *Satyrica*.

Introducing Petronius complicates rather than resolves the problem. Setting aside the perennial question about the relationship of Menippean satire to Petronius, as well as the not unnatural prejudice of Hellenists that Petronius "must have had" a Greek antecedent,[17] the options would

---

[16] The thoroughly Greek milieu of *Tinouphis* need not necessarily work against this hypothesis, Greek writers would presumably be as capable of adapting Roman models to Greek themes as Romans were of Greek models. In support of the opposite position, E. Courtney has argued cogently that Lucian was familiar with Juvenal (1980: 624–29).

[17] "Natural reason long ago revealed that Petronius had a Greek model" (Parsons 1971: 66). But a more salient question is, what kind of a Greek model? Greek novels of

appear to be as follows: (1) Petronius and *Iolaos* are descended from a common ancestor, (2) *Iolaos* represents a later copy of Petronius's direct antecedent, (3) *Iolaos* is descended from Petronius, or (4) the two are unrelated, there being sufficient variety of narrative type available by the first century C.E., that both Petronius and *Iolaos* could arrive on the scene independent of each other. How to decide?

Prosimetry is not all that common—only three examples (Petronius, *Iolaos, Tinouphis*) within a field of twenty-eight (seven complete or near complete novels, twenty-one fragments) suggests that there should be a link.[18] Further, prosimetry seems closer to the mainstream of literary composition in Latin (Varro, Seneca, Petronius) than in Greek. This might incline one to believe that Petronius, influenced by his native satire, injected prosimetry into the milieu of the Greek novel, rather than that prosimetric novellike texts (independently descended from Menippos?) enjoyed a subterranean existence in the Greek world. If *Iolaos* were alone, we would tend to this view, but *Tinouphis* changes things. Its milieu is more obviously that of the Greek as opposed to the Roman novels, its narrative affinities closer to Iamblichos than Petronius. And *Iolaos* and *Tinouphis* seem more like each other than like other Greek novels or novel fragments. Both focus on areas in which religion could and often did cross over into charlatanry, both mix in sex and low life in metrical form, both are written in a vigorous but hardly elegant Greek, both are full of textual errors,[19] neither shows a trace of serious purpose. Add to this the fact that fictional narratives in Greek with a reportedly

---

the historical or "idealistic" type, as well as salacious stories like Aristides' *Milesiaka* certainly preexisted the *Satyrica*, and Petronius, educated Roman that he was, would surely have read what existed. Did he adapt or satirize what had come to be a generic plot, did he have an individual serious novel in mind when he wrote the *Satyrica*, or was he writing a style of criminal-satiric fiction already well established in Greek?

[18] Stramaglia (1992: 136–42) takes a different tack, arguing that we should exorcise the ghost of Menippos from these discussions and that the mixture of prose and verse was a common feature of the writing of antiquity at all social levels. His argument is attractive in the abstract, but in actuality he can introduce only two more examples in the field of romance—the *Alexander Romance* and the "History of Apollonius, King of Tyre," both of which in their present condition, whether he wishes to concede the point or not, have been heavily influenced by the vagaries of their medieval transmission, and may not represent an Ur-form. Even if they do, five examples in a field of thirty is not a large number, although it does even the balance between Latin examples and Greek.

[19] We add this curious fact for what it is worth: only three of the fragments—*Iolaos*, *Tinouphis*, and *Daulis*—have serious textual problems, whereas the other novel fragments exhibit only minor difficulties.

salacious or criminal cast (or both) seem to have perished more completely than their more austere historical counterparts.[20] We are, therefore, inclined to (4) above—natural reason notwithstanding.

[20] Beginning with Aristides *Milesiaka*, including the *Sybaritica*, Arrian's life of Tillorobos the bandit (said to have been a juvenile effort), as well as a number of writings labeled as erōtika. See App. B below.

DESCRIPTION

P. Oxy. 3010 (measuring 13.2 × 23.5 cm) was found in Oxyrhynchus. It consists of one broad column from a book roll, nearly complete apart from the lower right corner. Upper and lower margins of about 2.5 cm survive. The first seven lines of text and the last nine are divided into two columns that read consecutively; the middle twenty lines present a single column of verse. These verses are set off by paragraphi; nu is written in suspension at lines 3 and 7; a caret is used as a space filler at line 2; a space left in text precedes the lines of Euripides quoted at lines 39–41. Note that these latter verses are written continuously within the prose text. The hand is a medium-sized upright, rounded type decorated with horizontal serifs. Ed. pr. compares it to the London Hyperides (*GLH*, pl. 13b) assigned to the second century C.E. There is one example of hiatus, lines 1–2: γάλλου ὀνομαζομένων. Like *Tinouphis*, *Iolaos* contains a number of vulgarisms and uncorrected errors in the both the prose and the verse sections of the text. The meter of lines 14–33 is Sotadean, according to the following scheme:

$$--\smile\smile \quad --\smile\smile \quad --\smile\smile \quad -- \quad \|$$
$$-\smile-\times \quad -\smile-\times \quad -\smile-\times \quad -- \quad \|$$

There is the usual anaclasis: a *longum* can be resolved, the *brevia* can be contracted. The third syllable of the first three metra may be anceps. According to Parsons (1971: 56), this scheme obtains for all lines certainly read or restored, though there are a number of peculiarities. For a fuller discussion of the verse of this piece, consult Parsons 1971: 56–59 or Merkelbach 1973: 90–94. Sotadean meter is usually associated with *galli*; see Demetrios *De eloc.* §189, Syrianus 1.47.9 (Rabe).

P. OXY. 3010

πορρήτων ὑπὸ τοῦ γάλ- 8 φορεῖν [ἐcθῆτα . . . . .]
λου ὀνομαζομένων   νον κληρω[. . . . .]
μανθάνει δι᾽ ὃν διδάcκειν   χηc δὲ πληρ[. . . . .]
4 ἔμελλεν ἵνα μήτε παρα-   ἐπῆλθε προ . [. . . . .]
πέcῃ τῷ cυμμύcτῃ, τε- 12 καὶ κατὰ τύχῃ[ν . . . . . .]
λεcθέντι δὲ πολλαχῶc   αὐτὸν εὑρω . [. . . . . . .]
καὶ διδαχθέντι θηλυκὴν

14 εὐγενῆ Ἰόλαε χαῖρε καὶ κίναιδε cιωπη·
μυcτικὸc λογο . [ ] . . cτικοιc παρηγορη[
16 γάλλοc γεγον[. . . . .] . Ἰόλαε δια . . . [
Νείκων μαν[   ]αδιαcεναπο . [
ἵνα γάλλον ἔχῃ[   ]ν εἰδότα πάντα [
οἶδα δὲ cὺ τίcι . [   ] πάντα δ᾽ οἶδα [
20 τὴν cυνήθεια[ν . . . .]ην τὸν ὅρκον [
νεκ[ρὸ]ν ἄταφο[ν   ]πειc τινοc π[
τὸν νόθον νο . [   ]ν πᾶν γεγον[
cμίλην θεμ[ὀλ]ολυγμὸν κα . [
24 οἰκίαν τε cὴν μ[ητ]έρα κοιτῶνα cὸν οἶδα [
θρήνουc πατρὸc Εὐρύκλειαν ὅτι cυνοιδ[
Νείκων᾽ ἄδολον κίναιδον καὶ τὰ γενέc[ια
οἶδα κλῆcιν καὶ κίναιδον cκω[

Supplements are those of Parsons unless otherwise noted. Henrichs's conjectures are in Merkelbach.

2. μενων⟩ pap.   3. δι᾽ ὃν, δι᾽ ὧν Par., δὲ ὃν Lloyd-Jones (in ed. pr.)   διδαcκῖ pap.
4–5. παρα|παίcῃ Merk.   7. και, θηλυκῆ pap.   8. [ἐcθῆτα] or [cτολὴν] Par.
8–9. [cτέφα]|νον Merk., [τύμπα]|νον or [τὸν κέρ]|νον Hen.   9. κληρω[θη Par., κληρώ[cηται Hen.   9–11. [διδα]|χῆc δὲ πλήρ[ηc γεγονώc (πληρ[ωθείc, δ᾽ ἐπληρ[ώθη)] | ἐπῆλθε πρὸc [τὸν Ἰόλαον] Par. (ed. pr.)   12. [ἔνδον] Merk.   13. ⟩αυτ pap., αὐτὸν εὑρὼν Par.   [ἄιδει τάδε] Merk.   15. παρηγορή[cω, -cει, -θην, or -ημαι Par., παρηγόρη[μα Merk.   16. γέγον[α, γέγον[εν, γεγον[ώc Par.   17. μ᾽ αν[Par., μάν-[τιc Merk.   18. τὸ]ν εἰδότα, cυ]νειδότα Par., ἔχῃ[c φίλον cυ]νειδότα Merk.   19. [πέφυκαc,] πάντα δ᾽ οἶδ᾽ ἀ[ληθῶc Merk.   20. τὸν ὅρκον Par., τὸν ὅρκον [οἶδα] Merk.   21. τίνι τυ]πείc Merk.   22. [αἰcχρὸ]ν πᾶν γεγον[ὸc Merk.   23. cμειλειν pap., cμίλην, C. Roberts, Merk., cμίλιν Merk.   25. θηρυκλειαν pap., read Εὐρύκλειαν, Reeve, M. L. West (in ed. pr.)   26. τὰ γενέc[ι᾽ οἶδα Merk.

P. OXY. 3010

He learns . . . of the things called ineffable by the *gallus*, by means of whom he was going to teach, (4) so that he would not fail his fellow-initiate and that to him, after he was initiated in many ways and had been taught to wear female (8) [dress,] would be allotted [. . . , when the instruction was] completed, he went to [Iolaos] and by chance (12) finding him [spoke as follows:]

[written as lines of Sotadean verse:]

14 "O noble Iolaos, hail, and shut up, *kinaidos*.
A mystic story [   ] consolation.
16 I have become a *gallus* [   ] Iolaos, through you [
Neikon [   ] through you,
that you may have a gallus [   ] who knows everything.
And I know your [   ] and I know everything—
20 the association [   ] the oath
unburied co[rpse] [   ] whose [
the illegitimate [   ] all that happened
knife [   ] wailing
24 and I know your house, your mother, your bedchamber,
your father's lamentations, Eurykleia, because I am [or you are] aware
that Neikon is a guileless [or tricky?] *kinaidos*, and the birth[day]
I know, the summons and the *kinaidos* mocking(?) [

28 πῶϲ πέπαιχεν, πῶϲ πέφευγε[
ἀνάλυϲιν, φάϲιν, κἀποκοπη μ[
ὅτι δόλῳ ϲὺ βινεῖν μέλλειϲ [
ὥϲτε μηδὲ ἕν με κρύβε πιϲτ̣[
32 καὶ τὸ ϲὸν θέλω Ἰόλαε ι̣ϲ . . . . [
γνώϲῃ δ᾽ · ὁ χρόνοϲ γὰρ με ̣ οϲ[

καὶ ὁ μὲν Ἰόλαοϲ ὑπὸ   44   ο[ὑ φίλου
τοῦ μυϲτικοῦ διδάϲκε-   κ[
36 ται ὅϲαπερ ἐμεμαθήκει,   μ[
ὁ] δὲ τέλειόϲ ἐϲτιν γάλλοϲ,   . [
τ]ῷ φίλῳ πεποιθὼϲ Νεί-   48   μ[
κ]ωνι · οὐκ ἔϲτιν οὐδὲν   και[
40 κ]ρε[ῖϲ]ϲον ἢ φίλοϲ ϲαφήϲ,   ραδ[
οὐ π]λοῦτοϲ ο[ὐδ]ὲ χρ[υϲόϲ ·   - - - - - - -
ἀλόγι]ϲτον δέ [τι τὸ πλῆ-
θοϲ ἀ]ντάλλαγμ[α γενναί-

---

30. βεινειν pap.   31. πιϲτ̣[οϲ ἔφυν φίλοϲ ϲοι Merk.   33. γνω pap.   perhaps
μέ[ϲ]οϲ Par.   34. υπο⟩ pap.?   36. μεμαθωκι pap., read (ἐ)μεμαθήκει? Par.

28   how he has joked, how he has fled [
      dissolution, affirmation, and amputation [
      that you intend a crafty fuck [
      so do not hide anything from me, faithful [
32   and your . . ., I wish, Iolaos, [
      and you will know . . . for time [

And Iolaos is taught by the mystic (36) all the things that he had learned, and he is a complete *gallus*, trusting of his friend Neikon. (40) "Nothing is greater than an unambiguous friend, not wealth or gold; the mob is a foolish substitute for a noble friend."

P. OXY. 3010

1. [ἀ]|πορρήτων: the restoration is almost inevitable. The word is usual to refer to secret lore of the initiated, regardless of the cult.

3. δι' ὸν: the antecedent is a puzzle. Is it γάλλου? Or a masculine accusative object of μανθάνει (now lost) on which [ἀ]|πορρήτων depends? Alternatively emend to δι' ὧν? ὅ̔απερ in line 36 suggests that this might be the correct course.

3–4. μανθάνει δι' ὸν διδάϲκειν | ἔμελλεν: the sense must be close to lines 34–36: καὶ ὁ μὲν Ἰόλαοϲ ὑπὸ | τοῦ μυϲτικοῦ διδάϲκε|ται ὅ̔απερ ἐμεμαθήκει. Here the subject of μανθάνει must be the mystic.

4–5. παρα|πέϲῃ: we accept Parsons's suggestion (1971: 55) that παραπέϲῃ + dative here must mean something like "fail his fellow initiate." Of παρα-πίπτω's usual meanings, "fall into sin" makes no sense here, and although "happen" or "befall" might do (e.g., "lest it befall his fellow initiate"), the rest of the sentence is not congenial to this approach.

5. ϲυμμύϲτῃ: usually a fellow initiate in both non-Christian and Christian writings. Also a confederate in evil (see Lampe, s.v. 2b).

5–7. The antecedent for τελεϲθέντι and διδαχθέντι would seem to be the mystic, not τῷ ϲυμμύϲτῃ.

371

7–8. θηλυκὴν | φορεῖν [ἐϲθῆτα (or sim.): for the wearing of female garments by *galli*, see above, introduction. Cataudella (1975b: 151–52) suggests ϲτόλην, citing Varro *Menippea*, frag. 120 (Büch): partim venusta muliebri ornati stola.

8–13. Approximate line lengths of fifteen to nineteen letters are based on those of lines 1–7.

9.]νον κληρω[: a form of κληρόω. The sense presumably is that after the mystic has been suitably initiated, some object is or will be alloted to him as a token of his new status. Objects suggested include [τύμπα]νον, [ϲτέφα]νον, [κέρ]νον. For the first compare Varro *Menippea*, frag. 132 (Büch):

> tibi tympanon inanis sonitus matris deum
> tonimus . . . tibi nos, tibi nunc semiviri
> teretem comam volantem iactant tibi galli.

9–10. [. . . .]|χηϲ : options are limited, and διδαχῆϲ suits both available space and sense.

14. εὐγενῆ Ἰόλαε χαῖρε καὶ κίναιδε ϲιωπη : the mystic couches his "instruction" to Iolaos in Sotadeans, the meter typical of *galli*. Either a second person, addressed as *kinaidos*, is present, or Iolaos is proleptically addressed by this term. In the former case, since *kinaidos* and *gallus* often function as interchangeable terms, this person is likely to be the instructor of the mystic, the friend named as Neikon below.

εὐγενῆ : the vulgar form of the vocative, but well attested for this period in funerary inscriptions and papyri (Parsons 1971: 56).

Ἰόλαε : the name of course is that of the nephew of Herakles. What weight it carries is impossible to guess. Parsons speculates: "It would not be surprising to find a grotesque Iolaus, at least in his uncle's company as on a famous Phlyax vase. Speculation would produce a mock-Iolaus, travelling with a cinaedus-Herakles whose femininity would recall the episode of Omphale" (1971: 62).

ϲιωπη : apparently intended to be scanned as a spondee (for details, see Parsons 1971: 61–62). Here it would appear to function as a parallel to the imperative χαῖρε; probably a noun (ϲιωπή) with an ellipse of ἔϲτω. Phrases like, e.g., ἐλπὶϲ ἔϲτω are not uncommon. Presumably an admonition to keep a ritual silence during the mystic's recitation.

15. μυϲτικὸϲ λογο . [ ] . . ϲτικοιϲ παρηγορη[: the syntax of these verses appears relatively straightforward, and grammatical units often seem to end with verse lines. At line end, a form of παρηγορέω, in the first person to judge from the number of οῖδαϲ below. Probably it is introducing the speech to come.

16. γάλλοϲ γεγον[ ] . Ἰόλαε διά . . . : "I became a gallus [ ], Iolaus, for you" (reading ϲε) or sim.? Lack of connectives seems standard in the poetic section of this piece. The ending of this line poses metrical difficulties (Parsons 1971: 57).

17. Νείκων: probably a name rather than νείκων or an itacism for νικῶν. Compare lines 26, 38 below.

21. νεκ[ρὸ]ν ἄταφο[ν : if the restoration is correct, the reference could be to Attis, whose corpse is mourned in the celebration of the Magna Mater. But Dodds's suggestion that it is a reference to the *gallus* himself is more attractive (Parsons 1972: 35 n. 1).

23. ϲμίλην : we have tentatively accepted Roberts' emendation. The knife by which the *gallus* castrates himself would be a suitable object to name in this company. Merkelbach suggests the possibility of a proper name, ϲμίλιϲ, "Schnitzler," linking it with a carver of wooden images. A man so named is mentioned by Pausanias for a shrine of Hera (Paus. 5.17.1, 7.4.4). If it is a proper name, a pun like that of "Carpe" in Petronius *Sat.* § 36 might have been intended.

   ὀλ]ολυγμὸν : the ritual lament for Attis? So Merkelbach 1973: 98. Or, following ϲμίλην, a lament for lost parts?

25. Εὐρύκλειαν: if this is indeed a proper name, is it the girl Iolaos intends to seduce? Or, as Parsons (1971: 58) suggests, his nurse, who like her Odyssean counterpart is in on the plot? Parsons would take Eurykleia as the subject of ϲυνοιδ[.

26. Νείκων᾽ ἄδολον κίναιδον : we assume that Neikon and the *kinaidos-gallus* are identical. If not, the plot is more complex. In that case, Neikon, the friend of the mystic (lines 38–39), will have somehow induced the *kinaidos-gallus* to initiate the self-styled "mystic," who in turn (and in Neikon's presence) initiates Iolaos. If the *kinaidos* has unsuspectingly revealed ἀπόρρητα to the mystic for the purposes outlined in line 30, ἄδολον would, of course, be preferable to δόλον.

   τὰ γενέϲ[ια : see above, note 5.

27. κλῆϲιν : as Parsons (1971: 67 n. 7) has it, either "vocation" or "invocation." Both meanings are well attested; either could be appropriate.

28. πῶϲ πέπαιχεν, πῶϲ πέφευγε[: Merkelbach tentatively suggests that the reference is to Attis fleeing the lion (see Cat. 63.74–89).

29. ἀνάλυϲιν, φάϲιν : possibly a reference to the formal rejection of the material world and assent to the new mode of life (MacLeod 1974). Alternatively, Parsons suggests "the freeing of the soul from mortality" (1971: 60).

   φάϲιν : for metrical reasons, rather than φαϲίν.

   κἀποκοπη μ[: most likely a form of the noun ἀποκοπή = "a cutting." The syntax is not immediately apparent.

30. δόλῳ ϲὺ βινεῖν μέλλειϲ : see above, introduction, for the pedigree of this plot.

36. ἐμεμαθήκει : we accept the easiest emendation of the papyrus's μεμαθωκι. Loss of pluperfect augment is common in this period.

37. ὁ] δὲ τέλειόϲ ἐϲτιν γάλλοϲ : if the supplement is correct, [ὁ] δὲ refers to the "mystic" from the line above. Prima facie, τέλειόϲ will mean "fully initiated,"

but John Rea's suggestion that it refers to a "complete" (i.e., unmutilated) *gallus* is hard to resist (Parsons 1971: 59).

39–41. Adapted from Euripides, *Orestes* 1155–57:

οὐκ ἔςτιν οὐδὲν κρεῖςςον ἢ φίλος ςαφής,
οὐ πλοῦτος, οὐ τυραννίς · ἀλόγιςτον δέ τι
τὸ πλῆθος ἀντάλλαγμα γενναίου φίλου.

The alteration of οὐ τυραννίς to οὐδὲ χρυςός probably signifies nothing more than the altered cultural circumstance, in which allusion to tyrants was no longer of interest.

Daulis

———— ❖ ————

The scene is Delphi. A dramatic and powerful exchange is taking place between one Daulis, leader of a barbarian army, and a prophet of Apollo whom Daulis intends to kill in an attempt to rid the world of the charlatanry of selling oracles. Daulis embellishes his threat with rhetorical intensity and grim detail, promising to pour out a libation of the prophet's blood to Ares (II.1–4). The prophet counters with an equally baroque prayer, climaxing in a triple (or quadruple) anaphora in which Daulis is imagined as a sacrifical offering of the Furies (III.16–22). The fragment breaks off before any of these events come to pass: did Daulis in fact kill the prophet and escape? Or was he prevented from doing so by a vengeful Apollo or the Furies? Since his objective seems not to have been the god, but the perversion of divine vision for human profit, we might suspect a more mundane resolution.

Previous editors have described this piece as an "aretalogy" of Apollo. The term is loosely applied by modern scholars to a number of ancient texts that incorporate some testimonial to the power of a deity.[1] Even if we assume that this fragment was intended as an anecdote that described Apollo's divine powers, all editors have been struck by the "romantic" tone of the interchange. In other words, the author of this piece seems far more interested in creating an atmosphere of wrath and terror— while, we might add, avoiding hiatus—than in producing evidence of Apollo's superior virtues. Stephanie West has described the piece as an "ugly duckling, an unobjectionable romance fragment which has been generally neglected on the assumption that it is a rather freakish specimen of some other genre" (1971: 96). We are inclined to agree. Daulis has many analogues in the novels: the tomb robbers of Chariton; Menelaos and Satyros in Achilles Tatius, who sham the blood sacrifice of Leukippe; Hippothoos in the *Ephesiaka* whose band is dedicated to Mars; and perhaps most interestingly, Thyamis, the former high priest who moonlights as the leader of the *boukoloi* in Heliodoros. Some of these men are unremittingly evil and come to a bad end, others are a

[1] The term does not in fact describe an ancient genre. For a discussion of its history and the historical reality, see Winkler 1985: 235–36.

blend, forced to crime by previous injustice. Daulis, to judge from the outraged tone of his indictment of oracles, is likely to fall into the latter category.

Previous editors have pretty much accepted the suggestion of Carl Robert, who identified this attack upon Delphi with a mythical assault of Phlegyas, a son of Ares.[2] The details are given in Pausanias 9.36.1–3. Phlegyas, the eponymous leader of the Phlegyans, a Boeotian people settled near Delphi and noted for aggressive behavior, apparently intended to loot the shrine. Pausanias lacks clear details about the success of that particular venture, but concludes by saying that the Phlegyans were completely overthrown by the god wielding thunderbolts and earthquakes.

But according to Pausanias 10.7.1 and Strabo 9.3.8, Delphi was plundered a number of times: by a Euboean pirate; the Phlegyans; Pyrrhos (Neoptolemos), the son of Achilles; a portion of Xerxes' army; the Phocians; the Gauls; and Nero. Further, the bare narrative bones, denuded of their rhetorical covering, have much in common with the Sacred War of 355/4 B.C.E., when Philomelos seized the sanctuary and forced the Pythia to prophesy to his liking.[3] The reason to connect this fragment with mythological rather than historical attacks against Delphi would seem to be Ares, the deity to whom Daulis dedicates himself. But this is hardly compelling. Hippothoos in the *Ephesiaka* is equally eager to sacrifice Antheia to Ares, whereas the robbers in Apuleius 4.22.1 sing songs to Mars. One suspects that "dedication to Ares" is no more than a literary shorthand for gruesome bad behavior.

Daulis is no help. This is the name of a Phocian state at the foot of Parnassos, named, according to Pausanias, after the nymph Daulis (10.4.7–10); Strabo (9.3.13) gives a slightly different version, but both confirm that it was also the home of Tereus (of Procne fame) and of an ancient sanctuary of Athene. There is no trace of Ares. Given the potpourri of details, none of which quite fit, it is reasonable to assume that this fragment represents not so much a particular mythological or historical event as a vague recollection of the type of thing that could happen, or often had happened, at Delphi.

---

[2] W. Crönert demurred, suggesting rather in a letter to Eitrem (1948: 176) that this was the work of an Hellenistic historian, treating the history of the Delphic oracle in a heavily adorned rhetorical style. In a private communication, E. Bowie observes that a barbarian attack against a Greek sanctuary would have gained a certain piquancy after the Costoboci overran Greece in the 160s (see Paus. 10.34.5).

[3] The main source is Diodoros's account, 16.23–40. For Philomelos's forcing of the prophetess, see §27.

Anaphora, hyperbaton, rhetorical questions, wordplay, and poetic language are all part of this writer's repertory. Note, for example, the chiastic arrangement of ὁ γὰρ Λατοῦϲ ἐκεῖνοϲ τὸν οὐρανὸν ἔχει, τὴν δὲ γῆν ἡμεῖϲ (II.18–19), the equal number of syllables in the two phrases ἐπὶ ϲοὶ νῦν ποῦ τὸ ἄδυτον and ἢ καὶ αὐτὸ καταδέδυκεν (23), or the imagery of δίκτυα χρηϲμῶν εἰϲ [ν]ε̣[ῦ]ρα ἐργαϲίαϲ πλέκτονταϲ (25), which would not disgrace Greek tragedy. The rhetorical polish of this piece, however, is in stark contrast to the carelessness with which it was copied. (The only other texts in this collection that display such poor workmanship are *Iolaos* and *Tinouphis*.)

DESCRIPTION

P. Berol. inv. 11517 (= P^2 2468, measuring 28.0 ×33.5 cm) contains three columns, of which only the middle is complete, from a papyrus roll written across the fibers on the back of an account; upper and lower margins of 2.5–3.0 cm survive, as well as intercolumnia of 2.5 cm. The complete column is unusually wide (around thirty-five letters), resembling, for example, a text of medical prescriptions far more than the formats of the known novels or of other literary texts; note in particular the spaces left between sections of text. The papyrus surface is in fair condition, with some abrading, a few holes, and a fair amount of random ink. The hand is an informal round style showing numerous cursive affinities, assigned by Wilcken to the end of the second century C.E. He remarks that the text has the appearance of a carefully written document. Punctuation includes dicola, paragraphi, and stops, but without consistency; elisions are also inconsistently marked. Iota adscript is regularly written, sometimes erroneously (lines 28, 44, 48). Corrections are made by deletion. There are at least six uncorrected errors, an unusually high number in comparision with other fragments of equal length found in this edition. Hiatus is avoided throughout.

377

DAULIS

COLUMN I

```
[..................] .ε[....]ον̣ . [..]επ[....
[............]ϲ[...]τι̣ [φ]οβεῖται γὰρ τ[....
[............] .ε̣[...]ν̣τοϲ ἰδιώτου λ̣ . [...
[space for two lines]
```

4   ```[..................] . .[...] λαβόντεϲ πρὸϲ```
    ```[.................. ὥρ]μηϲαν ἀϲεβείαϲ```
    ```[............. τοῖϲ χρ]ηϲμοῖϲ ἐπεχεί-```
    ```[ρηϲαν.............. τὴν γὰ]ρ Π[υ]θίαν ἀμή-```

8   ```[χαν-.................] ἀποθεϲπίζειν```
    ```[........... χρηϲ]μ̣ῳδ̣[....] μετατιθέντεϲ```
    ```[..............]κλέπ[τει]ν τὴν ἀπὸ τοῦ```
    ```[τρίποδοϲ Πυθίαν κ]α̣ὶ τοὺ[ϲ λ]ογιωτάτουϲ Δελ-```

12   ```[φῶν..............] . . ἀγ̣[ν]ὴν ἑϲτίαν καὶ```
    ```[..............]μύϲτῃ[ν] ἐβιάζοντο τρ .```
    ```[..............]μμένα [δ]εϲμοῖϲ ἀοράτοιϲ```
    ```[..............]ϲ κατοπτεῦϲαι καὶ τὴν```

16   ```[..............]ϲκευ . . . . ου λῦϲαι```
    ```[..............] . . . . εἴργ[ο]ντοϲ δὲ τοῦ```
    ```[..............]του . . . [.... ϲ]πα[ϲ]άμενοϲ```

Supplements are those of Schubart unless otherwise indicated. Conjectures of Bell, Powell, and Wilamowitz are in Schubart's ed. pr.

Col. I: 2. At end, τ . [.]ρ[. . pap., according to Schub., who conjectured Τ[η]ρ[εύϲ. The ρ is no longer present. **4.** [οἱ μὲν Φλεγύαι ?] Schub. **6.** [καὶ τοῖϲ τοῦ θεοῦ or τοῦ μαντείου χρ]ηϲμοῖϲ Schub. **6–12.** [καὶ ὀργιϲθέντεϲ τοῖϲ χρ]ηϲμοῖϲ ἐπεχεί|[ρηϲαν ἀνοϲιώτατον πρᾶγμα· τὴν γὰ]ρ Πυθίαν ἀμή|[χανα καὶ ψευδῆ φάϲκοντεϲ (λέγοντεϲ)] ἀπο-θεϲπίζειν | [καὶ ἅπερ ὁ θεὸϲ ἐχρηϲ]μ̣ῳδ̣[ηϲε] μετατιθέντεϲ | [οἱ ἄθεοι ἐπεχείρηϲαν (or ἐβου-λεύοντο)] κλέπ[τει]ν τὴν ἀπὸ τοῦ | [τρίποδοϲ ἀλήθειαν κ]α̣ὶ τοὺ[ϲ] ἁγιωτάτουϲ Δελ|[φῶν θεϲμοὺϲ καταλύειν (or ἀνατρέπειν)] Eit. **7–8.** ἀμή|[χανόν τι ἠνάγκαϲαν] Schub. **9.** χρηϲ]μῳδ[ία, χρηϲ]μῳδ[όϲ, or χρηϲ]μῳδ[εῖν? Schub. **11.** Either ἁγιο- or λογιο-τάτουϲ can be read, Schub. **12.** [καὶ πάϲηϲ τῆϲ Ἑλλάδοϲ ἔβ]ε̣ϲ[αν] τὴν ἑϲτίαν Mant. **13.** [τὸν τῶν ἀπορρήτων] μύϲτην Eit. **14.** [δεδε]μμένα or [κατεϲτε]μμένα Eit. [δ]εϲμοῖϲ better than [θ]εϲμοῖϲ Schub. **14–16.** [αὕτη δ᾽ ἐδήεϲαν τὰ ὄ]μματα δεϲμοῖϲ ἀοράτοιϲ, | [ἵνα μὴ δυνήθη ——— αὐτοὺ]ϲ κατοπτεῦϲαι καὶ τὴν | [κίϲτην, ἐν ᾗ τὰ ἱερὰ] Mant. **16.** [κίϲτην, ἐν ᾗ ———τὰ] ϲκεύη ἐνῆν Schub. **17–21.** εἴργοντοϲ δὲ τοῦ | [παρόντοϲ προφήτ]ου [τὸ ξίφοϲ ϲ]παϲάμενοϲ | [Δαῦλιϲ, ὁ τῆϲ βαρβ]άρου ϲτρατε[ι]ᾶϲ ἡγεμὼν | [ἔκφρων ὥρμηϲε]ν ἐπ᾽ αὐτὸν καὶ Γνώϲῃ, | [ἔφη, νῦν αὐτὸϲ] παθὼν Eit. **18.** Ini-tially [τοῦ προφή]του Schub.
    ```

] For he is afraid [
] of a private
4   ] attacking? [
] they urged an impious
[angered?] at the oracles, they undertook
] For the Pythia clueless
8   ] to prophesy
] oracular utterance, exchanging
] to steal the Pythia from the
] and the most eloquent of the Delphians
12   ] holy hearth and
] mystery they violated
] with eternal bonds
] to reconnoiter and the
16   ]
] was hastening
] drawing

[τὸ ξίφος ὁ τῆς βαρβ]άρου ςτρατε[ι]ᾶς ἡγεμὼν

20 [. . . . .]ν ἐπ' αὐτὸ[ν] · "καὶ γνώςῃ,"

[εἶπεν, ". . . . .]παθὼν κ̲[αὶ] βιάζῃ μάχ[ε-

[ςθαι . . . . υ]περέχ[ο]ντα. Ἄρης γὰρ

[. . . . .] ὧι νῦν ἐγὼ καθώπλιςμαι

24 [. . . . .]υτ . τ . . ἐμῆς ὅπλον ἐςτί

[space for four lines]

COLUMN II

χαίρει δὲ ςφαγαῖς ἀνθρ[ώ]πων, αἷς καὶ ἐγὼ τέρπομαι
τῶν ἐκείνωι καθοςιω[μέ]νων ςπονδῶν καταρ-
χόμενος. [blank]

4 καλὸν οὖν αὐτῶι θῦμα τὸν ςὸν ἐγὼ φόνον ςπείςω."
τοῦ δὲ ταῦτα μετὰ πικρᾶς ἀνατάςεως ἀπειλοῦντος,
⟨ὁ προφήτης⟩ ἐπὶ τὴν ἐν τῶι προδόμωι ςυμφυγὼν ἑςτίαν, ἐφ' ἧς
τὸ τῆς ἀθανάτου πυρᾶς τεθηςαυριςμένον φυλάτ-

8 τεται ⟨φ⟩ῶς. "φεῖςαι καὶ μὴ μιάνῃς," ἔλεγε, "Δαῦλι, τὸ τῆς
Θέμιδος ἀρχαῖον ἵδρυμα μηδὲ τὸν ἀναίμακτον
ςηκὸν ςφαγῆι φ[ύ]ρῃςαι." "οὐ προςιεμαι λόγον,"
εἶπεν ὁ Δαῦλις, "⟨οὐδ'⟩ ἱκέτην, ςὺ δὲ τοῖς ἄλλοις ἅπαςιν

12 ἃ δεῖ προλέγων ἃ̲ ς̲ὲ̲ δ̲ε̲ῖ̲ παθεῖν οὔτι ἔγνως.
παύςω δὲ πάν[τ]α[ς ἀνθρώπο]υς ψευδέςιν ἐξαπα-
τωμένους χρης[μ]οῖς. πο[ῖο]ς γὰρ ἐνθάδε νῦν

---

19. Initially, [τὸ ξίφος], [τὴν μάχαιραν], or sim. Schub.   21–22. [ὅτι] βιάζῃ μάχ[ε-
|ςθαι τὸν ςὸν θεὸν (or Ἀπόλλωνα or τὸν Δελφῶν θεὸν) πρὸς ὑ]περέχ[ο]ντα Schub.   ]ντα
αρης pap.   22–23. Ἄρης γὰρ | [τὸ ξίφος ἐμοὶ ἔδωκεν] or [τὸν θυμὸν ἔδωκεν] Eit.
Col. II: 1. χ̄ᾱιρει pap.   2. την pap., read τῶν   καθωςιω[μέ]νων Schub.   4. ςπει
ςωι pap.   6. προδ[όμ]ωι Bell   ςυνφυγων pap.   7. τὸ τῆς ἀθανάτου πυρᾶς ⟨πῦρ⟩
Schub.   8. ως pap., ⟨φ⟩ῶς Powell, ὦ Schub.   μανηςελπε pap., read μιάνῃς, ἔλεγε
Schub.   9. ἵδρυμα pap.   10. προςιεμεναι pap., προςίεμαι Eit., προςἵεμενος
Wilam., προςίε[με]ναι Schub.   11. ου pap., read ὁ   ἱκ pap.   ⟨οὐδ'⟩ ἱκέτην Eit.,
ἱκόμην Schub.   12. ουπεγνως pap., οὔτι ἔγνως Powell, corrected to οὐκ Schub., οὐδ'
ἔγνως or οὐδ' ἐπέγνως Eit.

380

his sword,] the leader of the barbarian army

20   ] against him, "you will learn,"

he said,] when you have suffered and you will be compelled to battle

        ] the one prevailing. For Ares

        ] by whom I am now armed

24   ] of my . . . is the shield.

COLUMN II

"And he [Ares] rejoices in slaughters of men, and I, too, take
                         pleasure in them
when I begin making the libations that are sacred to him.

. . .

4   Now as a worthy offering for him I shall pour out a libation
                        of your blood."
And when he had made these threats with a bitter intensity,
[the prophet] who had taken refuge at the hearth in the *prodomos*,
                        where

the treasure trove of sacred fire is preserved,

8   "Spare and do not pollute," he said, "Daulis, this
ancient seat of Themis, nor yet defile
with slaughter this unpolluted sacred enclosure." "I have no
                      wish for speech,"
said Daulis, "or entreaty, and you, although prophesying what
                      must happen to all the others,

12   do not know what must happen to you.
I will put an end to all men being deceived
by lying oracles. What sort of

Ἀπόλλων ἢ ποῖος ὀμφαλὸς γῆς δάφνηι καταστε-
16 φόμενος τὰ κοινὰ πάν[τω]ν ἀνθρώπων φόβητρα
καὶ τῆς ὑμετέρας ἐργας . . [. . .]εδ . . ατα;
ὁ γὰρ Λατοῦς ἐκεῖνος τὸν οὐρανὸν ἔχει, τὴν δὲ γῆν
ἡμεῖς · μισθοῦ δ' οὐ⟨ν⟩ μαντεύων θεὸς ἀνθρώποις
20 παυσάσθω πεινῶντος ἔργον ἐπιτηδεύων [. . . .] .
γόητος · ἀλλὰ ταῦτ' ἐστιν ὑμέτερα σοφίσματ[α πίς-
τιν ἀπὸ ληστείας κα[τα]σκευασαμένων.
ἐπὶ σοὶ νῦν ποῦ τὸ ἄδυτον ἢ καὶ αὐτὸ καταδέδυκεν;
24 μισῶ δὲ μάντεις ἀ[λ]λοτρίων προφήτας κακῶν
δίκτυα χρησμῶν εἰς [ν]ε[ῦ]ρα ἐργασίας πλέκτοντας."
ταῦτα δὲ αὐτοῦ λέγοντος, ὁ προφήτης, "μάντις Ἀπόλλων," εἶπε, "καὶ Δελφῶν ἑστία καὶ θείωι στόματι
28 προθεσπιζομένη χρησμ[ῶ]ν ἀψευδὴς ἀλήθεια
καὶ χάσμα γῆς, χθονίου πνεύματος στόμιον

COLUMN III

ἐξ οὗ τὴν ἀναφε[ρομένην ἀκούομεν
φωνὴν ἀθανάτω[ν
ὑβριζόμεθα δε[
4 ἀρρήτου χρησμω[
ται ξίφει καὶ ὀφ[
ὁ τῆς ἀσύλου Θέμ[ιδος
ὑπὸ Διὸς ἄνθρωπο[ς ?
8 ναὸν κα[ὶ τ]ὴν ὀροφ[ὴν
ἀγηράτοις ἀπόλ[υσθαι

---

17. καιτη pap.   ἐργάςεω[ς δ]ὲ δεῖλατα Mant., ἐργαςία[ς ἦ]ρε δίματα (= δείματα) Crön.,
δελέατα Eit., ἔκ[ριν]ε or ἔκ[τις]ε ? Schub.   19. δ' οὐ⟨ν⟩ Eit., δ' οὐ Schub.   ἀν-
θρώπῳ (or ἀνθρώποις) Eit., ἀνθρώπου Schub.   20. παυσασθωι pap.   παυσάσθωι,
⟨παυσάσθωι⟩ πεινῶντος ἔργον Eit.   at end, [καὶ] Schub.   21. γοητος αλλ pap.
22. τιν pap.   μενων : pap.   23. επι pap., read ἐπεὶ Wilam.   αδυτονον pap.,
read ἄδυτον Wilam.   δυκεν · pap.   24. μειςωι pap.   25. δι pap. [μ]έ[τ]ρα
Crön.   τοντας · pap.   29. της pap., read γῆς Wilam., Powell
Col. III: 2. φ pap.   5. ται pap.   ὀφ[θαλμ- Schub., ὄςιο[ν τὸν προφήτην] Mant.
9. ἀγηράτως Mant.

Apollo is here now, what sort of navel of the earth, crowned with laurel
16   ... the common objects of terror to all men and
the ... of your ... ?
For that offspring of Leto holds heaven, we hold the earth.
Let the god cease being a prophet to man for a profit,
20   <let him cease> playing the role of a poor
fortune-teller. But these are your contrivances,
for procuring yourselves a position of trust from theft.
Where now is the shrine under your control, or has it sunk away?
24   I loathe soothsayers, prophets of distress for others,
weaving webs of prophecy into the sinews of action."
After he said these things, the prophet replied, "Seer Apollo
and the hearth at Delphi and by your divine mouth
28   unlying truth of prophecies foretold
and the chasm of the earth, the opening of chthonic breath

COLUMN III

out of which [we hear
the voice of immortal [——] rising [
we are being abused [
4   of unspeakable [
with a sword and [
the [——] of inviolate Themis [
by Zeus man(?) [
8   a shrine and ceiling [
ageless is being destroyed [

καὶ καταϲβένν[υϲθαι
αἵματι τὸ ἀπὸ τῆ[ϲ
12 φῶϲ ἀλλ᾽ οὔ τι τ̣[
ἀϲεβείαϲ ἀφήϲε[ϲθαι
κυ̣η̣τοϲ τῆϲ ϲῆϲ η̣[
ἤδη γὰρ καὶ ὁ πα[τήρ ϲου . . . . τόνδε τὸν]
16 τ̣όπον ἐξύβριϲε[
θνητὸϲ παρὰ θε[ὸν . . . . ἤ-]
δη, Δαῦλ[ι], τέθηκται [τὸ ξίφοϲ
ἔϲτε[π]τα[ι ἡ] ἑϲτ̣[ία
20 κα[ὶ] καλλιερητ[
τὸν βωμὸν κει[
αἷμα · ἤδη γάρ ϲε [τίϲονται αἱ Ἐρινύεϲ τὸν]
ἐμὸν φόνον ἐγ[
24 δίκηϲ παιδὸϲ δ[
ἀπαραιτήτουϲ[
νυκτὶ πολλῇ κα[
α[ἱ] δ᾽ ἐ[γ]γὺϲ ἐφεϲτη[κυῖαι
28 καὶ γὰρ [ἀ]γορευον[
ἐκπλήττ̣ειϲ ἤδ̣[η

11–12. τὸ ἀπὸ τ[ῆϲ κοινῆϲ ἑϲτίαϲ] | φῶϲ Schub. [ἀγνῆϲ ἑϲτίαϲ ἀναλάμπον] | φῶϲ Eit.
14. κυη pap., ἀνό]|κυητοϲ Schub., καὶ ἴϲοϲ Mant.   15. ὁ πα[τήρ ϲου, Φλεγύαϲ
Eit.   17. θνη pap.   17–18. [καὶ ϲοὶ ἤ]|δη Eit.   18. δη pap.   20. καλ-
λιερῇ Schub.   23. εμον pap.   26. νυκ pap.   28. παρ[α]γορευον[Mant.

and quenched [
with blood [
12 the light, but not any [
impiety will be released(?) [
of your [
Now already your [father?] too [
16 outraged this place [
a mortal against a god [——— now already]
Daulis, [a sword] is whetted for you [
the hearth is wreathed [
20 and [if] the omen is favorable [
the altar [
blood. Now already [the Furies will take vengeance on] you
for my murder
24 of justice of a son(?) [
of implacable [
at darkest night [
The [Furies] who are standing near [
28 and speaking [
you?] have struck [

COLUMN I

1–3. There is a substantial space following these lines. Although it could indicate that a new section has begun, the large gaps between Columns I and II and after II.3 do not appear to be functional.

2. Schubart's conjecture of the proper name Tereus to fill out this line rests on the fact that Tereus was the king of Daulis; see above, introduction.

4–16. A description of an attack upon Delphi by a "barbarian army" (I.19) led by one Daulis (II.8). "They" are the subject of the verbs and participles until line 17. The reason for the attack does not appear to be straightforward theft; Daulis, in II.19ff., claims that he intends to rid the world of dishonest and profiteering prophets. In these lines, the attackers seem intent upon outrage to the Pythia as well as theft of some kind (if lines 10–11 are correctly read), when someone rushes in (I.17). At this point, the leader of the invaders threatens the interloper with death. The subsequent columns are taken up with speeches by the leader and his intended victim.

7–8. τὴν γὰ]ρ Π[υ]θίαν … ἀποθεсπίζειν : according to Strabo 9.3.5, φαсὶ δ᾽ εἶναι τὸ μαντεῖον ἄντρον κοῖλον κατὰ βάθουс, οὐ μάλα εὐρύсτομον, ἀναφέρεсθαι δ᾽ ἐξ αὐτοῦ πνεῦμα ἐνθουсιαсτικόν, ὑπερκεῖсθαι δὲ τοῦ сτομίου τρίποδα ὑψηλόν, ἐφ᾽ ὃν τὴν Πυθίαν ἀναβαίνουсαν, δεχομένην τὸ πνεῦμα, ἀποθεсπίζειν ἔμμετρά τε καὶ ἄμετρα. The invaders seem to have been harassing or suborning her in some way. Schubart supplements, e.g., ἀμή|[χανόν τι ἠνάγκαсαν. Compare DS 16.25.3: τὴν Πυθίαν ἠνάγκαсεν ἀναβᾶсαν ἐπὶ τὸν τρίποδα δοῦναι τὸν χρηсμόν.

9. χρηс]μῳδ[. . . .] : cf. DS 16.26.6: τὰ ἀπόρρητα τῶν χρηсμῳδουμένων, and below III.4.

10–11.]κλέπ[τει]ν τὴν ἀπὸ τοῦ | τρίποδοс Πυθίαν : the restoration is admittedly guesswork. But as is clear from the above passage, the most obvious feminine object in the temple would have been the Pythia herself, who is mentioned in the fragment only a few lines before. Eitrem (1939: 177) cites Plut. De Pyth. or. §407c as evidence for the disrepute into which the oracle had fallen: δοκοῦсα (sc. ποιητική) κοινὴν ἐμπαρέχειν ἑαυτὴν ἀπατεῶсι καὶ γόηсι ἀνθρώποιс καὶ ψευδομάντεсιν ἐξέπεсε τῆс ἀληθείαс καὶ τοῦ τρίποδοс.

11. λ]ογιωτάτουс : suits spacing and traces better than Schubart's ἁγιωτάτουс.

16. сκευ . . . . : Schubart's τὰ] сκεύη ἐνῆν admits hiatus, which is elsewhere avoided in this piece. Possibly]сκευην ἦν, but since the following οὐ λῦсαι is also odd, the ου may belong with the preceding, e.g.,]сκευαсμενου may have been intended.

17. εἴργ[ο]ντοс δὲ τοῦ : clearly προφήτου is to be restored somewhere in the next line. The function of the prophet at Delphi is not absolutely clear. He may have been identical with the *hiereis*, two of whom were appointed for life, who seem to have directed temple activity (see the discussion in Halliday 1928:

59–60), or with the poets who, according to Strabo 9.3.5 and Plut. *De Pyth.*
or. § 407b, rendered the utterances of the Pythia into verse.

22. Ἄρης: see above, introduction, for Ares as the patron saint of outlaws.

4. καλὸν οὖν αὐτῶι θῦμα: the thought is no doubt a product of rhetorical excess,
not intended to be an accurate description; θύματα are offerings of fruits or
animal victims, not liquids which cπείϲω would presuppose.

τὸν ϲὸν ἐγὼ φόνον: the hyperbaton is repeated in line 6: ἐπὶ τὴν ἐν τῶι προδόμωι ϲυμφυγὼν ἑϲτίαν, and in lines 7–8: τὸ τῆϲ ἀθανάτου πυρᾶϲ τεθηϲαυριϲμέ-
νον φυλάτ|τεται ⟨φ⟩ῶϲ.

6. The subject (ὁ προφήτηϲ) for ϲυμφυγών has dropped out. Compare lines
26–27 below for a similar construction: ταῦτα δὲ αὐτοῦ λέγοντοϲ, ὁ προφήτηϲ,
"μάντιϲ Ἀπόλλων," εἶπε, κτλ.

ἐν τῶι προδόμωι: the noun need not necessarily be emended to προδρόμωι;
the *prodomos* was a chamber leading immediately from the forecourt.

8. Δαῦλι: see above, introduction, for a discussion of the name.

9. Θέμιδος: for Themis's connection with Delphi, see Strabo 9.3.1–12.

10–11. "οὐ προϲίεμαι λόγον," | εἶπεν ὁ Δαῦλιϲ (ουδαυλιϲ pap.), "⟨οὐδ'⟩ ἱκέτην:
we accept Eitrem's emendation here. The trace above the μ of προϲίεμαι may
be intended to mark a correction, or it may simply be random ink. The reading ἱκέτην seems preferable from the traces. If οὐδ' originally stood before
ἱκέτην, it might account for the ουδαυλιϲ a bit earlier in the line well as its subsequent omission.

14–17. πο[ῖο]ϲ γὰρ ἐνθάδε νῦν | Ἀπόλλων ἢ ποῖοϲ . . . τὰ κοινὰ πάν[τω]ν ἀνθρώπων
φόβητρα | καὶ τῆϲ ὑμετέραϲ ἐργαϲ ⸏[. . .]εδ⸏ατα;: we take the question to
be, "What sort of Apollo, what sort of center of the earth [encourages,
exploits, or sim.] the common fears of men?" The obvious supplement, ἐργαϲίαϲ, does not fit the traces. The verb is now missing and, unless Schubart's
attempts to locate one after εργαϲ (ἔκ[ριν]ε or sim.) or at line end (read δέδιχα
= δέδειχα) are correct, it may never have been written in this copy. The final
words are hopeless. The traces before ατα fit no letters, and any solution
would have to be an inspired guess.

15–16. ὀμφαλὸϲ γῆϲ δάφνηι καταϲτε|φόμενοϲ: compare Strabo 9.3.6, ὀμφαλόϲ τιϲ
ἐν τῷ ναῷ τεταινιωμένοϲ.

19. μιϲθοῦ δ' οὐ⟨ν⟩ μαντεύων θεὸϲ ἀνθρώποιϲ: the original text needs help. The
negative before μαντεύων is almost impossible to construe, unless conditional
("if he is not a god who prophesies for a profit"); but in that case one expects
μή. Eitrem's correction to οὐ⟨ν⟩ seems the easiest solution. The final word is
broken at the end, and although the dative ἀνθρώποιϲ is clearly needed (μιϲθοῦ
must be genitive of price), οιϲ does not quite suit the traces.

20. παυϲάϲθω πεινῶντοϲ ἔργον ἐπιτηδεύων [....]. : if the imperative is not to be repeated, as Eitrem suggests, then this second participial phrase must be in apposition to the first, as a further qualification. Given Daulis's penchant for doublets, this seems a fair explanation. There is space, however, for a five-letter word at the end of the line, traces of the final letter of which are still visible at the edge of the lacuna.

21. γόητοϲ : the "fortune teller" was a generally seedy character, a habitué of low life.

23. τὸ ἄδυτον κτλ.: the thought seems forced, perhaps to accommodate word-play; ἄδυτον and καταδέδυκεν are both from the same root, δύω.

25. δίκτυα χρηϲμῶν : Crönert compares Aisch. *Ag.* 1115 and Eur. *Or.* 1315 (Eitrem 1948: 176).

28–III.2: these lines describe the chamber in which the Pythia uttered. See Strabo's remarks above, I.7–8 note.

29. χάϲμα γῆϲ : see the description in DS 16.26.2–5.

COLUMN III

4. ἀρρήτου χρηϲμω[: see above, note I.9.

9–10. The prophet is surely imagining his own slaughter, by which Daulis intends to quench the light from the sacred hearth. Compare above, II.7–8.

15. ἤδη or ἤδη γὰρ are repeated at least three times, possibly four (lines 17–18, 22, 29).

15–16. ὁ πα[τήρ ϲου ——τόνδε τὸν] | τόπον ἐξύβριϲε[: the restoration ὁ πα[τήρ seems almost inevitable. Eitrem conjectures that Daulis's father was Phlegyas, but there is no support for this.

18–20. The prophet imagines that Daulis is the sacrificial victim.

22. ἤδη γάρ ϲε [τίϲονται αἱ Ἐρινύεϲ τὸν] | ἐμὸν φόνον: Schubart's restoration depends on the α[ἱ of line 27. E. Bowie suggests that the *Oresteia* may have influenced this description of the behavior of the Furies at Delphi.

PART II

AMBIGUOUS FRAGMENTS

Apollonios

❖

What we have of the *Apollonios* consists in two small fragments, the larger of which opens at the Persian court, where the queen (*basilis*) is present, "adorned with a beauty suitable to the gods." The king offers a toast first to Dionysios, then to Apollonios, after which the fragment breaks off. The smaller fragment, marked as Column 14, contains a scene between Apollonios and a woman, who may be the queen. From the vocabulary, it appears that one party—probably the woman—is desirous of an assignation later that evening, whereas the other may be trying to dissuade. The banquet scene could belong to the beginning of the story, as do the banquets in *Metiochos* and *Parthenope* or in Achilles Tatius 1.5. Apollonios would seem to be present, and quite possibly it is during this banquet that the lady in the smaller bit first sets eyes on him, or he her. If it is the queen, the story may have the familiar ring of Potiphar's wife about it. The whole suggests a fictional work cast in the historical mode, but so little remains that it is impossible to rule out an "historical" work of the *Kyropaideia* variety.

A question of some interest is the relationship of these scraps to a piece of Latin romantic fiction known as the "History of Apollonius, King of Tyre" (= *Historia Apollonii regis Tyri*), for which a Greek original has often been posited.[1] Kortekaas offers the following summary of matters in his 1984 edition of the *Historia Apollonii*: "One may conclude that in its original form the *HA* was a typical representative of the Greek romance . . . and that it may be taken to have come into being at the end of the 2nd or the beginning of the 3rd century, most probably in Syria" (p. 130). Further, that original Greek version would have undergone substantial Christianizing revisions in the process of its translation and transmission. So the original may look quite unlike its offspring.

Certainly nothing prohibits the identification of these Greek scraps with the *Historia Apollonii*, but apart from the name of a single character, Apollonios, there is little to encourage it. True, both contain

---

[1] The debate over Greek origins has a long history. See, e.g., Rohde 1974: 436, or Merkelbach 1962: 160; see Klebs 1899: 295–322 and Perry 1967: 294–324 for the opposite opinion. See also Kussl 1991: 143–59.

banquet scenes, but in the Latin tale, Apollonius, unaccompanied, makes the acquaintance of the daughter of the king of Tarsus, who subsequently, and rather discretely, falls in love with him. In the Greek fragments, the wife of the Persian king figures prominently, and Apollonios appears to be propositioned. Given the insignificance of the Greek scraps, the fact that Apollonios was a common Greek name, the unclear status of his character (main or subordinate?) and the frequent appearance of banquet scenes in a variety of genres, we believe that it would be rash to label these bits as the ancestor of the Latin tale without much more persuasive evidence.[2]

---

[2] We note that neither Kortekaas nor Schmeling discuss these papyri in their recent editions of the *Historia Apollonii*. In fact, Kortekaas might be explicitly denying any connection when he writes, "Nor has any discovery among papyri . . . turned up yet to help us out of our quandary" (1984: 41).

DESCRIPTION

PSI 151 (= *P*² 2624, measuring 10.0 × 10.0 cm) and P. Mil. Vogl. 260 (measuring 4.8 × 16.4 cm) are two pieces from the same papyrus roll published separately. They were found in Oxyrhynchus. Writing is across the fibers on the back of a document. The former contains ends of lines and a portion of the right margin; from this fragment it is possible to determine that the lines were between twenty-seven and thirty letters long. The latter preserves a considerable upper margin, but is broken off elsewhere. The stichometric number 14 (ΙΔ), which occurs at the top of this column situates the piece relatively close to the beginning of the roll. The hand is a rather narrow, rapidly written upright with documentary affinities (note in particular the cursive epsilon), not unlike that of *The Apparition* (see below). We are inclined to assign it to the late third or early fourth century C.E. (although the original editors placed it in the third century). There are no lectional signs, but there are two supralinear additions. There are a number of itacistic spellings; iota adscript is not written. There is no attempt to avoid hiatus: notice in particular *PSI* 151.4–5: γυνὴ ὑπεράνω αὐτοῦ ἀνέκει|[το] .

PSI 151

[. . . . .] ̣ ϲατράπαι καὶ μεγι̣[ϲτᾶ]ν̣[εϲ καὶ]
[οἱ ἄλλ]οι, ἕκαϲτοϲ δὲ εἰϲ τὴν ϲυνήθη
[κλίνην] ἐκλίθη, ἡ δὲ βαϲιλὶϲ ἡ τού-
4 [του] γυνὴ ὑπεράνω αὐτοῦ ἀνέκει-
[το θε]οπρεπεῖ κάλλει κοϲμουμένη. τοῦ̣
[δὲ πό]του μεϲάϲαντοϲ, ὁ βαϲιλεὺϲ με-
[ταν]αϲτὰϲ ἐπὶ τὸν ἀγκῶνα, ὃν κατεῖ-
8 [χε ϲκύ]φον προέτεινεν τῷ Διονυϲίῳ
[. . . . .]βων καὶ τῷ Ἀπολλωνίῳ
[. . . . .] ̣ [. .]η ̣ ριον προπίνω
 ]πρεϲβύτηϲ ἀνα
12]ϲ εἰϲ τὴν βαϲιλίδ[α]
 ] ̣ δωρ ̣ ων προϲ
 ]ε[ῖ]πεν ἀληθ[. . .] ̣

Supplements are those of ed. pr. unless otherwise indicated.
2. [οἱ φίλ]οι Crusius   3. [τάξιν] Lav.   [κατ]εκλίθη Zimm.   βαϲιλειϲ pap.
τοῦ Zimm.   4. ὑπερανω pap.   5.]οπρεπι καλλι pap.   6–7. με|[ταν]αϲτὰϲ
Zimm.   7. ανκωνα pap.   9. [ὁ δὲ παραλα]βὼν Crus., [ὥϲπερ λεί]βων Lav., [ἅμα
δέ τι λεί]βων Zimm.   τῷ Ἀπόλλωνι · ὦ Zimm.   10. ῥονπροπεινω pap., [τὸ ποτή-]
ριον Crus., [λέγων ἅμα · "νικ]η̣[τή-]
ριον Lav.   14. ἀληθῶϲ,] ᾧ Zimm., ἀληθ[εία]ϲ Lav.

] satraps and nobles
[and the rest], each reclined in his usual
place, and the queen, his
4   wife, reclined above him,
resplendent in a godlike beauty.
In the midst of the drinking, the king,
heaving himself up onto his elbow,
8   extended the cup he held to Dionysios,
. . . and to Apollonios
[saying,] "I offer this cup [———]
elder above [———]
12   to the queen [———]
of offerings to . . .
he said. . . .

P. MIL. VOGL. 260

ΙΔ

το]cούτων τῆc βαcιλίδ[οc
Ἀ]πολλώνιοc ἔcτη βο[
]ηcη πότερον ἐπιδ[
4   ] cυνουcίαν ἢ ἀπορ[
]μνηcθει δὲ ὧν πρ[
εἶ]πεν εἰc πᾶν ὅ τι βου[λ
]cηc ἡ δὲ ὡc γυνὴ . [
8   ] πρότερον ἐπιcπαcαμε[
] . κατεφίληcεν τοῖc ε . [
]κτηρίοιc ἑαυτὴν ε . [
]c τὴν ἐπιθυμ[ίαν
12   "Ἀπο]λλώνιε κα . [
τῆc] νυκτὸc ταύτη[c
] . αμε ἐξου . [
] . α . [.] . . αcαμεν[
16   ] . . π . αν οδε[
. δ . . . ονεπι[
] . ρ[.]ε[.] . . ην . [
]. . [
20   ]τ . [
] . [

- -

_____

Supplements are those of ed. pr. unless otherwise indicated.
   1. βαcιλίδ[οc Bowman   5. Read]μνήcθη,]μνηcθῇ, or]μνηcθεὶ⟨c⟩   8. επιcπαᶜᵃμε[
pap.   9–10. τοῖc ἔρ[ωτοc μυ]ϲτηρίοιc Kussl   16. αν οδε[pap.

P. MIL. VOGL. 260

] of such as these, of the queen [
] Apollonios stood [
] . . . whether . . . [
4   ] intercourse which [
] And he, having recalled what [
] spoke against all that (s/he) plannned [
] And she, as a woman ? [
8   ] before having drawn out [
] s/he kissed to the [
] charms(?) herself [
] the desire [
12   [saying, "]Apollonios [
] on this night [

1–5. The presence of satraps would indicate the Persian court, though precisely where is moot. Though μεγι[cτᾶ]ν[εc is by no means certain as a reading, the remaining traces are not incompatible. For a description of Persian royal banquets, see Ath. 4.145c-d (said to be from Herakleides of Kumai). Note especially the presence of the queen (145d: ἐνίοτε δὲ καὶ ἡ γυνὴ αὐτῷ cυνδειπνεῖ καὶ τῶν υἱῶν ἔνιοι).

Compare, for example, the openings of AT 1.5, *Metiochos and Parthenope*, and *HA* (§§ 15–16), where women are present at dinner parties. Note also that in Chariton, Statira, the chief wife of the king of Persia, and in Heliodoros, Persinna, the wife of Hydraspes, the king of Ethiopia, as well as Arsake, the wife of the satrap Oroondates, are significant actors. Arsake actively attempts to sleep with the novel's hero, Theagenes.

2–3. Kussl (1991: 143), and Stramaglia (1992: 25) following him, read [τὸ]ν cυνήθη | [τόπον], on the grounds that the space in the lacuna is too small for η. But what they must be reading as ν is more likely to be the left vertical of η and the right vertical of ν respectively.

6. μεcάζω = a late form of μεcόω. Müller (1916: 361) observes that this and μεγι[cτᾶ]ν[εc (line 1) are evidence for the lateness of the Greek.

7. ἐπὶ τὸν ἀγκῶνα: ἐπ' ἀγκῶνοc is standard Greek for reclining on one's elbow while dining. Here the accusative is occasioned by the use of a verb involving motion.

8–9. The space available precludes Διονυcίῳ and Ἀπολλωνίῳ from being adjectives. So they are apparently the names of two dinner guests; perhaps comrades in misadventure, like Chaireas and Polycharmos. The names are too common in the ancient world to derive any particular significance from their occurrence together. Apollonios finds himself with the queen(?) in the later fragment.

9.]βων: Lavagnini's λεί]βων seems the best supplement. Here, surely, given the occurrence again in P. Mil. Vogl. 260, Ἀπολλωνίῳ is to be read, not Ἀπολλῶνι ω-.

10. Initially a verb of speaking, λέγων or sim., followed by direct address.

]η ριον: apparently a different word from P. Mil. Vogl. 260.10. Ed. pr.'s π[οτ]ήριον, with a wide space between η and ρ, seems the best choice; Lavagnini's supplement ([νικ]η[τή]ριον) is too long.

13.] δωρ ων: there appears to be a letter between ρ and ω; probably not δωρειῶν, but τ]ὰ δῶρα ὧν. Note that the king gives Apollonius gifts in *HA* § 15.

14. Although there appears to be space for several letters, ἀληθ[ῶ]c is a possible reading, if the horizontal of c was extended as far to the right as is the final letter of line 6 above.

P. MIL. VOGL. 260

2. There is a high trace before τῆc consistent with the ν of τοcούτων.

4. cυνουcίαν = intercourse, either social or sexual. In this context, the latter might be appropriate. Compare XE 3.12.4 or Lollianos Fragment A.2 recto 13–14.

η : ἦ or ἦ seems rather more likely than the article.

7. ἡ δὲ ὡc γυνὴ : alternatively, read ἡδέωc γυνὴ?

10.]κτηρίοιc : initially traces more suited to κ or c than η; possibly θελ]κτηρίοιc.

]κτηρίοιc ἑαυτὴν ε . [: since there is a τοῖc in the preceding line, a dative plural seems preferable to]κτηριοι cεαυτὴν ε . [.

12–13. Presumably the woman is speaking to Apollonios. His reply may begin at either 16 (read ὁ δὲ [?) or 17.

17. Read '] . δ' εῖπον ἐπι[or sim.?

Tinouphis

❖

Tinouphis is a tantalizing scrap of a narrative that involves a prophet apparently condemned for adultery but saved by the trickery of the executioner. There are three male characters—Tinouphis, Sosias, and Magoas—and an unknown number of females—the adulteress(?), the referent for a feminine participle in line 16, and Isias. Tinouphis is a magician (*magos*) who would seem to be identical with the prophet mentioned in line 14 and the "king's savior" of line 5. Though unattested, his name is clearly Egyptian in form (see below, line 16 note). Sosias is a name most familiar from New Comedy, often for the tricky slave. Here he is probably the executioner (line 15). Magoas is also unattested, but sounds like an intended reminiscence of the name Bagoas, the Persian eunuch who was active in leading a campaign against Nektanebos at the time of Artaxerxes III (DS 16.47–50). This multi-cultural combination—Egyptian, Persian, Greek—certainly points to Egypt at the time of the Persian invasion, but need not be confined to this period or place. The trio might as easily occur elsewhere in the Greek-speaking world. After all, Nektanebos fled to the Macedonian court when he left Egypt, and Antonius Diogenes' Egyptian magician Paapis seems to have spent the bulk of his novelistic life outside of Egypt. Stramaglia (1992: 13–16), noting a similarity with Chariton and *Apollonios*, would locate the action in the Persian court.

Magicians, prophets, and executioners are socially marginal, and the ambiguities inherent in this marginal status are often exploited in narrative fiction. *Magoi* were originally Persian priests of Ahura-Mazda, reputed for their astrological and other learning. As early as the fifth century B.C.E., such priests are often identified with unscrupulous behavior, undoubtedly because they held so much power in the Persian court that they were capable of influencing dynastic succession. There is, for example, the tale of Smerdis, who duped Kambyses and ruled for a brief time after him in place of another Smerdis, the son of Kyros and the legitimate heir (Herodotos 3.61–88); a similar tale of the duplicity of Sphendadates is found in Ktesias (Photios *Epit.* 37b6ff.). Iamblichos (Phot. *Epit.* 75b16), in discussing the kinds of magic in which the *magos* may special-

400

ize, lists "*magoi* who work with locusts," lions, mice, hail, serpents, necromancy, or ventriloquism—practices that no doubt contributed to the equation of *magos* with con artist. This equation grew more complex in the Christian period because the links between charismatic philosophy, the divine power of "holy men," and magic were closely intertwined. Every miracle worker who claimed a "legitimate" divine authority was in competiton with the unscrupulous *magos* who knowingly duped his gullible audience by performing equally marvelous feats.

Prophets do not fare much better. While *prophētēs* was the title for the highest priestly class in Egypt, and elsewhere usually a title of distinction and respect, not all prophets in fiction were morally upright. Daulis in his bitter attack on the Delphic *prophētēs* equates him with a dishonest fortune-teller. In Antonius Diogenes, Paapis' villainous use of magic spells is a prime mover for the novel's plot. Nektanebos fled to the court of Philip II, where he set up as a prophet, gaining the confidence of the queen Olympias. Predicting that she was fated to bear a son fathered by the Egyptian god Amon, he persuaded her to prepare herself in her bedchamber for the god's appearance. Then disguising himself on the awaited evening as the ram-headed god, he entered her room and slept with Olympias himself. Against these we might place the "good prophets"—Heliodoros's Kalasiris and possibly Apuleius's Zatchlas. Tinouphis, who is both prophet and magician, may belong in this latter category if he is the "king's savior."

The executioner was traditionally despised. For example, a courtesan in rejecting the embraces of a soldier claims that "he is no better than an executioner" (Lucian *Dial. mer.* 13.4.12). But Iamblichos features a priest, Soraichos, condemned to be a public executioner (Phot. *Epit.* 76a20), who is handed his own son for execution. The son then takes over his father's office, so that the priest will not be defiled by bloodletting (77b38). The son himself later escapes in the clothing of a farmer's daughter who was condemned to sleep with him, and she then acts as the executioner! Both Xenophon of Ephesos (4.6.4–7) and Apollonius of Tyre (§ 31) have characters who, out of sympathy for their victims, cannot perform the executions they were ordered to carry out. Like the characters in Iamblichos, Sosias would appear to add a dimension of cleverness to his role as executioner.

The low-status types, combined with adultery and a prison break, would seem to set this piece firmly in the area of criminal fiction. But it is wise to exercise caution. The whole may be no more than a witty and salacious anecdote within a longer and distinctly different type of work, not unlike that of Rhampsinitos and the thief in Herodotos (2.121)—a tale that turns on the clever strategy of a builder who contrives a secret, moveable block to the king's treasury. There is an aura of insouciance about *Tinouphis* with its frequent wordplay: the prophet is the "king's savior," which must be a deliberate play on the cult title of the Ptolemies, "king savior"; Magoas echoes *magos*, Sosias, whose name is from the same root, echoes *sōtēr* ("savior"), and with his trick of the brick he is the "savior" of the prophet (who in turn is the "savior" of the king). His "explanation" to an apparently dim-witted Magoas for building the execution or torture chamber "very large" (*megiston*) was that "Tinouphis happened to be a *magos*"— a pun on the similarity of sound of *megas* and *magos*. This is not unlike the kinds of explanations that occurred in Ptolemy Chennos's *Novel Research* (*Kainē historia*), such as the claim that Odysseus's real name was Outis, which he was given because at birth he had enormous ears, *ōta*.

Tinouphis, like *Iolaos*, is written as a combination of prose and verse, a form that is discussed above (see *Iolaos*). The verse section is iambic tetrameter catalectic, but with the break at mid-line apparently treated like the line end, permitting not only hiatus at this point, but *brevis in longo*. The scheme is ×– ◡– ×– ◡◡̲ ‖ ×– ◡– ×– ◡̲ ‖. Haslam argues that, although the closest extant analogues for the verse are currently to be found in Latin, its form is more likely to have been originally Greek, and possibly related to the Byzantine *versus politicus* (see Haslam 1981: 36–37). West (1982: 15) is not so certain that this peculiar form of Greek tetrameter is a native; he argues that it is a "typically post-Hadrianic manifestation." If it could be certainly demonstrated that this verse was Latin in origin, it would greatly strengthen an argument for prosimetric writing coming into later Greek from a Latin source. But if the verse is a Greek native, it does not prove the opposite thesis, namely that prosimetrum came originally from a Greek source like Menippos. Any Greek writer, although in the main imitating his Latin source, could choose to adopt a native meter.

DESCRIPTION

P. Turner 8 (= P. Haun. inv. 400, measuring 17.0 × 18.5 cm) holds remains of one column written along the fibers of light-colored papyrus, now stained in two places at upper and lower right. The column retains a bottom margin of at least 3.0 cm, and possibly 1.0 cm from an upper margin, though too little is left above the top line of extant writing to be certain. What are most likely traces from a preceding column lie opposite lines 6 (traces of one letter) and 23–24 (υφιν, i.e., Τινο]ῦφιν). Lines 9–17 are metrical and set in *ekthesis*; lines 18–25 are clearly prose. The nature of lines 1–8 is not clear, and evidence points in two directions: layout of these lines matches 18–25, and the final word of line 2, which appears to be καί, suggests prose; but βρότων (line 4) hints at poetry. In any case, lines 1–8 are not in the same meter as 9–17. The hand is a sturdily made informal round type, assignable to the second century C.E. It is not unlike the hand that copied Herodas's *Mimes* (*GMAW*[2] pl. 39), though the letters are less regularly formed. There are no marks of punctuation; in the prose section, there is elision at line 23. There is almost certainly one itacism (line 25), what appear to be scribal errors (lines 6, 16, 17), and possibly a supralinear correction at line 3. The back is blank.

P. TURNER 8

[The initial 3 lines are too mutilated to reproduce.]

4   [. . .] . ον ἄϲχετον καί τιϲ εἶπεν βροτῶν
     [. .] . οὗτοϲ, ὦ θεοί, βαϲιλέωϲ ϲωτὴρ φανείϲ
     . [. . . . . .]κα κατεκρίθη μοιχάδα . . . . λε[
     . . . . [. . .] . . ϲ ὁ νόμοϲ, ἂν γυνὴ μοιχὰϲ ᾖ
8   ἱερε[. . . . .] . .
     ×–◡–×–◡◡ καὶ τοῦ κατακριθέντο[ϲ
     ×–◡–×– βροτῶν οὐκ ἀγρότηϲ . [. . . . . .]
     ×–◡–× δαιμόνων μοίρηϲ γὰρ ἦν [τ]ροπα[ῖ]ον
12   ἐντεῦθεν ἦν πλίνθοϲ μία ϲώτειρα τοῦ προφήτου
     [ἀλλ'] οὐδὲ ε[ἷ]ϲ ἠπίϲτατο ἦν αὐτόϲοφον ὁ τέκτων
     ἐ[ν]ταῦθα γοῦν ὁ δήμιοϲ ἔϲτηϲε τὸν προφήτην
     ὁ δήμιοϲ δ' ὁ δυϲϲεβὴϲ ὁ τοῖϲ τρόποιϲι φαῦλοϲ
16   ἔϲωϲε τ[ῇ] ποθουμένῃ ζώοντα τὸν Τινοῦφιν
     πορθου γὰρ ἦν ὑπηρέτηϲ καὶ τῆϲ πικρᾶϲ [ἀν]άγκηϲ.
     ἐπὶ γοῦν μέγι[ϲ]τον οἶκον παρὰ [τὴν]
     ϲυνήθειαν οὗτοϲ ἐποίηϲεν, ἐπύ[θε]το
20   τὸ αἴτιον ὁ Μαγώαϲ καὶ ὁ Ϲωϲίαϲ ἀπε-
     κρίνατο ἔργῳ τοῦτο ἐπίτηδεϲ π[εποι-]
     ηκέναι διὰ τὸ τὸν Τινοῦφιν μάγον τ[υγ-]
     χάνειν· ὁ δ' εὖ λέγειν ὑπολαβὼ[ν τὸν]
24   δήμιον ἀπέϲτη· τελέϲαϲ δὲ πά[ντα ὁ]
     Ϲωϲίαϲ πρὸϲ τὴν Ἰϲιάδα ε . . . . [

The supplements are those of ed. pr. unless otherwise noted.
    4.] . οναϲχετον pap.   5. ἀλ]λ', οὐ]χ, or οὐ]δ' οὗτοϲ more likely than το]ιοῦτοϲ, Has-
lam   6. π[αραυτί]κα Luppe, [αὐτί]κα Haslam   κακαγεκριθη pap.   7. ἴϲον
ὁμόϲα Stramaglia   ηγ pap.   10. οὔτ' ἀγρότηϲ, οὔ[τ' ἀ]ϲ[τόϲ Luppe, but unmetri-
cal   13. ὃ δ'] Parsons   ⟨πλ⟩ὴν αὐτὸϲ ὁ φονοτέκτων? Kussl   16. εγωϲε pap.,
ἔϲωϲε or ἔγω ⟨γέ⟩ ϲε Haslam,   . [.]ποθημενη pap.   ἔγωγε ⟨δ' ἦν⟩ π[ε]ποθημένη
Luppe   17. πορθου pap.   18–19. παρα[ϲχὼν] | πλινθείαν, παρὰ [τὴν] | πλιν-
θείαν Haslam   21. κρεινατο pap.   24. πάϲ[αϲ τὰϲ Luppe   25. θυϲίαϲ
Luppe   ειϲιαδα pap.

4   ungovernable(?) and some mortal said:
    "But] this one, O gods, [who] seemed the savior of the king
    has been condemned . . . adulteress
    . . . the law states(?): if a woman is an adulteress
8   a priest(?)
    . . . and of the condemned man
    . . . of mortals, a not-unsophisticated [prophet?
    . . . of gods. For he was a trophy of fate.
12 There was one brick, the savior of the prophet
    but] no one knew; the workman was cleverness itself.
    There then the executioner stood the prophet
    —the executioner, the impious one, foul in his habits,
16 preserved Tinouphis alive for his beloved(?).
    For he was a servant of[?] and of bitter necessity.
            Now seeing as he had made the chamber very large
                                    contrary to
        custom, Magoas inquired
20   the reason for this, and Sosias
        replied that this was in fact appropriately done
        because Tinouphis happened to be
        magos. And when he realized that the executioner had
24   spoken well, he went away. When he had completed
                                    everything,
        Sosias [went?] to Isias. . . .

P. TURNER 8

4. καί τιϲ εἶπεν βροτῶν: most likely the introduction of a speech; for a similar start, see Chariton 2.2.6: καί τιϲ εἶπεν τῶν ἀγροίκων, also with a vocative following the first word of the quotation. Alternatively, articulate as John Rea suggests, "καί τιϲ," εἶπεν, "βροτῶν." For βροτόϲ in prose, see Luc. *Vit. auct.* 6.15: θεόϲ, οὐ βροτόϲ τιϲ εἶναι φαίνεται. Given the proximity of verse and the stilted or affected quality even of the prose of this piece, the fact that βροτόϲ does not normally occur in prose may not be significant. It may be intended to be proleptic of βροτῶν, below, line 10, or perhaps the quotation of part of a supposedly familiar line. Note, e.g., Sophocles OC 1663–64: εἴ τιϲ βροτῶν | θαυμαϲτόϲ.

If τιϲ εἶπεν βροτῶν serves as an introduction to the direct speech of the rest of the column, then ἄϲχετον must belong to the background information.

5. βαϲιλέωϲ ϲωτήρ: an inversion of the usual Hellenistic royal cult title—βαϲιλεύϲ ϲωτήρ.

6–7. If μοιχάϲ is the right word in these lines, there may again be a reversal; the usual legal prohibition is against men who corrupt women—the μοιχόϲ, not the μοιχάϲ. In any case, the term μοιχάϲ is rare, occurring in Ath. 5.220b (said to be from Aeschines Socratikos), Placit. 1.7.10, Vett. Val. 104.11. According to DS 1.80, Egyptian priests were normally confined to one wife, and in some cases (as with the priests of Isis in Apuleius) to sexual abstinence. What punishments the violator incurred is unknown, but they would presumably include loss of privileges. In Heliodoros, Kalasiris, the *prophētēs* of the temple of Isis in Memphis, flees his home rather than succumb to his desire for Rhodopis, out of fear not of legal punishment, but of pollution of the sacred temple and its rituals.

What is the syntax? Has he slept with or had contact with a μοιχάϲ? Is a masculine singular participle to be restored for which μοιχάδα is the object?

7–8. ἂν γυνὴ μοιχὰϲ ἦ | ἱερε[: a prohibition against a priest consorting with an adulteress? See DS 1.78.5 for penalties incurred by ordinary citizens for adultery in Egyptian law. Since the public executioner is involved, the offense must have been capital. It is possible that the prophet's crime may have been regarded as sacrilege, which at least in the Ptolemaic period could be punished by death. But in the extant novels, there is considerable arbitrariness about the imposition of the death penalty; there need not be any basis in actual legal practice for the prophet's crime and punishment. Stramaglia (1992: 16) notes that according to Herodotos (7.114), burying alive was a Persian custom.

10. οὐκ ἀγρότηϲ: the word is poetic; ἄγροικοϲ is more common in narrative fiction. Surely a noun is missing. Haslam suggests "no man nor god could help the condemned man" as the line of restoration. Alternatively, all four

phrases refer to the prophet, and, e.g., προφήτηϲ could be restored at the end of the line.

12. ἦν πλίνθοϲ μία ϲώτειρα τοῦ προφήτου: this, combined with the fact that the executioner builds a chamber of some kind for the prophet (below, lines 18–20), suggests that "one brick" was cunningly fitted to permit some type of escape.

14. For the executioner, see above, introduction. For the sympathetic executioner, see Photios' epitome of Iamblichos 76a and 78a (a priest condemned to be an executioner), and for the lover turned executioner, see Paus. 7.21.1.

16–17. Alternatively, the speaker is female: ἔγωγε ⟨δ᾽ ἦν⟩ π[ε]ποθημένη ζώοντα τὸν Τινοῦφιν | πορθου γὰρ ἦν ὑπηρέτηϲ καὶ τῆϲ πικρᾶϲ [ἀν]άγκηϲ. "I to be sure have longed for Tinouphis alive, for I was a servant of[?] and of bitter necessity."

The name Tinouphis does not occur elsewhere, though -ouphis/-nouphis names are common in Egyptian, and the forms Tenouphis and Tetnouphis are attested.

17. πορθου: this form is attested only in Hesychios as a variant of πτόρθοϲ, which makes no sense here. It could be a proper name, meant to sound enough like πόθοϲ to constitute a pun. (Though no examples of such a name occur, Parthos and Parthes do.) Against this is the fact that the article seems always to appear with proper names. Alternatively an error—the text is hardly a model of scribal accuracy. In this case, there are a number of possibilities: πόθου, πόρου, πόρνου. (1) If πόθου, the executioner might also be sexually involved with the adulteress (see also Stramaglia 1992: 10); (2) πόρου might be coupled with ἀναγκή as a reminiscence of the parentage of Eros in Plato's Symposium; (3) if πόρνου, was the foul demios "the servant of a fornicator and of bitter necessity," where πόρνοϲ = Tinouphis?

18. ἐπεὶ γοῦν: the combination is rare, but it does occur.

μέγι[ϲ]τον: it is tempting to restore μέγα[ν] τὸν οἶκον, but space does not permit.

18–19. παρὰ [τὴν] | ϲυνήθειαν: Haslam suggests that either πλινθείαν or ϲυνήθειαν might be read; it seems to us to fit somewhat better with Magoas's inquiry, if the chamber was built "contrary to expectation," rather than "by brickwork."

18–24. This prose section is an elaboration of the preceding tetrameters. The executioner's trick of the salvific brick is fleshed out in greater detail. In preparing the execution (or torture) chamber, he apparently built it large because the magos was megas. This kind of explanatory pun occurs elsewhere: cf. P. Oxy. 6.851, where the speaker says, "This man is not a magos, but perhaps his god is megas" (οὗτοϲ ὁ ἄνθρωποϲ οὔκ ἐϲτιν μάγοϲ, ἀλλὰ τάχα ὁ θ(εὸ)ϲ μέγαϲ ἐϲτίν). Or Clement 6.7.11.21: "a magos, being megas" (μέγαϲ ὤν, μάγοϲ).

407

20. ὁ Μαγώας : see above, introduction. Besides the historical Bagoas, Bagoas is the name of the eunuch servant of Oroondates in Hld. 8.13–15. The presence of Persian eunuchs should locate the action of the piece in an area controlled by Persian satrapies.

25. πρὸς τὴν Ἰςιάδα : probably a proper name, as in Hld. 6.4.1: ἐμοὶ δὲ ἐπὶ τὴν Ἰςιάδα ϲπευϲτέον, where Isias is the girlfriend of an incidental character. Is she identical with the adulteress, or τ[ῆ] ποθουμένῃ in line 16, or both?

The Apparition

❖

The Apparition is apparently a tale of sin and retribution, with overtones of the story of the rich man found in the New Testament (line 18: "feasting when I should have . . ."). Characters include the unnamed narrator, his companions, and the subject of his story, who speaks at lines 10–11 and 16ff. This last character has a vision ("he saw a god") that the narrator and his audience may or may not share, though they are affected by the terror. The fragment ends with the god departing, or the man who experiences the vision dying, or both.

The original editors, Grenfell and Hunt, assigned this scrap to "romance." Subsequently Zimmermann decided, on the basis of the rather fragile reading of *Til*[at the end of line 7, that it belonged to Arrian's life of a bandit named Tillorobos, the evidence for whose existence depends entirely on Lucian *Alex.* 2: "He [Arrian] saw fit to record the life of Tillorobos the bandit" (see App. B no. 3 below). Although Lucian mentions that Arrian took up the subject, to what extent and in what context is not stated. Unfortunately the identification of this fragment with Arrian's work is as dubious as the reading; nothing at all in the legible parts requires or even hints at the presence of Tillorobos, and Zimmermann's more than usually exuberant supplements neglect the margins and spacings of the papyrus.

Kerényi and Rattenbury preferred to assign this fragment to dream literature, the latter arguing that the events are more suited to "a religious tale of miraculous conversion" (Rattenbury 1933: 250). The presence of Asklepios tends to support this conclusion. Certainly there is much in this piece that is similar to, for example, Ailios Aristides' narratives of his dreams sent from Asklepios; as in our fragment, Aristides includes stories and dialogues embedded in the dream sequences. There is, however, one significant difference. In this piece the narrator and his companions are participants when the specter (Asklepios?) comes for a third party. In this respect, it seems more like a ghost story than a serious religious narrative. Such tales can occur in a wide variety of writings; for example, they are found in Ailian, Lucian, Philostratos, and Plutarch as well as in the novelists.

THE APPARITION

DESCRIPTION

P. Oxy. 416 (= P^2 168, measuring 12.0 × 9.5 cm) is written across the fibers on the back of a word list in sigma, the hand of which is a third century Severe style. One column with twenty-two lines remains, lacking all margins. The left break seems to have occurred at the beginnings of lines, however, so restorations along this edge are fairly certain. The right portion of the papyrus is now badly abraded and, to judge from lines 4–5, lacks between eight and ten letters per line. The text therefore can be made to yield little continuous sense. The column seems to have been rather wide, with at least forty letters per line, in its physical layout reminiscent of hypomnemata or of mimes. The hand is a fluently written upright with occasional eccentric flourishes, competent, but not particularly attractive, assigned by its original editors to the late third or early fourth century C.E. Punctuation includes high stop, apostrophe, and the occasional accent; paragraphi set off direct speech from surrounding narrative in lines 10–11 and 16ff. Elision is sometimes marked by the scribe; iota adscripts not written. There are two examples of hiatus: lines 9 and 18.

..]πο[.]εχεωβι[

ἀνθ' οὗ εἰς ἡμᾶς χ[ρ]ηςτὸς ἐφ[ά]νη [. . . .]ιτο[. . .]μ[

νευειν · cώματος μέχρι τέλους ὑμῖν τηςδε[

4   διάδοχον τὸν παῖδα καταλέγει · καὶ δη . οι παρα[

λ]ιπαρὸν ἐφήψιςται γέρας [ἑ]κατὸν καὶ δεκα . ε[

μηκυνόμενον ἐπ' ἀόριστον . . . . . . [

Ἀς]κλήπιον προςδοκᾷ ἐπιςπέρχοντα ιδ . . . . ιν . . ειλ[

8   ..]ων ἑώρα θεόν τινα ςκοτιαίῳ προϊόντα εἰ[δει καὶ

πενθικὴν καὶ φρικ[ώ]δη ἔχοντα [ὄ]φιν . . . [

τρομήςας · "ὦ," εἶπεν, "ἑταῖροι, τίς ἐςθ' οὗτος[.] . . [

πενθαλέος ἅμα καὶ καταγυκτικὸς [.] . . . . . [. "

12   καὶ δέος εἰςέρχεται εἰπόντων [. . . . . .] . . [

ὃ χρή · αὐχμηρὸν δ' ἐμφαίν[ω]ν ὄψ[ι]ν [. . .] . [.] . [

εἶναι · καταρρηξάμενος τὴ[ν] ἐςθῆ[τα .] . [. .] . [

προςεδραμεν αὐτῷ · κα . αρν . . . . . . [

16   "ὤμοι τῶν ἁμαρτηθέντων," ε[ἶπεν, " . . . .

τ]οῦ cώματος αἰκιζομένου . [. . . .] . [. .]γβ[

εὐ]ωχούμενος ἐν ᾧ ἔδει με κρειττον[. . . .

..]ε[ι]ν τὰς ἴcας ἀναδεδεγμ[έ]νας ὁλῳ[. . . . .

20   ..]μαντευτὰ ἡμῖν ἡ φύςις ξ . . . . . κα[.] . [.] . ε[

. . .]γεν ιμ[. . . .]εςτωτα . [. . .]α ἐπιτο[.]ε[.] . . δι[

. . . . .]αφ[. . .] ᾤχετο · καὶ ἅμ' εἶχεν . . αλλ[

---

3. νευειν · pap., Zimm. deletes punctuation of the papyrus   τελουcϋ pap.   4. λεγει ·
καιδη . οι pap., δη[λ]οῖ παρα[υτὰ ὅτι Zimm.   5. λι]παρὸν Zimm.   6. Initially
] . ειν deleted by scribe   ἐπήρι[ς]τον Zimm.   8. προ[ιό]γ[τα Stramaglia (by
letter) εἰ[δει Zimm.   9. πενθικην, φρεικ[.]δη pap.   10. τρομηςας · ὦ, εςθ'
pap.   11. καταγ[υκ]τικὸς Zimm., κατα[πληκ]τικὸc Lav., καταγ[οη]τικὸc Zimm.
12. καιδεος pap.   13. ὁχρη · αυχμηρον pap., read αὐχμηρὰν Zimm.   14. ειναι ·
pap.   15. προςεδραμεν αυτω · pap.   ἀ]ρν[ύομενος Zimm.   16. ὤμοι
pap.   ε[ἶπεν Garin   18. ενω pap.   κ[ρ]ε[ίτ]τογας Zimm.   19. ἴcας
pap.   21. ιμ[pap.   22.]ωχετο · pap.

[. . .]
. . . [he] appeared to be kindly disposed towards us [
of a body until the end for us [
4   he designates the boy as successor; indeed . . . [
110 . . . have already been granted as a rich reward [
being prolonged indefinitely [
he expects Asklepios hastening (or angry) [
8   he saw a god advancing with a shadowy form [and
having a mournful and frightening visage [
trembling, he said "O friends, who is this man [
sad and contrite . . . ["
12   and fear entered as [we?] spoke [
what was necessary. Showing a face withered [
to be, tearing his clothes [
ran towards him and denies(?)[
16   O my sins, [he said,
of the body being disfigured [
feasting while I should have better [
equivalent things received [
20   foretold to us, nature [
standing [
] departed, and at the same time he was holding [

P. OXY. 416

2. ἀγθ’ οὗ : there can be only one letter before νθου at the beginning of this line. It is unclear how the phrase fits with the preceding or the following sentence. εἰς ἡμᾶς χ[ρ]ηςτὸς : for the use of χρηςτὸς εἰς, see, e.g., Hld. 6.7.8, New Testament Eph. 4.32.

ἐφ[ά]νη : presumably this refers to the character within the narrative who is also the subject of καταλέγει, ἑώρα, and εἶπεν. This language could refer to the manifestation of a god; however, he does not actually appear until line 8.

3. νευειν· ςώματος μέχρι τέλους : if the punctuation is correct, then ςώματος must belong with μέχρι τέλους. This is certainly anomalous in word order, if not in thought. The high stop in this place does not look like the others found in this papyrus, however, and Zimmermann's inclination to disregard it may be correct. In that case, ςώματος will belong with the preceding infinitive ([μνη-μο]|νεύειν or sim., so Zimmermann 1935: 172), and μέχρι τέλους could either end or begin a phrase.

τηςδε[: the articulation of these letters is quite uncertain. Either τῆς δὲ begins a new thought or μέχρι τέλους begins the new phrase, and τηςδε[cannot τῆς δὲ[, but, e.g., τῆςδε [τῆς … with διάδοχον; alternatively, δε[might be the beginning of a noun. Options are limited to, e.g., δε[ςποίνης or δε[ςποτείας. Zimmermann suggests this is a prophet of Asklepios appointing his successor and restores τῆς δὲ [προφητείας (1935: 170).

4. δη . οι : either δή μοι or δηλοῖ … [ὅτι. Two different lines of restoration are possible: either the narrator—restoring δή μοι—has been granted a gift of 110 (years of life?) from the god or the Fates, or the character within the narration "makes clear"—restoring δηλοῖ—that a gift of some sort has been granted himself or another.

παρα[: this might be either παρὰ + the genitive—e.g., παρ’ Ἀςκληπίου, αὐτοῦ, or sim.; or an adverb—παρα[υτίκα or sim. For the former, compare Sacred Tales 2, quoted below, note 5.

5. [ἑ]κατὸν καὶ δεκα . ε[: there appears to be more ink between δε and ε than there should be for δέκα ἐ[, but no other reading suggests itself. Has the narrator been granted a gift of 110 years of life (restoring ἐ[τῶν), which is now ending? Compare, e.g., Ail. Arist. Sacred Tales 2 (2.398.26–27 Keil): ἔχεις, ἔφη [sc. Asklepios], δέκα ἔτη παρ’ ἐμοῦ καὶ τρία παρὰ Cαράπιδος….

6–7. [νῦν δὲ | Ἀς]κλήπιον προςδοκᾷ or sim.? This is part of the framing narrative that continues through ἑώρα in line 8. Either the third-person singular or an imperative can be restored; in the latter case, the addressee is uncertain.

7. ἐπιςπέρχοντα : the meaning of the participle is either "hastening" or, more likely, considering lines 16ff., "angry."

10. "ὦ," εἶπεν, "ἑταῖροι : the character within the narrative is now speaking; ἑταῖροι are probably meant to include the external narrator as well as his companions—ἡμᾶς, line 2 above—but they might also refer to another group.

414

13. αὐχμηρὸν δ' ἐμφαίν[ω]ν ὄψ[ι]ν: Zimmermann emends to a feminine form to agree with ὄψ[ι]ν; he may well be right, but given the extent of the lacuna, we hesitate. This and the following lines seem to describe the speaker of line 16, not the apparition. For connotations of a withered appearance, see Winkler 1980: 162.

15. κα.αρν....[: a form of ἀρνοῦμαι, καταρνοῦμαι, or ἄρνυμαι; the traces are too broken to determine much else.

16. "ὦ μοι τῶν ἁμαρτηθέντων," ε[ἶπεν: Garin compares the exclamation in XE 5.8.7: "οἴμοι τῶν κακῶν" λέγουσα (sc. Antheia).

18. εὐ]ωχούμενος ἐν ᾧ ἔδει με κρειττον[: is this a rich man regretting a life of self-indulgence?

20. ..]μαντευτὰ ἡμῖν ἡ φύσις: does μαντευτὰ belong with ἡ φύσις?

22. αφ[...]ᾤχετο: ἄφ[νω or sim. This could refer either to the apparition or to the speaker of line 16.

Goatherd and the
Palace Guards

❖

The narrator of *PSI 725* is apparently a goatherd (lines 5–6) who has witnessed or partaken in events in a palace (line 18), and who is quite possibly female. There is mention of someone (sex and species uncertain) with a recent wound closed up in the house. The torches mentioned in line 16 locate the time at night. Depending on the supplement to and translation of line 11, the action may be either a sneaky escape or a violent assault. There seems to be a chase by guards, who have interrupted someone's activities (lines 14–15). Action breaks off at the palace gates.

There are several characters in this tantalizing bit. (1) The narrator seems to belong to the group that is guarding goats (lines 5–6, 15). The singular "myself" is feminine in line 3. If the narrator remains the same thoughout the passage, then the narrator is a woman, but not identical with the woman mentioned in lines 13 and 17. Alternatively, there is only one woman, and the feminine pronoun, "myself," belongs to a reported speech. In this case, the narrator may be of either sex, though identification with goatherds makes a male more likely. (2) The guards (lines 14, 18) are conceivably identical with those watching the flocks (line 6), but more likely are palace guards. (3) A second woman (lines 13, 17) is probably distinct from the narrator. (4) The fractured Ωλε . . [of line 12 seems to indicate the presence of a male character, as do the broken participles in lines 14 and 19. But the name itself is problematic (see below, note 12).

The whole could well be a messenger speech, such as that in Apuleius 8.1–15, where a servant of Charite comes to the shepherds and rustics and relates the recent misadventures in the master's house. Since goatherds do not usually witness intimate events inside a palace, this one might need to explain how s/he happened to know what s/he now relates, as the slave-messenger in Euripides' *Medea* explains how he entered the women's quarters (1143ff.). One potential explanation: the "fresh wound" in line 8 is that of a goat, who must be tended in the stable of the

416

palace; the feminine participle in line 7 might refer to all the other nannies who have been "segregated all together" while the wounded one is being cared for in a different place. See below for another interpretation.

A key ambiguity in reconstructing the scene is the verb in line 11: either "the doors of the women's quarters were attacked" or "the doors were put in place," that is, for the night. Because there does not seem to be room for an agent phrase, we incline toward the latter. The layout of locked women's quarters, along with the plan to get inside, is described in Achilles Tatius 2.19. In that novel, the lovers escape to the city gates and an awaiting chariot (2.31). If the action is something that happens after the quarters are locked up for the night, someone might be feigning sleep, waiting for nightfall to make a move. Assuming Ωλε . . [to be a name, is he inside or outside the women's quarters? If he is inside, could he be disguised as a woman to be near his beloved? Or could he be quartered nearby recovering from a "recent wound"? He could be the subject of the verb in line 11: "He got up from his bed and went to her, she woke up at once."

DESCRIPTION

PSI 725 (= P^2 2626), measuring 5.0 × 9.7 cm, is a twenty-line fragment from a papyrus roll now lacking all margins. If γυν[αικωνίτιδος is correctly restored in line 10—and it is difficult to imagine another supplement—then the lines were at least thirty letters long. The text is written across the fibers; the front contains a document. The hand is a rapidly written informal mixed type assignable to the third century C.E., not unlike that of Chariton (P. Oxy. 7.1019; *GMAW* ^{2} pl. 66), though this hand is slightly taller and more narrowly written. The scribe marks elision whenever possible, but the text itself does not always avoid hiatus (note lines 9 and 19: punctuation might obviate the hiatus in line 19, but not those in 9). There are no other lectional signs or marks of punctuation visible. Iota adscript is not written at line 9.

PSI 725

- -

      ]εῳϲ[. .]
      ]ῆλθεν ἐμοὶ δεύτ[ε]ρο[
      ]υϲ ὅμωϲ δ᾽ ἐμαυτὴν θ[
    4 λ]άμβανον ἐκ τούτου ϲ[
      ]πάντεϲ πλὴν ἡμῶν[
      ] . φυλαττόντων αἶγα[ϲ
      ]ποτετμημέναι κοι[
    8 ν]εαροῦ τραύματοϲ τοιο[υτ
      ]νι οἴκῳ ἀποκεκλειμέν[
      ἐ]πεὶ δ᾽ αἱ θύραι τῆϲ γυν[αικωνίτιδοϲ
      ]ετέθηϲαν, ἀνιϲτη[
   12 τ]ῆϲ κλίνηϲ ὁ Ωλε . . [
      ]αϲ αυτη. ἡ δ᾽ εὐθὺϲ ἐ . [
      ]νταϲ εἶδον οἱ φύλακ[εϲ
      ]ἐκεῖθεν ἡμᾶϲ δια[
   16 λα]μπτῆραϲ φέροντ[εϲ
      ]ερε δ᾽ αὐτὴν δια[
      ]βαϲιλείων εὐθὺ[ϲ
      ] . αμένου ἐπὶ πύλα[
   20]υρε[. . . . .]ορ[

- -

Supplements are those of ed. pr. unless otherwise indicated.
4. ἀνε?λ]άμβανον ed. pr.   7. ἀ]ποτετμημέναι ed. pr., ὑ]ποτετμημέναι Zimm.
9. ἐν γείτο]νι οἴκῳ ed. pr., ἔν τι]νι οἴκῳ Zimm.   αποκεκλιμεν[pap., ἀποκελειμέν[η ed.
pr., ἀποκεκλειμέν[οϲ Zimm.   11. ἐπ?]ετέθηϲαν ed. pr., προϲ]ετέθηϲαν Zimm.   ἀνί-
ϲτη[ϲι ed. pr.   12. κλεινηϲ pap.   13. ἐγ[ερθεῖϲα] ed. pr., ἐπ[ακολουθεῖ] Zimm.
14. [ὡϲ δ᾽ ἐξελθό]νταϲ Lav., [ἐκτρεχό]νταϲ Zimm.   19. θεα]ϲαμένου Zimm.   ἐπὶ
πύλα[ιϲ? Vit.

418

```
        ] [it] came to me a second [
        ] but nevertheless myself [
 4      ] I [or they] grasped from this [
        ] all except us [
        ] tending goats [
        ] cut off from [
 8      ] from a recent wound, such as [
        ] chamber shut up [
        ] but when the doors of the women's quarters [
        ] were closed(?), s/he got up [
12      ] from the couch . . . [
        ] her(?). But she straightaway [
        ] them the guards saw [
        ] there us [
16      ] carrying torches [
        ] and carried her through [
        ] of the palace(?), straightaway [
        ] . . . at the gates [
```

PSI 725

5–6. καθεῦδον γὰρ] πάντες πλὴν ἡμῶν [———καὶ δι]αφυλαττόντων or sim.

6. αἶγα[ς : we have considered the possibility that they are not guarding goats, but the Achaian city Aigai, listed by Strabo along with Olenos (8.7.4), but in this case we would expect τὰς Αἰγάς. Strabo (quoting Aratos) mentions that an Olenian goat (Ὠλενίην ... αἶγα) nursed Zeus (8.7.5), but whether the collocation of Ὠλ . . and αἶγα[ς is significant or a coincidence we cannot tell. Certainly the rest of this fragment suggests a romantic escape, not a mythological digression on Zeus's nurse.

7. Either ἀ] or ὑ]ποτετμημέναι : if this refers to the sequestering of the nannies in the fold, it will indicate approaching night. [αἳ τῆς νυκτός εἰσι ἀ]ποτεμημέναι or sim.

8. ν]εαροῦ τραύματος : Zimmermann suggests that this is a "wound of love" rather than a real injury (cf. Ch. 1.1.17, AT 5.26.3); though attractive in the abstract, it is difficult to reconcile with the demands of the narrative. See above, introduction, for two ways in which the "recent wound" might be understood.

9. ἀποκεκλειμέν[: Zimmermann takes Ὠλε . . [as the subject of the participle. But if the name does not occur before line 12, it would seem to be too far away to be the referent.

10. γυν[αικωνίτιδος : the supplement is almost certain. This term for women's quarters occurs frequently in the novels; see, e.g, *Ninos* A.IV.23–24; Hld. 5.34.5, 7.22.3; Ch. 5.4.2, 6.1.7.

11. Either ἐπ] or προς]ετέθησαν can be restored; for the latter, compare Lys. 1.13: ἐκείνη δὲ ἀναστᾶσα καὶ ἀπιοῦσα προστίθησι τὴν θύραν.

ἀνιστη[: the subject could be the narrator, or Ὠλε . . [, or even the woman of line 13 (ἀνίστη or ἀνίστη[σι). The verb will probably be followed by μὲν to balance ἡ δ' εὐθὺς below (line 13).

12. Vitelli read ὁ Ὠλεω[, which Lavagnini and Zimmermann, ignoring the broken letters, were quick to restore as the attested name Ὠλένι[ος. From the photograph, however, the letter following ε looks more like μ plus a slightly angled vertical (i.e., η, ι, μ, ν). No name Olemios or Olemes is attested, a circumstance that brings to mind the possibility that the text contains an error. In spite of the reasonable precaution of not emending a text near a lacuna, we question whether οω might have been a scribal miscopying, either of πο (possible in some hands in which the verticals of pi are curled to a certain degree) or of οβ (β is formed in some cursive hands very like ω). Either Πολεμ . [or ὁ Βλεμμ would provide a slightly more promising beginning for a name. We also considered that δὲ might have been miscopied as ω, but ὁ δὲ Λεμ . [or ὁ δ' Ελεμ . is not an improvement.

13. αυτη : almost certainly αὐτῇ or αὐτῆ ; note that iota adscript is not written in line 9.

14. οἱ φύλακ[ες : probably the palace guards who appear to chase Ωλε . . [and the women.

15. ἡμᾶς : the narrator + Ωλε . . [and the woman?

16. φέροντ[ες : οἱ φύλακ[ες will be the antecedent. Surely they, not the escaping couple (if that is a correct conjecture), would be carrying torches.

17. Initially ἔφ]ερε or a compound seems unavoidable, in spite of the repetition "while the guards were carrying torches, he was carrying her."

19. παυ]ςαμένου or sim. Either Ωλε . . [or the narrator.

ἐπὶ πύλα[: either dative or accusative might be restored. If παυ]ςαμένου is the correct supplement for the preceding word, we prefer a dative. But compare AT 2.31.4: ὡς δὲ παρῆμεν ἐπὶ τὰς πύλας .

Nightmare or Necromancy?

❖

The recoverable plot of P. Mich. inv. 3378 is minimal but intriguing. An apparition urges the narrator to kill himself. This he does, "cheerfully and gladly, as if killing an enemy." After the narrating-I is dead, he recognizes the apparition as one Severis.

There are not many situations in which a narrator may say "I died," but enough exist to situate this piece comfortably in the tradition of Greco-Roman narrative. The dead Elpenor, for example, appears in Odysseus's trip to the Underworld claiming: "I fell down from the roof, I broke my neck and my soul went down to Hades" (*Od.* 11.64–65). Or a character in Lucian's *Dialogues of the Dead* can remark: "I . . . died suddenly when the roof fell on me" (18.359). More often, however, the spirits of the dead return to tell their stories to the living. Tlepolemus describes his death to Charite (Apuleius 8.8); the baker in the same novel appears to his daughter and reveals the manner of his death (9.30).[1] Both of these are real ghosts, but they appear in the night in the manner of dreams.

C. Bonner briefly entertained the possibility that this piece belonged to a collection of real dream narratives, like those recorded at Epidauros or the Serapeion, but rightly rejected it on the grounds that the high quality of the papyrus and writing was not typical of such texts. Further, the startling description of the narrator as he kills himself as "beaming and cheerful" is a famous line from Demosthenes' *On the Crown* (18.323). Such literary pretensions are unparalleled in extant dream narratives from shrines.

It remains possible that this is a report of a dream in a novel, in which case it might portend something good for the dreamer. At least, Artemidoros notes that dreams of death may portend marriage for the unmarried and freedom for the enslaved (2.49–51), a principle also observed by the robbers' cook in *The Golden Ass.*[2] Leukippe's mother dreams that a naked barbarian is thrusting a sword into her daughter at the exact

---

[1] Stramaglia (1990) makes the same point independently and in greater detail.

[2] denique flere et vapulare et nonnumquam iugulari lucrosum prosperumque proventum nuntiant (4.27).

moment when across the hall Kleitophon is preparing to have intercourse with Leukippe.

The name Severis is quite common in Greco-Egyptian documents of the Roman period, but the presence of one Egyptian character does not establish even a fictional Egyptian setting, much less an Egyptian source for this narrative: Paapis, the Egyptian magician in *The Incredible Things beyond Thule*, roams the known world, and then some. Barns, who argued that Greco-Roman fiction should be explained by a theory of immigration from Egypt, believed the piece to have a Demotic antecedent, but provided no secure evidence (1956: 34). S. West attempted to strengthen his argument by citing as a parallel an episode from the second Setne-Kemwe story in which the wife of Setne narrates her own death by drowning, her magical resuscitation, and her subsequent entombment, versions of which appear written in Demotic Egyptian during the Ptolemaic period. But there is nothing about our piece that requires such an explanation, even if Greek precedents were lacking. That this fragment betrays "an abnormal preoccupation with the macabre," for which there "is no parallel in the extant novels" (West 1983: 56 and n. 7), rests on the false equation of the entire field of ancient novels with the one type (historical dramas) that survived whole. If this fragment gives us, in West's nice phrase, "a ghost telling a ghost story," it is right at home in the category of criminal-satiric fiction.

Bonner provided an earlier parallel even less compelling than West: the dream of the pharaoh Merneptah, to whom Ptah appears, handing him a sword with the words, "Banish thou your fearful heart from thee." This dream belongs to the category of *Königsnovelle*, a regular feature of Egyptian dream literature in which the gods give advice to the pharaoh, often as he begins his reign. But the point of our piece is suicide and recognition, not the reception of advice.

A. Henrichs suggests that the piece describes a *Scheintod* in a mystery ritual (1972: 49 n. 11). But it would not seem to be a trick to fool anyone, since the narrator committing suicide is "beaming and cheerful." At most it could be a ritual act of pretended suicide. The suggestion of a mystery context has a certain appeal; criminal fiction displays considerable interest in orgies and violence, locating them in a conspirational context of outlaws or of mystery initiates. In any case, a fake apparition and feigned suicide, like the pretended eunuch of *Iolaos* or the false execution of *Tinouphis*, would suit a criminal-satiric narrative, as would an Egyptian magician or charlatan.

The key element in this piece, on which the rest must have been built, is not the Egyptian name, nor the apparition as such, but the recognition. The narrator describes two coincident transitions: his passage from life to death and his immediate realization of the identity of the phantom. At the moment of fading or vanished consciousness, the obscurity surrounding the beckoning image is illuminated—an *Aha-Erlebniss*. "So it was Severis after all!"[3] For our narrator, something at this point fell into place, but as with Edwin Drood we will probably remain mystified forever.

[3] This is known in the trade as the "imperfect of sudden realization."

DESCRIPTION

P. Mich. inv. 3378 (= P^2 2629), measuring 8.1 × 7.4 cm, contains part of a column of seventeen lines, lines 9 through 16 of which are virtually complete, from a papyrus roll of excellent quality. The fragment retains no margins beyond a small portion on the lower right. The hand is upright, informal, and round, of a type commonly dated to the second century C.E. Writing is between notional lines, except for phi, which regularly projects above and below. There is some contrast between narrow and broad letters, which suggests a date toward the end of the century or even early in the third. The format, with between sixteen and twenty letters per line, was probably similar to that of P. Oxy. 3.454, a roll of Plato's *Gorgias* (= *GMAW²*, pl. 62). There are no marks of punctuation or lectional signs; iota adscript is omitted; a correction or supralinear addition appears in line 7. Elision is everywhere neglected by the scribe. The back is blank.

P. MICH. INV. 3378

- -

]λ̣α̣[. . . .

]αυτῳ ου[. . .

] . ϲαϲ ἀλλο[. .

4   ]ἡμέραν [. .

] ωϲ τότε ε[. .

]ονιωϲ . [

. . . . .]απ[.] . [ἐ]μαυτοῦ [. .

8   . .] τό ξίφοϲ . διένευεν [δὲ

κα[ὶ] τὸ εἴδωλον ὠθεῖν κα[ὶ

προτρέποντι ἐῴκει. φα[ι-

δρὸϲ οὖν καὶ γεγηθώϲ, ὥϲ-

12   περ πολέμιον κτείνων,

ἐμαυτὸν ἀποϲφάττω.

ἐπεὶ δὲ ἔπεϲον καὶ ἀπέ-

θανον, γνωρίζω τὸ εἴδω-

16   λον, ϲευῆριϲ ἦν καὶ παρα

] . [

- -

---

6. [δαιμ]ονίωϲ Zimm.   7.]μαυτο ᴴ[pap. Apparently a correction above the line

7–8. [ἕλ|κω] Körte.

self [
] other [
4   ] day [
] then [
] like a god(?) [
] myself [
8   ] the sword. And he also signaled [me],
the apparition, to thrust and
seemed to be urging [me] on.
So beaming and cheerful, as
12   if killing an enemy,
I cut my own throat.
And when I had sunk down and
died, I recognized the ap-
16   parition. It was Severis, and by

5–6. ἐ[φά|νη] or sim.?

7. εἵλκυϲ]α π[α]ρ' [ἐ]μαυτοῦ or sim.? Since elision is neglected elsewhere, one expects the longer π[α]ρὰ [ἐ]μαυτοῦ, for which space is insufficient. But these texts are not necessarily consistent. Bonner's ἀπ[ὸ ἐ]μαυτοῦ is one letter too short for the space, but not impossible.

8–9. διένευεν [δὲ] | κα[ὶ] τὸ εἴδωλον ὠθεῖν: "and the phantom was signaling to thrust"; the injunctive sense that νεύω occasionally has is not found in the compound, which is rare in any case.

10–11. φα[ι]|δρὸϲ οὖν καὶ γεγηθώϲ: a reminiscence, conscious or otherwise, of Dem. 18.323. It indicates that the author (and his intended audience) would have had a rhetorical education and some pretensions to literary refinement.

12. κτείνων: the verb is rare in the uncompounded form in prose, though it does occur.

Staphulos

❖

The insouciant little narrative of *Staphulos* bears a superficial resemblance to the story of Moses or Oidipos. An infant named Staphulos ("Bunch of Grapes") is exposed in a vineyard, discovered and brought to the king, named Dryas ("Oak Tree"), who accepts him and rears him as the heir apparent. His mother, Hippotis ("Horsewoman"), is from Sardis and is some distance from home. She seems either to have been seduced by Dryas or married to him, and to have borne the child Staphulos. Staphulos could equally well be Dryas's son or the product of a previous liaison. In any case, his mother abandons him in a vineyard and returns to Sardis, where she apparently remains while the boy is growing up. Why she abandons her son in such unorthodox fashion is not clear.

There are three named characters: Hippotis, Dryas, and Staphulos. Hippotis is unattested as a proper name, though it occurs as an epithet of Dawn in Triphiodoros (670) and of Hore in Nonnos (1.172). Lydians, however, were noted for horsemanship (see, e.g., Hdt. 1.79), so the name would not be inappropriate for a well-born Sardian woman. Although a number of mythological heroes are named Dryas, no one of them is obviously identifiable with this episode. And, of course, Dryas is the name of a shepherd in *Daphnis and Chloe*. Staphulos was a son of Ariadne, either by Dionysos, conceived after she had been abandoned by Theseus, or in some versions by Theseus himself (e.g., Plut. *Thes.* §20). He figures as a character (along with Botrys and Ampelos) in Nonnos's *Dionysiaka*, Books 18–19. Whether this Staphulos is meant to be identified with the son of Dionysos is unknown, though Sardis might be regarded as a potential Dionysiac link. Mt. Tmolos, situated near the city, was the site of Dionysiac worship (see, e.g., Eur. *Bacchae* 55), and its slopes were famous for their vineyards.

A variety of suggestions have been made about the nature of this narrative. Zimmermann concluded that this piece was not a romantic narrative, but a "mythologischen Traktat."[1] Two points are in his favor:

---

[1] Although there are certainly points of similarity in style with the compressed erotic anecdotes of Parthenios, his argument that the story is a variant of the story of Lurkos, known from Parthenios's erotic *pathēmata*, is not persuasive.

(1) the narrative progresses rather too rapidly, encompassing, as it does, seduction, birth and exposure of a child, the child's discovery and rearing as heir to the throne, the mother's return to Sardis as well as her learning about her son's fate, all within about one and one-half columns; and (2) the name Staphulos. A. Körte (1935: 282–83) suggested that it might be a Milesian tale. But we do not really know what a Milesian tale was like; certainly none of the witty and salacious stories that Apuleius labels *Milesiae fabulae* dip into mythological-symbolic realms, as this piece appears to do. Pfeiffer suggested that this might be a euhemerizing version of the Theseus-Ariadne-Dionysos story, no doubt because of the name Staphulos (Zimmermann 1934: 29). Most recently, Merkelbach (1988: 143 n. 15) has claimed that the fragment belongs to a "dionysischen Roman" (though without elaboration). It might also suit an hypothesis of a tragedy, like those found in Hyginus, but no such play is known.

Still, it is unwise to dismiss less tendentious narrative fiction as the correct location for this fragment. Although it is difficult to imagine a character named "Bunch of Grapes," who is exposed in a vineyard, figuring in a serious romantic narrative,[2] he might well do in comic fiction. Or in a more serious context, the rapidity of the narrative and the symbolic names—just waiting to be an aetiology for some agricultural phenomenon—would suit a digression, like those in Achilles Tatius on the origin of porphyry (2.11) or the river Styx (8.12) or those in Longos on the cry of the ringdove (1.27) or the syrinx (2.34).

---

[2] We note, however, that there are characters named Mesopotamia, Tigris, and Euphrates (her twin brothers) in Iamblichos's *Babyloniaka*, which would *seem* to have been serious. On this, see "Iamblichos," above.

DESCRIPTION

PSI 1220 (= *P*² 2625), measuring 19.0 × 13.5 cm, consists of three columns from the upper portion of a papyrus roll written along the fibers. Two columns are complete for about thirteen lines; the initial column retains between one and nine letters from line ends. It is impossible to determine how much is missing between columns; although very little would seem to be missing from the narrative, at this period columns of forty or more lines would not be untypical. An upper margin of around 3.0 cm survives, as well as rather narrower intercolumnia. The columns show a pronounced tilt to the right. The hand is of an upright, informal round type that is usually assigned to the second century C.E. Only beta and phi project beyond notional guide lines. Lectional signs include rough breathing (III.1), circumflex accent (III.5), and apostrophe (III.6) to mark elision in the formula οὐκ οἶδ᾽ ὅ τι, though elsewhere it is unmarked or *scriptio plena* is used. Two errors were corrected by an expunging dot (III.1, 6), another was corrected by altering the form in text (II.8). All corrections and lectional signs could be the work of the original scribe. The papyrus in general presents an attractive, well-wrought appearance. The back is blank.

COLUMN I	COLUMN II

COLUMN I

```
   ]οι Cτάφυλοc
   ]τι ἀτιμᾶν
   ] . αμε
4  ]οc ᾔτει
   ]ν και
   ] . ημα
   ]αcθαι ω-
8  ]πεπον-
   ]ν
   ]ντυγ-
   ]η
12 ]εἶπε
   Ἱ]ππότιc
- - - - - - - - - - -
```

COLUMN II

```
   παιδὸc Cταφύλου, κολακεύcαc
   γυναῖκα λάβῃ. τρύ[του δ'] ὅραμα
   ἰδοῦcα ἡ Ἱππότιc μετενόει
4  ἐφ' οἷc εὔξατο· ἐφοβεῖτο γὰρ περὶ
   τοῦ παιδὸc μή τιc κίνδυνοc
   τὸν ἐκτεθέντα καταλάβῃ. ὅ-
   μωc δ' οὖν φέρουcα δίδωcί τε
8  τᾱῖc ἀμπέλοιc τὸν Cτάφυλον,
   καὶ αὐτὴ εἰc τὰc Cάρδειc ἐπο-
   ρεύθη. τὸν μὲν οὖν Cτάφυλον
   ἀνευρὼν ὁ τῶν ἀμπέλων
12 φύλαξ φέρων δίδωcι τῷ Δρύ-
   αντι, ὁ δὲ μέγα τι χρῆμα του
   . . . . . . ] . [ . ] . νῃ[ . . ] . . . ε
   . . . . . . . . αὐ]τὸν πόθοc λαμ-
- - - - - - - - - - - - - - - - - - - - - - -
```

Col. I: 2. τειμᾱ pap.   6.] . ημα⟩ pap.   8. πεπο̄ pap.
Col. II: 1. κολακεύcα[c]α ed. pr., κολακεύcα[c]α⟨ν⟩ Zimm.   2. γυν, λαβη·
pap.?   τοῦ[το δ'] ὅραμα ed. pr., τὸ δ[ὲ παρ]όραμα Zimm.   3. ἡ pap.   6. λαβη·
pap.   8. τοιc corrected to ταιc, cταφυλον· pap.   10. ρευθηι· pap.

COLUMN I

] Staphulos
] to dishonor ?
]
4   ] s/he asked
] and
]
]
8   ] I/he suffered
]
] meet
]
12   ] s/he said
] Hippotis

COLUMN II

of the child Staphulos, flattering
the woman, he took her [in marriage?]. [But]
   recognizing
[his] plan, Hippotis changed her mind
4   about what she had prayed for. For she was
   afraid
for the boy, lest some danger
overtake him after he was exposed.
But nevertheless she brings and gives
8   Staphulos to the vineyards(?),
and she herself went to Sardis.
Now Staphulos
a guard of the vineyard discovered,
12   and brings and gives him to Dryas,
who [thinks ?] it is a great thing
. . .
. . .] desire took him

COLUMN III

εχωϲ δὲ ἐμακάριζεν αὐτὸν
καὶ εὐδαιμόνιζεν ἐπὶ [τῷ
παιδὶ καὶ τὴν βίαν τοῖϲ φιλτά-
4 τοιϲ ἐξεῖπεν καὶ ὅτι τοῦ μὲν
παιδὸϲ ἡττοῖτο, τὴν δὲ μητ[έ-
ρα αὐτοῦ οὐκ οἶδ᾽ ὅ τι παθὼν
ἀποϲτρέφεται. καὶ Ϲτάφυλοϲ
8 μὲν ἐν τοῖϲ βαϲιλείοιϲ τοῖϲ
Δρύαντοϲ τρέφεται, ὡϲ νεώ-
τεροϲ βαϲιλεύϲ. Ἱππότιϲ δὲ
ἐν ταῖϲ Ϲάρδεϲιν ἀκούϲ[αϲα
12 τὴν τοῦ παιδὸ[ϲ κα]τάϲ[ταϲιν
ὑπερ[ή]δετο καὶ[
ἐν Ϲάρ[δ]εϲιν [
...[..].ιϲ[
- - - - - - - - - - - - - - - - - - - -

Col. III: 1. νεχωϲ pap.; presumably the scribe wrote [ϲυ]|νεχωϲ, then altered it to [ϲυν]|εχωϲ
by adding ν at the end of the preceding line and deleting it here   αυτον
pap.   5. ηττοῖτο pap.   6. ραν, οιδ᾽ pap.   7. αποϲτρεφεται·
pap.   10. τεροϲ pap.   12. κα]τάϲ[ταϲιν Vitelli 1935.

Ceaselessly he congratulated himself
and called himself blessed because
of the boy, and spoke about the rape
4   to his friends and that
he was won over by the boy, but
his [the boy's] mother, for some obscure reason,
he is abandoning. And Staphulos
8   is reared in
Dryas's palace, as the
heir apparent. Meanwhile, Hippotis
in Sardis, when she heard
12   of her son's situation,
rejoiced greatly and
in Sardis . . .

COLUMN I

8–9. πέπον||[θα or sim.

COLUMN II

1. κολακεύϲαϲ : what ed. pr. takes to be a second α (restoring the word as κολακεύϲα[ϲ]α) is far more likely to be a tipped ϲ. The masculine participle then belongs with the subject of λάβῃ. The meaning is probably similar to Ch. 1.3.7: ὁ Χαιρέαϲ ἤρξατο κολακεύειν (sc. Kallirhoe), or again 1.13.8. Zimmermann's reading κολακεύϲα[ϲ]α⟨ν⟩ γυναῖκα λάβῃ = "[so that he might] marry(?) a woman because she is flattering [him]" must depend on Column III below, where Dryas complains about his treatment at Hippotis's hands.

2. λάβῃ : this may mean "receive in marriage" rather than seduce (see LSJ, s.v. λαμβάνω 2.1c). Although it is the obvious inference, it is not explicitly stated that Staphulos was the son of Dryas and Hippotis. If he was, then the fact that she seems to have remained in the area (with Dryas) until the child was born points to marriage rather than the usual one-night stand so productive of offspring in Greek mythology. It is also possible that Hippotis foisted the child of another man on Dryas. The subjunctive presumes an initial ἵνα or ἐάν.

τού[του δ'] ὅραμα : ed. pr.'s τοῦ[το δ'] ὅραμα requires an article (so Körte); Zimmermann's τὸ δ[ὲ παρ]όραμα seems too long. The meaning of ὅραμα here must be "plan" rather than "vision"; see LSJ, s.v. 2.

3. For the name Hippotis, see above, introduction.

7–8. φέρουϲα δίδωϲί τε | ταῖϲ ἀμπέλοιϲ : the sense is unclear. If Hippotis is merely hiding the child among the grapevines, one expects a preposition and a different verb. Below, the same construction (lines 12–13) has a personal object, which led Vitelli-Norsa (PSI) to conjecture that the grapevines were personified (i.e., "Ampeloi"), for which there is no independent evidence. Further, lines 10–12 certainly suggest that the guard discovered the child untended, not in the arms of female attendants of some type. We have considered the possibility that the mother puts the child to the vines—no doubt a fitting wet nurse for an infant named Staphulos—as if in parody of a mother putting a child to the breast, but the usual verb for this is τίθημι.

For this idiomatic use of the participle of φέρω with a finite verb, see LSJ, s.v. 10.2.

7–12. The variation between present and past tenses is not uncommon in narrative fiction, at all levels of sophistication. Compare, for example, Lollianos B1 verso 10–12; AT 3.15ff.; [Lucian] Asin. §2; Longos 1.2ff. (so Henrichs 1972: 116).

13–14. τοῦ[το νομί]ζ[ων] (Vitelli 1935) is attractive, but the visible trace appears to extend higher than ζ does elsewhere in this hand.

COLUMN III

3. τὴν βίαν : presumably this is "the rape" of Hippotis. But the precise meaning is unclear—it could range from elopement (carrying a woman off from her father's home) to forceable rape. κολακεύcας (above II.1) would seem to rule out the latter, however.

7. ἀποcτρέφεται : does this mean "divorce"?

11–13. ἀκούc[αcα . . . ὑπερ[ή]δετο : the latter word is rare in Attic prose. For the expression, cf. Hdt. 1.90: ταῦτα ἀκούων ὁ Κῦροc ὑπερήδετο, which is imitated almost verbatim by Xen. (*Kyr.* 3.1.31). Possibly this passage is a conscious imitation of Herodotos or Xenophon, a phenomenon familiar from Chariton; see Papanikolaou 1964: 10ff.

Theano

❖

Theano is a straightforward, rapidly moving narrative where traumatic events are baldly described, without the evocation of passion found in, for example, *Kalligone* or *Chione*. The unprepossessing style, lacking variation or ornament, is reminiscent of *Staphulos*, an equally puzzling narrative. In the span of twenty-four lines we learn that the child of a woman named Theano had been taken captive; she attempts to recover it, having been informed in a dream by "the goddess" what she should do. There are three or four characters named in the column: the mother, Theano; a woman who seems to be her companion, Eunike; Hist.., the father of her child; and Hippasos (if the reading is correct; see below, note 7–8), the child's captor.

Both Theano and Hippasos have Pythagorean connections: Theano was the wife of Pythagoras and the daughter of a Pythagorean; to her a small collection of letters in the Pythagorean corpus is attributed. Hippasos, according to Pausanius (2.13.2), was the great-grandfather of Pythagoras. But what significance—if any—this has for our narrative is uncertain. A more interesting Theano was the mother of Pausanias, who, according to Polyainos (8.51), when her son was taken captive, fled to the temple of Athene Chalchioikos as a suppliant. In Polyainos, however, there are no dreams but clever strategies. Other Theanos include the daughter of Antenor, who was a priestess of Athene in Troy (*Il.* 5.70, 6.298, 302, 11.224), and the wife of Metapontus, the king of Ikaria (Hyg. *Fab.* 186). The last suggests the possibility that we might have an hypothesis to a tragedy, but the events in this fragment cannot be easily integrated into Hyginus's epitome. In fact, none of the known Theanos compels identification with our character.

The original editors thought the fragment looked "rather like . . . some romance . . . or perhaps the work of a scholiast or mythologer." Lavagnini includes it in his collection though with a disclaimer that it seemed from its narrative brevity to be rather a commentary on the divine. Zimmermann concurred, labeling it "Traktat περὶ θείων" (1935: 175). But the evidence for this is slender. This small bit is replete with divine paraphernalia, but so too was the Hellenistic and Roman period—landscapes abounded with temples, and supplication to the gods, temple incubation, and dream lore were part of the popular culture. In the extant novels, such elements frequently served as convenient stimuli for the narrative action. Although this piece seems more representative of the anecdotes that appear in Parthenios, Polyainos, or Hyginus than of longer fictional narratives, the names and the narrative details suggest that there is more to the story than a simple recovery of the child after a dream sent by "the goddess" to demonstrate the power of the gods in men's lives.

DESCRIPTION

P. Oxy. 417 (= P^2 2474) consists of one large fragment (measuring 14.3 ×9.7 cm) and three, too insignificant to reproduce, from at least two columns of a papyrus roll. Column I lacks upper, left, and lower margins, but preserves an intercolumnium of ±2.0 cm. Column II holds twenty-four lines, the majority complete, with a generous lower margin of ±4.0 cm. There are between fifteen and twenty letters per line. The hand is a rather small upright of the informal round type, which ed. pr. placed in the early third century C.E. (The parallel suggested in ed. pr.—P. Oxy. 404—is a third-century Severe style so different from 417 that it cannot have been intended. Probably a simple error was involved. The correct parallel was probably P. Oxy. 410—"a neat, rather small, round uncial hand"—which appears on the same plate as 404.) Punctuation includes high and middle stops and what appear on the broken surface to have been paragraphi at II.12 and 18; tremata occur on ἱκέτις, II.11; iota adscript was not written in II.20 (ηει = ᾔει), but it may have been added erroneously to the genitive Ἀμφιαρέω at II.22–23, though note that it does not appear on Θεανώ at II.5. Such hypercorrect iotas are not uncommon, even in carefully written texts. There are no errors or corrections (unless τὸ at II.21 = τὸν; see below, app. crit.), but two itacisms (II.4 and 20). The scribe observes elision at I.4, II.12, 16, and 21, but not at II.5 or 9. The text itself does not avoid hiatus in II.23 (if the reading is correct) and 24. Though the papyrus surface is now in poor condition, the impression from the hand and the ample margins is that of a well set out, carefully prepared roll. The back is blank.

COLUMN I   COLUMN II

```
- - - - - - - - - - - - -              - - - - - - - - - - - - - - - - - - - - - -
]κ[ . ] . [ . ]κ . . η                                      ] . .
]μενη καθ᾽ ἑκα-                                             ]νεν·
]ν ἀπὸ τοῦ ϲ                           [ . ]υτ[ . . . . . . ] . [ . . . . τὴ]ν
4   ]ᾳ· ὡϲ δ᾽ οὐδὲν        4   Εὐνίκην ἐποιήϲατο·
]νω τοὺϲ μὲν                            ἦν δὲ αὐτὴ ἡ Θεανὼ μή-
]                                       τηρ τ[ο]ῦ παιδὸϲ τοῦ Ἰϲτ . .
]ϲ                                      ὃν [τῶ]ν ϲκυθῶν ὁ ἱππα-
8   ]ϲκα                  8   ϲ[ . ]ϲ ᾳ[ἰχ]μάλωτον εἰλήφει.
]ᾳι                                     ἁρπαγέντοϲ δὲ αὐτοῦ οὐ-
]κη                                     κ ἐνεγκοῦϲα τὴν συμφο-
]εν                                     ρὰν ἱκέτιϲ ἐκ[ . . . ] . [κ]α-
12  ]ᾳειδε                 12  τ᾽ ὄναρ τῆϲ θεοῦ· [χ]ρόνον
]ειν                                    δ[ὲ . ] . [ . ] . [ . . . . . ] . [ . ]ενετρε-
]μοϲ·                                   ψαν· τελ[ε]υταῖον δὲ κε-
]ην                                     λεύει αὐτὴν ἡ θεὸϲ ἀπαλ-
16  ]κευ                   16  λάττεϲθαι τὴν ἐπ᾽ Ἀθή-
- - - - - - - - - - - -                 να[ϲ] ὡϲ [δ]ὴ τ[ὸ]ν πα[ῖ]δα
                                        ἀπ[ο]ληψομένη· ἡ δὲ πε-
                                        [ριχ]αρὴϲ οὖϲα παραλαβοῦ-
                       20  [ϲα τ]ὴν Εὐνίκην ᾔει
                                        [τὴ]ν ἐπ᾽ Α[θή]ναϲ· ἐπί τε
                                        [Ὠ]ρωπὸν καὶ τὸ το[ῦ Ἀμ-]
                                        [φι]αρέω ἱερ[ὸν . . ] . . [ . . . ]
                       24  [ . . ] ἐπεὶ ἐγέν[ετ]ο τ[ . . . . . ]
```

Three very small fragments have not been reproduced.

Col. I: 4.]ᾳ· pap.   14.]μοϲ· pap.

Col. II: 2.]νεν· pap.   3. τὴ]ν Zimm.   4. ευνεικην pap., read Εὐνίκην   εποιη ϲατο· pap.   5. αὐτὴ Lav., αὕτη Zimm.   6. ιϲτ . . pap., Ἰϲτ⟨ρ⟩ου Zimm. 7. [τῶ]ν ed. pr., [μετ]ὰ Calderini (in EGFP)   11. ἵκετιϲ pap.   εγ[έϲτ]η ed. pr., ἐϰ[άθιζε]ν Zimm.   12. θεου· pap.   13. δ[ὲ . τ]ὰ [ἐνύπνια Lav., δ᾽ [οὐ]κ [ὀλίγον οἱ θεοὶ οὐκ ?] Cald., δ[ὲ ἱ]ϰ[έτειαι (sic) οὐδ]ὲν Zimm.   13–14.]εγετρε|ψαν· pap.,]εγε- |τρεψαν ed. pr. in error,]εν ἔτρε|ψαν Zimm., ἐπέτρε|ψαν Lav.   16. ἐπ᾽ Wil., εἰϲ Fuhr   16–17. [Ἀθή]|ναϲ Lav.   17. ὡϲ [δ]ὴ ed. pr., ὡϲ ἔ[νθα] Zimm. 18. απ[.]ληψομενη· pap.   21.]ναϲ· pap.   22–23. τὸ το[ῦ Ἀμ|[φι]αρέω{ι} ἱερ[ὸν ed. pr., τὸ⟨ν⟩ το[ῦ Ἀμ|[φι]αρέω νε[ὼν] Cald.   23.]αρεωι ἱερ[pap.? 23–24. ἡ] Θ[εα|νὼ] Zimm.

4   . . . made Eunike;
       Theano herself
       was the mother of the child of Hist..,
       whom . . . of the Skythians
8   had taken prisoner.
       When he was seized,
       she did not accept the grievous loss
       but took her stand as a suppliant, in obedience
12   to a dream from the goddess. For a time
       . . . ,
       but finally
       the goddess orders her to depart
16   along the road leading to Athens,
       with a promise that she would certainly
       recover her child.
       Overjoyed, and taking
20   Eunike along with her,
       she proceeded to Athens.
       Oropos and the
       temple of Amphiareos, . . .
24   since . . . became . . .

COLUMN II

3. [.]υτ[: αὕτη or sim.? Punctuation dictates that the phrase run only from [.]υτ[to ἐποιήcατο. "This one made Eunike her [companion, servant or sim.?]." The subject of ἐποιήcατο is probably Theano.

3–4. τὴ]ν | Εὐνείκην: the definite article seems *de rigueur* with proper names in this piece. Eunike occurs as the name of a Nereid and as a nymph in Theokritos 13.45.

5. Θεανὼ: see above introd.

5–6. μή|τηρ τ[ο]ῦ παιδὸc τοῦ Ἱcτ . . : the word order seems to require the translation "mother of the child of Hist..," rather than "mother of the child, Hist..," as Calderini and Lavagnini have it.

Ἱcτ . . : the final letters are broken, and Ἱcται is as likely as Ἱcτου, in which case at least one syllable must have been omitted. For example, the scribe may have intended Ἱcταί⟨ου⟩ (a variant of Ἱcτιαῖοc), but omitted ου through haplography with the following ὃν. Kerényi (1962: 64 n. 80) connects the name with the region Histiaiotis in Euboia, suggesting a route for Theano's journey from Euboia through Oropos to Athens.

7. [τῶ]ν Cκυθῶν ὁ ἱππα|c[.]c : the papyrus appears to have ὁ Ἵππα|c[o]c, which is presumably a proper name. (For example, the Mytilenean general in Longos 3.1.2 is so named.) Cκυθῶν is preceded by either the definite article or a preposition. If [τῶ]ν Cκυθῶν, then the proper name following is anomalous. Ed. pr. attempted to solve the problem by reading the title ὁ ἵππα[ρ]|χ[o]c, but concluded that the traces did not suit. If μετ]ὰ Cκυθῶν, the word order seems unnatural. Does this mean "Hippasos, in the company of some Skythians, had taken the child captive"? Or does it mean, "Hippasos had taken the child captive as well as some Skythians"? On the whole, we are inclined to regard the text as corrupt and the correct reading to be [τῶ]ν Cκυθῶν ὁ ἵππα[ρ]|χ[o]c. In any event, this appears to be a military operation rather than a kidnapping.

11. ἱκέτιc ἐκ[. . .] . : the verb is a puzzle. Either ἐγένετο or Zimmermann's ἐκάθιζεν would be too long; ed. pr.'s ἐγ[έcτ]η is paleographically possible, but lacks parallel.

11–12. [κ]α|τ' ὄναρ: while this expression is rare in classical prose and was condemned by Phrynichos, it does occur with the meaning of "in accordance with a dream" in Ailios Aristides, so LSJ, s.v. ὄναρ II. See Hld. 2.16.2 for κατὰ τὸ ὄναρ.

12. τῆc θεοῦ: who is the goddess? Zimmermann suggests Artemis κουροτρόφοc. In AT 7.12.4, Artemis appears to Sostratos in a dream to tell him where he might find his daughter; in Hld. 3.11 Artemis and Apollo appear to Kalasiris. Since Theano's ultimate destination is Athens, the goddess might also be Athene.

13–14.]ενετρε|ψαν: the available space limits the options here: ἐνέτρεψαν can

442

mean either "alter" or "shame," and both meanings require an object, for which the space seems insufficient. ἐπέτρεψαν does not suit the traces; ἔτρεψαν, however, permits the preceding]εν to belong to an object or an adverb (e.g., οὐδὲν). The subject could be either Theano and Eunike, who have taken up positions as suppliants in a temple, or a word (now lost) at the beginning of the line. Presumably Zimmermann's restoration ἱ]κ[έτειαι (*sic*) οὐδ]ὲν ἔτρε|ψαν ("supplications accomplish nothing") adopts the latter course, but one might also try ἱ]κ[ε]τ[είαι ο]ὐ[δ]εν ἔτρε|ψαν ("by supplication they accomplish nothing"). For the Attic form ἱ]κ[ε]τ[εῖαι, compare ἀπαλλάττεcθαι below, lines 15–16.

16–17. τὴν ἐπ' Ἀθή|να[c] : sc. ὁδόν.

17–18. ὡc [δ]ὴ τ[ὸ]ν πα[ῖ]δα | ἀπ[ο]ληψομένη : the child must therefore be in Athens. If originally carried off by a Skythian as part of war booty, the child could have been sold into slavery to someone who either lived in or eventually traveled to Athens.

21–23. ἐπί τε | [Ὠ]ρωπὸν καὶ τὸ το[ῦ Ἀμ|[φι]αρέω ἱερ[ὸν : the Amphiareion at Oropos was famous, and associated with prophecy, though no particular goddess was connected with it (Paus. 1.34.1–5). If Oropos was not a side trip, a route from Oropos to Athens suggests that the women were traveling along the northern coast of Attika, possibly beginning their journey in Euboia, Aulis, or Kalchis.

The Festival

❖

This fragment appears to be a prose narrative of some kind written in the Attic dialect in a very formal, almost affected style. An unusually high number of rare or poetic words, strings of noun-adjective units with little syntactical variation, and an opacity of expression adorn—or indeed, overwhelm—the relatively straightforward events that are being described. These include an animal sacrifice, followed by an address by an officiating priest or a choral leader to begin the music: basic ingredients of a Greek festival. The following shape can be discerned:

line 1: the participants (or spectators) have taken their positions;
lines 2–5: description of the sacrifice and fire on the altar;
lines 6–8: prayers for the community are spoken;
lines 9–16: the hierophant(?) speaks to lead off the music and/or dancing.

Because of the language and apparent subject matter, the original editor thought this might be a comic chorus within a commentary, but there is little about it that looks like commentary, and no discernible metrical patterns emerge from the portions one might most easily imagine to have been poetry. Subsequently, Cazzaniga argued that it was an ekphrasis within a fictionalized narrative—a description of a rustic festival to Pan. We are inclined to agree with his basic premise: this is the kind of elaborate and artificial description of an event beloved by rhetoricians and epistolographers, and employed by Lucian and the Philostrati as well as the novelists. On our reading, however, the sacrifice and attendant performance are not necessarily rustic; the victim is of the bovine variety, not the kid or goat normally associated with Pan, and reed pipes may have been mentioned only to be dismissed. Beyond this, the text presents little more than the traditional components of a Greek festival, without anything sufficiently distinct to help locate the occasion.

Description

PSI inv. 516 (= P^2 2902) measures 11.2 × 9.0 cm. The fragment consists of ends of sixteen lines from one column and abraded traces of beginnings of lines from the next. The top is broken off, but there is a generous lower margin preserved (2.0–3.0 cm). Writing is across the fibers in a practiced, sloping Severe style that probably belongs to the middle or later part of the third century C.E. Letter spacing is uneven, and the occasional gaps are probably not significant. No lectional signs appear, and iota adscript does not seem to have been written. Insofar as it is possible to judge, hiatus has been avoided.

Although the previous editors do not seem to have noticed, a number of the suggested supplements for lines 11–16 produce a more or less satisfactory text, given the obscurity of language with which the piece seems to have been written. Further, these supplements will produce the tall, narrow column that, on the whole, was rather common for this period and handwriting style. To judge from Column II, left edges were slightly uneven, so estimates of missing letters may easily be off by one.

COLUMN I

COLUMN II

```
[......]χ[ . ]ρων τετ[αγμένων]
[......] εὐcύμβολα μυ[κή]μα-
[τα ...]ạν cφάδαcμα εὔτακτον
4 [.....ε]ὐχροοῦν cπλάγχνον
[.....]οι πῦρ ἀίδιον καον..
[.....] . [ . ] εὐθυφερηc εὐχὰc
[.....] . καὶ πανδήμουc εc-
8 [.... ἐ]πὶ ἀκοὰc ἀπλανεῖc
[προαγο]ρεύων· "ἀνῴδιον δ'," ἔ-
[φη, "ἐπιτ]ήδειον ἐπὶ ἱεροῖc τε-
[λείοιc ἐ]πιφέρωμεν οὐκ ἄcη-
12 [μον· .. κ]ạὶ τρητοῦ δόνακοc
[καὶ καλ]άμου φθόγγῳ προccυμ-
[βάλωμε]ν κρουμάτων ἐμμέ-
[λειαν κα]ὶ ἀγωγὴν πνεύματοc
16 [......]μένου, ἀλλὰ γλώττῃ
```

```
[...] . . [
...αν [
4 πραγ . [
προχει[
αξε .. [
... [
8 επιθ[
ρεπι .. [
κν ... [
εὐcυμβ[
12 τητα δε[
ενθα .. [
θειον .. [
τοcτ ... [
16 μα .... [
```

Bartoletti's conjectures are to be found in Cazzaniga; Kenneth Dover's are from personal communication.

Col. I: 1. χ[ω]ρῶν (sic) τετ[αγμένων] Bartoletti, χ[ο]ρῶ[ι] τετ[αγμένῳ? Terzaghi, χ[ώ]ρων Dover   2. μυ[κήμα]τα Terz., μυ[cτήρ]ιạ Cazz.   5. κάọντεc Cazz.   6. ευθυ φερηc pap., read εὐθυφερεῖc Terz.   7–8. ἐc|[χάραc], ἐc|[μούc, or [ἐc|[τίαc] Terz.   9. [προαγο]ρεύων Dover, [χο]ρεύων Bart., [νιγλα]ρεύων Terz.   10. [ἐπιτ]ήδειον Terz. επιϊεροιc pap.   11–12. ἄcη|[μον] Dover, ἀcή|[μωc] Cazz.   13–14. προc-cυμ|[βάλωμε]ν Dover, προccυμ|[φωνεῖ]ν or πρὸc cυμ|[φωνία]ν Terz.   14–15. ἐμμέ|[λεια] Cazz., ἐμμε|[λῶν] Terz.   15. [κα]ὶ Cazz., [δ]ι' Terz.   16. [κεκαθαρ]μένου Dover.

]
] well-omened lowings
] propitious spasm (of the sacrificial animal)
4   ] auspiciously colored entrails
] eternal fire burning
] prayers
] and for the whole community
8   for] steadfast ears
[proclaiming]: "a performance without song," he
[said], "suitable for holy
[rites], let us bring forth without blemish;
12   [. . .] with sound of perforate pipe
and hollow reed let us join together
modulation of sounds
and impulse of [. . .] breath,
16   but with tongue [of flute?]

COLUMN I

1. χ[.]ρων τετ[αγμένων]: the previous editors have restored χ[ο]ρῶν, and along with it [χο]ρεύων at line 9 below, on the supposition that the lower section of the column describes choral activity of some kind. The lacuna is large enough for either ω or ο, but lack of context makes restoration uncertain.

2–5. For the situation described in these lines, cf. Burkert 1985: 112–13: "Sacrifice . . . is followed with heightened attention; here everything is a sign: whether the animal goes willingly to the altar and bleeds to death quickly, whether the fire flames up swiftly and clearly. . . . The inspection of the livers of the victims developed into a special art: how the various lobes are formed and coloured is eagerly awaited and evaluated at every act of slaughter." Note that events are listed in correct temporal order—bellowing of the live animal, its death struggle, evaluation of entrails, and finally the burning of the offerings. But the accumulation of nouns and adjectives are static items in an inventory, not reported as actions in the process of being performed by an officiant.

2–3. μυ[κή]μα|[τα]: Terzaghi's conjecture is almost certainly correct, though the word cannot be fitted into one line. Cazzaniga's μυ[cτήρ]ια is too long for the lacuna. We take the phrase to describe the bellowing of the sacrificial animal, rather than inarticulate mumblings of the chorus (Terzaghi 1956: 384). μύκημα (and its cognate verb μυκάομαι) normally describes the bellowing of bulls (or sometimes lions), but it is not appropriate for the bleating of goats or kids (see LSJ s.v.).

A slightly less likely possibility is μνήματα. This rare word means "initiation." See Steph. Lex.

3. cφάδαcμα εὔτακτον: Dover suggests that this refers to the quivering of the sacrificed animal who indulges in no unseemly death throes; Cazzaniga (1956: 54) takes it to describe the movements of the dancers' bodies in harmony. The word occurs only once before (see Lampe s.v.), but its cognate verb cφαδάζω is commonly used to describe the death struggle (see LSJ s.v.).

4. ε]ὔχροουν cπλάγχνον: consultation of the entrails was a standard part of the sacrificial ritual. They are suitably colored, hence the omens are auspicious. See Burkert above, note 2–5.

5.]οι πῦρ ἀίδιον καον. . : presumably appropriate parts of the sacrifice are burned on the fire. Previous editors read κάοντος, but there is insufficient room for τ. More likely κᾶον. At the end of the line, possibly ὡc.

6–8. There are a number of ways to restore: (1) nominative adjective + accusative noun (εὐθυφερῆc εὔχαc), (2) accusative adjective + noun + another adjective (εὐθυφερεῖc εὐχὰc . . . καὶ πανδήμουc), or (3) two accusative adjective + noun units (εὐθυφερεῖc εὐχὰc . . . πανδήμουc εc-).

6. εὐθυφερηc: either a nominative describing the posture or attitude of the sup-

448

pliant, or an itacism for εὐθυφερεῖc, which would then be accusative plural modifying εὐχὰc = "prayers that go straight to their mark."

The adjective is quite rare: it occurs at Plato *Laws* 7.815b to describe a dance position.

7. καὶ πανδήμουc εc-: previous editors have attempted to supplement εc- as a noun, but if only five or six letters are missing from the beginning of the column, we are inclined to take πανδήμουc with the preceding εὐχὰc and restore a verb, e.g., ἔc|[τηκε], ἔc|[πευδε], ἔc|[πειcε], or sim.

8. ἀκοὰc ἀπλανεῖc: the phrase ἀπλανέεccιν ... ἀκουαῖc occurs elsewhere only in Nonnos, both in the *Dionysiaka* (1.4.251) and in his poetic version of the gospel of John (5.151), where it seems to mean "steadfast ears" or "hearing." Before it the traces suit ἐ]πί but not καί. We take this phrase to belong with the following participle, "proclaiming for steadfast ears." Thus lines 5–8 might be supplemented, e.g., ὡc | [δὲ ηὔξα]τ[ο] ... εὐχὰc | [πολλὰ]c καὶ πανδήμουc ἔc|[τηκε ἐ]πὶ ἀκοὰc ἀπλανεῖc | [προαγο]ρεύων = "When he had [prayed ... many] prayers on behalf of the whole city, [he stands], proclaiming for steadfast ears. . . ."

9. ἀνῳδιον: otherwise unattested, though ἄνῳδοc ("songless") occurs as an adjective in Arist. *Ha* 488a34. The meaning must be either a tune without vocal accompaniment or, as Cazzaniga understands it (comparing Longos 2.37), a dance without song (or pantomime).

11–12. Whether we restore ἀcήμωc or ἄcημον, there is space for two or three letters in the lacuna. [νῦν κ]αὶ or [μὴ κ]αὶ (see below, note 16)?

12–13. τρητοῦ δόνακοc | [καὶ καλ]άμου φθόγγῳ: τρητοὺc δόνακαc are pan pipes in Theokritos's epigram 2.3 (imitated by Eratosthenes Scholastikos, *AP* 6.78); κάλαμοc is a reed pipe associated with Pan in Eur. *IT* 1126 and *El.* 702. Cazzaniga inferred from the presence of these instruments that a rustic festival was being described, but pan pipes are solo, not choral instruments, and would be more appropriate for private performance.

13–14. προccυμ|[βάλωμε]ν: the verb is rare; it occurs elsewhere only in the middle.

14–15. κρουμάτων ἐμμέ|[λειαν]: κροῦμα is the sound produced when strings are strummed or a player blows into a wind instrument; ἐμμέλεια is a harmony, tune, or even a type of dance (for this last meaning, see Plato *Laws* 7.816b). The sense here appears to be "modulation of sounds (or strumming)," possibly meaning no more than "tune." Cf. AT 8.6.6: ἡ τοῦ κρούματος ἁρμονία.

15–16. ἀγωγὴν πνεύματοc | [. . . . . . .]μένου: the initial push of air through the wind instrument. A variety of participles will suit: Dover suggests [κεκαθαρ]μένου = "clear"; equally possible is [ἠθροιc]μένου = "gathered."

It is unclear whether the passage is contrasting the strumming of strings with the push of air through a wind instrument, or whether the two phrases are meant to describe different aspects of wind instruments (i.e., tune and initial intake of air, which functions as the downbeat).

16. ἀλλὰ γλώττῃ: the "tongue" is probably that of a flute or other reed instrument rather than the human voice (so Cazzaniga 1956: 55), and its case is surely dative to parallel φθόγγῳ above, line 13 (where iota adscript is not written). Note that both γλώττῃ and φθόγγῳ are used of the human voice.

ἀλλὰ suggests that a negative should be restored above, line 12—μὴ καὶ? The thought will then be that they should *not* employ the sounds of rustic instruments like the pan pipes and reed flute, but more appropriate instruments (like *auloi*?).

Inundation

———— ❖ ————

The intriguing piece in P. Michael. 4 presents an intricate and fanciful description of the annual flood of the Nile in the vicinity of Kanopos, coupled with a lyric account of the generation of new life that results. The geographic details have led editors to suppose that the piece was either scientific or historical in intent, and Merkelbach (1958: 114) even assigned it to Hekataios of Abdera, who is thought to have included a geographical section in his book on Egypt. But Oswyn Murray and Stephanie West, following him, have pointed out that the preciosity of the language is hardly in keeping with scientific writing. We agree. The apparent personification of the river (lines 17–19), the use of rare or unique words, and the elaborate and difficult sentence structure do not find their parallels in geographic treatises, so much as in the more rhetorically enhanced categories of prose.

Although Santoni (1991: 119) acknowledges its rhetorical excesses, she argues from the language of the piece that it must belong to the allegorizing tradition of Stoic philosophy.[1] This, coupled with what she considers to be a specialized knowledge of Egypt, inclines her to Chairemon of Alexandria, the Greco-Egyptian tutor of Nero, who was said to have written a book on Egypt. Her arguments do not persuade. Descriptions of the Nile flood, specific locations like Kanopos and Thonis, and even the devices used to measure the river's height hardly constitute knowledge so specialized that it could not appear in a fictional format. (Heliodoros is proof of this.) None of the rare words employed to describe the flood are technical terms. To the extent that they occur at all, they are to be found in well-known Greek authors of the Second Sophistic, but not in the documentary papyri, nor, for that matter, in what purport to be the fragments of Chairemon. The real question is to what extent the style must belong to an allegorizing Stoic tradition, the appropriation of that tradition by another fictional category, or to pretentious literary embellishment. Santoni herself cites Achilles Tatius 2.14, a speech containing considerable geographical description coupled

---

[1] I am grateful to A. Stramaglia for calling Santoni's edition to my attention.

with an allegorizing explanation of an oracle, in which "Hephaistos" equals "fire."

Of course, descriptions of the Nile have been part of Greek prose writing from at least the time of Herodotos. Isokrates, for example, waxing lyric in the *Busiris*, claims that the Nile has given Egyptians a godlike power over the irrigation of their land, freeing them from the tyranny of storms and droughts (§§13–14), and Diodoros opens his account of Egypt with an excursus on the Nile (1.10ff.). Ailios Aristides devotes an entire speech to the subject (36 Lenz-Behr), and Menander Rhetor mentions the Nile along with a few other rivers as a topic suitable for inclusion in a *lalia* or "chat" (2.392.26 Russell-Wilson). None of these writers, however, display the willful structural complexity of this scrap. The Greek novels provide further parallels—Achilles Tatius personifies the Nile (4.12), and Heliodoros digresses upon it on two separate occasions (2.28, 9.22).

The use of "it seems to me" (I.22) and the imperative "Come!" (II.7) almost certainly give us an ego-narrator; the "daughter" (II.12) could be his audience. Together these suggest that the Nile was not the main focus of this piece, but that it formed the subject of a digression or an ekphrasis within a larger narrative. Though novels are an obvious choice in which to situate this passage, it is also easy to imagine that it belongs in a narrative like the descriptions of paintings in Philostratos's *Imagines*, where the observers regularly stand outside the picture under scrutiny.

DESCRIPTION

P. Michael. 4 (= P^2 2271) measures 24.5 ×12.5 cm. It consists of one thirty-five-line column retaining considerable upper and lower margins (2.5 to 3.2 cm) and beginnings of twelve lines from the next column. There are also two small scraps, one of which Merkelbach (1958: 113) has located toward the bottom right of the first column, though Santoni (1991: 102–3 n. 9) questions the placement. We have tentatively accepted this, but not all his readings. The writing is along the fibers, with the column showing a pronounced tilt to the right; the back is blank. The hand is a rounded capital of medium size, not unlike $GMAW^2$, pl. 62, a text of Plato's *Gorgias*, assignable to the second century C.E. Punctuation consists of high and middle stops as well as paragraphi. In the right margin, written against I.2 and II.2 and 15, is the symbol χᵖ (= χρηϲτόν, χρῆϲιϲ, or χρήϲιμον), used by scholars to mark a passage for special attention. For a discussion of this siglum, see $GMAW^2$, pp. 14–15. Hiatus appears to have been avoided throughout, and iota adscript was not written. There are two itacisms (I.14, 19).

INUNDATION

COLUMN I

ζῴδιον, νη[. . .]βιοτευον, ἕ-
βδομον Αἰγ[υπτί]οιϲ ἱεροῖϲ
γράμμαϲιν, ὃ κατὰ ψῆφον
4 ἀναπεϲϲευόμενον ἐπιχω-
ρίαν τεϲϲαρεϲκαίδεκα δύ-
ναται πήχει[ϲ] · ὁ γ[ὰρ] ποταμὸϲ
αἱρόμενοϲ οἰκουμέν[η] Δή-
8 μητρα πομπεύει πολλ[ὴ]ν
ἐπιλιμνάζων τῶι Κανώβῳ
καὶ ἀναχεόμενοϲ πολ-
λὰ πεδία ϲυνωμβρεῖτο πί-
12 δαξι καὶ πολλοῖϲ ἕλεϲιν ἕ-
κολλα τόν τε Κάνωβον ὄν-
τα νηϲῖδα καὶ αὐτὸν Θῶνιν
λεγόμενον · τριάκοντά τε
16 ϲταδίοιϲ περιγραφόμενον
Αἰγυπτίοιϲ ἐδάφεϲιν ἡϲπά-
ϲατο καὶ κατὰ πρόχωϲιν
μελαίνηϲ ἰλύοϲ ϲυνύφη-
20 νεν · νῦν δ᾽ ἐϲτὶν ἀκρωτήριον ἀμφοτερίζον Ποϲει-
δῶνι καὶ Νείλῳ. δοκεῖ δέ μοι
περὶ τὸν τόπον ἀνθρώπει-

COLUMN II

- - - - -
δ[
[
[
4 . [
. [
ξατο[
ραϲ θυ[
8 ταϲδ[
αποτι[
του κα[
ἄγε γὰρ[
12 γατερ[
ενθα[
γ[
. [
16 . [
. [
ηφα[
λεγ[
20 νω[

Col. I: 1. νή[ϲῳ or νῆ[ϲον ἐ]βιότευον S. West, νή[ρῳ] or νή[κτῳ] βιότευον (sic) Roberts (in ed. pr.)   2. χ^ρ (or sim.) appears to have been written in the left margin (also in Col. II.2, 15)
3. ψηφον⟩pap.   6. ναται ·πηχ^{ει}[.] pap.   8. μητρα pap. 12–13. ἕ|κολλα pap., Merk. deletes   14. νηϲειδα pap.   15. λεγόμενον· pap.   16. περιγραφο μενον· pap.   19. ειλυοϲ pap.   22. δωνι, νειλω· pap.
Col. II: 18. ηφα pap.

454

. . . the sign, living

[———] being the seventh in the system of Egyptian

hieroglyphs, which

4   in the local method of calculation

marks fourteen

cubits. For the river

in its rising conveys to the inhabited land

8   much Mother Earth

by enswamping Kanopos

and flooding over it,

it was wont to deluge many acres

12   with its fountains, and with its many marshes

to join together both Kanopos

(which is an island) and the place called Thonis

itself. An area thirty

16   stades in circumference

it embraces with Egyptian soil

and weaves together with a piling up

of black mud.

20   Now this area is a promontory

with Poseidon (= ocean) and Nile on either side.

It seems to me that

around this area human

COLUMN I

24 οϲ π[ρῶ]τ̣ον ἀνατεῖλαι̣ τροφή·
    π[ολλο]ῖ̣ϲ γὰρ ἰκμαζομένη
    .[.]ε.[..]ϲ ἡ γῆ καὶ τὸ κ̣α̣[ῦμα]
    ἐντρέφει ῥίζαϲ ἀπαλ[ὰϲ]
28 καὶ γλυκὺν ἀνιείϲαϲ χυμ[όν,]
    ὅθεν καὶ βουνόμο̣ν τὸ ἔ[δα-]
    φοϲ, ἀφ᾽ ὧν γάλα δαψι̣λ̣[ὲϲ]
    ......]οιτη·ἐὰν δ̣ὲ κα[
32 ......]ι̣ ὑπὲρ βοταν...
    ......]η ταύταϲ ελε̣.φο[
    ....]νει ϲυν οικο[
    ......]εύϲατο καὶ κρατη̣[

---

25. π[ο̣λ̣λ̣ο̣ι̣]ϲ Drescher   26. κ[αῦμα Santoni   29–30. βουνόμο̣ν τὸ ἔ[δα]|φοϲ
Merk.

COLUMN I

24   nourishment came into being;
for the land being dried out by many
[——] and the [heat]
nourishes many tender shoots, and
28   exuding a sweet odor,
whence the soil even supports cattle,
from whose plentiful milk

. . .

32   beyond fodder. . . .

COLUMN I

1–6. We adopt the interpretation of S. West, following Roberts's suggestion (Crawford 1955: 11) that this is a description of a nilometer, the calibration of which is supposed to be in hieroglyphs, i.e., Αἰγ[υπτί]οιϲ ἱεροῖϲ | γράμμαϲιν. The seventh mark (ζῴδιον ἕβδομον) is equivalent to fourteen cubits. Compare Hld. 9.22.3–4: τὸ νειλομέτριον ... γραμμαῖϲ δὲ ἐκ πηχυαίου διαϲτήματοϲ κεχαραγμένον.

1. For the term ζῴδιον used of a hieroglyphic letter, West cites Sch. T on *Iliad* 6.168: ϲήματα λυγρά· τινὲϲ δὲ ὡϲ παρ᾽ Αἰγυπτίοιϲ ἱερὰ ζῴδια, δι᾽ ὧν δηλοῦται τὰ πράγματα.

νη[...]βιοτευον: the phrase is puzzling and has occasioned considerable debate. S. West would restore νή[ϲῳ or νῆ[ϲον ἐ]βιότευον, arguing that the original sentence read something like "[When the water reaches this] mark, they were living on an island." This very sentiment is expressed in Isokrates' *Busiris* § 14: διὰ τὴν τοῦ ποταμοῦ δύναμιν νῆϲον οἰκοῦϲιν· κύκλῳ γὰρ αὐτὴν περιέχων καὶ πᾶϲαν διαρρέων.... But νῆ[ϲον is too long, and νή[ϲῳ would introduce hiatus, which elsewhere in this text is avoided. Further, while its word order is complex, there are no examples of the extreme hyperbaton that would result from ζῴδιον, νή[ϲῳ ἐ]βιότευον, ἕβδομον κτλ. Even if the phrase were intended as an interjection, the placement would be odd; moreover, one would expect νήϲῳ γὰρ ἐβιότευον. Therefore, we are more inclined to understand the phrase as a modifier of ζῴδιον.

The two most famous nilometers were located in Memphis and on the island of Elephantine (see the account in Strabo 17.1.48). The phrase νή[ϲῳ] βιοτεῦον—"living on an island"—may have been intended as an allusion to the Elephantine nilometer, as opposed to that in Memphis (or in other locations).

Another possibility is Roberts's νή[ρῳ] βιοτεῦον, where the sign is being described as a "creature living in the water." Although a large number of water creatures (birds and fish) function as signifiers in the hieroglyphic writing system, no such hieroglyph is attested for the number seven.

Bernand (1970: 22), arguing that in artistic representation the cubits measuring the inundation are often shown as small children swarming about a bearded Nile figure, as described, for example, in Philostratos *Imagines* 1.5, would restore νη[πίου] βιοτεῦον, translating, "une statue de petit-infant, pleine de vie." Unfortunately for his ingenious conjecture, νη[πίου] is too long and βιοτεῦον means "dwelling," not "full of life."

Santoni (1991: 105) believes that the figure in question represents an animal that has special symbolic value in relation to the Nile flood. She suggests perhaps the phoenix, whose hieroglyphic signification is "to be inundated."

4. ἀναπεϲϲευόμενον: the word does not occur elsewhere. Since πεϲϲοί are counters in a board game, and the word may be used as a synonym for ψῆφοι,

458

it is not far-fetched to imagine that ἀναπεccεύω could mean "reckon up" (so West 1973: 76). Note, for example, the following remark in Philo: τύχης γὰρ ἀcταθμητότερον οὐδέν, ἄνω καὶ κάτω τὰ ἀνθρώπεια πεττευούcης (VM 1.31.1).

4–5. ἐπιχω|ρίαν: this should be understood with ψῆφον, so Roberts (Crawford 1955: 11).

6–15. We take the sentence to extend from ὁ γ[ὰρ] ποταμὸc through λεγόμενον, with πολ|λὰ πεδία cυνωμβρεῖτο πί|δαξι καὶ πολλοῖc ἔλεcιν ἔ|κολλα τόν τε Κάνωβον ὄν|τα νηcῖδα καὶ αὐτὸν Θῶνιν | λεγόμενον in a chiastic arrangement.

7–8. The use of Demeter for "earth" and Poseidon for "sea" (below, lines 21–22) led Merkelbach (1958: 114) to suppose that this piece was in keeping with Hekataios's theological system of explanations of the cosmos; but, as Oswyn Murray points out, these particular theomorphisms are rhetorical devices, not expressions of cosmological verities (1970: 148 n. 3).

8. The paragraphos at the beginning of this line suggests that there is full stop after πολλ[ή]ν, and that the two participles ἐπιλιμνάζων and ἀναχεόμενοc are intended to modify cυνωμβρεῖτο. This results in an asyndeton, however, which can be avoided only by ignoring the punctuation and attaching ἐπιλιμνάζων to πομπεύει and ἀναχεόμενοc to cυνωμβρεῖτο. Asyndeton notwithstanding, lines 9–15 do appear to form a coherent whole, describing the effects of the flood on specific locations—Kanopos and Thonis, in contrast to the generalized remark of lines 6–8. The phrase appears to be deliberately constructed with two participles (ἐπιλιμνάζων καὶ ἀναχεόμενοc), two imperfect verbs (cυνωμβρεῖτο καὶ ἔκολλα), and two proper nouns as objects (Κάνωβον καὶ Θῶνιν).

9. ἐπιλιμνάζων: the word is very rare, but it does occur. Steph. Lex. cites one example of active use + dative: ἐπιλιμνάζει τοῖc ἔλεcι. The passive occurs in Plut. Caes. §25: πεδία χειμάρροιc ἐπιλελιμναcμένα.

9–11. Presumably the imperfect tenses are chosen to describe the customary or repeated behavior of the river.

11. cυνωμβρεῖτο: another rare word, which occurs in Plutarch, frag. 157.7, to describe a flood of water.

13–14. τόν τε Κάνωβον ὄν|τα νηcῖδα: see Drescher 1949: 16–18 for a discussion of the relative locations of Kanopos and Thonis, as well as the island or near island status of the former in antiquity.

14. Θῶνιν: according to Steph. Byz. (s.v. Θῶνιc), Thonis was located at the Kanopic mouth of the Nile.

15. λεγόμενον· τριάκοντά τε: the punctuation of the papyrus indicates that λεγό-μενον is to be taken with Θῶνιν, a use often found with place names in papyrus documents. The τε following τριάκοντα will then introduce a new sentence. Drescher, however, takes τριάκοντά τε cταδίοιc περιγραφόμενον with καὶ αὐτὸν Θῶνιν. He would place a full stop after ἔκολλα, regarding the whole phrase from τόν τε Κάνωβον to περιγραφόμενον as the object of ἠcπάcατο. He translates: "It embraced and, by the deposit of black mud, knit together with

Egyptian soil Kanopos which was an islet and likewise called Thonis, being thirty stades in circumference."

18. πρόχωcιν: the word occurs elsewhere, but is often emended to πρόcχωcιc. The sense must be "by a heaping up" of the Nile mud.

19. μελαίνηc ἰλύοc: compare Hld. 9.22.5 where the name of the Nile itself is derived from "mud": νέαν ἰλὺν δι᾿ ἔτουc ἐπάγοντα καὶ Νεῖλον ἐντεῦθεν ὀνομα-ζόμενον.

21. ἀμφοτερίζον: the only other recorded example of ἀμφοτερίζω is in Julian, where it means "suitable for both." Here with a similar meaning—"accessible to both Ocean and Nile."

23–24. ἀνθρώπει|οc ... τροφή: the Nile as a nurturer of human life is a constant theme, especially for Greek writers, for whom the effortlessness of Egyptian agriculture and irrigation was in stark contrast to the difficulties engendered by the arid and rocky Greek countryside. See, for example, Isok. *Busiris* §§ 13–14 and Hld. 8.14.3–4.

24–25. Presumably these lines refer to the life that appears spontaneously created as the waters recede. Diodoros calls this τροφὰc αὐτοφυεῖc (1.10.1), and about the Nile he claims: ἐν μόνῃ ταύτῃ θεωρεῖcθαί τινα τῶν ἐμψύχων παραδόξωc ζωογονούμενα (1.10.3).

25. ἰκμαζομένη: the word is glossed by Hesychios as "to dry up," but in a passive form as "being moistened." It occurs only in a few late authors, including Plutarch §954e codd. (with the former meaning). Here, the drying out of the land should be the precursor to the sprouting of plants. Bowie suggests π[ολλο]ῖc γὰρ ἰκμαζομένη | ἀ[ν]εμ[οῖc] = "as the earth is being dried out by many breezes."

28. Again compare Diodoros on the subject of the Nile (1.10.1): τοῦτον γὰρ πολύγονον ὄντα καὶ τὰc τροφὰc αὐτοφυεῖc παρεχόμενον ῥᾳδίωc ἐκτρέφειν τὰ ζωογονηθέντα· τήν τε γὰρ τοῦ καλάμου ῥίζαν καὶ τὸν λωτόν....

γλυκὺν ... χυμ[όν: compare AT 4.12.3, where the Nile is described as a γλυκεῖαν θάλαccαν.

29. βουνόμο̣υ̣: the word occurs elsewhere infrequently and only in tragedy. For the lushness of the grazing land formed by the Nile, see Hld. 8.14.3.

COLUMN II

7. -ραc θυ[: a form of θυγάτηρ ? cf. below line II.12.

19. λεγ[: this might indicate dialogue, but note λεγόμενον at I.15.

Initiation

———— ❖ ————

P. Ant. 18 seems to give us an act of initiation into the mysteries: Triptolemos is invoked (line 3), followed by a rather standard recollection of Demeter and Kore. Apart from this, nothing is certain: the verb in line 5 may be either "I saw" or "they saw"; the whole may be a speech or prayer, or only the opening lines.

The reconstruction is complicated by the accepted restoration for line 8: all commentators restore "royal victors" (*nikēphorous basileis*), which is known to be a cult title of the Ptolemies. If correct, this would situate the action in Egypt and most probably in Alexandria, or at least guarantee that the speaker(s) has in mind an Egyptian experience. Roberts questioned whether the Eleusinian mysteries were ever celebrated in any form in Alexandria, but Delatte (1952a: 199ff.) links the festival of Hathor that was celebrated in late Epiph and early Mesore (late July) with that of the mysteries; he also provides considerable evidence for the identification of the Ptolemies with Triptolemos (= Osiris) as part of their political program to identify themselves with Egyptian deities through the readily available Greek parallels. Koenen and Thompson (1984: 120) argue that this kind of identification was such a normal part of Ptolemaic kingship that Gallus could expropriate it for his own dynastic ambitions, and that Gallus' attempt to identify himself as Triptolemos is portrayed on the Tazza Farnese (a carved dish assigned to the second or first century B.C.E.).

If the Egyptian connection is correct, then the speaker in the piece will be saying to Triptolemos, "I have [not] seen Kore or Demeter, but I have seen the victorious Ptolemies" (presumably participating in some fashion in an Alexandria-based version of the Eleusinian cult), that is, "I have not been initiated into the Athenian cult, but I have participated in the one in Alexandria." The occasion for such a statement is a puzzle. Delatte suggests either that the speaker is dead or that he is experiencing an ecstatic dream, although he is quick to observe that this text does not take the form of instructions given to the dead as found among the Orphic fragments (1952a: 208).

Roberts suggested three possibilities for the text: that it may have been (1) a fragment of ritual, (2) a fragment of romance, or (3) a rhetorical exercise. The text hardly qualifies as an actual ritual; apart from the prohibition against revealing the contents of the Eleusinian ceremonies under pain of death, the speaker (or speakers) seems to be saying that he (they) has not experienced initiation. Nor does anything in this piece resemble the extant material dealing with initiation into various of the mysteries. (Delatte 1952a: 200 provides a list of relevant texts.) If his suggestion of a dream is correct, then either (2) or (3) are distinct possibilities; a dream narrative could easily belong to the realm of narrative fiction. Alternatively, the dream might suit a rhetorical exercise; Sopatros, for example, lists the following exemplum: there is a law that anyone who reveals the mysteries is liable to death. A man saw the rites in a dream and asked one of those who had been initiated if these were the things that he had seen. The man agreed and was tried for impiety (Innes and Winterbottom 1988: case 20).

A final consideration: given the curious phrasing of the speech to Triptolemos, it is worth entertaining the possibility that the piece has to do with a fake ritual, like the false initiation into the priests of Cybele in the *Iolaos* fragment. In this case, it will very likely belong in the realm of criminal-satiric fiction.

D ESCRIPTION

P. Ant. 18 (= P^2 2466, measuring 5.3 ×6.0 cm) is a small fragment from the bottom of a column of a papyrus roll written along the fibers; the back is blank. The
hand is a quickly written type with documentary affinities, tilting slightly to the
right, assignable to the late second or the early third century C.E. The original
editor, Colin Roberts, remarked upon the shape of the nu as "almost of Ptolemaic type," and suggested that this could indicate that the writer was copying
from a Ptolemaic original (1950: 39). If true, a Ptolemaic date for the original
would almost certainly exclude it from the category of "romance." This form of
nu appears as archaizing feature in later hands, however, and becomes quite
common in the third century C.E. and after (Parca 1991: 7 and n. 19). The obvious supplements to lines 5–7 suggest that no more than eight letters are missing
between lines, and probably no more than one or two letters from the opening of
each line. Hiatus appears to have been avoided, and lines 5–7 at least, the restoration of which is virtually certain, display a very careful and balanced word
order.

P. ANT. 18

- - - - - - - - - - - - - - - - - - -

].λειμ‥[
μ]υρρίνην εἴλετ[
]ην· ὦ Τριπτόλεμε c[
4   ]υ coι νῦν μεμυηκ[
]τὴν Κόρην εἶδον η[
μ]ένην, οὐδὲ τὴν Δ[ήμητρα
λ]ελυπημένην· αλ[
8   ν]ικηφόρουc βα[
]ν μυcτικὸν τ[

1.]η λειμῳγ[Roberts   2. μ]υρρίνην εἴλετ[ε or εἴλετ[ο Roberts   3. τριπτολειμε pap.
4. ἡδ]ύ coι νῦν μεμυηκ[έναι Roberts   5–7. οὔτε] τὴν κόρην εἶδον ἡ[ρπαcμ]ένην (or
ἡ[ναγκαcμ]ένην), οὐδὲ τὴν Δη[ιὼ (or Δη[μήτερα) λ]ελυπημένην Roberts   8.]εικηφο
ρουc pap., ν]ικηφcορουc βα[cιλεῖc Roberts, followed by Delatte, Merk.

        ] . . . [
] he/you entwined the myrtle [
] . . . O Triptolemos [
4   ] . . . now have initiated [
] I/they saw Kore [
] nor yet [Demeter]
] grieving, but [
8   ] victorious [
] mystic [

P. ANT. 18

1. Delatte, and Merkelbach after him, regards λειμ . . [as a reference to the "prairies du paradis souterrain ou les mystes prennent leurs ébats, comme, par exemple, dans les *Grenouilles* d' Aristophane (326, 344, 374, 450)." Merkelbach (1958: 123) points out that Triptolemos is one of the judges of the dead in, e.g., Plato *Apol.* §41a, and that he is often identified with Osiris.
2. μ]υρρίνην εἰλετ[: not the crown of myrtle worn by initiates, but, as Delatte points out, a branch that is carried (hence the verb).
3. Bowie suggests ὦ Τριπτόλεμε ϲ[ωτέρ.
4. μεμυηκ[: the κ is clear. The perfect active form of this verb, however, is rare and difficult to understand in this context. Roberts supplements as ἡδ]ὺ ϲοι νῦν μεμυηκ[έναι, "It is now a pleasant thing for you to have initiated." Alternatively, it might be a participle with οἱ νῦν, i.e., μεμυηκ[ότεϲ = "the present initiators," in contrast to οἱ μεμυημένοι, the usual term for initiates. Note one of the few occurrences in Greek of the perfect active form of this verb is in the Sopatros exemplum mentioned above (introduction), where the subjects are Demeter and Kore: τί βουλόμεναι μεμυήκαϲι . . . (*RG* 8.122.5–6).
5–7. The sense of these lines appears to be "not A, nor yet B, but C." A and B certainly refer to the Eleusinian mysteries, the rape of Kore, and the grieving of Demeter; C is in question.
8. Roberts restores ν]ικηφόρουϲ βα[ϲιλεῖϲ, a cult title of the Ptolemies. If correct, then the sense of the passage must be a contrast between the Eleusinian mysteries and Alexandrian rites introduced by the Ptolemies. The speaker will be saying to Triptolemos, "I have not seen Kore carried off, nor yet Demeter grieving, but I have seen the royal victors (i.e., the Ptolemies)." Alternatively one might restore, e.g., ν]ικηφόρουϲ βα[ϲάνουϲ = "victory-bearing tests" (of initiation).
9.]ν μυϲτικὸν τ[: the ν suggests a masculine phrase, rather than τὸ μυϲτικόν.

466

APPENDIXES

APPENDIX A
ALSO KNOWN AS ROMANCE

I

It is wise to be suspicious of the category "romance," into which editors have dumped many unidentified fragments of prose. The following is a list of papyri that have been tentatively identified as "romance." All subsequently have been or should be assigned to other genres or to known authors.

1. P. Lit. Lond. 245 (= P^2 2638) was included in Zimmermann's collection (no. 12), largely on the presence of the word ληςτής, which means "brigand" or "robber," although the hand and the crosses serving as punctuation certainly indicated that the text was Christian in subject matter. M. Gronewald identified it as Pseudo-Eusebios *Sermo* 17 (Migne, *Patrologia Graeca* 62.723–24) in *Zeitschrift für Papyrologie und Epigraphik* 34 (1979): 22–25.

2. P. Hamb. 134 (= P^2 2811), thought by its original editors to be the fragment of a letter or dialogue or speech or possibly romance, was identified by J. Dingel, in *Zeitschrift für Papyrologie und Epigraphik* 14 (1974): 169–70, as a rhetorical exercise on a relatively popular topic: "the valiant in war receives whatever reward he requests."

3. O. Edfu 306 (= P^2 2447), which is in A. Zalateo's list of school exercises (*Aegyptus* 41 [1961]: 160ff., no. 173), was tentatively identified by C. Bonner in a personal communication to R. A. Pack as "a fragment of the Ninus Romance." D. Hagedorn, in *Zeitschrift für Papyrologie und Epigraphik* 13 (1973): 110–11, demonstrated that it was much more likely to be a private letter.

4. *PSI* 7.760 (= P^2 2639) originally appeared as "frammento di romanzo?" but C. H. Roberts in P. Oxy. 22 (p. 89 n. 4) argues rightly that the fragment is part of a prophecy, related probably to the material known as the "Oracle of the Potter."

5. P. Harris 13 (= P^2 2248) consists of portions of two fragmentary columns (with lower margins attached) written in an informal round hand assignable to the second century C.E. M. Gronewald in *Zeitschrift für Papyrologie und Epigraphik* 33 (1979): 1–5, demonstrated that the two pieces could be joined to form a fragment of a commentary on Euripides' *Kretans*, the exact nature of which is unclear.

469

6. P. Lit. Lond. 198 (= P^2 2640) is an illustrated text with writing above in what appears to be a sloping uncial of the fifth or sixth century C.E. There are three figures; the figure on the left is bearded and appears to hold a shield, the one on the right holds what appears to be a bowl and a scroll. Line 3 surely contains a nomen sacrum χρ̄ or π̄ρᾱ, however, and would therefore belong a Christian text of some kind.

7. Bibl. Nat. Cod. supp. gr. 1294 (= P^2 2641) is an unpublished papyrus roll that has nevertheless received considerable prominence as an example of an "illustrated romance" (see, e.g., Hägg, *The Novel in Antiquity* [Berkeley 1983], 94–95). It contains portions of three columns interspersed with small drawings, written in a small informal upright hand assignable to the third or perhaps early fourth century C.E. The discernible context indicates that the text is likely to be either a Jewish or Christian martyrology.

8. "Dream of Nektanebos" (UPZ I.81) (= P^2 2476) has been suggested as an Egyptian precursor to the Greek novel, but its real function is that of *Königsnovelle*, an admonitory narrative addressed to the pharaoh that often foretells disaster for the kingdom, if certain conditions are not rectified. For a discussion of this text, see L. Koenen, *Bulletin of the American Society of Papyrologists* 22 (1985): 171–194, and above, General Introduction.

9. Tefnut (P. Lit. Lond. 192 = P^2 2618), published by S. West in *Journal of Egyptian Archaeology* 55 (1969) 161–83, is a Greek version of an extremely popular Egyptian tale. It is discussed in the General Introduction, above.

10. P. Oxy. 42.3011 was published as "a narrative about Amenophis." Although it is conceivable that this belongs to a novellike narrative about this Egyptian king, along the lines of *Sesonchosis*, it seems rather to us to be a *Königsnovelle*, like the "Dream of Nektanebos" above.

11. P. Mich. inv. 3793, published by T. Renner in *Proceedings of the XVI International Congress of Papyrology* (Chico, 1981): 93–101, was assigned to romance almost by default. The piece is more likely to be mime or a fable or even a declamatory exercise. We suggest restoring Column II.11–13 as follows: ὁ δέ, "ἄγε καὶ cάρκα[——," ἔφη,] διανοηθεὶ⟨c⟩ Εὐρρυδ[ί]κη[ν ——] θηριόβρωτον γεγον[έναι] or γεγο[νυῖαν] (And he [says]: 'Come, and [consume my?] flesh, having supposed that Eurydike had been devoured by beasts'"). This passage may be reminiscent of Ovid *Metamorphoses* 4.112–14, where Pyramus, after he has found Thisbe's bloodied veil, invokes the lions dwelling in the area to kill him: "nostrum divellite corpus | et scelerata fero consumite viscera morsu, | o quicumque sub hac habitatis rupe, leones!"

12. A fragment—apparently without inventory number—published by M. Norsa in *Aegyptus* 1 (1920): 154–58, was subsequently identified as a

fragment of a new Greek romance about Troy(?) by B. Lavagnini in *Aegyptus* 2 (1921): 192–99. In reality, it is a rhetorical exercise cast as a contest for the arms of Achilles.

13. P. Oxy. 6.868 (= P^2 2630), which seems to be from a speech of some kind, was assigned to "romance" on the basis of reading the name of an historical character, Tithraustes, in line 2. If this articulation is correct, there is no a priori reason to assign this scrap to a fictionalized narrative in preference to history or oratory. The relatively early date of the piece, first century B.C.E., has inclined us to exclude it from consideration.

14. P. Gen. inv. 187 was listed by C. Wehrli in "L'État de la collection papyrologique de Genève," *Actes du XVe Congrès international de papyrologie*, pt. 3 (Brussels, 1979), as "un fragment romanesque." No complete edition has been published, but Kussl (1991: 1973–75) assigned the fragment to Antonius Diogenes' *The Incredible Things beyond Thule*, because it appears to describe a number of sights in the Underworld. He believes the subject to be the *katabasis* of Derkyllis. Kussl does not provide a transcript of the whole, but what he does provide is far too lacunose even to identify as prose fiction, let alone as part of *The Incredible Things*.

II

The following fragments, all of which have been tentatively identified as "romance" by earlier editors or commentators, have so little context remaining that we have not included them in the main text.

1. P. Harris 23 (= P^2 2827) is a narrow strip of papyrus that retains only a few letters per line. Körte originally assigned it to "romance," observing that the only other occurrence of ὑποβαϲταϲα[was in Chariton. J. Lenaerts, in *Chronique d'Égypte* 55 (1980): 211, bolstered his argument by restoring line 12 as ἔρ]ωτοϲ ἀτυχ[οῦϲ (or ἀτυχ[οῦντοϲ) and line 13 as ἐνθύμιο[ν]. The only other words to suggest a context, "wagon" (in line 21) and "the satrapy" (in line 27), are not inconsistent with this supposition. But the strip might just as easily belong to history or rhetorical exercise.

2. P. Fouad 4 (= P^2 2632) consists of two small scraps written in a Biblical uncial, assignable to the fourth century C.E. The context is a storm at sea. As such, the narrative might belong to narrative fiction, though it might equally well occur in pagan or Christian *acta* or as a topos in rhetorical literature, history, or patristic writing.

3. P. Oxy 45.3218 consists of two small papyrus scraps that should be assigned to the late first or early second century C.E. There is little to suggest context

beyond the occurrence of the rather tantalizing verb ἐπηρώθη, mention of a goddess, and a reference to Alexandria.

4. P. Harris 18 (= P^2 2633) consists of scraps from the top of two columns of a papyrus roll. Ed. pr. assigned it to the first century C.E., but we are inclined to a slightly earlier date. Surviving vocabulary suggests intrigue and betrayal. Ed. pr. assigned it to "romance" on the basis of lines 2.4–6, which have vocabulary in common with a scene in Heliodoros in which a slave is summoned to bring a light for travelers (8.2). But it might as easily be the narrative section of a trial speech; one need only recollect the details of Andocides *On the Mysteries* to find similar language of betrayal and nocturnal activity.

5. P. Harris 19 (= P^2 2634) and 20 (= P^2 2635), and P. Frei. 4.47 have so little discernible context that it is impossible even to speculate on their natures.

III

An equally salubrious lesson can be learned from the following fragments, which were originally identified as other than prose fiction.

1. P. Oxy. 7.1014 (= P^2 2258) was originally identified as "an historical work, apparently not extant," and included the description of a battle that took place along a sea coast. Gronewald identified it as Achilles Tatius 4.14.2–5 in *Zeitschrift für Papyrologie und Epigraphik* 22 (1976): 14–17.

2. P. Amh. 2.160 (= P^2 2797) was simply "prose," until Gronewald identified it as Heliodoros 8.16.6–7, 17.3–4 in *Zeitschrift für Papyrologie und Epigraphik* 34 (1979): 19–21.

3. P. Oxy. 2466 (= P^2 2259) was originally "Egyptian history," but was reassigned to the Sesonchosis "Romance" when another piece of the same papyrus roll was found on which the name Sesonchosis was written.

4. P. Lit. Lond. 194 (= P^2 2637), Zimmermann's no. 13, is a fragment from an attractive fourth-century codex. Assigned by the original editors to "romance," A. D. Knox preferred to "regard it as part of a speech of Lysias, rather than a novel" (*Journal of Egyptian Archaeology* 15 [1929]: 139). J. Lenaerts, in *Chronique d' Egypte* 49 (1974): 115–120, identified it as [Lucian] *Asinus* §§ 47.2–4, 5–7.

APPENDIX B
TESTIMONIA

We include the following references to lost prose narratives that may be said to have been fictional, whatever the genre their authors intended, and which share features, in some measure, with the fragments we have printed above. Our list does not aim at completeness.

1. Antiphanes of Berga (see above, introduction to "Antonius Diogenes")

  A. He [Antonius Diogenes] mentions an older Antiphanes, whom he says devoted himself to the recording of such bizarre matters (Photios *Bibl.* cod. 166: [112a])

  B. Now all this does not fall very far short of the fictions of Pytheas, Euhemeros, and Antiphanes (Str. 2.3.5 [C102])

  C. How, then, can we avoid thinking that Eratosthenes has surpassed in foolishness Antiphanes of Berga and rendered it impossible for any subsequent writer to excel him in absurdity? (Polybios 34.6.15)

  D. Strabo says it is the village from which the comic writer Antiphanes of Berga came. This man wrote about marvels, as they say. From here comes also the saying "to *Bergaize*," to speak the truth in no respect. (Steph. Byz., s.v. Βέργη)

  E. The Strymon is a great river flowing
      alongside this land as far as the sea, sweeping down
      to those who are called there the choruses of Nereids.
      On the middle section of this river the country of Antiphanes
      is located, called Berga; he of course is the writer
      of an unbelievable mockery of mythic history.
                    ([Skymnos] 650–55 *GGM* 1:221)

2. Aristides *Milesiaka*; Eubios, *Sybaritika*

  A. Aristides linked himself with Milesian vices,
      yet Aristides was not exiled from his city.
      Nor was the man who described mothers' seed being destroyed [i.e.,
                                                                  abortion],

473

Eubios, a writer of impure history.
Nor did he go into exile, who recently composed the *Sybaritika*,
nor those who talked about their own couplings.

(Ovid *Tr.* 2.413–16)

B. When he had gathered the Seleukid council of elders, he brought to their notice the licentious books of Aristides' *Milesiaka*, and he was not making this up. For they were found in the gear of Rustius, and afforded Surena with a great opportunity to mock and pour scorn on the Romans, on the grounds that not even when they were off to war could they put aside such business and such writings. (Plut. *Crass.* § 32 [Ziegler])

3. Arrian, *Life of Tillorobos the Bandit*

For Arrian, the pupil of Epiktetos, a Roman of the first rank, and devoted to education his whole life, experienced the same thing [sc. the accusation of frivolity in writing such a work], and so might speak in my defense too. He thought it appropriate to record the life of Tillorobos [one ms. reads Tilloboros] the bandit. But I shall commemorate a bandit who was much more savage, because he plied his trade not in forests and mountains but in cities, overrunning not just Mysia and Mt. Ida and plundering a few of the more deserted regions of Asia, but filling the whole Roman Empire so to speak with his banditry. (Lucian *Alex.* § 2)

4. Damaskios, Book 2: *Marvelous Stories concerning Spirits*

The second (book) of *Marvelous Stories* is about spirits, in forty-two chapters. In all of these are impossible, unbelievable, and ill-conceived tales of marvelous and foolish things, truly worthy of the godless and impious Damaskios, who even when the light of piety had filled the world, continued to sleep in the deep darkness of idolatry. His style in these stories is summarizing: it is neither unadorned nor lacking in clarity as in such tales. (Photios *Bibl.* cod. 130 [96b–97a])

5. Eubios, *Sybaritika* (see above, 2.A)

6. Hemitheos, *Sybaritika*

A.   The most libidinous books of Mussetus,
which vie with the Sybaritic books
and rolls tinged with prurient wit,
read, Instantius Rufus; but
let your girlfriend be with you, lest
you pollute the hymeneal with your lustful hands

474

and become a husband without a wife [i.e., masturbate].
(Martial 12.95 [Heraeus])

B. Hemitheos of Sybaris is mentioned twice in Lucian.
Pseudologista § 3: [the greatest of asses] beyond the Sybarite Hemitheon
Adversus indoctum § 23: the catamite Hemitheon the Sybarite, who has
written those wonderful rules for you, that you should wear makeup and
pluck out your body hair and do or have done to you those things . . .

7. Hegesianax

A. The Troad, the land of Ilium, which is called "Teukris" and "Dardania"
and "Xanthe." The ethnic designation is "Troadeus." Also from there
came Hegesianax, an elementary school teacher, who wrote one book on the
style of Demokritos and also about poetic expressions. He was a Troadeus.
(Steph. Byz., s.v. Τρῳάς)

B. Hegesianax of Alexandria, who composed *The Trojan War* attributed to
Kephalion, says that Kyknos [= Swan], too, who fought against Achilles in
single combat, was reared in Leukophrys by the bird whose name he bore.
(Ath. 9.393d [Kaibel])

C. Hegesianax says that when the Galatai crossed from Europe they went
up into the city because they needed a stronghold, but left it immediately
because it was unwalled. (Str. 13.27)

8. Kadmos of Miletus

Kadmos, the son of Archelaos, a Milesian, a more recent historian. Some
have recorded Lukinos as Kadmos. Perhaps there is another. He wrote
these things: A *Deliverance from Erotic Passions* (*erōtikōn pathōn*) in four
books, *Attic Histories* in sixteen. (*Souda* s.v.)

9. Kapito of Alexandria, *Erotika*

Some record Harmonia as the wine pourer for the gods, according to the
account given in Kapito the epic poet, an Alexandrian, in the second book of
his *Erotic Tales* (*erōtikōn*). (Ath. 10.425c)

10. Klearchos of Soli

Klearchos's *Erotika* is well attested: for complete testimonia, see F. Wehrli,
Die Schule des Aristotles (Basel, 1948), vol. 3, frags. 21–35. One example
will suffice here.

Klearchos in his first book of *Erotic Tales* says: "Gyges, the king of Lydia, became notorious for his mistress, not only during her lifetime, entrusting himself and his whole empire to her; but also when she died, he gathered all the Lydians of the country together and erected a monument that to this day is still named after his Companion, raising it so high that when he made his royal progress on that side of Mt. Tmolos, he would be able to see the monument wherever he happened to turn, and it would be visible to all who lived in Lydia." (Ath. 13.573 [Wehrli 29])

11. Lykophron, *Letters*

[Read] the letters of Lykophron, especially for his plain good sense and his diction. (Joseph Rhakendytos *Rhetores Graeci* 3.521.26–27 [Walz])

12. Philip of Amphipolis, *Rhodiaka, Koaka, Thasiaka*

A. Philip, from Amphipolis, an historian. *Rhodian Matters*, nineteen books—and they are about wholly shameful things; *Koan Matters*, two books; *Thasian Matters*, two books. (*Souda* s.v.)

B. Meanwhile they [the sexually dysfunctional] should rest not only the whole night long but also the whole day; they should use feathers and softer coverlets or blankets. Meanwhile, the services of pretty girls or the similar services of boys should be procured. With discretion they should employ readings that stimulate their minds sexually, like those of Philip of Amphipolis or Herodian or of course the Syrian Iamblichos, or others who tell erotic tales (*amatorias fabulas*) charmingly. (Theodor. Prisc. 133.5–12 [Rose])

13. Xenophon of Antioch

Xenophon, an Antiochene, an historian. *Babylonian Matters*. These are erotic tales (*erōtika*). (*Souda* s.v.)

14. Xenophon of Cyprus, *Kypriaka*

Xenophon, a Cypriot, an historian. *Cypriot Matters*: these consist of erotic stories (*erōtikōn hypotheseōn*), including the history of Kinyra and Myrra and Adonis. (*Souda* s.v.)

15. *Araspes the Lover of Pantheia*

Those who attribute to Dionysios the work called *Araspes the Lover of Pantheia* have no ear for his rhythms, nor for the rest of his expression, and they know nothing of the art of ratiocination. For this is not the thought of Dionysios, but of Celer, the writer of technical works on rhetoric. While Celer was a good imperial secretary, he was unskilled in declamation, and he quarreled with Dionysios from the time of young manhood. (Philostratos *Vit. Soph.* § 524; see above, introduction to *Lollianos*, for a discussion of this passage.)

16. *Memoirs of Pilate and Christ*

Having forged indeed Memoirs of Pilate and our Savior, full of every blasphemy against Christ. (Eusebios *HE* 9.5.1 [G. Bardy, ed., *Eusèbe de Cesarée, Histoire ecclesiastique, Sources chrétiennes,* vol. 55 (Paris, 1958).

APPENDIX C
CHART OF PROVENANCES
AND DATES

Name	Date	Provenance	Format
Achilles Tatius	150	Oxyrhynchus?	papyrus codex
Achilles Tatius	150	Oxyrhynchus	roll
Achilles Tatius	250	Hermoupolis Magna	2-col.? codex—papyrus
Achilles Tatius	250	Oxyrhynchus	roll
Achilles Tatius	250	unknown	roll
Achilles Tatius	300	Oxyrhynchus	roll
Antheia	175	unknown	roll
Antonius Diogenes?	150	Arsinoe	roll
Antonius Diogenes	200	Arsinoite nome?	roll
Antonius Diogenes	200	Oxyrhynchus	roll
Apollonios	300	Oxyrhynchus	roll
Apparition	300	Oxyrhynchus	roll
Chariton	150	unknown	roll
Chariton	200	Oxyrhynchus	roll
Chariton	200	Karanis	roll
Chariton	600	Thebaid?	2-col. codex—parchment
Chione?	150	unknown	roll
Chione	600	Thebaid?	2-col. codex—parchment
Daulis	175	unknown	roll
Diktys	200	Oxyrhynchus?	roll
Diktys	225	Tebtunis	roll
Festival	275	Oxyrhynchus	roll
Goatherd	250	Oxyrhynchus	roll
Heliodoros	550	unknown	codex—parchment
Initiation	200	Antinoopolis	roll
Inundation	150	unknown	roll
Iolaos	150	Oxyrhynchus	roll
Kalligone	150	Oxyrhynchus	roll
Lollianos	250	Oxyrhynchus	roll
Lollianos	175	unknown	papyrus codex
Love Drug	150	Fayum	roll
[Lucian], *Ass Tale*	300	unknown	codex—parchment
Metiochos & Parthenope	150	Karanis	roll
Metiochos & Parthenope?	200	Oxyrhynchus	roll
Nightmare	150	Karanis?	roll
Ninos	75	Karanis?	roll
Ninos	75	Oxyrhynchus	roll
Sesonchosis	250	Oxyrhynchus	roll
Sesonchosis	300	Oxyrhynchus	papyrus codex
Staphulos	150	Oxyrhynchus	roll
Theano	200	Oxyrhynchus	roll
Tinouphis	150	unknown	roll

Letters per line	Lines per column	Other side of text
unknown	unknown	codex
16–20	42–44	back is blank
unknown	unknown	codex
24–29	26+	front is a survey list
40–48	40–42	back is blank
19–25	41–42	back is blank
27–30	60?	front is Demosthenes
30–35	60	front is accounts, Demosthenes
29–31	unknown	front is accounts
14–16	unknown	back is blank
27–30	unknown	front is a document
40	unknown	front is a word list
18–22	18	back is an astrological text
19–26	49–50	back is blank
20–25	57	back is blank
14–16	28	codex
18–20	unknown	back is blank
14–16	28	codex
32–36	29	front is an account
unknown	unknown	blank
38–44	53	front is a document
18–22	unknown	back is blank
28–32	unknown	front is a document
35–40	30+	codex
17–20	unknown	back is blank
18–23	35	back is blank
metrical	43	back is blank
17–22	42	back is blank
20	29+	back is a register
50–63	59+	codex
16–19	23+	back is blank
16–18	27	codex
33–37	38	fron is an account of rents
18–22	unknown	back is blank
16–20	unknown	back is blank
20–24	38	back is a document
15–19	50	back is blank
20–24	23–28	back is blank
unknown	15+	codex
20–23	unknown	back is blank
15–20	unknown	back is blank
metrical	25	back is blank

BIBLIOGRAPHY

This Bibliography begins with references to the General Introduction, followed by sections for the individual fragments, arranged alphabetically by author (where known) or title.

GENERAL INTRODUCTION

Anderson, G. 1984. *Ancient Fiction: The Novel in the Graeco-Roman World.* London.

Bakhtin, M. 1981. *The Dialogic Imagination.* Translated by C. Emerson and M. Holquist. Austin, Texas.

Barns, J.W.B. 1956. "Egypt and the Greek Romance." Akten des VIII. Internationalen Kongresses für Papyrologie, edited by H. Gerstinger. *Mitteilungen aus der Papyrussammlung der Nationalbibliothek in Wien,* n.s. 5:34.

Bowie, E. L. 1985. "The Greek Novel." In *Cambridge History of Classical Literature I: Greek Literature,* edited by P. E. Easterling and B.M.W. Knox, pp. 683–99. Cambridge.

Grumach, E. 1949. *Goethe und die Antike.* Vol. 1. [Berlin]. [Pp. 316–320.]

Hägg, T. 1983. *The Novel in Antiquity.* Berkeley.

Harris, W. V. 1989. *Ancient Literacy.* Cambridge, Mass. [p. 283.]

Hennecke, E., and W. Schneemelcher. 1963. *New Testament Apocrypha.* Vol. 2. Translated by R. M. Wilson. Philadephia. [Pp. 498–504.]

Hermann, A. 1938. *Die altägyptische Königsnovelle.* Hamburg and New York.

Kemp, B. 1989. *Ancient Egypt: Anatomy of a Civilization.* London. [Pp. 198–200.]

Koenen, L. 1985. "The Dream of Nektanebos." *Bulletin of the American Society of Papyrologists* 22:171–94.

Lichtheim, M. 1975–80. *Ancient Egyptian Literature.* Vols. 1–3. Berkeley and Los Angeles.

Reeve, M. 1971. "Hiatus in the Greek Novelists." *Classical Quarterly,* n.s. 21:514–39.

Samuel, A. E. 1983. *From Athens to Alexandria: Hellenism and Social Goals in Ptolemaic Egypt.* Studia Hellenistica, vol. 26. Louvain. [Pp. 109–110.]

Selden, Daniel. 1994. "Genre of Genre." In *The Search for the Ancient Novel,* edited by James Tatum, pp. 39–64. Baltimore.

Smith, J. Z. 1978. *Map Is Not Territory.* Leiden. [Pp. 67–87.]

Stephens, Susan A. 1994. "Who Read Ancient Novels?" In *The Search for the Ancient Novel,* edited by James Tatum, pp. 405–18. Baltimore.

Vanderlip, V. 1972. *Hymns of Isodorus.* American Studies in Papyrology, vol. 12. Toronto.

Walsh, P. 1970. *The Roman Novel.* Cambridge.

Watt, I. 1957. *The Rise of the Novel.* Berkeley.

Wesseling, B. 1988. "The Audience of the Ancient Novels." In *Groningen Colloquia on the Novel*, vol. 1, edited by H. Hofman, pp. 67–79. Groningen.

Wilson, D. de A. 1991. *Allegories of Love: Cervantes' Persiles and Sigismunda*. Princeton.

INDIVIDUAL FRAGMENTS

Antheia and a Cast of Thousands

Bürger, K. 1892. "Zu Xenophon von Ephesos." *Hermes* 27:36–67.

Garin, F. 1920. "I papiri d'Egitto e i romanzi greci." *Studi italiani di filologia classica* 1:180–82.

Körte, A. 1924. Review of literary papyri. *Archiv für Papyrusforschung* 7:253, no. 661.

Lavagnini, B. 1922. *Eroticorum graecorum fragmenta papyracaea*. Leipzig. [Pp. 29–30.]

Norsa, M. 1920. *Papiri greci i latini. Pubblicazioni della Società Italiana*. Vol. 6. Florence. [726: 163–65.]

Papanikolaou, A. 1964. "Chariton und Xenophon zon Ephesos. Zur Frage der Abhängigkeit." Χάρις Κ.Ι. Βουρβέρῃ. Athens.

Rattenbury, R. M. 1933. "Romance: The Greek Novel." In *New Chapters in the History of Greek Literature*, edited by J. U. Powell, 3d ser., pp. 247–248. Oxford.

Reeve, M. 1971. "Hiatus in the Greek Novelists." *Classical Quarterly*, n.s. 21:531.

Schmeling, G. 1980. *Xenophon of Ephesus*. Twayne World Author Series. Boston. [Pp. 75–79.]

Zimmermann, F. 1931. Review of Lavagnini 1922. *Philologische Wochenschrift* 51:230–31.

———. 1936. *Griechische Roman-Papyri und verwandte Texte*. Heidelberg. [No. 9: 78–84.]

Antonius Diogenes

Anderson, G. 1976. "Antonius Diogenes." In *Studies in Lucian's Comic Fiction*, *Mnemosyne* suppl. 43: 1–7.

Anderson, W. 1907. "Eine Märchenparallele zu Antonius Diogenes." *Philologus* 66:606–8.

Boll, F. 1907. "Zum griechischen Roman. I. Lychnopolis." *Philologus* 66:1–11.

Borgogno, A. 1975. "Sulla struttura degli apista di Antonio Diogene." *Prometheus* 1:49–64.

———. 1979a. "Antonio Diogene e le trame dei romanzi Greci." *Prometheus* 5:137–56.

———. 1979b. "Sul nuovo papiro di Antonio Diogene." *Grazer Beiträge* 8:239–42.

Bürger, K. 1903. *Studien zur Geschichte des griechischen romans*. vol. 2, *Die litteraturgeschichtliche Stellung des Antonius Diogenes und der historia Apollonii.* Wissenschaftliche Beilage zum Programm des Herzoglichen Gymnasiums. Blankenburg am Harz.

Burkert, W. 1962. *Weisheit und Wissenschaft: Studien zu Pythagoras, Philolaos und Platon.* Nürnberg. [P. 88.] = *Lore and Science in Ancient Pythagoreanism*, trans. E. L. Minar [Cambridge, Mass., 1972], 99 n. 9.)

Burton, R. F. 1887. *Supplemental Nights to the Book of the Thousand Nights and a Night.* Vol. 5. London. [Pp. 281–90.]

Cary, M., and E. H. Warmington. 1929. *The Ancient Explorers.* London. [Pp. 33–40.]

Chatzis, A. 1914. *Der Philosoph und Grammatiker Ptolemaios Chennos: Leben, Schriftstellerei und Fragmente.* Studien zur Geschichte und Kultur des Altertums 7.2. Paderborn.

Davies, M. 1988. *Epicorum graecorum fragmenta.* Göttingen. [Pp. 149–53.]

Di Gregorio, L. 1968. "Sugli apista hyper Thoulēn di Antonio Diogene." *Aevum* 42:199–211.

Dihle, A. 1957. "Der Platoniker Ptolemaios." *Hermes* 85:314–25.

Dion, R. 1965. "La Renommée de Pythéas dans l'antiquité." *Revue des études latines* 43:443–66.

———. 1966. "Pythéas explorateur." *Revue de philologie* 40:191–216.

Fauth, W. 1978a. "Astraios und Zamolxis: Über Spuren Pythagoreischer Aretalogie im Thule-Roman des Antonius Diogenes." *Hermes* 106:220–41.

———. 1978b. "Zur Kompositorischen Anlage und zur Typik der Apista des Antonius Diogenes." *Würzburger Jahrbücher für die Altertumswissenschaft*, n.s. 4:57–68.

Fusillo, M., ed. 1990. *Antonio Diogene: Le incredibili avventure al di là di Tule.* Palermo.

Gallavotti, C. 1930. "Frammento di Antonio Diogene?" *Studi italiani di filologia classica*, n.s. 8:247–57.

Genette, G. 1980. *Narrative Discourse: An Essay in Method.* Trans. J. E. Lewin. Ithaca, N.Y. [Pp. 244–45; French orig., 1971.]

Gronewald, M. 1976. "P. Oxy. 3012 (Antonios Diogenes?)." *Zeitschrift für Papyrologie und Epigraphik* 22:17–18.

Gurney, O. R. 1956. "The Tale of the Poor Man of Nippur." *Anatolian Studies* 6:145–64.

Hallström, A. 1910. "De aetate Antonii Diogenis." *Eranos* 10:200–201.

Henry, R. 1960. *Photios, Bibliothèque.* Vol. 2. Paris. [166: 140–49.]

Hercher, R. 1855–56. "Über die Glaubwürdigkeit der neuen Geschichte des Ptolemaeus Chennos." *Jahrbücher für classische Philologie*, suppl. 1: 269–93.

Jacoby, F. 1940. "Die Überlieferung von Ps. Plutarchs Parallela Minora und die Schwindelautoren." *Mnemosyne*, 3d ser., 8:73–144.

Jäger, H. 1919. "Die Quellen des Porphyrios in seiner Pythagoras-Biographie." Diss., Zürich.

Kerényi, K. [1927] 1962. *Die griechisch-orientalische Romanliteratur in religions-geschichtlicher Beleuchtung.* Darmstadt. [Pp. 239–40.]

Knaack, G. 1906. "Antiphanes von Berge." *Rheinisches Museum für Philologie* 61:135–38.

Körte, A. 1932. Review of literary papyri. *Archiv für Papyrusforschung* 10:233–34, no. 775.

Lacôte, F. 1911. "Sur l'origine indienne du roman grec." *Mélanges d'indianisme S. Lévi* (Paris): 249–304.

Lasserre, F. 1963. "Ostiéens et Ostimniens chez Pytheas." *Museum Helveticum* 20:107–13.

Merkelbach, R. 1962. *Roman und Mysterium in der Antike.* Munich and Berlin. [Pp. 225–33.]

Mette, H. J., ed. 1952. *Pytheas von Massalia.* Kleine Texte für Vorlesungen und Übungen 173. Berlin.

Migne, J. P. 1857–66. *Patrilogia Graeca.* Paris.

Morgan, J. R. 1985. "Lucian's *True Histories* and the *Wonders beyond Thule* of Antonius Diogenes." *Classical Quarterly* 35:475–90.

Nauck, A. 1886. *Porphyrii philosophi Platonici opuscula selecta.* Leipzig.

Neumann, G. 1953. "Thruskanos." *Beitäge zur Namenforschung* 4:53–55.

Nicols, J. 1987. "Indigenous Culture and the Process of Romanization in Iberian Galicia." *American Journal of Philology* 108:129–51.

Parsons, P. J. 1974. Vol. 42. Egypt Exploration Society. London. *The Oxyrhynchus Papyri.* [3012: 43–46.]

Pisani, V. 1940. "Riflessi Indiani del romanzo ellenistico-romano." *Annali Pisa,* ser. 2, vol. 9:145–54.

Reyhl, K. 1969. "Antonius Diogenes: Untersuchungen zu den Roman-Fragmenten der *Wunder jenseits von Thule* und zu den *Wahren Geschichten* des Lukian." Diss., Tübingen.

Riess, E. 1894. "Aberglaube." In *Real-Encyclopädie der klassischen Altertumswissenschaft,* edited by A. Pauly, G. Wissowa, and W. Kroll, 1:39–41. Stuttgart.

Rohde, E. 1871–72. "Die Quellen des Iamblichus in seiner Biographie des Pythagoras." *Rheinische Museum für Philologie* 26:554–76, 27:23–61 (= *Kleine Schriften,* vol. 2 [Tübingen 1901], 102–72.)

——. [1876] 1974. *Der griechische Roman und seine Vorläufer.* 3d ed. Hildesheim.

Ronconi, A. 1931. "Per l'onomastica antica dei mari." *Studi italiani filologia classica,* n.s. 9:193–242, 257–331, esp. 298–331.

Rzach, A. 1913. "Homeridai." In *Real-Encyclopädie der klassischen Altertumswissenschaft,* edited by A. Pauly, G. Wissowa, and W. Kroll, 8:2150–52. Stuttgart.

Schissel von Fleschenberg, O. 1912. "Die komposition der Apista des Antonius Diogenes." *Novellenkränze Lukians* (Halle): 101–8.

Sinko, T. 1940–46. "De ordine quo erotici scriptores Graeci sibi successisse videantur." *Eos* 41:25.

Tomberg, K.-H. 1967. "Die Kaine Historia des Ptolemaios Chennos." Diss., Bonn.

Treadgold, W. T. 1980. *The Nature of the "Bibliotheca" of Photius.* Washington, D.C.

Vallauri, G. 1956. *Evemero di Messene*. Università di Torino, Pubblicazioni della facoltà di lettere e filosophia, vol. 8/8. Turin.

Vitelli, G. 1932. *Papiri greci i latini. Pubblicazioni della Società Italiana*. Vol. 10. Florence. [1177: 156–61.]

Weinreich, O. 1942. *Antiphanes und Münchhausen: Das antike Lügenmärlein von den gefroren Worten und sein Fortleben im Abendland*. Sitzungs-berichts der Akademie der Wissenschaft in Wien. [Pp. 220–24.]

Winkler, J. J. 1985. *Auctor et Actor: A Narratological Reading of Apuleius's "The Golden Ass."* Berkeley. [Pp. 73–75.]

Wünsch, R. 1898. *Joannes Laurentius Lydus liber de mensibus*. Leipzig.

Zimmermann, F. 1935. "Ein stumme Myrto: Ein Szene aud der Antonius Diogenes "τὰ ὑπὲρ Θούλην ἄπιστα." *Philologische Wochenschrift* 55:474–80.

———. 1936a. "Die APISTA des Antonios Diogenes im Licht des neuen Fundes." *Hermes* 71:312–19.

———. 1936b. *Griechische Roman-Papyri und verwandte Texte*. Heidelberg. [No. 10: 85–89.]

Antonius Diogenes?

Burkert, W. 1985. *Greek Religion*. Translated by J. Raffan. Cambridge. [Pp. 213.]

Crönert, W. 1903. "Ein neuer griechischer Roman." *Archiv für Papyrus-forschung* 2:365–66.

Crusius, O. 1897. "Die neuesten Papyrusfunde." *Beilage zur Allgemeinen Zeitung*, no. 145 (July 3): 1–2.

Gallavotti, C. 1931. "Frammento di Antonio Diogene?" *Studi italiani di filologia classica* 8:257.

Garin, F. 1920. "Su i romanzi greci." *Studi italiani di filologia classica*, n.s. 1:170–71.

Kussl, R. 1991. *Papyrusfragmente griechischer Romane*. Classica Monacensia, Band 2. Tübingen. [Pp. 103–40.]

Lavagnini, B. 1921. "Integrazioni e congetture a frammenti di romanza greci." *Aegyptus* 2:200–206.

Mahaffy, J. P. 1897. "Papiro greco inedito." *Rendiconti della reale accademia dei Lincei*, ser. 5, vol. 6:91–96.

Rattenbury, R. M. 1933. "Romance: The Greek Novel." In *New Chapters in the History of Greek Literature*, edited by J. U. Powell, 3d ser., pp. 234–37. Oxford.

Schmid, W. 1907. *Bursians Jahresbericht über die Fortschritte der klassischen Altertumswissenschaft*. Leipzig. [Band 129:286–87.]

Smyly, J. G. 1909 "Fragment of a Greek Romance." *Hermathena* 9:322–30.

Stephens, S. 1989. "Recycled Demosthenes." *Zeitschrift für Papyrologie und Epigraphik* 77:271–72.

Vogliano, A. 1925–26. "Per il testo dei romanzieri greci." *Bolletino di filologia classica* 32:86.

West, S. 1971. "Notes on Some Romance Papyri." *Zeitschrift für Papyrologie und Epigraphik* 7:95.

Wilcken, U. 1901. "Eine neue Roman-Handschrift." *Archiv für Papyrusforschung* 1:268–71.

Zimmermann, F. 1931. Review of Lavagnini 1922. *Philologische Wochenschrift* 51:225–26.

———. 1935. "Aus der Welt der griechisches Romans." *Die Antike* 1:299–300.

———. 1936. *Griechische Roman-Papyri und verwandte Texte.* Heidelberg. [No. 8:68–77.]

Apollonios

Bowman, A. 1979. Review of P. Mil. Vogl. 6.260. *Classical Review*, n.s. 29:188–89.

Conca, F. 1977. *Papiri della Università degli Studi di Milano.* Vol. 6. Edited by C. Gallazzi and M. Vandoni. Milan. [No. 260: 3–6.]

Crusius, O. 1913. *Literarisches Zentralblatt* 64, no. 50 (Dec. 13): 1725–26.

Garin, F. 1920. "I papiri d'Egitto e i romanzi greci." *Studi italiani di filologia classica* 1:l80.

Jacoby, F. 1923–58. *Die Fragmente der griechischen Historiker.* Berlin and Leiden. [Dritter Tiel C, 544–45.]

Klebs, E. 1899. *Die Erzahlung von Apollonios aus Tyrus.* Berlin. [Pp. 295–322.]

Kortekaas, G. 1984. *Historia Apollonii Regis Tyri: Prolegomena, Text Edition of the Two Principal Latin Recensions, Bibliography, Indices and Appendices.* Groningen.

Körte, A. 1924. Review of literary papryi. *Archiv für Papyrusforschung* 7:253, no. 659.

Kussl, R. 1991. *Papyrusfragmente griechischer Romane.* Classica Monacensia, Band 2. Tübingen. [Pp. 141–59.]

Lavagnini, B. 1922. *Eroticorum graecorum fragmenta papyracea.* Leipzig. [Pp. 32–33.]

Lodi, T. 1913. *Papiri greci i latini. Pubblicazioni della Società Italiana.* Vol. 2. Edited by G. Vitelli. Florence. [No. 141:82.]

Merkelbach, R. 1962. *Roman und Mysterium in der Antike.* Munich. [P. 160.]

Müller, B. A. 1916. "Ein neuer griechischer Roman." *Rheinisches Museum für Philologie* 71:358–63.

Perry, B. E. 1967. *The Ancient Romances.* Berkeley. [Pp. 294–324.]

Rattenbury, R. M. 1933. "Romance: The Greek Novel." in *New Chapters in the History of Greek Literature*, edited by J. U. Powell, 3d ser., pp. 248–49. Oxford.

Rohde, E. [1876] 1974. *Der griechische Roman und seine Vorläufer.* 3d ed. Hildesheim. [P. 436.]

Schmeling, G. 1988. *Historia Apollonii Regis Tyri.* Leipzig.

Stramaglia, A. 1992. "Prosimetria narrativa e 'romanza perduto': PTurner 8 (con discussione e riedizione di PSI 151 [Pack^2 2624] + PMilVogliano 260)." *Zeitschrift für Papyrologie und Epigraphik* 92:121–49.

Zimmermann, F. 1931. Review of Lavagnini 1922. *Philologische Wochenschrift* 51:231.

———. 1936. *Griechische Roman-Papyri und verwandte Texte.* Heidelberg. [No. 5: 50–52.]

The Apparition

Blass, F. 1906. Review of literary papyri. *Archiv für Papyrusforschung* 3: 296 (no. 246).

Fuhr, C. 1903. Review of P. Oxy. 3. *Berliner Philologische Wochenschrift* 23:1479.

Garin, F. 1920. "I papiri d'Egitto e i romanzi greci." *Studi italiani di filologia classica* 1:177.

Grenfell, B. P., and A. S. Hunt. 1903. *The Oxyrhynchus Papyri.* Vol. 3. The Egypt Exploration Society. London. [416: 60–61.]

Kerényi, K. [1927] 1962. *Die griechisch-orientalische Romanliteratur in religions-geschichtlicher Beleuchtung.* Darmstadt. [Pp. 169 n. 62.]

Kussl, R. 1991. *Papyrusfragmente griechischer Romane.* Classica Monacensia, Band 2. Tübingen. [Pp. 161–62.]

Müller, B. A. 1916. "Ein neuer griechischer Roman." *Rheinische Museum für Philologie* 71:359, nn. 5 and 6.

Rattenbury, R. M. 1933. "Romance: The Greek Novel." In *New Chapters in the History of Greek Literature*, edited by J. U. Powell, 3d ser., pp. 249–50. Oxford.

Winkler, J. J. 1980. "Lollianos and the Desperadoes." *Journal of Hellenic Studies* 100:162.

Zimmermann, F. 1931. Review of Lavagnini 1922. *Philologische Wochenschrift* 51:232.

———. 1935. "Verkannte Papyri." *Archiv für Papyrusforschung* 11:165–75.

Chione

Crönert, W. 1900. "Ein neuer griechischer Roman." *Beilage zur allgemeinen Zeitung* 259:6.

———. 1901. "Literarische Texte." *Archiv für Papyrusforschung* 1:529, no. 63.

Dieterich, K. 1906. "Neugriechische Sagenklänge vom alten Griechenland." *Neue Jahrbücher für das Klassische Altertum und für Pädagogik* 9:88.

Garin, F. 1909. "Su i romanzi greci." *Studi italiani di filologia classica* 17:424 n. 2.

———. 1920. "I papiri d'Egitto e i romanzi greci." *Studi italiani di filologia classica*, n.s. 1:174–77.

Lavagnini, B. 1921. "Integrazioni e congetture a frammenti di romanzi greci." *Aegyptus* 2:204–5.

———. 1922a. "Le origini del romanzo greco." *Annali della R. Scuola Normale Superiore Universitaria di Pisa* 28:89–97.

———. 1922b. *Eroticorum graecorum fragmenta papyracea.* Leipzig. [Pp. 24–27.]

Naber, S. A. 1901. "Chariton." *Mnemosyne* 29:99.

Rattenbury, R. M. 1926. "A New Interpretation of the *Chione* Fragments." *Classical Quarterly* 20:181–84.

———. 1933. "Romance: The Greek Novel." In *New Chapters in the History of Greek Literature*, edited by J. U. Powell, 3d ser., pp. 230–234. Oxford.

Reeve, M. 1971. "Hiatus in the Greek Novelists." *Classical Quarterly*, n.s. 21:536.

Schmid, W. 1902. *Bursians Jahresbericht über die Fortschritte der klassischen Altertumswissenschaft*. Leipzig. [Band 108:276.]

Wilamowitz-Moellendorf, U. von. 1909. "Lesefrüchte." *Hermes* 44:464–66.

Wilcken, U. 1901. "Ein neue Roman-Handschrift." *Archiv für Papyrusforschung* 1:227–64.

Zimmermann, F. 1931. "Der Chione-Roman ernuet untersucht." *Aegyptus* 11:45–56.

———. 1936a. "Ein Vermutung zum Chione-Roman." *Hermes* 71:236–40.

———. 1936b. *Griechische Roman-Papyri und verwandte Texte*. Heidelberg. [No. 3: 40–46.]

Chione?

Gronewald, M. 1979. "Ein neues Fragment zu einem Roman." *Zeitschrift für Papyrologie und Epigraphik* 35:15–20.

Lucke, C. 1984. "Bemerkungen zu zwei Romanfragmenten." *Zeitschrift für Papyrologie und Epigraphik* 54:41–47.

Zimmermann, F. 1935. "Ein neuer griechischer Roman." *Forschungen und Fortschnitte* 11:319–20.

———. 1936a. "Der P. Berol. 10535." *Atti del IV Congresso Internazionale de Papirologia di Firenze, Aegyptus* 5:383–93.

———. 1936b. *Griechische Roman-Papyri und verwandte Texte*. Heidelberg. [No. 7: 64–68.]

Daulis

Bell, H. I. 1921. Survey of literary papyri published in 1919–1920. *Journal of Egyptian Archaeology* 7:87.

Eitrem, S. 1939. "Daulis in Delphoi und Apollons Strafe." *Dragma Martino P. Nilsson ... Dedicatum*. Skrifter utgivna av Svenska Institutet i Rom, ser. 2.1:170–80.

———. 1948. "Varia." *Symbolae Osloenses* 26:175–76.

Halliday, W. R. 1928. *The Greek Questions of Plutarch*. Oxford. [Pp. 59–60.]

Körte, A. 1924. Review of literary papyri. *Archiv für Papyrusforschung* 7:252–53, no. 657.

Manteuffel, G. 1930. *De opusculis Graecis Aegypti e papyris, ostracis lapidibusque collectis*. Travaux de la Société des Sciences et des Lettres de Varsovie, Classe 1, no. 12. Warsaw. [No. 66: 28–29, 95–99.]

Schubart, W. 1920. "Aus einer Apollon-Aretologie." *Hermes* 55:188–95.

West, S. 1971. "Notes on Some Romance Papyri." *Zeitschrift für Papyrologie und Epigraphik* 7:96.

Winkler, J. J. 1985. *Auctor et Actor: A Narratological Reading of Apuleius's "The Golden Ass."* Berkeley. [Pp. 235–36.]

The Festival

Burkert, W. 1985. *Greek Religion*. Translated by J. Raffan. Cambridge. [Pp. 59–64, 112–113.]

Cazzaniga, I. 1956. "Intorno al pap. fiorentino inv. 516." *Acme* 9:53–56.

Terzaghi, N. 1956. "Commentario ad un' opera poetica? Dai papiri inediti della Società Italiana." *La parola del passato* 50:378–86.

Goatherd and the Palace Guards

Körte, A. 1924. Review of literary papyri. *Archiv für Papyrusforschung* 7:253, no. 660.

Lavagnini, B. 1922. *Eroticorum graecorum fragmenta papyracaea*. Leipzig. [Pp. 36–37.]

Rattenbury, R. M. 1933. "Romance: The Greek Novel." In *New Chapters in the History of Greek Literature*, edited by J. U. Powell, 3d ser., p. 248. Oxford.

Stramaglia, A. 1992. "Fuga dal gineceo? PSI 725 (Pack² 2626)." *Zeitschrift für Papyrologie und Epigraphik* 94:64–76.

Vitelli, G. 1920. *Papiri greci i latini. Pubblicazioni della Società Italiana*. Vol. 6. Florence. [725: 163.]

Zimmermann, F. 1936a. "Ein verklungene Novelle: zur Deutung des PSI 725." *Symbolae Osloenses* 15–16:101–10.

———. 1936b. *Griechische Roman-Papyri und verwandte Texte*. Heidelberg. [No. 11: 90–92.]

Iamblichos

Adler, A. 1928–. *Suidae Lexicon*. Leipzig.

Barigazzi, A. 1961. Review of Habrich 1960. *Athenaeum* 39:368–71.

Borgogno, A. 1975a. "Sui *Babyloniaca* di Giamblico." *Hermes* 103:101–26.

———. 1975b. "Sopra un *Excerptum* di Giamblico Siro." *Istituto Lombardo (Rend. Lett.)* 109:162–72.

Braun, M. 1938. *History and Romance in Graeco-Oriental Literature*. Oxford.

Bruhn, E. 1890. "Suidea." *Rheinisches Museum für Philologie* 45:273–83.

Cataudella, Q. 1973. *Il romanzo Antico Greco e Latino*. Florence. [Italian translation.]

Di Gregorio, L. 1963. "Su alcuni frammenti delle *Storie Babilonesi* di Giamblico." *Aevum* 37:390–405.

———. 1964. "Sulla Biografia di Giamblico e la fortuna del suo romanzo attraverso i secoli." *Aevum* 38:1–13.

Habrich, E., ed. 1960. *Iamblichi Babyloniacorum Reliquiae*. Leipzig.

Halfmann, H. 1979. *Die Senatoren aus dem östlichen Teil des Imperium Romanum bis zum Ende des 2. Jahrhunderts n. Chr*. Hypomnemata 58. Göttingen. [Pp. 175–76.]

BIBLIOGRAPHY

Hefti, V. [1940] 1950. *Zur Erzählungstechnik in Heliodors Aethiopika.* Vienna. [P. 455.]

Henry, R. 1960. *Photios, Bibliothèque.* Vol. 2. Paris. [94: 34–48.]

Hercher, R. 1858–59. *Erotici scriptores Graeci.* Vol. 1 (1858), 33–34, pp. 217–20; vol. 2 (1959), 64–67. Leipzig.

———. 1866. "Zu Iamblichus Babyloniaca." *Hermes* 1:361–66.

———. 1867. "Zu Iamblichus Babyloniaca." *Hermes* 2:95.

———. 1875. "Über einige Fragmente bei Suidas." *Monatsbericht der königliche preussische Akademie der Wissenschaften* (Jan. 1–).

———. 1876. "Zu Griechischen Prosaikern." *Hermes* 11:361–62.

Hinck, H. 1873. *Polemonis declamationes.* Leipzig.

Hunger, J. 1909. *Babylonische Tieromina nebst griechisch-römischen Parallelen.* Mitteilungen der Vorderasiatischen Gesellschaft 14. Berlin. [Pp. 37–39, 40–42.]

Innes, D., and M. Winterbottom 1988. *Sopatros the Rhetor: Studies in the Text of the Διαιρέcειc Ζητημάτων.* University of London Institute of Classical Studies, suppl. 48. London. [Pp. 93–101.]

James, M. R. 1924. *The Apocryphal New Testament.* Reprint. Oxford.

Macurdy, H. [1932] 1985. *Hellenistic Queens.* Chicago.

Münscher, K. 1920. *Xenophon in der griechisch-römischen Literatur. Philologus* suppl. 13: 146.

Naechster, M. 1908. *De Pollucis et Phrynichi controversiis.* Leipzig.

Reardon, B. 1982. "Theme, Structure and Narrative in Chariton." *Yale Classical Studies* 27:1–27.

Reeve, M. 1971. "Hiatus in the Greek Novelists." *Classical Quarterly,* n.s. 21:534–35.

Rohde, E. [1876] 1974. *Der griechische Roman und seine Vorläufer.* Hildesheim.

Schneider-Menzel, U. 1948. "Jamblichos' Babylonische Geschichten." In *Literatur und Gesellschaft im ausgehenden Altertum,* edited by Franz Altheim, 1:48–92. Halle/Saale.

Thompson, R. C. 1971. *Semitic Magic.* Reprint. New York. [Pp. 24–27.]

Trencsényi-Waldapfel, I. 1969. "Das Rosenmotif ausserhalb des Eselromans." In *Festschrift für Franz Altheim,* edited by R. Stiehl and H. E. Stier, 512–17. Berlin.

Winkler, J. J. 1980. "Lollianos and the Desperadoes." *Journal of Hellenic Studies* 100:160–65.

———. 1985. *Auctor et Actor: A Narratological Reading of Apuleius's "The Golden Ass."* Berkeley. [Pp. 257–73.]

Wüst, E. 1938. "Pharnouchos." In *Real-Encyclopädie der klassischen Altertumswissenschaft,* edited by A. Pauly, G. Wissowa, and W. Kroll, 19.2: 1856–57. Stuttgart.

Wuthnow, H. 1930. *Die semitische Menschennamen in griechischen Inscriften und Papyri der vorderen Orients.* Leipzig. [Pp. 56, 148.]

Ziegler, K. H. 1964. *Die Beziehungen zwischen Rom und dem Partherreich.* Weisbaden.

Initiation

Delatte, A. 1952a. "Le Papyrus d'*Antinoopolis* relatif aux mystères." *Bulletin de la Classe des lettres de l' Académie Royale de Belgique*, ser. 5, 38:194–208.

———. 1952b. "Le Papyrus d'*Antinoopolis* relatif aux mystères." *Comptes rendus de l'Académie des Inscriptions et Belles-Lettres*: 251–58.

Innes, D and M. Winterbottom. 1988. *Sopatros the Rhetor: Studies in the Text of the Διαιρέςειc Ζητημάτων*. University of London Institute of Classical Studies, suppl. 48. London. [Pp. 93–101.]

Koenen, L., and D. B. Thompson. 1984. "Gallus as Triptolemos on the Tazza Farnese." *Bulletin of the American Society of Papyrologists* 21: 111–53.

Merkelbach, R. 1958. Survey of literary papyri. *Archiv für Papyrusforschung* 16:123–24, no. 1141.

Parca, M. 1991. *Ptocheia, or Odysseus in Disguise at Troy*. American Studies in Papyrology 31. Atlanta. [P. 7 n. 19.]

Roberts, C. H. 1950. *The Antinoopolis Papyri*. Vol. 1. London. [18: 39–40.]

Inundation

Bernand, A. 1970. *Le Delta Égyptien d' après les textes greces*. Mémoires publié par les membres de l'Institut français d' Archéologie orientale. Cairo. [Pp. 225–28.]

Crawford, D. S. 1955. *Papyri Michaelidae: Being a Catalogue of the Greek and Latin Papyri, Tablets and Ostraca in the Library of Mr. G. A. Michailides of Cairo*. Aberdeen. [Pp. 10–13.]

Drescher, J. 1949. "Topological Notes for Alexandria and the District." *Bulletin de la société archéologique d' Alexandrie* 38:13–22.

Merkelbach, R. 1958. Survey of literary papyri. *Archiv für Papyrusforschung* 16:112–14, no.1117.

Murray, O. 1970. "Hecataeus of Abdera and Pharaonic Kingship." *Journal of Egyptian Archaeology* 56:148 n. 3.

Santoni, A. 1991. "Una descrizione di Canopo in P. Michael. 4." In *Studi e testi per il corpus dei papiri filosofici greci e latini*, edited by A. Santoni, vol. 5. Florence. [Pp. 101–20.]

Stramaglia, A. 1993. "Sul frammento di romanzo(?) PMichael 4 (Pack^2 2271)." *Zeitschrift für Papyrologie und Epigrafik* 93:7–15.

West, S. 1973. "P. Michael. 4: Fact or Fiction?" *Zeitschrift für Papyrologie und Epigraphik* 10, pt. 1:75–77.

Iolaos

Astbury, R. 1977. "Petronius, *P. Oxy.* 3010, and Menippean Satire." *Classical Philology* 72:22–31.

Boyancé, P. 1935. "Sur les mystères phrygiens." *Revue des études ancienne* 37:161–64.

Burkert, W. 1987. *Ancient Mystery Cults*. Cambridge, Mass.

BIBLIOGRAPHY

Carcopino, J. 1942. *Aspects mystiques de la Rome païenne*. Paris.
Cataudella, Q. 1975a. "Ultime da Oxyrhynchos." *Cultura e scuola* 54:42–48.
————. 1975b. "Un frammento di Menippo di Gadara?" *Sileno* 1:143–54.
Courtney, E. 1980. "Juvenal and Lucian." In Courtney, ed., *Commentary on Juvenal*, pp. 624–29. Oxford.
Duthoy, R. 1965. *The Taurobolium: Its Evolution and Terminology*. Études préliminaires des religions orientales dans l'empire romain 10. Leiden.
Graillot, H. 1912. *Le Culte de Cybèle Mère des dieux à Rome et dans l'empire romain*. Paris.
Helm, R. 1906. *Lucian und Menipp*. Leipzig and Berlin.
Hepding, H. [1903] 1967. *Attis, seine Mythen und sein Kult*. Religionsgeschichtliche Versuche und Verarbeiten 1. Giessen.
McCarthy, B. P. 1934. "Lucian and Menippus." *Yale Classical Studies* 4:3–55.
Macleod, C. W. 1974. "A Note on P. Oxy. 3010.29." *Zeitschrift für Papyrologie und Epigraphik* 15:159–61.
Merkelbach, R. 1973. "Fragment eines Satirischen Romans: Aufforderung zur Beichte." *Zeitschrift für Papyrologie und Epigraphik* 11:81–100.
Neumann, G. 1953. "Menanders *Androgynos*." *Hermes* 81:491–96.
Oden, R. A. 1977. *Studies in Lucian's "De Syria dea."* Harvard Semitic Monographs 15. Cambridge, Mass.
Parsons, P. 1971. "A Greek Satyricon?" *Bulletin of the Institute of Classical Studies* 18:53–68.
————. 1974. *The Oxyrhynchus Papyri*. Vol. 42. Egypt Exploration Society. London. [3010: 34–41].
Perry, B. E. 1967. *The Ancient Romances*. Berkeley. [Pp. 208–9.]
Richard, L. 1966. "Juvénal et les galles de Cybèle." *Revue de l'histoire des religions* 169:51–67.
Sanders, G. 1972. "Gallos." *Rivista di archaeologica cristiana* 8:984–1034.
————. 1978. "Les Galles et le gallat devant l'opinion chrétienne." In *Hommages à Maarten J. Vermaseren*, edited by Margreet de Boer and T. A. Edridge, Études préliminaires des religions orientales dans l'empire romain 68/3, pp. 1062–91. Leiden.
Schmidt, Richard O. 1886. *De Hymenaeo et Talasio dis nuptialibus*. Kiel.
Sfameni Gasparro, G. 1985. *Soteriology and Mystic Aspects in the Cult of Cybele and Attis*. Études préliminaires des religions orientales dans l'empire romain 103. Leiden.
Stramaglia, A. 1992. "Prosimetria narrativa e 'romanza perduto': PTurner 8 (con discussione e riedizione di PSI 151 [Pack² 2624] + PMilVogliano 260)." *Zeitschrift für Papyrologie und Epigraphik* 92:121–49.
Thilo, G., and H. Hagen, eds. 1961. *Servius*. Vol. 2, pt. 2. Reprint. Hildesheim. [P. 336.21–24.]
Vermaseren, Maarten J. 1977. *Cybele and Attis: The Myth and the Cult*. London.
————. 1982. *Corpus cultus Cybelae Attidisque II. Graecia atque insulae*. Études préliminaires des religions orientales dans l'empire romain 50. Leiden.

BIBLIOGRAPHY

Kalligone

Harmatta, J. 1950. *Studies on the History of the Sarmatians.* Budapest.
Kretschmer, K. 1921. "Sarmatae" and " Sarmatia." In *Real-Encyclopädie der klassischen Altertumswissenschaft,* edited by A. Pauly, G. Wissowa, and W. Kroll, ser. 2, vol. 1.2:2542–50 and vol. 2.1:1–11. Stuttgart.
Körte, A. 1927. Survey of literary papyri. *Archiv für Papyrusforschung* 8:271, no. 699.
Norsa, M. 1927. *Papiri greci i latini. Pubblicazioni della Società Italiana.* Vol. 8. Florence. [981: 196–99, aided by C. C. Edgar.]
Rattenbury, R. M. 1933. "Romance: The Greek Novel." In *New Chapters in the History of Greek Literature,* edited by J. U. Powell, 3d ser., pp. 240–44. Oxford.
Rostovtzeff, M. 1931. *Skythien und der Bosporus* I. Berlin. [Pp. 98–99.]
Sulimirski, T. 1970. *The Sarmatians.* New York.
Zimmermann, F. 1935. "Lukians Toxaris und das Kairener Romanfragment." *Philologische Wochenschrift* 55:1211–16.
———. 1936. *Griechische Roman-Papyri und verwandte Texte.* Heidelberg. [No. 4: 46–50.]

Lollianos

Browne, G. M. 1973. "On the Text of the *Phoinikika* of Lollianos." *Zeitschrift für Papyrologie und Epigraphik* 10:77.
———. 1982. "Ad Lolliani *Phoenicica.*" *Zeitschrift für Papyrologie und Epigraphik* 46:135–43, pls. 5–7.
———. 1989. "Notes on Literary Papyri." *Zeitschrift für Papyrologie und Epigraphik* 76:239.
Fischer, E. 1974. *Die Ekloge des Phrynichos.* Berlin. [Nos. 140, 141, 152 (= pp. 15, 170, 180 Lobeck).]
Garin, F. 1920. "I papiri d' Egitto e i romanzi greci." *Studi italiani di filologia classica,* n.s. 1:181.
Graf, F. 1986. "ΒΟΥΚΟΛΟΙ." *Zeitschrift für Papyrologie und Epigraphik* 62:43–44.
Grenfell, B., and A. Hunt. 1915. *The Oxyrhynchus Papyri.* Vol. 11. Egypt Exploration Society. London. [1368: 119–21.]
Henrichs, A. 1969. "Lollianos, *Phoinikika*: Fragmente eines neuen griechischen Romans." *Zeitschrift für Papyrologie und Epigraphik* 4:205–15.
———. 1970a. "Nachtrag zu Lollianos, *Phoinikika.*" *Zeitschrift für Papyrologie und Epigraphik* 5:22.
———. 1970b. "Pagan Ritual and the Alleged Crimes of the Early Christians: A Reconsideration." In *Kyriakon, Festschrift Johannes Quasten,* edited by P. Granfield and J. A. Jungmann, 1:18–35. Munich.
———. 1970c. "Lollianos und P. Oxy. 1368." *Zeitschrift für Papyrologie und Epigraphik* 6:42–43.
———. 1972. *Die "Phoinikika" des Lollianos.* Papyrologische Texte und Abhandlungen, no. 14. Bonn.

Husson, G, 1983. OIKIA: *Le vocabulaire de la maison privée en Égypte d' après les papyrus grecs.* Paris.

Jones, C. P. 1980. "Apuleius' *Metamorphoses* and Lollianos' *Phoinikika.*" *Phoenix* 34:243–54.

Keil, J. 1953. "Vertreter der zweiten Sophistik in Ephesos." *Jahreshefte des Österreichischen Archäologischen Instituts, Wein* 40:7–12.

Kerényi, K. [1927] 1962. *Die griechisch-orientalische Romanliteratur in religions-geschichtlicher Beleuchtung.* Reprint. Tubingen.

Koenen, L. 1979. "Notes on Papyri. P. Cologne Inv. 3328: Lollianos' *Phoinikika.*" *Bulletin of the American Society of Papyrologists* 16:109–14.

Kohl, R. 1915. "De scholasticarum declamationum argumentis ex historia petitis." Diss. Paderborn. [no. 210.]

Körte, A. 1924. Survey of literary papyri. *Archiv für Papyrusforschung* 7:253, no. 658 (reporting an incorrect number for papyrus).

Lavagnini, B. 1922. *Eroticorum graecorum fragmenta papyracaea.* Leipzig. [Pp. 33–34.]

Merkelbach, R. 1962. *Roman und Mysterium in der Antike.* Munich and Berlin.

Nowicka, M. 1969. *La Maison privée dans l' Égypte ptolemaïque.* Warsaw.

O'Sullivan, J. N. 1983. "Some Thoughts on Lollianus Fr. B1." *Zeitschrift für Papyrologie und Epigraphik* 50:7–11.

Rattenbury, R. M. 1933. "Romance: The Greek Novel." In *New Chapters in the History of Greek Literature*, edited by J. U. Powell, 3d ser., pp. 246–247. Oxford.

Rohde, E. [1876] 1974. *Der griechische Roman und seine Vorläufer.* 3d ed. Hildesheim. [Pp. 369–72.]

Sandy, G. N. 1979. "Notes on Lollianos' *Phoenicica.*" *American Journal of Philology* 100:367–76.

Scarcella, A. M. 1981. "Metastasi narratologica del dato storico nel romanzo erotico greco." In *Materiali e contributi per la storia della narrativa greco-latina*, edited by Luigi Pepe, 3:341–367.

Schissel von Fleschenberg, O. 1926. "Lollianos aus Ephesos." *Philologus* 82, n.s. 36:181–201.

Selden, Daniel. 1994. "Genre of Genre." In *The Search for the Ancient Novel*, edited by James Tatum, pp. 39–64. Baltimore.

Stramaglia, A. 1992. "Covi di banditi e cadaveri 'scomodi' in Lolliano, Apuleio e [Luciano]." *Zeitschrift für Papyrologie und Epigraphik* 94:59–63.

Szepessy, T. 1978. "Zur Interpretation eines neu entdeckten griechischen Romans." *Acta Antiqua Academiae Scientiarum Hungaricae* 26:29–36.

Tatum, J. 1989. *Xenophon's Imperial Fiction.* Princeton. [Pp. 163–188.]

Triantaphyllopoulos, J. 1988 "Virginité et défloration masculines." In *Proceedings of the XIIIth International Congress of Papyrology*, edited by B. Mandalaras, 2:327–33. Athens.

Winkler, J. J. 1980. "Lollianos and the Desperadoes." *Journal of Hellenic Studies* 100:155–81.

———. 1990. *The Constraints of Desire: The Anthropology of Sex and Gender in Ancient Greece.* New York and London. [Pp. 189–93 and n. 1.]

The Love Drug

Barns, J.W.B. 1956. "Egypt and the Greek Romance." Akten des VIII. Internationalen Kongresses für Papyrologie, edited by H. Gerstinger. *Mitteilungen aus der Papyrussammlung der Nationalbibliothek in Wien*, n.s. 5:34.

Bell, H. I. 1924. Survey of literary papyri published in 1922–23. *Journal of Egyptian Archaeology* 10:156.

Bonner, C. 1921. "A Papyrus Describing Magical Powers." *Transactions of the American Philological Association* 52:111–18.

Daris, S. 1986. "Prosa (Romanzo?)." *Aegyptus* 66: 110–14.

Dodds, E. R. 1952. "A Fragment of a Greek Novel." *Phoenix*, suppl. 1 (Studies in Honor of Gilbert Norwood): 133–38.

Eitrem, S. 1924. "Varia," *Symbolae Osloenses* 2:71.

Körte, A. 1927. Survey of literary papyri. *Archiv für Papyrusforschung* 8:128.

Merkelbach, R. 1958. Survey of literary papyri. *Archiv für Papyrusforschung* 16:122–23.

Preisendanz, K., ed. 1931. *Papyri graecae magicae: Die griechischen Zauberpapyri*. Vol. 2. Leipzig. [No. 34.]

Reyhl, K. 1969. "Antonius Diogenes: Untersuchungen zu den Roman-Fragmenten der *Wunder jenseits von Thule* und zu den *Wahren Geschichten* des Lukian." Diss. Tubingen. [Pp. 14–20.]

Stramaglia, A. 1991. "Innamoramento in sogno o storia fantasmi?" *Zeitschrift für Papyrologie und Epigraphik* 88: 73–86.

West, S. 1971. "Notes on Some Romance Papyri." *Zeitschrift für Papyrologie und Epigraphik* 7:95.

Metiochos and Parthenope

Coquin, R.-G. 1981. "Le Roman de Παρθενόπη/Bartanuba (ms. IFAO, Copte 22, ff° 1^{r-v} 2^r)." *Bulletin de Centenaire*, supplément au Bulletin de l'institut français d' archaeologie orientale 81:343–58 and pl. 42.

Dihle, A. 1978. "Zur Datierung des Metiochos-Roman." *Würzburger Jahrbücher für die Altertumswissenschaft*, n.s. 4:47–55.

Garin, F. 1920. "I papiri d' Egitto e i romanza greci." *Studi italiani di filologia classica*, n.s. 1:168–70.

Gronewald, M. 1977. "Ein neues Fragment aus dem Metiochos-Parthenope-Roman (Ostracon Bodl. 2175 = P^2 2782)." *Zeitschrift für Papyrologie und Epigraphik* 24:21–22.

Hägg, T. 1984. "The Parthenope Romance Decapitated?" *Symbolae Osloenses* 59:61–92.

———. 1985. "Metiochus at Polycrates' Court." *Eranos* 83:92–102.

———. 1987. "Callirhoe and Parthenope: The Beginnings of the Historical Novel." *Classical Antiquity* 6:184–204.

———. 1989. "Hermes and the Invention of the Lyre: An Unorthodox Version." *Symbolae Osloenses* 64:36–73.

Hoffmann, H. 1970. *Ten Centuries that Shaped the West: Greek and Roman Art in Texas Collections*. Mainz. [Pp. 112–115.]

Kaladze, I. 1983. *Epiceskoe nasladie Unsuri*. Tbilisi. [Russian edition of *Wamiq and 'Adhra'*.]

Kerényi, K. [1927] 1962. *Die griechisch-orientalische Romanliteratur in religions-geschichtlicher Beleuchtung*. Darmstadt. [Pp. 59–60, 202–3.]

Kokolakis, M. 1959. "Pantomimus and the Treatise ΠΕΡΙ ΟΡΧΗΣΕΩΣ." *Platon* 11:47–51.

Körte, A. 1933. Survey of literary papryi. *Archiv für Papyrusforschung* 11:283, no. 846.

Krebs, F. 1895. "Metiochos und Parthenope." *Hermes* 30:144–50. [With an addendum by G. Kaibel and C. Robert.]

Lavagnini, B. 1921. "Integrazioni e congetture a frammenti di romanzi greci." *Aegyptus* 2:200–206.

———. 1922a. "Le origini del romanzo greco." *Annali della R. Scuola Normale Superiore Universitaria di Pisa* 28:82–89.

———. 1922b. *Eroticorum graecorum fragmenta papyracaea*. Leipzig. [Pp. 21–24.]

———. 1950. *Studi sul romanzo greco*. Florence. [Pp. 222–224.]

Levi, D. 1947. *Antioch Mosaic Pavements*. Princeton. [1:118–19, 2: pl. 20c.]

Maehler, H. 1976. "Der Metiochos-Parthenope-Roman." *Zeitschrift für Papyrologie und Epigraphik* 23:1–20.

Münscher, K. 1911. *Bursians Jahresbericht über die Fortschritte der klassischen Altertumswissenschaft*. Leipzig. [Band 149:188.]

Rattenbury, R. M. 1933. "Romance: The Greek Novel." In *New Chapters in the History of Greek Literature*, edited by J. U. Powell, 3d ser., pp. 237–40. Oxford.

Reitzenstein, R. 1906. *Hellenistische Wundererzählungen*. Leipzig. [Pp. 167–68.]

Ritter, H. 1948. Review of Diwan-i Abu l-Qasim Ḥasan b. Aḥmad 'Unṣuri (Tahran 1323/1945). *Oriens* 1:134–39.

Schmid, W. 1902. *Bursians Jahresbericht über die Fortschritte der klassischen Altertumswissenschaft*. Leipzig. [Band 102:274.]

Shafi, M. 1967. *Wamiq-o-'Adhra' of 'Unsuri*. Lahore. [Pp. 1–8 (English preface).]

Stilwell, R. 1938. *Antioch-on-the-Orontes*. Vol. 2. Princeton. [Pp. 203, No. 99.]

Tait, J., and C. Préaux, eds. 1955. *Greek Ostraca in the Bodleian Library at Oxford and Various Other Collections*, Vol. 2: *Ostraca of the Roman and Byzantine Periods*. London.

Utas, B. 1984–86. "Did 'Adhra' Remain a Virgin?" *Orientalia Suecana* 33–35:429–41.

Wilcken, U. 1901. "Eine neue Roman-Handschrift." *Archiv für Papyrusforschung* 1:264–67.

Wilhelm, A. 1909. "Parerga." In *Wiener Eranos*, edited by A. Hölder, pp. 134–35. Vienna.

Ziegler, K. 1949. "Parthenope." In *Real-Encyclopädie der klassischen Alter-*

tumswissenschaft, edited by A. Pauly, G. Wissowa, and W. Kroll, 18.4: 1935–36. Stuttgart.

Zimmermann, F. 1933a. "Ein unveröffentliches Bruchstück des Metiochos-Parthenope-Romans." *Aegyptus* 13:53–61.

——. 1933b. "Zu Pap. Berol. 7927." *Archiv für Papyrusforschung* 11:114–16.

——. 1935a. "ΔΕΥΤΕΡΑΙ ΦΡΟΝΤΙΔΕΣ: Ein Nachwort zu P. Berol. 9588." *Aegyptus* 15:277–81.

——. 1935b. "Papyrologisches und Philologisches zu P. Berol. 7927: Metiochos-Parthenope-Roman A." *Aegyptus* 15:405–14.

——. 1936. Griechische Roman-Papyri und verwandte Texte. Heidelberg. [No. 6: 52–63.]

Metiochos and Parthenope?

Blass, F. 1906. Survey of literary papryi. *Archiv für Papyrusforschung* 3: 282, no. 221.

Fuhr, K. 1903. Review of papyri. *Berliner Philologische Wochenschrift* 23:1478.

Garin, F, 1920. "I papiri d' Egitto e i romanzi greci." *Studi italiani di filologia classica* 1:179–80.

Grenfell, B. P. and A. S. Hunt. 1903. *The Oxyrhynchus Papyri.* Vol. 3. Egypt Exploration Society. London. [435: 76–78.]

Kussl, R. 1991. *Papyrusfragmente griechischer Romane.* Classica Monacensia, Band 2. Tübingen. [Pp. 165–67.]

Lavagnini, B. 1922. *Eroticorum graecorum fragmenta papyracaea.* Leipzig. [Pp. 28–29.]

Maehler, H. 1976. "Der Metiochos-Parthenope-Roman." *Zeitschrift für Papyrologie und Epigraphik* 23:1–20.

Rattenbury, R. M. 1933. "Romance: The Greek Novel." In *New Chapters in the History of Greek Literature,* edited by J. U. Powell, 3d ser., p. 245. Oxford.

Ritter, H. 1948. Review of Diwan-i Abu l-Qasim Ḥasan b. Aḥmad 'Unṣuri (Tahran 1323/1945). *Oriens* 1:138.

Zimmermann, F. 1935. "Neues zum Metiochos-Parthenope-Roman PO435." *Philologus* 90:194–205.

——. 1936. *Griechische Roman-Papyri und verwandte Texte.* Heidelberg. [No. 6c: 62–63.]

Nightmare or Necromancy?

Barns, J.W.B. 1956. "Egypt and the Greek Romance." Akten des VIII. Internationalen Kongresses für Papyrologie, edited by H. Gerstinger. *Mitteilungen aus der Papyrussammlung der Nationalbibliothek in Wien,* n.s. 5:29–34.

Bonner, C. 1933. "A Fragment of a Romance." *Aegyptus* 13:203–7.

Henrichs, A. 1972. *Die "Phoinikika" des Lollianos.* Papyrologische Texte und Abhandlungen, no. 14. Bonn. [P. 49 n. 11.]

Körte, A. 1935. Survey of literary papyri. *Archiv für Papyrusforschung* 11:283, no. 845.

Longo, v. 1969. *Aretologie nel mondo greco. I: Epigrafi e papiri*. Università di Genova, Facoltà di lettere, Instituto di filologia classica e medievale. Genoa. [Pp. 181–83.]

Stramaglia, A. 1990. "Due storie de fantasmi raccontate di fantasmi?" *Zeitschrift für Papyrologie und Epigraphik* 89:19–26.

West, S. 1983. "P. Mich. 3378: A Voice from the Grave?" *Zeitschrift für Papyrologie und Epigraphik* 51:55–58.

Zimmermann, F. 1934. "Romanpapyri." *Münchner Beiträge für Papyrusforschung* 19:30–41.

Ninos

Braun, M. 1938. *History and Romance in Graeco-Oriental Literature*. Oxford.

Brinkmann, A. 1910. "Lückenbüsser." *Rheinisches Museum für Philologie* 65:319–20.

Castiglioni, L. 1926. "Communicazione." *Bollettino della Filologia classica* 33:147.

Dihle, A. 1978. "Zur Datierung des Metiochos-Romans." *Würzburger Jahrbücher für die Altertumswissenschaft*, n.s. 4:47–55.

Garin, F. 1920. "I papiri d' Egitto e i romanzi greci." *Studi italiani di filologia classica* 1:162–68.

Gaselee, S. 1916. "The Ninus Romance." In *Daphnis and Chloe by Longus*, edited by J. M. Edmonds, Loeb Classical Library, pp. 382–99. London and Cambridge, Mass.

Gronewald, M. 1993. "Zum Ninos-Roman." *Zeitschrift für Papyrologie und Epigrafik* 97:1–6.

Herrmann, L. 1939. "La Date du roman de Ninus." *Chronique d' Égypte* 28:373–75.

Hopkins, K. 1978. *Conquerors and Slaves*. Cambridge. [P. 199.]

Jenistové, R. 1953. "Nejstatsi Romàn Svetové Literatury (Ziomky reckého románu o Ninovi)." *Listy Filologické*, n.s. 1:30–54, pl. 4, 210–28 (English summary, 319).

Kussl, R. 1991. *Papyrusfragmente griechischer Romane*. Classica Monacensia, Band 2. Tübingen. [Pp. 13–101.]

Lavagnini, B. 1921. "Integrazioni e congetture a frammenti di romanzi greci." *Aegyptus* 2:200–203.

———. 1922. *Eroticorum graecorum fragmenta papyracea*. Leipzig. [Pp. 1–15.]

———. 1950. *Studi sul romanzo greco*. Florence. [Pp. 221–22.]

Lehmann. C. F. 1901. "Die historische Semiramis und Herodot." *Klio* 1:256–81.

Levi, D. 1944. "The Novel of Ninus and Semiramis." *Proceedings of the American Philosophical Society* 87:420–28.

Levi, L. 1895. "Sui frammenti del 'Romanzo di Nino' recentemente scopteri."
Rivista di filologia e di instruzione classica 23:1–22.

MacCormack, S. 1985. *Art and Ceremony in Late Antiquity.* Berkeley. [P. 24.]

Merkelbach, R. 1958. Survey of literary papyri. *Archiv für Papyrusforschung*
16:122, no. 1139.

Müller, B. A. 1917–18. "Zum Ninosroman." *Rheinisches Museum für Philologie* 72:198–216.

Norsa, M. 1945. "Un frammento del romanzo di Nino." In *Scritti dedicati alla
memoria di Ippolito Rosellini nel primo centenario della morte*, pp. 193–97.
Florence.

———. 1949. *Papiri greci i latini. Pubblicazioni della Società Italiana.* Vol. 13.
Florence. [1305: 82–86.]

Perry, B. E. 1967. *The Ancient Romances.* Berkeley. [Pp. 153–73.]

Piccolomini, E. 1893a. "Supplementi ed osservationi ai frammenti del romanzo
di Nino." *Rendiconti dell' accademia dei Lincei* 5, 2:313–32.

———. 1893b. "Sui frammenti del romanzo di Nino . . ." *Nuova Antologia* 3,
46:490–99.

Piotrowicz, L. 1953. "Ninus i Semiramida w legenzie i historii." *Meander*
8:197–98.

Rattenbury, R. M. 1933. "Romance: The Greek Novel." In *New Chapters in the
History of Greek Literature*, edited by J. U. Powell, 3d ser., pp. 213–219.
Oxford.

Scheuchzer, A. 1863. "Die Lage der verschiedenen Ninus-Städte." *Rheinisches
Museum für Philologie* 18:329–41.

Stadtmüller, H. 1896. Review of Levi 1895. *Berliner Philologische Wochenschrift* 16:1285–89.

Vitelli, G. 1894. "L'iato nel romanzo di Nino." *Studi italiani di filologia classica*
2:297–98.

Wehrli, C. 1970. "Un Fragment du roman de Ninos." *Zeitschrift für Papyrologie
und Epigraphik* 6:39–41.

———. 1986. *Les Papyrus de Genève.* Geneva. [2.85.]

Weil, H. 1893. Review of Wilcken 1893. *Revue des études grecques* 6:140.

———. 1902. "La Ninopédie." *Études de littérature et de rythmique grecques:*
90–106.

West, S. 1971. "Notes on Some Romance Papyri." *Zeitschrift für Papyrologie
und Epigraphik* 7:95.

Wilcken, U. 1893. "Ein neuer griechischer Roman." *Hermes* 28:161–93.

Zimmermann, F. 1931. Review of Lavagnini 1922. *Philologische Wochenschrift*
51:193–202.

———. 1932. "Zwei zerstörte Columnen des Ninos-romans." *Hermes*
67:91–116.

———. 1936. *Griechische Roman-Papyri und verwandte Texte.* Heidelberg.
[No. 1:13–35.]

———. 1953–54. "Das neue Bruchstuck des Ninos-Romans (PSI 1305)."
*Wissenschaftliche Zeitschrift der Univ. Rostock, Gesellschafts- und sprach-
wissenschaftliche Reihe* 3/4:171–81.

BIBLIOGRAPHY

Sesonchosis

Barns, J.W.B. 1956. "Egypt and the Greek Romance." Akten des VIII. Internationalen Kongresses für Papyrologie, edited by H. Gerstinger. *Mitteilungen aus der Papyrussammlung der Nationalbibliothek in Wien*, n.s. 5:29–34.

Braun, M. 1938. *History and Romance in Graeco-Oriental Literature.* Oxford.

Grenfell, B., and A. Hunt. 1922. *The Oxyrhynchus Papyri.* Vol. 15. Egypt Exploration Society. London. [1826: 228–29.]

Jacoby, F. 1923–58. *Die Fragmente der griechischen Historiker.* Berlin and Leiden. [Dritter Teil C, no. 194, 272. Reprints Zimmerman's text of P. Oxy. 1826.]

Körte, A. 1924. Survey of literary papyri. *Archiv für Papyrusforschung* 7:253–54, no. 662.

Lloyd, A. B. 1988. *Herodotus, Book II: Commentary 99–182.* Études préliminaires des religions orientales dans l'empire romain, vol. 43, pt. 2, no. 2. Leiden and New York.

Luppe, W. 1981. "Das neue Bruchstück aus dem Sesongosis-Roman." *Zeitschrift für Papyrologie und Epigraphik* 41:63–66.

Merkelbach, R. 1954. *Die Quellen des griechischen Alexanderromans.* Munich.

Murray, O. 1970. "Hecataeus of Abdera and Pharaonic Kingship." *Journal of Egyptian Archaeology* 56:141–71.

O'Sullivan, J. N. 1984. "The Sesonchosis Romance." *Zeitschrift für Papyrologie und Epigraphik* 56:39–44.

O'Sullivan, J. N., and W. Beck. 1982. "P. Oxy. 3319: The Sesonchosis Romance." *Zeitschrift für Papyrologie und Epigraphik* 45:71–83.

Perry, B. E. 1967. *The Ancient Romances.* Berkeley. [Pp. 167–69.]

Rattenbury, R. M. 1933. "Romance: The Greek Novel." In *New Chapters in the History of Greek Literature,* edited by J. U. Powell, 3d ser., pp. 253–54. Oxford.

Rea, J. 1962. *The Oxyrhynchus Papyri.* Egypt Exploration Society. London. Vol. 27. [2466: 134–36.]

Ruiz-Montero, C. 1989. "P. Oxy. 2466: The Sesonchosis Romance." *Zeitschrift für Papyrologie und Epigraphik* 79:51–57.

Tatum, J. 1989. *Xenophon's Imperial Fiction.* Princeton. [Pp. 9–12.]

Weil, H. 1902. "La Ninopédie." *Études de littérature et de rhythmique greques:* 90–106.

West, S. 1980. *The Oxyrhynchus Papyri.* Egypt Exploration Society. London. Vol. 47. [3319: 11–19.]

Wuthnow, H. 1930. *Die semitische Menschennamen in griechischen Inscriften und Papyri der vorderen Orients.* Leipzig.

Zimmermann, F. 1936a. "Ein Bruchstück aus einem historischen Roman." *Rheinisches Museum für Philologie* 85:165–76.

———. 1936b. *Griechische Roman-Papyri und verwandte Texte.* Heidelberg. [No. 2: 36–40.]

BIBLIOGRAPHY

Staphulos

Henrichs, A. 1972. *Die "Phoinikika" des Lollianos.* Papyrologische Texte und Abhandlungen, no. 14. Bonn. [P. 116.]

Körte, A. 1935. Survey of literary papyri. *Archiv für Papyrusforschung* 11:282–83, no. 844.

Kussl, R. 1991. *Papyrusfragmente griechischer Romane.* Classica Monacensia, Band 2. Tübingen. [Pp. 168–70.]

Merkelbach, R. 1988. *Die Hirten des Dionysos: Die Dionysos-Mysterien der römischen Kaiserzeit und der bukolische Roman des Longus.* Stuttgart. [P. 143 n. 15.]

Papanikolaou, A. 1964. "Chariton und Xenophon zon Ephesos. Zur Frage der Abhängigkeit." Χάρις Κ.Ι. Βουρβέρῃ. Athens. [P. 10.]

Vitelli, G. 1935. *Papiri greci i latini. Pubblicazioni della Società Italiana.* Vol. 11. Florence. [1220: 149–52.]

Vitelli, G., and M. Norsa. 1933. "Da papiri della Società italiana." *Bulletin de la société archéologique d' Alexandrie* 28:135–37.

Zimmermann, F. 1934. "Romanpapyri." *Münchner Beiträge für Papyrusforschung* 19:22–29.

Theano

Blass, F. 1906. Survey of literary papyri. *Archiv für Papyrusforschung* 3:296, no. 247.

Calderini, A. 1913. *Caritone e il suo romanzo.* Turin. [P. 63 n. 2.]

Fuhr, C. 1903. Review of P. Oxy. 3. *Berliner Philologische Wochenschrift* 23:1479.

Garin, F. 1920. "I papiri d'Egitto e i romanzi greci." *Studi italiani di filologia classica* 1:178–79.

Grenfell, B. P., and A. S. Hunt, eds. 1903. *The Oxrhynchus Papyri.* Vol. 3. Egypt Exploration Society. London. [417:61–63].

Kerényi, K. [1927] 1962. *Die griechisch-orientalische Romanliteratur in religions-geschichtlicher Beleuchtung.* Darmstadt. [P. 64 and n. 80.]

Lavagnini, B. 1922. *Eroticorum graecorum fragmenta papyracea.* Leipzig. [Pp. 31–32.]

Longo, V. 1969. *Aretologie nel mondo greco. I: Epigrafi e papiri.* Università di Genova, Facoltà di lettere, Instituto di filologia classica e medievale. Genoa. [Pp. 183–84.]

Müller, B. A. 1916. "Ein neuer griechischer Roman." *Rheinisches Museum für Philologie* 71:359 and n. 8.

Rattenbury, R. M. 1933. "Romance: The Greek Novel." In *New Chapters in the History of Greek Literature,* edited by J. U. Powell, 3d ser., pp. 245–46. Oxford.

Zimmermann, F. 1931. Review of Lavagnini 1922. *Philologische Wochenschrift* 51:231.

———. 1935. "Verkannte Papyri." *Archiv für Papyrusforschung* 11:175–82.

503

Tinouphis

Haslam, M. W. 1981. *Papyri Greek and Egyptian: Edited by Various Hands in Honour of Eric Gardner Turner on the Occasion of His Seventieth Birthday.* Graeco-Roman Memoirs 68. Oxford. [8: 35–45.]

Kussl, R. 1991. *Papyrusfragmente griechischer Romane.* Classica Monacensia, Band 2. Tübingen. [Pp. 171–72.]

Stramaglia, A. 1992. "Prosimetria narrativa e 'romanza perduto': PTurner 8 (con discussione e riedizione di PSI 151 [Pack^2 2624] + PMilVogliano 260)." *Zeitschrift für Papyrologie und Epigraphik* 92:121–49.

INDEX OF PASSAGES CITED

Ancient sources are cited by English title where in common use, elsewhere usually by Latin title. Abbreviated titles used in the main text, if not obvious, are included in parentheses, e.g., *Lives of the Sophists* (= *Vit. Soph.*).

INDEX OF PASSAGES CITED

Souda (cont.)
4.691.17, s.v. φαγήματα: 212–13
4.703.20, s.v. φάϲμα: 202–3
4.739.7, s.v. φιμοῖ: 216–17
4.826.7, s.v. χρηϲτουργία: 216–17
frags. 11, 14, 16, 55: 180n.5
s.v. Iamblichos: 180
s.v. Kadmos of Miletus: 475
s.v. Lollianos: 316n.4
s.v. Xenophon of Antioch: 476
s.v. Xenophon of Cyprus, Kypriaka: 476
Statius
Thebaid
5.162–63: 351
Stephanus of Byzantium
s.v. Ἄρνη: 276
s.v. Βέργη: 105n.6, 473
s.v. Germara: 124n.45
s.v. Θῶνιϲ: 459
s.v. Neapolis: 77n.13, 123n.43
s.v. Ninoe: 26
s.v. Troas: 475
Strabo
Geography
1.2.13: 77n.13
1.2.35: 105
1.3.4: 69
1.4.3: 106–7
2.3.4: 105, 105n.5
2.3.5: 105, 106, 473
2.4.1: 106
2.4.2: 105n.6, 106n.10, 107
2.5.8: 104, 106n.9
2.5.18: 104–5n.4, 122n.35
3.2.9: 124n.47
3.4.15: 124n.46
5.4.5: 123n.41
5.4.7: 77n.13
7.3.1: 106n.10
7.3.5: 125n.52
8.6.8: 276
8.7.4: 420
8.7.5: 420
9.3.1–12: 387
9.3.5: 386, 387, 388
9.3.6: 387
9.3.8: 376
9.3.13: 376
10.5.16: 171

11.3.4: 68
11.6.3: 105
11.8.2: 245
11.13.7: 227
11.14.9: 227
13.27: 475
14.2.19: 171
16.2.10: 181
16.2.12–22: 319
16.2.29: 363
16.4.7: 288
17.1.48: 458
Synesios
Letters
148: 120
Syrianus
1.47.9 (Rabe): 367

Tacitus
Annals
11.4: 229
Histories
1.36: 170
Tertullian
Apologeticum
15.2: 362n.12
TGrF
1: 76 F12 [Dion., tyrant of Sicily]: 194n.29
Themistios
Orationes
22.268c: 94
Theodorus Priscianus
133.5–12 [Rose]: 476
Theokritos
Epigrams
2.3: 449
11.2: 178
13.45: 442
Thucydides
2.44: 170
3.83: 353
Tibullus
1.2.43: 178
Timotheos
Fragmenta
2 Kock: 94
Triphiodoros
Halosis Troiae
670: 429

518

INDEX OF PROPER NAMES
FROM THE FRAGMENTS AND
TESTIMONIA

This index contains references to proper names where they occur in the novel fragments and testimonia. See the general index for references to discussions of people, characters, and places.

GENERAL INDEX

Orphic fragments, 461
Osiris, 190–91n.16, 461, 466
Osroes (king of Armenia), 183
Osroes (king of Parthia), 183
Ostiaioi, 106n.10
Ostimnioi, 106n.10
Outis, 108, 402
outlaws. *See* bandits
Ovid, 112, 170
Oxyrhynchus, 7, 63, 268, 322, 367, 393, 480
Ozymandias, 246

P. Amh. 2.160, 472
P. Dubl. C3, 101
P. Fouad 4, 471
P. Frei. 4.47, 472
P. Gen. inv. 187, 471
P. Hamb. 134, 469
P. Harris 13, 469
P. Harris 18, 472
P. Harris 19, 472
P. Harris 23, 471
P. Hordeonius Lollianos, 316, 324. *See also* Lollianos
P. Lit. Lond. 194, 472
P. Lit. Lond. 198, 470
P. Lit. Lond. 245, 469
P. Mich. inv. 3793, 470
P. Oxy. 2.435, 72
P. Oxy. 3.454, 425
P. Oxy. 6.868, 471
P. Oxy. 7.1014, 472
P. Oxy. 22.2330, 25n.3
P. Oxy. 42.3011, 470
P. Oxy. 45.3218, 471
P. Oxy. 404, 439
P. Oxy. 410, 439
P. Oxy. 2466, 472
P. Oxy. ined. 112/130 (a), 268
Paapis, 101, 110, 115, 122n.39, 123n.40, 124n.49, 126n.54, 148, 154, 160, 174, 400–401, 423
paideia of princes, 26, 246–49. *See also* coming of age; military apprenticeship
paidotrophia, 133–34n.69
pais, 321–22, 324
Palaistra, 324
Palestine, 259
Palmyra, 181

Pamounis, 247–48, 264–65
Pan, 444, 449
Panchaia, 106n.8
panegyrics, imperial, 60
Panopolis, 13
Panotioi, 106n.11
Pantheia, 26, 160n.5, 184, 275, 287, 317, 476
pantomime, 449. *See also* actors; mime
Parnassos, 376
parody, 107n.12, 108–9, 119
Parthenios, 429n.1, 439
Parthenope, 72–73, 76–80, 89, 91–93, 95
Parthenope, the Siren, 123n.43
Parthia, 183
Parthian, 182
Pasiphae, 178
passion, 219n.74, 267–69
Patrokles (Seleucid admiral), 122n.35
Pausanias, 376, 438
Pelasgian, 26
Pelusium, 319
Pergamum, 359
Perilaos, 278
Persephone, 114. *See also* Kore
Perseus, 109n.15, 322
Persia, 78, 183; king of, 76–77, 227, 392, 398
Persian conquest, 248
Persian court, 227, 391
Persian Empire, 319
Persian invasion, 246
Persian lexica, 73
Persian narrative patterns, 12
Persian origins of the novel, 11n.16. *See also* origins of the Greek novel
Persian royal banquets, 398. *See also* banquets
Persian short sword, 276
Persian version of *Metiochos and Parthenope*, 72
Persians, 190n.15, 228, 301
Persika. See Ktesias
Persinna, 398
Persis, 321–22, 324, 329–30, 345–48, 354
Persius, 318n.13
Petesis, 15
Petronius, 3, 5, 7, 108, 363–65
Phaidra, 78, 80
phalloi, 362